THE COMPLETE
BOOK OF CREATIVE
GLASS ART

THE COMPLETE BOOK OF CREATIVE GLASS ART

by Polly Rothenberg

CROWN PUBLISHERS, INC., NEW YORK

Also by the Author

METAL ENAMELING
THE COMPLETE BOOK OF CERAMIC ART
CREATIVE STAINED GLASS

Library of Congress Catalog Card Number:
74-80319
ISBN: 0-517-51690X
ISBN: 0-517-516918 pbk.
Printed in the United States of America
Published simultaneously in Canada by General
Publishing Company Limited
Designed by Shari de Miskey

Third Printing, May, 1978

Acknowledgments

I AM indebted to the talented and friendly individual glass artists and members of professional glass studios who have contributed the photographs of their inspired works that appear in this book. Many of them have attained an impressive standing in their special fields. I sincerely thank Helene Weis of the Willet Stained Glass Studios for her courteous assistance in supplying fine process photos of members of the studio's large staff of talented and skilled artists at work on actual projects.

Thanks also go to the staff of *Ceramics Monthly* for permission to include in the book material of mine that has appeared in their publication. My appreciation is extended to the Toledo Museum of Art for allowing me to select photographs from the "American Glass Now" exhibition for the section of the book relating to contemporary glassblowing. And Bob Brodecki of Etmans Lab thank you again for your fine custom prints made from my negatives.

My deep appreciation goes to Vernon Brejcha who generously demonstrated for the book photo-sequences of his glassblowing specialties and to Sherry Brejcha who captured the essence of the action with her camera.

I especially thank again all the fine and friendly folks at the Georgian College of Applied Arts and Technology in Barrie, Ontario, for the courtesies extended me during the time I spent in their Glass Design Department summer workshop. Roman Bartkiw's watchful guidance through the basics of glassblowing made it possible for me to have some experience in this fascinating art. Sandblasting, etching, and engraving, as well as other "cold glass" techniques made the workshop a rewarding experience. My thanks go to Georgian College staff members Wayne Cunningham, David Phillips, Jack Hunt, and Charles McManus. Marc Robillard's stunning photographs of Roman Bartkiw "blocking" a blown glass bubble with a wet newspaper and photos of other activities in the glass department are valuable additions to the book. Finally, I sincerely thank my husband, Maurice, for his patient and helpful cooperation in this project.

Contents

7 BLOWN GLASS

8 GLASS SCULPTURE AND ARCHITECTURAL ART

Preface

GLASS art has been endowed with mystery and glamor since the prehistoric days when the first shining beads were molded from silica sand, potash, and lime. Although archaeologists have unearthed crude glass objects in Egypt that presumably were made over 3,000 years ago, there is evidence among the findings that many of the older glass articles uncovered came from Asia. Discoveries also reveal that during those early years, glass in the form of jewelry and small statues was owned by the wealthy and the noble. Glassmakers were under strict supervision of the ruling Pharaohs. To the common people, glass was mysterious, glamorous, and unattainable.

Until the advent of the blown glass bubble, colored beads, small amulets, and statues were the most cherished glass forms, not only for personal adornment and pleasure but also for use as trade currency and tax payments. The discovery, just prior to the Christian era, that glass can be blown was a major achievement. As time passed and glass became more plentiful, Phoenician traders carried it throughout the Mediterranean area. Glass beads became available to others besides the wealthy and high-born. But across the Mediterranean a newer, more imperious empire was stirring. Eventually Egyptian power and pre-eminence in glassmaking fell to the Romans. By the beginning of the Christian era, the Roman Emperor Tiberius had transported captive Egyptian glassworkers to Rome and had settled them there and in his vassal colonies over Europe wherever sand and fuel were available. He was so enamored with glass that it is said he even learned how to make it himself.

The first four centuries of the Christian era became the first golden age of glass. Glassblowing created a thin wall that could be seen through, an amazing accomplishment to the ordinary Roman citizen who attributed strange powers to the master glassmakers. The Romans began to experiment in earnest to produce thinner, clearer glass. They decorated this fragile, clear glass with applied colored glass threads, painted it with gilt and enamel, added "prunts," or pressed lumps of molten glass, and used many of the methods contemporary glass craftsmen employ today to enrich the surface of their blown forms. But with the rise and fall of the Roman Empire, the development of glass rose and fell also. A succession of powerful barbarian tribes from the north overpowered and pillaged the western Mediterranean. During the next four hundred years, Roman glory and the first golden age of glass grew dim.

The savage hordes that ravaged Europe left destruction and decay. But the secrets of glassmaking did not perish. Constantinople became more than a caretaker political and cultural power for all the Mediterranean world. Glass mosaic-making flourished in Byzantium. By the twelfth century, Christian missionaries emigrating from Constantinople established monasteries all over Europe and glassmaking was one of their important arts.

As the years passed, the City of Venice was destined to replace Constantinople as the center of the glass arts. Founded in the sixth century by refugees from the plunderers of Rome, the marshy islands of sand where they achieved safety proved to be ideal for making glass. Beech forests nearby just across the Gulf of Venice yielded the fuel and potash. With these advantages, Venice needed only to acquire the techniques of glassmaking; she brought in master glassworkers from her captured colony of Syria. The secrecy of Venetian glassmaking techniques and the intrigue surrounding glass art became legendary. By the end of the thirteenth century, to protect their glass secrets, Venetian authorities had moved all their glassworkers to the small offshore island of Murano. Their movements were closely restricted, although from time to time freedom-loving Venetians managed to slip away. But again glassmaking was shrouded in mystery.

With the spread of Christianity, glass mosaics had become a major art. But a newer form in colored glass was emerging. A development in religious architecture, the Gothic cluster of arches with their supporting columns, niches and spaces between them, became ideal for cloistering colored glass windows. Wealthy nobility supplied the materials with which artisan monks were to design and construct them. The twelfth and thirteenth centuries became the second golden age of glass. Glass art in all its forms developed and flourished as never before or since that time until the twentieth century. Some of the mystery of glass has lessened, but man's ability to create new forms with this exciting material has scarcely begun.

This book concerns the glass art of our time, its craftsmen, and the many ways it is formed. Now more than ever, people with leisure to enjoy all the arts yearn to create decorative works that are uniquely their own. Anyone who loves beauty can learn how to make decorative glass objects by following easily understood but precise directions. The illustrated and detailed step-by-step instructions in the book offer both simple and complex projects that are exciting to follow. As your skill develops, your own confidence and creativity will emerge. Once you have conquered the processes, you can develop unusual and creative ideas of your own. Throughout these pages there are beautiful photographs of the works of skilled and talented professional glass artists, illustrating the amazing variety of their styles. Their works will be an inspiration to experienced craftsmen, to collectors, and to those who are just discovering the joyful world of glass.

1
Introduction

STAINED GLASS

FOR centuries stained glass has richly adorned the churches of the world, uplifting the spirits of millions of worshipers. Except for brief historical interludes when stained glass was used in private dwellings, it was associated almost entirely with religious architecture. Today, the classical art of designing with this beautiful transparent material has swept aside the last restraints of its ancient role. Although it is still very important in religious architecture, stained glass has moved into the modern world of secular construction and home workshop creations. With new attitudes and new ways of utilizing the vibrant beauty of its colors, enthusiastic craftsmen are creating delightful glass panels, windows, beautiful lanterns, jewelry, whimsical hangings, sculptures, and countless accessories.

Stained glass as an artistic creation depends for its beauty on the transmitted light that illuminates it from moment to moment.

Moving daylight sends its rays through each bit of glass in ever-changing hues. Simple shapes become alive the moment they capture a gleam of sunshine. The origin and force of the light are phenomena that form the basis of stained glass designing. Not only must the glass artist reckon with light coming through the glass, but also with the changing color effects of whatever is seen beyond the glass. These modulating elements may themselves be in full sunlight, in shadow, or dappled with light and shadow. All these effects are heightened by the texture and undulations in the stained glass itself.

COLOR IN GLASS

Light moving through vibrant stained glass is influenced by many factors: the time of day; the types and sources of lighting; highlights and shadows; the effects of halation due to the juxtaposition of certain colors; the transparency, texture, and luminosity of the glass itself

◀

Bonded exhibition panel. Louis Moses. A prismatic display of stained glass color overlaid with areas of colorless glass strips set on edge to diffuse the underlying hues in third dimension. *Photo by courtesy of Willet Stained Glass Studios.*

1

as well as the personal interpretation of these factors. When you stand before a great stained glass window shimmering with color, your emotions will differ from those of any other person. Scientists have learned that color originates in the human brain, stimulated by light rays of varying lengths that are transmitted from objects to the eye of the beholder. Hence, color as experienced by each individual is personal and involves the mind as well as the eyes. The blue pattern one person sees may not be the same blue pattern as experienced by another.

Although no direction can be given on how to select glass colors that will satisfy all persons, it is suggested that early in the work of the serious glass art student, a good book on color should be studied, especially before important amounts of money are invested in glass. The beginner or amateur can discover beauty and emotion in color by observing nature. The subtle overtones and harmonies of translucent flower petals, butterflies, or glistening tropical fish glowing in sunlight are often enhanced by adding startling contrasts, such as bright pink spots on the pale chartreuse wings of a moth or purple splotches in the cup of a yellow tulip. Books filled with color plates of these and other natural forms are in every public library. They can yield rich and inspirational ideas to help the beginner select rewarding color combinations for his initial projects. The final selection of stained glass colors should be made by viewing them in bright natural daylight, whether you are developing an impressive stained glass wall or a decorative glass butterfly. Certain color subtleties in the glass can be discerned only by transmitted natural light. Black, which stands out so forcefully in paintings and natural forms, is overpowered by dazzling patches of light streaming through brilliant colored glass. Frequently, dark passages are desirable in a stained glass composition. But the subtle use of a dark hue already employed in the design can give more pervasive overtones to the glass composition than black glass could offer.

KINDS OF STAINED GLASS

Antique stained glass is the costliest and most exciting of the colored glasses. Spectacular stained glass church windows, panels, and windows in public and private buildings, and charming functional and decorative art objects are fashioned from this handmade glass. Despite its name it is not old glass; but it is made in nearly the same way glass was formed by early glassmakers. Skilled craftsmen employ simple tools and methods to produce hand-formed sheet glass in hundreds of new colors developed by modern chemistry. Antique glass has random streaks, ripples, undulations, bubbles, or other irregularities whose seeming imperfections catch light transmitted through them to bring character and beauty to your work. Areas of preferred thicknesses in this glass are cut and sold from larger sheets, which results in a considerable waste or "curious" glass that is sometimes sold by glass supply stores at a discount. This scrap sheet glass is useful for projects in basic glasscraft. Although it may not fit easily into a large leaded glass composition, it is suitable for bonding with epoxy resin, for grouted projects, jewelry, mobiles, and other decorative hangings.

Flashed stained glass denotes a variety of antique glass with a light colored glass base and thinner skins of rich deep contrasting colored glass. By examining the edges of a piece of flashed glass, you can see these separate color layers. Light passing through flashed glass mixes the separate color effects much the way a painter mixes his pigments. Flashed glass is useful in any project where it will not be transformed by heat: etched glass, lead came project, glass bonded with epoxy or combinations of these methods. If flashed glass is fired, the thin layer of colored glass will likely pull back from the edges, leaving a colorless or white rim around the glass piece. Flashed glass should be *cut* on the unflashed side, but it should be *etched* on the flashed side.

Cathedral glass is a machine-rolled stained glass with medium to heavy texture on one side and a smooth surface on the reverse side. It is passed between rollers that impress a variety of textures on it while the glass is still hot and pliable. Because the glass is generally of uniform thickness of ⅛ inch, there is less waste than from cutting antique glass. It is sold in a wide variety of delightful colors and textures. Rolled patterns in this glass are called hammered, rippled, seedy (containing tiny bubbles), and antique texture. Cathedral glass is cut on the smooth surface.

Slab glass (faceted glass) is the name given to an extra-clear-colored antique glass cast in thick slabs. An unusual cutting procedure called "faceting" gives them reflective sparkle and leaves a myriad of small thick glass chips, which have many decorative uses. The glass slabs are generally 8 by 8 inches, 8 by 12 inches, or 12 by 12 inches; they may vary from ½ to 1 inch in thickness. A steel wedge, a dalle

cutting hammer, and special skills are required to cut these extra-thick slabs. But the novice can make wonderful projects with broken segments of this glass. Most glass suppliers sell broken slab glass segments.

Rondels are round disks of antique glass made by blowing a bubble, then twirling the hot molten glass bubble on the end of the blowing rod to flatten it by centrifugal force. Rondels are made in many sizes and beautiful colors. These very decorative forms are useful in leaded and bonded compositions.

Jewels are small novelty stained glass forms used decoratively either singly or as part of a larger composition. In addition, jewels are made by firing small glass bits into balls or cabochon shapes according to the temperature at which they are fired. They are especially effective when they are bonded on stained glass lanterns.

Opalescent glass is a milky semitranslucent glass in one or more colors and white, swirled together while the glass is still molten and finally rolled into sheets. The glass is somewhat brittle and difficult to cut.

Layered three-dimensional stained glass panel. Fredrica Fields. *Photo by Kenneth Fields.*

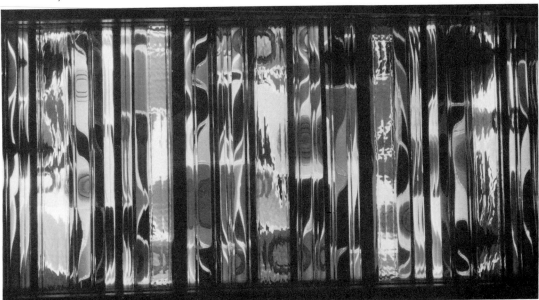

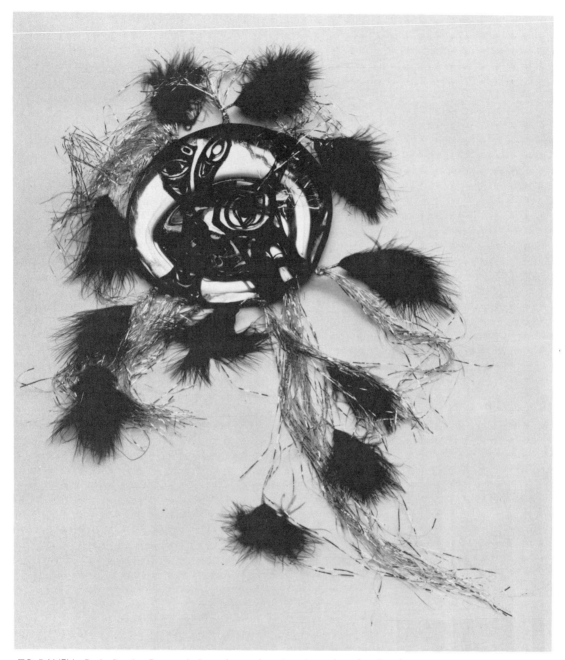

TO RAVEN. Beth Beede. Bent colorless sheet glass is mirrored and painted with black designs. Loops of wire are soldered to a lead camed edge to hold threads and fibers of Mylar. Black downy feathers are fastened into the fibers. *Photo by Erik Redlich.*

Off-hand blown bottles. Kent Ipsen. Mr. Ipsen is Chairman of the Craft Department of Virginia Commonwealth University in Richmond.

CUTTING THE GLASS

Although your first project may be confined to compositions made from glass scraps, you will find random shapes that can be improved by a little nipping and cutting here and there as you visualize how you can combine them into attractive designs. "Cutting glass" is a term that does not adequately describe the process. When glass is scored with a tiny sharp metal wheel set into a metal handle, only the surface of the glass is fractured. The cut encourages glass molecules to open up along a scored line, *when adequate pressure is applied.* This pressure must be applied at once, if you would make a clean separation. If more than a couple of minutes elapse, the separated molecules of glass will "close ranks" so that a clean separation is not achieved, even though the scored line is still visible. This characteristic of glass is unknown to the average novice. It may exlpain why a clean scored line does not always result in a clean separation of the glass when you are first learning to cut it.

Certain safety precautions must be followed when you work with glass. Always wear gloves when you transport large glass sheets. Keep glass bins on the floor so you need not elevate the glass above your head; it may have fine cracks that will make it break suddenly as you move it. If a sheet of glass begins to fall, do not grab it; step back and let it fall. If a choice piece is partly buried beneath other pieces of glass, remove the upper glass, starting from the top. If you try to shuffle the glass around with bare hands, you are likely to receive multiple gashes. Always scrape or sand the edges of newly cut glass to remove the thin sharp slivers that often appear along a freshly cut edge. The most common cause of small aggravating and painful cuts is absentmindedly brushing or pressing the bare hands on the minute glass shards that litter the cutting table's cutting surface after a session of glass cutting. If you receive a few of these painful (although usually not severe) cuts, you will automatically discontinue this careless practice. Happily, very few glass craftsmen cut themselves severely.

An inexpensive *glass cutter* with a hard steel cutting wheel is adequate for general use and it will give long service when proper care is exercised. Tungsten carbide cutting wheels, a little more expensive, give longer service and greater separation of the glass surface when it is scored. Commercial diamonds set into glass cutters are costly and they are not easy for the inexperienced craftsman to control, although many professional glass craftsmen like the flexibility they provide in cutting intricate shapes. The cutters used for projects in this book have tungsten carbide cutting wheels.

The *cutting table* must be firm, flat, and level. To maintain good arm leverage, it is advisable to stand while you cut glass. The table should have a comfortable height for this standing position. About 34 to 36 inches from the floor is adequate working table height for the average person. If the table is too low, your back will begin to feel the strain. Short-pile carpet makes a good cutting surface for the table top. Tiny slivers from glass cuttings drop into the pile where they do not interfere with subsequent cutting or scratch the glass when it is being shifted. Carpet is resilient enough to "give" under the pressure exerted to separate the scored glass. Vacuum the carpet occasionally, or if it is a very small piece shake it gently over a broad trash container to rid it of accumulated glass scraps. Some craftsmen prefer to place layers of paper or a sheet of pressed cork on the cutting table instead of carpet, especially when a limited amount of glass cutting is done.

Although rulers or other *straightedges* can guide the cutter when straight lines are scored, they have the annoying propensity of shifting suddenly or sliding on the glass (especially on uneven antique stained glass). Until you become adept at cutting glass, you can control this slippage by gluing a long strip of thin rubber to the underside of the straightedge. "Rug grip," sold in carpet stores, is excellent for this purpose. Before cutting begins, clean the glass with detergent water to remove all soil that may cause the cutter to "skip" and make separation of the scored glass difficult or ragged. Lubricate the cutting wheel with kerosene. When you score glass, hold the cutter perpendicular to the table top. It can lean slightly toward you, but if it tilts sideways one edge of the score may be undercut and make a rough separation of the glass.

Position the glass on the table *smoothest side up*. Dip the cutter into kerosene and dab it on a paper towel to remove excess oil. Beginning about ⅛ inch from the edge of the glass to avoid chipping it, make a firm continuous stroke from one edge of the glass to the other *without pausing or lifting* the cutter. Score either toward you or away from you, whichever is easier and allows you to see where you are going. Hold the cutter close to the straightedge but not pressed against it. The cutter must not wander away from the line you are scoring. Press it firmly against the glass. It should make a soft steady scratching sound as it bites into the glass but does not roughen the score line. Long straight cuts against a guide stick are not automatically easy to control; they require strict concentration. If the cutter begins to lean sideways, the cutting wheel may curve away from the straightedge. Some craftsmen prefer to lay a straightedged sheet of paper under the glass and guide the cutting wheel above it. Only experience can teach you how firmly pressure must be applied. In spite of a few false starts, it is surprising how quickly you will gain confidence after a session of practice on glass scraps or inexpensive window glass.

As soon as the glass has been scored, lay one end of your glass cutter under the near end of the score line and immediately press firmly down with your thumbs on each side of the line at the end nearest you. The scored glass should separate evenly. If it doesn't, lay the glass over the table edge so the scored line comes just beyond and parallel to the table top; with one hand pressing the glass firmly against the top of the table, snap the glass in two with the other hand bending it down and away from the table. Hang onto the glass as you force it down so it does not fall suddenly to the floor and shatter. After these two tries, if you have not separated the glass, another procedure must be tried. Hold the glass in one hand and with the end of the cutter in the other hand, tap firmly but gently all along the scored line underneath the glass. Tap first at one end, then at the other end and along the middle of the line. You will soon see a fracture developing under the scored line. Hold the glass over the table in case it should fall apart suddenly, which it frequently will do. Apply equal pressure to the two sides of the fractured score line and snap them apart. Long curved lines are cut the same way if they are not too sharply curved. Glass thicker than ⅛ inch is difficult for beginners to cut.

To cut out a shaped piece of glass, a different method is employed. Select a pattern template and lay it on a piece of glass with at least a ¾-inch margin around the shape. With the fingers of one hand spread out on the template, hold it firmly against the glass, taking care that it does not slip while you are scoring around it. One side of the glass shape will be scored and separated at a time. Dip the cutter into kerosene and dab it lightly on a paper towel. Begin at one edge of the glass and score along one side of the pattern, continuing beyond it to the opposite edge of the glass without pausing or lifting the cutter. Lay down the cutter at once and pick up the glass before the score line heals, as described earlier; applying firm equal pressure on each side of the scored line, snap the glass down and out. If you are cutting off a thin strip of glass, grasp it on the narrow side of the score line with glass pliers or other flat end pliers and on the other side with the other hand or another pair of pliers. If you wrap narrow masking tape or a thin cloth strip around the plier's jaws, you can avoid splintering the glass when the hard metal clutches it. It may be necessary to tap sharply along the underside of the score line to *start* the fracture; then press down and out on each side of the fracture line as described for straight cuts. If you try to complete the glass separation only by tapping it until it falls apart, you will have a ragged cut. Each side of the shape is cut by scoring and separating the same way, before the next side is cut. Remember to sand its edges lightly with fine sandpaper or scrape them with another piece of glass to remove sharp border slivers. By meticulous attention to this precaution, you can avoid painful cuts.

When you have cut out the curved shape as best you can, you will likely be left with unwanted small projections along its edges. They must be chipped, or "grozed," away. Although the notches in glass cutters are meant traditionally to be used for grozing, today many craftsmen prefer to use the tips of the jaws on a pair of grozing nippers or ordinary small pliers to pinch off small projections of glass. If the thickness of the glass will fit closely into one of the notches on the cutter, with care you can successfully chip off irregularities. But if the notch is a bit wider than the thickness of the glass, the projection may take too much glass with it when it separates; you may be left with an unwanted jagged notch instead of an unwanted projection. To pinch off irregularities, grasp only the portion you want to remove from the glass edge and squeeze or pinch the nippers with quick firm pressure until you literally bite off the glass protrusion with the nipper jaws. Because the glass cutting process is fundamentally quite simple, the novice can pass from nervous frustration to easy skill in a relatively short time. Occasionally you will encounter glass bubbles and other surface irregularities when you are cutting antique stained glass. Ease the cutter over them gently without lifting it from the glass; try to avoid forcing a ragged cut through the irregularity. These bubbles and thick areas give beauty and character to the glass. After a little experience you will ride the cutter smoothly over them.

A circle cutter is required for cutting out perfect circles of glass; or you can have them cut by your local glass supplier. To cut your own, position the pivot of the cutter on a square sheet of glass, allowing about ¾ inch clearance all around. Follow exactly the instructions that accompany the circle cutter. If the cutter's rubber disk, which clamps against the glass, tends to let go of the glass while you are cutting it, wipe it with a film of water, then clamp it down again. You should have no further difficulty with it. To facilitate scoring, before you begin, hold a small brush dipped in kerosene in the hand that will swing the cutter around; lift the cutter wheel off the glass but hold the brush against it so it brushes a band of kerosene onto the glass in the path where the cutting wheel will score. Then lay the brush down and score the circle by pressing the cutting wheel against the glass as you score it in a complete circle without pausing until you hear a light click as the cutter joins the starting end of the score line. Remove the circle cutter from the glass and score four straight lines radiating out from near the circle to the edge of each side of the glass sheet. Tap gently but persistently all along the underside of the scored circle until a crack develops in it. Tap under the four radiating lines in the same way. The glass should separate easily. Hold the glass above the table and close to it while you tap so it does not fall to the floor. Regardless of how awkward you may feel initially, do not become discouraged. (Read these cutting instructions over several times until you feel ready to begin the fascinating experience of cutting glass.)

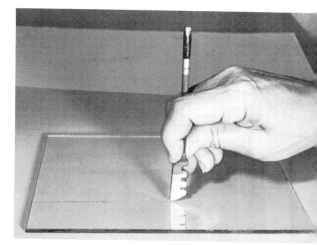

Hold the glass cutter perpendicular between your first and second fingers. The thumb supports the cutter on the underneath side of the flat surface just above the cutter notches. The tiny cutting wheel rides on the glass.

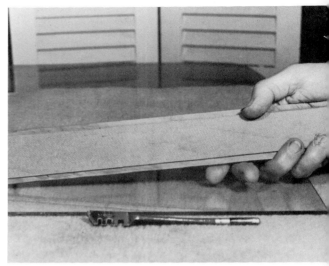

Before you start, clean the glass with liquid cleaner. Begin scoring about 1/16" from the edge of the glass and make a firm, even, continuous stroke from one edge to the other without pausing or lifting the cutter. Do not retrace the stroke. As you reach the end of the score line, relax your hand so the cutter does not chip the glass edge.

When you score straight lines along a guide stick, keep the straightedge from slipping by gluing a wide strip of thin rubber "rug grip" to the underside of the guide stick. It can be bought in rug stores.

As soon as the glass has been scored, lay one end of the cutter under the near end of the score line and immediately press down firmly on each side of the line. The glass should separate evenly.

Another method of separating the glass. With one hand pressing the glass against the table top, and with the score line extending over the edge and parallel to it, snap the glass down and out.

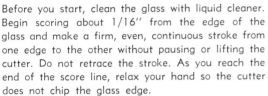

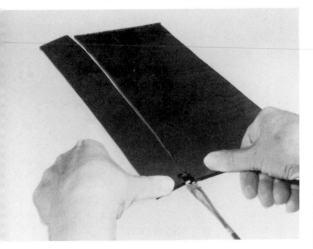

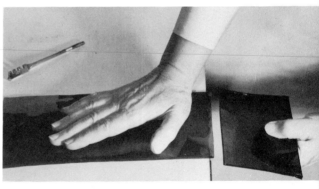

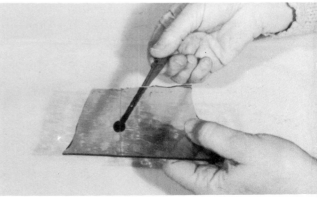

Tap firmly but gently all along the scored line underneath the glass for another way to separate it. You will see a fracture developing under the scored line.

Apply equal pressure to the two sides of the *fractured* score line and snap them apart.

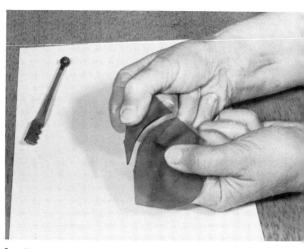

Small pieces are snapped apart on the score line with the thumbs and curled forefingers pressing down and outward.

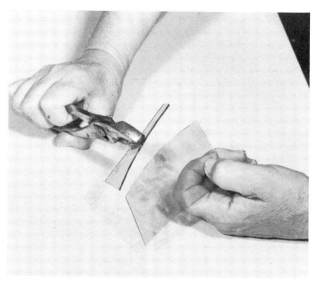

To separate a thin strip of glass from a wider section, grasp the glass on the narrow side of the score line with regular pliers or glass pliers and on the other side with your hand. Notice that the glass is always held between the thumb and curled forefinger to provide safe leverage for parting the glass.

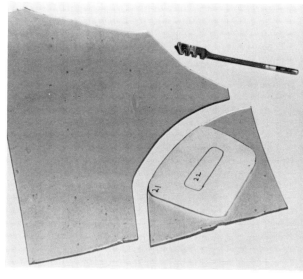

The first cut for a shaped piece is made by scoring along one side of the pattern from one edge of the glass to the other.

With the fingers of one hand spread out to hold the pattern firmly against the glass, cut along the second side from edge to edge of the glass.

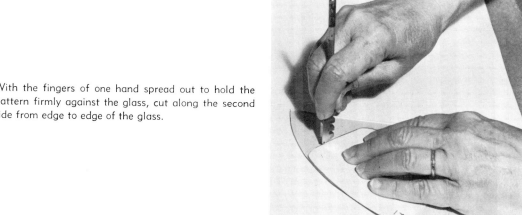

A rounded shape is cut out in a series of short curved strokes.

Corners and unwanted projections are "grozed," or nipped off, with small flat-nosed pliers or grozing pliers.

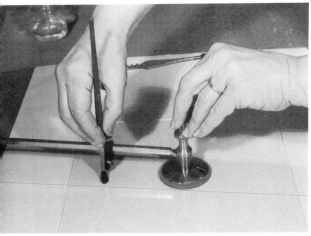

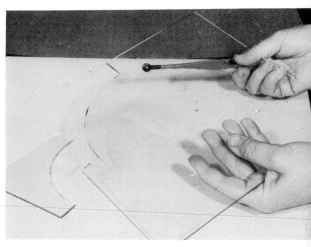

Lift the cutting wheel and swinging arm of the cutter off the glass while you hold a kerosened brush against the cutter. Scribe a full circle with the brush (not with the cutter) to put kerosene where the cutter will score the glass. Put down the brush, press the cutter against the glass, and score it on the kerosened path made by the brush.

If the glass has not separated, light tapping under the score lines should complete the separation.

When the circle has separated, sand the edge lightly with wet carborundum paper.

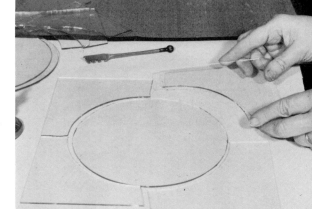

Rondels and flat marbles.

A glass storage cabinet. The top section for holding small pieces is set back to leave space for a shelf.

LEAD CAME

The slender channeled lead stripping that becomes the chief skeletal support in a leaded stained glass composition is called "lead came" (came), or just "lead." In addition to holding the glass construction together, lead came becomes a dynamic linear pictorial or abstract design with its lead lines and colorful glass being of equal importance to a successful composition. Structural strength requires that leads run vertically, horizontally, and/or diagonally, not in parallel lines alone. Avoid running several lead ends together at one point. What to do with all these ends where they meet would become an aesthetic as well as a structural problem. The lead lines are designated first on the original cartoon (drawing), then glass colors are selected.

To achieve interest and avoid monotony, lengths and widths of lead should vary. The chief structural lines of the design may be composed of heavier leads than the ones chosen to delineate delicate details, which can be worked out with narrower leads. Important lines are sweeping and rhythmical with lesser details being more subtle; they should not dart or wander aimlessly across the glass composition.

Lead widths are measured across the top surface rather than across the channeled sides. This top surface may be flat or rounded. Lead is usually available in six-foot lengths of varying styles and widths. H-shaped leads have double channels and a $\frac{1}{16}$-inch-thin wall or heart between channels. From an end view, the lead is shaped exactly like a capital H. The crossbar on the H represents the thin lead heart. H cames are employed for joining pieces of stained glass to one another within the composition and for border leads where the unused outside channel will be framed or puttied into a window. The H-leads used for the projects in this book are in the range of $\frac{1}{8}$ to $\frac{1}{4}$ inch wide, with the exception of the wider flat border leads.

U-shaped lead has one channel and is rounded or flat on the opposite side. It is intended for perimeter leading where a more finished effect is preferred. However, most professionals who usually make large compositions split a wide H-lead down through the center heart with a chisel or leading knife and bend the wide strips lengthwise to make their own U-leads if they want to use them; but this does take some skill. A $\frac{1}{8}$-inch U-lead with a flat side is a versatile and flexible lead commonly employed to finish free-form hangings or "light catchers" so dear to the hobbyist. However, the more delicate U-leads can be used in the construction of a quite professionally executed glass design. These ⅛-inch flat U-leads are employed in the construction of intricate patterns in glass lampshades to give them a sturdy but fragile-looking form.

Although the creative craftsman of today uses whatever tools he desires, whether traditional, personally designed, or improvised, the artist who devotes considerable time to stained glass work eventually acquires professional tools. A glazier's knife with a curved thin blade of top-quality steel has a thick wooden handle, useful for tapping glass pieces into the leads. Glazier's knives, lead stretchers, grozing pliers, and other glazing tools can be bought from major supply sources found in art glass publications.

Frequently, lead must be stretched and straightened before it can be used. Fasten one end of a lead strip in a vise or lead stretcher and pull firmly on the other end with pliers until you feel it stretch. Take hold of the lead with the other hand so that if it should break suddenly, you will not fall backward. If the lead is kinked or twisted, straighten and untwist it, then slide the flattened and waxed end of a dowel stick or glazier's lathekin between its flanges to open them. With a sharp knife such as a regular glazing knife or matt knife, cut the lead into usable lengths by rocking the knife from side to side through the lead. (For additional information about using lead came, see the section "Leading a Rectangular Panel.")

A set of stained glass doors. Jack A. Landis. Colors are purple, red, green, gold set against a light green hammered cathedral glass background. From the home of Mr. and Mrs. R. M. Graf, Dayton, Ohio. *Photo by Kathy Clark.*

Rounded and flat H leads have double channels. An end view shows the lead shaped like an H. A crossbar represents a thin wall, or "heart," between channels. Glass pieces fit into the channels, which hold them securely in place.

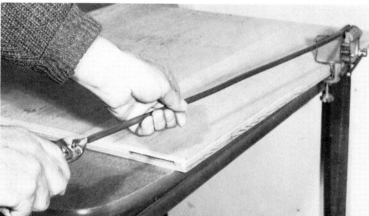

To stretch lead, fasten one end of the strip in a vise and pull firmly on the other end with pliers until you feel it stretch.

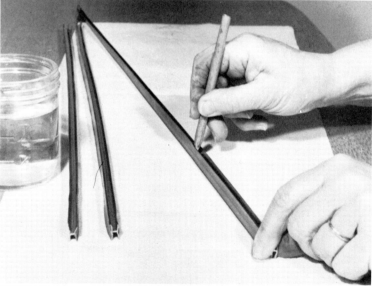

Draw the flattened end of a length of dowel stick, ¼" thick, along the lead channels to open them.

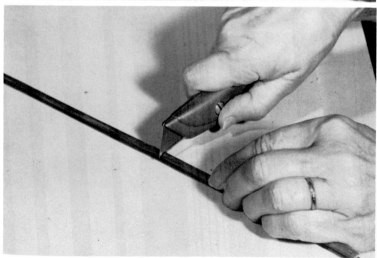

To cut lead, first score it to mark the location of the cut, then rock the knife blade gently as you press through the lead.

Lead camed stained glass panel. Herbert Tepping. The leading gives charm to a very simple statement in stained glass.

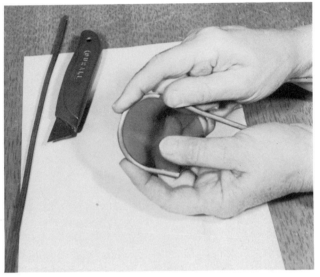

Rounded H lead is bent snugly around a curved shape without crimping it.

To trim lead ends so they form a sharp angle, hold the knife blade so it continues an imaginary line running through the center of the corner angle. The leads will form a neat juncture when they are mitered.

SOLDERING

Each separate length of lead came in a stained glass work must be soldered to adjoining pieces of lead. A 100-watt soldering iron with a copper tip and wooden handle heats up readily and is lightweight to hold. The kind of tip you use is a personal choice to some extent and may be limited to whatever is available. Examine the various soldering irons and tips at a reliable hardware store. You will find that there are three basic shapes to the tips and many variations of these: chisel, conical, and pyramidal. A small tip is convenient for soldering small delicate works or the inside of angles on three-dimensional objects. An iron with changeable tips is very useful. Try different size irons to see how they feel in your hand.

To avoid the nuisance of unplugging the cord when the iron gets too hot, a simple and inexpensive "on-off" line switch should be installed on the cord about 12 to 14 inches from the handle of the iron. If you want to spend extra money, you might invest in a more professional rheostat control unit. A small stand to rest the hot iron on when it is not in use is imperative.

Before a new soldering iron is used, its copper tip must be "tinned." For this procedure, the first step is to clean it by filing the tip to remove all traces of oxidation and soil. Stroke it smoothly in one direction until it is copper pink and shiny, taking care to maintain the original planes of the tip. Brush liquid soldering flux over the tip when it is clean. The flux used for all solder work in this book is liquid oleic (ō-lā-ic) acid. Soldering flux promotes close adhesion between solder and metal; without it the melted solder will roll off the metal in balls. Flux also deters the formation of oxides on the hot surface while solder is applied. Over a period of use, some pitting will accumulate on the iron's tip. Tinning must be repeated from time to time, always starting with a clean filed tip. Solder will not adhere to tarnished or soiled metal. The solder employed both for tinning the copper tip and for joining leads in stained glass work is 60/40 solid-core ⅛-inch wire solder. It contains 60 percent tin and 40 percent lead. The percentage of tin is always placed first in designating solder content. Resin core solders are not suitable for leading stained glass work. They will gum up the glass to the extent that it will be difficult to clean it.

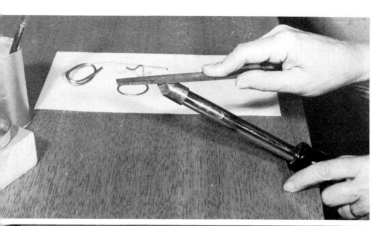

Clean the soldering iron by filing the tip to remove oxidation and soil.

Flux the tip of the iron with oleic acid.

When the iron's tip has been cleaned and fluxed, plug in the iron and heat it. As soon as solder that has been touched to the tip begins to melt, run the solder all over the planes of the tip to cover it with a thin solder coating. If the solder does not adhere to the tip, it may be the iron is too hot. Cool down the tip to the temperature at which it will accept the solder. Keep the tip clean by brushing it with flux occasionally while you are using it. Avoid inhaling the hot flux fumes.

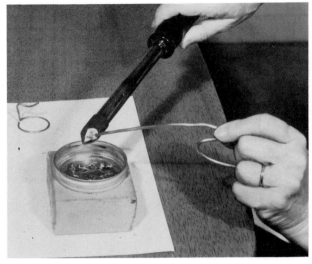

Run the solder over the planes of the working tip on the iron to cover it with a coat of solder. This is called "tinning" the iron.

The melting point of the same 60/40 solid core solder used for tinning the iron's tip is just right to use with lead came. The solder melts approximately 10 degrees lower in temperature than lead, which provides an adequate working range. The leads around the juncture area must be cleaned before flux is applied. Scrub the leads carefully at the juncture with a copper wire brush or fine sandpaper. When the joints are shiny, dip the solder wire into oleic acid and dab a few drops on each lead joint with a small brush. To apply solder to the lead, position the tip of the heated iron near the end of the solder wire as it approaches the lead joint and bring them together as they touch the joint. Use the minimum amount of solder, about ⅛ inch, and press it against the joint with the iron's tip riding on top of the bead of solder. Hold it there for a second, then lift it up *before it melts the lead.* It should leave a tiny flat solder puddle. Practice soldering on lead scraps before attempting to solder a cherished project. Fill any gaps between lead joints with little slivers of lead before you attempt to solder them. When you have soldered all the joints between leads, check the junctures one by one to be sure none have been missed; then support the panel carefully with one hand beneath it, turn it over and solder the joints on the reverse side.

It is imperative to rest the hot iron on a special small stand when it is not in use. Otherwise you may burn a table or start a fire.

The four most common reasons solder does not adhere to lead are: the wrong kind of solder; insufficient or incorrect flux; incorrect soldering iron temperature; and soiled lead.

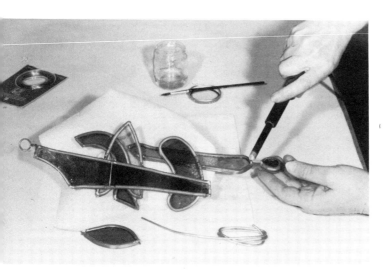

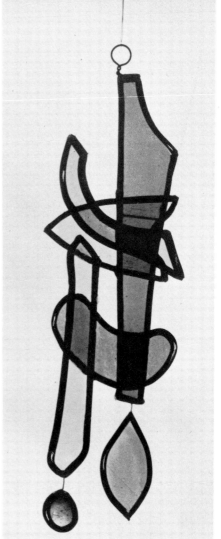

Single glass shapes are leaded as units in a complex construction. The units are soldered together. They are propped on a cushion of folded paper toweling to hold the assemblage in position while the final pieces are soldered to it.

A stained glass suspension. The pieces can be made into a mobile by wiring them separately.

2
Leaded Stained Glass

A BEGINNING

IT IS advisable to make a very simple initial leaded stained glass project before you attempt something more complex. A four-piece colorful stained glass suspension is easy to make, and it requires only a minimum of materials. Creating it will involve many of the techniques you will encounter in fashioning almost any free-form leaded stained glass object. But most important, your own successfully designed and executed stained glass ornament will inspire you to create many other delightful glass objects to beautify your home; and they make wonderful gifts for all ages.

Before you begin, read carefully the introductory sections on cutting glass, applying the lead, and soldering. Make a sketch you like and enlarge it to a full-size drawing divided into three or four sections that are drawn with gently curving or straight lines. Each space will represent a piece of colored glass; each line will represent a strip of lead. Make two carbon

copies of the full-scale drawing, one on firm paper that is cut into small patterns for cutting glass. A second copy is a work drawing on which you will assemble the project. When the glass pieces are cut out, they will be placed on the original drawing nearby to keep them organized and accessible.

Cut out the pattern pieces from the firm paper drawing, using shears to remove a $\frac{1}{16}$-inch paper strip between sections. The narrow space it leaves will represent the place to be occupied by the heart of the lead. With these small paper templates as guides, cut out the glass pieces by following detailed instructions under "Cutting the Glass." To assemble your glass, you will need a three- or four-foot strip of $\frac{1}{4}$-inch rounded H lead, a sharp knife for cutting lead, some blue steel lath nails, and a hammer. In addition, you need a soldering iron, some 60/40 solid core wire solder, and oleic acid for a soldering flux.

Tape the work drawing to a workboard and cut a piece of lead came a little longer than necessary to go completely around the glass

composition. It can be trimmed later. The first glass piece is positioned on its matching space in the work drawing. Its outer edge is inserted into the border lead, which is positioned so it abuts the drawn border line of the design, along its outside. Lath nails are driven into the workboard (right through the paper drawing) close against the outside of the lead; more nails go along the inside bare glass edge to hold the lead and glass securely together while the work proceeds. Cut and fit another lead along one side of the glass with an end trimmed to abut the border lead. Insert the remaining glass pieces into the composition, fitting them one by one with leads that abut the border lead snugly. Lengths of lead fitted between the sides of two glass pieces are always cut about $\frac{1}{16}$ inch shorter at each end than the glass sides, to allow for fitting the remaining bare glass sides into cross-leads. After each glass is inserted, tap it gently into the lead with a small block of wood held between the glass and the hammer. Never strike the bare glass; you may shatter it. As you continue to bend the border lead around the outside of the assemblage, keep it in position with lath nails. Check to assure that they do not press too tightly against the lead and make unsightly dents in it. The nails will all be pulled out when the leads have been soldered.

Once the border lead is in place around the completed composition, trim its two ends for a close fit. Butt them together carefully and anchor them with lath nails. Make certain all pieces are tight and that lead joints fit flush. If you have left any gaps between junctures, fill them with bits of lead that can be soldered over when you apply solder to each joint. When the first side is soldered (follow directions in the "Soldering" section), remove the lath nails, turn the piece over, and solder leads on the reverse side.

To make a hanger for your stained glass composition, double a three- or four-inch length of 18-gauge copper wire, insert the rounded handle of a small brush into the bent loop end and twist it three or four times. Clean and flux the copper wire. Spread the free wire ends apart and solder them to the fluxed leading on top of your hanging. The leaded glass piece can be anchored in a can of sand or vermiculite so both your hands are free to solder. When the oleic acid flux has been cleaned off the glass and lead, your stained glass composition is ready to be hung wherever moving sunlight will infuse it with shimmering beauty.

◀

FLOWERS. Old Dominion Stained Glass Studio. Leaded antique stained glass window. From the Designers' Corner of The Blenko Glass Company, Milton, West Virginia.

Make a full-scale drawing divided into four sections that are drawn with gently curved or straight lines. Trace over it to make two carbon copies, one of which is heavy drawing paper or construction paper.

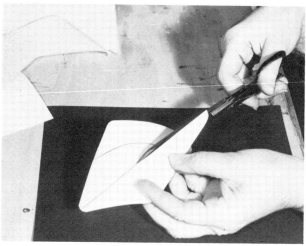

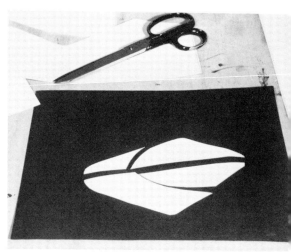

On the heavy paper copy, cut along each side of the inside lines to remove a 1/16″ paper strip between sections. The narrow space remaining represents the place to be occupied by the lead heart.

These four sections of paper are the patterns around which the glass shapes are cut.

The first glass piece is inserted into the border lead. Lath nails temporarily hold the glass and lead in place.

Another lead is cut and fitted along the side of the first glass, and a second glass is inserted. Tap the glass firmly into the lead with a small block of wood.

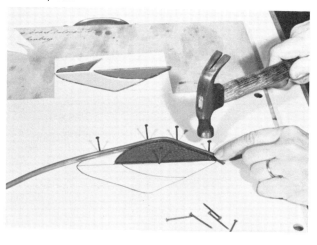

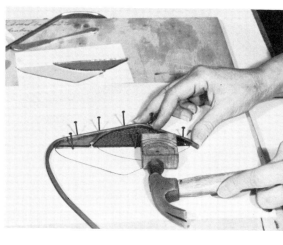

Cut a long lead strip and fit it along the inside edge of the first two glass pieces. To cut the lead, rock the knife gently as you press down. If you press the knife too hard, it will collapse the channels.

Fit lead along a curved edge by holding the glass piece and pressing the lead firmly around the curve.

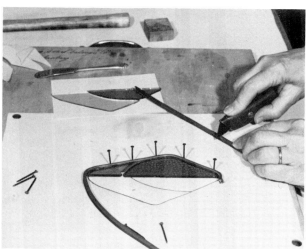

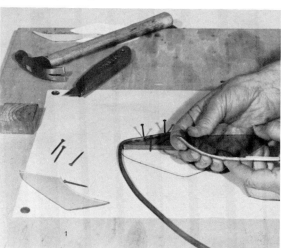

Lengths of lead are always marked and cut a little shorter than the glass edge to allow for insertion of the glass into cross leads. When the location of the cut has been marked, *remove* the lead to cut it. Trim all lead ends so they abut cross-leads snugly parallel.

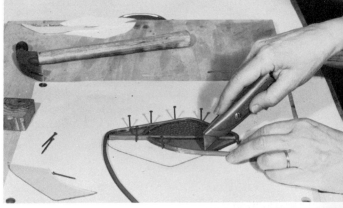

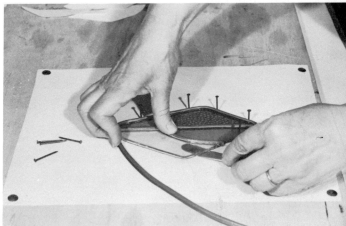

A small gadget for lifting and working a glass piece securely into the lead is made by bending a short butter knife an inch from the end. Support and brace the assemblage with one hand while the other hand works the knife and glass.

When the last piece is in place, bend the border lead around the completed composition and trim its two ends for a close fit. Hold them in place with lath nails.

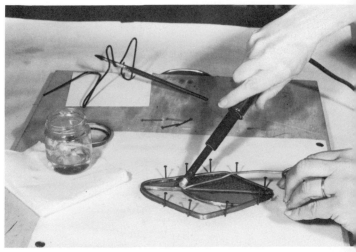

Apply flux and solder to each lead joint, then remove the nails and solder the joints on the reverse side.

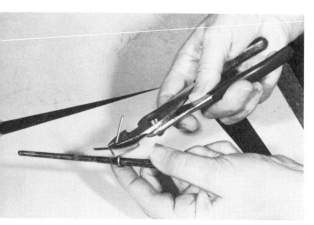

Make a hanger by doubling a 4" length of copper wire, then twist the loop around a small brush handle.

Clean and flux the wire and lead. Anchor the glass form in a can of sand to hold it so both hands are free to solder the copper wire in position. Pick up some solder with the hot iron tip and run it over the hanger ends while you are pressing them against the lead came. A wooden snap clothespin is convenient for holding the wire hanger in position.

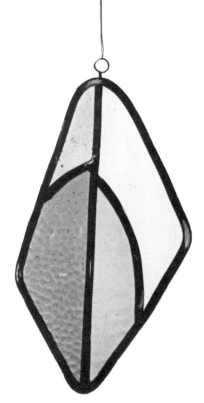

The completed stained glass ornament.

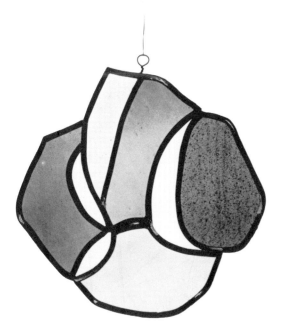

Four units leaded separately and soldered together with open spaces between them.

THE LIGHT TABLE

Although stained glass appears at its best when it is viewed by natural sunlight, this is not always possible in a studio or home workshop situation. As you begin to work with a greater number of stained glass shapes, a good light table can enable you to see relationships of glass colors and their values. It permits you to view colors spread out together. In addition, it is a most important aid for painting on glass. The light table illustrated here is so simple it can be assembled by anyone if the side and end boards and the legs are precut by a lumber company. The table has ball bearing casters installed on the bottom of each leg. These casters with special fixtures for installing them are available at most large hardware stores. When the table is in use, its legs must be anchored in shallow coasters. Casters on the legs are extremely useful when you want to push the light table out of the way. If you prefer a light box instead of a light table, the same specifications can be used by substituting short posts instead of legs. A light box can be set on a table or shelf. Dimensions for the light table are: side walls, 30 by 15 by ¾ inches; end walls, 22½ by 15 by ¾ inches; legs, 30¼ by 1¾ by 1¾ inches.

Nail the side and end boards together to form a box frame. To brace them securely, the legs are held in place in the corners of the box with two large C-clamps while bolts are being installed through holes drilled into the legs as well as the sides and ends of the corners, as shown. The bolts are staggered to prevent interference with one another when they are bolted through the legs to anchor the sides and ends firmly in position. Notice that a space is left at the top of each leg to accommodate ½-inch strips that will be fastened in place with screws ¼ inch below the top edge of the table, to support a sheet of ¼-inch frosted plate glass. Frosted glass is regular plate that can be sandblasted by any large glass company. A heavy plywood bottom for the box or table has corners cut out so it can be slipped over

the legs (the table is upended) and fastened in place with screws. The entire interior of the light box part of the table is painted white to give good light reflection and increase illumination under the glass.

Artificial light does not approximate natural daylight for selecting glass, but warm white fluorescent lights help to identify colors and values. Wire the lights together across the bottom of the box. Run the wire through the end wall to a single switch on the outside. A ten-foot cord is a great convenience.

Freestanding stained glass form. Jack Landis.

Freestanding stained glass forms. Jack Landis.

A space is left at the top of each leg to leave room for wood strips to support the frosted glass top of the table.

Nail together side and end boards of the light table. To brace them securely, two C-clamps hold them in place while holes are drilled for bolting the legs to the corner.

A plywood bottom for the light box is slipped over the legs and fastened in place with screws.

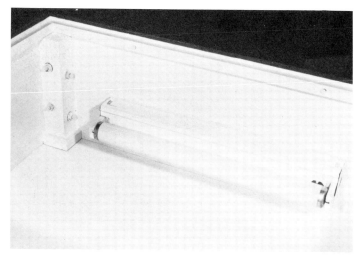

Notice that leg bolts are staggered to allow a leg to be bolted to a side and end board. Lights are installed across the bottom of the box. The interior is painted white.

Illumination shines through to identify colors and values.

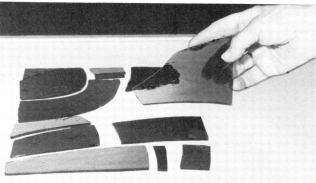

CHRYSANTHEMUM. Edward J. Byrne. Three-dimensional glass sculpture. Red, orange, and yellow. 36'' diameter.

Edward Byrne works over a stained glass composition on a light table in his Doylestown, Pennsylvania, studio. *Photo by courtesy of* The Philadelphia Inquirer.

PATTERNS AND CARTOONS

A stained glass window or panel begins with a small-scale drawing transposed into a full-size precise pattern or *cartoon*. Two additional copies of the full-size drawing are made: a work drawing and a pattern on heavy paper to be cut into templates. This latter paper must be sturdy but not too thick. Firm drawing paper or smooth heavy wrapping paper will do for these small patterns around which each individual glass piece is cut. Cardboard is too thick; it can prevent the cutting wheel from riding smoothly around each pattern piece.

The cartoon for a leaded stained glass panel must include three important measurements around the border: the full-size line that represents the outer perimeter of the panel's wide border lead; the cut-size line indicating where the glass pieces next to the border will abut the heart of the border lead; and the sight-size line showing the inside edge of the border lead. If you are making a panel or window that must fit into a specified opening, these measurements must be accurate so the outside edge of the perimeter lead will fit exactly.

Because leads may tend to sag, a leaded window that is much higher than three feet tall, should have supportive horizontal one-inch iron T-bars fastened into the window opening at regular intervals to carry the weight of glass and lead. In addition, it requires ½-inch-round horizontal reinforcement bars every foot to brace it against bulging. Five-inch metal ties made of 18-gauge copper wire soldered to the leads of the window can be fastened around the bars. These supports are all designated on the original cartoon. (The making of large stained glass windows is not covered in this book.)

When the full-scale drawing is completed, retrace over the lines of the design with a felt tipped marker to make thick lines that represent the leads of the panel. The heart of each lead forms a thin wall between contiguous glass pieces as they are inserted into the stained glass panel. Space allotted to the lead heart must be allowed for in cutting out the pattern pieces and their subsequent matching glass shapes.

The next step is to make two copies of the cartoon. First, lay down the firm paper (from which patterns will be cut). On top of it, place a large sheet of good quality carbon paper, carbon side down. If large sheets are not available, lap or butt several small sheets and tape them together on the back with cellophane tape. On top of the carbon paper lay a sheet of paper for the working drawing (to be explained later.) Next comes another large sheet of carbon paper. Finally, the precisely drawn cartoon is positioned on top of all. Thumbtack them all securely to the workboard, pressing each tack firmly through the corners of all these layers to prevent slippage. Some craftsmen prefer to tape each layer to a worktable instead of tacking them to a workboard. When all the layers of paper and carbons are securely in position, take a sharp pencil and trace through the *center* of the thick lines of the design with enough pressure to reach the bottom layer of paper. From time to time as you are tracing, take out one or two thumbtacks to check whether your tracings have gone through all paper layers. Before you take the papers apart, number each space that represents a piece of glass.

When tracing is completed, separate the papers. The *working drawing* will be positioned on the workboard when glazing begins. The *original cartoon* is located nearby so it can be consulted when necessary. Spaces representing pieces of glass are numbered the same on all three drawings. Colors can be written in pencil in case of future changes. The *third heavier drawing* will be cut into small patterns representing the glass pieces. If you have access to a pair of cartoon shears, this is the best tool for cutting out pattern pieces. The shears have a double blade and a single blade; as they cut along the lines of the drawing, a narrow paper strip is removed, leaving a thin space between each pattern to indicate where the heart of the lead goes between glass pieces. Cartoon shears are not always available. A substitute cutting device used by beginners is made by sandwiching a piece of $1/16$-inch cardboard between two single-edged razor blades. They are taped together in two directions. Of course small sharp scissors can be used to cut along each side of the black line to remove it, if you prefer.

To use the razor blade cutting device, position the heavy paper pattern on smooth-topped corrugated cardboard or several sheets of paper to cushion it so the blades of the tool can sink through the pattern and actually cut into it. Draw the blades firmly along so they straddle the pattern lines. Note: the middle, or *cut-size,* line in the *border* of the composition represents the edge of border glass pieces. No narrow paper strip is removed between it and the remaining border area, which is entirely cut away with ordinary scissors. If you use the

razor blade tool for cutting out pattern pieces, be sure to use new blades or blades that are sharp. When they are pressed firmly and held perpendicular, both razor blades should cut through the paper. You may find that only one blade seems to be cutting, due to a tendency of most persons to hold the tool on a slant; the other blade will at least leave an indented line that can be cut through with ordinary scissors.

Position each cutout template on the original cartoon over matching numbered spaces. As each template is picked up and a glass shape is cut out around it, both the glass and the template are repositioned on the cartoon. This is the best way to keep all these shapes organized and easily accessible. When all glass pieces for a stained glass composition have been cut, it is time to begin leading them or *glazing* the panel.

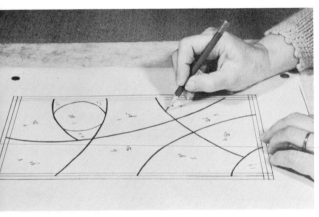

When a design has been drawn full-scale between the three outside lines, trace over the lines of the design with a felt-tipped marker.

To use the razor-blade cutting device, position the paper pattern on smooth-topped corrugated cardboard, which cushions it so the blades can sink through the pattern and cut it.

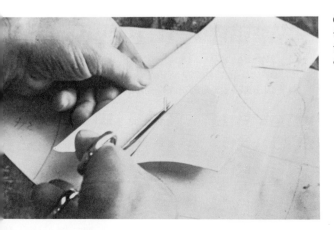

Cutting patterns with a regular pattern shears to allow for lead caming. The single top blade sinks between two lower blades to remove a narrow strip. *Photo by courtesy of Willet Stained Glass Studios.*

LEADING A RECTANGULAR PANEL

When all the glass shapes have been cut for a rectangular panel, tape the work drawing to a workboard that is made of soft wood. Most plywood is too hard to receive the small nails that will hold your work in place temporarily while you are leading it. These nails must be removed from the workboard when leading (glazing) is completed. It is difficult to remove the nails from hard wood without bruising your fingers. Cut two half-inch lath strips, one a little longer than the length of the work drawing and one a little longer than its width. They will guide the placement of the glass and strips of lead. Position them at a right angle to each other on a lower corner of the work drawing with their *inside* edges abutting the *outer full-size* lines of the drawing; this allows room for the flat border leads. Space for these border leads must be included in the original cartoon measurements of the window opening or the frame if you are making a panel. One wood strip runs along the vertical edge of the drawing from top to bottom; the other strip runs along the horizontal lower edge of the work drawing with one of its ends firmly abutting the vertical wooden strip. When both of these strips are nailed into place (with nails going through the paper drawing), it is time to begin leading.

Remember that lead must be stretched and its flanges must be opened before it is used. Stretching it straightens out kinks, firms up the lead, and takes up slack in the soft lead so it fits snugly around the stained glass shapes. If you neglect to stretch it, the lead and glass composition may become wobbly and insecure. When you construct a hanging panel, its hangers should be installed directly above perpendicular lengths of lead in the design; otherwise the border lead to which the small wire hangers are soldered may begin to sag and "let go" the glass after it has hung for a while if the lead is not vigorously stretched before it is used.

To stretch lead, fasten one end of a strip in a strong vise or lead stretcher, grasp the other end of it with pliers and pull firmly until the lead is taut and its channels are straightened. If it is twisted, untwist it between pulls. When you pull on the free end with pliers, hold the lead near the pliers with your other hand and brace yourself with one foot behind you so you do not fall backwards if the lead should break suddenly. Pull firmly until you can feel the lead stretch and become taut. When two persons are working together, each one can pull on an end of the lead until it is stretched. Draw the wet and flattened end of a ¼-inch dowel stick (or glazier's lathekin) along the channels to open them up so different thicknesses of stained glass will fit easily between the flanges. If you are using antique glass, you will find that it has varying thicknesses in one glass sheet, which accounts for its handsome lighter and darker shading of color. When you have stretched a long strip of lead, cut it into shorter convenient lengths and lay it out on a table without doubling or kinking it.

To cut the lead, first score it to mark location of the intended cut; then rock the knife blade gently as you press down cautiously through the lead. Too much or sudden pressure will collapse the channels. It is wise to practice on scraps of lead. The lead-cutting knife used for projects in this book is a standard matt knife with removable blades that can be replaced or sharpened. They are sold in most art supply stores. If you have access to a glazier's curved knife, of course that will be fine; these knives are not always available to the novice.

Place the cartoon beside your workboard with the glass pieces temporarily in place over corresponding drawn spaces. Give it a final check before glazing begins; any changes after this point may waste time and lead. For the border of your panel, cut two stretched and open lengths of ⅜-inch flat H-lead and fit them into the angle of the wooden lath boards you have nailed to the workboard. One lead strip should run along the top of the lower *horizontal lath strip.* The length of the second lead is pressed against the *vertical lath strip* with its bottom end butting down against the horizontal *lead* strip. (Read these instructions again as you follow them in the illustrations on these pages.) Cut the free ends of the leads a little longer than necessary; they will be trimmed when they have been worked into the glass composition. To hold these border leads in place while the first glass pieces are inserted, you may tack the free ends to the workboard temporarily. Make sure the two lengths of lead are butted firmly together in the lower corner. Some craftsmen prefer to pinch the lower end of the vertical lead and slip it into the horizontal lead instead of butting them. Either way, avoid leaving gaps between lead joints that will create problems when you are soldering them.

When the two border leads are securely in place, check their flanges to see whether they are still open along their lengths. If they are not, they can be opened with a handy gadget called a "stopping knife," which you can make by bending a short butter knife about an inch from the end. Or a slender steel table knife can be shortened, ground smooth, and bent near the end. When you have cleared the lead channels, press the first glass piece into the channels where they meet at the corner. Here again, the stopping knife is useful. Slip it under the glass to lift and work it deeper into the corner channels.

The next important step is to place a small block of wood against the glass piece and tap it firmly but gently into the leads. This procedure must be followed after every piece or two are placed, if you would have a snugly fitting firm leaded glass composition. Fit a lead piece into place along each side of the corner glass piece, butting one end of the lead against the border lead. When you have evaluated how much to cut that end of lead so it will abut at an angle parallel to the border lead for a snug fit, remove it and trim it. Trim the other lead end just a little shorter than the glass to allow for insertion of the glass into the cross-lead that divides it from the next row of glass shapes. Build up pieces of glass contiguous to the first corner glass, fanning out from it and supporting it. As each piece of glass is fitted with lead and inserted into bordering leads, tap it gently with the wood block.

As you are building up the glass design,

check the drawing under your work to be sure each piece coincides with drawn lines. Sometimes a piece may need a minor amount of grozing (chipping) before it will fit into its designated space. But first tap it in firmly to be sure it is seated and really needs grozing; pieces that are cut accurately and tapped into the leads securely should need very little or no trimming. When you are inserting the glass, avoid surrounding an empty space to the point that the next glass piece cannot be slid into it without requiring the removal of some of the glass already in position.

After each glass is fitted with lead and seated, secure it in place *temporarily* with thin sharp blue steel lath nails driven close beside the lead and bare glass sides, two or three nails to the piece. Take care not to press the nails into the lead or you may have a ragged-looking lead when the nails are removed. The nails are pulled out along the working side of each piece as adjoining leads and glass are positioned. The traditional and useful leading nails (or horseshoe nails) used by professional craftsmen are not easy for the novice to locate. They are nonexistent in some localities. Steel lath nails will serve our purpose very well for simple projects.

Once the glass and leads are all in place, it is time to fit the last two border leads into position. Inspect each glass edge and lead end where they abut the border. If any glass protrudes over the middle line (cut-size line) of the border, it should be tapped in firmly with the wooden block to determine whether looseness in the assemblage caused the bulge. If there is still some glass extending over the line, remove the piece and groze it to fit, or better yet, replace it with a new piece redesigned to fit. Trim the lead ends to make a smooth border juncture. Finally, the wide flat border leads are positioned over the glass and smaller lead ends; two more lath strips are nailed into position against them to hold them in place. When you have inspected your work and filled any lead joint gaps with bits of lead, it is time to solder the work. Do not remove the nails from the lath strips until the first side of the panel is completely soldered. (Read carefully the instructions detailed in the section "Soldering.") Then remove the nails, support the panel with one hand braced under it, and when you have turned it over carefully solder the second side.

When both sides of the panel have been soldered, push gray glazing compound (putty) against the leads with your thumb and work it under them wherever possible. It holds the glass tight and makes a window weatherproof. Clean up excess putty by running a pointed stick along the leads. The flat border leads are pressed firmly with a putty knife to work out excess glazing compound. To absorb and remove the remainder of putty and the oleic acid, sprinkle a couple of handfuls of whiting (calcium carbonate) over the panel and scrub it around with a stiff brush. Brush away the dust and dirt with a soft brush and rags. The glass is cleaned in the usual way with detergent water or regular glass cleaner.

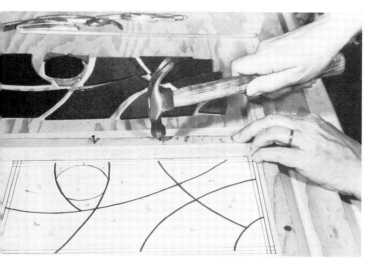

Two ½" lath strips guide the placement of the glass and lead. Nail them at right angles to one another on a lower corner of the work drawing. The glass pieces are laid out in correct sequence on the paper patterns beside the work.

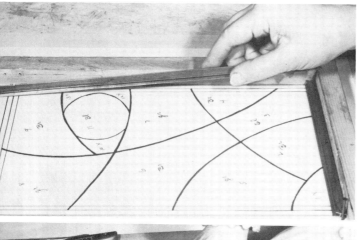

Fit two lengths of lead into the angle of the wood lath boards. The first glass pieces will be inserted into the corner of the leads.

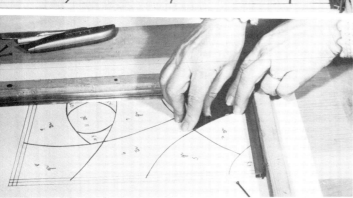

Press the first glass piece into the lead channels where they meet at the corner.

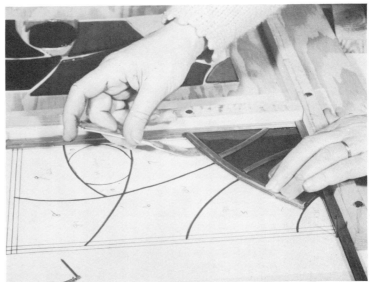

A short bent knife (stopping knife) lifts up the glass to help seat it into the channels of the leads.

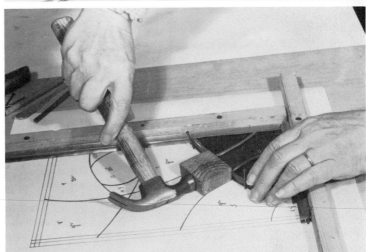

Place a small wood block against the leaded glass and tap it firmly to make a snug-fitting composition.

Small lath nails hold the composition in place temporarily. The leads and glass follow lines in the drawing.

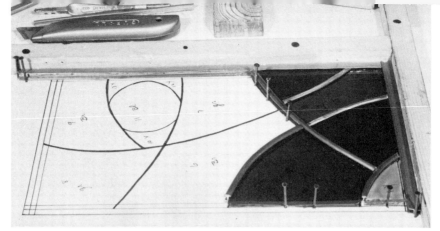

Additional glass pieces and leads are inserted. The bare glass edge borders the middle cut-size line.

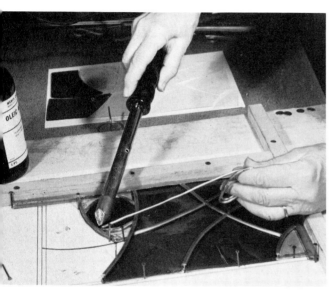

Although a rectangular or square panel is usually leaded up completely before it is soldered, a small grouping of pieces in a larger composition is sometimes soldered into place to hold it secure as the panel is assembled.

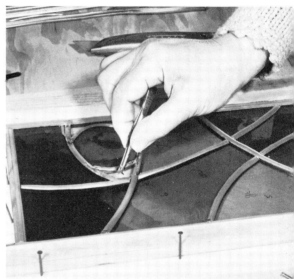

All glass and leads are in place; the final border leads are positioned and anchored with nails and a third lath strip. Fill any gaps in lead junctures with bits of lead.

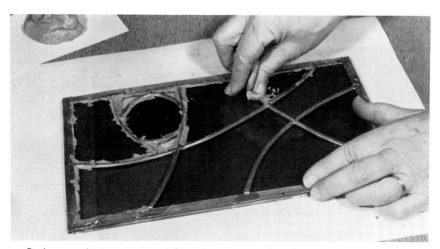

Push gray glazing compound (putty) against and under each lead with your thumb. It holds the glass tight and will make a window panel weatherproof.

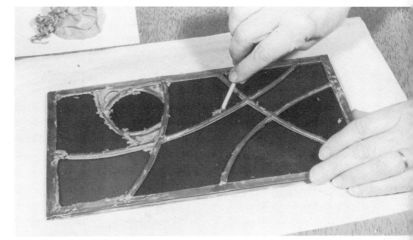

Remove excess putty by running a pointed dowel stick, meat skewer, or pencil along all the leads.

Flat border leads are pressed smooth with a putty knife to work out excess compound.

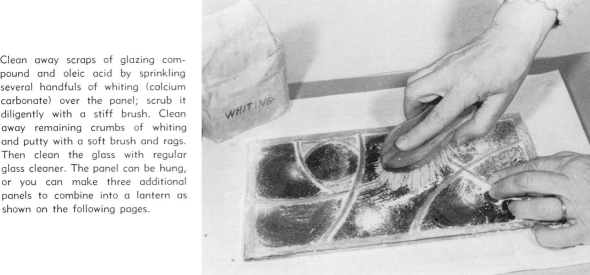

Clean away scraps of glazing compound and oleic acid by sprinkling several handfuls of whiting (calcium carbonate) over the panel; scrub it diligently with a stiff brush. Clean away remaining crumbs of whiting and putty with a soft brush and rags. Then clean the glass with regular glass cleaner. The panel can be hung, or you can make three additional panels to combine into a lantern as shown on the following pages.

A FOUR-PANEL LANTERN

The panels for a four-sided lantern are individually formed before they are assembled. Follow the instructions given in the preceding section. Designs may be similar for all four panels, or they may alternate. They can, of course, be different in all four panels, but this would be a more complex undertaking. It is advisable to keep them simple and to employ medium and light colors. The electric bulbs used in stained glass lanterns do not transmit the kind of illumination that comes from a sunny sky. Dark glass transmits very little light.

To shield the light fixture from sight, the lantern top can be formed of metal or opalescent glass. A top made from glass sections is not the easiest kind for an initial project. The top for the demonstration lantern is an upside-down copper tray, the kind sold in metal enameling supply shops. You will be delighted to find a variety of copper trays in many sizes and shapes: square, round, octagonal, and others. A $3/8$-inch hole must be cut in the metal top to accommodate electric wiring and a top ring for holding the chain or rope hanger. If you cannot cut the hole, any metalwork shop will do it for a nominal fee.

Panel dimensions for the demonstration lantern are $6\frac{1}{2}$ by 11 inches. Border leads are $3/8$-inch flat H-leads; leads for the panel design are $\frac{1}{4}$ inch, with the exception of the rounded glass piece, which is fitted with $3/16$-inch lead. The copper tray top is $7\frac{1}{2}$ inches square. On each panel side edge, the border lead flange, which faces toward the *inside* of the lantern, is bent to about a 90-degree angle to the panel, permitting the *outside* flanges at each corner to butt together. Stand the first two panels on end at a right angle to one another, as illustrated in the accompanying photograph. Prop them in position with any straightedged blocks such as bricks. Pinch the bent lead flanges together down the inside of the corner and solder them along the edge. A small soldering iron tip is very convenient for inside corners.

Set the third panel in position and support it with additional bricks. Once it is soldered in place, lay the assemblage down with the remaining open side toward the table top. Brace the two panels that rest on the table with bricks laid against their outside surfaces while the fourth panel is positioned between them and soldered, first from one end, then from the other end. At this point, the lantern is set upside down so 8-gauge copper wire that has been annealed can be soldered into the bottom lead channels and around corners to brace them. The wire is annealed by heating it red hot, then dousing it in water. Annealing metal makes it pliable and easy to work. If it stiffens as you work it, anneal it again. Until the square top is soldered to the lantern, care must be exercised in handling the work to keep the four joined panels in a right-angled position. Once the firm metal top is soldered in place, it will keep the lantern squared.

If you want to conceal the outside juncture crack between the leads that run down the length of each outside corner of the lantern, split some $3/8$-inch or $\frac{1}{2}$-inch flat H-leads down through the heart with a chisel or shears to make flat lead strips. Tack a strip to each corner with solder, top and bottom. Press the soft lead smoothly against and around each corner with your fingers and solder it in several additional places along the edges. Set the completed body of the lantern aside while the square copper top (with a $3/8$-inch hole cut in it) is scrubbed clean with scouring powder, rinsed, dried, and set upside down on a bench wheel.

The solder used for bonding the copper top to the lantern is 40/60 low fusing self-fluxing paste solder called "Fast." This type solder is doubtless available under other trade names. Copper oxidizes so quickly when heat is applied that the 60/40 solid core wire solder used for leading cannot be used for soldering copper to lead. An exception is when copper wire (which heats up rapidly) is soldered to make hangers for suspending stained glass mobiles. Self-fluxing paste solder excludes air from the metal surface, which deters oxidation and allows bonding readily. Set the lantern upside down on the copper top and mark its intended location with a pencil. Then remove the lantern and brush paste solder along each section of the inverted top (copper tray) over the pencil marking.

Set the lantern upside down again on the metal top, carefully matching the lantern to the brushed solder. There are bound to be a few crevices between the lantern and the metal top. Cut some small flat slivers of lead and brush solder on both surfaces of the little lead pieces. For extra reinforcement, insert two or three of them securely against the juncture between the lantern and the metal top on each side. Once all the small lead bits are in place, it is time to apply the heat. Low heat is sufficient to melt this solder; a propane cylinder torch, the kind bought in hardware stores, will

work very well. Hold a length of asbestos paper in front of the stained glass and leads of the lantern to protect them while you apply gentle heat from below the copper as illustrated. Hold the flame under the area to be soldered and *play it back and forth slowly*. The tip of the flame should be held about an inch from the metal. Keep close watch over it. As soon as the solder turns silver and shiny, *remove the torch*. Leave the lantern undisturbed for several minutes before you set it upright so the solder can harden.

Most electric lamp and fixture stores carry an assortment of accessories for lanterns. The parts used for the four-panel lantern shown here are a lamp ring (also called a *loop*), a threaded *nipple,* a *light socket,* and a *separator plate* that fits between the metal lantern top and the threaded nipple. Decorative chain is used to hang the lamp or lantern.

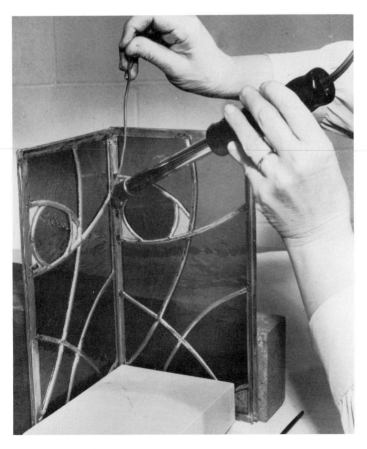

Stand the first two panels on end at a right angle. Prop them securely in place with any straight-edged blocks such as bricks. Solder them along the inside of the corner angle.

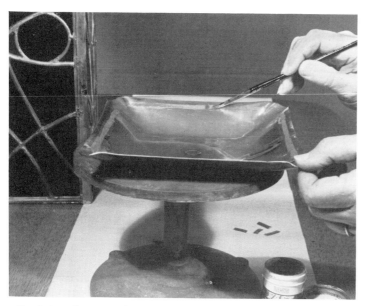

Brush low fusing 40/60 paste solder along each section of the copper top where the lantern will be positioned. Notice the small lead pieces that will be soldered into the juncture between the lantern and its top.

Hold asbestos in front of the glass and lead to protect them from the torch as you play it slowly along under the solder.

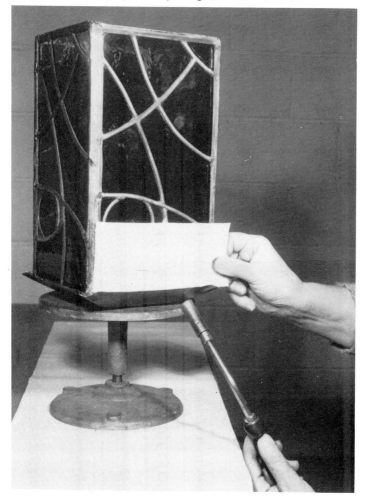

The completed lantern with electric fittings. Antique stained glass provides shimmering color.

The interior leads in this free-form design extend outward to become part of the border glass lead, then they curve into the interior again. There is no continuous framing lead.

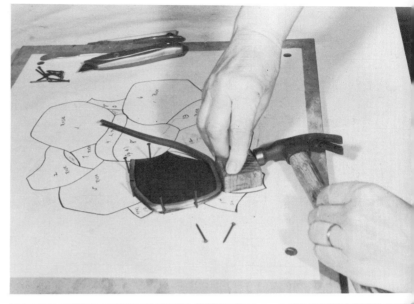

Small leaf shapes have well-defined corners. The lead is cut apart at each corner and ends are mitered together again.

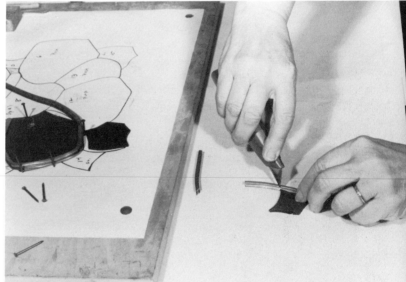

Lead joints in a free-form design are soldered as the leading progresses.

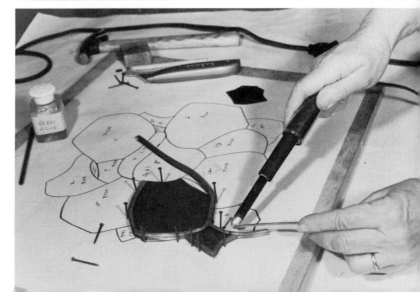

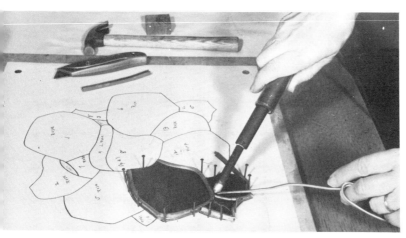

Apply and solder the leads straight across the panel. Include the center glass piece with the first row.

As you work, anchor the leads all around the edge of the assemblage with lath nails until the project is complete, then remove the nails.

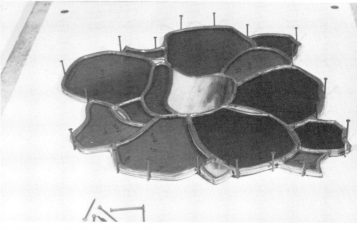

A colorful antique glass panel makes a decorative and striking window treatment against the sun or snow. Colors are opalescent rose and green for the center and one leaf. Rose, amethyst, olive, and green for the rest of the flower.

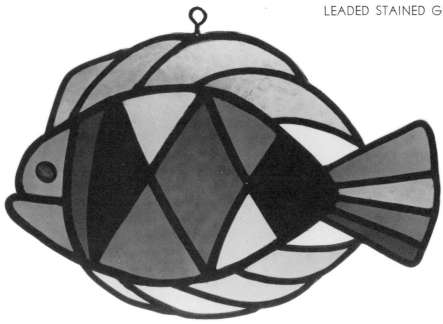

Lead camed antique glass fish. Bright blue, green, and red. The body is leaded first, then the tail and fins beginning with the rear fins. Open spaces are left between the rear fins and body.

COMBINING STAINED GLASS TECHNIQUES

Colored glass is an exciting medium for craftsmen. Although a form may be simple, the moment sunlight floods through it, brilliant shimmering color delights the eye. Pieces of contrasting bonded stained glass and crushed glass sparkle and glow. You can provide a subtle layered effect with small shapes fused to glass that will be bonded, leaded, or bent. Add an exotic touch to dull leads by rubbing metallic paste finishes over them to transform them with rich coloring. For an exciting way to create with glass, make use of a variety of materials and methods to add color and texture wherever you want them.

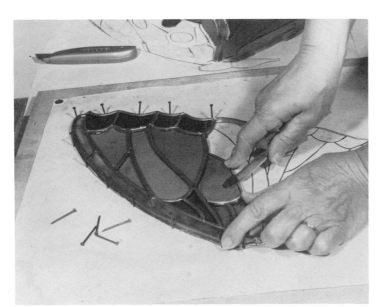

A LARGE BUTTERFLY HANGING

Leading for a large stained glass butterfly begins at the border of the top right wing and progresses down the panel.

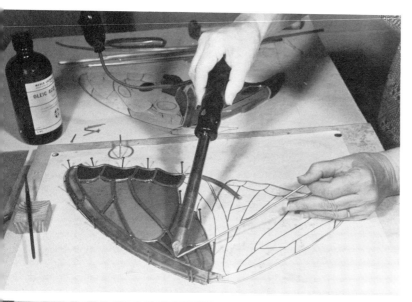

Leading along each side of the wing sections is continuous; it is soldered together at each wing tip. After every two or three glass pieces are inserted, they are tapped securely into the lead and soldered.

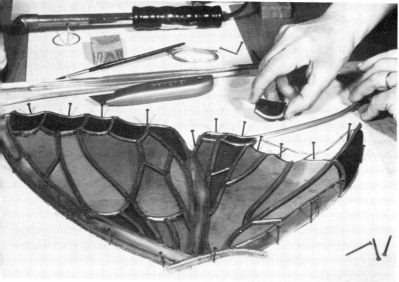

One piece of lead is bent around two sides of each border scalloped piece before it is inserted into the border leading.

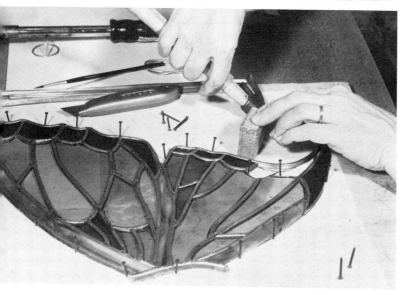

Tap each piece firmly so it lines up with the drawn design underneath it.

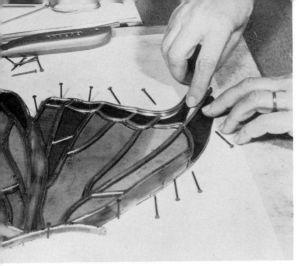

Final wing pieces are inserted. Notice that some of the nails are removed so border leads can be fitted.

The last lead is fitted along a wing edge. Glass shapes are worked into the leading with the small knife. An end of lead is left extending one-half inch long at wing tip and is curved to give a decorative effect and to provide a hanging hook at each upper wing tip.

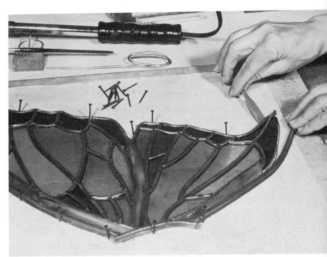

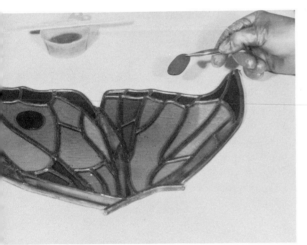

After the glass has been thoroughly cleaned, wing spots are epoxied into position. The epoxy is dried completely. Finally, the wing is turned over and soldered at each joint. The leads are puttied to give added firmness to the composition. Scrub away the soil and putty with whiting as described earlier. A second wing is prepared in reverse, identical to the first.

A hammered, contoured copper body is made in two sections. Brush 40/60 low-fusing paste solder along the edges of each half, inside and outside. Bind them securely with regular jeweler's binding wire around the head and tail and insert the body into the leading of the wings where they normally join the body.

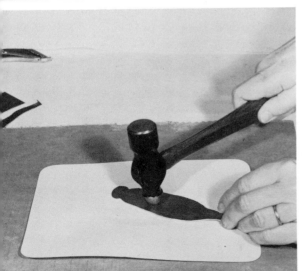

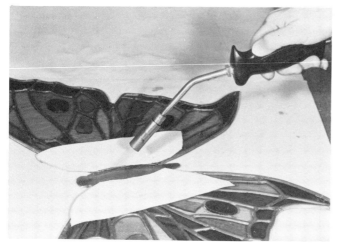

Two pieces of asbestos paper protect the glass and lead while a propane torch applies the low heat required to melt this solder.

Achieve a final rich effect on any of your leaded stained glass creations by rubbing the leads and solder with any of the nontoxic lustrous metallic paste finishes. They come in dozens of beautiful metallic colors. The butterfly leading is covered with bronze wax paste. The antennae are made from a doubled wire soldered to the head with 40/60 solder.

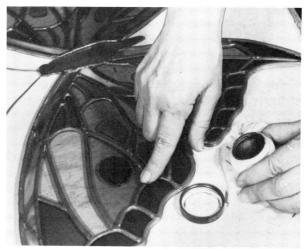

The completed butterfly is 26" from wing tip to wing tip. It is 16" deep. It can be made strong by soldering slender steel rods on the back side that cross the body diagonally behind the opalescent edges of the wings. This butterfly is adequately supported with very fine steel wires that suspend it from the small lead "hooks" at the tips of the upper wings. It is deep blue, green, orange, and lavender, and a very light blue glass over most of the butterfly gives it a gossamer fragile appearance, even though it is such a large composition.

SMALL WINDOW PANELS

Glass for a small leaded window panel is spread out on the light table for a final check of color relationships. The separate glass piece that has been removed from the composition will be painted and fired before it is leaded into place.

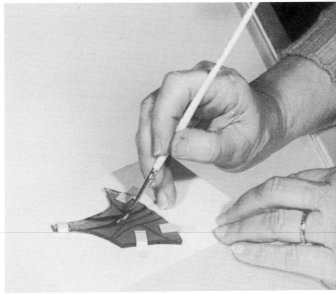

The glass piece is taped to a design over the light table so it can be revolved as painting progresses. A wood bridge is not needed for this one glass piece.

A complex design with irregularly shaped pieces must be braced securely with one hand while they are tapped firmly into position in leading. Otherwise they will slide out of place when they are tapped with the wood block. Geometric compositions are easier to control. Glass pieces must coincide with the drawn design beneath them.

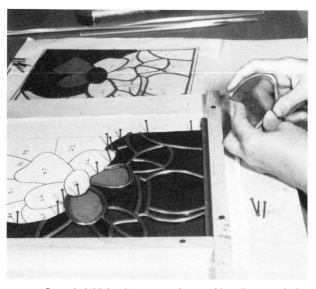

Rounded H lead is pressed smoothly all around the curved piece before it is inserted into the assemblage.

When the panel is completely leaded and soldered on both sides, the glass is cleaned thoroughly to remove oil from the oleic acid. Several small glass shapes are epoxied into place for a sparkling effect. It is wise to wear gloves when you use epoxy products. Avoid inhaling the fumes.

The panel gleams with color against the sunlit snow. It is puttied into place against the regular window glass.

3
Bonded Glass

INTRODUCTION TO BONDING

A BONDED glass panel begins with a sheet of colorless double-strength window glass or plate glass for a base. When it has been cleaned carefully, small stained glass shapes in various sizes, thicknesses, and colors are epoxied to it. Because the bonded glass composition does not have the supportive dark linear design quality of leaded glass, some definite variation in value must be provided with dark glass accents or dark grouting worked between the applied glass shapes. When you become bolder, you may add small chips of faceted glass, segments of clear glass adhered flat or on their edges, and even materials other than glass. Although your first efforts may produce a few cracked and shivered glass assemblages, you should be rewarded eventually with exciting and delightful ideas for design. Improved technical mastery will soon translate them into successful glass art.

The undulating quality that gives beauty to antique glass makes it difficult to bond without creating some irregular bubbles be-

tween it and the clear glass base, an effect that can be quite decorative. However, if you do not care for this effect, it is suggested that you use rolled cathedral glass, which has one smooth surface suitable for bubble-free bonding. The glass must be prepared *before the epoxy is mixed.* For safety's sake, all glass edges are sanded smooth under water. Wash stained glass and clear glass base with hot detergent water, rinse it in warm water, and dry it completely. Take care to support the glass by its edges to avoid transferring skin oil to the clean surfaces. Epoxy will not bond securely to damp or soiled glass.

Epoxy adhesives come in two containers: one is the resin and the other is the hardener. The two components must be blended thoroughly before use. For very small projects, epoxy can be bought in tubes. Epoxy is bought in quarts or gallons for large important projects. Be sure to use *epoxy* resin and hardener especially formulated for glass on glass bonding.* *Polyester* resins usually shrink when

* Epoxy used for *sheet glass* bonding projects in this book is Thermoset Resin #600 with Thermoset Hardener #37.

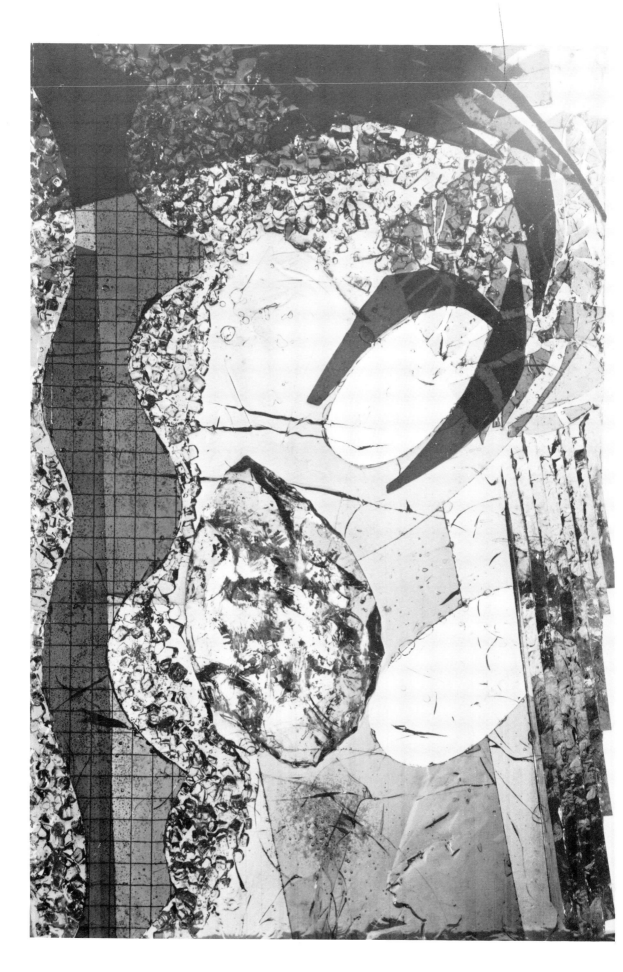

they dry and they may set up stresses in the glass that can cause large bonded glass projects to crack.

Before epoxying begins, clear the table top and the surrounding area where the work will be done. The table *must be level*. Otherwise pieces may slide out of position while the adhesive is drying. Mix only the amount you can apply in 30 to 40 minutes. Work diligently so all pieces are epoxied and pressed into place before the adhesive starts to set. The resin, the hardener, the pieces of glass, and the working room temperature should all be kept between 75° and 85°F throughout the process. Make certain the area is well ventilated and avoid inhaling the fumes. It is advisable to wear thin plastic gloves that can be bought in hardware or paint stores, when you work with epoxy resins; some skins are sensitive to resin.

A thin film of the epoxy cement provides the greatest adhesive strength. Epoxy has a different coefficient of expansion from glass. When stained glass is bonded to plate glass or double-strength window glass in large windows or panels, stresses are set up in the glass if it is exposed to bright sunlight for long periods of time. A large stained glass panel will absorb heat faster than clear colorless glass and it will tend to expand; the darker the color of the glass, the greater is the strain. If large sheets of stained glass, or even large segments, are encased entirely in resin top and bottom, they are almost certain to crack when the stained glass begins to expand. But a thin layer of the adhesive applied beneath stained glass pieces causes less strain and less hazard of breaking when the pieces are no longer than eight inches. If a design calls for a long piece of dark glass, use a series of shorter pieces spaced $\frac{1}{16}$ inch between segments. Follow the epoxy manufacturer's instructions. Remember, *other resins may mix differently*. Do not mix up more epoxy than you can apply in 30 to 40 minutes. A half ounce of resin and a half ounce of hardener make a considerable amount. The beginner tends to mix too great a quantity at one time.

Once the epoxy ingredients have been blended the required amount of time, pick up a clean piece of glass, spread it evenly and thinly with epoxy, position it exactly and press it firmly in place on the clear sheet of glass, following the drawn design underneath the window glass. Continue epoxying and applying glass pieces and pressing firmly. If you plan to apply grout between the glass shapes when the epoxy has dried, the resin that oozes out between glass pieces when you press them down must be removed with a toothpick or other means and wiped on paper toweling. If the epoxy is left to fill the cracks, there will be no place for the grout. By this time you may have smeared some epoxy on the pieces of stained glass. Do not be too concerned; as soon as the epoxy has started to set and become rubbery, but before it hardens, it can be scraped away with a single-edged razor blade and removed completely with epoxy solvent. Moisten the cloth lightly so solvent does not run under the epoxied glass and ruin the epoxy's adhesive qualities. Always wear plastic gloves when you use any kind of solvent; if this is neglected, the solvent may carry chemicals deep into your skin. And of course do not clean your hands with solvents.

◀

Bonded stained glass exhibition panel. Willet Stained Glass Studios. Farbigem process.

BONDING GLASS—RANDOM SHAPES

Shaped glass remnants obtained from a glass studio or an art glass supply company often make interesting and beautiful compositions when they are bonded to window glass with epoxy resin. Studio glass scraps separated from actual glass designs have exciting and useful shapes. For a first project, it is advisable to select light colorful hues until you are experienced in using darker glass for accents in a composition.

Lay a sheet of double-strength window glass on the light box or on white paper so the glass colors are easily seen. Spread a number of glass pieces directly on the glass sheet; move them around until you have a pleasing arrangement. They may be laid closely together or with spaces between them. Some of them may require minor trimming with short straight cuts or grozing. (See "Cutting the Glass.") When you have made a final selection of glass shapes, wash, rinse, and dry them as explained earlier. The clean colored glass pieces are positioned on clean paper to one side of the window glass in the same order they will have when they are bonded to the clear glass. It is helpful to make a full-size drawing of the final arrangement of the pieces, and to put it under the window glass to guide placement of the epoxied stained glass.

Read carefully all the directions on epoxy containers before you mix the resin and hard-ener as specified. The two parts must be blended thoroughly. As soon as you apply the adhesive in a thin coat to the underside of a glass shape, press it firmly into position on the clear glass pane. If you use a spreading stick, it can be wiped clean with a rag or paper towel that you can discard at little cost. Should you apply epoxy with a brush, in a short time your brush may accumulate a mass of resin in various stages of hardening and it may have to be discarded. When all the glass is in place, let the panel dry for at least 24 hours. If any pieces are moved after the epoxy starts to set, the epoxy will show up as cloudy distortions in the glass. When the adhesive has set, grout may be applied between the glass.

Mix powdered grout with water to damp clay consistency. Pack it between glass pieces with a tiny spatula or cardboard edge, then smooth it evenly. Remove all surplus grout from the tops of glass pieces immediately; it will be very difficult to remove after it sets. *To keep grout from cracking* while it dries, cover the panel closely with plastic sheeting for eight hours. White grout in small projects can be painted with India ink when it is dry. Grouting for projects in this book is ceramic tile grout bought in commercial tile stores. Companies that make this grout also sell a coloring material to blend with the dry powder before it is mixed with water.

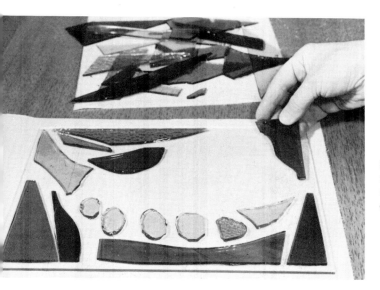

Spread random stained glass pieces directly on the clear glass sheet and move them around until you have a pleasing arrangement.

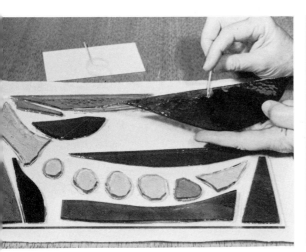

Apply epoxy in a thin even coat to the underside of each glass piece and press it firmly into place.

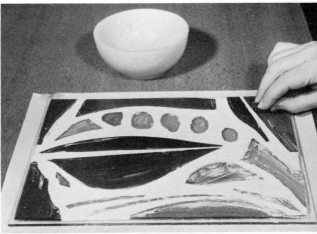

As soon as grout is packed into all spaces between the glass, remove all excess grout with water and a sponge before the grout dries. It is difficult to remove after it has set.

The grout can be painted with coats of India ink. Grout is also mixed with grout color before it is used.

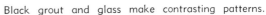

Black grout and glass make contrasting patterns.

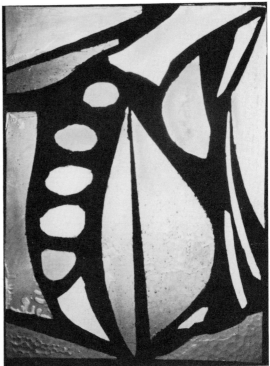

A design is drawn full-scale in color for a small bonded panel.

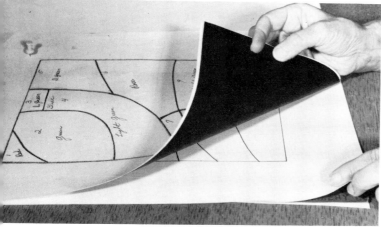

Three identical drawings are made of the panel design.

BONDING GLASS—CUT SHAPES

Three identical drawings are made for a project in bonded glass that is designed and cut to a definite pattern. Unlike a leaded glass project, only one border line is made on each copy. This line indicates the outer limits of applied stained glass shapes. One drawing, on firm paper, is cut into small templates representing glass pieces that will be applied to the clear glass base. The glass shapes are cut out around the small patterns, carefully washed and dried, and arranged in their correct sequence on the cartoon. The work drawing is taped to the workboard. A sheet of clean double-strength window glass is positioned on top of it so extra drawing paper extends beyond the clear glass. The window glass base must be the size of the drawn design *plus a margin of at least ¼ inch* all around the edge

to allow clear space for mounting the finished panel. Tape the glass sheet securely to the drawing so the masking tape extends over this ¼-inch margin all around the glass edge; no stained glass or epoxy is applied to this margin. Putty or thin wood strips can cover the edge when the completed panel is installed or framed. The masking tape must be removed when the epoxy begins to set and become rubbery, but *before it hardens*. Otherwise the epoxy will seal it firmly to the glass.

A heavy cardboard or plastic container, plastic measuring spoons, two plastic ¼-cup measures, a small scale such as a postage scale, stirring sticks, spreaders, and a can of epoxy solvent that should be bought at the same time the resin is purchased are placed on a nearby shelf. If the instructions on the resin container specify equal amounts of resin and hardener by volume rather than by weight, the scales are

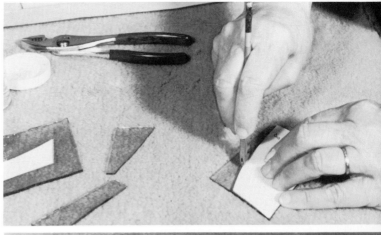

One drawing is cut into small patterns. Glass shapes are cut out around the small patterns, one side at a time.

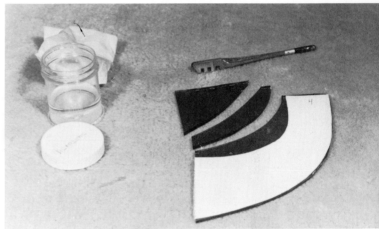

Deep curves are cut in shallow sections, one at a time.

not necessary. For large projects, the scale would be proportionately larger if it is required. When the entire amount of resin and hardener in the containers is mixed at one time, no scale is necessary. But remember, when the two components are blended, they must be used up in the brief length of time specified on the containers. Clean rags or paper toweling are needed to clean up after the epoxying is completed.

When everything is ready, don your plastic gloves and prepare to mix the epoxy. The success of your bonded project will depend on *following exactly* the manufacturer's instructions, so read them again. Mixing directions will vary for different resin-hardener combinations. Thermoset Resin #600 and Thermoset Hardener #37 were used for these bonding projects. This resin becomes cloudy when it is first mixed with hardener due to tiny bubbles

formed through chemical action. The two components are mixed very thoroughly. About twenty minutes after they have been mixed, the cloudiness begins to disperse and then the epoxy is applied. As it dries it becomes quite clear and colorless, unless it has been applied too thick.

Check the epoxied stained glass pieces from time to time to make certain they have not shifted. As long as they move quite easily, they can be slid gently back into place. If some pieces touch one another at certain points and are farther apart at others, it adds a pleasing casual effect, typical of bonded glass work. Do not move the glass shapes once the epoxy begins to set. When all the glass pieces are pressed into place, leave the panel undisturbed (except for cleaning up) for a minimum of 24 hours. The bonding achieves its greatest strength after seven days.

The narrow piece of glass is separated with pliers while one hand bends the larger section outward.

Each cut piece of glass is positioned on the cartoon along with its pattern piece, to keep all these small shapes organized and convenient.

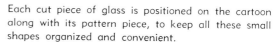

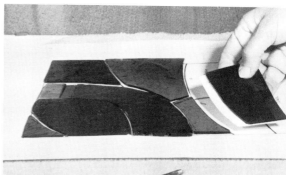

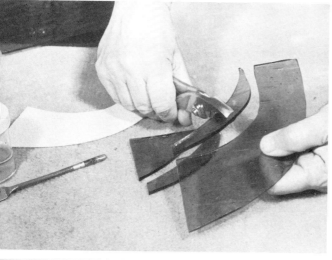

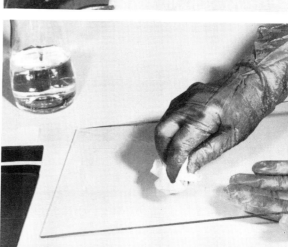

Sand the edges of newly cut glass to remove thin sharp slivers that appear along new cuts.

The glass is cleaned and dried. It is wise to wear gloves whenever you work with chemicals.

Tape the work drawing to the work-board. Tape the glass sheet securely to the drawing with masking tape extending over a ¼" margin all around the glass edge.

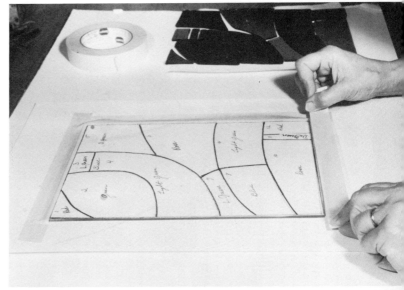

Spread epoxy thin and even over each glass shape and press it firmly in place on the clear glass sheet following the drawn design under the glass.

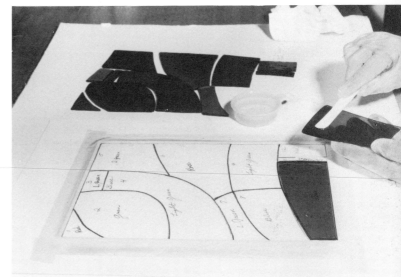

Dry black grout colorant is mixed with white grout before water is added. The colored grout will be lighter when dry.

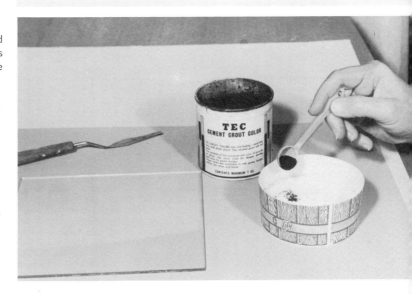

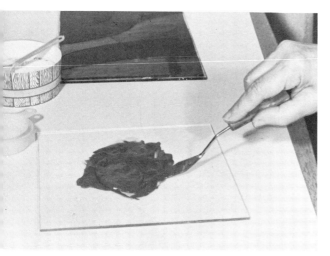 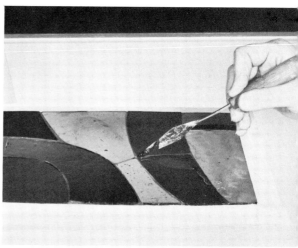

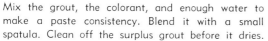

Mix the grout, the colorant, and enough water to make a paste consistency. Blend it with a small spatula. Clean off the surplus grout before it dries.

Work the grout into each crevice until it is even with the glass surface. Then press it smoothly with a spatula. Clean off the surplus grout before it dries.

Textured antique glass panels are decorative and cheery in any window.

BONDED GLASS MOSAICS

Few glass methods are simpler yet more effective than making a colorful glass mosaic. This ancient art form fits easily into today's life style, providing aesthetic beauty and often structural reinforcement to a surface that may be as great as a wall or as diminutive as an ear ring. Glass, unlike other mosaic materials, is often transparent, although it may be translucent or opaque as well. The glass is cut into small shapes called tesserae (pronounced tesserī). The professional mosaic artist may skillfully mix unusual shapes and materials. By far the most mosaics are made with fairly uniform, more or less rectangular shaped tesserae that are from ½ to 1 inch long, usually laid side by side in rows to form a design. Glass is seldom mixed with other mosaic materials. Because glass is usually transparent or translucent, its true beauty is realized when the base or backing for the mosaic is either transparent, as sheet glass or plastic, or if it is opaque it must be finished in a very light reflective neutral color or white. Plywood, masonite, glass, and plastic are materials commonly used for the base or backing of a glass mosaic.

The base for the illustrated project is the top of a previously discarded small table. It is completely refinished and prepared before the mosaic is begun. Old varnish is stripped from the entire table. The top is sanded, then given a coat of light cream-colored house paint. After it has dried, it is sanded lightly for better bondage with the adhesive that will hold the glass tesserae in place. The rest of the table is sanded smooth, then given a coat of cherry wood-stain, topped with clear shellac and rubbed with paste wax. Care must be taken to keep wax and oil off the surface where the mosaic will be applied to ensure that the adhesive will hold the tesserae firmly attached. Regular household glue will not work for this project. It adheres to wood and other porous materials but not to glass which is too smooth, hard, and nonporous. An excellent glass adhesive is two-component epoxy resin made especially for bonding glass as discussed in the section "Bonded Glass." Narrow spaces are left between the tesserae for grouting.

Grout is a very fine durable mortar used in all kinds of mosaics. To bond a grouted glass mosaic, epoxy the glass pieces individually to the base, leaving narrow spaces for the grout between the tesserae. When the adhesive is quite dry, the grout mixture is worked into the cracks with a rubber spatula. Regular bathroom and kitchen tile grout is excellent for glass mosaics, and it is water-resistant.

Begin the mosaic by making a sketch that exactly fits the planned mosaic area. Spaces for individual pieces are not drawn in exact detail because colors and ideas may inspire changes as you go along. It is helpful to think of both the design and the background as consisting of broad strokes of color rather than lines because they will be developed chiefly in rows of glass tesserae. If the rows are smooth and flowing, they will give strength and unity to the mosaic design. These rows can be developed in the design. Some areas may depart from a pattern of rows; they are filled with odd-shaped small pieces placed at random, making an interesting contrast to rows of tesserae.

When the pattern is completed, trace it onto the surface prepared for the mosaic. Thicken the lines on both the pattern and the prepared surface by tracing over them with a felt tipped marker. These broad lines represent narrow spaces between glass pieces. Use a light gray marker or pencil for the traced design on the prepared mosaic base because you may make a few changes as you arrange the tesserae. Gray is not likely to show through the glass after it is applied. Black lines are traced over the original pattern. The glass is cut over this pattern. It will be cut into strips that fit between these thick lines; the small tesserae are cut from the strips.

Detail of a 20' X 47' stained glass mosaic. By Glass-art Studio of Phoenix, Arizona. Installed in the Sunland Mausoleum in Sun City, Arizona.

Some are cut individually to fit into odd spaces. It is well to be flexible and adapt the glass to the design.

To retain smooth lines and the unity of the design, the glass strips should conform closely to the widths of the rows where they are designated in the pattern. It is advisable to read again the section on cutting glass. Remember, too many lines should not be scored on the glass before it is separated. Score and separate each strip, then score and break apart the small glass tesserae individually. If you score a grill-type pattern of lines and then try to separate a lot of little uniform pieces at once, it will only make cutting more difficult, not easier, By cutting them individually from strips of glass, you can angle edges slightly to fit along curves. It is very helpful to examine illustrations of mosaics in magazines and books to see how different mosaic artists worked out their problems by subtly shaping the small tesserae.

The glass pieces for the demonstrated project are washed in detergent water, a few at a time, then rinsed, dried, and *replaced* on the pattern. At this point, care must be taken to avoid mixing up the pieces lest a discouraging amount of time be required to relocate them on the working pattern. The edges of glass mosaic pieces must be either sanded or fired to 1350°F in a small kiln to just blunt the sharp edges but retain shape. All glass colors must be test-fired to find out whether they change color. In testing colors for the illustrated project, it was found that the brown glass fired to opaque black and the orange fired red. The edges of those glass pieces were lightly sanded for the mosaic.

To fire glass tesserae, lay them in their original order on the kiln shelf, which has been coated with sifted kiln wash for a separator. After the pieces are fired, they are replaced on the pattern. If you cannot fire the glass, all cut edges are sanded with fine emery paper, preferably under water, to remove dangerous sharp slivers and corners. Protect your eyes from flying bits. The small table for the project is moved near the tesserae so they can be easily transferred to it before they are epoxied. Changes in the arrangement of the glass design are made before epoxying begins. Once started it must proceed smoothly without interruption. If the border around the planned mosaic area is wood or metal, protect it with masking tape before bonding begins.

Following directions in the section "Bonded Glass," each piece is picked up, epoxied on the back and placed on the table design that has been drawn directly on the table top. Begin with main design features, then work in the lesser areas and the background. Most projects require several mixings of the resin and hardener. Mix only the amount you can use in 30 to 40 minutes, following exactly the directions that accompany the epoxy. Leave a ⅛-to ¼-inch margin all around the edge. It will be filled in with grout. When all the glass is applied, remove the masking tape carefully. Bits of resin that get on the glass must be removed with epoxy solvent on a cloth. Do not let the solvent run between the tesserae. It will weaken the adhesive that holds the glass in place. Leave the work undisturbed overnight. When it is dry, it is time to mix the grout.

All spaces for individual pieces are not drawn in exact detail because ideas may inspire changes as you work. Trace heavy black lines over the drawing to indicate narrow spaces that will be filled with grout after the glass is bonded.

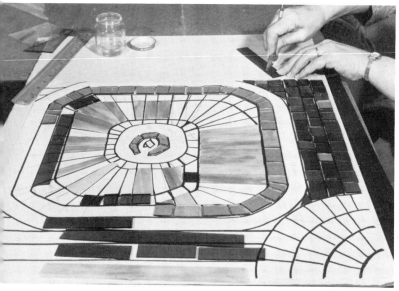

Small tesserae are cut from long strips of glass that are cut to fit between parallel lines in the design. They are positioned on the pattern.

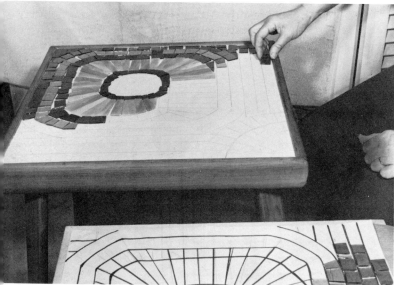

When all the glass is cut, transfer the glass tesserae from the paper drawing to the traced design on the painted white table top so you do not lose them or mix them up.

Mix small amounts of epoxy at a time. Spread a thin coat of adhesive to the back of each glass piece and press it firmly into position on the table top until all are glued.

Thoroughly blend the dry tile grout with coloring powder before you add water, unless you are using it white. A cup of dry white tile grout mixed with brown coloring powder to medium brown was used for the demonstration project. The grouted area is 20 by 20 inches. Color all the dry grout you think is necessary for a project and blend it well; then mix small amounts of it with a water and glue solution (three parts of water to one of glue) to work over a small area at a time. When you have mixed it to toothpaste consistency, let it sit for a few moments and then it should be just about right for working into spaces between the glass pieces. Force it into the cracks with a flexible rubber spatula pressed flat against the glass. Lightly scrape most of the excess grout from the tesserae with the spatula, but do not disturb the grout in the cracks until it has set. Then clean up with damp rags. Do not wait too long before you clean the grouted area completely. If it dries on the glass, it can be stubborn to remove. It can be sprayed *very lightly* with water to assist the cleanup. Cover the mosaic with plastic wrapping sheet for eight hours to assure slow drying that will prevent fine cracks from forming in the grout. When it is quite dry, polish the wood, grout and glass with liquid wax or marble polish.

When the epoxy has dried for 24 hours, mix enough grout and water paste to fill crevices in a limited area at one time. With a very flexible rubber spatula, work it into the cracks and lightly scrape away some of the excess grout. When it is firm but not dry, clean the glass with damp rags. Cover it with plastic wrapping sheet for eight hours to prevent cracks from forming.

After several days of "curing," the mosaic is rubbed with steel wool, and the entire table and mosaic are waxed with liquid wax.

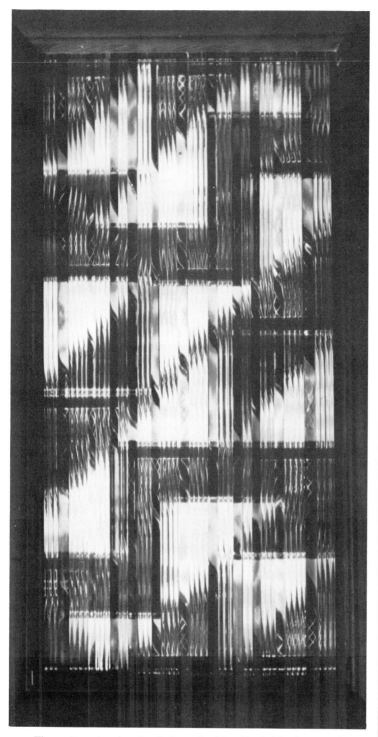

Three-dimensional stained glass. Fredrica H. Fields. Layers of stained glass in many colors in a shadow box panel, 26½" X 13". *Photo by Kenneth E. Fields.* (See Fredrica Fields's Work, Section 8).

►

Layered three-dimensional stained glass panel. Fredrica H. Fields. National Cathedral, Washington, D.C. *Photo by Kenneth E. Fields.*

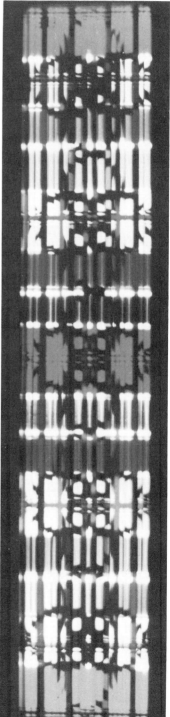

A SMALL BONDED WINDOW

A sketch is drawn for a small bonded window to be made from antique stained glass bonded to $\frac{3}{16}$-inch plate glass. Three full-scale copies are made, one on heavy paper to be cut into patterns. In measuring for the clear glass base, allow at least ¼ inch around the edge to be free of stained glass so there will be a space for framing the window. When the patterns are cut, space is allowed for grout between each glass shape. Tape one drawing to the table and tape the plate over it, masking off the ¼ inch around the edge. After the glass has been washed, dried, and laid out on the third drawing, it is time to mix just the amount of epoxy you can apply in thirty minutes. Spread a thin coating of adhesive to each glass and press it firmly into position. Make sure the table is level or the glass will likely slide out of position before it can dry. Continue to mix and apply epoxy until all the glass is in place. Clean up the glass with a rag dampened with epoxy solvent and a razor blade, after the epoxy has become rubbery. Do not let the solvent seep into the cracks between glass pieces. When the glass has dried overnight, fill all the cracks with grout. When excess grout has been cleaned away, cover the glass with a plastic sheet for eight hours to prevent cracks from forming in the grout.

A small scale sketch for a bonded window, "Stems and Flowers." Dark areas indicate grouted work.

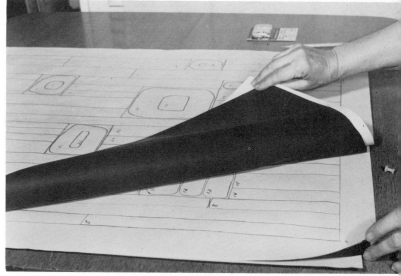

Three copies are made of the full-scale drawing. Only one border line is required for the bonded window.

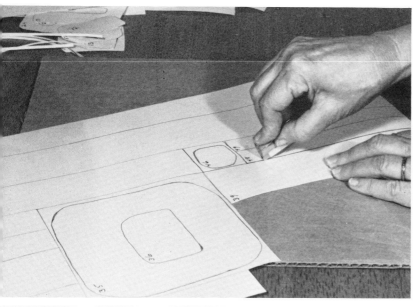

Individual patterns are cut out. Use pattern shears if they are available.

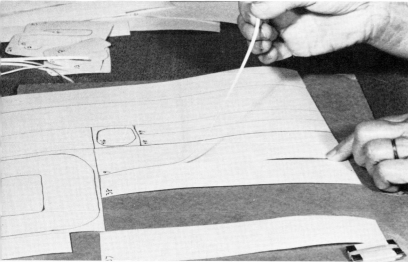

The removed strips leave spaces that indicate where grouting will be applied instead of leads.

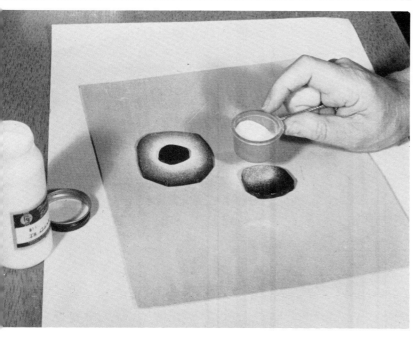

Abstract flower shapes will be fused and bonded, both singly and in layers. To facilitate fusion, sift glass flux over the glass before it is fired. (For directions on how to fuse small glass pieces, refer to the section "Fused Glass Windchimes.")

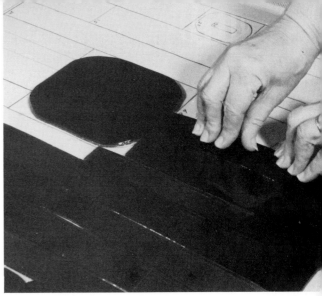

Read again the instructions under "Glass Bonded with Epoxy Resin," before you begin work on a large project. If only one person is bonding the glass, no more than one-fourth of the total amount of glass in this window can be bonded before the epoxy begins to set. Remove the masking tape along the edge as soon as the epoxy becomes rubbery.

The third application of resin begins.

A section of the completed window, STEMS AND FLOWERS.

Faceted glass window. First Presbyterian Church, Bartlesville, Oklahoma. Willet Stained Glass Studios.

FACETED STAINED GLASS

The imaginative use of thick segments of sparkling antique stained glass has formed a major contemporary glass craft in this country and in Europe. It is reminiscent of an old art first developed by the Egyptians and the Byzantines when thick colored glass was the only kind available to them for creating mosaics and windows. Segments of the semi-transparent blocks of glass imbedded in walls and window openings transformed medieval churches from gloomy caverns to jeweled shrines of mysterious beauty. As time passed and glass became thinner, painters covered areas of it with pictorial delineations, hiding the real beauty of the glowing glass colors. Stained glass reached a plateau of development where it remained for centuries.

Near the end of the nineteenth century, French glass artists traveling to ancient shrines "rediscovered" the beauty of simple primitive works. They developed a thick, unusually clear and vibrantly colored stained glass cast into thick slabs that they called "dalles-de-verre" (flagstones of glass). They chipped the glass in a special way to make light reflective, sparkling facets. Soon glass artists in many countries were experimenting with faceted glass. They began to recapture with pure color and symbolic form the emotional and psychological elements of spiritual truths, which they built primarily into religious architecture. Detailed realistic representations are not needed in this mingling of light and color. Sensitive juxtaposition of colors, subtle faceting and expert arrangement of vibrant glass in a contrasting sober matrix, suffice to modify the bold glass forms. When the eye encounters the rich hues in a faceted glass mural wall or window, the viewer does not engage in interpreting the various shapes, colors, and textures of the composition. His emotions become deeply involved with its pervasive spell, stilling any inclination to identify realistic pictorial details.

Glass dalles are made in a wide variety of vibrant and subtle colors developed by modern chemistry. The slabs may be sized 8 by 8 inches to 12 by 12 inches, and ½ to 1 inch thick. Shaped segments of faceted glass can be bonded into panels of cement in warm or moderate climates or interior installations. Weather fluctuations make cement-bonded glass impractical for exterior use in cold or variable climates. Cement shrinks at a different rate than glass in cold temperatures; the glass can loosen. In some instances it has even fallen out of its matrix. Professional craftsmen are bonding faceted glass with a special adhesive usually mixed with sand. The epoxy employed in the demonstration project is Thermoset #16 Epoxy and Hardener, available in several appropriate colors: black, charcoal, limestone, mortar, and adobe. The adhesive is formulated to give structural strength, durability, and weather resistance to interior and exterior slab glass installations. It is easy to to use if the manufacturer's directions are followed exactly.

A predesigned faceted panel usually begins with a color sketch enlarged to a full-size cartoon representing glass segments that will be cut to a pattern. But cutting slab glass requires special tools and skills. Because of the high cost of individual glass slabs, it is recommended that the beginner make his initial projects from broken slab glass segments, available from stained glass suppliers. They are sold by the pound at smaller cost. Select some pieces of the glass that have interesting shapes and arrange them in a composition on a sheet of paper; trace around each glass segment to make a cartoon and a carbon copy for the work drawing.

Before the project begins, all the glass pieces must be washed in hot detergent water, rinsed in warm water, and dried. Four boards are nailed together to make a frame of correct dimensions into which the panel is cast. Varnish the frame's interior surface and seal its inside corners with masking tape. Then rub it with paste wax. The next step is the preparation of the base of the frame. The full-size work drawing, indicating the position of the glass segments for the planned panel, is spread out on a sheet of ¾-inch plywood. Cover it with a transparent parting sheet such as polyethylene sheet, fiberglass laminate, or other plastic. For an initial project, space the glass pieces far enough apart to facilitate pouring the epoxy without dribbling it over the glass. To anchor the wood frame in position over the plastic parting sheet, nail small blocks of wood against the outside of the frame. The nails go into the plywood through the parting sheet and drawing paper that extend beyond the frame. Coat the parting sheet with paste wax.

The bottom of each slab glass segment must be sealed off to prevent epoxy from running underneath it. A material such as latex (Thermoset #529 was used for the demonstration project) acts as both a sealant for the glass and a release agent for the parting sheet and the frame, when the epoxy in the panel has set. Brush some latex over the inside of the wooden frame; then paint the bottom of each glass piece with the latex before you set it inside the frame in its designated position on the parting sheet. When all the glass is in place, pour a very thin layer of latex over the plastic parting sheet between glass pieces. To keep the glass clean, wear gloves if you must touch it. After 24 hours, if the latex is dry, it is time to prepare the epoxy resin and hardener. If any glass pieces are deeply faceted around their top edge, you may fill in the facets temporarily with putty to shield them from the epoxy. It can be dug out when the epoxy has set. If you should see a slight buckling of the plastic parting sheet after the latex is dry, do not be dismayed. It may impart a shallow ripple to the surface of the epoxy matrix between glass pieces that can be interesting and attractive. The shallow buckling is caused by air trapped beneath the plastic parting sheet. Some craftsmen pierce the plastic sheet in several places to release the air as the poured epoxy settles.

Epoxy resin is always supplied with a hardener as a unit. They must be mixed together thoroughly. If you have access to a paint shaking mixer, use it as a good blending device, but remember, the epoxy begins to activate as soon as it is blended with its hardener! If you must travel some distance to use a mixer, it is best to forget it! The epoxy compound can be mixed by hand. Should you plan to mix less than the entire amount in the container, the resin and the hardener must be mixed in exactly the same proportions specified in the manufacturer's instructions. A can containing the correct amount of hardener is supplied with each container of epoxy resin. Space is provided in the container for the hardener to be mixed in the same can. It is simple to combine the entire amount of compound for one pouring. An additional project can be planned at the same time should you blend the entire amount of epoxy and then discover you have a surplus left over. Once the ingredients are mixed, they cannot be stored for future use. Be sure the pouring table is level; the slightest slant will cause the glass pieces to slide gently out of place. The epoxy levels out completely, although slowly, so take care not to pour so much that it runs over the shorter glass.

The resin and hardener for the demonstrated project, charcoal gray Thermoset #116 Resin and Hardener, was hand-mixed with a stout stick for five minutes. It was scraped down the sides of the container and *stirred from the bottom up* continually, which brought up very thick dark sandy material. When you first begin to stir the thick mixture, you may have some misgivings about being able to pour it smoothly. Do not be too concerned. Once the thin hardener is added to it and blended vigorously for five minutes, it acquires a wonderful texture and pourable viscosity that will make you marvel at the manufacturer's skill! Be sure to stir it from the bottom up, and do not mix it longer than the time specified on the container.

For the demonstration project, several kinds of pouring vessels were considered in order to find one that could be easily manipulated by the novice. A clean half-gallon milk carton was selected. It was partly filled for each pouring, then it was refilled. You can control a thin stream of the mix by squeezing a corner of the container to make a spout for pouring the compound into narrow spaces between the glass. Pour it to a level approximately ⅝ inch thick. If you inadvertently spill some of it on the glass, remove it with a cloth dampened with epoxy solvent. Should you want a sand-finished surface, sift sand evenly over the setting epoxy *15 to 20 minutes after* the casting to prevent too much sand from sinking out of sight into the matrix. If too much sand sinks into it, the level of the epoxy may rise and cover some of the glass.

In order to use up surplus epoxy that might be left over when the entire gallon container of epoxy was blended, an extra free-form panel was prepared at the time the rectangular demonstration project was planned. Heavy waxed linoleum was employed for a frame instead of wood. To make this kind of frame, set a strip of linoleum on

edge with the smooth side facing in, and bend it to the desired shape. Wrap and fasten heavy twine around it, then press a roll of moist clay into the outside angle where the linoleum meets the plastic topped base. Follow the same preparatory procedure outlined for the larger panel. A short length of copper pipe ⅞ inch wide and ¾ inch long was set into the latex release agent one-half inch from the edge of the linoleum strip at the time glass pieces were positioned, to provide for a hanging device.

Panels cast with this kind of special epoxy resin should cure for 24 hours at normal room temperature. After that time, the latex sealant is stripped from it. Allow several days before installation. If a faceted glass panel will be set into an exterior wall, it should be secured on setting blocks (such as lead blocks) with enough clearance on all sides to provide for expansion and contraction during changes in the weather. It should be sealed with permanently flexible caulking compound. In a construction where many panels are stacked, adequate reinforcement must be provided, of course.

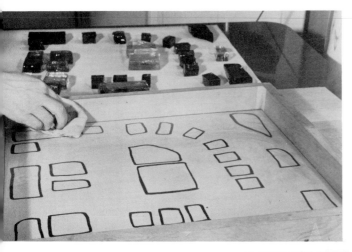

A full-size drawing is laid out on a sheet of plywood and covered with a transparent parting sheet. The wood frame is anchored over it. The base and the inside of the frame are coated with hard paste wax.

Liquid latex brushed over the inside of the wood frame provides a release agent for the epoxy panel.

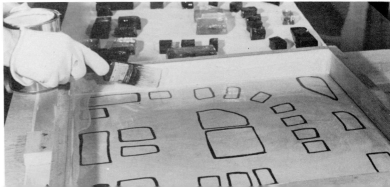

The bottom of each glass is coated with latex before it is set in place. The latex turns translucent and light tan as it dries.

When all glass is positioned, the thin latex is poured over the parting sheet between glass pieces. If it is poured over ⅛'' thick it may crack as it dries.

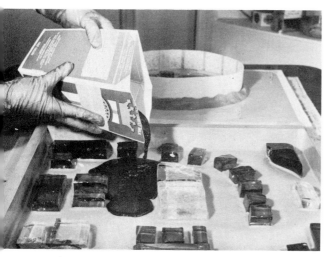

A half-gallon milk carton provides an excellent pouring vessel for the heavy dark epoxy that is poured over the dry latex.

The top of the carton is cut so it slants away from one corner, which provides a good spout for pouring into narrow spaces.

An oval of linoleum with clay pressed around it provides the mold frame for a smaller panel.

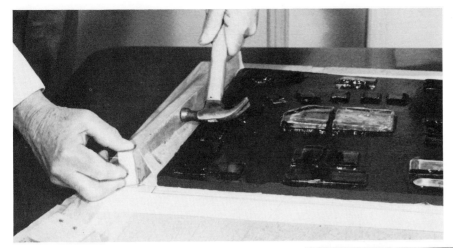

When the resin has set, the frame is knocked loose from the panel. Notice the thin sheet of latex pulling away from the wood.

The latex release sheet offers no resistance when it is pulled away from the panel.

One completed panel for a divider.

THREE FACES. Old Dominion Stained Glass Company. The black epoxy matrix gives dynamic definition to this simple faceted glass design.

CREATION. Laws Stained Glass Studio. Faceted glass in a black epoxy matrix.

Faceted walls, windows, and dividers have gained phenomenal acceptance by architects, artists, and laymen alike. Reflection, refraction, and transmission of light in a mélange of vibrant color produces emotion of depth and power particularly suited to religious architecture. In our time, however, faceted glass is not limited to ecclesiastical settings, but it enriches the durable planes and volumes of modern secular architecture everywhere with shimmering color and lasting beauty.

Faceted window. Chapel of Warren State Hospital, Warren, Pennsylvania. Willet Stained Glass Studios.

Jan selects glass dalles. Each slab of glass is numbered according to color.

Jan Ozog designs a faceted lumiere (design in full color) for the Willet Stained Glass Studios.

Mike Caputo patterns a faceted glass cartoon at the Willet Stained Glass Studios.

James Harris chops a knobbed (scored) glass dalle. The individual pattern is held against the glass. Willet Stained Glass Studios.

Detail of James Harris chopping.

Pouring epoxy in a faceted window section at the Willet Stained Glass Studios.

Jan Ozog pours resin for a gemmaux panel. A mélange of richly colored glass segments are imbedded in transparent resin for this method.

Faceted glass crucifixion. Saint Mark's Lutheran Church, Glastonbury, Connecticut. Willet Stained Glass Studios.

BURNING BUSH. Willet Studio. Designed for and installed in Temple Shalom, Levittown, Pennsylvania. Faceted glass.

Kiln-fired laminated glass suspension. R. Bruce Laughlin.

4
Fired Glass

GLASSES FOR KILN-FIRING

WINDOW Glass. Colorless transparent sheet glass has many uses besides windowmaking. But glass sources know just what kind of glass is indicated when you ask for it as window glass. It is available in single-strength ($\frac{1}{16}$ inch), double-strength ($\frac{1}{8}$ inch), and in $\frac{3}{16}$- and $\frac{1}{4}$-inch thicknesses. Glass pieces that will be laminated together should be made by the same manufacturer. If you are not sure that they are of identical composition, test-fire a lamination of small pieces. If they do not fracture upon cooling, it may be assumed they are identical. Should you want to laminate circles or ovals before you become adept at cutting glass, or if you are pressed for time, you can have them cut where you purchase glass. For initial projects, single-strength glass is suitable for pieces up to six inches wide in one-layer projects. Pieces of wider diameter should be cut from glass that is double-strength, again specifically one-layer compositions. Two layers of single-strength glass are satisfactory for laminations up to 12 inches across.

Plate Glass. Window glass and plate glass are sold in the same thicknesses. Because of its strength, clarity, and freedom from imperfections, it is useful as a base for bonded assemblages. Plate glass is sometimes very hard and may tend to separate erratically when it is cut. It is also more expensive than the same thickness in window glass. For standard use, the window glass serves very well for fired projects. A few of the colorless sheet glasses tend to devitrify when they are fired; within a certain temperature range they crystallize if they are held too long at a sustained high temperature (usually just below the liquefication point). This temperature is usually reached only when glass is cast, blown, or otherwise manipulated by the experienced craftsman. A complex technical explanation is not in the scope of this book. But it is well to know that a glass that tends to devitrify will acquire a frosted effect. It may be considered desirable in some instances, of course.

Stained Glass. Antique stained glass varies in thickness in each sheet of glass. It can be used successfully for bending or slumping in single sheets. The results of laminating or of fusing together different colors of stained glass cannot be accurately predicted. Many colors are not compatible when they are fused together because of differences in their composition resulting from their various metallic oxide colorants. Reds, oranges, and red golds are not usually successful when they are fused to other colors, although they may sometimes fuse to one another. On rare occasions a colored glass may not remain fused to another piece of the same color. But very lovely objects are made of single sheets of stained glass bent into shape over a mold. These characteristics of antique glass apply to cathedral glass as well as antique, except that cathedral glass is rolled between steel rollers when it is still hot and flexible. It is sold in ⅛-inch even thickness. Various stained glass colors should be test fired before they are used in fired projects. (For more on stained glasses, see the section "Stained Glass.")

Preformed Shapes. Bottles, fruit jars, glass plates, old glass ornaments, ashtrays, and combinations of these and other preformed glass objects are usually easy to find and cost very little. Much molded old glass is soft and fires to a sparkling clarity. As with any material, whether or not it is excellent depends upon the manner of its treatment. It can be fired on a mold like any flat glass.

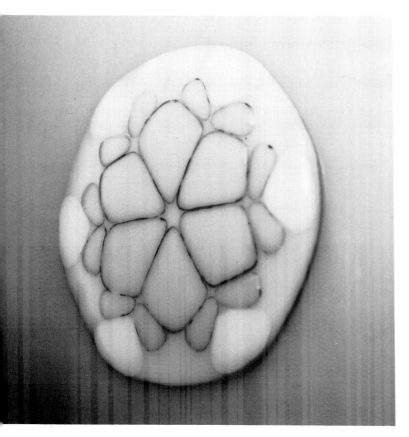

Fused glass. R. Bruce Laughlin. The panel is deep pink with yellow triangular shapes around the edge.

Fused glass. BoBo Zinn. The smaller circle of glass with added small glass shapes was covered with a combination of blue and green glass ices and opaque enamels. It was fired flat separately on the kiln shelf until glowing red and molten. Edges were manipulated and pleated with a firing tool while in the kiln. The clear glass background panel was fired to attach the hanger and round glass edges. The two panels were cemented together with R-TV glue. *Photo by Drew Henery.*

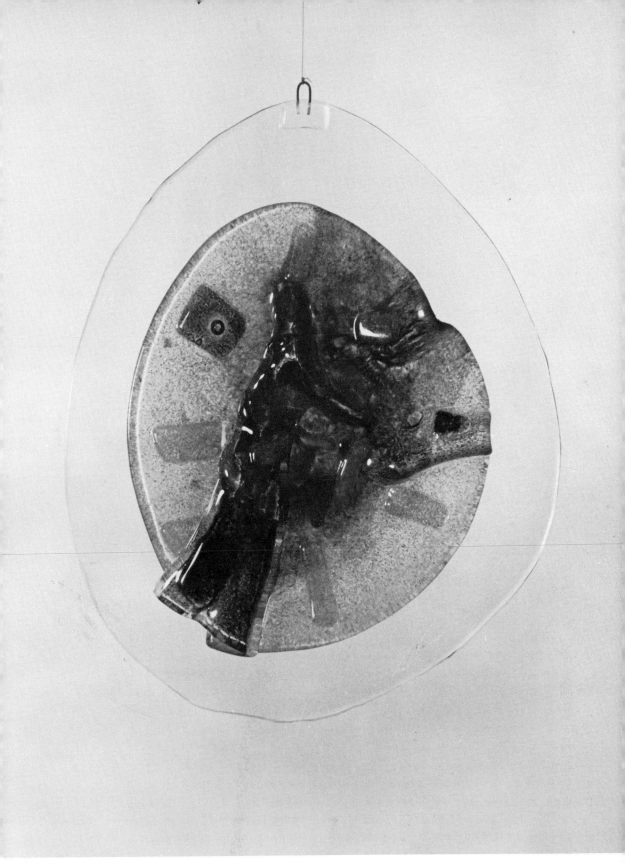

Fused glass. R. Bruce Laughlin. Circular panel with applied shapes and colors fused in one firing with nichrome wire hanger.

KILNS

Individual kilns do not all fire the same; specific firing results are therefore difficult to forecast for all kilns. The kiln-fired glass projects in this book were fired in either a front-loading electric enameling kiln, 12 by 12 by 7½ inches high, or a top-loading electric ceramic kiln, 13½ by 14½ inches. Kilns such as these, which have pyrometers and temperature controls, will fire almost any kind of glass fusing or bending projects for the average craftsman who has a small studio. The front loader is wired around the walls and across the floor. Ideally, a glass-firing kiln is also wired in the door. But if you refrain from opening the door or vents after the temperature has climbed to 1,000°F, until firing is completed, even without door-wiring, glass can be fired successfully. In a front-loading kiln, glass pieces should be set back from the door a few inches; the kiln's interior temperature may be cooler near the door, especially if the door is opened during the firing process. The edges of the glass nearest the door may be somewhat angular when the rest of the glass has fired to maturity, if positioned too near the door.

For accurate glass firing, the kiln should be equipped with a pyrometer. Kiln switches are operated several times during one glass firing. The use of a number of pyrometric cones to indicate different heating adjustments for one firing is awkward; it permits only partial temperature control. The serious glass craftsman, whether amateur or professional, will make the extra expenditure required for this important piece of equipment. Accurate temperature control is imperative for the successful firing of any glass.

KILN FURNITURE

High-fired ceramic kiln shelves, usually available in square, round, and half-round shapes and in different sizes, retain heat for quite a while longer than the glass, after the switches are turned off. It is advisable to elevate molds from the shelf with short kiln posts, sections of insulation brick, or a square of acoustical insulation board treated as described under "Molds for Firing Glass."

Whatever elevation prop is used should support the mold level, or the glass will bend at an angle.

To keep insulation brick posts from crumbling, dip them in a solution of equal parts of water and sodium silicate (water glass), dry them and fire them to 1500°F on a kiln shelf sifted with dry kiln wash for a separator.

MOLDS FOR FIRING GLASS

Refractory molds are a requirement for fusing, bending, or contouring glass. The glass is positioned on top of the mold and both are put into a cool kiln. After the kiln switches are turned on, the heat is increased gradually until the glass fuses or bends to fit the contours of the mold. Glass that will be fused flat can be fired directly on the kiln shelf, but this method becomes awkward if you fire glass continually over a period of time. Glass can be fired flat on sections of Marinite, Armstrong Ceramiguard, or other fireproof acoustical board. These fireproof sheets must be heat treated in the kiln before they can be employed as supports for firing glass. They have been low-fired, and are soft and porous.

To strengthen the insulation boards, fire them with the rough side down to 1600°–1800°F on a regular kiln shelf that has been covered with a coating of kiln wash. The kiln and the room must be ventilated for the preliminary firing of these insulation sheets. They give off pungent fumes during the first firing that could cloud the glass if they are not prefired. Fire them for one hour at *low* with the door ajar ½ inch. Then turn the switch to *high* for ½ hour with the door still ajar. At this time the increased temperature will bring fumes and smoke from the insulation

board. A door or window must be opened so smoke can disperse during this first firing. The smooth white top side of the board will turn to a light caramel color temporarily, then it will turn white again. After ½ hour, close the kiln door and continue firing to about 1600°F with the switches still on *high*. Finally turn off the kiln and let it cool naturally. The ceramic material in these boards can cause them to crack if the kiln door is opened while they are still hot or if they are not fired perfectly flat on the kiln shelf. When they have cooled, fill all the pits by rubbing a paste of whiting and water into them. After the boards are fired, they will be firm and somewhat brittle; but if they are handled with reasonable care, they should give good service. In addition they are lightweight and inexpensive. Sift kiln wash over them as a separator.

One of the most common kinds of material for making shaped molds is ready-prepared white sculpture clay (cone 04) bought moist from the supplier. The molds are fired to cone 08, which leaves the clay somewhat porous and less likely to crack when glass is fired on it. Simple greenware shapes can be used for molds if there are no undercut details that may prevent the fired bent glass from releasing from the clay

One of the most common kinds of mold material is white sculpture clay. This is a 25-pound plastic bag of the clay as it comes ready-to-use from the supplier.

Roll out some clay between two sticks about ¼″ thick.

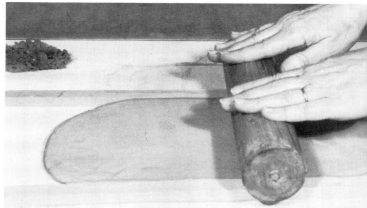

Lay out a cardboard pattern the size and shape of the mold you plan and cut the clay around it.

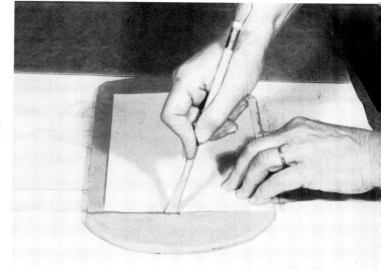

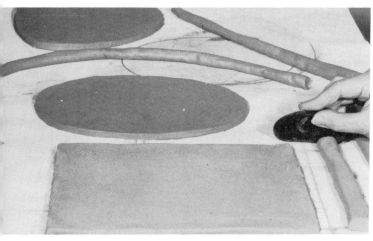

Roll thick clay coils that will prop up the rim of each slab that will become a mold.

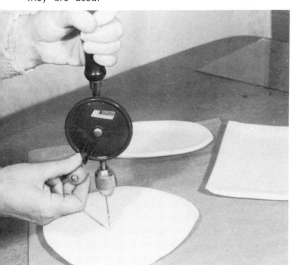

When the clay shape has become slightly firm but not stiff, lift up each edge and prop it into position with coils. Do not remove them until the tray has become leather hard or it will slowly flatten out before it is dry.

As soon as the clay is bone dry, the molds are fired to cone 08. Several small holes are drilled in the center and along the base edge of each mold before they are used.

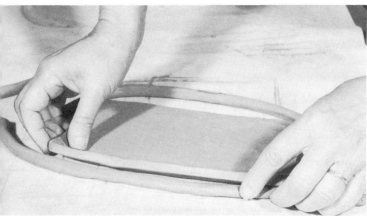

Rub whiting (calcium carbonate) over the surface of each mold to fill in any rough spots.

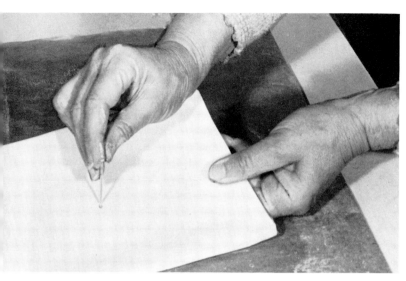

Push whiting out of each clogged hole with a toothpick so air can pass through when glass slumps into the mold. Otherwise, a huge bubble may be formed by trapped air.

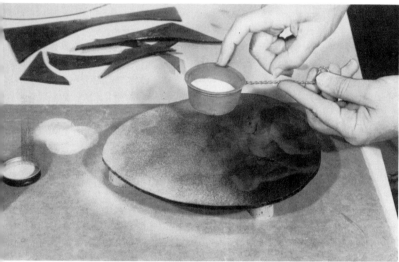

A piece of red stained glass is cut to fit the shape of a free-form mold. Clear glass flux is sifted over it very lightly to make a fine texture in the glass when it is fired.

Kiln wash was sifted over the mold for a separator before the glass was lowered into position. The glass must not extend beyond the edge of the mold.

The glowing red of ruby antique glass with its natural streaks of lighter and darker color could not be improved with surface designing.

Certain powdered castable refractories such as Kastolite (or other castable refractories), used for chimney and furnace linings, make excellent molds for glass bending. This kind of material is cast over a model of the desired shape. Place a form such as a bowl upside down on a square of ¾-inch plywood board. Snip off the heads of some tacks or brads and drive them into the board all around the bowl's perimeter to hold it in position. A strip of linoleum should be cut at least an inch wider than the deepest measurement of the model and a little longer than its circumference. Wrap the strip, smooth side in and standing on edge, around the model and headless tacks with the ends of the linoleum lapped. Tie it temporarily with string wound around it while you drive long slim nails all around close against it. Brush vegetable oil over the outside of the inverted model so the mold will release from it easily.

When the model is ready, it is time to mix the Kastolite. Because this material is composed of small variably sized particles, over a period of time the finest dustlike grains sift to the bottom of the bag container. The entire dry bagful must be mixed thoroughly before it is used. To make stronger molds,

blend in a cupful of powdered alumina to a 2½-gallon bucketful of the dry material, then mix it with water to lava consistency. Scoop it over the top of the greased model, pushing it well down the sides. When the mold enclosure is half filled, lift the plywood base at one end and *gently* rap it down against the table several times to bring air bubbles to the surface. Sprinkle a little dry Kastolite over the surface to absorb moisture rising to the top. Add some of the dry material to the remainder of the mixture, stir it well, and fill the mold to the top with this dryer mixture. Rap the plywood again and soak up surface water with layers of paper toweling. The mold should set for at least 24 hours without being disturbed; then carefully remove the linoleum strip and let the mold dry another 12 hours. Remember that the mold is fragile until it is fired. Remove the model and put the mold into a cool kiln with its door open about an inch; turn switches to *low* for an hour to drive off remaining moisture or oil. When the door has been closed, turn the switches to *high* and fire to 1400°–1500°F. After the kiln is turned off, let it cool before you remove the mold.

Drill some air holes in the mold with a

hand drill. They will prevent large bubbles of air from becoming trapped under sagging glass. Seal the mold by brushing it generously inside and outside with a thin solution of sodium silicate (water glass). To fill all the pits in the top of the mold, rub a paste of whiting and water into them and wipe a thin film of the paste over the surface. This paste will also clog the drilled air holes; to reopen them, pierce each one with a needle or tooth-

pick. The mold should be refired to 800°F before the first time glass is bent over it.

Unusual and exciting shapes in bent glass are formed over nichrome wire, high-fire clay stilts, plate pins, insulation brick forms, and other materials that can withstand heat high enough to bend glass. Molds made from these materials are all coated with a separator such as kiln wash before glass is bent over them.

Slumped or sagged glass. BoBo Zinn. An eight-inch circle was decorated by brushing strokes of enameling gum on the glass, sifting on several enamel colors, then tapping off excess. It was slumped into a mold. *Photo by Drew Henery.*

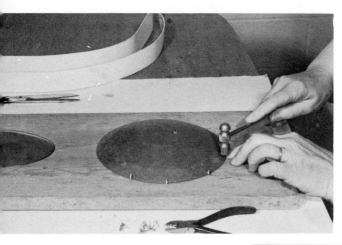

A raised metal form is the model for casting a mold. Place any bowl form upside down on a square of ¾'' plywood board. Snip off the heads of some tacks or brads and drive them into the board around the bowl's edge to hold it in position.

A strip of linoleum is wrapped, smooth side in, around the model and headless tacks. Linoleum ends are lapped.

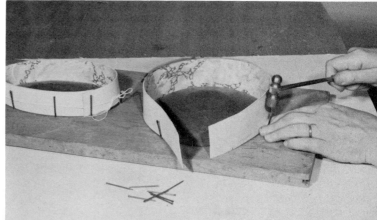

Drive long slim nails all around the outside of the linoleum and press a roll of clay against it. Brush or pour vegetable oil over the outside of the inverted model so the mold will release from it later.

Scoop the mold mixture over the top of the greased model.

Sprinkle dry Kastolite over the surface of the mold mixture to absorb moisture rising to the top.

Soak up surface moisture with layers of paper.

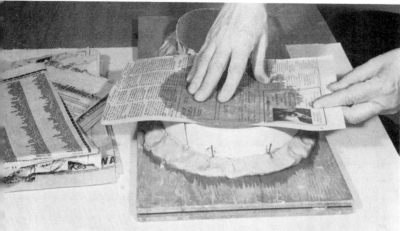

Rap the plywood against the table occasionally to level the Kastolite mix and bring bubbles of air to the top.

After 24 hours, remove the linoleum strip and the model. Let the mold continue to dry in a warm place. Place it in a cool kiln to fire at 1400°–1500°F.

When the cooled mold has been removed from the kiln, bore several holes in it and fill all pinholes by rubbing the mold surface with whiting. Push whiting out of each bored hole with a toothpick. Sift it with fresh kiln wash each time it is used.

A circle of single-strength window glass with a soft-edged stencil pattern of low-fusing glass ice and enamels was slumped into the mold in one firing. The heat was brought to 1350°F to fire the colors and blunt the edges of the form.

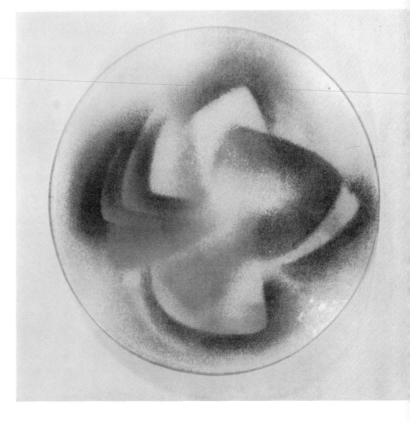

KILN WASH

The ceramic shelves in any kiln are given at least three coats of kiln wash to protect them from drippings of glaze, enamel, or melted glass. Mix the dry kiln wash (equal parts of kaolin and flint) with water to thin cream consistency. Brush the shelf first with plain water, then in quick long strokes brush on three even coats of the kiln wash crosswise to one another. For best results, let the shelf dry completely and slowly for a day or two in a warm (not hot) place. When the shelf is in use, if enamel, glaze, or glass drippings fall to the shelf and melt, they can be cleaned away easily. Just scrape off the spots and patch the scraped areas with additional kiln wash.

Dry kiln wash sifted through 80-mesh screen is an excellent separator between glass and any mold used for fusing or bending glass. It leaves a fine texture in the glass and protects the mold from molten glass that could otherwise stick to it. After every two or three firings, brush off the used kiln wash and sift a new layer over the mold.

MAKING A KILN WASH SIFTER

A practical sifter for applying kiln wash as a separator can be made from a 13-ounce tuna can (not the regular smaller size). Clean it thoroughly with detergent water, rinse it and dry it. Remove both ends of the can. Cut a circle of 80-mesh brass sieve cloth a little larger in diameter than the can, turn up the edge, and solder it to the *rim* of the tuna can. It will likely not adhere to the side of the can, which usually has a coating that does not accept most solder. Use either low-fusing paste solder or 60/40 solid core solder that must be fluxed. (For the soldering process, see "Soldering" in the stained glass section.)

When the sifter has been soldered, wash it well in detergent water to remove any oil from the solder flux, then press narrow self-adhering plastic tape firmly around the edge of the brass sieve cloth to cover rough wire ends that could scratch your fingers. Use a soft dry two-inch nylon paintbrush to apply the powdered kiln wash by whisking it back and forth to push the powder through the sifter. Move the sifter around above the mold surface as you brush a fine sifting over every part of the mold surface.

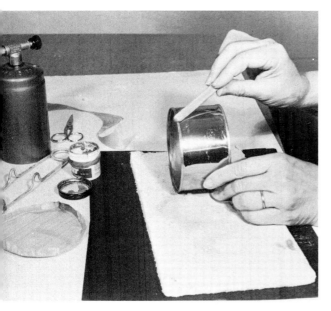

Low-fusing paste solder called Fast (trade name) is spread along the rim of the tuna can. Notice the circle of brass sieve-cloth with its edge turned up ready for soldering to the can.

Spread more paste solder on the edge over the sieve cloth, which has been positioned on the rim of the can.

The brass sieve material is held tightly against the rim with a nichrome rod as the torch moves around the edge and melts the solder. Let the solder cool before you disturb it.

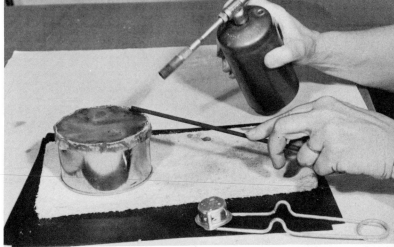

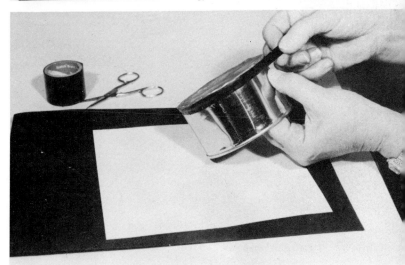

Press narrow self-adhering plastic tape firmly over the wire ends that could scratch your fingers.

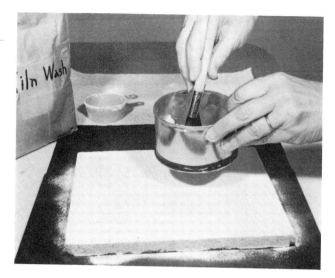

Use a soft nylon paintbrush to whisk the kiln wash through the sifter in a thin layer over any surface on which glass will be fired.

Slumped glass bowl. R. Bruce Laughlin. Laminated and decorated with glass enamels. (See section "Bubbles in Laminated Glass.")

THE FIRING SCHEDULE

General kiln-firing procedures are given here for fusing glass flat. Specific requirements for bent or sagged glass are discussed separately. When glass is ready for firing, it is placed in a cool kiln on its prepared mold or shelf. Position it away from the kiln door and from the electric elements. The temperature controls are turned to *low* and the door is left ajar for a gentle preheating period of two hours or longer, depending upon the size and the number of pieces to be fired. By the end of that period, the temperature should be approximately 400° to 500°F. In a large fully loaded kiln, the preliminary heating period can be several hours.

All glass firing requires the kiln to be vented until the temperature reaches approximately 950°F (or cone 022). Atmospheric moisture in the kiln, the mold, and in the room, as well as gases from chemicals in materials fired into the glass, can cloud the heating glass if they cannot escape from the kiln quickly. By venting the kiln while it is heating to approximately 950°F, you can assure that all these gases escape from the kiln. This means opening a peephole and leaving the door or lid ajar. To vent a top-loading kiln during the preliminary heating period, prop its lid open about ½ inch and leave the lower peephole open. The door of a front-loading kiln is left open ½ inch. After two or more hours on *low,* turn the switches to *high* and adjust the kiln door to be only slightly ajar until the temperature reaches 950°F. In a top-loading kiln, the lid props must be lowered so there is only a slight opening. Peepholes are closed. Protect your eyes, face, hands, and arms from the intense heat that emanates from the top loader while you are changing lid props.

In addition to allowing fumes and moisture to escape readily, venting slows down the temperature rise and deters the hazard of glass breakage in a kiln that tends to heat too fast. The *medium* switch is rarely used because in many kilns it turns off half the elements which can cause uneven heating that sets up stresses in glass. When the pyrometer indicates approximately 950°F, close the kiln vents and door. After that time, maintain a close watch over the rising temperature. Check the glass visually from time to time, beginning at 1200°F. When the glass edges are gently rounded and the glass becomes red, flat glass is mature. This will occur at a lower temperature for stained glass than for window glass. When the temperature reaches 1400°F, if you are firing window glass (1300°F for stained glass), turn off the switches and vent the kiln for a few moments. Venting the kiln at this time prevents a continued rise in temperature that may result from heat stored in the kiln walls even after it has been turned off.

After two or three minutes, close the vents again and let the kiln cool to the annealing point of the glass you are firing, or to 950°–1000°F if you do not know the exact annealing range of your particular glass. Then turn the kiln switches on again to low and keep all the vents closed. Hold the temperature between 950° and 1000° for at least an hour or longer to anneal, then let the kiln cool slowly. (An important detailed explanation of the cooling cycle of glass and of annealing continues in the following paragraphs.)

ANNEALING GLASS

Glass has a cooling cycle as well as a firing cycle. If strain, which may cause fracture, is to be avoided, this cycle must be followed. Most kiln-fired materials expand somewhat as their temperature rises and contract as it falls. Glass undergoes this normal thermal expansion and contraction, and in addition, above a certain *transformation* temperature, it undergoes coincidentally a second unique *configurational* change. An intermolecular rearrangement of glass atoms that takes place creates a less open structure in the glass. The change continues at a rate set by the viscosity of the glass as it heats.

No kiln heats evenly throughout. Since most glass is a poor conductor of heat, when the temperature rises in the kiln, warm and cool areas of the glass expand unevenly, causing uneven stresses to form throughout the glass. If the kiln is shut off immediately after firing, the cooling glass will shrink unevenly as it becomes more viscous. Shrinkage is arrested first in the more rapidly cooled areas. Viscosity increases unevenly as the temperature continues to descend, until the intricate internal stresses have become fixed and rigid throughout the glass. The scientific reasons for this behavior of glass are complex. A complete understanding of them is not required of the glass artist, but there should be an awareness that glass does react to high temperature in this manner and that rapidly cooled glass becomes brittle and tends to fracture easily some time after removal from the kiln. This tendency can be controlled by a simple heat treatment called "annealing."

Annealing stabilizes movement within cooling glass so stresses are relieved. As the kiln cools, maintenance of a controlled slow and even temperature gradient (rate of descent) in the hot glass, between certain upper and lower temperature limits known as the *annealing range,* allows time for both configurational and thermal changes to take place. This heat soaking spreads the heat evenly throughout the pliant glass form until flowing glass molecules can gradually realign themselves in an orderly fashion. Strain and brittleness are relieved. The highest point in the annealing range is called the *annealing point;* the lowest temperature is the *strain point.* (Some specific temperatures are given later.) Glass that has cooled without being annealed can and should be reheated above the annealing point and then annealed.

When the temperature has descended to approximately 1000°F, or to the annealing point if it is known, the switches are turned to *low* to hold the temperature stationary for about an hour or longer, according to the kiln load and the size of individual glass objects. Then the switches are turned off. Vents are closed tight during this important period so cooling proceeds slowly and evenly through the annealing range until the temperature descends to 650°F. After that point it can cool more rapidly to room temperature before the glass is removed from the kiln. The rate of descent through the annealing range should be about *20°F every seven minutes* for glass up to ¼ inch thick, and more slowly for large or thick pieces. Two or three layers of glass fused together should be allowed a temperature decrease as slow as *20°F every 10 to 12 minutes* of annealing time. If the temperature drops too fast when your kiln is turned off, switches must be turned back to *low* for five to eight minutes from time to time to slow it down.

The annealing range of different glasses varies as the coefficient (rate or measure) of their expansion varies. The annealing range of stained glass from one manufacturer is 1000°F to 700°F; the annealing range for most window glass falls somewhere between 1070°F and 934°F. It is clear that these different glasses, if fused together, would fracture some time after fusion takes place because they expand and contract at different rates. Temperatures of the annealing range of a specific glass may be obtained from the manufacturer. However, if you cannot get this information, you can determine the rate yourself with a simple test firing. Support a piece of the glass, 6 inches by 1 inch, between two insulation brick posts (across their tops) placed in the kiln so you can observe them through the peephole. Turn the switches to *high.* When the kiln temperature nears 900°F, begin checking the glass closely. The moment a very slight bending of the glass begins, note the exact temperature indicated. Subtract 50°F from that number and you will have the approximate annealing point or top limit of the annealing range of that glass.

FUSED GLASS WINDCHIMES *

Long segments of fused stained glass with silver wire hangers make a colorful set of windchimes that are easy to form. Cut the glass into long rectangular and triangular shapes, two for each chime. When all the planned pieces are cut out, washed and dried, prepare lengths of either nichrome or fine silver wire, 18- or 20-gauge, by curving the ends with small round-nosed jewelry pliers or other shaping tool. Then bend the wires double to make hanging loops for suspending the chimes. Flatten the wire ends gently with a small hammer. The wire ends will be laminated between the top ends of the glass chime layers. Brush each completed wire hanger with alcohol or acetone to remove all traces of soil that could prevent fusion of the glass laminated over them.

Flat molds on which the chimes will be fused are sliced from soft insulation brick with a fine-toothed hacksaw. The top surface of each brick section is rubbed gently with whiting (calcium carbonate) to fill in the pores of the brick and make a smooth surface, as well as to provide a separator between the glass and the insulation brick. It will also prevent the glass from melting into the brick when the kiln is fired. Finally, sift a layer of kiln wash over the whiting. When the glass segments, the wire hangers, and the sections of insulation brick have been prepared, it is time to assemble everything ready for the kiln.

Each chime will be put together on a separate section of brick. Sift clear glass enamel *flux* over the top surface of the *bottom glass segment* of each chime and position it on a section of the prepared brick. Flux will assist the glass fusing process. Pick up one of the wire hangers with tweezers and position it on one end of the glass so the loop extends beyond it. Hold it in place with the

* From an article by the author that appeared in *Ceramics Monthly*.

small tweezers while a second glass shape, cut from the same color of glass, is positioned on top of the wire hanger. The edges of some of the glass chimes may be offset very slightly for an interesting variation. The small offset glass edge should not slump over the edge of the glass beneath it if the heat is turned off at the indicated temperature.

If you want to fuse different stained glass colors together, you will find some colors do not remain fused but crack apart some time after the glass cools; the different oxides and other chemicals that determine stained glass colors result in differences in expansion and contraction as the glass heats and cools, or even when draughts in the room drift over the glass some time after it has fired and cooled. Glasses colored with similar oxides, such as blues, greens, and turquoises are less likely to crack apart when they are fused together. But colors should be test-fired before they are used in an important fused glass project.

When all the glass chimes with their wire hangers in place are assembled on the insulation bricks ready for firing, they are positioned in the cool kiln. Switches are turned to *low*. The door or lid is left open ½ inch to allow fumes and any moisture to escape. After an hour of venting (for these small shapes), the switches are turned to *high* until 950°F is reached, when vents are closed. The best way to check the progress of fused glass is to observe it visually. The differences in kilns, kinds and sizes of glass forms, and other possible factors make firing times variable. Begin checking when the kiln temperature reaches 1200°F; when the edges of the glass are rounded, switches are turned off and the kiln is vented immediately to halt further heat rise. After three minutes of venting, close vents and let the kiln cool slowly, following the annealing procedure as outlined earlier.

When the kiln has cooled completely and the chimes are removed, if some residue of whiting and kiln wash still clings to the glass, sponge it off carefully with warm water. A piece of striated weathered wood makes a support for these windchimes whose long glass strips make a pattern of vertical striations. Colors for the chimes are blue, green, purple, and amber. Fishline cords strung through the silver wire loops are tied to small staples driven into the back of the weathered wooden support. Touch a drop of glue to each cord knot to ensure it against unraveling when wind moves the chimes. The wooden support can be hung with chains or leather thongs.

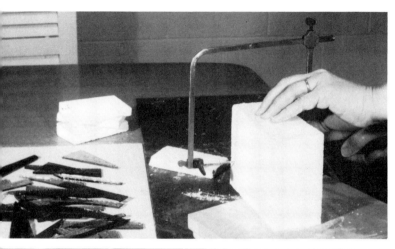

Slice sections of soft insulation brick to make flat molds for fusing the chimes.

The top of each brick section is rubbed with whiting to fill pores and provide a separator. Sift a thin film of kiln wash over it.

Position the wire on one end of the lower glass piece and hold it there with tweezers while the second glass is placed on top of it.

Fishline cords strung through the wire loops are tied to small staples driven into the back of a wood support.

Sponge off any residue of kiln wash that clings to the fired glass.

The completed windchimes are green, blue, purple, and amber, suspended from weathered wood.

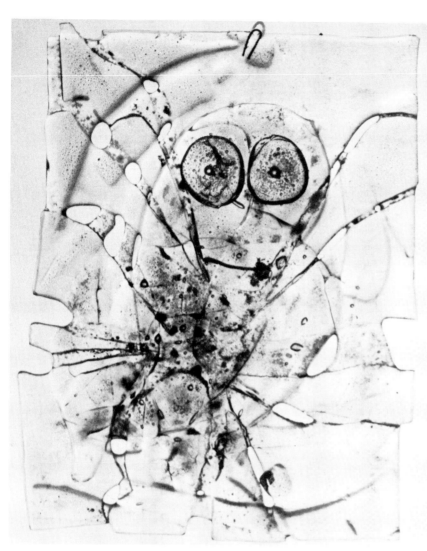

Owl panel. Glenda Davis. Three layers of fragments and sprinklings of transparent green, yellow, and tan glass ices and enamels are fused in one firing.

Fused pendants. Glenda Davis. Clear window glass fragments laminated to glass backgrounds and colored with glass enamels.

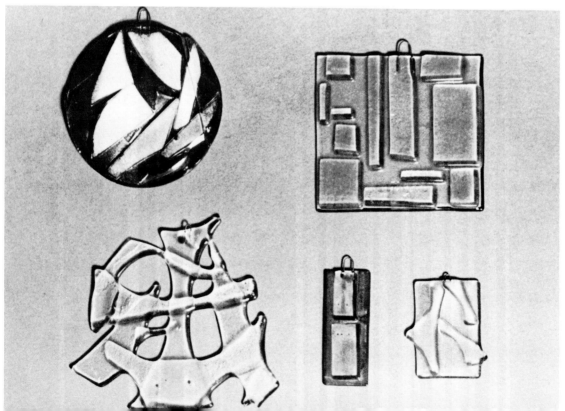

BENT AND LAMINATED GLASS

Bent glass is fired over a three-dimensional mold to a temperature at which glass softens, bends, and takes on the contours of the mold. A fired glass object made from two or more glass pieces fused flat or bent together with some decorative material encased between them is *laminated*. Correct firing procedures are a requirement for successfully fused, bent, or laminated glass. A variation of more than 25° from the ideal temperature required to bring a fired piece to *maturity* may prevent it from attaining its full potential beauty. Because of the wide variation in glass manufacturing formulas, various glasses expand and contract at different rates when exposed to heat; therefore the separate parts of a laminated glass object should be cut from a single piece of glass, if possible. They should at least be cut from similar glass made by the same manufacturer. Otherwise the fired piece may eventually crack apart due to the differences in expansion of its separate glass components.

Beautiful bent and laminated glass objects can be formed with stained glass, but window glass and stained glass cannot be fused or bent together by heat. Inevitably they crack apart because of the wide difference between their coefficients of expansion. Window glass can be given color with glass ices, glass enamels, overglazes, and metallic lusters developed especially to be compatible with all glass when it is fired. Some different colors of the same type stained glass do not remain fused together without cracking. This is especially likely to occur when reds, oranges, and red golds are fused to other colors of glass, but they may fuse to one another successfully. All glass should be test-fired before a fused project is begun. Metallic oxides, carbonates, and other chemical ingredients added to the glass batch to color it, to lower its melting point, to control viscosity, or to attain a workable temperature range give each glass color, type, and thickness its individual rate of expansion. However, stained glass shapes can be fired separately to round their edges and they can then be bonded together, to double-strength window glass, or to plate glass with an epoxy resin made especially for bonding glass to glass.

Most window glass begins to sag almost imperceptibly at 1100°F and settles into its mold at 1250°–1300°F, depending upon the glass thickness. It reaches the top heat required to round its edges at 1400°–1450°F. Both blanks of glass for a lamination may be fired flat separately to the heat required to round the glass edges and thereafter be combined and positioned on the mold to settle into it together. Or they can be laminated flat together before they are positioned on the mold and sagged. If the glass has not been given this prefiring treatment to round the edges, it is left in the kiln on its mold to complete the firing after it has sagged. Glass that has prefired must fire just long enough to settle completely into the mold. It must be annealed after each firing to assure that it will not split or crack between operations.

Stained glass begins to sag at 1000°F and settles into the mold by 1150°F. The edges become softly rounded by 1300°–1350°F. The color variations in each sheet of antique stained glass are so vibrant they need no other embellishment than the form they take when they are contoured over a mold.

Whenever the top glass for a lamination is decorated with powdered glass colorant on the surface that will be turned over and positioned against the lower glass, it must be given an extra spraying with enameling gum. Otherwise some of the glass ice or enamel is sure to drop off the glass when it is turned over. Hold the glass at arm's length and spray it gently so the spray does not blow off the enamel. Dry it completely before the glass is reversed and lowered onto the bottom sheet of glass. (See Section 5, "Decorating Methods and Projects," for additional information on decorating laminations.)

GLASS BENT BY DRAPING

A small disc mold is positioned on top of a column of insulation brick and a 10-inch glass circle is centered over it and fired for an exciting bent glass project. To make the mold, bend a strip of linoleum, shiny side in, to make a 3½-inch circle; tie a string around it to hold it temporarily. Set it on a section of formica board or a sheet of glass and press a clay coil all around the base to secure it and to prevent the mold mix from running out. Paint the inside of the linoleum and the base with a light oil, such as baby oil or vegetable oil, so the mold will release easily. Consult the directions under "Glass Casting" for making the mold mixture. When the glass bends around the disc mold in the heat of the kiln, it may prevent the disc from being removed easily. To facilitate removal, implant a flat coil of nichrome wire into the small mold

circle before the mixture sets. After the glass is bent and cooled, a firm tug on the wire will crumble the expendable mold and make it easy to remove.

When the glass is positioned on its "pedestal" mold and set into a cool kiln, follow regular firing procedures. The glass will begin to bend down in an arc at 1200°F. Watch it closely through the peephole. At about 1300°F, it will form gentle curves around the edge. The kiln is shut off and vented. It is important to avoid opening the door unnecessarily or too often because this will lower the temperature near the door and slow the bending in that area. Gold or silver luster or painted designs can be applied to the glass before it is bent or for a second firing. Fire the luster to 1000°F if the glass has already been bent.

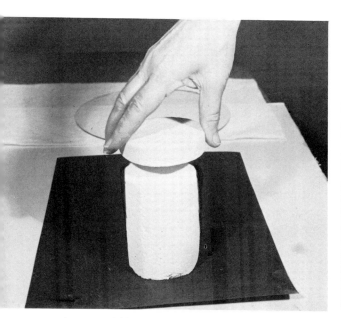

An expendable disc shaped mold made of equal parts of plaster and Plicast Verilite is positioned on top of a column of insulation brick cut with a hacksaw. The disc and the column were rubbed with kiln wash.

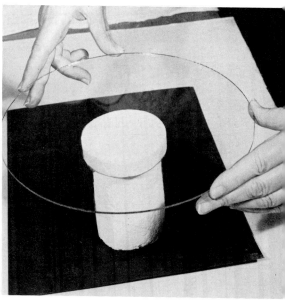

A 10" circle of double-strength window glass is centered over the disc mold. Gold luster can be brushed on the very edge of the glass circle for decorative effect. When the luster dries, the assemblage is transported to the kiln and set back from the door in a front-loading kiln.

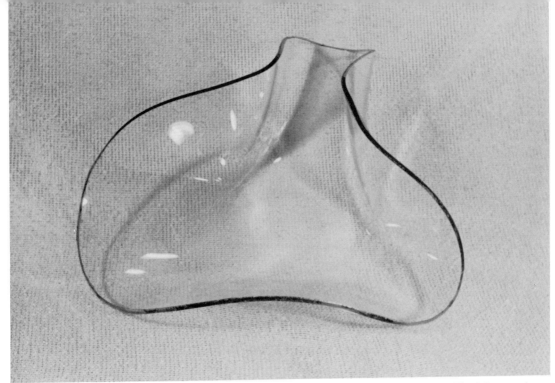

The glass begins to arc at 1200°F. It must be watched closely through the peephole. The kiln was shut off and vented for a few moments at 1300°F. The completed glass form has a gold luster edge.

A small circle of light blue cathedral glass bent further at 1250°F. Stained glass softens at lower temperature than window glass.

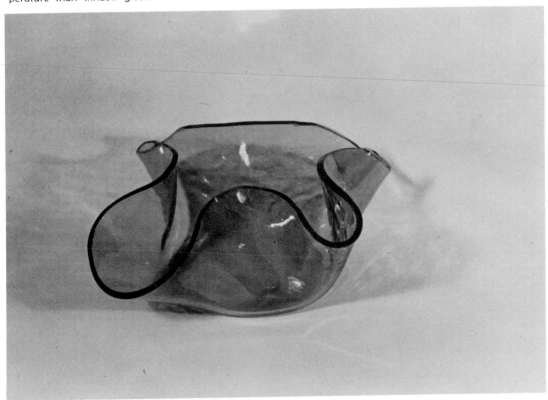

BUBBLES IN LAMINATED GLASS

The bubbles that frequently appear in laminated glass are an accepted and usually beautiful characteristic of fused glass, although large bubbles caused by incorrect firing may not be decorative. Bubbles form in laminations when air spaces are enclosed by powdered glass colorants or any materials that do not leave escape routes for trapped air to travel to the edge of the laminated glass as it fuses. If a bowl has steep sides, bubbles may be entrapped at the point where the base meets the sides of the mold. Included material may continue to hold the glass elevated for a while after the surrounding glass starts to fuse;

small bubbles clustered around the inclusion can be exciting.

Bubbles are induced in a lamination if you add tiny dots of fresh baking soda to the lower glass wherever you want them. A general bubble effect is achieved if a pinch of baking soda is blended in some powdered colorant and sifted over the lower glass. Whenever an even layer of powdered glass color is sifted over the glass in a lamination, to avoid unwanted bubbles, sift a little extra layer of the powder or colorless glass flux in the center area; the centers will fuse first and force air to the outside edge where it can escape.

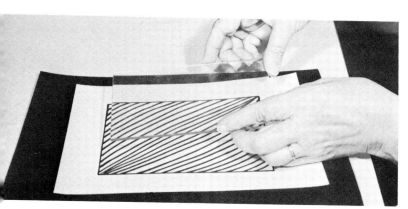

A square of single-strength window glass is laid over a design of freehand drawn lines.

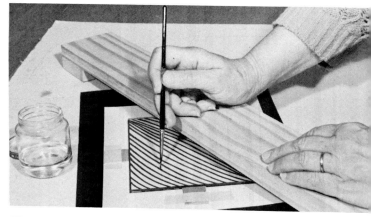

Small squares of thick cardboard are taped against each side of the glass to hold it in place. A wood "bridge" supports the hand to steady it while lines of squeegee oil are traced over the drawn lines.

Dark enamel is sifted generously over the drawn lines.

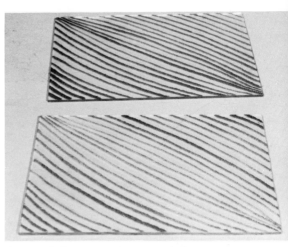

Excess enamel is tapped from the glass.

A second glass square is prepared the same way. The glass must be "baked" on aluminum foil in a warm oven at 350°F to drive off gases from the oil before it is fused.

One glass square is turned over and lowered carefully onto the other glass. They are fired to 1450°F to fuse the glass.

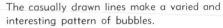

The casually drawn lines make a varied and interesting pattern of bubbles.

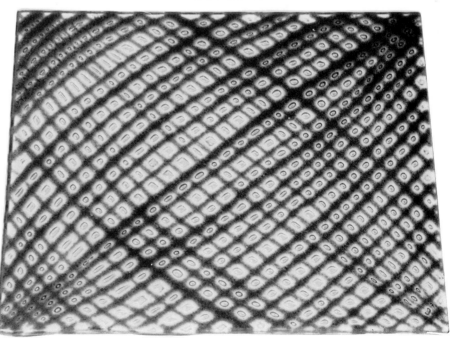

Laminated plate. Glenda Davis. The two circles of glass were enameled and sprayed with enameling gum. Lines were scratched through the powder on each circle and the two were laminated for this attractive effect.

Light transparent enamel is sifted all over the glass. A tiny sifter dusts red opaque enamel in a trailed design.

A pointed wooden skewer scratches holes in the red design.

A second clear glass circle is positioned over the enamel-covered glass.

The two are lowered carefully and exactly centered on the prepared mold, which has been sifted with fresh kiln wash.

The glass has slumped and edges are fused at 1450°F.

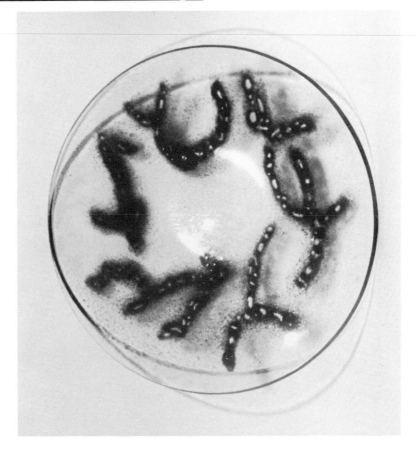

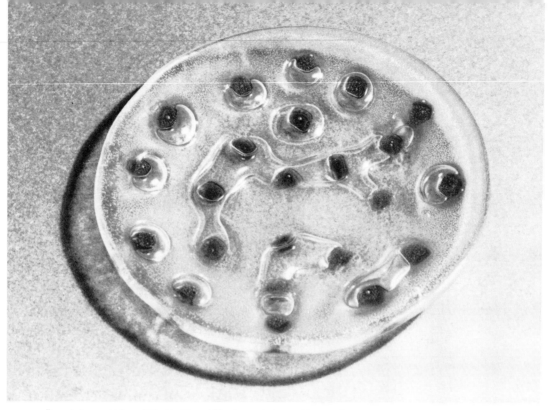

Fused tray. Alden Abbott. Two 7" glass circles with small squares of colored bottle glass laminated between them and slumped.

Two glass circles laminated. Alden Abbott. Lines were drawn through enamels in a gentle arc on each circle of glass. They were sprayed with enameling gum and dried, then fused together.

PREFORMED GLASS OBJECTS

Discarded glass bottles have endless possibilities as potential decorative objects; fired rings cut from bottles make wonderful units in mosaics or for jewelry. Most commercial bottles are made of "soft" glass that is low fusing. Since many of them are very thick however, especially wine bottles, they must often be fired as high as 1550°F to 1600°F to fuse them flat. The glass fires to a lovely silken gloss that gives them great depth of color. The bottom of a bottle is very bulky and can be massive when it folds or collapses toward the top of the bottle, which it always does in firing flat. It is advisable to remove this unwieldly section of glass before the bottle is slumped into a mold. A round bottle that is laid horizontal in its mold tends to roll sideways. To prevent it from rolling, sift an extra amount of kiln wash at the point of contact, then sink the bottle on it. This should hold it.

Bottle cutting should be practiced on any available ordinary bottles before you risk an especially attractive specimen. It requires considerable practice to make a clean severance. Although theoretically bottles can be scored and separated by adhering masking tape around the bottle, then scoring an unbroken line along the tape with a glass cutter, when you start to score, the cutter tends to skitter off on a path of its own choice as you press it against the slick curved glass. There are several excellent types of bottle cutters on the market and they are accompanied by detailed instructions and suggestions for their use. The one in the demonstration project can be used to cut various sizes of glass bottles and jugs; and it costs only a few dollars. Investing in one of these gadgets is more rewarding than trying to improvise a cutter.

For the illustrated project, the bottom and threaded top of the green wine bottle were removed. A slab clay mold was made to follow the contours of the bottle but leaving extra inches to allow for the glass stretching

Wall hanging. BoBo Zinn. All segments of glass are laminated with enamels sgraffitoed and bubbles achieved with seven parts enamel mixed with one part baking soda. *Photo by Drew Henery.*

out as the bottle flattened. Coils of clay were laid under the edges of the slab to give it a shallow contour as the clay dried. It was fired slowly to cone 08 (or 1800°F). Then the kiln was turned off and left to cool completely before the mold was removed.

The wine bottle was fired to 1600°F to flatten it as it slumped into the mold. It was annealed for two hours because of the thickness of the glass. When the bottle tray cooled, long stripes of gold metallic luster were brushed from one end to the other on the tray. The luster was fired to 1000°F.

Almost any kind of bottle or jar can be made attractive when it is mosaicked with very small glass tesserae. Flat-sided bottles or flasks are easy to decorate, but curved ones require a little patience. Because it takes some time for epoxy to set, only one row can be affixed at a time on a curved surface. Additional glass would slide off before it adhered. On this kind of surface, the glass pieces should be narrow. A round jar or bottle is laid horizontal and anchored between two sticks that are tacked to a board. Epoxy the tesserae and apply a row along the ridge of the horizontal plane and let it set before you begin the next row. Be sure to use special glass adhesive. When the board and bottle are set up in a convenient out-of-the-way place, the rows can be applied while other activities are going on. If the epoxy is mixed correctly (and the room temperature is not below 70°F), it should set firm in three hours. Three or four rows can be applied in one day. For additional instruction on mosaics, see "Mosaics" in Section 3.

The left hand swings the cutter toward the right hand, which holds the bottle firm at the top. The bottle is rotated clockwise as the left hand continues to score it with the cutter.

A tapper that comes with the cutter taps under the score line. As soon as a crack appears, the glass is tapped just ahead of the crack on the scored line until the crack has developed all around the bottle. The glass should separate with a final sharp rap of the tapper.

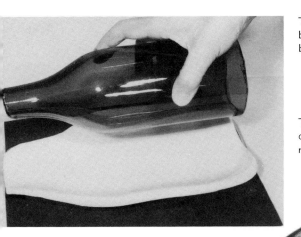

The prepared clay slab mold is sifted with kiln wash before the bottle is positioned. The bottle's top and bottom have been removed.

The fired bottle tray is decorated with long stripes of gold luster. The shape of the mold has given the narrow end a gentle curve.

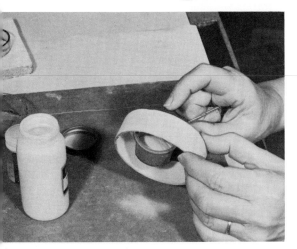

To give color to glass rings cut from colorless bottles, spray them with enameling gum and sift high-fire transparent or opaque glass ices or enamels over inside and outside of a ring before it is fired flat.

A colorless small bottle ring was given coats of imperial blue and light turquoise transparent enamels, then it was fused flat. Fused glass jewels made from scraps of colored glass were epoxied to the ring and to one another only at *points of contact.* The open spaces between them give a delicate effect. (For making the little glass "Jewels," see Section 6.)

A round lidded candy jar is laid horizontal and anchored between two
sticks tacked to a board. Stained
glass tesserae are epoxied along the
ridge of the horizontal plane. The
epoxy must set before the next row
of glass is applied.

Grout is applied with a very flexible
rubber spatula.

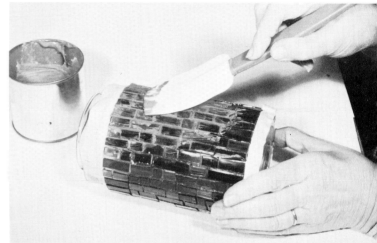

The completed mosaicked candy jar.
Notice that a few additional glass
pieces were cemented on top of the
glass in several places to give a more
sculptural effect.

RECYCLE YOUR BOTTLES INTO "STAINED GLASS"

The countless methods and objects that
are made from emptied bottles alone comprise a fascinating glasscraft. Glass artist Bruce
Laughlin, known for his beautiful fused and
bent glass, suggests a way to recycle colored
and clear glass bottles by making "stained
glass" for use in leaded, bonded, or bent work.
The clear glass is colored with sifted glass ices
and enamels after it is flattened.

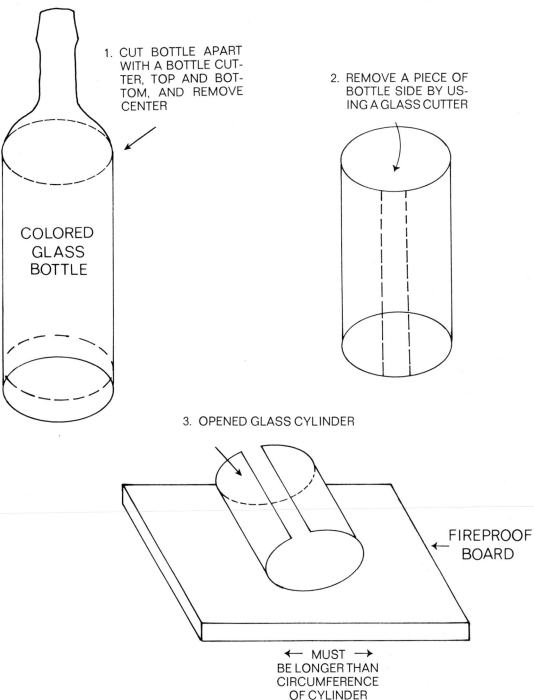

1. CUT BOTTLE APART WITH A BOTTLE CUTTER, TOP AND BOTTOM, AND REMOVE CENTER

COLORED GLASS BOTTLE

2. REMOVE A PIECE OF BOTTLE SIDE BY USING A GLASS CUTTER

3. OPENED GLASS CYLINDER

FIREPROOF BOARD

← MUST →
BE LONGER THAN CIRCUMFERENCE OF CYLINDER

Bruce Laughlin's make-your-own stained glass idea. A section of bottle is cut open and fired flat. The small colored glass rectangles can be used for leaded or bonded glass. If the narrow strip is not removed from the glass before it is fired flat, the glass will fuse shut again instead of opening out flat in the kiln heat. The glass should flatten at 1200°F. It is annealed for two hours if it is thicker than ⅛".

Mold-blown jar, designed, sandblasted, and etched by Polly Rothenberg.

5
Decorating Methods and Projects

DECORATING LAMINATIONS

THE objective in laminating two or more layers of glass is to entrap materials that will give decorative effects between the layers that could not be fired to the top surface of the glass. For example, the enamels fired to metal are not always compatible with glass, but they can be fired between glass layers if they are not applied too thickly. Other materials such as flattened silver wire, underglazes, stenciled patterns in glass ices and enamels, very fine glass crushings, enamel threads, and combinations of these materials can be laminated safely.

Laminated materials must be thin, flat, and dispersed over the surface of the lower glass so bare glass spaces are left between them. The bare spaces fuse to the covering glass and seal the lamination together. Small bubbles form around these entrapped designs and add to the decorative effect. Both sheets of glass must be clean and of identical glass. Small dabs of Elmer's Glue-all will hold the material to the glass and should keep them in place until they can be safely positioned in the kiln. The materials to be laminated must be completely dry before you combine both sheets of glass on the mold, ready for firing.

COLORANTS FOR BENT AND LAMINATED GLASS

Special glass ices, enamels, and painting colors are formulated with the correct coefficient of expansion to fit glass that will be fired. Glass ices are available in *high-fire* and *low-fire* colors designated as HF and LF. The high-fire ice colors are fired on the surface and between flat or contoured laminated glass by firing them to 1500°F–1600°F. The glass must be annealed after the colors are fired on it. Low-fire colors will fuse to the surface of glass objects at about 1050°F–1100°F. These low-fire colors are useful for decorating glass that will not be bent or laminated. Each series includes a clear glass flux that is sifted lightly over glass surfaces to assure a sparkling finish and subtle texturing. A small amount of regular metal enamels can be used *in combination* with high-fire glass ices for laminations where additional or intensified colors are wanted. Most metal enamels are generally unsatisfactory when they are used alone on glass surfaces, but they can be laminated between two glass sheets if they are not applied too thick. In combination with glass ices, a ratio of four parts glass ice to one part metal enamel is suggested.

The glass ices and enamels used for

projects in this book are 80-mesh powders. To apply them to glass, a thin layer of adhesive such as light oil or enameling gum is applied to the glass surface before the glass colors are sifted in a thin layer with an 80-mesh sifter. When the glass has been cleaned thoroughly with a thin solution of detergent water, brush it with squeegee oil or lavender oil. Or agar, Klyrfire, or other enameling gum can be applied with a power sprayer or aerosol spray unit in a solution thinned with water so it will go through the sprayer. Spray guns or atomizers manipulated by hand may give erratic distribution of the spray that makes droplets or other disfigurations in the enamel layer. Once the two glasses are laminated, these unwanted marks cannot be eliminated. Dry the glass thoroughly before it is fired. Oils must be baked off at 300°F before the glass is laminated.

Decorating colors for *painting on glass* are easily mixed with one of several mediums, depending on the decorating problem. The powdered kind should be mixed with squeegee oil or other light painting oil where slow drying is desirable. The powders should be mixed with water, Klyrfire, or other enameling gum for painting, spot decoration, or laminated color. The decorating colors are bought in *low fire* (1100°F) and *high fire* (1500°F). The low-fire series are used either for glass surfaces where no distortion is planned or where bending has already taken place. The high-fire series are used for surface decoration of glass that will be slumped or laminated. Moisture or oils must be driven off by slow drying in a warm place before colorants are laminated between glass layers. Otherwise the fumes may be trapped and may discolor the glass. *Ready-mixed moist colors* are applied with a fine pointed brush.

Glass ices, enamels, and dry and moist painting colors used in projects in this book were from Thomas C. Thompson Company. Other companies that sell glass colorants are listed in Supply Sources. Eighty-mesh sifters with convenient handles are available at metal enamel supply stores.

Glass bowl. R. Bruce Laughlin. Enamels and glass ices are laminated between two glass circles and slumped in a mold. Lines were sgraffitoed through a design for this stunning effect.

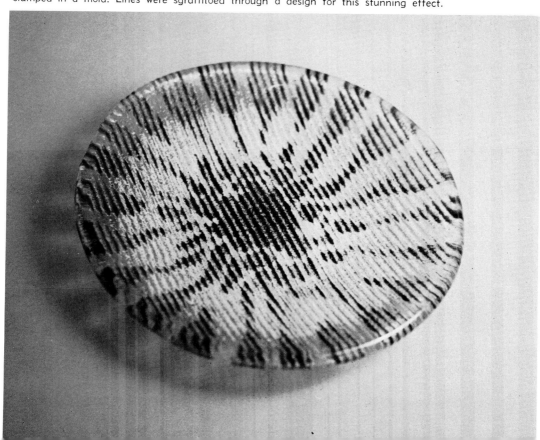

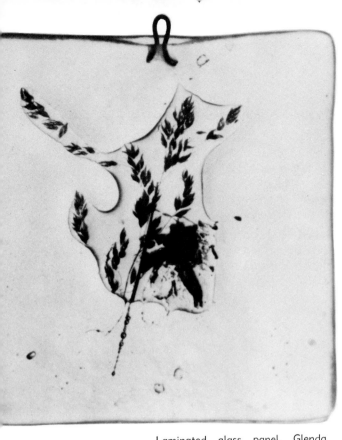

Laminated glass panel. Glenda Davis. Weeds fused between two panels of window glass become black and charred but retain their forms. The gray area is smoked glass resulting from the fumes of the weeds as they were heated.

Ragweed fused in glass. Glenda Davis.

Weed fused in glass. Glenda Davis.

EMBOSSED GLASS

When small glass shapes are fired to a glass base, all the applied pieces and the base must be cut from one variety of glass made by the same manufacturer. Clean all the glass with detergent water, rinse it well and dry it. Dabs of Elmer's Glue-all will hold the small pieces in position until they are fused. Colored glass decorating powders are sifted over them either before or after they are positioned, depending upon the desired effect. Fire the assemblage until the edges of the applied glass and the base are rounded, about 1350°F for window glass. Although stained glass cannot be fired successfully to window glass, a beautiful effect can be achieved when stained glass shapes are fired flat separately to round their edges and are subsequently epoxied to the window glass base.

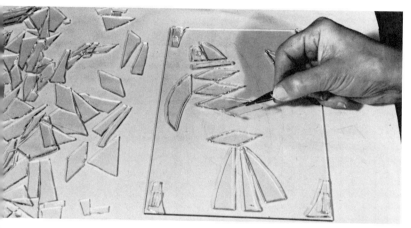

GLASS SEASCAPE

Clear glass fragments are tentatively positioned on a rectangle to develop a design.

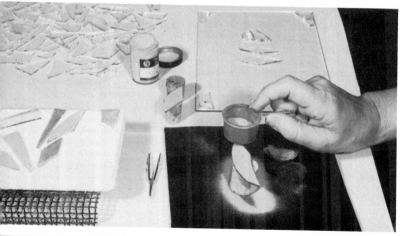

Individual pieces are sifted with low-firing powdered glass colors and placed on a slice of prepared insulation brick to fire the colors.

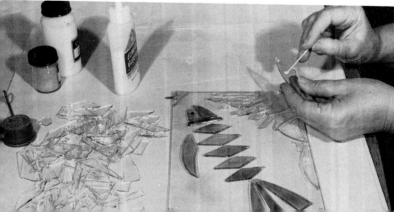

All the glass pieces are stuck to the glass panel with dabs of Elmer's Glue-all to keep them from shifting before they are fired.

Siftings of blue, green, and aqua transparent glass ices are applied to the background and glass "seaweeds." It does not matter if some of the color drifts onto the fish design.

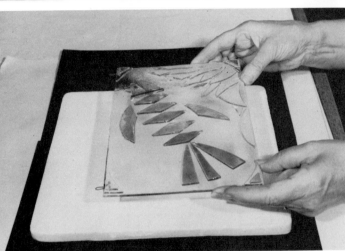

A kiln shelf has been prepared with a light sifting of kiln wash as a separator. The glass panel is lowered carefully onto the shelf. The glue holds everything secure. It will fire out in the kiln and leave no ash.

Glass seascape in blue, aqua, turquoise, and purple.

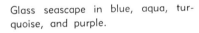

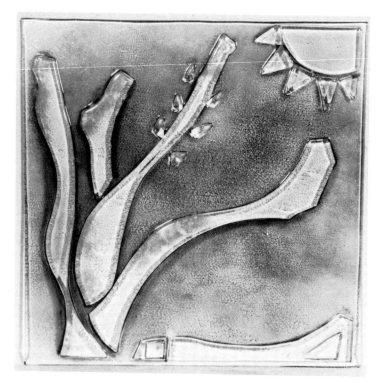

Glass landscape. The embossed shapes are glued in place with bits of Elmer's glue before glass ices are sifted over them. Chartreuse is sifted on the applied shapes and transparent red over the background with the colors merging. The panel is given one firing to 1350°F.

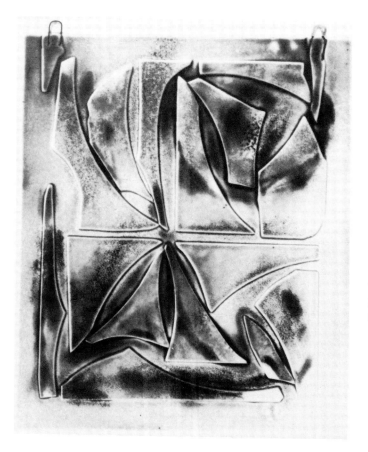

THE SAILBOAT. Glenda Davis. Transparent and opaque blues, transparent green, opaque orange, and white.

Fused panel. BoBo Zinn. A wedge of glass with added smaller pieces of glass is covered with a combination of blue and green glass ices and opaque enamels. It is fired until it is glowing red and molten on the kiln shelf. Edges are pulled up and pleated with a firing tool while the glass is still in the kiln. (Gloves must be worn for this method.) A clear glass panel is fired without color to achieve rounded edges and attach the hook. The two panels are bonded with R-TV Glue. Overall size: 10″ X 4″. *Photo by Drew Henery.*

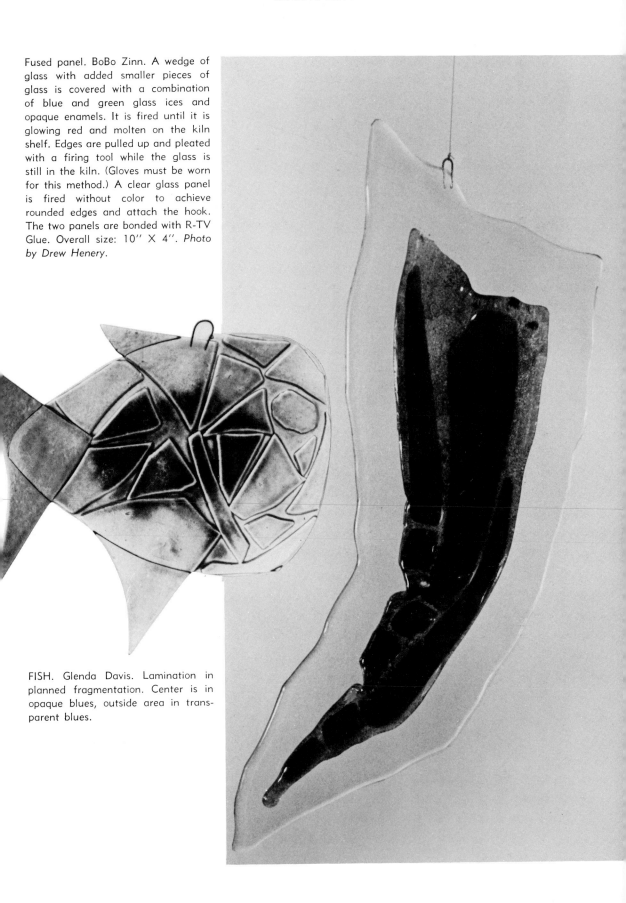

FISH. Glenda Davis. Lamination in planned fragmentation. Center is in opaque blues, outside area in transparent blues.

BOTTLES. Glenda Davis. Fused fragments. Transparent colors in green, blue, pink, and tan.

3D Form. Alden Abbott. Small single-strength triangles are fused flat on the circle. Extra-thick triangles are fused on edge.

Brown stained glass geese heads were fired to round their edges. They are traced on paper to locate their position for a panel design.

The panel was prepared with stenciled heads of flying geese and corner hangers fired on it. The stained glass shapes are epoxied to the background glass.

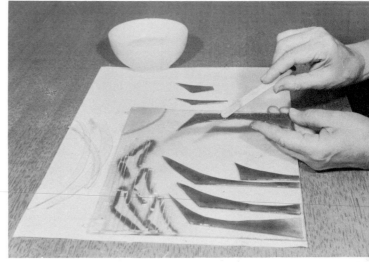

FLIGHT OF THE BROWN GEESE. The thin strips of clear glass epoxied over stenciled heads of flying geese are drifting clouds. Colorless glass waves epoxied over the brown geese are a third layer of bonded glass. Part of an orange moon is bonded to the upper right corner. This is an example of both fused and bonded glass to develop an idea.

PAINTING ON STAINED GLASS— FIRED

The lavish painting of stained glass cathedral windows during the final stages of the Renaissance cast the art into controversy for centuries, but today the restrained and thoughtful use of fired paints can add variation and emphasis to stained glass designs. In leaded glass, the leads form the chief linear expression. Glass paint should not interfere with the integrity of the lead line design nor obscure the pervasive beauty of transparent stained glass.

This demonstration project does not include leads. Small squares of green gold antique glass depend on the black painted lines for decorative design. Although the complex professional painting applied to large windows requires methods and skills beyond the simple treatment described here, linear patterns and judicious brushstrokes applied with glass paint are another of the many techniques well within the ability of the serious amateur.

Prepare glass in the usual way by washing it with a thin solution of detergent water. Rinse it with warm water and dry it. Tape it over a design drawn on paper that extends beyond the glass. The square of glass and the pattern taped to the underside of it are rotated together on the light box as the work progresses. Apply your brushstrokes in the direction that is easiest for you to control, by simply turning the paper. An armrest or "bridge," made from a board with flat wood blocks nailed under each end, will elevate your hand and wrist above the glass surface while you work. It will prevent them from smearing the paint or soiling the glass with oil from your skin, which can cause the paint to "skip." It is advisable to make the bridge long enough that the blocks rest on the frame of the light box rather than on its glass top where undue pressure could crack the glass.

The paint employed in this project is one of Thompson's glass colors. It should fire smooth, shiny, and permanent at 1100°F. These dry powdered paints can be mixed with oil or water-based binders. Lavender oil or squeegee oil do not leave an ash when they are fired. If you prefer a water-based binder, try an agar solution in the proportion of one part liquid agar to three parts water. A commercial medium called Klyrfire can also be used effectively for mixing glass paints. Water-based binders dry rapidly. Oils dry more slowly and should be dried with some mild heat such as 300°F in an oven or on top of a warm kiln. Oil promotes a smooth-flowing application of the paint that does not dry it out on the palette while you are using it. Whether you use water or oil is a matter of personal preference. Several manufacturers make and sell glass paints and binders.

Liner brushes (pure red sable) are excellent for painting fine, long, smooth lines and details. The brush used for this project is a #4 red sable liner. Its bristles are long, thin, and flexible. To mix the paint, heap a small mound of dry powdered glass paint on the palette and add a few drops of paint medium as you blend it with a small palette knife. Work it into a smooth homogeneous mix of good brushing consistency. To load the brush, roll it into the paint to work plenty of pigment into the bristles; then stroke the brush lightly two or three times on the bare glass palette to relieve it of excess paint. It must retain enough paint to flow smoothly through a complete stroke without suddenly going dry. Movement of the brush is controlled with the fingers rather than with the arm or wrist as in oil painting. Rest the palm of your hand on the bridge and make the strokes without too much pressure. Vary the width of lines by rolling the brush as you stroke it. Let the paint dry before you carve away irregularities with a pointed round toothpick, a sliver of pointed bamboo or other scriber.

The paint must dry completely before it is fired. If you are firing only one or two glass pieces, set them on a prepared section of insulation brick that has been rubbed with dry whiting to fill its pores, then sift kiln wash over it. If you are firing several pieces or a large glass shape, they can be fired directly on the kiln shelf. It must be prepared in the usual way with a separator to prevent the glass from sticking to the shelf when it is fired. Lower the glass into position and put it into a cool kiln before you turn on the heat. Keep the glass away from the electric elements; if the kiln loads from the front, position the glass away from the door opening. Turn the switch to *low* and leave the kiln door ajar ½ inch to permit glass paint fumes and any remaining moisture to escape. After a half hour, close the door or lid, but leave vents open and turn the heat to *high*. At 950°F close vents; keep a close watch over the temperature rise. Turn off the kiln when the thermostat indicates 1100°F, or when the paint becomes shiny and smooth. Vent the kiln to halt heat rise. After two or three minutes, close the vents again and let the kiln cool normally, making sure to keep it tightly closed so it does not cool too rapidly. When it has cooled, if the fired paint seems too thin, add a second coat and refire the glass.

Painted effects made with brushes, scratching tools, masking tape, rubber cement, stencils, crumpled toweling, and other texturing devices are possibilities for the craftsman who wants to add this dimension to his glass works. It is for the artist himself to decide.

The ends of a wooden "bridge" rest on the light table frame. A design is outlined, not filled in solid, so work can be observed as painting progresses. Paint one coat and fire it; additional coats can be added.

After the first firing, thin areas will be apparent. If a perfectly opaque design is preferred, paint a second coat and fire it again.

Four small gold antique glass windows in a Colonial door are painted in opaque black.

The demonstration of painting small stained glass panes for a Colonial door is quite simple. Although this book does not cover the painting of large stained glass windows as developed in a large studio, a few words should be said about it here. In one method of painting a window, an easel of plate glass is laid over a design and the stained glass shapes are positioned on the plate. Hot beeswax is spooned on junctures and between joints to secure each glass in the relative position it will occupy in the completed window, allowing for an even spacing between segments that will be filled by the leads. This assures that painted details are carried smoothly across the glass. When the wax is hard, the easel may be placed upright and secured in a window where daylight exists. With a variety of brushes, the skillful glass artist applies details to complete a subject already defined by the vibrant glass colors and the leads.*

* Patrick Reyntiens, *The Technique of Stained Glass.* Watson-Guptill Publications, New York.

Fred Conese waxing up stained glass for painting. *Photo by courtesy of Willet Stained Glass Studios.*

A selection of artist's brushes for painting glass. *Photo by courtesy of Willet Stained Glass Studios.*

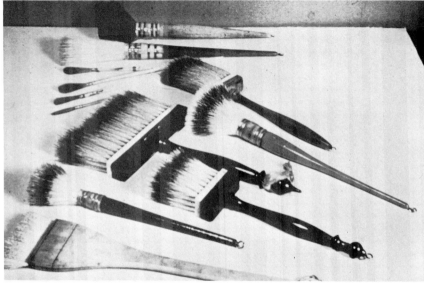

Ray DiHaven painting a waxed-up window with monotone for Willet Stained Glass Studios. The paint is dried and kiln-fired. *Photo by Ted Koepper.*

GLASS PAINTS—UNFIRED

If you prefer to use a glass paint that does not require firing, it is well to select one of the epoxy paints made especially for painting on glass.* The paint usually is sold in large paint stores. At present, it comes in both two-component and ready mixed form in quarts and gallons that are available in several colors. Unless you plan to use all the paint when it is first opened, it is best to select the two-component variety and mix it in the exact proportions indicated on the container.

* Epoxy paint used in the demonstrated project is two-component O'Brien Mira-plate epoxy coating.

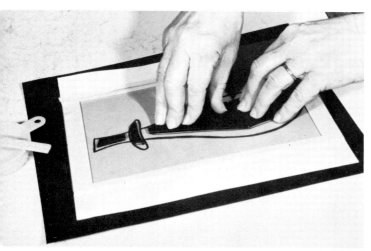

An outline sketch is taped under the glass base. Sections of stained glass are spread with epoxy and pressed firmly in place. Dry it overnight.

Unfired paint with stained glass bonded to clear glass.

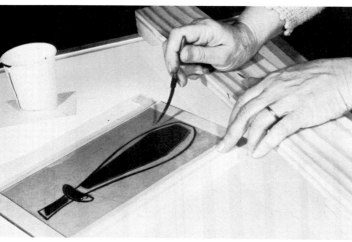

A flexible Mack Sword Striper brush #0 with black epoxy paint is traced over the yellow glass, following the bottle sketch underneath it. The light in the table shows up the sketch clearly. Dry the paint for several hours, but do not fire it.

SANDBLASTING AND ENGRAVING

Growing enthusiasm for decorative and functional glass art of all kinds has aroused new interest in surface enrichment of this dramatic transparent material. Increased zeal among craftsmen for etching glass with a sandblaster is prompting large and small colleges to install major sandblasting equipment for use in their regular art programs. Today large art glass studios include sandblasted glass in their commissioned works. Although the equipment represents a substantial investment, especially for the small glass studio, commercial sheet and plate glass companies have begun to offer sandblasting services to their customers. They may etch your properly prepared glass for a fee.

Sandblasting on glass achieves a frosted effect of translucent to transparent contrast. Almost any kind of glass is suitable: sheet crystal, window glass, preformed shapes such as bottles, vases, goblets, and glass sculptures. Stained glass of the "flashed" variety is beautiful when it is etched. Mirrored glass is another favorite for this method. Contemporary artist-craftsmen have a special fondness for etching blown glass sculptures.

To begin, cover the glass all over with masking tape, lapping the strips and making sure the tape is pressed closely against the glass so sand is not forced under it. Be careful to cover all the edges. Draw a simple design on the tape with a sharp pencil point. Using a sharp stencil knife or single-edge razor blade, cut around and peel away sections of the tape to reveal areas to be etched. Now the glass is ready for the sandblaster.

The equipment must include an exhaust fan for drawing off silica dust that is harmful to the lungs. A compressor is required to blast out the stream of special cutting sand. A coarse sand called flint shot, made from St. Peter's sandstone quarried in the Midwest, and carborundum grains are two abrasives commonly used on glass. Heavy gloves sealed

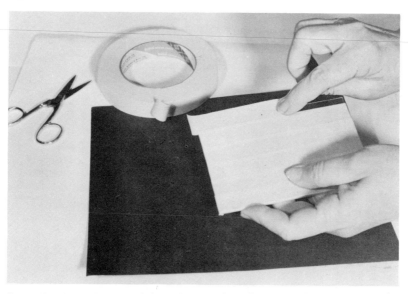

Cover the glass all over with lapped strips of masking tape. Be sure to cover the edges.

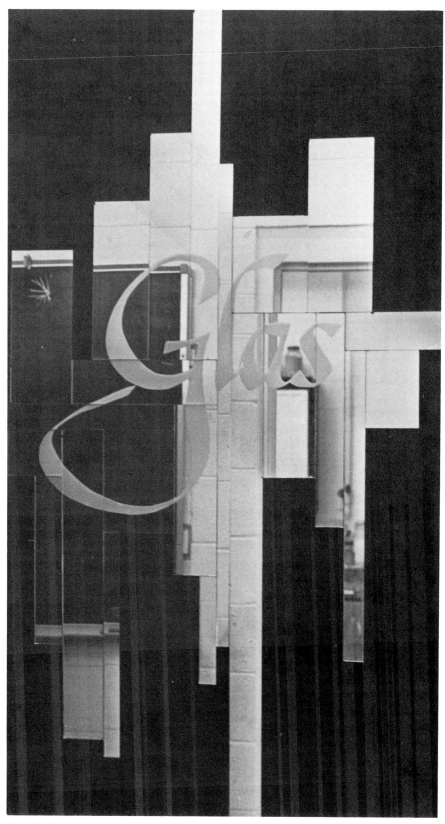

Mural of mirrored glass with designs etched by sandblasting. The Georgian College of Applied Arts and Technology, Barrie, Ontario. *Georgian College photos by Marc Robillard.*

into openings in the front wall of the sand-blasting machine allow you to thrust your hands into the gloves that project into a lighted airtight interior. You can view the interior through a window while you manipulate the glass, constantly turning and revolving it under the forced sand, controlled by a foot switch outside the machine. There are different-sized machines to suit a variety of requirements.

When the frosted glass is removed from the machine, parts of the design can be. taken further. If tape is peeled from the glass to reveal clear areas, new tape can be masked over certain sections of the etched and clear glass and it is returned to the sandblaster to achieve deeper or lighter carving and shading. In addition, a combination of sandblasting and engraving can give the glass design an airy lightness.

Linear designs are drawn into the glass surface with an engraving tool. There are many types of engravers; the one described here is a small hand-held electric tool. A dental drill with a variety of tips is excellent for engraving on glass. The artist who is adept with freehand sketching may be able, with practice, to engrave directly and freely. Others will need to tape a pattern to the underside of the glass and engrave over its guiding lines. It is advisable to practice on scraps or small rectangles of glass to work out ideas for strokes before embarking on any glass engraving projects. Fine lines are incised by holding the engraving tool as vertical as possible. For matting broad areas, tilt it on the side and skim or vibrate it lightly over the glass. To engrave deeply, inscribe a succession of light strokes, one over the other. Above all, do not be disheartened by your initial shaky strokes. With practice, you will find that instead of striking small blows that take your tool off on a tangent, you are beginning to achieve firm skillful strokes. Engraving glass will become a delight.

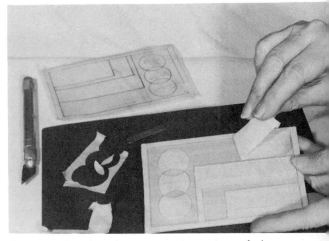

Cut around and peel away certain sections of the tape to reveal the areas of the glass you want to etch.

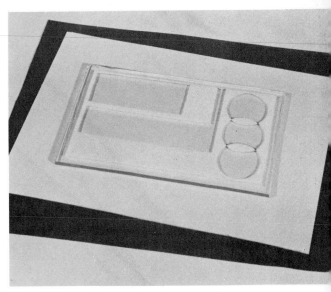

The sandblasted areas cast shadows along their edges, which become part of the design.

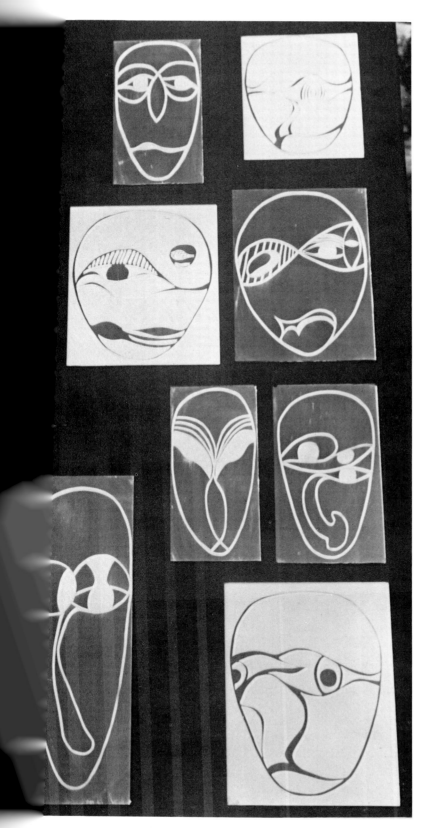

FACES. Glass Design Department of Georgian College. Sandblasting combined with etching on mirrored glass.

▶

Designer Kornelia Meszaros and artist Robin Clarke plan a design for engraving a bowl of blown glass. Glass Design Department, Georgian College.

▶

Engraved strokes are practiced on a glass scrap before the tool is applied to a glass form. To matt broad areas, the tip of the engraver is tilted on its side and skimmed lightly over the glass. Robin Clarke, *left*, and Kornelia Meszaros, *right*.

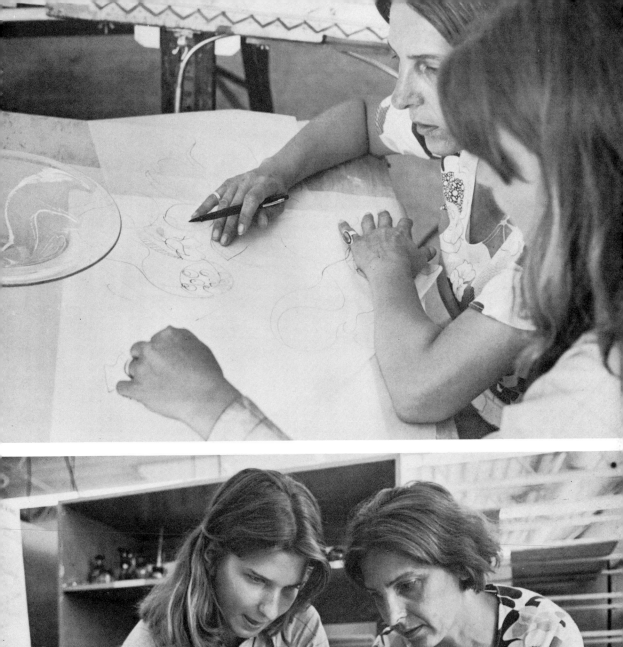

SGRAFFITO

Spray or paint over a glass sheet with enameling gum, then sift colored glass powder over the gum. When it has dried, use any scratching tool to remove lines or spaces in the glass ice or enamel to create a design. The glass can be positioned over a drawn design or you can work it out freehand if you can sketch. A light table is useful if you are using dark powders. In drawing your lines, remember, lines that do not lead off the edge of the glass will likely trap bubbles in the lamination, but not on a top surface. Fired sgraffito lines drawn in light transparent colors are not as pronounced as lines scratched in dark or opaque colors. Metal enamels come in many beautiful and intense colors. They can be used for sgraffito work if they are laminated *between* two glass sheets. If oil is used for the adhesive, it must be baked off in an oven at 350°F before the enamel is sgraffitoed or combined for lamination.

In the demonstrated project, glass rectangles are cut from single-strength window glass. They are washed with detergent water, rinsed and dried. One glass is sprayed with diluted agar solution of one part liquid agar to three parts water, a consistency that will go through a sprayer without clogging it. Deep blue transparent enamels are sifted over the gummed surface and dried. The enamel is sgraffitoed with two combs in a pattern of crossed lines that lead off the glass edges. The enamel is sprayed again with gum and *dried*. A clear glass rectangle is lowered gently onto the prepared glass that has been positioned on a kiln shelf sifted with kiln wash. The combined glass sheets will be fused flat before they are slumped on a clay mold. If you have a steady hand, they can be positioned together on the mold and fired in one operation to slump them.

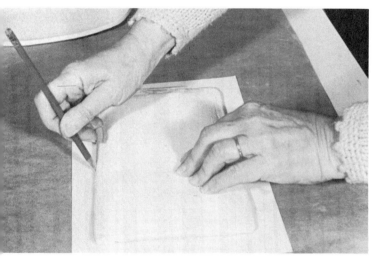

The outline of a mold for a rectangular tray is traced on thin cardboard for a pattern.

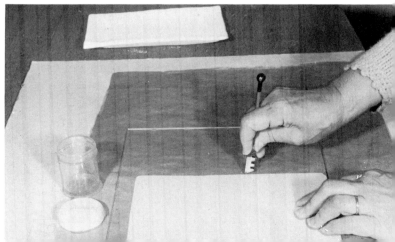

Two individual sheets of single-strength window glass are cut around the pattern.

One glass is sprayed with a solution of three parts water to one part agar.

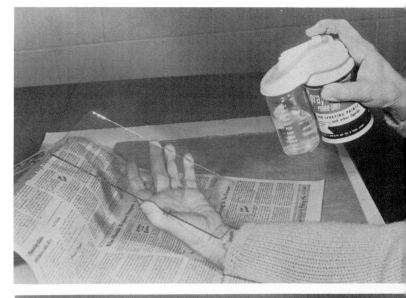

The glass is propped on corks so it can be picked up easily. Transparent blue enamels and glass flux are sifted over it. It is dried and sgraffitoed.

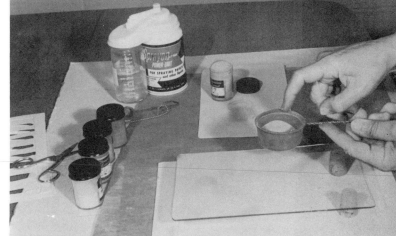

Because regular metal enamels have been used, a second clear glass sheet is laminated to it and fired flat on the kiln shelf. Notice the small combs on the left that were the scratching tools. Firing temperature is 1400°F to blunt edges and fuse the enamels.

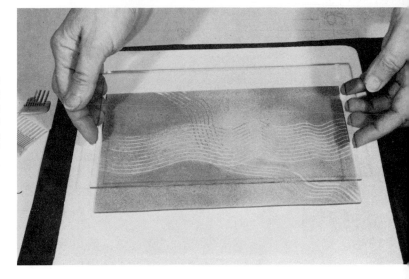

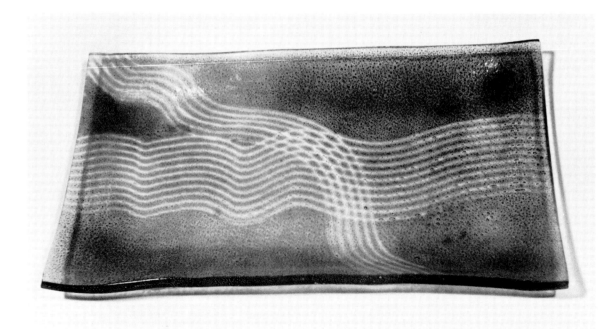

The laminated glass is slumped on a clay mold to 1300°F.

Sgraffitoed glass panel. Alden Abbott.

LAMINATED SILVER FOIL AND STENCIL

To laminate powdered glass colorants or other materials between two layers of glass that will be decorated and slumped, preparatory processes are planned in a workable sequence. In the demonstrated project employing silver foil and stenciled glass enamels, the silver foil areas are applied and fired first.

Clean the glass and dry it. Position the bottom glass layer over a drawn design. The design area that will become foil is transferred to tracing paper. Place a foil sheet between the traced design and another sheet of tracing paper. Cut out the design through the two sheets of tracing paper and the silver foil. The foil is too fragile to be cut by itself. With the foil still held between the tracing paper, lay it on a firm surface and prick holes all over it with a sharp needle. These holes will permit gases and moisture to escape as the foil is fired.

Brush enameling gum on the planned foil location on the glass; immediately press a damp brush on the foil cutout and transfer it to the gummed area on the flat glass. A long piece of foil should be cut and applied in sections. Smooth it out with the brush, stroking it from center to edge to work out excess gum and smooth away wrinkles. After you have dried it in a warm place for at least an hour, insert the glass into a cool kiln and follow regular glass firing procedures to 1350°–1400°F. When the glass is annealed and cooled, mask off the glass on each side of the silver foil with pieces of firm paper towel (the kind in commercial paper towel dispensers, not the soft stretchy kind), spray it with enameling gum, and sift transparent glass ice or enamel over the silver. In the project illustrated, paper towel strips also mask off the glass around the center rectangular area, and light green transparent enamel is sifted over the center. When the stencil is removed, the glass is set aside while the second glass is prepared.

Because the two glass sheets must *register* or match their designs, it is important to reverse the design on the second glass, which will be placed upside down over the first glass with their enameled sides together for firing and fusing them. Trace the design on regular translucent tracing paper with a fine-pointed felt tipped marker so it is easily seen when you turn it upside down under the second glass as a guide for decorating it. The second glass is also reversed because it is a free-form design and must register with the shape of the lower glass when they are positioned one over the other. Place the second glass over the reversed design.

String is the stencil for a linear design that appears as a sgraffitoed pattern in the completed tray. To give the string some body and make it manageable, it is soaked with enameling gum. Then it is laid out on the glass following the drawn lines on the design under the glass. A stencil of firm paper toweling blocks off the rectangular area in the center while enameling gum is sprayed over the glass, the strings, and the paper stencil. Green transparent enamel is sifted quickly over all before the adhesive gum dries out. When the paper stencil and the strings have been removed, spray the enamel again, holding the enameled glass at arm's length from the sprayer so the enamel already applied does not blow off the glass. An adequate amount of adhesive will ensure that the enamel does not fall off when the glass is reversed over the lower glass section. Set the prepared piece aside to dry.

It is advisable to assemble the glass sheets near the kiln to avoid the hazard of disturbing the work enroute to the kiln. Place the lower glass on its mold before you reverse the top glass and gently lower it into position. It must be perfectly registered at the moment it touches the enamel surface below it. Fire the lamination to 1450°F so the edges are firmly combined and rounded. Anneal it for at least an hour as it cools because of the thickness of two laminated glass layers. Gold luster accents are applied and fired to 1000°F. The tray is annealed as it cools.

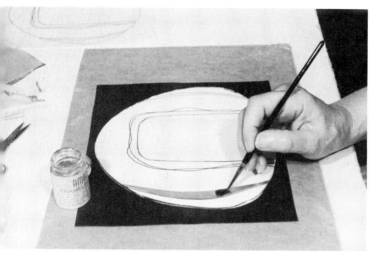

Smooth out the foil with a damp brush, stroking it to work out wrinkles. It is dried and fired to 1350° F.

Mask off the glass on each side of the foil with paper toweling stencils, then spray it with gum and sift transparent glass enamel over the silver foil.

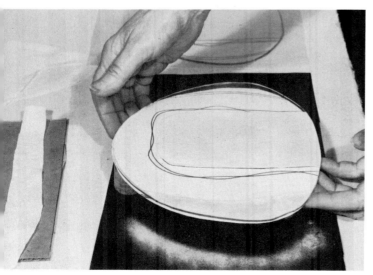

Enamel is sifted over the center area; when the stencils are removed, the glass is set aside while the second glass is prepared.

String is the stencil for a linear design that appears as a sgraffitoed pattern in the composition. Or the lines may be sgraffitoed with a pointed tool after the enamel is sifted.

A stencil is placed over the center area; enameling gum and enamels are sifted over-all. The paper stencil is removed.

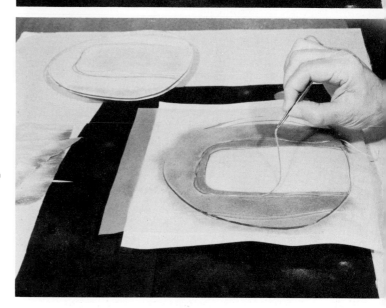

The string stencils are picked off with tweezers.

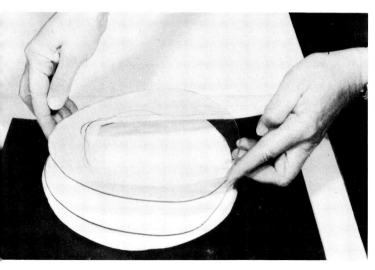

Place the lower glass on its mold before you reverse the top glass and gently lower it into position. Be sure it is registered perfectly before it touches the enamel surface beneath it. The glass is laminated and slumped at 1400°F.

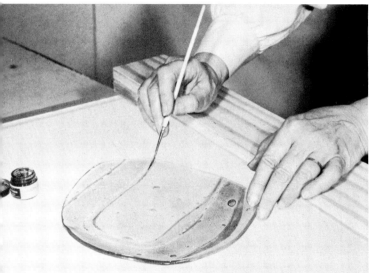

The design is emphasized with gold luster lines applied with a #4 sable liner. A wooden "bridge" steadies the hand with the brush. When the luster dries it is fired to 1000°F.

The completed tray.

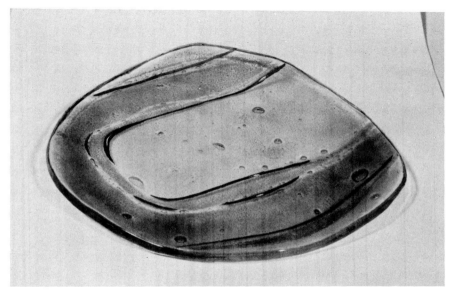

METALLIC LUSTERS

Liquid gold and platinum metallic over-glazes (lusters) add glamor to fired surfaces when they are applied with restraint. Clean the glass with detergent water, rinse it well and dry it. Use a good-quality thin flexible brush such as a china painting tracer or liner or a small Oriental watercolor brush. A brush of poor quality may shed hairs on the luster and spoil the finish when the hairs burn out. Luster essence should be bought when the luster is purchased. Only a drop or two is required to keep the metallic paint flowing smoothly. The lusters are applied and fired as the final touch to a completed bent or fused piece. During the application, if any luster is smeared on the glass, remove it at once with alcohol, wiping it off two or three times. Let the piece dry in a warm place for several hours before you fire it.

Position the glass in a cool kiln and turn the switches to *low*. Leave the door partly open for at least ½ hour to slowly drive off fumes from the luster oils. Then continue with regular firing procedures until the temperature reaches 1000°F. Follow the regular cooling and annealing schedule.

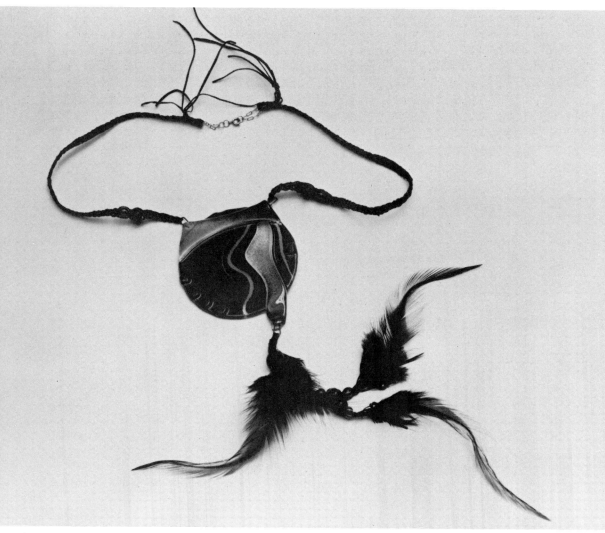

Sculptured necklace. Beth and Larry Beede. Constructed of single-strength window glass colored with glass powders in black, brown shading to orange, and clear glass combined with stencils. Nichrome wire loops are fused in place with tabs of glass. Braided strands of leather, handmade beads, and black feathers complete the composition. *Photo by Erik Redlich.*

6
Glass Jewelry

THE methods and materials that can be combined with glass to make delightful jewelry are endless. Small glass jewelry shapes with laminated silver wire or nichrome wire hangers have great versatility as units for constructing all sorts of objects such as bracelets, bolos, pendants, necklaces, and other articles of personal adornment. Use either stained glass or single-strength window glass colored by firing glass decorating powders over the shapes after they have been cut.

All the techniques discussed so far can be adapted in miniature to making jewelry. Contoured or bent glass, laminated fine silver wire designs, alone or in combination with other materials, crushed glass fused to glass and also combined with enameled copper, melted glass jewels, glossy glass chunks tumbled in a lapidary tumbler and combined with wire, hammered metal, leather and feathers, are some of the possibilities explored here. As you work with these materials, you will discover other additional methods of making imaginative jewelry for yourself and for others.

CONTOURED GLASS PENDANTS

To make clay molds for the glass shapes, model white ungrogged sculpture clay (cone 06) so the top surface of each mold contour is broadly shallow and the bottom is flat and level. Avoid undercuts that will prevent the release of glass pieces when they have sagged into the molds. Carve a tiny channel through the *top* of the side wall on each mold to allow air to escape when the hot glass slumps into the mold cavity. If this is neglected, when the glass is fired a large unwanted trapped air bubble may rise under the sagging glass and distort it. Dry and fire the clay molds to cone 06. When they have cooled, paint their tops with whiting (calcium carbonate) dissolved in water to thin cream consistency. Then sift dry kiln wash lightly over the top of the mold. Let the molds dry completely before they are used. Kiln wash should be brushed off and fresh siftings added before each time the molds are used. When they are completed, it is time to prepare the glass.

Some glass pendant shapes are cut to match the top perimeter outlines of the small molds. Wash them in detergent water and dry them. If you are using window glass, apply a light film of adhesive oil or enameling gum and sift colored glass powder over each shape before you fire it. Before the glass is positioned on its matching mold, place each mold on a nichrome mesh firing rack (the kind used for enameling); it will facilitate setting them into the kiln and removing them after they are fired and cooled. It is practical to assemble the pendants on a table near the kiln to avoid the hazard of having pieces slide to the floor when they are transported.

A lightweight hanger for each glass unit is made of silver or nichrome wire, 18–20 gauge, bent double and shaped with its ends curled decoratively and flattened. Position it on one end of the glass shape with the bent loop end extending beyond the glass. The wire should not be flattened at the point where it extends beyond the end of the glass; it may weaken and break. A dab of glue will hold it until it is in the kiln. Lay a very small piece of glass over the wire where it rests on the glass unit, but not covering the loop extension. This wire hanger and small glass piece will fuse onto the glass jewelry shape when they are fired together. When everything is in place, check once more to see that the small hangers are still in position and extending beyond the glass edge.

Set the firing rack with its assembled pieces into the cool kiln, which has not yet been turned on. Position it well toward the rear in a front loading kiln or near the center of the shelf in a top loader. Turn the switch to *low* for at least a half hour with the door or lid open about one-half inch to dry out the kiln as the glass warms gradually. Then close the door but leave vents open and turn switches to *high*. Close vents at 950°F. When the temperature reaches 1250°F, check visually to see whether the little pendant shapes are settling into their molds. Stained glass will slump earlier than window glass. As soon as the glass has settled into the molds, turn off

the kiln and open vents for two or three minutes to halt the heat rise. Then close vents and let the kiln cool. The glass is decorated with gold luster or black overglaze and re-fired to 1000°F.

A solution of kiln wash is brushed over small clay molds.

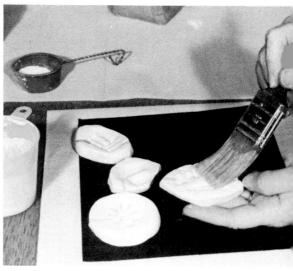

Glass-fluxed pendant shapes are positioned on the clay molds. Notice the wire hangers with tiny glass tabs over them on one end of each pendant form.

The glass is removed from the kiln with a handy firing fork. Each glass has settled into its small mold.

The contoured pendants are decorated with Liquid Gold luster. Dry the gold in a warm spot. Fire it to 1000°F.

The completed pendants.

GLASS AND WOOD JEWELRY

Glass combines attractively with other materials. The illustrated bracelet is formed of yellow stained glass and wire links with polished rosewood units. Cut small rectangles of stained glass, twice as many as the required number of glass links. Sift colorless glass flux on half the links and position them on sections of prepared insulation brick. On top of each of these glass rectangles, position a fine silver or nichrome wire that is long enough that you can bend a loop in each end and also curve the wire decoratively through the glass rectangles that make up each link. If you gently flatten the wires they will stay in place more readily. But do not flatten them where they extend beyond the glass or they will thin too much and will surely break at that point.

Cover each wire on its glass rectangle with one of the remaining small glass rectangles. To hold the top glass pieces in place, dab a bit of Elmer's Glue-all to their underneath surfaces before you position them over the wires. Set the brick support with its glass and wire assemblages on a mesh firing rack and insert it into the cool kiln with a firing fork. Follow regular firing instructions until the glass edges appear to be slightly rounded, 1350°–1400°F. Finally, close the vents and let the kiln cool.

To complete the bracelet, drill small holes in the wood links that have been cut and polished; join them alternately to the wire loops of the fused glass rectangles with silver jump rings. Use regular jewelry clasps on the ends of the bracelet or make your own with silver wire or sheet.

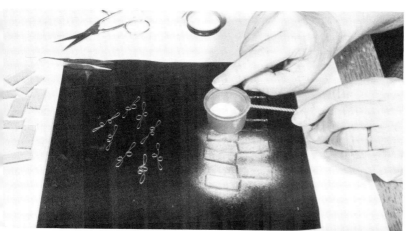

GLASS AND WOOD BRACELET

Glass flux is sifted over half the glass links.

Position small wire hangers on the glass with a pair of tweezers. A dab of Elmer's Glue-all will hold them in place. When each wire is covered with a second glass piece, they are positioned on a slice of insulation brick covered with whiting and kiln wash and placed in a cool kiln.

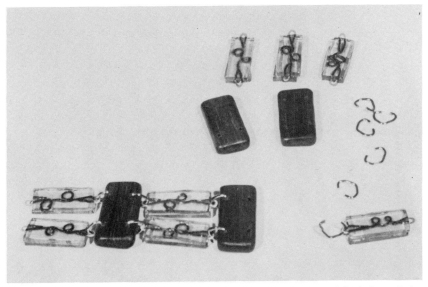

After firing, to complete the bracelet, join polished wood pieces (which have holes drilled in them) to the wire loops of the fused glass units with jump rings.

Units such as these fused links can be combined to make all sorts of jewelry, alone or combined with other materials.

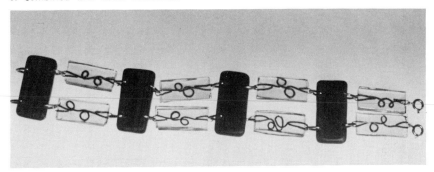

GLASS AND WOOD PENDANT

Three glass units in red and yellow stained glass have single silver loops to combine with wood for a pendant.

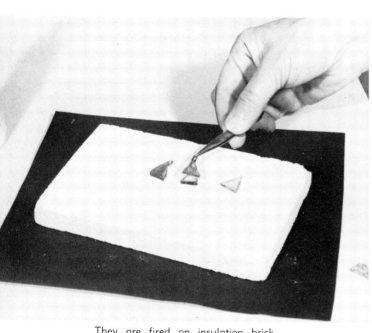

They are fired on insulation brick.

Laminated glass and wire "drops" combined with polished walnut and a leather thong.

LAMINATED WIRE DESIGNS

Laminated wire has been discussed chiefly as it is used for wire loop hangers. It can also be effective for larger designs. Fine silver is the best kind of wire for decorative laminations. It almost always retains its clean silver color, although when it is combined with pink glass or pink powdered glass colors, it turns an attractive gold. It may turn a copper color when it is combined with yellow glass. Reds should be tested; they are unpredictable. Sterling silver or nichrome wire turn a dull gray when they are laminated, which does not matter too much when they are used for hangers, but they are disappointing as decorative laminations. Copper wire will turn black before it fuses to the glass because of heavy oxidation in the heat of the kiln. All wire works best if it is lightly tapped and flattened. Avoid flattening it at the point where it passes from between the glass layers. It can become weakened if it is bent frequently and it may break. The bubbles that tend to form around the small wires in a lamination can be most attractive.

Cast silver combined with glass links and silver wire loops in a bracelet. Maurice Rothenberg.

To clean wire for lamination, brush it with alcohol or lighter fluid over paper toweling. 18–20 gauge wire is suitable for decorative lamination, 18-gauge or two twisted strands of thinner wire for loops.

Pick up wires with tweezers, touch them with a bit of glue, and position them on the glass.

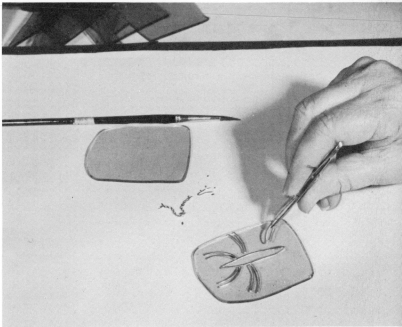

Sift glass flux over the wires. It will assist fusing. Cover it with a second glass.

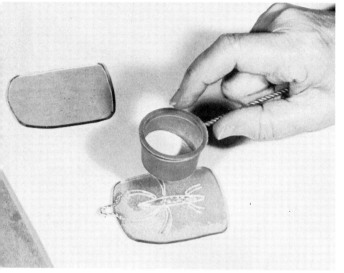

The pendant was fired to 1425°F to completely round the glass edges and fuse the wires. Interesting bubbles have formed around angles in the wires. Blue cathedral glass.

A pendant of laminated wires in window glass colored with pink glass ice. Fired to 1425°F.

Fused glass and wire units with macramé
and woven collars. Bette Warner.

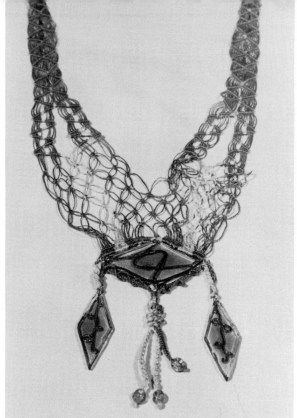

Woven collar and earrings with fused glass and silver wire. By Bette Warner.

CRUSHED GLASS FUSED TO ENAMELED COPPER *

Pieces of stained glass fused to enameled copper must be quite small and of fairly uniform size to fuse successfully. For good results, the glass should fuse at temperatures compatible with the melting temperature of the enamel. Cathedral glass (commercial stained glass) fuses to enamel at about 1400°F. The crushed glass applied to the illustrated pendants is blue and green cathe-

* See *Metal Enameling* by Polly Rothenberg. Crown Publishers Arts and Crafts Series.

dral glass. For the demonstration pendant design, transparent turquoise enamel is wet-packed and fused over silver foil with over-glaze accents of fine-line black painted with a very small brush.

A preformed slightly convex round copper shape is selected for the pendant. Convex shapes are not likely to flex and fracture the glass while it is cooling. Cut a hole near the edge for the jump ring to fasten through; then scour the copper and rinse it well. A thick coat of enamel must be fired to the back of the copper disc. This counter-enamel will hold the metal from flexing when crushed glass is fired to the top side. Paint or spray the back of the disc with enameling gum and sift 80-mesh enamel over it. Dry and fire this counter-enamel, then clean the top surface of firescale and apply enamel flux to it. Fire the enamel before crushed glass is applied.

Free-form pieces of silver foil are cut out between leaves of thin tracing paper and are pierced all over with a needle, right through the tracing paper. These holes will let gases escape when the foil is fired and will help keep the foil flat. It may rise up in a few places while it is firing, but if it has been pierced, it will soon flatten again. Brush enameling gum over the enameled surface. Pick up the foil pieces with a damp brush, then press them into position on the pendant surface. Press moisture from the foil with a tissue and let it dry. Fire the piece at 1400°F until the foil is red hot and flat. When it has cooled, wet-pack *transparent* enamel over the foil areas; dry and fire them. After they are cool, it is time to prepare the crushed glass.

Glass must be crushed against a firm surface. A piece of cabinet top with a laminated plastic surface, such as Formica, makes an excellent surface for crushing glass. Formica board remnants are usually obtained at cabinetmaker or woodworking shops. Place some pieces of one color of cathedral glass between folds of heavy canvas and pound them with a hammer to break them up. Protect your eyes and hands from sharp glass

segments; never scoop up crushed glass with bare hands! Some of the crushed glass and enameling gum are mixed together in a small container. Pick out the large pieces of glass, leaving only the very small bits for this project. Spoon the glass and gum mixture onto the edge of the pendant surface with a small spatula, patting it down firmly.

The next important step is to sift glass flux enamel or ice over the crushed glass. Flux will bind the glass particles together and assist the fusing process. After a final light spraying with diluted enameling gum, the pendant is dried and fired at 1400°F or until the glass particles are fused together. Do not overfire it. Turn off the kiln and open vents to allow the temperature to drop to 1000°F before you close the door or peepholes and let the kiln cool naturally. If painted black lines are added, they are fired to only 1100°F. When the pendant is completed and has cooled, the edge can be cleaned of firescale by a gentle rubbing with fine steel wool. Care must be taken lest protruding glass is struck and broken off when the copper edge is polished. If all procedures are followed carefully, the glass will not fracture.

Cathedral glass is crushed between layers of heavy canvas, with a ball peen hammer.

A preformed convex round copper shape is enameled on both surfaces with clear metal-enamel or glass flux. Brush the pendant with enameling gum and position the silver foil shapes on the enameled surface. When dry, fire to 1400°F to *fuse* the silver.

Black overglaze lines are applied last and fired to 1000°F.

The pendant's loop is turned back with round-nosed jewelry pliers. Light transparent turquoise and blue.

Wet pack or sift transparent turquoise enamel over the foil. It can be fired separately or with the crushed glass. Very fine pieces of the crushed glass are mixed with gum (agar or any enameling gum) and the mixture is packed around the edge of the pendant. When dry, fire it to 1450°F to fuse and round the glass bits.

When the pendant is completed, metal for a handmade loop (jump ring) is cut from 18- or 20-gauge copper. Cut the small copper segment narrow enough to go through the hole that was drilled through the copper disk near its edge, before it was enameled. When you have cleaned and polished it with fine steel wool to remove rough edges, thread it through the hole and bend it to shape with jewelry pliers.

JEWELRY MADE FROM GLASS SEGMENTS

Flashlight lenses are fused for the demonstrated glass pendant. The smaller lens was fractured between two layers of canvas. The larger lens was brushed with enameling gum, and clear glass flux was sifted in a thin layer. After the pieces of the smaller lens were positioned on it, gum was sprayed and yellow *high-fire* glass ice and yellow transparent enamel were sifted over all. A pinch of opaque black in the center sharpened the design. Because of the hardness of the lens glass, firing was to 1600°F.

Two flashlight lenses were combined for a simple crushed-glass designed pendant. The smaller of the lenses was fractured with blows of the hammer. The pieces of glass are glued to the larger disc; one small piece is laid over a wire loop hanger.

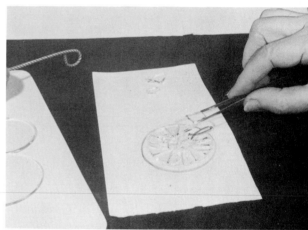

Glass flux and bright yellow transparent enamel are sifted over the entire assemblage. Bits of opaque black enamel are sprinkled in the center. Colors are high-fire.

Lucky blows on the smaller glass disc made this interesting fracture. Because of the hardness of flashlight lenses, firing was 1600°F.

Small pieces of colored glass make wonderful "jewels" for pendants and other jewelry. They are fired to 1400°F to just blunt the edges; when fired to 1450°F the glass draws up to round the edges more fully; when fired to 1500°F, the glass becomes cabochon or fully rounded. After they are fired, brush all mica off their base. Residue of mica can prevent fusion or bonding. Shards and other fragments of glass make charming small suspensions and pendants when they are sifted with glass colorants and fused together.

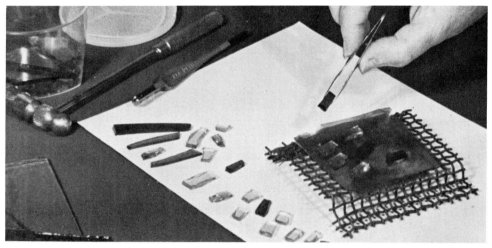

To make glass "jewels" that have many uses in glass work, cut small pieces of glass and spread them on a sheet of mica placed on a mesh trivet for firing.

Test panel for stained glass jewels. *Left to right:* 1. Unfired glass; 2. pieces fired to 1400°F.; 3. pieces fired to 1450°F.; 4. pieces fired to 1500°F.

1   2   3   4

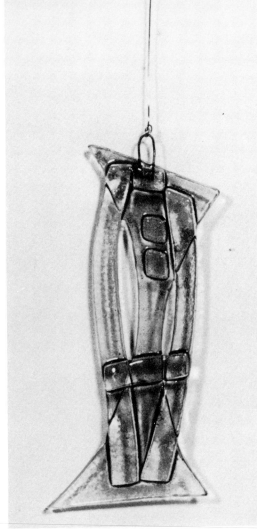

Segments of window glass with siftings of blue transparent enamels and ices fused together in one firing.

Fused pendant. BoBo Zinn. Enamels were fired on a sheet of single-strength window glass. Small rectangles of the colored glass were fused with clear glass. 2″ X 4″. *Photo by Drew Henery.*

JEWELRY FROM TUMBLED GLASS

A most exciting method of preparing small segments of thick antique slab glass for jewelry making is to tumble facet chips or larger chunks in a lapidary tumbler. Pieces as large as walnuts are easily polished in a small "beginner's" tumbler. The glass chunks are tumbled through the regular succession of rock tumbling grits to a final mix of tin oxide, cork, and water for a lovely satiny gloss. The glass is combined with metals or other materials just like any polished stones.

Chips of faceted glass before they were tumbled *(left)*. After tumbling *(right)*.

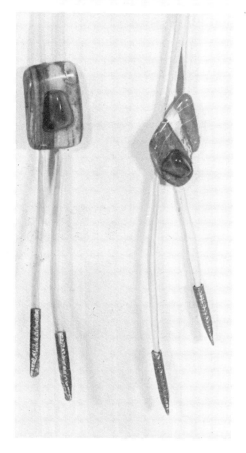

Bolos. Polished stones with tumbled glass lumps epoxied to them. Hand-formed and tooled bolo tips. Maurice Rothenberg.

A 2½" round copper disc is tooled over a pitch pot.

Four wire "posts" are flattened and soldered into four drilled holes. They serve as prongs to hold the glossy tumbled glass nugget. Bright turquoise on copper. Maurice Rothenberg.

Amber tumbled glass with twisted and hammered copper wire. Maurice Rothenberg.

Pendant. Audrea Kreye. Ruby red transparent segment of dalle glass, tumbled and wrapped with electroplated copper wire.

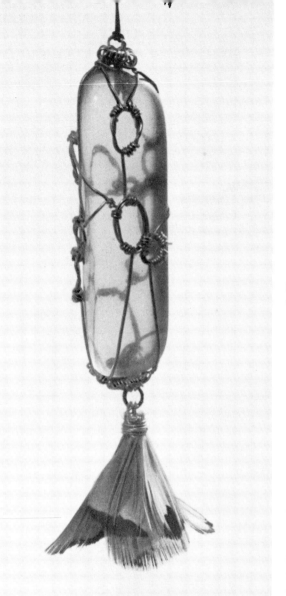

Pendant. Audrea Kreye. Tumbled segment of blue dalle glass with 24-gauge wire macramé and feathers.

Pendant. Audrea Kreye. Blue glass with electroplating directly on the glass.

Silver collar with electroplated emerald green glass nuggets. Audrea Kreye. Audrea is a talented silversmith and enamelist.

7
Blown Glass

THE invention of blown glass, developed at the beginning of the Christian era, was without a doubt one of man's finest achievements. We do not know exactly how nor where it was discovered that molten glass could be blown into a bubble; but it revolutionized glass forming. Every facet of man's life today involves blown glass: science, industry, medicine, construction, containers (seven million tons of them), electronics, and visual art. As a direct aesthetic form created entirely by the individual artist, it is receiving a phenomenal acceptance as a serious sculptural medium. Fluid free blown glass is barely at the threshold of its artistic development. Dozens of colleges and universities are establishing glass-working facilities in their regular art programs.

"Glass blowing," as discussed in this book, means taking a gather of hot glass from a furnace and manipulating it on the end of a metal blowpipe, as distinguished from "lampworking," or starting with a glass tube, one end of which is heated with a torch and becomes the softened and manipulated glass object. A blowpipe (also called a blowing iron or rod) is an iron or steel tube four to six feet long with a tapered end or nose of heatproof alloy. The bore, which is the interior lengthwise cavity of the blowpipe, is about 1/4 inch across. The diameter of the blowing rod's nose is usually selected according to the personal preference of the blower, although too large a nose may gather too much glass, resulting in a thick form and a waste of glass.

◀

#6. David Hopper. Two off-hand blown, hot-tooled white glass figures, each composed of two parts joined with epoxy. From the "American Glass Now" exhibition. *Photo by courtesy of The Toledo Museum of Art.*

Many kinds of glass for offhand blowing are made by mixing and liquefying exactly proportioned materials according to a formula whose basic ingredient is pure silica sand. Silica by itself is difficult to melt and work; it must be modified by other chemicals such as soda (Na_2O) and sometimes potash (K_2O), lime (CaO), and others, along with coloring oxides if colored glass is to be used. These modifications make silica glass more workable and give it a predictable working temperature as well as achieve other desirable qualities. The dry batch mix, compounded according to the purpose for which the glass is to be used, along with some glass cullet of the same kind, is fed into a white-hot melting furnace. When the mass fuses and begins to flow, some impurities rise to the top. Refractory rings may be anchored in a position near the working hole. They float on the molten glass surface, excluding scum from the glass that is being gathered from within the rings.

In a large operation, the impurities that rise to the top of the huge "continuous tank" are held back by a bridge wall that allows the clean glass to flow beneath it through a submerged opening into a clean glass area. From an opening above the clean glass level, glassworkers may gather glass for hand manipulation and blowing; or it may flow into forehearths where it is fed into forming machines. In such a complex operation, glassworkers organized into small groups of six or seven men work together from one reheating furnace or "glory hole." The glassworker who extracts molten glass from the furnace on the end of a blowing iron carefully heats the pipe's nose before inserting it into the molten glass in the furnace. It must be heated to a dull red, just hot enough for the glass to adhere, but not so hot that the glass slides off the iron. The blowpipe is held horizontal in both hands, then tilted downward until its tip just touches the surface of the glass. As it is rotated, it is moved slightly in a horizontal direction away from the direction of rotation, which brings a

Roman Bartkiw gathers glass on his blowing iron. Roman heads the Glass Design Department of Georgian College of Applied Arts and Technology in Barrie, Ontario.

flow of molten glass over the nose of the blowing iron and winds up a gather of glass without collecting unwanted bubbles. After at least one or two full rotations, the pipe is withdrawn from the furnace. The hot glass is a soft viscous mass that must be controlled by continuous rotation of the blowing iron, during and after its removal from the furnace, to prevent the force of gravity from pulling it off the iron. The gatherer must know just how much glass he will need; he must avoid trapping unwanted air bubbles; and he must obtain a symmetrical gather.

When the first gather has been taken from the furnace, it may be rolled on a steel-topped table, to cool it slightly, and "marvered," or rolled, into a cylindrical shape; or the glass-worker may move very quickly to his bench, position the blowing iron across its arms (all the while rotating the iron), pick up a wet scoop-shaped wooden "block" from a tub of water near the bench and shape a sphere from the hot glass while he works it to the end of the rotating blowing iron. While he manipulates the hot material, he sits close against the side of his bench. One hand keeps the iron rotating while the other hand gently cradles the glass with the block. The glass gather rides on a cushion of steam rising from the wet wood block, not on the bare wood.

Marvering, or blocking, the molten glass has cooled it down just enough for a skin of glass to form on the sphere, and it is against this skin that the first bubble of air is blown. Now with just the right amount of molten glass on the blowing iron, with gentle puffs of breath, the blower traps air inside the glass. Because the blowing iron will be returned to the furnace to pick up a second gather, the first bubble must be small, Too large a bubble in the first gather will result in a very thin layer of glass around the bubble. The thin glass may melt off when the second gather is taken from the furnace. It is important to cool the surface of the first gather after the bubble has been blown, so slightly stiffened glass will give stability to the second gather, but not so cool it can break off the iron.

The hot glass is a soft viscous mass that must be controlled by continuous rotation of the blowing iron, during and after its removal from the furnace, to prevent gravity from pulling it off the blowpipe.

A glassworker's bench is simple and functional. The shelf at one side of the bench holds handle-shears, with blades that form opposing right angles that can hold or guide the punty into place or cut off masses of viscous glass; steel-bladed jacks and other forming tools are arranged in convenient order to be readily accessible. Wooden blocks in a tub or bucket of water are at hand when needed.

Blocking the molten glass has cooled it down just enough for a "skin" of glass to form on the gather. With gentle puffs of breath, Roman traps air inside the glass in a small bubble.

As soon as the second gather is taken from the furnace, it is blocked again and inflated further. With a doubled tong called a jack, or pucella, the glassworker may grove or neck his glass by circling it just beyond the blowpipe's nose. Periodically, the glass is returned to the reheating furnace so it is kept hot enough to be necked, worked, shaped, or trimmed with glass shears while it is pliable. A great part of a glassworker's time is spent in warming up his material and cooling down his work. To achieve a form of larger size, additional gathers and blockings must be made, one over the other. Subsequent manipulation depends upon the kind of glass article to be made. Gravity exerting its pull stretches the glass. Sometimes it is swung back and forth while it is still hot and flexible to bring the glass lower on the blowing iron or to elongate it. At this point it may be lowered into a waiting mold. It may be flattened by spinning or shaped with moist wooden paddles. The wood blocks and tools are made from apple, cherry, or other wood that does not cause sap problems.

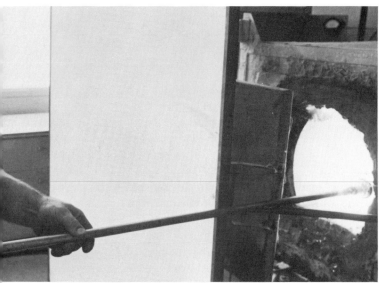

Periodically the glass is returned either to the furnace to gather more glass or to the reheating furnace (glory hole) to keep it hot and pliant enough to be worked, necked, shaped, or trimmed.

The base of a form may be flattened in one of several ways. Roman taps the hot glass with the end of a jack. He sits close against the side of his bench; his left hand continues rotating the blowpipe to prevent the hot soft glass from sagging.

Artist David Lucas holds a punty with a hot glass trailing for Roman to manipulate onto the form.

When the blowing and preliminary shaping are achieved, the glass is cooled slightly so the partly formed piece can be transferred to a four-foot solid pontil rod (punty) tipped with a small bit of hot glass. The tip of the punty is heated a dull red before the bit of glass is gathered, but it must not get so hot that the glass form will melt off it. The hot bit of molten glass is marvered or pulled into a point that is pressed against the center of the bottom on the blown glass bubble. Once the punty is attached to the blown glass piece opposite the blowing iron juncture, the glass is chilled with water at the point where it was grooved (necked) after the second gather. The point of intended severance is scratched with a large file or small handsaw; the glass-worker raps the blowing rod, *not the glass object,* and the glass is cracked off the iron's tip. Now that the glass is free of the blowing iron and attached at its opposite end to the punty, it is again inserted into the reheating furnace just far enough to heat it without overheating the punty. After each manipula-

tion of the glass, the form must be returned to the furnace for reheating.

All the separate portions of the glass form are joined and shaped with shears and simple tools. For decorative work, extra small gathers of hot glass from the furnace are applied with another punty. The ragged edge of the glass form where it was separated from the blowing iron is reheated by being inserted into the furnace just far enough to heat the glass edge red-hot. When it is returned to the bench, it may be opened with a wet tool, trimmed with glass shears, stretched into a necked form or spread into a more open form while the glass is still pliable. The skillful finisher knows just how to utilize the pull of gravity to maintain clean flowing lines on the glass form. The completed hot glass object is removed from the punty with a gentle blow to the rod; it falls on an asbestos bed or asbestos-covered pronged fork and is quickly inserted into the annealing lehr where it remains until all strain is removed from the glass as described under "Annealing Glass."

David scores the glass with a saw preparatory to severing it from the iron.

Under Roman's watchful eyes, David cracks off the glass form with a sharp blow to the rod. With asbestos gloves, he will transfer it immediately to an annealing oven.

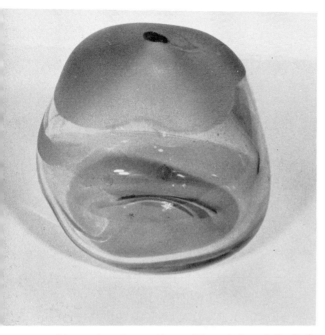

Blown glass open form with palladium luster fired later to 1000°F. Polly Rothenberg.

Blown glass form with sandblast design. Polly Rothenberg.

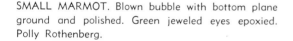

SMALL MARMOT. Blown bubble with bottom plane ground and polished. Green jeweled eyes epoxied. Polly Rothenberg.

Although the methods described concern glassworking in a large operation, the series of processes in a small one- or two-man situation are similar but adapted to a greatly modified scale. The independent craftsman dedicated to working creatively today must plan a strict disciplinary routine for himself because of the very high temperatures involved. Once a familiarity with proved and safe glassblowing procedures is acquired, the artist is free to explore the tantalizing world of molten glass. The art of glassworking is evolving at an exciting pace today. A phenomenon of the current resurgent interest in blown glass is the burgeoning number of individual glassworkers who either maintain their own studios and equipment or who work independently in a college workshop after class hours. On these pages are illustrations of some of these talented professional artists at work along with the astonishing variety of their glass forms. Because off-hand blown glass sculpture is an important development of our time, examples of these sculptural works are shown in this special blown glass section rather than with the glass sculpture and architectural glass group.

ROMAN BARTKIW HAND-BLOCKS A BLOWN GLASS BUBBLE

The glass craftsman who is experienced in glassblowing can achieve subtle variations in a blown form by "hand-blocking" it with a soaked folded wet newspaper. The conventional wood blocks are used in conjunction with this interesting process, before or during the wet paper blocking process. The folded paper is fully soaked before the blocking begins. Because the hot glass bubble is cradled on a layer of rising steam, the paper (12 to 16 layers) does not catch fire. This method is recommended only for the experienced glassblower.

Roman Bartkiw demonstrates daily in his glass workshop. He blocks the glass with wet newspaper. Heat does not penetrate to his hand; the glass form rides on a layer of steam. The paper is quite wet.

The glass is reheated and blocked gently from the end. The shape of the form can be felt through the wet paper, which does not burn.

Roman may alternate blocking with a wood block if he feels the form may require it. He continually reheats the glass.

Back to the newspaper and more manipulation of the glass form.

With the wet folded newspaper, subtle contours are defined that are not possible with a wooden block. The paper is somewhat tattered at this point. Additional refinements may be made with tools, but the form subtleties are retained. All photographs of Georgian College activities in the Glass Design Department were taken by Marc Robillard.

Artist Robin Clarke grinds the base of her blown glass form. Water drips on the rotating grinder stone from a long tapered trough. Georgian College.

The glass is held firmly. Eyes must be kept on the form as the wheel rotates, for the slightest movement of the hand can change the glass position and scar the smooth glass surface.

The ground surface is refined with sand belts from coarse to fine. Final polishing is achieved with a cork belt. The belts are kept on numbered pegs.

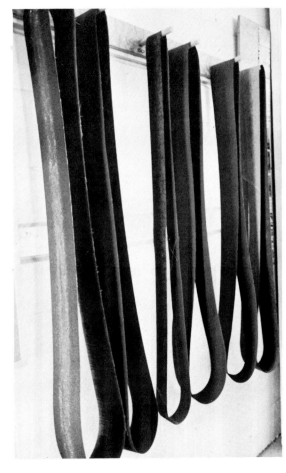

MODERN GLASS OVENS AND SOME WOOD BLOCKS

Although glass is blown today in much the same way it was formed centuries ago, there are some modern gas and oil furnaces and ovens for the glassworker who is not interested in constructing them. The wooden blocks, mostly hand formed, are still like those primitive ones. Other forming tools are shown in use in accompanying illustrations.

Reheating furnace, or "glory hole." Courtesy A. D. Alpine, Inc.

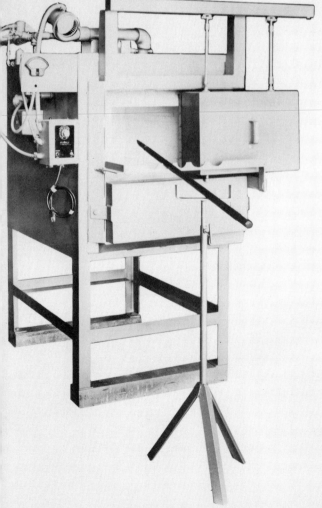

Although many glassworkers build their own furnaces, glassblowing equipment is available on the market now. A gas-fired glass tank melting furnace, constructed of pure zircon firebrick. Movable stand for blowpipe and punties. Designed for studio artists and schools. *Photo courtesy of A. D. Alpine, Inc., California.*

Annealing oven, or lehr (lare), of welded sheet steel, lined with 4½" firebrick insulation. Courtesy A. D. Alpine, Inc.

Wooden block of cherrywood for shaping blown glass.

Cherrywood shaping paddle.

Wood mold for pressing blown glass forms.

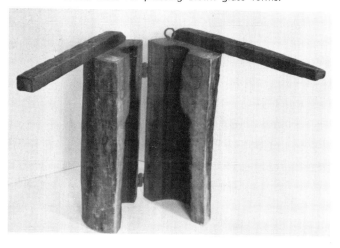

A.

C.

B.

D.

A. Three-dimensional layered stained glass. Fredrica Fields.

B. Blown glass vase. John Nickerson. Artist in residence, Blenko Glass Company.

C. **RED JEWEL.** Edris Eckhardt. Bronze cast over glass relief sculpture.

D. Hand-formed silver collar with electroplated stained glass nuggets. Audrea Kreye.

A.

A. Section of 65-foot faceted glass skylight in California mart of Los Angeles. By the Glassart Studio.
B. Stained glass mosaic table top. Polly Rothenberg.
C. Fused stained-glass wind chimes with weathered walnut. Polly Rothenberg.

B.

C.

A.

B.

A. Lighted Farbigem bonded glass sculptures. Van Tetterode Studio, Amsterdam, Holland. *Courtesy of Willet Studio.*

B. Bent glass sculpture. Louis La Rooy, for Willet Stained Glass Studios.

A.

A. **STONEY PATH.** Edward J. Byrne. Leaded and painted stained glass powder-room window. Carnwath residence.
B. One panel of Farbigem bonded mural wall, *World History of Medicine*. Willet Studio. Installed in the Ohio State University Medical Center.

B.

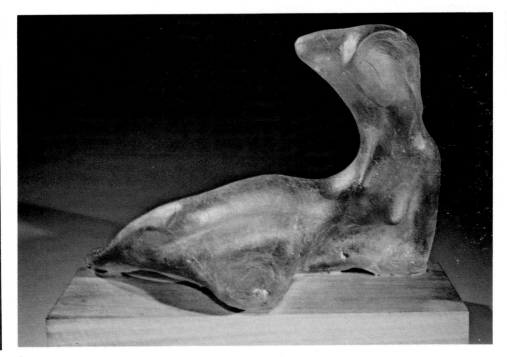

A.

B.

A. **PINK NUDE.** Edris Eckhardt. Cast glass.
B. **HOLY FAMILY.** Don Shepherd. Cast glass relief sculpture.

A.

A. **FLOWERS.** Old Dominion Stained Glass Studio. Leaded antique glass. *Courtesy, Blenko Glass Company.*
B. Suspended panel. Edward J. Byrne. Leaded stained glass.

B.

A.

A. **CREATION.** Laws Stained
Glass Studio. Faceted glass
in epoxy resin matrix. *Cour-
tesy, Blenko Glass Company.*
B. Three-dimensional layered
stained glass. Fredrica
Fields. *Photo by Kenneth
Fields.*

B.

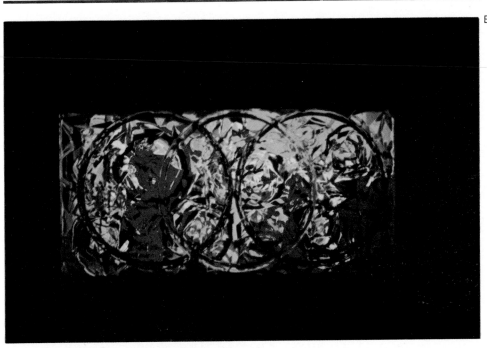

A.

B.

A. Leaded antique glass butter-
fly. Polly Rothenberg.
B. Blown glass bottle with tooled
design. Steven Zachofsky.
C. Antique glass lantern. Bette
Warner.

C.

VERNON BREJCHA'S WORK AND PHILOSOPHY

"Annually, as the hot south wind is forming waves over the golden high plains, I return to the flat lands for the wheat harvest. Atop the grain combine, one's hands have to become a part of the machine. The Kansas sun shows no mercy as the grain flows into the bin as if it were a yellow liquid. Over the constant roar of the engine, chains, belts and gears, the ear tries to detect how the grain and straw are separating.

"The roar is not too different from the burners on a glass tank as the melt gives off an intense heat like the prairie sun. Here the hands tune themselves to primitive tools to master another golden flowing liquid—molten glass giving off light only for the artist to enjoy before it stiffens into a statement that had to be made."—Vernon Brejcha

Vase and bowl. Vernon Brejcha. Clear glass with copper blue applied designs. Vase 8½'' tall. Bowl 6'' diameter.

TORNADO CLOUD. Vernon Brejcha. Blown glass wall sculpture. 11'' X 19''.

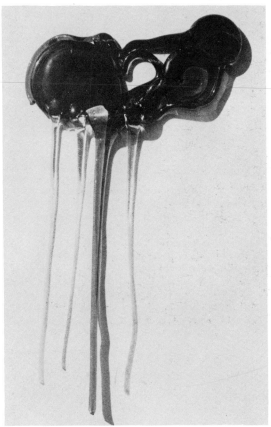

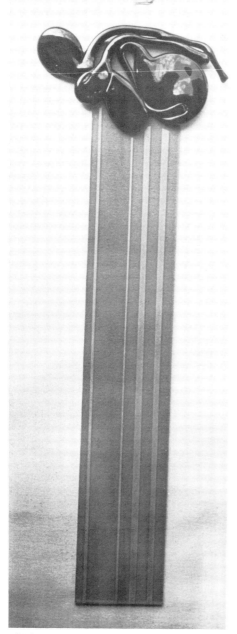

PRAIRIE STORM. Vernon Brejcha. Blown glass with gray plate glass. 13″ X 17″.

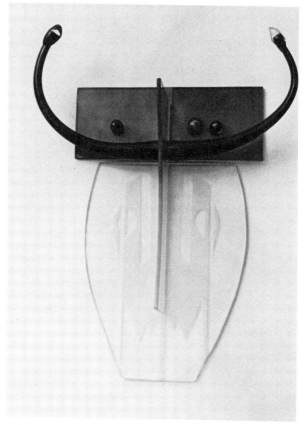

WHY THE BUFFALO! Vernon Brejcha. Wall sculpture of blown and plate glass with sandblasting. 16″ X 17″ X 5″.

ONE LAST TROPHY FOR JACKSON SUNDOWN. Vernon Brejcha. Glass wall sculpture of mirror, blown glass, gray plate glass with sandblasting. 20″ X 24″.

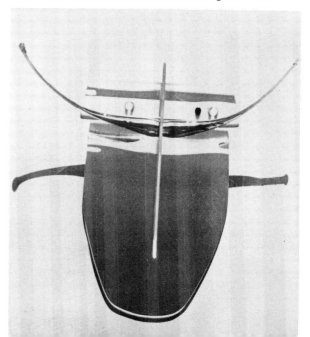

VERNON BREJCHA
GLASS BLOWING

The first gather of glass is marvered (blocked).

The gather is inflated with gentle
puffs of breath.

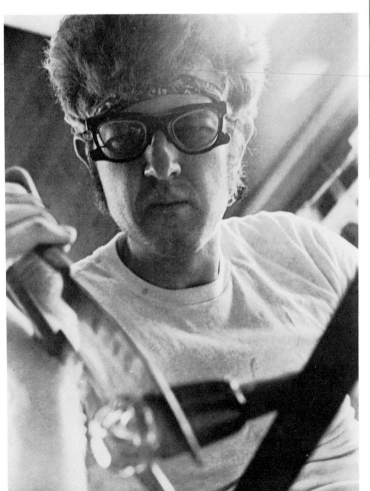

Vernon Brejcha necks the first
gather of clear glass. The clear
glass will stay warmer on the pipe
than the black glass that will case
the bubble.

A second gather is cradled in a wet wood block. Blocking is very important. The glass is red hot.

The bubble grows in size from repeated gathers and blowings. The third gather is blocked. It is a very gentle process, with little if any pressure being applied. The dark area on the bubble indicates that it is cooling toward the pipe end first.

With extra glass on the punty, a design is threaded on the bubble.

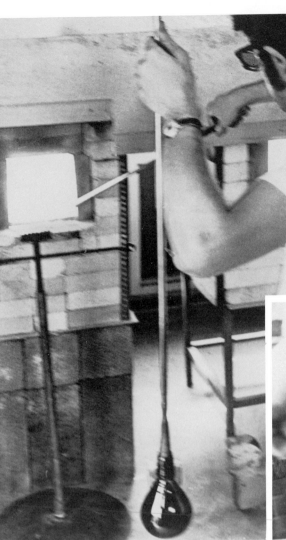

Vernon can work alone when necessary. He gathers a bit of glass on the end of a punty.

The punty is attached to the base of the glass form.

With a blow to the pipe, he breaks off the bubble.

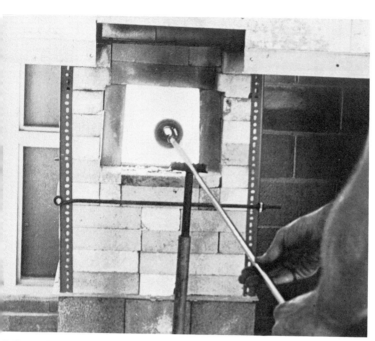

He returns the glass to the fire and inserts it into the furnace just far enough to heat the open end until it is red, but not so far as to collapse the bubble.

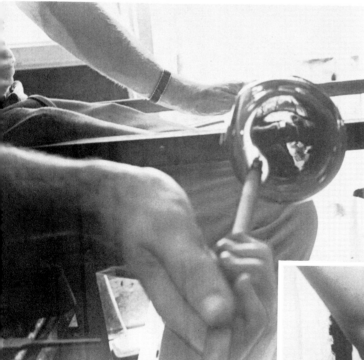

Pressing with a wet wood stick in his right hand, he opens the glass into a bowl form as his left hand rotates the iron.

While the glass is still very hot, it is broken off the punty into the annealing oven.

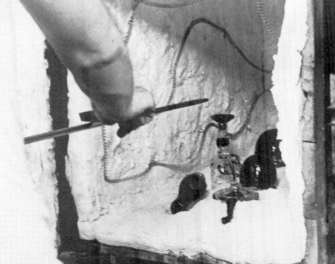

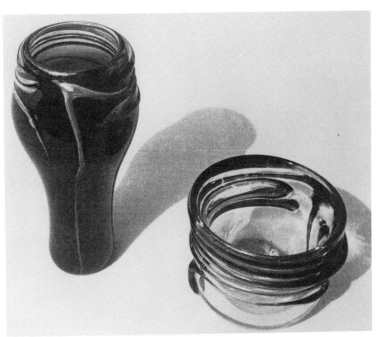

Blown vase and bowl with applied glass designs. Vernon Brejcha.

WALL FLOWER. Vernon Brejcha. Blown and plate glass wall sculpture. 10½″ X 15″.

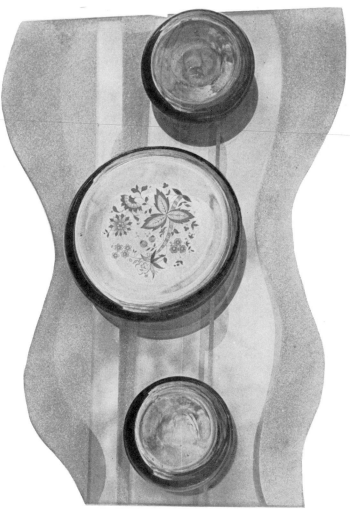

VERNON BREJCHA DEMONSTRATES
BLOWING A GLASS GOBLET

Gathers are taken for Vernon's demonstration of blowing a glass goblet. All photos of Vernon Brejcha's work are by Sherry Brejcha.

Blocking the second gather.

Vernon makes decorative cuts at the base of a hot bubble.

He adds a small bit of color between two of the decorative cuts.

Glass is added, pulled out to the desired length and cut off to make a stem.

The stem is added to a hot paddy of glass to make a foot.

Glass is added to attach the punty to the foot of the goblet.

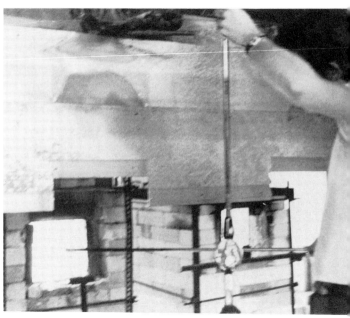

After the punty is attached, the neck is broken from the blowpipe with a light tap to the pipe. Where the glass was separated from the pipe, it is reheated in the furnace and it is opened with a wet stick.

The completed goblet. Dark areas are green. The cup of the goblet is amber with trailings of color. Stem is clear glass. 7½'' tall. In the author's collection. Vernon Brejcha is Assistant Professor of Art at Tusculum College, Greeneville, Tennessee. *Photos by Sherry Brejcha.*

SOME OF TODAY'S GLASS ARTISTS AND BLOWN GLASS WORKS THAT APPEARED IN THE "AMERICAN GLASS NOW" EXHIBITION

Off-hand blown forms. Kim Newcomb. Bottle with applied decoration and fumed surface, 11" X 3⅝" X 3⅝". Vase with applied decoration and fumed surface, 6½" X 4⅛" X 4⅛". Bowl with applied foot and fumed surface, 7½" X 5⅛" X 5⅛". From the "American Glass Now" exhibition. *Photo by courtesy of The Toledo Museum of Art.*

JUMPING TROUT. Kim Newcomb. Off-hand blown glass with applied glass parts.

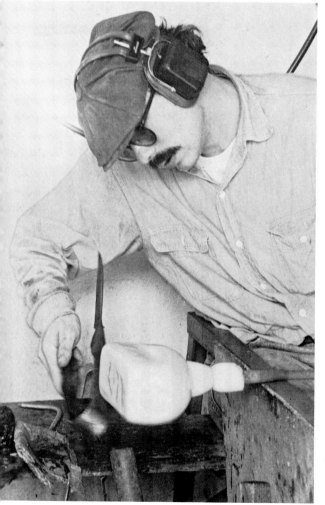

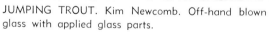

Kim Newcomb works on one of his blown glass Bread Bottle forms while listening to FM radio. He feels the rhythm of the music inspires a rhythm in his work. Mr. Newcomb is Assistant Professor of Fine and Applied Arts at the University of Illinois, Urbana-Champaign. *Photo by Jennifer Manning.*

CLUSTERFORM II. Eriks Rudans. Cluster of off-hand blown forms on a base of epoxy-painted fiber glass reinforced polyester. 11½" X 31" X 24". From the "American Glass Now" exhibition. Mr. Rudans teaches at Saint Cloud State College, Saint Cloud, Minnesota. *Photo by courtesy of The Toledo Museum of Art.*

Eriks's workbench and tools after a busy workshop demonstration.

Eriks Rudans during a workshop demonstration.

TRANSFUSION. Curtis C. Hoard. Off-hand blown form with flocked metal, rubber, Plexiglas, and flocked parts. 12" X 16½" X 24¼". From the "American Glass Now" exhibition. Mr. Hoard is Associate Professor of Art, University of Minnesota, Minneapolis. *Photo by courtesy of The Toledo Museum of Art.*

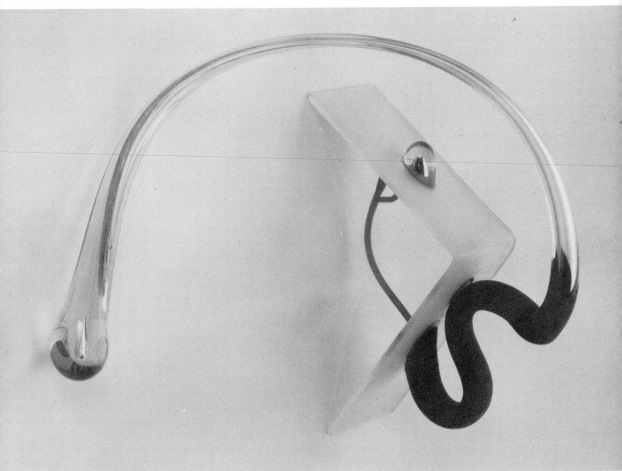

SPACE CUP #4. Michael Cohn. One of a series of nonfunctional cups. Blown, cut, and fabricated glass with sandblasted contrasting areas. From the collection of Mark Graham, Baltimore.

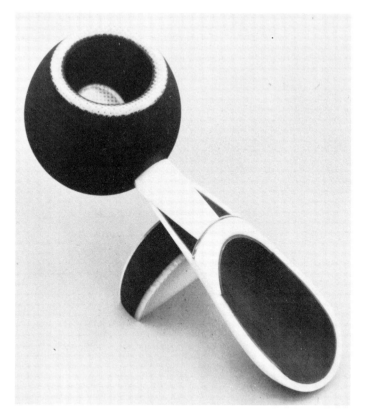

Blown glass cups. Paula Bartron. Part of a series. *Left to right:* Untitled #13, blown cup with applied foot and handle and fumed surface; Untitled #3, blown cup with trailed decoration and applied handles; Untitled #8, blown cup with applied foot and handle. From the "American Glass Now" exhibition. Courtesy of The Toledo Museum of Art.

VENINI SERIES #1. Marvin B. Lipofsky, assisted by Gianni Toso, Murano, Italy. Off-hand blown, hot-tooled form. 11½″ X 15″ X 17″. From the "American Glass Now" exhibition. *Photo by courtesy of The Toledo Museum of Art.*

Untitled. Michael Edward Cohn. Blown, cut, and polished glass form with mirrors. 3⅞'' X 10⅞'' X 5½''. From the ''American Glass Now'' exhibition. *Photo by courtesy of The Toledo Museum of Art.*

Glass jar. Kent Ipsen. Off-hand blown jar with trailed surface design. 14'' X 10''. From the ''American Glass Now'' Exhibition. *Photo by courtesy of The Toledo Museum of Art.*

Kent Ipsen constricts a large blown form with a wet wooden jack. Mr. Ipsen is Chairman of the Crafts Department at Virginia Commonwealth University, Richmond.

8
Glass Sculpture and Architectural Art

HISTORY abounds with examples of glass art, but today glass is climbing to notable levels of aesthetic approval as a serious sculptural and architectural art medium. New uses of old methods, such as sandblasting, mirroring, bonding, bending, glassblowing and more, are encouraging further extensive experimentation to discover what else can be done with, to, and on glass. This glamorous material depends for its beauty on the light rays that journey through it and illuminate it with ever-changing effects from moment to moment. Glassworkers, investigating their material in its relation to light, are evolving new and unusual processes to exploit this property. Not only does the sculptor and architectural artist work with light as it directly affects the glass, but also with whatever is seen through the glass, around it and reflected in it, and with the light that illuminates these elements. Although individual artists are finding new ways with glass, the professional glass studios, large and small, with their extensive resources and contacts, actively advance and improve appreciation and understanding of glass art among art lovers, collectors, and the public in general. They enrich the lives of all of us with their devotion to the creation of lasting beauty.

◀

Mosaic Cross. Glassart Studio. Architectural sculpture of antique sheet stained glass and dalle glass with gold lamination. In the United Church of Christ, Scottsdale, Arizona. *Photo by Glassart Studio, Phoenix, Arizona.*

Three-dimensional stained glass. Fredrica Fields. In the main lounge of the YWCA, Green-wich, Connecticut. *Photo by Kenneth Fields.*

◄

MADONNA AND CHILD. Edris Eckhardt. Cast glass in turquoise, aqua, and blue with transparent gold surface touched with rose tones from the copper reduction during fusion. Collection of Gates Mills. *Photo by The Cleveland Museum of Art.*

Three-dimensional stained glass panel. Fredrica Fields. Main lounge of the YWCA, Greenwich, Connecticut. *Photo by Kenneth Fields.*

Three-dimensional stained glass panel. Fredrica Fields. Main lounge of the YWCA, Greenwich, Connecticut. *Photo by Kenneth Fields.*

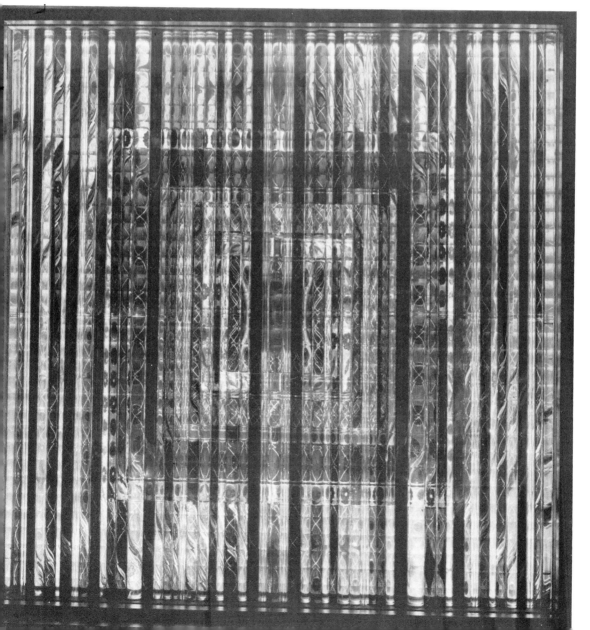

The boxlike frame that holds one of Fredrica's panels is built with reinforced corners. The frame's back edge has strong molding to support the glass. Fitted wood strips along the interior of the frame sides hold the composition secure.

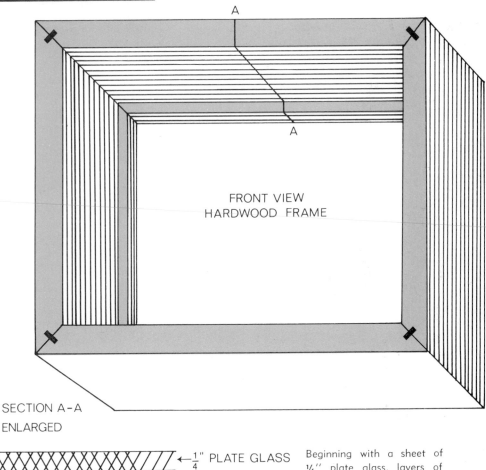

A

A

FRONT VIEW
HARDWOOD FRAME

SECTION A-A
ENLARGED

$\frac{1}{4}''$ PLATE GLASS

COLORED GLASS
INTERMEDIATE LAYERS

$\frac{1}{4}''$ PLATE GLASS

HARDWOOD FRAME

Beginning with a sheet of $\frac{1}{4}''$ plate glass, layers of colored glass are built up, one over the other. The assemblage is completed with another sheet of $\frac{1}{4}''$ plate, secured with a wood molding screwed into the frame.

FREDRICA FIELDS'S WORK

The glass of Fredrica Fields is three-dimensional construction in pure glass. She does not in any way change the character or brilliance of the original glass by fusing, bending, or laminating it.

The boxlike frame that holds one of her panels is built with reinforced corners. The frame's back edge has a strong molding to support the glass. Fitted wood strips along the interior of the frame sides hold the composition secure. She lays the hardwood frame with its back edge flat against the top of a strong iron light-table so she may see the composition while she builds up the colorful layers.

Beginning with a sheet of ¼-inch plate glass, layers of colored glass are built up, one over the other. When light is transmitted through these layers it is diffused and refracted into a mélange of color. Fredrica works with an endless variety of glass materials: antique sheet, rods, tubes, marbles, glass rings, jewels, beads, rondels, and faceted glass chips. She designs as she builds, taking apart and putting together each layer many times before she completes the assemblage with another sheet of ¼-inch plate, secured with a wood molding screwed into the frame.

This talented artist comments: "My work is entirely a construction of glass fitted together bit by bit, sometimes solid, sometimes with air spaces, sometimes in layers, but never the same in any two panels. Occasionally, I use commercial epoxy to hold a piece in a certain position, as I do not use leads internally for this purpose. I do use "drop-in" holding frames in the layered work, but they are not visible as they fit the inner contour of the frame that is holding the work. It is a long demanding process—truly a work of love.

"As to colors, I use all colors. They are spattered about; no one color predominates. There is not a green panel, a blue panel, and so on. They are multicolor. Sometimes I use black and white opaque glass in combination; sometimes I make use of engraved flashed glasses. This allows wonderful glints of light and color to come through."—Fredrica Fields

Three-dimensional stained glass interior wall panels in the lobby of the Marie Cole Auditorium, Greenwich Library, Connecticut. Fredrica Fields. *Photos by Kenneth Fields.*

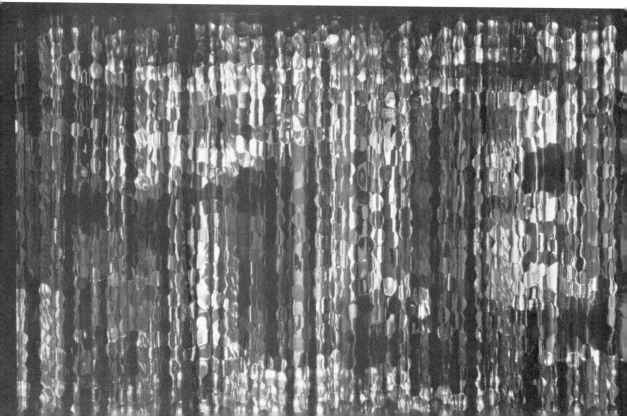

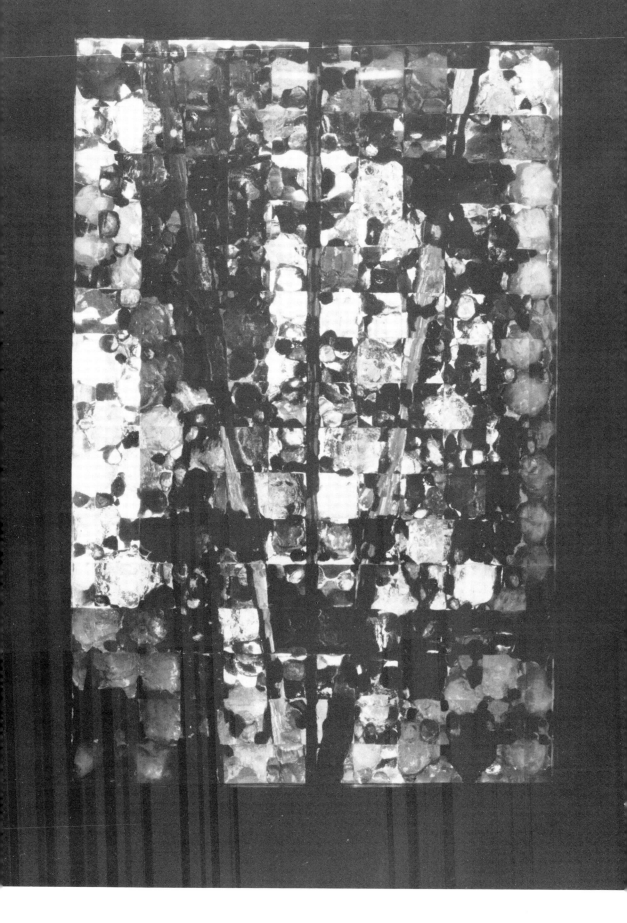

ee-dimensional stained glass interior wall panels in the lobby of the Marie Cole Auditorium, Green-
Library, Connecticut. Fredrica Fields. *Photos by Kenneth Fields.*

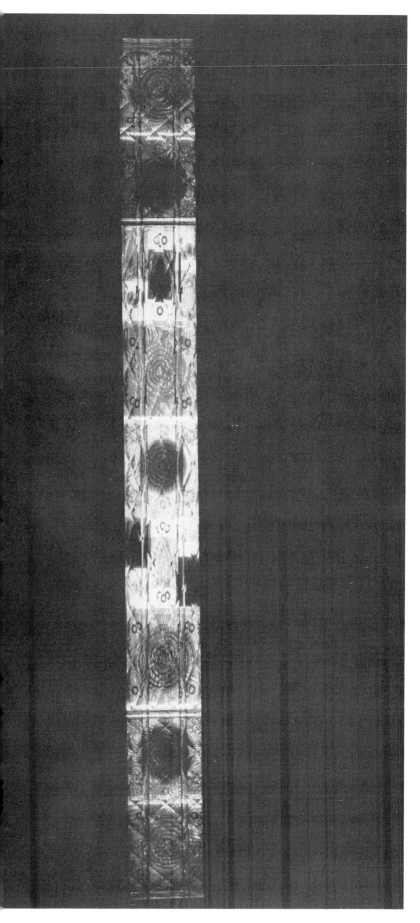

Exhibition Panel. 5'' tall X 5½'' wide.
Fredrica Fields.

Exhibition panel. 20½'' tall X 5'' wide. Fredrica Fields.

WINTER'S NIGHT. Fredrica Fields. Exhibition panel. 17" tall X 14" wide. *Photo by Kenneth Fields.*

Exhibition panel. 5½" tall X 5" wide. Fredrica Fields.

THE WORK OF LUCIEN DEN AREND

Lucien den Arend of Zwijndrecht, Holland, is an eminent architectural sculptor. The sophisticated appearance of his bent glass work is deceptively simple. With rectangles of glass supported on steel molds that he shapes on a hand roller, he bends the forms in a large kiln.

Lucien says modestly: "I have only to bend the steel; the furnace shapes the glass. I rolled the molds out of 4mm steel and bent the glass on these in the large kiln of Bruining Glass Company in Dordrecht, Holland. For the line, I covered the glass with adhesive vinyl, cut out the space for the line and sandblasted it. The line is rubbed with oil paint."

Lucien den Arend's sculptural work is usually quite large. He is well known in Europe for his environmental sculptures. The glass sculptures shown here will be models for future commissioned work of six to eight feet.

Lucien den Arend inserts the steel sheet into a hand-worked roller. He shapes the first large curve, then reverses the sheet in the roller to form the smaller curves.

Turning the roller to bend the sheet.

The steel sheet must be controlled.

The curves are subtle. Lucien sights
the arch of the form.

Applying oil color to the etched line.

Rubbing in the paint.

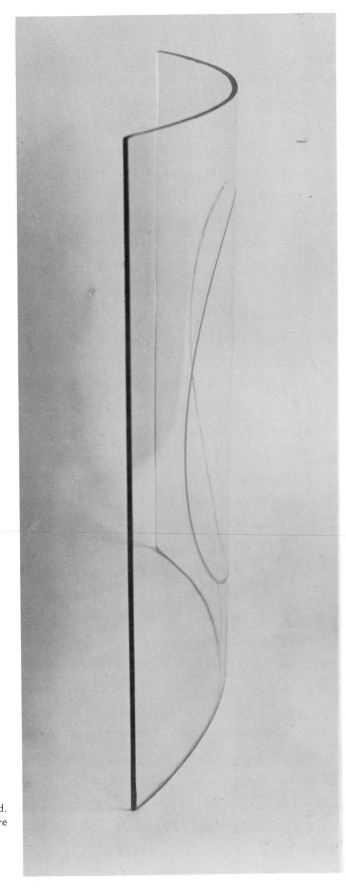

MONOLINEAR I. Lucien den Arend.
¼″ bent plate glass. Size before
bending 27″ X 26″.

MONOLINEAR II. Lucien den Arend. ¼'' bent plate glass. Size before bending 20'' X 28''.

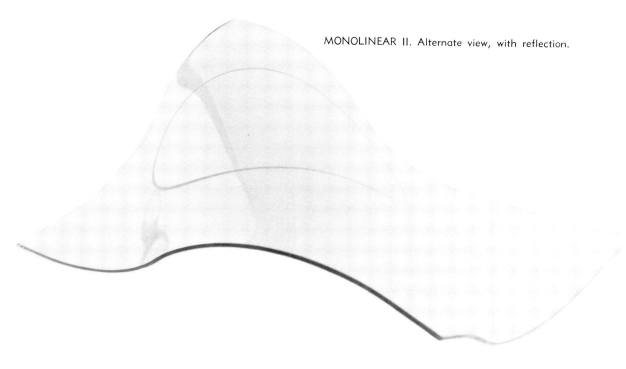

MONOLINEAR II. Alternate view, with reflection.

CONTOURING GLASS OVER NICHROME WIRE

A new and exciting technique in glass-bending requires 16-gauge or heavier nichrome wire. The demonstration sculpture project "White Peaks" also calls for insulation board such as Ceramiguard, Marinite, or other porous fireproof acoustical board that has been prefired as described under "Molds for Glass Fusing and Bending." Dry kiln wash is sifted over the board, then wires are inserted. Do not push them so far through the board that points of the wire project out the underneath side of the board and cause problems. The nichrome wire lengths are stuck into the board and bent in projecting patterns over which double-strength window glass will be positioned and sagged in the kiln. No pointed ends of the wires should project upward; they should be bent so the glass rests only on curved or horizontal wires. At least three of the tallest bent wire projections should be of nearly equal height to hold the glass sheet horizontal so it does not slide off the wires in the kiln before it can bend.

The next step is very important. Make a thin creamy solution of kiln wash and water, and paint all the nichrome wires wherever the glass can possibly touch them as it slumps in the heat of the kiln. The kiln wash protects the wires from adhering to the glass. Dry the wires before you position glass over them.

The glass should be cut wide enough that it extends beyond the outermost wires farther than the distance between the tops of the wires and the board, if you want some of the glass to flatten out around the perimeter of the composition. When the glass begins to bend in the hot kiln, first the entire sheet bends in a broad shallow arc before it sags between the individual wire projections. The edges of the glass touch the fireproof board and then slump flat, making a base for the sculpture. Glass ices and enamels can be sifted over the flat glass before it is positioned on the wires. (Always clean any glass that will be kiln-fired.)

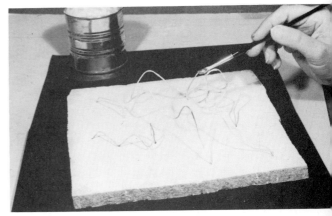

Nichrome wires are given a coating of kiln wash.

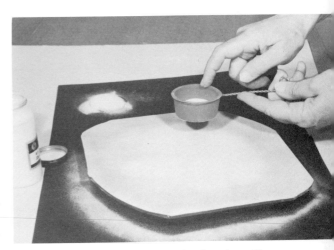

Sift glass ices and enamels over the flat glass. Clear colorless sheet glass can be very attractive when bent like this.

The glass is positioned over the shaped wires.

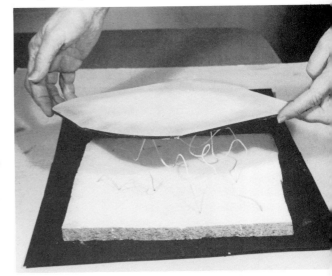

When the glass has been positioned carefully over the assemblage, it is time to insert it into a cool kiln well away from the door if it is a front-loading kiln. Switches are turned to *low* position. *Leave the door vented* one-half inch for an hour, then turn the switches to *high* position until the temperature climbs to 950°F. At that temperature the kiln door is closed. The final firing temperatures are all-important in contouring glass over nichrome wire. The illustrated project, "White Peaks," made of **PPG** Pennvernon double-strength window glass showed a definite contour at 1250°F. By 1400°F, it had arced and had begun to flatten out around the edges of the glass. It had slumped between the wires as far as desired at 1450°F, and the glass ices and enamels had melted and matured. The kiln was shut off and the door was vented for 2 to 3 minutes to completely halt further softening of the glass; otherwise the softened glass would have continued to stretch over the wires, which could allow them to protrude through the soft glass. Although this could be an interesting development, it would not be the effect that was planned. After brief venting, the kiln door was closed while the glass cooled slowly through the annealing cycle. (See the section "Annealing Glass.")

For a very different nichrome wire proj-

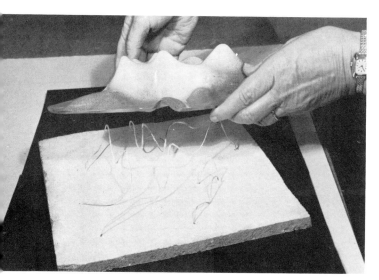

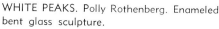
When firing is completed, the glass is lifted off the wires.

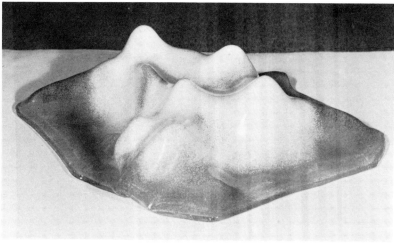
WHITE PEAKS. Polly Rothenberg. Enameled bent glass sculpture.

Sculpture fired over the same wires at 25°F higher temperature. The glass has sagged deeper between the wires. One of the wires pushed through the glass. The ragged edge was ground off in an interesting variation.

ect, a three-inch square piece of nichrome mesh, the kind used as a firing rack for copper enameling, is the base for drape-bending glass to form a square tray. Although this is a fascinatingly simple method, it must nonetheless be done precisely to achieve the desired result. Brush a thin creamy solution of kiln wash and water over the mesh and dry it. The square of wire mesh is positioned flat and centered on a thick ceramic kiln-post or a slim section of insulation brick. A five-inch square of clean double-strength window glass, placed on the mesh and extending evenly beyond the edges all around it, must clear the kiln-floor when it sags around the perimeter of the nichrome mesh. The assemblage is positioned on a prefired insulation board and inserted into a cool kiln well away from the kiln door. The switches are turned to *low* position. Follow firing instructions for nichrome wire project "White Peaks" until the temperature reaches 1300°F. Then take a quick look inside the barely opened door (if the kiln is front loading) to check the progress of the bending glass. The glass that extends beyond the edge of the wire mesh will slowly begin

to bend down around the edges in a subtle ripple effect. Just how far you want it to bend is a personal decision. Avoid opening the door very far or too often; the glass nearest the door will not sag as much as the glass around the other three sides of the piece if the door was shut off at 1350°F and the door vented about two minutes for this project. The glass was cooled and annealed.

If your kiln is a top loader, the bending glass is observed through a peephole. There is too great a surge of intense heat into your face when an attempt is made to lift up the lid of a top-loading kiln while it is firing. A first experimental firing could be made by shutting off the switches at 1350°F and removing peephole plugs to halt the rise in temperature, if you have difficulty seeing the glass through a peephole in a top loader. After the fired glass has become cool, it can be refired to a slightly higher temperature for further bending. If you are using nichrome mesh, it is well to halt the bending process before the glass sags to the point that the mesh becomes entrapped and cannot be removed from the glass after it has cooled.

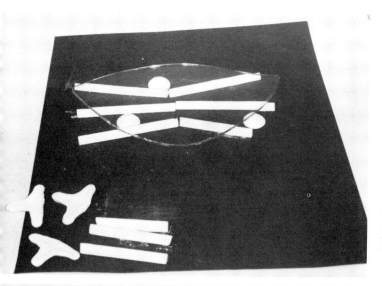

Clay-firing accessories make interesting glass bending designs. They are painted with kiln wash and dried before the glass is positioned over them.

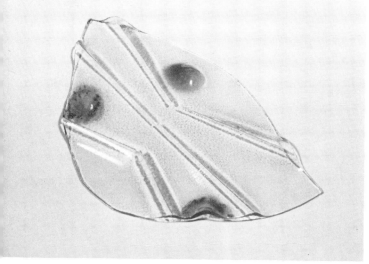

The glass was sifted with yellow glass coloring powder, with brown, orange, and light green spots.

A three-inch square piece of nichrome wire mesh is painted with kiln wash solution for a separator.

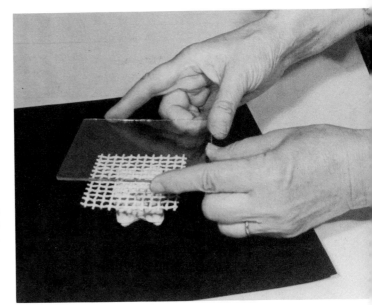

A five-inch square of clean double-strength window glass will clear the kiln floor when it sags around the perimeter of the mesh. It has been raised on small clay stilts.

Units like this can be epoxied to plate glass backgrounds repetitively for dividers.

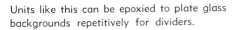

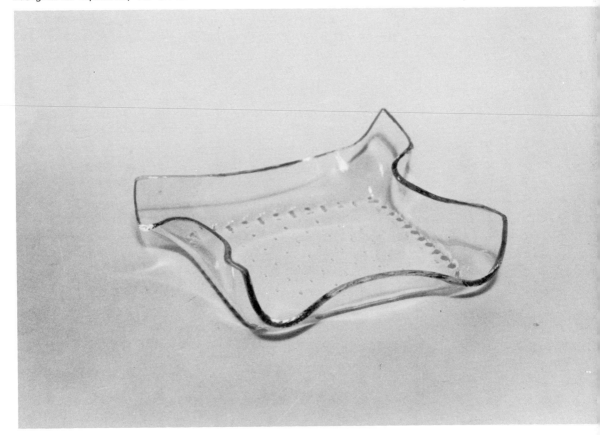

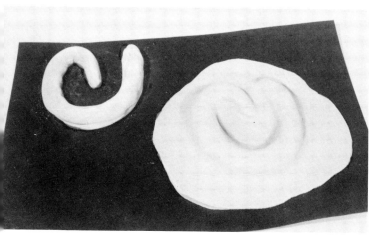

Moist white sculpture clay was rolled out and pressed over a curled clay coil that was leather-hard. The clay form is used for a mold.

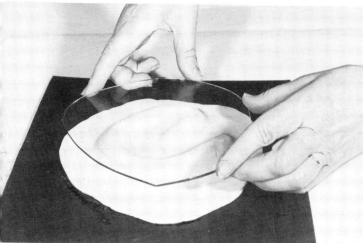

Double-strength window glass is cut to a size that will not extend beyond the mold perimeter when it is fired.

The completed sculptural unit.

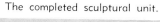

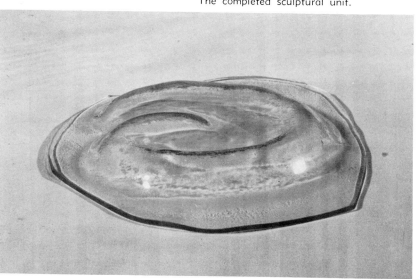

BETH BEEDE'S WORK

Beth Beede's craft designs reflect her years of study and teaching in the far Northwest and in Alaska. Although her work appears in many materials, the best known are her fine designs in fibers and in combinations of glass with other materials. Inspiration for some of her compositions comes from ancient Northwest Indian designs and their historical masks made from carved wood with grasses, walrus whiskers, eagle down, and fibers.

Beth comments on her work in glass: "I feel the possibilities of combining glass and fibers have to do with the contrasts and likenesses between them, for instance, the smooth solid and yet fluid forms of the glass as opposed to the textured, soft suppleness of fibers. The varying degree of permanency between materials has its roots in some of our earliest traditions in Europe, Africa, and the Americas; the use of clay, stone, metal, or glass contrasts with the more perishable materials like dry grasses, hair, fur, feathers, leather, fibers, and wood.

"The reflective qualities of glass and its transparency possibilities, with or without the formation of new colors in transitional areas are really exciting. Even though I feel pulled to natural materials as a satisfying complement of glass, I would be missing a lot if I ignored the possibilities in exploring man-made materials."—Beth Beede.

In her exotic hanging panel, MORNING SUN, Beth combined fused glass with wire, dyed wool, and beads. Two 8-inch single-

Beth Beede constructs one of her designs of fiber and feathers combined with glass.

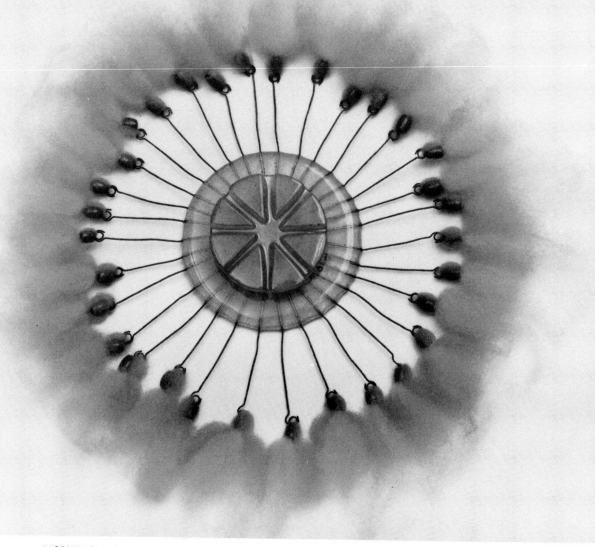

MORNING SUN. Beth Beede. Fused glass colored with transparent yellow and orange glass powders. Nichrome wires, orange handmade beads and dyed top Merino sheep fleece are combined in the exotic wall sculpture. *Photo by Erik Redlich.*

strength window glass discs were fused together with laminated lengths of nichrome wire fanning out from near the center of the glass and extending beyond it. One of two additional smaller glass discs was divided into wedges with a glass cutter. The small full circle was coated with transparent glass enamel and the wedged sectons were sifted with orange to red orange toward the center. When the wedge-shaped sections had been fused to the small full circle, this assemblage was set out from the two fused large glass discs by a small piece of glass glued between them with G.E. Silicone Cement. Handmade orange

glass beads from Pakistan and fluffs of top Merino sheep fleece dyed yellow and orange were fastened into the ends of the extending wires that were twisted into loops.

For a fused glass and macramé suspension, identical large glass shapes were fused together with laminated transparent blue and turquoise glass enamels flowing into one another. Small air spaces made in the enamel and bits of baking soda form the planned bubbles. Silver wire loops for hangers were fused between the glass layers at their lower edge and a double wire twisted loop at the top for the macramé suspensions. The small

Sculptured wall pendant. Beth Beede. Two large single-strength window glass shapes with blues and turquoise glass ices and silver wire loops laminated between them. Bubbles are from tiny dots of baking soda. Smaller discs, laminated flashlight lenses, are colored with blue and turquoise glass powders. They are suspended on macrame cords of monofilament.

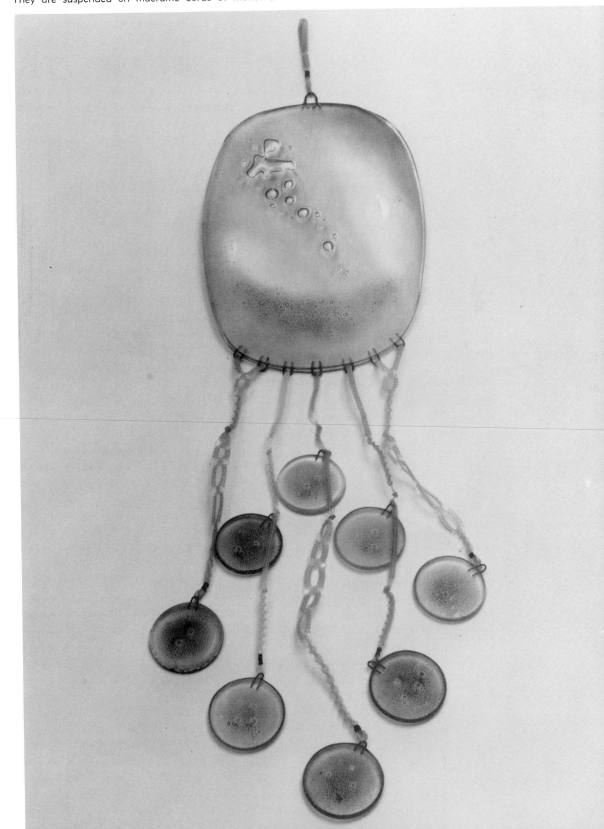

Detail of sculptured wall suspension.

suspended glass discs are made from fused flashlight lenses. They are in turquoise and blue hues, two each color. The bubbles were formed by the same method as those in the larger glass shape. Macramé done with monofilament (fishline) in blue and turquoise tints is finished with silver wire wound around the turned-up ends.

COPPER FOILING

Copper foil experimentation with segments of faceted glass, to make mobiles and sculptures, is creative and alluring. Sun streaming through these thick chunks of stained glass gives them a wondrous jewel-like glitter.

The copper foil is pliable and easy to use. To attain rigidity and durability once it has been applied to the glass segments, it must be coated with solder. Copper foil can be bought in ¼- and ⅜-inch rolls, 36 feet long, with an adhesive backing. If you want to use wider, less expensive copper foil that is nonadhesive, unroll it and cut off a strip about twenty inches long. Mark off ¼- or ⅜-inch intervals along each end of the strip. Lay a straightedge along a length of the foil and begin scoring with a nail or other scriber between marked intervals from one end of the strip to the other. With small sharp scissors, cut off *only a few* strips at one time along scored lines; if you cut too many at once they may tangle. Lay the strips on paper so they do not touch one another. Apply one of the new spray adhesives over the surface of a few strips. When the adhesive feels tacky but not sticky, it is time to begin applying the foil. The purpose of the adhesive is to hold the foil in place until it is soldered.

The copper foil applied in the demonstrated project is an adhesive-backed ¼-inch kind. The glass is broken faceted stained glass segments. Narrow ready-coated foil has paper backing that is peeled away as you apply the foil to a glass edge. You must keep foil and glass clean and free of oil from your skin; after it is cleaned, handle it gingerly. Alcohol or acetone will clean off oils.

To begin, pick up a clean glass piece, peel away some paper backing and wrap the foil along a glass ridge so an equal amount of foil is pressed to each side of the ridge. Press it firmly into all crevices and cut off the foil strip so it fits flush with the starting end. Apply soldering flux (oleic acid) to the ends of the copper strip and solder them together. If the solder does not cling to the copper, it may be soiled or the soldering iron may not be hot enough. Because the melting point of copper is much higher than that if tin or lead, there is little danger of melting the copper strip. Apply a few foil strips in different directions over the glass lump along its ridges, then cover the copper generously with 60/40 solid core solder to create a firm tight "cage" around the glass (Don't forget the soldering flux!). To suspend the glass as a mobile, solder an 18-gauge wire hanger to it. For exciting sculptures, solder foiled glass chunks together and epoxy them to a base.

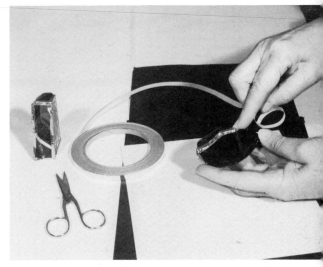

Pick up a clean glass piece as lightly as possible to keep skin oil from soiling it. Peel off some paper backing and press the narrow copper foil along a glass ridge.

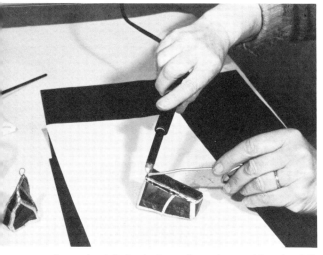

Press the foil firmly into all crevices; solder the foil ends together. Apply soldering flux and run solder over the entire copper foil area. Twisted wire hangers are soldered into place.

Small copper-foiled hanging sculptures made with dalle glass segments.

Faceted glass sculpture. Jean Abbott. Four three-dimensional stained glass pyramid shapes foiled and soldered together. 12" tall. *Photo by Alden Abbott.*

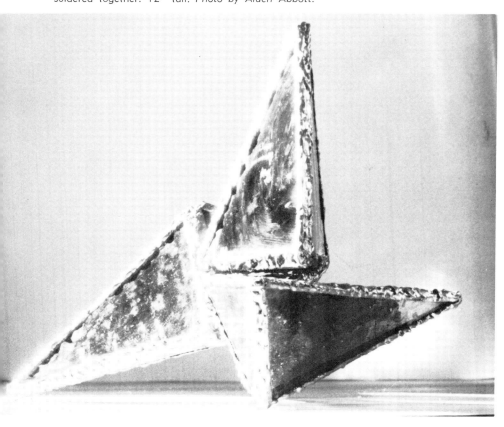

GLASS CASTING

Cast glass is an ancient art form dating back as far as the fifteenth century B.C. Shallow bowls, relief sculptures, and small figurines of remarkable detail have been found in ancient Egyptian tombs. The Egyptians valued small colored glass bits as highly as gemstones. Precious jeweled body ornaments from archaeological findings reveal handmade glass beads and small glass amulets. Glass casting continued intermittently throughout the southern Mediterranean area right up to the advent of blown glass around the first century A.D. Thereafter, the old method of casting glass seems to have been neglected until the beginning of the twentieth century, when Décorchemont, Rousseau, and other Frenchmen began to create sizable cast glass bowls and strong glass relief sculptures.

The formation of a small cast glass relief requires a model and a mold mixture that will be expendable after it is fired. The model for the relief can be made in either clay or wax. For the first basic sculptural relief project, the model is clay. Almost any clay will do, because it will not be fired. The small crucifix for the demonstration project is made from white sculpture clay, bought moist from the supplier. The model is placed flat on a sheet of glass or Formica-covered board; position the model with the front side facing up. Cut a strip of linoleum a little more than an inch wider than the deepest measurement of the clay model and several inches longer than its circumference. Wrap the strip around the model, smooth side facing inward and standing on edge; allow at least 1½ inches between the model and the linoleum. A string tied around the linoleum will hold it while you press clay all along the crack where the linoleum meets the sheet of glass or Formica board. Brush some vegetable oil or soap size over the inside of the linoleum strip and the base so the mold will release from it easily. The next step is to prepare the mold material.

The mold must be strong enough that it does not crack while it is being fired, but friable enough that it can be broken away from the glass object when it has been removed from the kiln. Most glass-casting molds today have a base of some form of plaster, combined with materials such as calcined refractory clay or silica sand and vermiculite or pulverized asbestos. The mold mixture developed especially for the demonstration project is made of equal parts of builder's plaster and a castable refractory powder called Plicast Verilite (trade name). This material is commonly used for commercial furnace linings. Kastolite is another satisfactory material. By consulting the telephone book classified advertisements, you may locate a local source of castable refractory material.

Blend thoroughly equal parts of dry plaster and the powdered material. Wear plastic gloves if you mix it by hand; plaster is very drying to the skin. Sprinkle the dry mixture over the surface of water in a plastic basin until it begins to pile up above the water just as though you were mixing plaster by itself. For one or two molds, two cups of water are sufficient for mixing adequate mold material. Be sure to add dry powder to water, not water to dry material. *Let it stand* for several minutes to slake or absorb, then blend it with a large wood or plastic spoon until it begins to thicken like heavy cream. Pour it immediately over the clay model in the prepared linoleum strip mold form to at least ¾ inch above the clay model. The mix will seem thin at first, but it will thicken and set in ten to twenty minutes. After it sets about an hour, the linoleum can be removed and soon the clay model is pulled from the mold. See that every bit of clay is removed from the mold and bevel the edges carefully. The mold is very fragile until its preliminary firing, so handle it gingerly. The inside of the mold cavity is painted with a thin solution of kiln wash for a separator. Set the completed mold in a warm place to dry for 24 hours. In the meantime completely scrub the plastic basin and tools used to mix and form the mold. If they are not cleaned at once, it is difficult to remove residue of mold material. After the fresh mold dries for 24 hours, set it into a cool kiln with the door or lid cracked ½ inch and turn switches to *low*. Fire it slowly to 400°–500°F to remove gases from the plaster that could cloud the glass. *When the kiln cools,* remove the mold with care.

For the demonstration piece, small fragments of washed antique glass were carefully positioned in the mold. Avoid scratching the mold cavity lining so bits of plaster or kiln wash (with which the lining is painted) are not mingled with glass particles. The filled mold was set gingerly into the kiln and fired until it reached 1650°F. The glass was cooled and annealed for 4 hours. Tests made for this project suggested that in certain colorless sheet glasses, devitrification (crystallization) tended to occur just *below* the temperature of liquefication if held there for a protracted period of time. When the rate of rise or descent was increased between 1650°F and 1450°F, crystallization did not occur. It did not occur when stained glass was used. Window glass has a higher liquefication temperature than stained glass.

When the glass was annealed and cooled, the casting was removed and the mold was broken away from it. After the glass sculpture was scrubbed with a stiff brush and water to clean off bits of kiln wash and mold material clinging to it, roughness around the edge was stoned smooth under water with a fine carborundum stone. The sculpture was dried and cemented to a section of granite rock with epoxy resin.

Preparation is made for casting molds; a large mold will be made for casting a glass cross and two smaller molds for glass draping. It is practical to make more than one mold at a time when the mixture is made up.

After the mold has set for an hour or more, the linoleum strip and clay model are removed from it. The clay is dug out easily with a loop end modeling tool.

Paint the mold's interior with a solution of kiln wash. Handle the fragile mold with care until it dries.

Small chunks of antique dalle glass fill the mold to rounding. The level will sink as the glass liquefies.

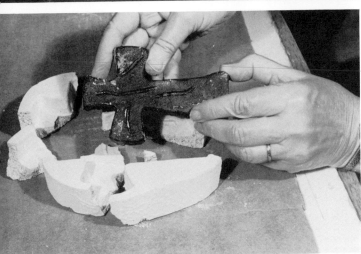

After the casting is fired, annealed, and cooled, break away the mold and scrub off the residue of kiln wash.

Cast glass cross. Polly Rothenberg. Deep ruby red antique glass mounted on natural unpolished red granite.

Regardless of how smooth the inside surface of a casting mold may be, the surface of a cast glass form takes on a slight graininess from the mold lining. You may prefer a more highly reflective surface for your cast glass. Although the procedure of fire-polishing rough glass is not usually available to the average individual craftsman, another method can be employed. Clean the glass with detergent water and dry it. Wipe a *thin* film of squeegee oil or other enameling oil over it, or spray it with enameling gum. Sift a very thin coating of low-firing glass flux over all but the back surface of the glass and dry it in a warm place. Fire it again *slowly,* back side down, following regular firing procedures to the temperature at which the flux is shiny. Vent the kiln from time to time if the temperature rises too rapidly. Be sure to anneal it as it cools! Because of the thickness of cast glass, reheating, cooling, and annealing *must be slow enough* to prevent the glass from cracking. Specific timing is not given due to variations in kilns and glasses.

EDRIS ECKHARDT'S SCULPTURES

Edris Eckhardt, talented ceramic and glass sculptor, combines glass casting with fusing and lamination for her sensitive sculptures. Her cast glass is formed in the lost-wax process; she formulates her own glasses with special oxide colorants and casts them in compatible investment molds.

STRANGE BLOSSOM. Edris Eckhardt. The preformed glass was inserted in the wax model to be cast in bronze. High temperature glass to withstand 2300°F bronze when the metal was cast. Colors: metal, golden bronze to dark brown; glass, iridescent. Mounted on black marble. Photo by Ray Sommer.

Cast glass group. Edris Eckhardt. *Left:* JUNE MORNING, emerald green, turquoise, crystal, amber, chartreuse. Head, SUMMER, peach color glass. NUDE, pink. All pieces from Edris's retrospective exhibition at the Corning Glass Museum. *Photo courtesy The Corning Museum of Glass.*

CHERUBIM. Edris Eckhardt. Low relief. Glass fused into investment. Colors: jade green, semiopaque. Transparent gold over raised surfaces.

◄

AND THOU BESIDE ME. Edris Eckhardt. Relief panel mounted for indirect light. Glass fused into investment material. Colors: emerald, turquoise, chartreuse with transparent gold over all raised surfaces.

THE SOURCE. Edris Eckhardt. The story of water from a drop to the Delta. Illuminated low-relief sculpture. Made of fused laminated glass. Colors: emerald and moss greens, cobalt and turquoise blues, pink and crystal white. Edris Eckhardt is an eminent sculptor who works in several mediums. She makes all her own glass, from the sands to the coloring oxides. *Photo courtesy The Corning Museum of Glass.*

▶

Cast and fused glass squares set into fences. At the Blenko Glass Company Visitors Center, Milton, West Virginia.

BLENKO GLASS

Fused and Cast Glass Fences at The Blenko Glass Company Visitors Center.

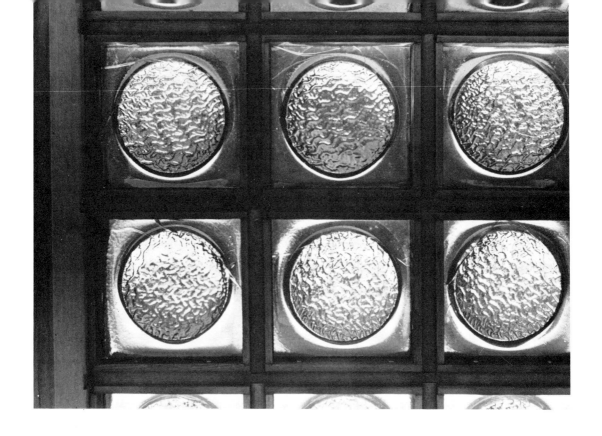

GLASSART STUDIO'S CALIFORNIA MART SKYLIGHT

The Glassart Studio of America in Phoenix, Arizona, completed in 1973 the magnificent 2,200-square-foot faceted stained glass skylight of the California Mart in Los Angeles. It is the largest single stained glass skylight in the United States: 65 feet long, 35 feet wide, with 126 panels that are 2 feet by 7 feet.

Faceted stained glass skylight at the California Mart, in Los Angeles. Completed by Glassart Studio, Phoenix, Arizona, in 1973. The skylight contains over 2,200 square feet; 65 feet long, 35 feet wide; 126 panels, each 2 feet by 7 feet. *Photo by courtesy of Glassart Studio.*

Top of the faceted glass skylight at California Mart as it appears from four stories above. One vertical side of the skylight can be seen along the right edge.

View from beneath the California Mart skylight. The sides of the skylight can be seen.

Detail of the skylight from below center.

Detail of the skylight design from below the portion near one end. See color plate. *Photos of the California Mart faceted stained glass skylight by courtesy of Glassart Studio.*

One of twelve windows in Saint Ambrose Catholic Church, Salt Lake City, Utah. Glassart Studio. A combination of faceted stained glass dalles and leaded glass in concrete.

Leaded stained glass window in Paradise Valley Methodist Church, Phoenix, Arizona. Glassart Studio.

Close view of Paradise Valley Methodist
Church window.

Distinctive faceted stained glass skylight
in a residential home. Glassart Studio.

Leaded stained glass residential bathroom window. Glassart Studio.

Faceted stained glass residential door. Glassart Studio.

Leaded stained glass arched window. Glassart Studio.

Faceted stained glass doorside panel. Glassart Studio.

◄

Clerestory windows of faceted stained glass. Glassart Studio. Eliminates the need for draperies above doors leading to an Arcadia patio.

EDWARD J. BYRNE STUDIO

Edward Byrne glazes (leads) etched glass panels.

Upper right:
Lead camed window with metallic overlay. Edward J. Byrne Studio.

Detail of camed window with overlay.

THE CUMMINGS ARCHITECTURAL WINDOW

"The window is 36 feet by 13 feet and the sill is 11 feet off the ground. The photograph shows only five of the six sections. . . . It is in the Officers' Open Mess, Fort Lewis, Washington. The problem to solve: 'A stained glass window to hide the brick wall outside . . .' well, look! In the final analysis, the brick wall became an integral visual part of the window; lights are projected on the brick wall at night to add a third dimension to the window. Another problem was that there is clear plate glass, glazed into each of the six sections, that was there to stay. Our window was to be placed on the inside of the plate glass at a distance of 6 inches; in order to avoid problems of condensation, we built our window with holes in it. The black areas are not glass at all, but black acrylic . . . The areas that appear as gray in the photo are a commercially made stained glass called 'Pentacore' by Mississippi Glass. The clear areas are the 'holes' in our window. They allow for plenty of air circulation so there will never be any problem of moisture buildup between the two windows. Lastly, the 'leads' are not leads at all, but are 1¾-inch bronze anodized aluminum with snapon beads." —Judy Cummings.

A window beautifully planned to cope with a major architectural problem. Designed by Hilda Sachs and H. M. Cummings. Executed by Cummings Studio, San Rafael, California, for the Officers' Open Mess, Fort Lewis, Washington.

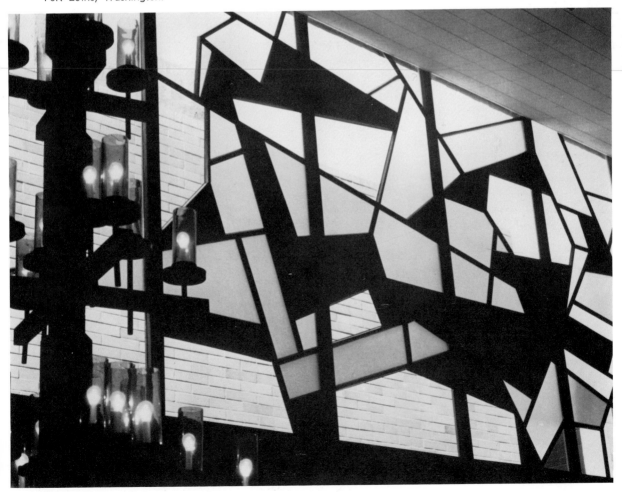

FARBIGEM AND THE WILLETS

"Exploration on the part of several stained glass studios, both American and European, into the possibility of locating colored glass works of art in commercial buildings and homes, necessitated moving away from leaded glass of the medieval style found in traditional churches and cathedrals. This lead to a certain amount of experimentation with new techniques.

"A most revolutionary method of using glass as an art form was originated in Holland by Florin Van Tetterode. His striking installations in banks, hotels, shops, and office buildings came to the attention of Mr. and Mrs. Henry Lee Willet in 1965. An arrangement was soon made whereby they would have exclusive rights to the process in the United States . . . At the Willet Stained Glass Studios it was given the name Farbigem.

"Farbigem is a technique making possible an art form in which whole walls can be designed in decorative thicknesses of glass. Starting with a base of two thicknesses of plate glass with plexiglass between, areas of colored glasses and/or masses of clear crystal can be laminated layer on layer on either or both sides. The permanence and safety of the resulting sculptured effect, in spite of its great weight, is assured through the use of special adhesives.

"The medium is especially successful in nonrepresentational abstract designs, although the two panels telling the history of medicine in the Ohio State University Medical Center are full of accurate portraits. The versatility of Farbigem is evident. It is used for small freestanding sculptures, gigantic three-dimensional effects on exterior facades as well as in window walls and room dividers. It has been successfully combined with faceted glass and sandblasted glass. It is effective with either a daylight or artificial light source from the back, and also when surface lighted."—Helene Weis.

The Willets' splendid Ohio State University Medical Center Farbigem murals depict great milestones in the advance of medicine around the world and medical services to humanity. Bonded layers of flat glass set vertically, varicolored spheres, cylinders, faceted chunks, and gemmaux backgrounds, together with heads, lettering, and other special representations acid-etched on flashed glass, create an aesthetic effect of scintillating imagery and storytelling.

WORLD HISTORY OF MEDICINE. Willet Studio. Designed for and installed in Ohio State University Medical Center, Columbus, Ohio. Illuminated Farbigem glass wall. Bonded in layers of colored stained glass and clear glass.

▶

Finished Farbigem for Ohio State University. Close view showing depth and laminated textures.

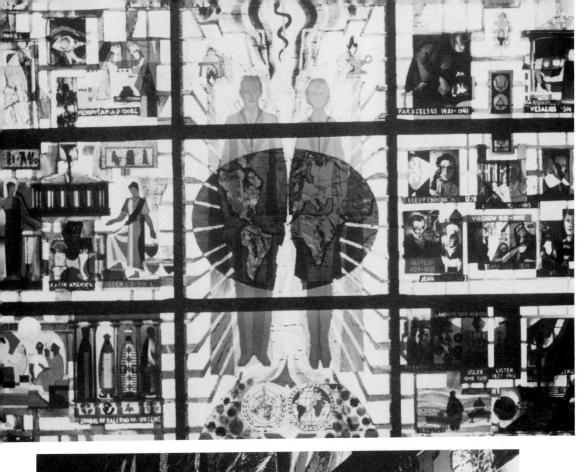

Detail of Ohio State University glass mural with its intricate layering and texture.

Additional detail of Ohio State University Farbigem mural.

View from beneath the Ohio State Farbigem freestanding mural showing intricate variety and depth of individual applications.

Farbigem panel on a bank building in Dordrecht, Holland, executed by Van Tetterode's Studio, Amsterdam, Holland.

Many skilled glassworkers are required to plan and construct one of these truly heroic compositions. Vincent Sirrianni of the Willet Studios lays out glass for the Farbigem mural in Ohio State University Medical Center.

Edgar Williams prepares glass for lamination of the mural wall at the Willet Studios.

Detail of the Farbigem Teilhard de Chardin window in Riverside Park Methodist Church, Jacksonville, Florida. Made by Willet Stained Glass Studios.

TABLETS OF THE LAW. Willet Stained Glass Studios. Bonding in the Farbigem process can be combined with any other glass method. It is combined here with faceted glass. Greenborough Hebrew Congregation, Dobbs Ferry, New York.

The Willet Stained Glass Studios has an illustrious experience in faceted glass applications as well as in Farbigem. Henry Willet selects glass dalles for a faceted window.

Marguerite Gaudin designs a black and white for a faceted lumiere. Willet Stained Glass Studios.

Donald Consul selects and knobs dalles for a faceted window at Willet Stained Glass Studios.

Phillip Tate faceting stained glass dalles at Willet's.

Willet Studio personnel installing a faceted window in the Zion Lutheran Church, Anaheim, California.

St. Mark's Episcopal Church, New Canaan, Connecticut. The interior of the church and faceted windows, both by Willet Stained Glass Studios.

Glossary

Annealing Glass: The heating and controlled cooling of glass to relieve stress and brittleness. The temperature range for annealing varies, depending on characteristics of the glass.

Antique Glass: Sheets of stained glass made by blowing.

Batch: Glass ingredients put into a furnace to be melted.

Bending: Softening and sagging of glass during kiln-firing.

Blank: A piece of glass cut to basic shape for use in creating a bent glass object.

Blocking: Shaping a gather or bubble of glass with a wooden block or other object.

Blown Glass: Glass objects that have been formed by blowing air into a gather of molten glass. The resultant glass bubble is shaped into many forms.

Blowpipe: An iron or steel pipe with a nose of heatproof alloy for gathering molten glass from a furnace. Air is blown through the pipe to inflate the gather into a glass bubble.

Bonded Glass: Pieces of glass cemented together or to a glass sheet with transparent adhesive.

Bridge: A flat wooden strip elevated with end blocks to support the hand while it is painting glass over a light table.

Bridge Wall: A wall across the top section of a tank beneath which molten glass flows, to trap impurities.

Bubble: 1. Air pocket trapped in glass when it is fused. 2. The large pocket of air intentionally formed when glass is blown.

Calcine: To heat inorganic substances to a high temperature (without fusion) to pulverize or oxidize.

Calcium Carbonate: Whiting. A separating powder used between glass and molds or kiln shelves to prevent adhesion when fired.

Came: Lead strips that join pieces of stained glass.

Carborundum Stone: A silicon carbide stone for hand-grinding rough spots on glass. Should be done under water.

Cartoon: The layout design of a stained glass composition in actual size.

Cathedral Glass: Machine-rolled stained glass with medium to heavy texture on one side and a smooth surface on the other side, ⅛-inch thickness uniformly.

Caulk: To stop up seams and make them watertight.

Coefficient of Expansion: The rate at which glass (or other material) expands during heating and contracts during cooling.

Collage: An assemblage of fragments of glass to create an art composition.

Conchoidal: Having swirled elevations and depressions in form, such as one-half of a conch shell.

Contoured: Glass sagged or slumped over a mold in the kiln to bend it to the shape of the mold.

Crazing: A mesh of fine cracks in glass caused by too rapid or imperfect cooling.

Cullet: Broken or refuse glass usually added to new material to facilitate melting of a glass batch in a furnace.

Curious Glass: Fragments of sheet glass sold as scrap glass.

Cut-size Line: Cutline. The border line of the stained glass composition against which the border lead will be placed.

Cutting: A term often used for scoring and separating glass; the glass is not actually cut.

Dalles: From the French *dalles* [doll] *de verre* (flagstones of glass). Slabs of antique stained glass measuring ¾ inch to 2 inches in thickness. Usually cast in squares or rectangles with dimensions of 8 inches to 12 inches.

Embossed: Surface with raised designs.

Etching: Chemical or mechanical erosion of surface to make designs.

Faceted Glass: Slab glass chipped to produce sparkling light-reflective small planes in a conchoidal fracture.

Ferrier's Nails: Horseshoe nails for securing glass and leads together; blue lath nails are often substituted.

Fine Silver: Pure silver. Does not oxidize when it is fired.

Firebrick: A hard refractory brick with extremely high heat resistance. Not to be confused with insulation brick.

Flashed Stained Glass: Denotes a variety of antique, having a light-colored glass base with thinner skins of richer, deeper contrasting colored glass.

Flux: 1. Colorless glass ground to fine mesh. 2. A substance for promoting fusion in soldering. See Oleic Acid.

Foil: An extra-thin metal sheeting.

Fracture: Breaking or splitting and cracking of glass.

Fusing: Combining glass pieces through heat by melting together.

Gather: The molten glass picked up on the end of the blowpipe from the hot furnace melt.

Gemmaux: An application of many small colored glass chunks and bits bonded together for a scintillating effect.

Glass Cutter: A small hand-held steel or wood-handled tool with a tiny cutting wheel set into one end. The tool is used to score glass so it can be separated or cleanly broken apart. Some cutters have minute commercial diamonds instead of steel wheels.

Glazier: A craftsman who sets glass and putties its edges to weatherproof it.

Glazing: Enclosing window openings or other areas with glass by puttying, cementing, leading.

Glazing Compound: Putty used to secure glass in a leaded composition.

Glory Hole: A furnace for reheating glass on a rod or punty when blowing glass.

Greenware: Unfired bone-dry ceramic objects sold by ceramic suppliers. They can often be fired for use as glass bending molds if they have no undercuts.

Grout: A creamy mortar filled in between ceramic or glass tiles.

Grozing: Chipping away irregular projections to refine the edge or to improve the fit of glass.

Halation: The spread of light beyond the boundaries of a lighted object to create a diffused ring or imagery of light or color on adjoining objects.

Heart: The thin crossbar between channels of lead came.

H-lead: H-shaped double channeled lead came.

Hardener: One of two components in epoxy resin. It causes the hardening of the resin.

Ices or Ice Colors: Colored glass powder used for decorating glass surfaces when they are fired.

Impervious: Impenetrable or unaffected by moisture, light rays, chemicals, etc.

Incise: To cut.

Insulation Brick: A soft porous brick with high heat resistance; may be carved to make glass-bending molds. Sometimes incorrectly called firebrick.

Jack: A steel or waxed wood two-pronged spring tool for shaping molten glass that is being formed.

Jewels: Small lumps of colored glass that have been fired and then adhered to glass objects for decoration.

Kastolite: Brand name. A castable refractory sometimes used for making molds to be used for glass bending. Its primary use is for furnace lining.

Kiln: A high temperature oven, ideally equipped with a pyrometer, used for firing glass, enamels, clay, and refractory molds.

Kiln Wash: Equal parts of kaolin and flint in powdered form or creamy solution.

Lamination: Two or more glass pieces fused flat or bent together with materials entrapped between them.

Lath Nails: Small thin hard carpenter's nails that may be employed to hold glass and leads together during construction of a stained glass composition.

Lathekin: A small smooth bluntly pointed or almond shaped tool for opening the channels of lead came.

Lavender Oil: An oil derived from the lavender plant. It can be used as a binder for application of enamels.

Leading: Joining pieces of stained glass together with lead came strips.

Lehr: An oven designed for annealing stained glass.

Light Table: An enclosure with frosted glass (ground glass) top through which artificial light is transmitted.

Lumiere: A design in color for a stained glass window.

Luster: A metallic overglaze.

Marver: A steel or marble-topped table on which a molten glass gather is rolled and cooled slightly.

Matrix: The base in which another form is developed. In a faceted glass panel, the cement or epoxy surrounding each glass segment is the matrix.

Matting: Applying glass paint to a glass surface, then tapping it with a badger brush to give a translucent surface.

Maturity: The temperature at which fired glass attains its full beauty.

Mica: A fireproof silicate that separates into thin sheets.

Nichrome: An acid-resistant refractory alloy of nickel, iron, and chromium.

Oleic Acid: A fatty oil used for a flux in soldering lead.

Opalescent Glass: Milky semitranslucent rolled glass in one or more swirled colors and white. It is somewhat brittle and is difficult to cut.

Oxidize: To combine chemically with oxygen. Metals, when weathered, darken or change color by oxidation.

Punty: A slender steel rod for picking up extra bits of molten glass to decorate a blown form or to attach to the base of the form so the blowpipe can be removed. Also called pontil rod.

Pyrometer: An instrument for measuring and indicating kiln temperatures.

Refractory: Hard and resistant to high temperatures.

Release Agent: A separator for preventing glass or mold material from adhering to one another.

Repoussé: A hammered, pressed, or raised design in metals.

Rheostat: Device for regulating electric current temperatures by variable controls.

Resin Core Solder: Solder with an invisible resin core that does not require flux. Not suitable for leaded glass.

Rondel: Round disc of stained antique glass.

Sagging: Loss of rigidity as fired glass slumps into the shape of its supporting mold.

Sandblasting: Engraving with a high-velocity stream of sand on areas not protected by tape to create surface patterns.

Seedy Glass: Contains tiny bubbles that create a texture.

Sgraffito: Designs created by scratching into enamel or glaze before firing.

Shard: A fragment of a brittle substance such as glass or pottery.

Shears, Cartoon: Scissors for cutting out individual stained glass patterns. They have a single-edged blade and a double-edged blade. When a cut is made, the blades remove a strip of paper between pattern pieces to make room for the lead heart that separates glass pieces.

Slab Glass: Clear colored antique glass cast in thick slabs used for facet glass.

Soldering: Joining metals with solder by heating with a soldering iron.

Square Shears: When they close, the shears form a square hole for cutting or clasping molten glass rods or gobs.

Stained Glass: Glass colored with oxides and other chemicals incorporated into the batch while it is molten.

Stencil: A design pattern around which colors are sifted or painted to transfer the design to glass or other surfaces.

Stopping Knife: A short-bladed knife with a rounded bent end. Useful for lifting and inserting glass shapes into lead channels.

Strain Point: The lower limit of the annealing range, which varies with the type of glass being annealed.

Stress: Inner strain of glass caused by improper annealing or by fusing incompatible glasses together.

Striations: Random threadlike lines or grooves in surfaces of glass.

Subsurface: The bottom side of a piece of glass.

Temperature Gradient: The uniform or graded rate of rising or lowering of temperature.

Template: A pattern cut from thin material to an exact shape.

Tesserae: Glass cut into small pieces for making mosaics.

Tinning: Coating the copper tip of a soldering iron with tin-lead solder.

Translucent: Diffused transmission of light rays.

Transmitted Light: Light that passes through glass or other material.

Transparent: Full transmission of light rays with clear vision of objects through the glass.

Undercut: A cut that slants inward, preventing bent or cast glass from releasing from its mold.

U-lead: Single channeled U-shaped lead came, used especially for border leading.

Vent: An opening to permit passage of heat,

fumes, or gases from a hot kiln. It may be either a door, lid, or peephole.

Viscosity: Resistance to flow, increased as molten glass cools and thickens. The property of a fluid to resist internal flow.

Vitreous: Pertaining to glass. Vitreous enamels are ground glass and they must be fired to maturity.

Vitrified: Changed into glass, as when sand fused with chemicals is converted into glass.

Volatile: Readily changed into vapor or gas.

Waterglass: Sodium silicate in powdered form, mixed with water to form a thick liquid. It is sometimes used as a protective coating for molds or insulation brick.

Waxing Up: Hot wax is dropped on corners of stained glass pieces that are being temporarily affixed to a sheet of clear glass to hold them in proper sequence so they may be painted decoratively.

Bibliography

Anderson, Harriette. *Kiln-fired Glass.* Philadelphia, New York, and London: Chilton Book Company, 1970.

Birren, Faber. *Creative Color.* New York: Reinhold Publishing Corporation, 1961.

Diamond, Freda. *The Story of Glass.* New York: Harcourt, Brace and Company, 1953.

Duval, Jean-Jacques. *Working with Stained Glass.* New York: Thomas Y. Crowell Company, 1972.

Kinney, Kay. *Glass Craft.* Philadelphia, New York, and London: Chilton Book Company, 1962.

Koch, Robert. Louis C. Tiffany. *Rebel in Glass.* New York: Crown Publishers, Inc., 1964.

Littleton, Harvey. *Glassblowing: A Search for Form.* New York: Van Nostrand Reinhold Company, 1971.

Lloyd, John Gilbert. *Stained Glass in America.* Jenkintown, Pennsylvania: The Religious Publishing Co., 1963.

Maloney, F. J. Terrence. *Glass in the Modern World.* Garden City, New York: Doubleday & Co., Inc., 1968.

Reyntiens, Patrick. *The Techniques of Stained Glass.* New York: Watson-Guptill Publications, and London: B. T. Batsford Ltd., 1967.

Rothenberg, Polly. *Creative Stained Glass.* New York: Crown Publishers, Inc., 1973.

———. *The Complete Book of Ceramic Art.* New York: Crown Publishers, Inc., 1972.

———. *Metal Enameling.* New York: Crown Publishers, Inc., 1969.

Schuler, Frederic and Lilli. *Glassforming.* Philadelphia, New York, and London: Chilton Book Co., 1970.

Sowers, Robert. *Stained Glass: An Architectural Art.* New York: Universal Books, Inc., 1965.

PERIODICALS

Ceramics Monthly, Columbus, Ohio; *Craft Horizons,* New York; *Glass Art,* Oakland, California; *Stained Glass,* St. Louis, Missouri.

Supply Sources

UNITED STATES AND CANADA

(Check local art, craft, lapidary, hardware stores, and yellow pages of the phone book; write these manufacturers for their brochures and names of nearest dealers.)

ADHESIVES:

Epoxy systems, cements, compounds

Benesco Co.
40 North Rock Hill
St. Louis, Missouri 63119

H & M Plastics
129 S. Second Street
Philadelphia, Pennsylvania 19106

Resins Research Corp.
1989 Bayberry Road
Huntington Valley, Pennsylvania
    19006

Thermoset Plastics, Inc.
5101 E. 65th Street
Indianapolis, Indiana 46220

CASTABLE REFRACTORIES:

A. P. Green Refractories Co. (Kas-
    tolite)
Mexico, Missouri 65265

Plibrico Co. (Plicast Verilite)
1600 Kingbury
Chicago, Illinois 60614

COLORANTS:

Ices, stains, enamels, lusters
(for glass)

Blythe Colours Ltd.
34 Brydon Drive
Rexdale, Ontario

B. F. Drakenfeld & Co.
45 Park Place
New York, N.Y. 10007

O. Hommel Co.
Hope Street, Carnegie
Pittsburgh, Pennsylvania 15106

L. Reusche & Co.
2 Lister Avenue
Newark, New Jersey 07105

Standard Ceramic Supply Co.
P.O. Box 4435
Pittsburgh, Pennsylvania 15205

Thomas C. Thompson Co.
1530 Old Deerfield Road
Highland Park, Illinois 60035

UNFIRED PAINTS FOR GLASS:

Fuller O'Brien Corp.
South San Francisco, California
    94080
(Write for nearest dealer and a
    color chart.)

Mira-Plate Epox Paint
The O'Brien Corp.
South Bend, Indiana 46628

FURNACES, KILNS, GLASSBLOWING EQUIPMENT:

A. D. Alpine, Inc.
353 Coral Circle
El Segundo, California 90245

Drykiln Design
P.O. Box 7527
Oakland, California 94601

GLASS:

Antique, rondels, dalles
(stained glass)

The Blenko Glass Co.
Milton, West Virginia 25541

Antique and cathedral

S. A. Bendheim Co., Inc.
122 Hudson Street
New York, N.Y. 10013

Bienenfeld Industries, Inc.
1541 Covert Street
Brooklyn, New York 11227

Cathedral (stained glass)

Advance Glass Company
Newark, Ohio 43055

Kokomo Opalescent Glass Co., Inc.
P.O. Box 809
State and Market Streets
Kokomo, Indiana 46901

Cullet

Consumers Glass
Islington Avenue
Toronto, Ontario

Drykiln Design
P.O. Box 7527
Oakland, California 94601

Keystone Cullet Co.
R.F.D. 8, Box 344
Greensburg, Pennsylvania 15601

Window glass and plate
(for bending and sagging)

Libbey-Owens-Ford (LOF)
Pittsburgh Plate Glass Co. (PPG)
(These glasses available locally;
    check phone book)

GLAZING COMPOUND:

Dap 33 Gray, for leaded glass

Dap, Inc.
5300 Huberville Road
Dayton, Ohio 45431

GROUT AND GROUT COLORANTS:

G. E. Kaiser Co.
Houston, Texas 77008

Technical Adhesives
Division of H. B. Fuller Co.
315 S. Hicks Road
Palatine, Illinois 60067

KNIVES AND CUTTERS:

Lead cutters

S. Camlott
520 Hollywood Avenue
Salt Lake City, Utah 84105

Matt knives

Local hardware and art supply
  stores

Glass cutters

The Fletcher-Terry Co.
Spring Lane
Farmington, Connecticut 06032

LEAD CAME AND SOLDER:

G. A. Avril Co.
Langdon Farm Road & Seymour
  Avenue
Cincinnati, Ohio 45237

Crown Metal Co.
117 E. Washington Street
Milwaukee, Wisconsin 54204

Gardner Metal Co.
4820 S. Campbell Avenue
Chicago, Illinois 60632

PATTERN SCISSORS:

S. A. Bendheim Co.
122 Hudson Street
New York, N.Y. 10013

SAFETY GLASSES:

(Glassblowers' safety glass
with G-20 lenses)

Bausch & Lomb Optical Co.
Lindsay Street
Midland, Ontario

Bausch & Lomb Optical Co.
635 St. Paul
Rochester, New York 14605

TOOLS:

For slab glass

Bienfeld Industries, Inc.
1541 Covert Street
Brooklyn, New York 11227

For glassblowing

Drykiln Design
P.O. Box 7527
4317 Howard Street
Oakland, California 94601

MISCELLANEOUS:

Nitschke Products, Inc.
P.O. Box 104
Oak Park, Illinois 60303

Oxyweld Ltd. (asbestos mitts)
156 John Street
Barrie, Ontario

Stained Glass Club
482 Tappan Road
Northvale, New Jersey 07647

Copper Foil

Glenside Glass
West Mt. Carmeil Avenue
Glenside, Pennsylvania 19038

The Hidden House of Crafts
44 Encina Avenue
Palo Alto, California 94301

M & C Specialties Co.
Philadelphia, Pennsylvania 19135

Glass Globs and Marbles

Peltier Glass Co.
518–524 De Lean Street
Ottawa, Illinois 61350

Hammers for Facet Glass

William Howard
c/o Willet Studio
10 East Moreland Avenue
Philadelphia, Pennsylvania 19118

Glass Masters Guild
621 Avenue of the Americas
New York, N.Y. 10011

ENGLAND

COLORANTS:

James Hetley & Co. Ltd.
Beresford Avenue
Wembley, Middlesex

Johnson Matthey
Hatton Gardens
London EC1

Wengers Ltd.
Stoke-on-Trent, Staffs

GLASS:

Claritude Ltd.
19 Dunraven Street
Park Lane, London W1

James Hetley & Co Ltd.
Beresford Avenue
Wembley, Middlesex

KILNS AND FURNACES:

Wild Barfield Ltd.
Elecfurn Works
Otterspool Way
Waterford By-pass, Hertfordshire

Catterson Smith Ltd.
Adam Bridge Works
Exhibition Ground
Wembley, Middlesex

LEAD:

British Insulated
Callender Cables Ltd.
21 Bloomsbury Street
London WC1

Bruntons Ltd.
5 Miles Street
Vauxhall SW8

PLASTER OF PARIS:

Gyproc Ltd.
Ferguson House
Marylebone Road
London NW1

PUTTY & WHITING:

Dussek Brothers
Thames Road
Crayford, Kent

SOLDER & SOLDERING IRONS:

James Hetley & Co. Ltd.
Beresford Avenue
Wembley, Middlesex

TOOLS:

Buck & Ryan Ltd.
101 Tottenham Court Road
London W1

Alex Tiranti Ltd.
72 Charlotte Street
London W1

Sharratt & Newth Ltd.
287 Goswell Road
London EC1

VISES:

Johnson Matthey
78 Hatton Gardens
London EC1

Index

California Real Estate Principles

Walt Huber
Glendale Community College

™

12th Edition

COPYRIGHT 1976, 1977, 1978, 1979, 1985, 1989, 1994, ,1995, 2003, 2004, 2005, 2006, 2008 12th Edition
Educational Textbook Company, Inc.
P. O. Box 3597
Covina, California 91722
(626)339-7733
(626)332-4744 (Fax)
etctextbooks.com or etcbooks.com

Library of Congress Cataloging-in-Publication Data

California Real Estate Principles - Walt Huber

Summary: Covers all material in Real Estate Principles classes with special emphasis on California real estate laws. Very clear and simple language, easy-to-read format with photographs, charts, and graphs. Includes glossary and index. Suitable for consumers, students, and teachers wishing information about personal real estate transactions. This textbook is designed to fulfill the course requirement necessary to take the California Real Estate Salespersons and Broker's Exams.

ISBN 0-916772-08-X
       978-0-916772-08-6

Preface

The Real Estate Market Has Taken a Dramatic Turn!

The Great Credit Crunch of 2007-2009 is upon us nationally, and the economic/real estate slump has affected California. Credit terms and lending criteria will no doubt continue to change due to the so-called "meltdown." This book offers options to avoid the "crisis" mentality of the less educated, and help focus on the opportunities presented in these difficult times. Borrowers, in order to save their credit and homes, are appealing to lenders to "renegotiate" loan payments, and there will be an increasing need for alternatives to traditional financing—for example, short sales, land contracts, and sellers taking back second deeds of trust—all of which are detailed in this 12th Edition of *California Real Estate Principles*. We also provide forms and explanations for other alternatives such as a Leases, and Leases With an Option to Buy.

Whether you're an owner with high monthly payments, or a buyer looking for a bargain, or a salesperson looking to best help his or her client and make a commission, this book draws your attention to alternatives that you should explore.

I want to express my appreciation to the many people who helped to make this text possible. I received advice and helpful suggestions from the **California Department of Real Estate** (www.dre.ca.gov) and advice and forms from the **California Association of REALTORS®** (www.car.org).

We would also like to thank Levin P. Messick, IFAC, President, AC Appraisals, Inc. and instructor at Mt. San Antonio College, and Arlette Lyons, CRS, GRI, President and owner of Lyons and Associates, Inc. REALTOR®, and instructor at Mt. San Antonio College. We would also like to thank Fred Martinez, instructor at City College of San Francisco.

Special thanks for the valuable assistance given by the people who helped design and produce this book: Philip Dockter, art director; Melinda Winters, cover design; Colleen Taber, executive editor; Troy Monroe Stacey, graphics; Linda Serra and Andrea Adkins, editors; and Rick Lee, pre-press editor and layout.

Meet our charming trademark character "Hubie, the Internet Mouse." But don't let his quirky good looks fool you—he's one heck of a businessman! Let this little "mouse about town" guide you to all the best websites on the Internet, and maybe help make the learning experience a little more fun in the process.

Acknowledgments

This book contains the input of many prominent educators and real estate professionals. Their involvement as contributing advisors has made it possible for us to cover a wide range of material in detail and, at the same time, offer practical perspectives based upon their extensive classroom and industry experience. Their contributions were invaluable and merit our most sincere thanks.

Hal Madson
Allan Hancock College

Alfred J. Guetling
American River College

Steve Sodergren
Antelope Valley College

Joe Newton
Bakersfield College

Thurza B. Andrew
Butte College

Donald T. Brown
Butte College

Carol A. Jensen
Cabrillo College/CCSF

Joseph F. Belohlavek
Cabrillo College

Robin Sherman
Cabrillo College

Melvin Brady
Cerritos College

John T. Martinez
Chabot College

Richard McCartney
Chabot College

John A. Culver
Chabot College

Robert Andersen
Chabot College

Earl H. Bond
Chaffey College

J. O. Wright
Chaffey College

Keith H. Kerr
City College San Francisco

Fred Martinez
City College San Francisco

Hal Bouley
Coastline College

Allen C. Shute
College of The Canyons

Ken Determan
College of The Canyons

Stan Reyburn
College of The Desert

Jeff Eddy
College of The Sequoias

John A. Miller
Contra Costa College

Ronald G. Rueb
Contra Costa College

Corina D. Rollins
Contra Costa College

D. Blazej
Cuesta College

Fred C. Hoey
Cuesta College

Rick Chehab
De Anza College

John R. Morrissey
Diablo Valley College

Tim Murphy
Diablo Valley College

Leo Saunders, GRI, CRB
Diablo Valley College

Dr. Elliott J. Dixon
East Los Angeles College

Olivia Vasquez Anderson
East Los Angeles College

Michael Botello
El Camino College

Dr. Donna Grogan, GRI, CPM
El Camino College

Bud Zeller
Folsom Lake College

Charles Krackeler
Foothill College

Dr. Eugene C. Azamber
Fresno City College

Dr. Robert J. Bowers
Fullerton College

Peter Kirianoff
Fullerton College

Karen Obuljen
Golden West College

Dino Vlachos
Golden West College

Frank Pangborn
Irvine Valley College

Alex Yguado
Los Angeles Mission College

John J. Meichtry
Los Angeles Mission College

Thomas Morehouse
Los Angeles Pierce College

Harold Lerner
Los Angeles Pierce College

Robert R. Enger
Los Angeles Pierce College

Bernard Grabois
Los Angeles Valley College

Patricia Moore
Los Medanos College

Frank Coon
Los Medanos College

R. Joseph Banuat, CRS, CRB
Los Medanos College

Ignacio Gonzalez
Mendocino College

Harvey Rafel
Merced College

Tom Gee
Merritt College

Edward L. Culbertson
MiraCosta College

Frank Diaz
Mission College

Gerald A. W. Haight
Modesto Junior College

Joseph G. Ansel
Monterey Peninsula College

Mary Ann Zamel
Mt. San Antonio College

Arlette A. Lyons
Mt. San Antonio College

Glenn Vice
Mt. San Antonio College

Paul Guess
Mt. San Jacinto College

Charles C. Van Zee
Mt. San Jacinto College

Heli Sairanen
Napa Valley College

Bruce Gold
Orange Coast College

Edwin Estes, Jr.
Palomar College

David Kemp
Palomar College

June Ann Reese
Rio Hondo College

Gilbert Mosqueda
Rio Hondo College

Michael Bernston
Riverside Comm. College

William A. Mcgrath
Sacramento City College

Nick Zoumbos
San Bernardino Valley College

Paul Grutsis
San Bernardino Valley College

Michael Durrett
San Bernardino Valley College

Dr. Shad Jefferies
San Diego Mesa College

John Wallace
San Diego Mesa College

Norma F. Hurley
San Joaquin Delta College

Raymond O' Connor
Santa Barbara City College

Steve Herndon
Santa Rosa Junior College

Jim Michaelson
Santa Rosa Junior College

Dr. Evelyn D. Winkel
Santiago Canyon College

William Rawlings
Santiago Canyon College

Kim Tyler
Shasta College

Marty Carrick
Shasta College

M. Wurschmidt
Shasta College

Mike Walker
Sierra College

Joseph A. McNeill, Jr.
Solano Community College

Robert C. Cass
Southwestern College

Chris Grover
Victor Valley College

Carl W. Hefke
West Hills College

Jerome L. Fox
West Los Angeles College

Abraham H. Farkas
West Los Angeles College

Faz Elahi
West Los Angeles College

Don Holman
West Los Angeles College

George H. Miller
West Valley College

Lance Shoemaker, J.D.
West Valley College

James R. Overton
Yuba College

Real Estate Specialists

Charles Ellis

James Short
San Diego State University

Reginald Woolfolk
West Valley Occupational Cntr.

Evan Morris
North Valley Occupational Cntr.

Claudia Wagner
North Valley Occupational Cntr.

Lorraine Abrams
West Valley Occupational Cntr.

Stan Hechinger
CAL-LAND International

Hugh C. Damon
TMH Home Mortgage Co.

Table of Contents

Chapter 3:   *Encumbrances*   *49*

Chapter 4: *Agency and Its Responsibilities* 71

Chapter 5:   Contracts   *113*

Chapter 6:   *Landlord and Tenant*   155

TABLE OF CONTENTS

Chapter 7: Escrows and Title Insurance   185

Chapter 8:   Real Estate Finance　　　　*217*

Chapter 9: *Financial Institutions*   **263**

Chapter 10: Appraisal Basics   *303*

Chapter 11: Appraisal Methods   333

Chapter 12: Subdivisions and Government Control   361

Chapter 13: Taxation of Real Estate   *399*

Chapter 14: Licensing, Education, and Associations 431

Chapter 15: Real Estate Math 473

TABLE OF CONTENTS

SUNSET BROKERS

Scott Chapin

http://www.bankhomes.com

9/493-4357

CHAPTER 1
Introduction to Real Estate

I. California's Real Estate Market

A. CALIFORNIA DEPARTMENT OF REAL ESTATE (DRE)

In California, real estate licensing laws are regulated by the Department of Real Estate (DRE), which is headed by the Real Estate Commissioner. The California DRE is widely recognized as a progressive organization whose example is followed by other states. The most current and accurate information from the DRE can be found at their website: **www.dre.ca.gov**.

B. HIGH COST OF REAL ESTATE

Due to increased job opportunities, higher birthrates, immigration, and migration, California's population growth rate is expected to practically double that of the national average in the next decade. For a variety of reasons, the number of new houses and condominiums being constructed is low. As a result, demand is already outpacing supply.

With the state's abundance of community colleges and universities generating so many educated professionals, is it any wonder the personal incomes in California are the envy of the rest of the nation?

California's remarkable expansion is due no doubt to our dominance in the areas of: 1) high technology and biotechnology; 2) foreign trade; 3) tourism and entertainment; 4) agriculture; as well as 5) professional services. Projections indicate that California will nearly double the national average in: 1) population increases; 2) job creations; 3) income increases, and 4) household formation. This has created a demand for housing, and a scarcity of buildable land close to urban areas, which means the price of real estate will continue to be higher than almost any other state, regardless of any fluctuations in the market.

A home is an expensive venture that includes a home loan payment. This payment usually equals 25 percent to 28 percent of the wages earned monthly by the homeowner, although this percentage may be higher in California. The monthly payment is only part of owning a home. Property taxes, fire insurance, repairs, and furnishings are expenses that will further increase the monthly cost of maintaining a home.

The credit crunch of 2007-2009 offered buyers lower priced homes and potential bargains for investors.

CHAPTER 1

CHAPTER OUTLINE

California Department of Real Estate (DRE)

The California Department of Real Estate (DRE) is on the Internet at **www.dre.ca.gov**. Their website provides all the information you need to know about obtaining a license, for example, the latest educational requirements needed to take the salesperson's exam. We advise you to look at the section called "Examinees."

The DRE is constantly improving their website and adding valuable services via the Internet. Now, not only can you research what's new at the DRE and access valuable information on most subjects involving real estate, you can conduct DRE licensing transactions online as well! The following transactions can now be performed online, using the "eLicensing" system:

1. Acquire Testing Schedules
2. Check Test Results
3. Salesperson and Broker License Renewals
4. File Mailing Address Changes
5. Salesperson Changes of Employing Broker
6. Continuing Education Extension/Exemption Request

It doesn't get much easier than this! Check out DRE's website for further improvements!

www.dre.ca.gov (Your main source of information)

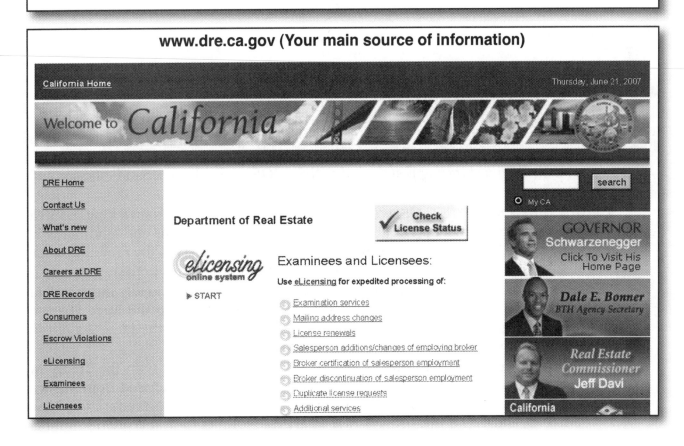

C. REAL ESTATE: A PROFITABLE PROFESSION

With the high cost of real estate comes the potential for high profits in the selling of real estate. A purchase as important as a home requires a great deal of knowledge and usually entails the services of a real estate professional. Because brokers and real estate salespeople are paid by commission, the higher the cost of housing, the higher the price of their services. A *COMMISSION is an amount paid, usually as a percentage of the selling price, to a broker for services.* The broker is responsible for paying his or her salespeople their part of any commissions.

The maximum commission that can be charged by a real estate broker in the sale of residential income property is negotiable between the principal and broker.

Real estate brokers in California normally receive around five or six percent of the sales price of a home as their commission. For example, if a home sells for $500,000 and the broker involved in the sale receives a 6 percent commission, he or she would collect a total of $30,000 ($500,000 x .06).

As you can see, the real estate business is a profitable one. It requires a person who is helpful, ambitious, willing to work and familiar with computer programs and the Internet. There is always a need for knowledgeable, well-trained salespeople and professionals in related fields, such as loan brokers, appraisers, and escrow officers.

II. Historical Influence

www.ca.gov
Welcome To California
www.calhist.org
California History

A. CALIFORNIA'S COLORFUL HISTORY

California's colorful history gives a unique flavor to its customs and lifestyles. The first Europeans to actively settle in California were Spaniards. In 1769, they began the famous mission system along El Camino Real, now known as U.S. Highway 101 and California 1. They established *fortified trading posts, called* **PRESIDIOS**, at San Diego, San Francisco and Monterey.

The *first cities, called* **PUEBLOS**, were Los Angeles and San Jose. Spain's king granted vast ranchos to favored civil and military officers. Many streets, towns and landmarks in California still bear their names. The state's distinct architectural style, the rambling, cool, thick-walled adobe structure with red tile roof, dates from the Spanish period.

In the early 1800s, California became a self-governing province of newly independent Mexico. The ruling government attempted land reform, breaking up the huge Spanish ranchos and giving ownership to Mexican citizens. This disturbed the large American population in California and led to war with Mexico.

The United States' war with Mexico ended on February 2, 1848, with the **Treaty of Guadalupe Hidalgo**. As part of the settlement, the United States purchased from Mexico more than 500,000 square miles of land, including the present states of Nevada, Utah, New Mexico, Arizona, and California. In an extraordinary example of political-economic timing,

Mexico deeded over all rights to this province within weeks of John Sutter's explosive discovery of gold near Sacramento.

The **Gold Rush** brought thousands of new citizens swarming to the west coast. Many settled permanently, founding towns and businesses, and expanding the already well-established orchards, vineyards and cattle ranches. Foreign trade crowded the coastal cities with goods and increased immigration. **California achieved full statehood on September 9, 1850**, and from that time on the state's population increased until it could boast of having the largest population in the nation (over 12.5%). The newly established legislature adopted a land ownership recording system that recognized and protected the early land grants. This recording system provides an interesting and complete history of the ownership of California lands and their subsequent division and subdivision.

38 million Californians now make up 12.5% of the U.S. population.

In 1917, California passed the first real estate licensing law in the nation. Although this first law was declared unconstitutional, the Real Estate Act of 1919 was upheld by the State Supreme Court. Licensing laws are a reasonable exercise by the state to regulate the conduct of its citizens in the interest of the public good.

III. Real and Personal Property

A. OWNERSHIP IS A BUNDLE OF RIGHTS

"Property" is defined as the "rights and interests that a person has in the thing owned."

Commonly referred to as a "bundle of rights," some of these rights include possession, enjoyment, control, and disposition (see **Figure 1-1** for more details). There are two types of property: **Real Property** (immovable) and **Personal Property** (movable), formerly called "chattel" or "chattel real."

Real property is "immovable" by law.

Figure 1-1   **OWNERSHIP IS A "BUNDLE OF RIGHTS"**

Bundle of Rights Theory

The bundle of rights theory views property ownership rights as a large bundle of sticks, where each "stick" is a property right. Individually, these rights represent various, specific forms of ownership; the more of these you hold, the more completely you own the property. So if you lease the property to someone, you give up one of your "sticks" (the right of possession). The basic rights of ownership include the rights of:

1. **Possession** – the right to occupy, rent, or keep others out.
2. **Enjoyment** – the right to "peace and quiet" without interference from past owners and others.
3. **Control** – the right to physically change or keep the property the way you like it.
4. **Disposition** – the right to transfer all or part of your property to others as you see fit.

B. REAL PROPERTY

REAL PROPERTY is the right or interest that a person has in the land or anything attached to the land.

Real property is legally defined as:

1. Land
2. Anything permanently attached or affixed to the land
3. Anything incidental or appurtenant to the land
4. Immovable by law

1. Land

LAND OWNERSHIP is commonly thought of as owning the surface of the earth; in other words, the ground we walk and build upon. But ownership also gives us rights to the space that is above our land and extends below our feet to the center of the earth, as **Figure 1-2** illustrates.

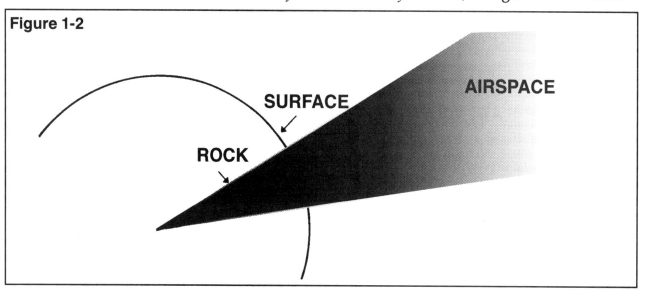

Figure 1-2

SURFACE

ROCK

AIRSPACE

An *AIRSPACE RIGHT is the right to the use of the airspace above the surface of the earth.* It is real property. In reality, the courts have restricted, to a reasonable height, the right of the property owner to use this space. An example for allowing only reasonable use of airspace is the need for airlines to have public "air highways" to provide us with transportation.

This airspace above the ground can be leased or sold in the same manner that mineral rights can be leased or sold. Airspace is an effective way to fully utilize the prime construction sites in many of our larger cities by building "up" instead of "out." An example of effective airspace use is storage space leased under our freeway overpasses by Caltrans, our state highway maintenance division.

Condominiums are another good example of airspace use. Inside a condominium, one only owns the airspace (area within the finished walls). The owner also owns a fractional share of the entire project (common area). Each owner may use the airspace within his or her unit in any manner he or she wishes, unless it violates the bylaws of the homeowner's group.

Generally, all that is beneath the surface of the earth belongs to the owner as real property. *MINERAL RIGHTS are the rights to unmined minerals (solids), such as gold, silver, and borax, that are part of the real property, but can be removed.* However, there are some exceptions: oil and other minerals can be claimed by the owner as personal property when removed from the ground. This is because they are considered, by law, to be "fugitive (meaning moving) substances." As an owner, you may sell your mineral rights below 500 feet; or you may exercise your "right of surface entry" above the 500-foot level.

A *RIPARIAN RIGHT is the right of a landowner to the reasonable use of moving, free flowing water on, under, and adjacent to his/her land (like a river or stream within the watershed), provided that its use does not infringe on the rights of any neighboring landowners.*

Riparian rights can be severed by condemnation or prescription.

A *LITTORAL RIGHT is the right of a landowner to the reasonable usage of a nonflowing body of water (with a shoreline) abutting his/her land.*

Riparian rights refer to moving water (rivers and streams), and littoral rights refer to bodies of water with a shoreline (oceans and lakes). Remember "R" for rivers and "L" for lakes.

APPROPRIATION OF WATER is the private taking and use of water flowing on the public domain from its natural course.

Riparian rights include the right to reasonably "appropriate" water as needed.

PERCOLATING WATER refers to underground water not found in a defined channel (natural water course). A spring that originates underground and seeps up through the soil is an example of percolating water. A landowner has the right, in common with others, to take his/her share of underground (percolating) waters for beneficial use. The *ALLOCATION (taking) by the state (not city or county) of surplus underground water for beneficial use of non-owners is also referred to as APPROPRIATION.*

POTABLE WATER refers to water that is suitable for human consumption.

SURFACE WATER RIGHTS prohibit the diversion of runoff from rain unless confined to a channel (river or stream) to the property of another. An owner can use reasonable means to protect against floodwater, but not at the expense of his/her neighbor.

2. Attached to the Land ("Improvements")

Anything attached to the land, such as buildings, fences, walls, walks and shrubs, are called IMPROVEMENTS, and become **real property** when they are permanently incorporated, integrated in, affixed or attached to the land. Buildings that rest on the land or anything attached by cement, nails, screws, and plaster are examples of real property, as is a **bearing wall** that supports the upper part of a structure.

Real property is the land and anything attached to the land (called "improvements").

3. Incidental or Appurtenant to the Land

Anything that is incidental or appurtenant to the land is real property. *APPURTENANT means ownership transfers with the land automatically without the need of a separate conveyance*

(runs with the land). Certain things that are a part of the land must be sold with the land or else the usefulness of the land is reduced.

For example, **MUTUAL WATER COMPANIES** *are organized by water users in a given district to supply ample water at a reasonable rate.* They are usually corporations in which the owners of each parcel of land are given a share of stock. The stock is appurtenant to the land; that is, each share of stock is attached to the land and cannot be sold separately.

Easements that allow the use of someone else's land, such as a driveway to enter your land, also go with the land being sold if it is the only way to access the land.

Stock in a mutual water company is real property and appurtenant (runs with the land) and thus automatically transfers to the buyer.

4. Immovable by Law

That which by law is considered immovable is real property. Under California law, established crops and trees are a part of the land. The only exception is when a contract of sale for these items is made before the land is sold. If you have such a contract, it is a good idea to record it at the appropriate county recorder's office to assure that everyone has notice of the sale.

Natural growth (vegetation attached by roots) is real property as are cultivated crops (like unpicked fruit or corn) until they are severed, mortgaged, or sold.

C. PERSONAL PROPERTY

PERSONAL PROPERTY is any property that is movable and cannot be properly classified under the definition of real property. Items such as clothes, furniture, and automobiles are tangible and easily movable. Personal property can also be documents that represent value, such as stocks, bonds, or leases.

Minerals, oil, and gas, when extracted, are also considered personal property.

EMBLEMENTS *are planted growing crops that are cultivated annually by a tenant farmer on leased land.* Unlike landscaping, these crops belong to the tenant even after the expiration of the lease.

If previously contracted for sale, the "fruit" of a commercial orchard may be personal property, but the trees upon which it grows are real property.

When buying personal property, your receipt is called a "**Bill of Sale.**" The Bill of Sale states that the goods have been paid for and that no outstanding loans exist on the personal property. It is always considered good practice to obtain a Bill of Sale. **Figure 1-3** is an example of a Bill of Sale.

The ownership of personal property is transferred with a "bill of sale." An instrument used to secure a loan on personal property is called a "security agreement."

D. FIXTURES

FIXTURES are items of personal property that are attached to, or incorporated into, the land in such a manner as to become real property. The courts use these five tests to determine if an item is a fixture:

Figure 1-3   **TRANSFERS TITLE OF PERSONAL PROPERTY**

BILL OF SALE

In consideration for the sum of *Three hundred fifty and no/100*

_____*$350.00*_____ as payment in full is hereby acknowledged from

(Mr John Q. Smart   *for the purchase of*   *(a Maytag washer*

and dryer, serial numbers #H02257 and #D376240).

Executed on *April 19, 20XX*

in the county of   California.
Sacramento

Robert Seller

Signature of Seller

M **1. Method of attachment**
A **2. Adaptability**
R **3. Relationship of the parties**
I   **4. Intention**
A **5. Agreement**

> We sometimes use an acronym (in this case, **MARIA**) to help you remember!

1. Method of Attachment

If an item can be removed by simply being unplugged, it is probably personal property. On the other hand, if it is attached by cement, plaster, screws, nails or plumbing, it is probably real property. If removal of an item would leave permanent damage or an unusable area, it is surely real property. A rug lying in a living room would be considered personal property; carpet affixed to the floor would be considered real property.

Cost and time installed are NOT tests in determining if something is a fixture (real property).

2. Adaptability

The adaptability of personal property refers to ordinary use in connection with the land. If property is well adapted for the land or building, it is probably a fixture.

3. Relationship of the Parties

If a fixture is not mentioned in a contract, and is affixed to the property, most courts will give the seller the benefit of the doubt. A refrigerator that is just plugged in would be considered personal property and would remain with the seller. To protect yourself, any questionable

9

fixtures should be mentioned in the purchase agreement. **Real estate salespeople remember: your client should secure a bill of sale for personal property items.** In the case of a tenant and landlord, the court usually rules in favor of the tenant. There are, however, no set rules. A court decision is dependent upon the facts of each individual case.

4. Intention

If you plan to remove an item of personal property, you may not permanently attach it to the land.

5. Agreement

Disputes between buyers and sellers often arise regarding what items remain with the property. It is advisable to secure, in writing, any personal property that you want to remain as personal property. If you are buying a house, list all items you want to accompany the house, such as light fixtures, drapes or a fireplace screen. If you are selling, list only the items that will remain with the house. Remember: if in doubt, put it in writing!

Any item can be specifically identified as being included or excluded as part of the sale. It is advisable to identify, in writing, any personal property that is to be included as part of the sale.

E. TRADE FIXTURES (Always Personal Property) (Removable – Exception to the Rule)

TRADE FIXTURES are personal property used in the normal course of business, such as shelving or refrigeration units. A tenant may remove any trade fixture he or she installed provided the real property is left in the same condition as he or she found it. In this sense, trade fixtures are an exception to the rules of personal property.

A "bill of sale" transfers trade fixtures because they are personal property.

IV. Methods of Land Description

In California, every parcel of land must be properly described or identified. If the property is to be sold, financed or leased, a recognized legal description is required. The following three methods are accepted as means of property identification.

A. Metes and Bounds (Surveyor's Maps – Irregular Parcels)
B. Sections and Townships (U.S. Government Survey – Rural)
C. Lots, Blocks, and Tracts (Recorded Subdivision – Cities)

The legal description of a property is the minimum legal description of real property that appears in a listing.

A. METES AND BOUNDS (Surveyor's Maps)

METES AND BOUNDS (measuring boundaries) is the method of identifying (describing) property by its boundaries, distances, and angles from a given starting point. In the past, surveyors often used natural objects as a starting point in their descriptions. *A MONUMENT is a fixed object and point set in the earth by surveyors to establish land locations.* An outdated surveyor's report might read:

"Starting at the old oak tree at the stream, go 300 feet north along the river bed, then make a 90 degree right turn and proceed 100 feet. . ."

The weakness in this type of description is that when natural objects are used as starting points, there is a chance that time, or man, may move or destroy these objects. Modern day surveying is a complicated method of property description better left to the professionals. It is also unnecessary for the average real estate salesperson to study this method in depth, but a basic working knowledge can be helpful. **Figure 1-4** is an example of how a simple surveyor's report might look.

Figure 1-4

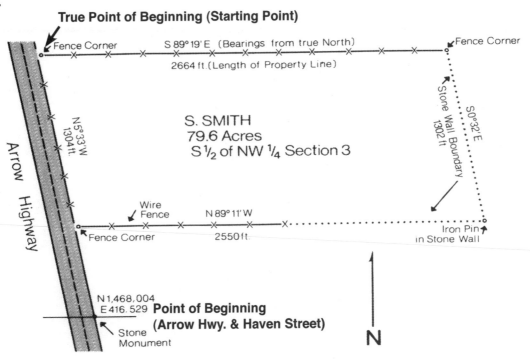

B. SECTIONS AND TOWNSHIPS (U.S. Government Survey)

The United States Government Survey system was established to identify all public lands by the use of "base lines" and "meridian lines" starting from a precise surveying point. California has three principal base and meridian line intersections (see **Figure 1-5**):

1. **Humboldt Base Line and Meridian** in Northern California;
2. **Mt. Diablo Base Line and Meridian** in Central California; and
3. **San Bernardino Base Line and Meridian** in Southern California.

From these three starting points, all of California may be described using sections, townships and ranges to define any given parcel.

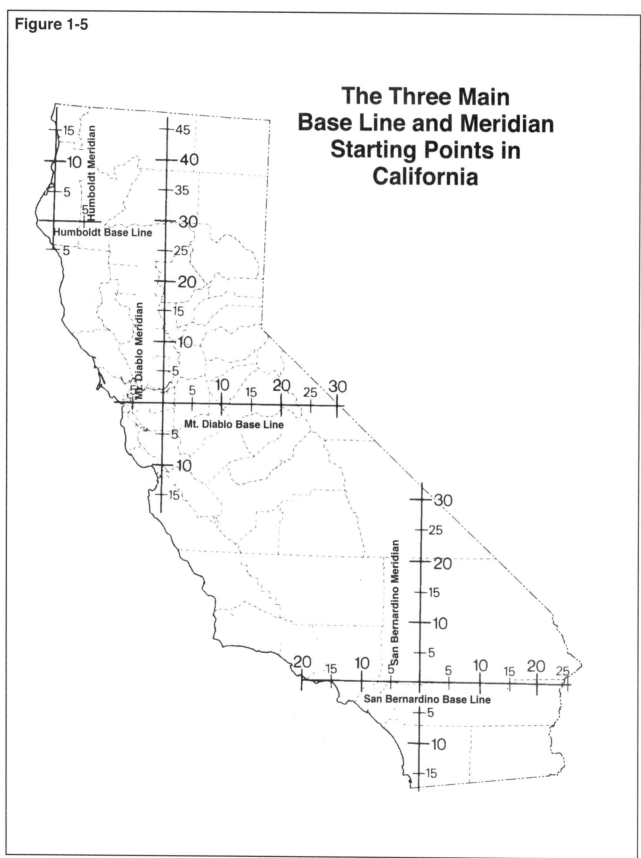

Figure 1-5

The Three Main Base Line and Meridian Starting Points in California

1. Base Lines and Meridian Lines

A *BASE LINE is a horizontal line that* **runs east and west** *from any one of three starting points in California.* Each base line is marked in six-mile increments. Every six-mile increment is called a range and each range is six miles in length. It is possible to move east or west a designated number of ranges from any starting point.

MERIDIAN LINES are vertical lines that **run north and south** *from any one of the three starting points in California.* Meridians are also marked off in increments of six miles each, but each six-mile increment north or south on a meridian is called a township or tier.

2. Tiers, Ranges, and Townships

Each rectangular survey grid consists of a series of lines that run parallel to the principal meridian and the base line, at intervals of six miles. *The east-west lines (running parallel to the base line) are called* **TIER LINES**. *The north-south lines (running parallel to the principal meridian) are referred to as* **RANGE LINES**.

Township lines divide the land into a series of east-west strips, called **TIERS**. *Range lines divide the land into north-south strips called* **RANGES**. *Where a tier intersects with a range, the result is a six-mile by six-mile square of land known as a* **TOWNSHIP**. Thus, each township contains 36 square miles. Townships are the main divisions of land in the rectangular survey system. Each township is identified according to its distance from the principal meridian and base line.

The location of any township is determined by its distance from the nearest base line and meridian line. For example, see **Figure 1-6** to determine the location of a township northeast of the San Bernardino Base Line and Meridian (T. 4N, R. 3E). The following steps are used:

First, move east along the San Bernardino Base Line three ranges. This is the range located between the 2nd and 3rd range lines east of the San Bernardino Meridian. Second, move north from the San Bernardino Base Line four tiers (townships). This is the township located between the 3rd and 4th tier (township) lines north of the base line.

a. Reading Tier (Township) and Section Descriptions

The above description would be written:

T. 4N, R. 3E San Bernardino Base Line and Meridian.

In this form "R" represents the word range and "3E" tells you to move three ranges east of the meridian. Likewise, "T" means township (a tier), and "4N" tells you to go four townships (tiers) north of the San Bernardino Base Line.

To locate a property, work backwards on the description. When reading a description, read it from right to left. A verbal interpretation of our above description would read: "Starting from the San Bernardino Base Line and Meridian, go three ranges east and four townships north." You have located the township in which the property is located.

CHAPTER 1

Figure 1-6

Tiers, Ranges, and Townships

				Fig. 1-7	Tier 4 North
	MERIDIAN LINE				Tier 3 North
		6 Miles x 6 Miles			Tier 2 North
					Tier 1 North
San Bernardino		BASE LINE			Tier 1 South
Range 1 West	Range 1 East	Range 2 East	Range 3 East	Range 4 East	

N

3. Sections (A Section is One Square Mile)

Each township is divided into 36 sections. A *SECTION is one square mile of land consisting of 640 acres.* There are 36 sections in a township.

A section contains 640 acres; 1/2 section, 320 acres; 1/4 section, 160 acres.

These sections are numbered in sequential order starting at the upper right-hand corner. Since each township is six miles square and consists of 36 sections, each section measures one mile square (see **Figure 1-7**).

Each section measures one square mile and consists of 640 acres. A section can be broken down into halves or quarters (see **Figure 1-8**).

a. Section Problem

The SW¼ of the NW¼ of section 11 sells for $800 per acre, while the S½ of the NE¼ of Section 12 sells for $500 per acre. What is the difference in the values of the two parcels?

b. Section Answer

1 section = 640 Acres
NW¼ of Section 11 = 160 acres
SW¼ of NW¼ of Section 11 = 40 acres
40 acres x $800/acre = $32,000

NE¼ of section 12 = 640 acres x ¼ = 160 acres
S½ of NE¼ of section 12 = 160 acres x ½ = 80 acres (continued on page 16)

Figure 1-7 Township is divided into 36 sections

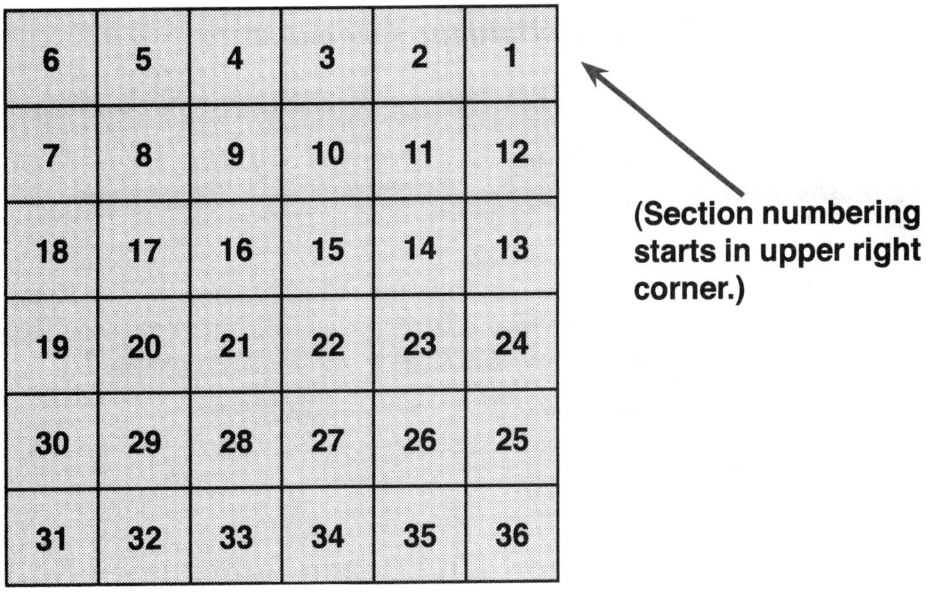

(Section numbering starts in upper right corner.)

Figure 1-8 Section by acres

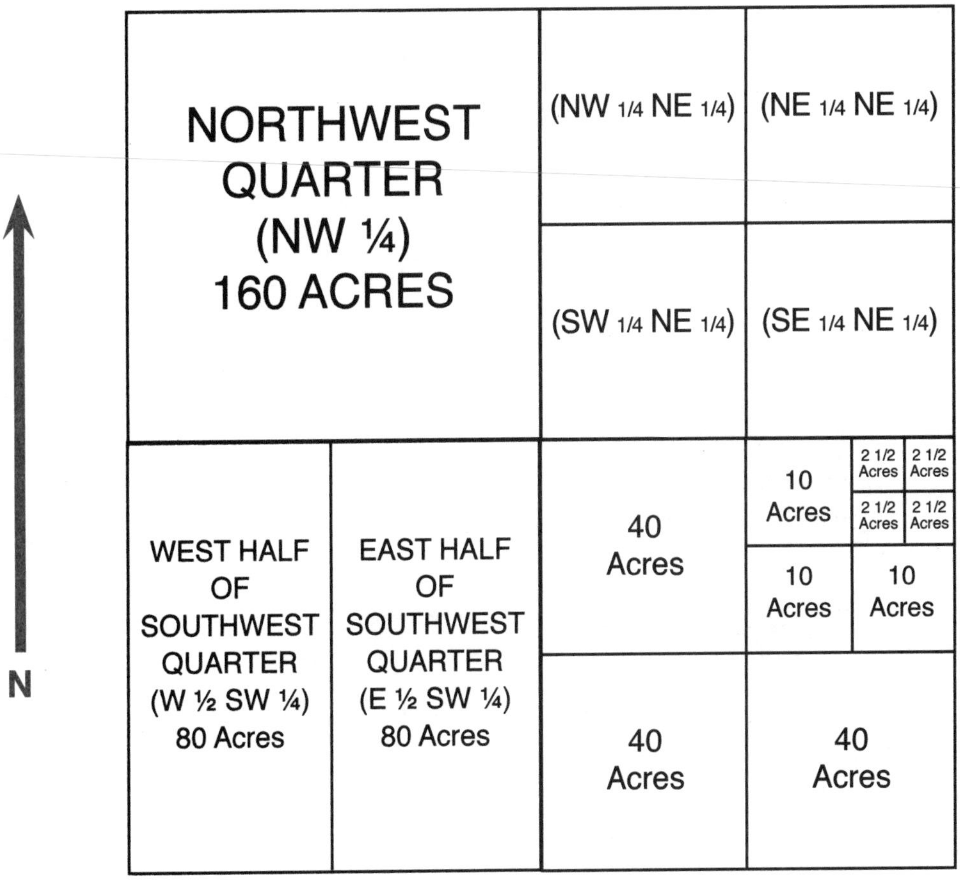

80 acres x $500/acre = $40,000
$40,000 - $32,000 = **$8,000 difference**

Work backwards and multiply the denominators.

C. LOTS, BLOCKS, AND TRACTS (Recorded Subdivisions)

In California, subdivisions are granted by the Department of Real Estate. The subdivision map, however, is approved by the county or city in which the property is located.

The approved subdivision map is recorded at the County Recorder's Office, and given a book and page number. Once it is recorded, all future transactions can be referenced to that map. *This subdivision map is also referred to as a **PLAT MAP**.* As an example, **Figure 1-9** is a description of a home located in Venice, California.

See **Figure 1-10** for math problems and **Figure 1-11** for a handy reference table.

Figure 1-9

Short Line Beach Subdivision No. 2

LOT 22 in BLOCK 21 of Short Line Beach Subdivision No. 2, as per map recorded in Book 4, Page 42 of Maps, in the office of the County Recorder of Los Angeles.

Figure 1-10

Doing the Math – Acres and Area

An **ACRE** *is an area of land that contains 43,560 square feet.* So, if the area of a lot has more than 43,560 square feet, there is more than an acre of land. On the other hand, if there is less than 43,560 square feet in a lot, it is smaller than an acre.

AREA *is a definite amount of space within a shape.* In America, area is usually measured in square feet, but may also be measured in square yards or square meters in other parts of the world. Most test questions about area refer to a rectangular or square shape. The area of a rectangular or square shape is obtained by multiplying length x (times) width. The answer is in square feet. The area of a square lot 100 feet x 100 feet is 10,000 square feet.

Example (1): How many acres is a parcel of land that measures 330 feet by 660 feet?

Answer:

Area   =   Length x Width
217,800   =   330 feet x 660 feet

Note: 1 acre = 43,560 square feet

$$\frac{217,800}{43,560} = \textbf{5 ACRES (Round if necessary)}$$

Example (2): If an acre is divided into four equal lots, with each lot placed parallel to the other and having a depth of 240 feet, what is the width of each lot?

Answer:

Area   =   Length x Width
43,560   =   240 feet (x 4 lots)   x ? feet
43,560   =   960 feet   x ? feet

$$\frac{43,560}{960} = \textbf{45.375 feet wide (Round to 45.4 feet wide)}$$

See Chapter 15 (Real Estate Math) for more problems.

Figure 1-11

Reference Table

One **ACRE** is 43,560 square feet; 4,840 square yards.

One **SQUARE ACRE** is 208.71 feet on each side, but this number is generally rounded off to 209 feet.

One **MILE** is 5,280 feet long.

One **SQUARE MILE** contains 640 acres.

One **SECTION** is one mile square, containing 640 acres.

One **TOWNSHIP** (standard) is six miles square (36 square miles).

One **COMMERCIAL ACRE** is an acre minus any required public dedications.

One **ROD** is 16.5 feet long (5.5 yards). There are four rods, or 66 feet, to one chain, and 320 rods to a mile.

V. CHAPTER SUMMARY

In California, real estate licensing laws are regulated by the **Department of Real Estate (DRE)**. Commission rates are fully negotiable between broker and buyer/seller, with the broker responsible for paying his or her salespeople their part of any commission.

California was purchased by the United States from Mexico as part of the **Treaty of Guadalupe Hidalgo** in 1848, just weeks before the discovery of gold by John Sutter, and became a state on **September 9, 1850**. California's Legislature passed the nation's first real estate licensing law in 1917.

Real property is generally immovable, passed by deed, and includes the right or interests in: 1) the land; 2) anything permanently attached or affixed to the land; and 3) anything incidental or appurtenant to the land. Anything attached to the land, like fences, walls, etc., become real property when they are permanently incorporated or integrated in, affixed, or attached to the land (called **improvements**). Land ownership is not only the surface of the earth but the **airspace** above it and that which is below, like mineral rights. Real property can be thought of as a **bundle of rights**, which includes the rights of possession, enjoyment, control, and disposition.

Personal property is movable, like a refrigerator or washing machine, but can include **emblements** (annually harvested crops) and some substances beneath the land, like oil and minerals when they have been removed from the land.

Anything that is **appurtenant** to the land means it is transferred with the land (runs with the land). An example is stock in a mutual water company. (Water suitable for drinking is referred to as **potable water**.) **Title** to real property is passed with a **deed**, while title to personal property is passed with a **bill of sale**.

A **fixture** is an item of personal property that is attached to or incorporated into the land in such a way as to become real property. The courts use the **MARIA** method to determine if an item is a fixture: **Method of attachment**, **Adaptability**, **Relationship of the parties**, **Intention**, and **Agreement**. **Trade fixtures** are personal property used in the normal course of business, such as shelving or refrigeration units which can be removed by tenants, who are responsible for any damage caused by their removal.

In California, every parcel of land must be properly described and identified. The three methods of identification include the **Metes and Bounds method**, the **Section and Township method**, and the **Lots, Blocks, and Tracts method**. Metes and Bounds is the method of identifying property in relationship to its boundaries, distances, and angles from a given **starting point**.

Sections and Townships are used in a government survey system used to identify public and private lands. This system uses **base lines** (running east and west) and **meridian lines** (running north and south), as well as defining **townships** (36 square mile sections of land, where each section is 640 acres). **Lots, Blocks, and Tracts** make up subdivisions, which are approved by the Department of Real Estate and the city, and then recorded on a **Subdivision Map** in the County Recorder's Office.

VI. TERMINOLOGY

A. Acre
B. Admission Date
C. Airspace
D. Base Lines
E. Bill of Sale
F. Bundle of Rights
G. Chattel or Chattel Real
H. Commission

I. Condominium
J. Emblements
K. Fixtures
L. Meridian Lines
M. Metes and Bounds
N. Personal Property
O. Potable Water
P. Range

Q. Real Property
R. Riparian Rights
S. Rod
T. Section
U. Township
V. Trade Fixtures

1. _P_ A column of land six miles wide, determined by a government survey, running in a north-south direction, lying east or west of a principal meridian.
2. _K_ Personal property that has become permanently attached to the land or improvements that are legally treated as real property; examples: plumbing fixtures, or built-in range, etc.
3. _V_ Personal property used in a business, attached to the property, but removable by the tenant.
4. _I_ A structure of two or more units where the interior airspace of each unit is individually owned; the balance of land and improvements is owned in common by all the owners.
5. _L_ Imaginary north-south lines used in U.S. government surveys.
6. _N_ Property that is movable and not real property.
7. _E_ A written instrument that passes title of personal property from vendor (seller) to the vendee (buyer).

8.__H__ An amount, usually a percentage, paid to a broker as compensation for his or her services.

9.__M__ A legal description of land, setting forth all the boundary lines with their terminal points and angles.

10.__F__ All of the legal rights relevant to ownership of property including rights of use, possession, encumbering and disposition.

11.__U__ In the survey of public lands, a territorial subdivision six miles long, six miles wide and containing 36 sections, each one square mile.

12.__Q__ Land, improvements, items permanently attached to the land, appurtenances and that which is immovable by law.

13.__G__ A personal property interest in real property; an old term meaning personal property.

14.__A__ An area of land equaling 43,560 square feet, or a tract about 208.71 feet square.

15.__R__ The right of a landowner, whose land borders a stream or waterway, to use and enjoy the water, provided such use does not injure the rights of other owners.

16.__T__ A square of land (U.S. government survey) that contains 640 acres and is one square mile.

17.__S__ This old unit of measurement is 16 1/2 feet long (5.5 yards).

18.__C__ The reasonable space above a parcel; or in a condominium, the cubic area of a space within the walls.

19.__D__ Imaginary east-west lines that intersect meridian lines to form a starting point for the measurement of land.

20.__O__ Water that is suitable for human consumption.

21.__J__ Crops (produced on leased land by a tenant farmer) from an annual cultivation considered personal property.

22.__B__ September 9, 1850.

Answers to the matching terminology are found on page 550.

VII. CHAPTER QUIZ

1. Property is defined as:
   a. the rights or interests that a person has in the thing owned.
   b. freehold estates.
   c. only personal property.
   d. things that buyers and sellers own.

2. Riparian rights generally:
   a. are detailed in the trust deed.
   b. concern the use of moving water from a river or stream within the watershed.
   c. are detailed in the public records of all counties affected by surface waters.
   d. are absolute and universal.

3. "Potable water" refers to:
   a. well water on the property.
   b. water suitable for irrigation.
   c. water suitable for drinking.
   d. water suitable for cooking.

4. Which of the following would normally be considered real property?

    a. Trade fixtures
    b. Chattel reals
    c. Vegetation
    d. Deeds of trust

5. The ownership of personal property is transferred by using a:

    a. grant deed.
    b. financing statement.
    c. trust deed.
    d. bill of sale.

6. A loan secured by personal property usually consists of:

    a. a financing statement and trust deed.
    b. a promissory note and a trust deed.
    c. FHA or VA insurance.
    d. a security agreement.

7. Which of the following is NOT a test for a fixture?

    a. Adaptability
    b. Agreement
    c. Cost and size of the item
    d. Intention

8. California has how many principal intersections of base lines and meridian lines?

    a. One
    b. Two
    c. Three
    d. Five

9. A township contains:

    a. one square mile only.
    b. a six-mile by six-mile square of land.
    c. 36 square miles.
    d. both b and c.

10. A commercial acre is:

    a. an acre of land used only for agricultural purposes.
    b. an acre of land where an industrial building is situated.
    c. an acre of land where retail buildings are situated.
    d. an acre less the amount of land dedicated for public improvements (sidewalks, alleys, etc.).

ANSWERS: 1. a; 2. b; 3. c; 4. c; 5. d; 6. d; 7. c; 8. c; 9. d; 10. d

CHAPTER 2
Estates, Transfers, and Titles

In the previous chapter, we explained the differences between real and personal property. In this chapter, we will illustrate the types of estates (ownership) that you may have, the ways in which you can hold title and the methods of transferring real property.

I. Estate Ownership

Estates Freehold & Less-Than-Freehold	
Freehold (Real Property)	**Less-Than-Freehold (Personal Property)**

A. ESTATES (Ownership Interest in Land)

An **ESTATE** *is an interest, share, right or equity in real estate that varies from the minimal right of a renter to the maximum right of a full owner.*

An estate is an ownership interest in land.

Estates are either **(1) freehold** or **(2) less-than-freehold**, depending upon the degree of ownership and the duration of interest. Freehold estates are real property and less-than-freehold estates are personal property. Less-than-freehold estates come with certain rights for the use of real property (see **Figure 2-1**).

B. FREEHOLD ESTATES (Real Property)

The two major types of freehold estates are: 1) fee simple estates and 2) life estates.

The two types of freehold estates are the greatest degree of ownership you can have under the law.

1. Estates in Fee

A fee simple estate is the most complete form of ownership and the most common in California. This can be referred to as fee, fee ownership, or fee simple. *FEE SIMPLE*

CHAPTER OUTLINE

Figure 2-1

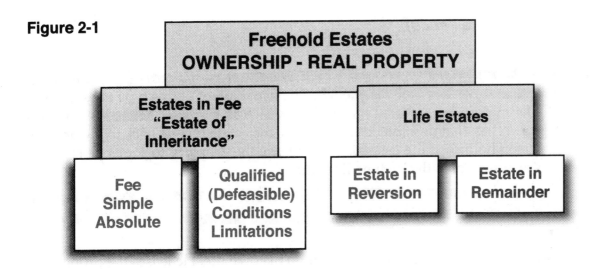

means an owner has transferred all rights of a property to a new owner for an indefinite duration of time (perpetual). All transfers are assumed to be fee simple unless the grant part of the deed limits, by the use of conditions, the property's use.

An estate in fee (also called "fee simple" or "fee") is the greatest interest a person can hold; it is of "indefinite duration" (perpetual), "freely transferable," and "inheritable" (referred to as an estate of inheritance). An estate in fee is a freehold estate.

a. Conditions That Restrict a Fee Estate (Fee Simple Defeasible Estate)

A *FEE SIMPLE DEFEASIBLE ESTATE (or qualified fee estate) is a fee estate that is subject to particular limitations imposed by the grantor of the estate.* **Breaking any condition of the transfer may be grounds for terminating or revoking the property transfer.**

Example: Duke sold his property to Jane with the condition that Jane must never use it for any purpose other than as a private residence. However, after owning the property for several years, Jane decided to start a board and care facility for handicapped adults. The estate may revert to Duke because it is a fee simple defeasible estate.

Example: A buyer agrees not to sell alcoholic beverages on a property. This condition is included in the deed. The buyer has taken fee simple defeasible title to the property. If a person takes title subject to a condition (subsequent) that liquor not be served on the premises, and then turns around and breaks this promise, the previous title holder has grounds to reclaim title through a court action.

In this chapter we have briefly discussed conditions, as in CC&Rs (Covenants, Conditions, & Restrictions). For a more complete discussion of other types of private restrictions, please see Chapter 3.

2. Life Estate (Indefinite Period)

A life estate is an example of a freehold estate.

A **LIFE ESTATE** is an ownership interest in real property that only exists for the life of any designated person or persons (often the grantee). The usual intent of this type of estate is to provide a lifetime residence for an individual. A life estate can be created by either a will or a deed. When that designated person dies, the estate reverts back to the original owner. A person holding a life estate is free to lease the property to someone else, but this lease is also subject to the lifetime limitation.

A life estate holder may lease the property to someone else, but if the designated person dies, the estate ends and all rights, including any tenant rights, revert back to the original owner/grantor.

Example: John owns a life estate based upon his own life. He leases the property to a tenant on a five-year lease. John, the life tenant, dies two years later. The lease is terminated.

The life tenant usually has certain interests and obligations as long as the life estate is in effect. The life tenant:

1. has the right of physical possession of the property;
2. has the right to all rents and profits, but this terminates when the life estate holder dies;
3. can usually lease the property, but not beyond the time frame of the life estate;
4. is obligated to keep the property in good repair, although he or she is not required to make improvements;
5. may not damage or destroy any permanent part of the property to the detriment of succeeding interests, and
6. is usually responsible for all annual costs and expenses.

The party (grantor) granting a life estate is said to hold an **ESTATE IN REVERSION**.

If I give you a life estate, you hold "possession" for as long as you live. You can lease it out. However, if you lease it out, when you die, possession reverts back to me, or any specified person (estate in remainder).

If an owner granting a life estate names another person to receive title upon the death of the current life estate holder, that other person claims an **ESTATE IN REMAINDER**. The holder of an estate in remainder or estate in reversion has no right to the use and enjoyment of the property until the current life tenant dies.

"Pur autre vie" (often used in life estates) means "for another's life."

C. LESS-THAN-FREEHOLD ESTATES (No Title to Real Property) (A Leasehold is Personal Property)

A less-than-freehold estate is also called a leasehold estate, and is considered personal property.

LESS-THAN-FREEHOLD ESTATES are personal rights to the use of real property for a period of time. They are more commonly referred to as **leases** or rental agreements, which give tenants various rights to use real property for a specified period.

A similarity between owning a condominium and renting an apartment is the occupier of each unit has an estate in real property.

The tenant (renting the apartment), however, only has possession of the property (see **Figure 2-2**).

Figure 2-2

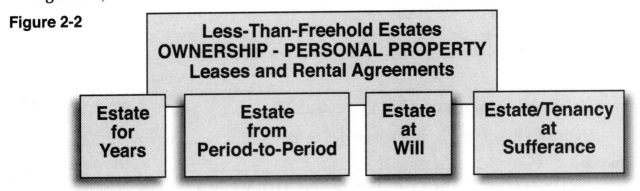

1. Estate For Years (Tenancy for a Fixed Term)

An *ESTATE FOR YEARS is a lease for a fixed period of time, agreed to in advance.* This period can be from a few days up to 99 years. No notice to terminate is necessary.

Whether a lease is for two months or seven years, it is considered an "estate for years," personal property, and chattel real.

2. Estate From Period-To-Period (Periodic Tenancy)

An *ESTATE FROM PERIOD-TO-PERIOD is a renewable agreement to rent or lease a property for a period of time, where the rental or lease amount is fixed at an agreed to sum per week, month, or year.* A notice to terminate must be given (usually 30 days).

3. Estate At Will

An *ESTATE AT WILL is a rental agreement that can be terminated by either party at any time,* although by California law, there must be at least a 30-day notice to vacate (so there is no true "estate at will" in California).

An estate at will can be terminated by either the lessor or the lessee.

4. Estate At Sufferance/Tenancy At Sufferance

An *ESTATE AT SUFFERANCE occurs when the person renting or leasing a particular property remains after the expiration of the stated term.*

A *TENANCY AT SUFFERANCE occurs when a tenant remains in the property after expiration of a lease without the owner's consent.*

The four main types of less-than-freehold estates are explained in further detail in Chapter 6, "Landlord and Tenant."

II. Acquisitions and Transfers

Alienation is the opposite of acquisition. "Acquisition" means to acquire, buy, or pull in, whereas "alienation" means to transfer, sell, or push away.

A. TRANSFERS

A sale is the means by which real estate is usually transferred. A sale is the most familiar way of transferring property, but it is not the only way. The seven basic ways to transfer real property are:

1. Deed
2. Will
3. Probate
4. Intestate Succession (no will)

5. Accession
6. Occupancy
7. Dedication

Figure 2-3 illustrates the seven methods of transferring real property.

Figure 2-3

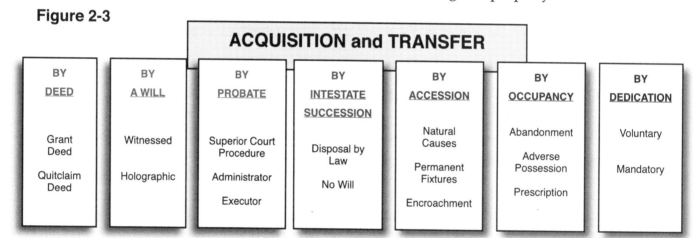

ACQUISITION and TRANSFER						
BY DEED	BY A WILL	BY PROBATE	BY INTESTATE SUCCESSION	BY ACCESSION	BY OCCUPANCY	BY DEDICATION
Grant Deed Quitclaim Deed	Witnessed Holographic	Superior Court Procedure Administrator Executor	Disposal by Law No Will	Natural Causes Permanent Fixtures Encroachment	Abandonment Adverse Possession Prescription	Voluntary Mandatory

1. Transfer by Deed

The deed is NOT the title, but is "evidence" of the title.

The most common method of acquiring title to a property is by deed transfer. In California, **CONVEYANCE** *is the document used to effect the transfer of title to property from one person to another.* This is usually accomplished by a simple written document known as a deed. **A DEED** *is a written instrument that conveys and evidences title.*

The **GRANTOR** *is the person who grants property or property rights (seller).* The **GRANTEE** *is the person to whom the grant is made (buyer).* A grantee cannot be a fictitious person (i.e., Batman or Catwoman), but it can be a person with a fictitious name (i.e., Microsoft, Inc.).

Grant deeds must have a "granting" type clause (action clause). The grantor is the person transferring real property. Both grant deeds and quitclaim deeds are signed only by the grantor, at which time they are considered to be "executed."

There are two basic types of deeds: (1) grant deed and (2) quitclaim deed. All other deeds are versions of these two deeds.

A **GRANT DEED** *is a document that transfers title (evidence of property ownership), with the key word being "grant"* (see **Figure 2-4**). The grant (or warranty) aspect of the deed is a promise that:

a. The owner (grantor) has not conveyed title to the property to any other person (grantee).

b. The property is free of any encumbrances (liens or other restrictions) other than those already disclosed to the grantee. A grant deed also transfers any **after-acquired title**, meaning that rights obtained after the sale has been completed are also conveyed.

These warranties are part of the grant deed, although they are not written into the deed. They are called **IMPLIED WARRANTIES** *because they are not expressed in writing, but are present.*

Grant deeds contain "implied warranties" that are NOT expressed in writing.

It should be noted that the grant deed does not necessarily give one all the rights to a property. Easements, rights of way, mineral rights, building restrictions and other types of restrictions may still restrict the use of the property.

A person who transfers title to real property is the grantor; therefore anyone who signs a grant deed or a quitclaim deed is a "grantor." The person receiving property is the "grantee."

A **QUITCLAIM DEED** *is a deed that conveys all the present rights or interest that a person may have in a property, without any warranty, title, or interest.*

Quitclaim deeds make NO "covenants" (promises); they guarantee nothing. They only convey any rights the grantor may have.

A quitclaim deed can give absolute ownership or only such title as one may hold. If there is no ownership interest, then nothing can be acquired. Read the quitclaim deed in **Figure 2-5**. Note that there are no warranties; just the clause, "do hereby remise, release, and forever quitclaim to…" This deed is used primarily to clear a cloud on title from the records. A **CLOUD ON TITLE** *is a claim, encumbrance or condition that impairs the title to real property until disproved or eliminated, as, for example, through a quitclaim deed or a quiet title legal action.*

A **QUIET TITLE ACTION** *is a court proceeding to remove a cloud on title to real property.* It is usually a minor defect that requires a quitclaim deed before a title insurance company will clear the transfer. A quitclaim deed is often used in divorce actions, so that one party may have clear title.

The ownership of real property may best be determined by a quiet title action.

Example: For three generations the Mendez family has owned the mining rights to mine gold on Diego's land. Last month, Diego sold his land to a developer who promptly enclosed the land with a large chain-link fence that had only one access, a locked gate. The Mendez family should institute a quiet title action.

If a buyer purchases a property on an installment plan and abandons that property after a few payments, then there will likely be a "cloud on the title" if the contract was recorded.

Figure 2-4

827367

WHEN RECORDED MAIL TO

NAME Philip S. Dockter
Street Address 1212 Lincoln Avenue
City & State Pomona, California 91767

#61638

RECORDED IN OFFICIAL RECORDS
OF LOS ANGELES COUNTY. CALIF.
FOR TITLE INSURANCE & TRUST CO

MAY 19 1971 AT 8 A.M.

Registrar-Recorder

FEE $2 C

MAIL TAX STATEMENTS TO

NAME SAME AS SHOWN ABOVE:
Street Address
City & State

— SPACE ABOVE THIS LINE FOR RECORDER'S USE —

DOCUMENTARY TRANSFER TAX $33.00
...Computed on full value of property conveyed
...Or computed on full value less liens and encum-
brances remaining at time of sale.
WILSHIRE ESCROW COMPANY
Signature of Declarant or Agent determining tax. Firm name

Grant Deed

FOR A VALUABLE CONSIDERATION, receipt of which is hereby acknowledged,

HENRY W. SPLITTER, a widower, who acquired title as HENRY SPLITTER, , does hereby

GRANT to   Philip S. Dockter , a single man,

the real property in the   City of Los Angeles   County of   Los Angeles
State of California, described as:

Lot 22 in Block 21 of Short Line Beach Subdivision No. 2, as per map recorded in
Book 4 Page 42 of Maps, in the office of the County Recorder of said County.

RESERVING UNTO THE GRANTOR 50% of all oil, minerals, coals, petroleum, gas and
kindred substances in and under said land, from a depth below 500 feet from the
surface of said land, but without the right of entry of the surface thereof.

SUBJECT TO:
1. General and Special Taxes for the fiscal year 1971-72.
2. Covenants, conditions, restrictions, reservations, easements, rights and rights
   of way of record, if any.
3. Trust Deed to file concurrently herewith.

Dated____April 15, 1971_____

Henry W Splitter
Henry W. Splitter

STATE OF CALIFORNIA
COUNTY OF____Los Angeles_____ }SS.
On____May 4, 1971_____before me, the under-
signed, a Notary Public in and for said State, personally appeared
Henry W. Splitter

_____, known to me
to be the person___whose name__is__subscribed to the within
instrument and acknowledged that__he___executed the same.
WITNESS my hand and official seal.

Signature_____

Donald R. Shewfelt
Name (Typed or Printed)

OFFICIAL SEAL
DONALD R. SHEWFELT
NOTARY PUBLIC — CALIFORNIA
PRINCIPAL OFFICE IN
LOS ANGELES COUNTY
My Commission Expires Aug. 17, 1971

(This area for official notarial seal)

320

MAIL TAX STATEMENTS AS DIRECTED ABOVE

Figure 2-5

Title Order No.   Escrow No.

———— SPACE ABOVE THIS LINE FOR RECORDER'S USE ————

Quitclaim Deed

The undersigned declares that the documentary transfer tax is $ .... and is

☐ computed on the full value of the interest or property conveyed, or is

☐ computed on the full value less the value of liens or encumbrances remaining thereon at the time of sale. The land, tenements or realty is located in

☐ unincorporated area   ☐ city of ....

FOR A VALUABLE CONSIDERATION, receipt of which is hereby acknowledged,

do   . hereby remise, release and forever quitclaim to

the following described real property in the   county of
state of California:

Dated _____

STATE OF CALIFORNIA

COUNTY OF _____ } SS

On this the _____ day of _____ 19 __, before me,
the undersigned, a Notary Public in and for said County and State,
personally appeared _____
_____
_____
_____, personally known to me
or proved to me on the basis of satisfactory evidence to be the
person____ whose name____ subscribed to the within instrument
and acknowledged that _____ executed the same.

_____
Signature of Notary

FOR NOTARY SEAL OR STAMP

MAIL TAX STATEMENTS TO PARTY SHOWN ON FOLLOWING LINE; IF NO PARTY SO SHOWN, MAIL AS DIRECTED ABOVE

| Name | Street Address | City & State |

SAFECO Stock No. CAL-0011A

A **VALID DEED** has all the following essential elements:

    a. It must be in writing.

    b. The parties (grantee and grantor) must be properly named and have legal capacity.

    c. The property must be adequately described (need not be legal description).

    d. There must be a granting clause (action clause).

    e. It must be signed by the granting party (grantor).

A valid deed passes title when the deed is recorded (which is a form of delivery), thereby giving constructive notice.

    A deed does not take effect until it is delivered and accepted. In order for title to be transferred, the grantor must sign the deed and deliver it with the intention of passing title immediately.

Some subtypes of grant or quitclaim deeds used in California are:

GIFT DEED – *Granted as a gift of love and affection.* No other consideration is necessary, but is void if given to defraud creditors.

TAX DEED – *Given if property is sold as payment of past-due property taxes.*

ADMINISTRATOR'S DEED or EXECUTOR'S DEED – *Given to the purchaser of the deceased person's real property.*

SHERIFF'S DEED – *Granted to the purchaser at a court-ordered sale.*

TRUSTEE'S DEED – *Given to the purchaser of property at a trust deed foreclosure sale.*

GUARDIAN'S DEED – *Used by a guardian to transfer the real property of minors or incompetents.*

LAND PATENT – *Used by the government to grant public land to an individual.*

A deed does NOT have to be acknowledged to be valid. Delivery and acceptance of the deed is presumed with recording.

    The following are the three basic methods of delivery:

    1. *MANUAL DELIVERY is a direct transfer of the deed from the grantor to the grantee.*

    2. *DELIVERY THROUGH RECORDING is the act of putting the title of record in the grantee's name at the county recorder's office.* The grantee must have agreed to the recording.

    3. *CONDITIONAL DELIVERY requires that a specific event take place before title can be passed, and must be handled by a disinterested third party.* The deed is then delivered manually.

A "trust deed" is NOT a deed, but rather a conveyance; it gives bare (or naked) legal title to a trustee with the power to sell.

2. Transfer by Will (Testate)

A *WILL is a document, created by a person, stating how that person's property is to be conveyed or distributed upon his or her death.* It also leaves instructions as to the disposition of the body upon death. This is known as dying *TESTATE, which means having made and left a valid will.* A *TESTATOR or TESTATRIX is one who makes a will.* To *BEQUEATH is to transfer personal property by will;* to *DEVISE is to transfer real property by will.* There are two types of wills that can legally dispose of real and personal property:

a. Witnessed will (typed)
b. Holographic will (handwritten)

A *WITNESSED WILL is a typed document usually prepared by an attorney, dated, signed by the property owners and declared to be a will by at least two witnesses (**three signatures total**).*

A *HOLOGRAPHIC WILL is entirely handwritten by the owner, dated, and signed.* Since it is in the owner's own handwriting, no other formalities and no witnesses are required, unless the will is signed with an "X," in which case it must be witnessed.

A holographic will is NOT a printed form.

A *CODICIL is a change in a will before the maker's death.*

Note: A *REVOCABLE LIVING TRUST is a trust that is effective during the life of the owner, rather than upon his or her death.* It can eliminate probate (to prove a will) cost and serve the same function as a will. The property is placed in a trust created for the heirs and may consist of both real and personal property. It is revocable at the discretion of the benefactor (owner), but becomes fully enforceable upon that person's death. There can be a considerable estate tax savings under this arrangement, depending on the size of the estate. At the very least, a revocable living trust protects the interests of everyone involved while avoiding the time and expense of probate. This type of trust is, however, rather complicated to set up, so an attorney specializing in this field should be consulted.

3. Transfer by Probate (Superior Court Approval)

PROBATE is a Superior Court procedure to determine a will's validity, any creditors' claims, and establish the identity of the beneficiaries. There are charges for the court probate action and fees for any related attorney costs.

The real estate commission for a property that is in probate is set by court order.

After a person dies, an **administrator (male)** or **administratrix (female)** is appointed by the court to temporarily take possession of the property until probate is finalized. An **executrix** is a female person appointed by will to administer the estate of the deceased person (**executor** is a male).

The minimum length of time for probate is six months. A party has four months to file a claim for probate.

Note: Wills and living trusts are legal devices for transferring property at death. To protect yourself, have an attorney draw up a will or living trust that reflects your desires, or leave your own handwritten (holographic) will.

Customarily, the court confirms a probate sale and sets the broker's commission.

4. Transfer by Intestate Succession (No Will)

If there is no will, the procedure used for transferring the deceased's property to his or her heirs is called INTESTATE SUCCESSION. The law of intestate succession provides for the disposition of the property. The rules for dividing the property are complex and dependent upon the relationship of the kin.

Separate property: If the decedent has no will and leaves a spouse and one child, property is divided equally, 50-50. If there is a surviving spouse and two or more children, 1/3 goes to the spouse and 2/3 to the children. If there is no surviving spouse, property is divided equally among the children.

ESCHEAT is the term used if there is no will and there are no heirs; the property will go to the state of California. This is not automatic. There is a **five-year period** during which heirs can make claims to the state for the property.

If a person dies intestate and leaves no heirs, his/her estate will go to the state of California if no heirs are found during a five-year period. Individuals do NOT acquire property by escheat.

5. Transfer by Accession (Natural Causes)

ACCESSION occurs when an owner acquires title to additional land by natural causes, that is, additions to the property by natural growth. The addition to land from natural causes, such as earthquakes, volcanoes, or the action of moving water is known as ACCRETION. For example, a river, over time, may slowly deposit soil on one of its banks. *These deposits of earth made through the natural action of water, called ALLUVIUM,* become the real property of the landowner who holds title to the river bank. *AVULSION is the sudden, violent tearing away of land by, for example, a river.* Title to that land is lost by the property owner.

The owner of property adjacent to the water flow can acquire title to additional land by accession or accretion.

Permanent fixtures attached to the land or buildings by residential tenants must be left with the building. Any improvements that are mistakenly placed on the property must also remain. *Placement of improvements and permanent fixtures on property that do not legally belong to the person who placed them is called ENCROACHMENT.*

A fence built over the property line onto a neighbor's lot is a form of encroachment. The neighboring landowner has three years from discovery to take action for its removal.

6. Transfer by Occupancy

Ownership of real property, or the use of real property, can be gained through three types of occupancy:

   a. Abandonment
   b. Adverse Possession
   c. Prescription (by use)

a. Abandonment

ABANDONMENT is the relinquishing of a right or interest with the intention of never again reclaiming it. One cannot acquire title to abandoned real property without court action, but a landlord can acquire possession of a property that is left (abandoned) by a tenant simply by gaining full control of the property. In the case of a lease, a financially troubled tenant might negotiate a release or abandon the property, thereby forfeiting part of the deposit.

When a tenant voluntarily moves out of an apartment and never returns, this is called abandonment or vacating.

b. Adverse Possession

ADVERSE POSSESSION is acquiring title to another's property through continuous and notorious occupancy for five years under a claim of title. It is the legal way to acquire title without a deed. Title may be obtained through adverse possession only if certain conditions are met:

1. **Open and notorious occupancy** – The adverse possessor must live on, or openly use, the property in such a way that the titled owners might easily detect his or her presence.

2. **Hostile and adverse** – The adverse possessor must possess the property hostile to the legal owner, without his or her permission or any rental payment (consideration).

3. **Uninterrupted use for five years** – The adverse possessor must use the property continuously for at least five consecutive years.

4. **Right or color of title** – The adverse possessor must have some reasonable claim of right or color of title (perhaps a defective written instrument) as a basis for his or her assertion. For example, a person could claim that his uncle gave the property to him before he died, but the deed is missing.

5. **Property taxes** – The adverse possessor must have paid all taxes levied and assessed on the property for five consecutive years.

The courts will require substantial proof before ruling there is an adverse possession. To obtain marketable title, or before a title insurance company can insure a property, clear title must be obtained by a court decree. This essentially means that a "quiet title" action is brought in court to prove that all requirements have been fulfilled. In the peoples' interest, adverse possession is not possible against public or government lands, but only against privately owned lands.

c. Easement by Prescription

PRESCRIPTION is an easement, or the right to use another's land, which can be obtained through five years of continuous use. Its requirements are similar to those of adverse possession, the differences being that by prescription: 1) only the use of the property has been obtained, and 2) taxes are still paid by the property owner (paying the property taxes is not a requirement for an easement by prescription).

Unlike "adverse possession," "prescription" is the "use" of a property, NOT the transfer of the title.

7. Transfer by Dedication

DEDICATION is the gift (appropriation) of land, by its owner, for some public use. To be fully dedicated, the land must be accepted for such use by authorized public officials. Dedication may be either (1) **voluntary or (2) mandated by statute.**

III. Title (Forms of Ownership)

A. TITLE

TITLE is the right to ownership of land and the evidence of that ownership. There are six distinct methods of holding title. **Figure 2-6** displays the six ways a person, or persons, may hold title to real property and whether a single title holder has the right to will or sell his or her share independent of the other owners. *VESTING is the placing of a person's (or persons') name on the deed and the description of the method by which that person will hold title.*

Figure 2-6 **Methods of Holding Title (Vesting) Concurrently or in Severalty**		
A SINGLE TITLE HOLDER	**WILL**	**SELL**
SEVERALTY ("Sole Ownership")	YES	YES
TENANCY IN COMMON	YES	YES
JOINT TENANCY	NO	YES
TENANCY IN PARTNERSHIP	NO	NO
COMMUNITY PROPERTY	YES	NO
COMMUNITY PROPERTY (w/Right of Survivorship)	NO	NO

Vesting is the method by which one holds title. A deed to a fictitious name is valid; a deed to a fictitious person is void.

1. Severalty (Sole Ownership)

SEVERALTY is the sole and separate ownership of property by one individual or by a corporation. The word "severed" means to sever, to cut off or separate. The name severalty is misleading; it means single.

Severalty means "sole ownership."

Property held by corporations is owned in severalty, as if by a single individual. A *CORPORATION is a body of persons treated by law as a single "legal person," having a personality and existence distinct from that of its shareholders.* A corporation can go on forever; it does not die.

Examples to show ownership by severalty are:

as a natural person, a real person

"Mary Smith, a single woman"
or
"Mary Smith, an unmarried woman"

or as a legal person; charter granted by the state

"Urban Analysis Inc., a corporation"

Sometimes married people wish to keep ownership to certain properties as separate property (in severalty). They may then use the phrase:

"Mary Smith, a married women, as her sole and separate property"
or
"Jim Smith, a married man, as his sole and separate property"

2. Tenancy In Common (Unity of Possession)

*When two or more people own property together with the right to will or sell it (however, without survivorship rights or community property rights), it is called **TENANCY IN COMMON**.* If there is no other agreement, they will each share an equal interest in the property. All tenants in common have **UNITY OF POSSESSION**, *which means they each have the right to occupy the property.* Often, the property is rented to one of the owners or to a tenant. Tenancy in common gives all owners a share of the income and expenses of the property.

Each owner may sell or transfer his or her interest separately from the others. For example, if one of the four owners of a building were to sell his/her one-quarter interest, there would be no restrictions. More commonly, if one of the owners dies, his/her heirs would inherit a one-quarter interest in the property.

If the owners do not agree on the ownership or management, and persistent disagreements exist, it would probably be best to sell the property and divide the profits accordingly. If an agreement cannot be reached by the owners, a court of law will sell the property and decide what is best for all concerned. *When the courts have the responsibility of physically dividing or selling the property, it is referred to as a **PARTITION ACTION**.* It is obviously better for the owners to sell the property themselves, as attorney's fees and court costs would be involved. Furthermore, the court would probably sell the land at a lower price to expedite the sale.

3. Joint Tenancy (Right of Survivorship)

JOINT TENANCY *occurs when two or more people have identical interests in the whole property with the same right of possession and the right of survivorship.* If one of the joint tenancy owners should die, his or her interest is then split evenly with the surviving owners. Joint tenancy can never be willed.

Joint tenants have the right of "survivorship." A joint tenancy cannot be willed.

Example: Dick and Jane, brother and sister, own an apartment building in joint tenancy. Dick needs $10,000 to cover unexpected medical expenses, so he borrows the money from a lender, signing a trust deed on the property that was soon recorded in the public records. Forty-five days later, Dick dies. Jane now owns the apartment free and clear of the brother's $10,000 debt.

Example: Al and Betty are brother and sister and own an apartment building in joint tenancy. Al having a trust deed or mortgage recorded against his ½ interest in the property would not terminate this joint tenancy.

A joint tenancy in real property can legally be created with the execution of a deed by a husband and wife to themselves as joint tenants, existing joint tenants to themselves and others as joint tenants, and existing tenants in common to themselves as joint tenants.

When a joint tenancy is established, there are four necessary unities (**T-Tip**):

T 1. **Title** – All owners are granted title by the same instrument.
T 2. **Time** – All owners obtain title at the same time.
I 3. **Interest** – All owners share an equal interest.
P 4. **Possession** – All owners have an equal right to possess the property.

To create joint tenancy, there must be intention by the owners. If it does not "state" that it is a joint tenancy, joint tenancy does not exist.

If one of the parties should die, the property is automatically transferred to the remaining parties without having to go through the superior court procedure known as **PROBATE** *(to prove a will)*. The transferred portion conveys the ownership and all debts on the property at the moment of death. Upon death, that debt does not transfer to the surviving joint tenants until it is foreclosed. Although probate costs may be avoided in joint tenancy, the surviving owners may end up paying higher income taxes later.

Joint tenancy is free of "unsecured debts."

A joint tenant can sell or transfer his or her ownership interest. Any portion of joint tenancy transferred or sold to a nonowner will bring the nonowner into tenancy in common with the other owners, who remain as joint tenants. If A, B and C own a property together and C sells his interest to D, then D gets only the tenancy in common interest with A and B (who continue to be joint tenants).

Because a corporation could, conceivably, go on forever, it is not permitted to enter into joint tenancies. Such a situation would give corporations an unfair survivorship advantage.

4. Tenancy in Partnership

TENANCY IN PARTNERSHIP refers to two or more people who are co-owners in a business. In a *GENERAL PARTNERSHIP, the partners share all profits and losses and share management responsibilities.* All partners must agree to a sale or transfer of real property. Each has a right to possess the partnership property. If a partner should die, his or her interest passes to any heirs who then have a right in the partnership, but not in any particular property. If an agreement cannot be reached with the heirs, the partnership may have to be dissolved.

The amount invested in a partnership need not be equal, but must be agreed upon mutually. The partnership agreement states the amount of money to be contributed by each, the duties of each, and sets the proportional distribution of profits or losses.

A *LIMITED PARTNERSHIP (tax shelter) is one consisting of one or more general partners and limited partners.* A limited partner's losses are limited to the amount of his or her investment. A limited partner does not share management responsibilities.

5. Community Property

COMMUNITY PROPERTY refers to all the property acquired by a husband and wife during their marriage. California is a community property state, which means that any property acquired during a marriage is shared equally. This practice is derived from Spanish law and became incorporated into our legal system when California was a part of Mexico. Both husband and wife must sign all transfer documents to convey community real property. If only one spouse signs a transfer document, the "injured" spouse could void the sale within a one-year period. **As a salesperson, you should make certain that both husband and wife sign all real estate documents, such as listings, purchase agreements, and escrow instructions, if the property being transferred is community property. Both signatures are required when selling, borrowing money, or leasing community property for more than one year.**

Both husband and wife's signatures are needed to transfer property deeded "Mary Smith, a married woman."

The right to manage the community property is shared by both the husband and wife. Each can will his or her respective half to whomever he or she wishes. **If there is no will, the half belonging to the deceased would go to the surviving spouse. If willed to an heir, the heir and the remaining spouse would then be tenants in common.**

Community property (husband and wife) vesting has equal interest.

Debts can become a liability if they are incurred after marriage. Debts incurred by either spouse before marriage cannot be converted to the debts of the community property. The law also allows some community property to be transferred without going through probate. Questions about debts or probate should be directed to an attorney, as this issue is quite complex.

Wages (paychecks) earned by either spouse during a marriage are considered "community property."

Any property obtained by either the husband or wife before marriage may remain as *SEPARATE PROPERTY.* Both may inherit or receive gifts of property during the marriage, which can remain as separate property. **However, any proceeds from the property held separately, such as rents or profit, cannot be commingled with community property, as this would cause them to become community property.**

Do not advise a buyer on how to hold title—that is giving legal advice. However, you can explain the different ways to take title. How a person holds title has a big impact upon income tax planning and estate planning.

A real estate agent who advises a buyer on how to take title to real property may be liable for practicing law, giving tax advice, and discrimination.

6. Community Property with Right of Survivorship

The California Legislature enacted legislation that allows married couples in California to hold title to real and personal property as "community property with right of survivorship." *COMMUNITY PROPERTY WITH RIGHT OF SURVIVORSHIP transfers ownership to the spouse at death, with income tax benefits.* The goal of the legislation was to combine the right of survivorship benefit of joint tenancy with the favorable tax status of community property under federal tax law. The survivorship benefit allows title to pass to the surviving spouse at the death of one spouse. The surviving spouse also gets the benefit of a stepped-up basis for 100% of the property upon the death of a spouse. The surviving spouse may use an affidavit of death of spouse to satisfy title company underwriting requirements to convey or encumber title. Probate proceedings are not necessary to transfer title to the surviving spouse.

IV. Recording and Acknowledgment

A deed does NOT have to be "acknowledged" or "recorded" to be valid, although it is wise to do both.

A. RECORDING

RECORDING is the legal process of making an instrument an official part of the records of a county, after it has been acknowledged. Instruments that affect real property are legal documents, such as deeds, mortgages, trust deeds, leases and contracts of sale. **Recording gives constructive notice** of the existence and content of these instruments to the public.

CONSTRUCTIVE NOTICE is notice of documents presumed by law to have been acquired by a person whether or not they have actually examined them. It can be accomplished by recording a deed or taking possession of the property. Any recorded notice that can be obtained from the county recorder's office can be considered constructive notice (and therefore public knowledge).

ACTUAL NOTICE is knowing (or one's responsibility for knowing) that a transaction has taken place. If you have found, for example, that someone other than the owner is living in a house you are buying, you should have been aware of the existence of a signed lease. This is actual notice, whereas public records are representative of constructive notice. The act of taking possession (holding an unrecorded deed) gives constructive notice.

The recording process is a privilege rather than a legal requirement. **Some documents have to be recorded to be valid. These include mechanic's liens and declarations of homestead.** You may record an acknowledged instrument at any time. However, failure to utilize the privilege of recording at the earliest possible date can result in a question of legal or rightful title.

If the same property is sold to more than one party, the individual who has given constructive notice first (by possession or recordation) will usually be recognized as the rightful owner.

Example: When selling his home to John, Bert negotiated a leaseback arrangement in order to continue renting and occupying the property for the next two years. John immediately placed the unrecorded grant deed into a safe deposit box for ultimate security. Two days later, Bert "sold" the home a second time to Julie, who promptly recorded her deed. Julie is the likely owner of the property by virtue of recording her deed first.

In order to establish priority, the documents affecting real property must be recorded by the county recorder in the county where the property is located. If the property is located in two counties, the documents should be recorded in both counties.

B. PRIORITY OF RECORDING

Under the recording system in California, "The first in time is the first in right." If an owner sells his or her house twice, the first deed recorded usually is considered the valid deed. This person must not have knowledge of the rights of the other party. This is the reward granted in California for recording any real estate transaction. However, there are four exceptions to the rule, including:

1. Government liens, property taxes, and special assessments.
2. Actual or constructive notice of another person's prior rights.
3. Mechanic's liens.
4. Agreements to the contrary.

C. ACKNOWLEDGMENT (or Notary)

All documents must be acknowledged before they are recorded by the county recorder. *ACKNOWLEDGMENT refers to a signed or verbal statement by the named person that he/she has*

signed that document of his/her own free will. In other words, that person "acknowledges" his or her signature. This acknowledgment must be performed in the presence of a witness, usually a notary public, authorized by law to witness acknowledgments.

A *NOTARY PUBLIC is a person who is authorized by the Secretary of State to witness the acknowledgment of documents.* All notarized documents must be stamped with a notary seal. The seal must contain the following information:

1. The word "Notary Public"
2. The name of the county
3. The name of the notary
4. The state seal
5. The expiration date

In order to be notarized, any person signing a **grant deed**, **quitclaim deed**, or **trust deed** is required to place a right thumb print on the notary's sequential journal. This is because of a high rate of fraud by the use of false deeds. Additionally, a notary must immediately notify the Secretary of State if the notary's sequential journal is stolen, lost, misplaced, destroyed, damaged or otherwise rendered unusable.

A deed does NOT have to be acknowledged to be valid, but must be acknowledged to be recorded.

VERIFICATION is an oath or affirmation made before a notary public that the content of an instrument is true. Notices of completion, nonresponsibility, and the statements used in filing a mechanic's lien are among instruments that must be verified rather than simply acknowledged.

An *AFFIRMATION is a solemn and legally binding declaration made under penalty of perjury by a person whose religious or other beliefs prohibit the taking of an oath.*

An *AFFIDAVIT is a verified written statement of facts.*

A notary public does NOT acknowledge a document, but "witnesses" an acknowledgment.

D. DO NOT GIVE LEGAL ADVICE

A real estate salesperson or broker may not give legal advice, because the law is a highly complex and specialized profession that requires years of preparation and training. In the state of California, only a licensed attorney who is a member of the State Bar is allowed to practice law. A broker cannot give legal advice, unless he or she is also an attorney.

It is illegal for an agent, except an attorney, to draw up legal documents. For this reason, real estate brokers use preprinted fill-in forms. These standard forms are drawn up by licensed attorneys who are familiar with the legalities involved in contracts.

V. CHAPTER SUMMARY

An **estate** is an interest, share, right or equity in real estate, and can be either **freehold** (real property) or **less-than-freehold** (personal property). Freehold estates include fee simple estates or life estates.

A **fee simple** (or estate in fee) is the most complete form of ownership as it is of indefinite duration, freely transferable, and inheritable. If a **condition precedent** (before) or **condition subsequent** (future) **condition** is attached to a property's use, it is a **fee simple defeasible estate**.

A **life estate** is a freehold estate with a limited duration based upon someone's lifetime, with the property reverting back to the original owner (who holds an **estate in reversion**) upon the death of the life estate holder. If someone other than the owner is to receive title, that person is said to hold an **estate in remainder.**

A property owner may reserve a life estate for the duration of his or her lifetime. Although the estate is deeded to a designated party, he or she doesn't take possession until the death of the owner.

A **lease** or **rental agreement** is a less-than-freehold estate, where the tenant is given rights to use the real property for a period of time. It's personal property because no real ownership exists. An **estate for years** is a lease for a fixed period of time, agreed to in advance. Other less-than-freehold estates include **estates from period-to-period**, **estates at will**, and **estates at sufferance.**

Property can be sold or transferred by: 1) **deed** (grant deed transfers title); 2) **will** (witnessed or holographic); 3) **probate** (after death through the courts); 4) **intestate succession** (no will, divided among family or state); 5) **accession** (land increases through natural causes); 6) **occupancy** (**abandonment, adverse possession,** and **prescription**); and 7) **dedication** (gift to public).

A **grant deed** is a document that transfers title (evidence of the right to possess property). The method of holding title concurrently or in severalty is called **vesting**. The methods of tenancy include **severalty, tenants in common, joint tenancy, tenancy in partnership, community property**, and **community property with right of survivorship.**

Although **severalty** means separate ownership, title can be held by an individual or a corporation and can be willed or sold. When two or more people own property concurrently, it is called a **tenancy in common,** and it, too, can be willed or sold (although there are no survivorship or community property rights).

If there is the right of survivorship it is called **joint tenancy,** and that title cannot be willed. The four unities for joint tenancy are: 1) **title**, 2) **time**, 3) **interest**, and 4) **possession** (**Remember: "T-TIP"**).

Tenancy in partnership refers to two or more people who are co-owners in a business, and can be a **general partnership** (losses and management duties shared) or **limited partnership** (losses limited and no management duties).

Community property refers to all the property acquired by a husband and wife during their marriage, and it can be willed, but if no heir exists, it goes to the remaining spouse. **Community property with right of survivorship** allows the property to pass to the surviving spouse without probate administration, and the property will receive a full step-up basis, which means no capital gains tax to the surviving spouse if the property is sold.

All deeds should be **acknowledged** in the presence of a notary public and recorded with the county. **Generally, the deed recorded first has priority over any that follow**.

VI. TERMINOLOGY

A. Abandonment	**K.** Dedication	**U.** Life Estate
B. Accession	**L.** Delivery	**V.** Notary Public
C. Actual Notice	**M.** Encroachment	**W.** Prescription
D. Adverse Possession	**N.** Escheat	**X.** Probate
E. Affirmation, Affidavit, Verification	**O.** Freehold Estate	**Y.** Quitclaim Deed
F. Community Property	**P.** General and Limited Partnerships	**Z.** Recording
G. Condition Precedent	**Q.** Grant Deed	**AA.** Remainder
H. Condition Subsequent	**R.** Holographic Will	**BB.** Reversion
I. Constructive Notice	**S.** Intestate Succession	**CC.** Severalty
J. Corporation	**T.** Joint Tenancy	**DD.** Tenancy in Common
		EE. Witnessed Will

1.____ The giving of private land by its owner for a public use; most commonly, the developer who gives it to a city.

2.____ The reverting of private property to the state when there are no valid heirs.

3.____ A voluntary association between two or more people to carry on a business with general and limited partners.

4.____ A deed using the word "grant," or like words, containing warranties against prior conveyances and encumbrances. This is the most commonly used deed in California.

5.____ An estate of indeterminable duration, e.g., fee simple or life estate.

6.____ Undivided ownership of a property interest by two or more persons, each of whom has a right to an equal share in the interest and a right of survivorship.

7.____ It is notice that is actually and expressly given or implied.

8.____ A person authorized by the state to witness the signatures of persons executing documents, sign the certificate and affix the official seal.

9.____ An event that must happen before title is passed.

10.____ Documents filed with the County Recorder in such a way as are considered open notice to the world.

11.____ Co-ownership of property by two or more persons who hold undivided interest, without right of survivorship. The interests need not be equal.

12.____An unlawful intrusion onto another's property by making improvements to real property, e.g., a swimming pool built across a property line.

13.____A legal entity, sanctioned by the state, with rights and liabilities, distinct and apart from those of the persons composing it.

14.____The intentional and voluntary relinquishment of any ownership interest (such as an easement) or possession of real property.

15.____The means of acquiring interests in land, usually an easement, by continued use.

16.____A condition attached to an estate whereby the estate is defeated or changed through the failure or non-performance of the condition.

17.____A process of law by which the state lays out the correct succession of inheritance when a person dies without leaving a valid will.

18.____Many different types of statements made before a professional witness.

19.____An estate that reverts back to the grantor after the life of the tenant expires.

20.____The court procedure of proving that a will is valid.

21.____A method of acquiring title to real property, through possession of the property for a statutory period under certain conditions, by a person other than the owner.

22.____A deed to relinquish any interest in property, that the grantor may have, without any warranty of title or interest.

23.____An estate that is transferred to a third party (anyone other than the grantor) upon the death of the life estate holder.

24.____A formal expression of a person's desires, witnessed by others, as to the disposition of his or her property after death.

25.____Property acquired by husband and/or wife during marriage that is not acquired as separate property. Each spouse has equal rights of management, alienation and disposition.

26.____An estate of a single entity held by a single person alone.

27.____An estate or interest in real property that is held for the duration of the life of some certain person. It may be the person holding title to the estate or some other person.

28.____A handwritten expression of a person's desires as to the disposition of their property after death.

29.____Placing a document in the official records of the county.

30.____The act of receiving a deed.

31.____The acquiring of additional property.

VII. CHAPTER QUIZ

1. Which of the following is a type of freehold estate?

    a. Probate estate
    b. Fee simple defeasible
    c. Estate in fee
    d. Estate in sufferance

2. Duke sold his property to Jane with the condition that Jane must never use it for any purpose other than as a private residence. However, after owning the property for several years, Jane decided to start a board and care facility for handicapped adults. What is the status of the estate?

    a. It may revert to Duke because it is a fee simple defeasible estate
    b. It may revert to Duke because it is a fee simple absolute estate
    c. Duke has no claim because his condition is unlawful
    d. Duke has no claim because the statute of limitations ran out on the condition

3. Which of the following is an example of a freehold estate?

    a. The interest created by a trust deed
    b. An estate at will
    c. A life estate
    d. A leasehold estate

4. A seven-year lease would be considered:

    a. an estate for years.
    b. personal property.
    c. chattel real.
    d. all of the above.

5. A tenancy at sufferance would occur when:

    a. a tenant remains in the property after the end of an estate for years and continues to pay rent.
    b. a tenant remains in the property after expiration of a lease without the owner's consent.
    c. a landlord who delivers a 30-day notice to vacate the premises cannot find the tenant.
    d. a landlord cannot obtain a writ of execution from the courts.

6. The owner of property adjacent to the water flow can acquire title to additional land by:

    a. avulsion.
    b. alluvium.
    c. percolation.
    d. accession.

7. Dick and Jane, brother and sister, own an apartment building in joint tenancy. Dick needs $10,000 to cover unexpected medical expenses, so he borrows the money from a lender and signs a trust deed on the property that was soon recorded in the public records. Forty-five days later, Dick dies. Which of the following is most correct?

   a. Jane is now responsible for the entire $10,000.
   b. Jane is now responsible for $5,000.
   c. Jane now owns the apartment building free and clear of her brother's $10,000 debt.
   d. If the loan is not repaid, the lender can foreclose only on Dick's 1/2 interest in the property.

8. Which of the following is needed to transfer property deeded "Mary Smith, a married woman"?

   a. Husband's signature only
   b. Wife's signature only
   c. Both husband and wife's signature
   d. Husband's signature only, if the wife gives verbal consent

9. If a real estate agent advises a buyer how to take title to real property, he/she may be liable for:

   a. practicing law.
   b. giving tax advice.
   c. discrimination.
   d. all of the above.

10. When selling his home to John, Bert negotiated a leaseback arrangement in order to continue renting and occupying the property for the next two years. John immediately placed the unrecorded grant deed into a safe deposit box for ultimate security. Two days later, Bert "sold" the home a second time to Julie who promptly recorded her deed. Which of the following is most correct?

   a. John is the rightful owner of the home provided he can produce this first deed to the property.
   b. Julie is the likely owner of the property because she recorded her deed first.
   c. Bert still owns the home until he vacates.
   d. The title company will decide who is the rightful owner of the property.

ANSWERS: 1. c; 2. a; 3. c; 4. d; 5. b; 6. d; 7. c; 8. c; 9. d; 10. b

THE GREAT SEAL OF THE STATE

THE MIN

CHAPTER 3
Encumbrances

I. Encumbrances – An Overview

The term encumbrance is usually new to the beginner in real estate. An *ENCUMBRANCE is a right or interest in real property other than an ownership or tenancy interest.* It is a burden to the property that limits its use and may lessen its value. The two main types of encumbrances, shown in **Figure 3-1** and **Figure 3-3**, are: (1) liens and (2) items that affect the physical condition or use of the property.

Figure 3-1

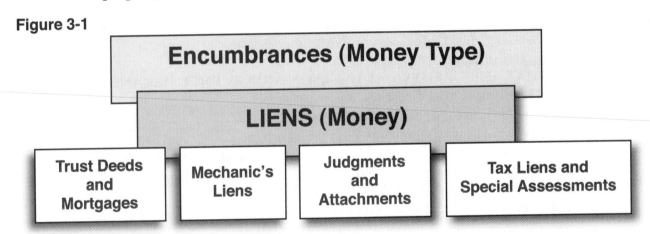

All liens are encumbrances but NOT all encumbrances are liens.

When an owner encumbers more than one lot under a single lien, that owner has created a blanket encumbrance. A *BLANKET ENCUMBRANCE is a voluntary lien (for money owed) placed over more than one parcel.* A *RELEASE CLAUSE releases portions of the property.*

II. Liens (Money Owed)

A *LIEN is a document that uses a property to secure the payment of a debt or the discharge of an obligation.* It is money owed for one reason or another on a property. Liens include trust deeds or mortgages, tax liens, special assessments, mechanic's liens, judgments, and attachments.

CHAPTER OUTLINE

Liens are either:

1. voluntary or
2. involuntary; and
3. specific or
4. general

A. VOLUNTARY AND INVOLUNTARY LIENS

VOLUNTARY LIENS are money debts that an owner agrees to pay. A lien is created when the buyer takes out a loan to finance the purchase of real estate. He or she voluntarily agrees to allow liens to be placed on the property.

A voluntary lien does NOT have to be recorded.

INVOLUNTARY LIENS are money obligations that create a burden on a property by government taxes or legal action because of unpaid bills. Both involuntary liens and voluntary liens must be paid, or assumed, in full before the owner can sell or refinance the property.

B. SPECIFIC AND GENERAL LIENS

SPECIFIC LIENS are liens against just one property. Property taxes assessed against real property automatically become a specific lien on only that property on **January 1** of each year.

GENERAL LIENS are liens on all the properties of the owner, not just one. Federal or state income taxes and judgment liens can become a general lien on all your real property.

C. TRUST DEED (Security Device – Voluntary and Specific)

A *TRUST DEED is a written instrument that makes real property collateral for a loan.* The evidence of debt is created by the promissory note that accompanies the trust deed. The trust deed pledges (hypothecates) the property as collateral, or security, for the note. In California, the trust deed is the usual security device for real property. In eastern states, the mortgage is the typical financing instrument. See Chapter 8 for details on trust deeds.

A promissory note (which accompanies the trust deed) is evidence of the debt. Trust deeds and mortgages are personal property.

D. MORTGAGE (Security Device – Voluntary and Specific)

A *MORTGAGE is a lien that secures real property for the payment of a promissory note (debt).* Mortgages are rarely employed in financing California homes, but because of their wide use in other states, they are emphasized in the real estate licensing examination. In California many people use the term "mortgage" to mean a property loan, but they usually are talking about trust deeds. Therefore, it is essential to understand the difference between mortgages and trust deeds since almost every property transfer in California is financed through a trust deed. Details on mortgages are discussed further in Chapter 8.

E. MECHANIC'S LIENS (Involuntary and Specific)

MECHANIC'S LIENS are liens that may be filed against a property by a person who was not paid after furnishing labor or materials for construction work on that property. The form used to

enforce a mechanic's lien action must be recorded to be valid. A mechanic's lien is a lien against the property itself. The property cannot be transferred until the obligation is paid and the title cleared. This gives a subcontractor, craftsman or general contractor, employed by an owner, the right to protect his or her interest. The same right applies to material suppliers who furnish such items as lumber, plumbing or roofing supplies. To determine the start time, the mechanic's lien dates back to the commencement of the project.

A mechanic's lien is filed against a property and must be recorded to be valid.

1. Preliminary Notice

A *PRELIMINARY NOTICE is a written notice that must be given before filing a mechanic's lien and within 20 days of supplying labor or services.* This notice must be given, either by mail or in person, to the owner, general contractor and the lender. The notice must contain a general description of the labor or materials furnished, who supplied them and the person who contracted for these services. Failure to give the preliminary notice within 20 days does not restrict a supplier's right to file, but he or she may have allowed other claimants to file before him or her, which gives those claimants priority. As a matter of good practice, most suppliers include a preliminary notice as part of the original contract.

If a contractor files a mechanic's lien, it takes priority over all other liens except taxes, special assessments, and trust deeds filed prior to the "start of work."

2. Determining the Start Time for Mechanic's Liens

An important determination when considering a mechanic's lien is the **date that work started on the property**. Mechanic's liens, once recorded, have priority over all other liens, except property taxes, special assessments, and trust deeds. To lenders, this is critical because lenders want their trust deeds recorded before any work starts. Before they will lend money, lenders will conduct a physical inspection of the property to make sure no construction has started.

A mechanic's lien dates back to the time work began on the project.

A mechanic's lien (labor or materials) dates back to the beginning (commencement) of work on the project. This is known as the SCHEME OF IMPROVEMENTS.

3. Notice of Completion and Notice of Cessation (Limits Time to File)

A **"Notice of Completion"** (see **Figure 3-2**), in order to be valid, should be recorded by the owner within 10 days of completion, thereby limiting the general contractor to **60 days** to file a claim and subcontractors to **30 days**. This gives everyone constructive notice. Completion technically occurs when the owner accepts the finished work of the contractor, but in some instances, the job is never completed. **Guidelines have been set up by the state to allow suppliers of services and materials a filing period of up to 90 days if the owner doesn't file a valid notice of completion.** If one of these four alternatives occurs, the work is considered to be complete:

1. Occupation or use by owner after cessation of labor.
2. Acceptance of work improvements by owner.

Figure 3-2

RECORDING REQUESTED BY

AND WHEN RECORDED MAIL TO

```
Name
Street
Address
City &
State
```

———— SPACE ABOVE THIS LINE FOR RECORDER'S USE ————

INDIVIDUAL FORM

Notice of Completion

Before execution, refer to title company requirements stated on reverse side. A. P. N. _ _ ___ _ _____

TO 1927 CA (3-75)

Notice is hereby given that:

1. The undersigned is owner of the interest or estate stated below in the property hereinafter described.
2. The full name of the undersigned is _____
3. The full address of the undersigned is _____
4. The nature of the title of the undersigned is: In fee. _____
   (If other than fee, strike "In fee" and insert, for example, "purchaser under contract of purchase," or "lessee".)
5. The full names and full addresses of all persons, if any, who hold title with the undersigned as joint tenants or as tenants in common are:

   NAMES   ADDRESSES
   _____
   _____
   _____

6. The names of the predecessors in interest of the undersigned, if the property was transferred subsequent to the commencement of the work of improvement herein referred to:

   NAMES   ADDRESSES
   _____
   _____
   _____

   (If no transfer made, insert "none".)

7. A work of improvement on the property hereinafter described was completed on _____
8. The name of the contractor, if any, for such work of improvement was _____

   (If no contractor for work of improvement as a whole, insert "none".)

9. The property on which said work of improvement was completed is in the City of_____
   _____, County of_____, State of California, and is described as follows:
   _____
   _____
   _____
   _____
   _____
   _____

10. The street address of said property is _____
    (If no street address has been officially assigned, insert "none".)

Signature of owner named in paragraph 2

Dated: _____

(Also sign verification below at X)

STATE OF CALIFORNIA, } SS.
COUNTY OF_____

The undersigned, being duly sworn, says: That ___he is the owner of the aforesaid interest or estate in the property described in the foregoing notice; that ___he has read the same, and knows the contents thereof, and that the facts stated therein are true.

Signature of owner named in paragraph 2 X_____

SUBSCRIBED AND SWORN TO before me

on _____

Signature_____
   Notary Public in and for said State

Title Order No._____
Escrow or Loan No._____

SEE REVERSE SIDE FOR
TITLE COMPANY REQUIREMENTS AS TO NOTICE OF COMPLETION

(This area for official notarial seal)

3. A cessation of labor for 60 continuous days.
4. A cessation of labor for 30 continuous days if the owner files a "Notice of Cessation" with the county recorder's office.

A "Completion Bond" may be required by a lender to ensure that an insurance company will complete the job if the contractor cannot.

4. Filing Time (Limited)

The filing period is very important because the rights of a person filing a mechanic's lien are valid for only a short time. A suit can be filed later, but it would not automatically become a lien against the real property. A mechanic's lien may be filed any time after the preliminary notice and until 30 days after completion, if you are a supplier or subcontractor, and 60 days after completion if you are the general contractor. **If there is no notice of completion recorded for the project, all parties have 90 days after completion of the job to file.**

Filing time = 30 days (subcontractor), 60 days (general contractor), and 90 days (all parties, if no notice of completion).

5. Notice of Non-Responsibility (Must be Recorded and Posted)

An owner may file a notice of non-responsibility within 10 days of discovering that an unauthorized person is performing construction service on his or her property. A recorded and verified **NOTICE OF NON-RESPONSIBILITY** *is posted on the property stating that the owner is not responsible for the work being done.* This action releases an owner from any liability caused by the unauthorized activity and prevents suppliers from filing a valid mechanic's lien. If a tenant is installing carpet in your apartment without your authorization, filing a notice of non-responsibility with the county recorder's office protects you against the claims of the carpet supplier.

F. TAX LIENS (Specific or General Liens)

If any government tax is not paid, it may become a lien, through law or a court action, on real property. If the lien is not settled, the property can be sold to pay back-taxes. Tax liens are either: (1) specific liens or (2) general liens.

The difference between property taxes and special assessments is that special assessments are levied for the cost of specific local improvements, while property tax revenue goes into the general fund.

G. SPECIAL ASSESSMENTS

Local improvements are paid by the property owners in a given district through SPECIAL ASSESSMENTS. Improvements such as streets, sewers, street lighting and irrigation projects are generally paid for by the property owners who have benefited from the work. If these assessments are not paid, they become a lien against the property. Most special assessments are 10-to-30-year bonds. This allows the property owner a reasonable amount of time to pay them off. The property can be transferred without the assessment being paid. It is best that buyer and seller agree that the buyer will assume the assessment.

Developers finance roads, schools, and other off-site improvements with "Mello-Roos Bonds," which become a special tax levied against homeowners. Sellers must disclose if their property is subject to a Mello-Roos lien.

H. JUDGMENTS (Involuntary and General Liens)

A *JUDGMENT is a court decision determining the rights of the parties involved and the amount of compensation.* A judgment can be appealed, and is good for ten years.

For a judgment to become a lien, an *ABSTRACT OF JUDGMENT, or formal filing of the judgment,* must be recorded. The judgment then becomes a lien upon all nonexempt property of the debtor. It also becomes a lien on all future property he or she later acquires until the lien is paid. A judgment lien is good for ten years. So, if any property is transferred within this ten year period, the lien must first be paid off. Under additional court action, the judgment holder may be able to force the debtor to sell the real property to pay off the lien.

1. Small Claims Court

At this point, it is important that you understand the use of the Small Claims Court. Anyone can take someone else to court regarding civil cases for a $6 filing fee plus the fee for serving the subpoena. Neither party is allowed to be represented in the courtroom by legal counsel. The current maximum amount of a judgment is $7,500. This limit will be adjusted periodically by the state legislature to meet inflationary trends. Night court is also available in some districts, making this process even more accessible. You should be aware, however, that for a plaintiff, the judge's decision in a small claims action is final. The defendant, though, has the right of appeal. This is an excellent way to settle a dispute with a minimal amount of time and expense.

I. TERMINATION OF JUDGMENT LIEN

Most judgment liens are terminated by the satisfaction of the judgment. A *JUDGMENT IS SATISFIED by the payment of money or the return of property.* A notice that the judgment has been satisfied should be filed with the clerk of the court. It clears the lien from the record. Sometimes certain properties may be released from the judgment, but only with the judgment holder's consent. This partial release enables an owner to sell a property to satisfy a part of the judgment. A judgment may also be terminated if a bond is posted or if the judge grants a new trial.

J. ATTACHMENT (Court-Seized Property)

ATTACHMENT (LIEN) is a process of the law that creates a lien. It gives custody of real or personal property to the court to assure payment of a pending lawsuit in that county. This is to assure that there will be enough property to satisfy the judgment should the plaintiff prevail. The *PLAINTIFF is the person filing a court action to obtain an attachment lien.* The *DEFENDANT is the person who is being sued.* During an unlawful detainer action for collection of past due rents, for instance, it may be advantageous for a plaintiff to obtain an attachment against the defendant. This type of lien is good for three years, and is extended only if the plaintiff wins the court case. Use of the attachment lien is not very common because there are many rules and formalities involved in obtaining this type of lien. This is another area that requires the help of an attorney.

An attachment is a prejudgment process that creates a lien, good for three years, which does NOT terminate on the death of the property owner.

K. LIS PENDENS ("Lawsuit Pending")

LIS PENDENS *is the recording of a notice with the county recorder's office warning all persons that a certain type of lawsuit is pending concerning a particular property.* Attorneys often file a lis pendens before a court date is set in order to stop the transfer of the property. A lis pendens places a cloud on the title, and is effective when filed. The property is not marketable until the lis pendens is removed.

A lis pendens is notice of a pending lawsuit that may affect (cloud) title to real property based on the lawsuit outcome. It remains on the public record (is effective) until the lis pendens is removed, the action is dismissed, or final judgment is rendered.

L. SHERIFF'S SALE (Court Order to Sell – Execution)

A **WRIT OF EXECUTION** *(sale) is a court order requiring the sale of certain property to satisfy a judgment.* The writ of execution extends the lien against the real property for one year. If the judgment has already been recorded as a lien on the property, the writ of execution will not create a new lien. The county sheriff, or other local officials, are then ordered to secure and sell the real or personal property to satisfy the lien.

If a person refuses to pay off the judgment, the sheriff's sale is the next step. A **SHERIFF'S SALE** *is the forced sale of a debtor's property to satisfy a judgment under a writ of execution.* In California, the sheriff's sale is the usual method of forcing the sale of property to pay off a judgment.

Mechanic's liens and any previously recorded judgments have priority over paying the expenses of the sale. If these expenses are paid, a first trust deed is next to be satisfied. Any amount left over is applied toward a second trust deed and any subsequent liens, in the order of their recording, until the proceeds are exhausted.

M. INJUNCTION (Court Order to Stop)

An **INJUNCTION** *is a court order which can restrict a party from doing an act such as violating private deed restrictions.*

Example: Mr. Crawford has been burning rubbish on his own property. The neighbors have complained and have secured a court order, ordering Mr. Crawford to stop the offending practice. The court order is called an injunction.

III. Items That Affect Physical Use (Non-Money Encumbrances)

A. ITEMS THAT AFFECT PHYSICAL USE

ITEMS THAT AFFECT PHYSICAL USE *are non-money encumbrances that affect the physical use of real property.* They include: easements, building restrictions and zoning (such as setback requirements), and encroachments and leases, which are conditions that limit the physical use of the property (see **Figure 3-3**).

Figure 3-3

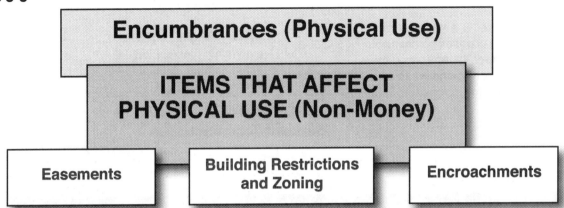

Some encumbrances affect the physical use of the property. They are:

1. Easements
2. Building Restrictions and Zoning
3. Encroachments
4. Leases (see Chapter 6)

1. Easements (The Right to Use Another's Land)

An easement is the right to use another's land; it is an "interest," but NOT an estate. An easement is a non-money encumbrance, but NOT a lien.

An *EASEMENT is an interest in land owned by another person consisting of the right to use or control the land, or an area above or below it, for a specific, limited purpose. The right to enter is called* ***INGRESS*** *and the right to exit is* ***EGRESS***. Included in this definition is the right to profit from the easement, such as the right to take minerals, oil and gas.

Easements are of two types: (1) easements appurtenant and (2) easements in gross.

a. Easement Appurtenant (Runs With the Land)

An *EASEMENT APPURTENANT is an easement "created for and beneficial to" the owner of adjoining or attached lands. An easement is real property, not personal property, but it is not an estate. In this case there are two parcels of land, with one owner giving another owner an easement. The* ***DOMINANT TENEMENT*** *is the land that obtains the benefits of an easement.* **Figure 3-4** *is an illustration of a driveway easement. Owner A's land is the dominant tenement and Owner B's land is the servient tenement.*

The owner of the servient tenement CANNOT terminate the easement; it must "serve" the dominant tenement.

Example: Able has leased Blackacre for a ten-year term. Baker owns Whiteacre, which is adjacent to Blackacre. Baker requests an easement over Blackacre from Able. Able, the tenant, can legally grant such a right for an indefinite period. A lessee can grant an easement over leased property, but only for the term of the lease. After the lease expires, the easement is no longer valid.

Figure 3-4

Property owner B owns the land the easement crosses but cannot block or hinder in any way the right of property owner A to use the driveway for access to his property.

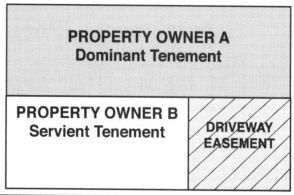

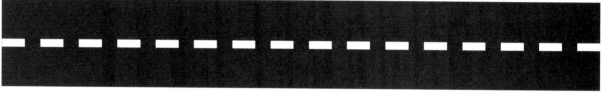

A *SERVIENT TENEMENT is the land that gives the easement (use of the land) for the benefit of another*. The appurtenant easement belongs to the land and is transferred with the land. This easement cannot be transferred separately from the land.

The dominant tenement and the servient tenement do NOT need to physically abut (touch) each other.

b. Easement in Gross (Does Not Benefit Adjoining Landowner)

An example of an easement in gross would be an easement for the telephone company (utility company) to enter the property to run telephone lines.

An "appurtenant easement" goes with the land, whereas an "easement in gross" goes to a person.

An *EASEMENT IN GROSS is not attached to any particular land or dominant tenement. It is an easement created for the benefit of others who do not own adjoining or attached lands.* It is a personal property right. Even though it is a personal right, it is still a servient tenement. An example of an easement in gross would be a utility company or person obtaining the right to run natural gas lines across your land. In this instance your land would become a servient tenement.

Example: Landowner Jacobs granted the telephone company the right to erect telephone poles on his land. This easement in gross is an **encumbrance**.

Other not-so-common easements are: rights to take water, wood or minerals; rights to transact business or conduct sports upon the land; rights to receive light, air or heat from the land, and the right to use a wall as a common party wall.

An easement that does not specify a special area for a right-of-way is also valid. *A property owner could give the right to cross his or her land and not limit how or where a person would have to cross. This is known as an UNLOCATED EASEMENT.*

A "license" is permission to use another's property for a certain purpose and period of time. Unlike an easement in gross, it can be revoked at any time.

c. Creation of an Easement

Easements are created in three basic ways:

1. Express Grant (in writing)
2. Implication of Law (implied easement)
3. Long Use (prescription)

1. EXPRESS GRANT (IN WRITING), AS IN A DEED OR CONTRACT. If a property is transferred as part of the deed, an easement appurtenant to the land would be included in the grant. The same thing is accomplished by transferring a property, but **reserving an easement** over the land. A written contract can create an easement between the parties. For legal protection, this contract should be acknowledged and recorded.

> **Example:** Daniel, who owned two pieces of adjacent land, sold one of them to Charles, reserving an easement for himself at the time. Daniel soon left the state for 21 years, during which time he did not use the easement. When Daniel finally returned to the state, he discovered that the easement was still valid and enforceable.

2. IMPLICATION OF LAW (IMPLIED EASEMENT). If an easement is implied in a transfer, or if it is necessary for use of the land, then the easement is said to be implied by law. The right to use the land for obtaining minerals implies that you have the right of surface entry in order to extract the minerals.

EASEMENT BY NECESSITY (LANDLOCKED) is an easement granted by the court if it is absolutely necessary for access. If a person is sold property that landlocks that person, he or she may acquire an easement by necessity. When the grantor transfers a portion of his or her land that leaves the grantee totally surrounded by the grantor (transferor), the grantor can be forced to give an easement of access to the grantee. An easement by necessity does not have to be the most convenient way of entering the property. If the grantee later acquires another access to his or her property, the easement by necessity is then terminated.

3. LONG USE (EASEMENT BY PRESCRIPTION). *PRESCRIPTION is an easement to continue using land by virtue of having used it for a long period of time.*

Possession for five continuous years can create a prescriptive easement, as long as the use is:

1. Open and notorious;
2. Uninterrupted for five years;
3. Under a claim of right or color of title, and
4. Hostile (without permission of the owner).

An easement obtained by prescription can be terminated if not used for five years.

d. Transfer of an Easement

Easements are transferred automatically if they are easements appurtenant. Easements in gross can be transferred only by express agreement, providing the easement is not made to a specific individual. An easement should be recorded. If it is not recorded, and the purchaser does not have knowledge of an easement, then the easement may not be considered to have been transferred with the property.

e. Termination of an Easement

Easements may be terminated in several ways:

1. EXPRESS RELEASE – Any written agreement can terminate an easement, but the usual form is a quitclaim deed or release.

Only the owner of the dominant tenement can release (terminate) an easement, usually by recording a quitclaim deed.

2. MERGER OF DOMINANT AND SERVIENT TENEMENTS – An easement is automatically terminated when the dominant and servient tenements merge into a common, or single, ownership. The easement can be created again if any part of the property is later transferred to a "separate owner."

3. EXCESSIVE USE – The courts have held that excessive use of an easement that increases the burden on the servient tenement may be forfeited through a court injunction. If the dominant tenement refuses to correct the excessive use, and misuses of the easement can be established, the easement can be terminated. An example would be a dominant tenement owner allowing the entire neighborhood to use the easement as a through-street.

4. ABANDONMENT AND NON-USE – If there is an obvious intent of an easement holder to abandon his or her easement, then that person may lose the easement through court action. In this way, an easement gained through prescription may be extinguished if non-use exists for a period of five continuous years.

Non-use can only terminate an easement created by prescription.

5. DESTRUCTION OF SERVIENT TENEMENT – When a governing body, by exercising the right of eminent domain, takes servient tenement property for its own use, the dominant tenement easement is considered automatically terminated.

2. Building Restrictions (Public and Private)

PRIVATE DEED RESTRICTIONS limit the use or occupancy of the land. A typical restriction limits the types of buildings on a given piece of land to single family residences. Also, a restriction might require future construction to meet specific standards. For example, all houses erected on a property must be at least 5,000 square feet.

There are three types of private building restrictions: Covenants, Conditions, and Restrictions (CC&Rs). They are usually included in the deed at the time the property is subdivided, or may be created by a written contract and are listed in the recorded "Declaration of Restrictions." Their main purpose is to keep use of the land uniform throughout certain tracts of land. Subdivisions and condominiums usually include deed restrictions as a method to promote the aesthetics and economics of the project. These private deed restrictions and bylaws are usually recorded separately, and are only referenced in the original grant deeds.

Private restrictions on the use of land may be created by private land use controls, written agreement, or a developer's general plan restrictions for a subdivision.

a. Covenants (Promise Broken, Sue for Damages)

A *COVENANT is a promise to do or not to do a certain thing.* For instance, a property could sell with a covenant stating that the property shall never be used to sell alcoholic beverages. If the covenant is broken, the usual court remedy would be an action for money damages. A court may also grant an injunction requiring compliance with the covenant.

Only SOME covenants "run with the land," but ALL conditions "run with the land."

b. Conditions (More Stringent Than Breaking a Covenant – Can Lose Title)

A *CONDITION is a future and uncertain event which must happen to create an obligation to extinguish an existing obligation.* **The penalty for not following the set conditions is the reversion of the property to the grantor.** This penalty is so stiff that most courts will treat a condition as a covenant unless the terms are clearly stated in the deed or other contract. For a complete discussion of conditions, refer back to Chapter 2.

A condominium's CC&Rs may prohibit "for sale" signs, but an owner may place a reasonably sized "for sale" sign on the property.

If a condominium owner breaches a "condition" in the CC&Rs, this would be more stringent than breaching a covenant.

With regard to CC&Rs, violating a condition can result in loss of title to property, which is more stringent than breaching a covenant.

c. Public/Governmental Restrictions (Zoning)

PUBLIC RESTRICTIONS are limits made by governmental agencies, usually by cities and counties, in the form of zoning.

"Public restrictions" promote health, safety, morals, and general welfare of the public. This is the use of "police power."

Private restrictions are made by the present or previous landowners and are created only for their benefit. On the other hand, **zoning restrictions** are created by and for the benefit of the general public to insure its health, safety, comfort, and morals.

ZONING is the restriction on the use of private property by the local government agency. Zoning dictates how the property can be used, the **setbacks required,** and the height limit on any structures.

CHAPTER 3

If public restrictions (zoning) and private restrictions (CC&Rs) differ, the more stringent or rigid will apply.

> For example, if a developer sets a deed restriction of **at least** 15,000 square feet to a lot, but zoning only allows 10,000 square feet per lot, the deed restriction is more restrictive and would prevail. This area is covered in depth in Chapter 12 under "Government Control."

d. Race Restrictions (Illegal)

> In 1961, the California State Legislature enacted a law that voided all restrictions as to race. Any race deed restriction before that law or after that law is now void. It is illegal to restrict the right of an individual to sell, rent, lease, use or otherwise occupy a property because of race or membership in a certain ethnic group.

Race restrictions on a property by a grantor (past or present) are unenforceable and illegal. The courts can remove race restrictions from a deed.

3. Encroachments (Three Years to Act)

> As stated earlier, an **ENCROACHMENT** *is the wrongful, unauthorized placement of improvements or permanent fixtures on property by a nonowner of that property.* You must pursue the right to have an encroachment removed within three years or lose your right. If someone encroaches on your property, he or she is limiting the use of your property.

> **Example:** If your neighbor builds a driveway over your property, it is considered an encroachment, which is a form of "trespass." You have three years to sue your neighbor to have the encroachment removed.

> Often fences, walls, or buildings may extend over the recognized boundary line. The encroaching party may possibly gain legal title to the property through adverse possession, or legal use through an easement by prescription, if there is legal justification. In any event, an encroachment may legally limit the use of your property.

IV. Homesteading Your Residence (Protects Against Judgment Liens)

A lease is an encumbrance and a homestead is NOT considered an encumbrance.

Although a homestead **is not an encumbrance**, it is appropriately discussed at this point. A **HOMESTEAD** *is a special provision of the California law that allows homeowners to protect their homes from forced sale to satisfy their debts, within certain limits.* There are two types of homesteads: (1) Head of the household and (2) Federal Homestead Act of 1862, whereby the government encouraged settlements (gave land free to those who made certain improvements—this is not discussed here). It is basic to our society that a homeowner should have some protection against losing his or her home because of debts. A homestead consists of the house and adjoining dwellings in which the owner resides. This can include condominiums, farm and life estates.

A homestead cannot include "unimproved" land such as vacant lots or a residence under construction.

A. DECLARATION OF HOMESTEAD

The first $75,000 of a home's value may NOT be used to satisfy a judgment against a head of household.

A **DECLARATION OF HOMESTEAD** *is the recorded document that protects a homeowner from foreclosure by certain judgment creditors* (see **Figure 3-5**). This protects you for $75,000 if you are the head of a family. Persons who are mentally or physically disabled, over the age of 65, or 55 or older with a specific low income, are entitled to protection for up to $150,000. Any resident who does not qualify under one of these conditions has a homestead valued at $50,000. If the equity exceeds the exemption, the home may be sold to satisfy creditors, but the exemption amount is protected for six months for reinvestment in another home.

A homestead does NOT protect a homeowner against foreclosure on a trust deed, mechanic's lien, or lien filed prior to the filing of the homestead.

In order for a declaration of homestead to be valid, there are certain requirements that must be met. Omissions of any one of these will make the homestead void. The requirements are:

1. A statement showing the claimant is the head of a family and stating the name of the spouse. "Head of family" may be anyone who lives in the home and provides for any relative living in the same house.

2. A statement that the claimant is residing on the premises and claims it as his or her homestead.

3. A description of the premises and an estimate of cash value.

4. It further provides that the declaration of homestead may need to contain a statement as to the character of the property; that no former declaration has been made and that it is within the limits prescribed by law.

The homeowner has time to file a declaration of homestead prior to court approval for a writ of execution. As part of the judicial process, the defendant must be informed of his or her right to file a declaration of homestead. This law, in effect, reduces the necessity of filing a homestead declaration until the homeowner is in financial trouble.

A recorded homestead would have the least impact on property taxes.

B. TERMINATION OF HOMESTEAD

The usual methods for termination of homestead are the sale of the property or the filing of a declaration of abandonment.

A homestead may be terminated by a **DECLARATION OF ABANDONMENT**. The declaration of abandonment must be acknowledged and recorded by the involved parties. A sale or other conveyance of the property also terminates the homestead. The removal or destruction of the dwelling does not terminate the homestead. The reason for abandoning

Figure 3-5

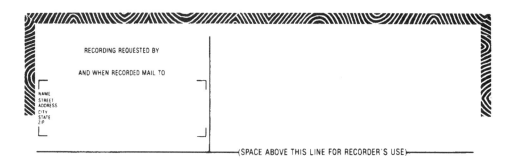

HOMESTEAD DECLARATION

◄ ►

I, _____
(Full Name of Declarant)

do hereby certify and declare as follows

(1) I hereby claim as a declared homestead the premises located in the City of _____.

County of _____. State of _____ commonly known as

_____
Street Address

and more particularly described as follows [Give complete legal description]

(2) I am the declared homestead owner of the above declared homestead

(3) I own the following interest in the above declared homestead:

(4) The above declared homestead is [strike inapplicable clause] my principal dwelling, the principal dwelling of my spouse, and
[strike inapplicable clause] I am my spouse is currently residing on that declared homestead.

(5) The facts stated in this Declaration are true as of my personal knowledge

Dated: _____, 19____ _____
(Signature of Declarant)

STATE OF _____ }
COUNTY OF _____ } ss.

On _____ before me, _____
(Name, title of officer, i.e. "Jane Doe, Notary Public")

_____

personally appeared _____

personally known to me (or proved to me on the basis of satisfactory evidence) to
be the person(s) whose name(s) is/are subscribed to the within instrument and
acknowledged to me that he/she/they executed the same in his/her/their authorized capacity(ies), and that by his/her/their signature(s) on the instrument the
person(s), or the entity upon behalf of which the person(s) acted, executed the
instrument.

WITNESS my hand and official seal.

_____
Signature

(Seal)

WOLCOTTS FORM 756—HOMESTEAD DECLARATION — Rev 1-93
(price class 3)

© 1993 WOLCOTTS FORMS, INC.

This standard form is intended for the typical situations encountered in the field indicated. However, before you sign, read it, fill in all blanks, and make
whatever changes are appropriate and necessary to your particular transaction. Consult a lawyer if you doubt the form's fitness for your purpose and use.

a homestead is to allow the homeowner the privilege of obtaining another homestead on a new residence.

A homestead is terminated by 1) Declaration of Abandonment or 2) the sale of the homesteaded property.

While the typical homeowner need not file a declared homestead to enjoy basic homestead protection, homeowners who are in financial trouble, or who expect to be in financial trouble, probably should file a homestead declaration, just to be on the safe side.

V. CHAPTER SUMMARY

An **encumbrance** is a burden to a property that limits its use by either 1) money owed (liens) or 2) items that affect the physical use of the property (non-money). All liens are "encumbrances," but not all encumbrances are liens. A **blanket encumbrance** is a voluntary lien placed over more than one property, and usually has a **release clause** for one or more of the parcels.

A **lien** is a document that uses a property to secure the payment of a debt or the discharge of an obligation. Liens are either 1) **voluntary** or 2) **involuntary**, and 3) **specific** or 4) **general**.

Trust deeds and **mortgages** (mortgages are rare in California) are security devices that make property security for a debt and are considered personal property. The accompanying **promissory note** is the evidence of the debt.

If the people who supply labor or materials for construction on a property are not paid, they can file a **mechanic's lien** against that individual property. It is a **specific and involuntary lien** and, once recorded, has priority over all other liens except taxes, special assessments, and trust deeds filed prior to the "start of work." Before filing a mechanic's lien, **Preliminary Notice** must be given (within 20 days of supplying labor or services).

It is important to establish the starting time and completion date of the work or materials supplied. A **Notice of Completion** should be recorded by the owner within ten days of completion, or a **Notice of Cessation** within 30 days of cessation of labor.

If a person is unauthorized to do construction on a property, an owner needs to file and post a **Notice of Non-Responsibility** on the property, releasing him or her from liability and preventing suppliers from filing a valid mechanic's lien.

Property taxes and mechanic's liens are **specific liens**, meaning liens against just one property, whereas income taxes and judgments are **general liens**, covering all the properties of an owner. A **judgment** is a **general and involuntary lien** against all real property in the county in which the judgment is recorded, and is good for ten years. A **satisfaction of judgment** is made by payment of money or return of property and clears the lien from the record.

CHAPTER 3

An **attachment (lien)**, which is good for three years, creates a **specific and involuntary lien** on one property to assure payment of a pending lawsuit. A **lis pendens** is a notice of a pending lawsuit that affects (**clouds**) title and remains on the public record until the lis pendens is removed, the action is dismissed, or final judgment is rendered. If a person does not pay off a judgment, he or she may be forced to sell the property in a **sheriff's sale** under a court order called a **Writ of Execution**.

Items that affect **physical use** of a property are **non-money encumbrances** and include: 1) **easements**, 2) **restrictions**, 3) **encroachments**, and 4) **leases**.

An **easement** is the right to enter, use and exit another person's land for certain purpose. If it runs with the land it is an **easement appurtenant**. The **dominant tenement** is the land that benefits from the easement that the **servient tenement** gives up. An **easement in gross** benefits others who do not own adjoining or attached lands (like a utility company running a gas line across a property).

Easements can be created by 1) **deed** (writing), 2) **implication of law** (implied easement or easement by necessity), or 3) **prescription** (long use). They can also be terminated in several ways, including: 1) **express release**, 2) **merger** of dominant and servient tenements, 3) **excessive use**, 4) **abandonment and non-use**, and 5) **destruction of servient tenement**.

Restrictions can be private deed restrictions, or public restrictions. **Covenants, conditions, and restrictions (CC&Rs)** are private building restrictions. **Public restrictions** are limits made by governmental agencies and are meant to promote health, safety, morals, and general welfare of the public (**police power**). **Zoning** is a public restriction dictating how property can be used, including setback requirements. An **encroachment** is the wrongful, unauthorized placement of improvements or permanent fixtures on a property by a non-owner, which must be removed by the owner within three years.

A **homestead** is not an encumbrance, but a special provision of California law that allows homeowners to protect their homes from forced sale to satisfy their debts. A homestead is terminated by: 1) **declaration of abandonment**, or 2) **the sale of the homesteaded property**.

VI. TERMINOLOGY

A. Abstract of Judgment
B. Attachment
C. Blanket Encumbrance
D. Conditions
E. Covenant
F. Declaration of Abandonment
G. Declaration of Homestead
H. Defendant
I. Dominant Tenement
J. Easement

K. Easement Appurtenant
L. Easement in Gross
M. Encroachment
N. Encumbrance
O. General Lien
P. Homestead
Q. Lien
R. Lis Pendens
S. Mechanic's Lien
T. Mortgage

U. Notice of Non-Responsibility
V. Plaintiff
W. Preliminary Notice
X. Restrictions
Y. Satisfaction
Z. Servient Tenement
AA. Sheriff's Sale
BB. Specific Lien
CC. Trust Deed
DD. Writ of Execution

1.____ A right, limited to a specific use, that one party has in the land of another.
2.____ A statutory protection of a home from the claims of certain creditors and judgments up to a specified amount.
3.____ Anything that affects or limits the fee simple title to, or value of, property, e.g., mortgages or easements.
4.____ A notice, recorded and posted by the property owner to relieve them of responsibility for the cost of unauthorized work done on his or her property or materials furnished.
5.____ A limitation on the use of real property. These limitations fall into two general classifications: public and private. Zoning ordinances are public, while a clause in the deed requiring the roof to be made of Spanish red title would be a private limitation.
6.____ The process by which real or personal property is seized by the court for the purpose of assuring payment.
7.____ A form of encumbrance that usually makes specific property security for the payment of a debt.
8.____ Discharge of a mortgage or trust deed from the records upon payment of the debt. Make sure you receive a Deed of Reconveyance to prove that you paid off the deed of trust.
9.____ A limiting restriction stating that upon the happening or not happening of some stated event, the estate shall be changed in some manner.
10.____ A promise to do or not to do a particular thing.
11.____ A person against whom a civil or criminal action is taken.
12.____ An instrument, recognized by law, by which property is hypothecated to secure the payment of a debt. This instrument is not commonly used in California, but is popular on the east coast.
13.____ In a court action, the one who sues; the complainant.
14.____ A recorded document of the essential provisions of a court judgment.
15.____ A lien, created by statute, which exists against real or personal property in favor of persons who have performed work or furnished materials for the improvement of real property.
16.____ A legal document by which a borrower pledges certain real property as collateral for the repayment of a loan. In addition to the buyer and seller, there is a third party to the transaction known as a trustee.
17.____ A formal statement that protects the head of the household from losing the property to the claims of creditors, usually up to a set maximum amount.
18.____ A lien, usually a trust deed in California, covering more than one property of the borrower.
19.____ A notice that informs or warns owners, lenders and general contractors that subcontractors have been hired, or materials have been supplied to a particular job site.
20.____ A statement declaring the intent to give up a homestead, usually to declare a homestead on a new residence.

21.____A court ordered sale of real or personal property by the sheriff pursuant to the execution of a judgment.

22.____The construction of improvements on the property of another.

23.____An easement for the benefit of the owner of an adjacent parcel of land.

24.____Real property that benefits from an easement.

25.____A writ to carry out a court order, usually arising from a judgment.

26.____A property that is burdened by an easement.

27.____An easement for the benefit of a person or utility company rather than for the benefit of adjacent landowners.

28.____A notice filed or recorded for the purpose of warning all persons that the title to certain real property is in litigation.

29.____A lien such as a tax lien or judgment lien that attaches to all property of the debtor rather than a specific property.

30.____A lien that attaches to a specific property rather than all the property of the debtor.

VII. CHAPTER QUIZ

1. When a project of improvement on real property has been completed and the owner has not filed a "notice of completion," how many days do claimants have to file mechanic's liens?

  a. 30 days
  b. 60 days
  c. 90 days
  d. Unlimited

2. The difference between property taxes and special assessments is that:

  a. assessment liens are always subordinate to property tax liens.
  b. assessment liens can only be levied by local improvement districts.
  c. foreclosure of assessment liens can only be achieved by court foreclosure.
  d. special assessments are levied for the cost of specific local improvements, while property tax revenue goes into the general fund.

3. A lis pendens:

  a. may affect title to the property, based upon the results of the lawsuit.
  b. allows real property to be reassessed when it is sold.
  c. means "and wife."
  d. none of the above.

4. Which of the following is a court order restricting a party from doing an act such as violating private deed restrictions?

  a. Writ of execution
  b. Writ of possession
  c. Injunction
  d. Quiet title action

5. Which of the following will terminate an easement?

a. Dominant tenant records a quitclaim deed
b. Servient tenant records a grant deed
c. The owner of the servient tenement records a grant deed
d. The owner of the dominant tenement records a quitclaim deed

6. Landowner Jacobs granted the telephone company the right to erect telephone poles on his land. Which of the following best describes this situation?

a. An encroachment
b. An encumbrance
c. An appurtenance
d. Accession

7. Daniel, who owned two pieces of adjacent land, sold one of them to Charles reserving an easement for himself at the time. Daniel soon left the state for 21 years during which time he did not use the easement. When Daniel finally returned to the state he discovered that:

a. the easement was terminated after 5 years of non-use.
b. the easement was still valid and enforceable.
c. the owner of the servient tenement had died leaving Daniel with no easement rights at all.
d. easements cannot be created by "reservation."

8. A condominium's CC&Rs prohibit "for sale" signs. The owner may:

a. sue the condo assocation.
b. place a reasonably sized "for sale" sign on the property.
c. not place a "for sale" sign on the property.
d. none of the above.

9. If a condominium owner breaches a "condition" in the CC&Rs this would be:

a. enforced by the local building department.
b. the same as violating a health code regulation.
c. more stringent than breaching a covenant.
d. the same as breaching a public restriction.

10. Which of the following would have the least impact on property taxes?

a. Selling price
b. Market value
c. A recorded homestead
d. Tax deferment

ANSWERS: 1. c; 2. d; 3. a; 4. c; 5. d; 6. b; 7. b; 8. b; 9. c; 10. c

CHAPTER 4
Agency and Its Responsibility

www.dre.ca.gov
California Department of Real Estate
www.car.org
California Association of Realtors
www.inman.com/index.asp
Inman News Features

I. Agency – An Overview

A. AGENT, PRINCIPAL, AND THIRD PARTY

The seller gives the right to sell and the broker agrees to use diligence in obtaining a purchaser. This is called "agency."

1. Agent

AGENCY is the authority (or power) to act in place of another, a principal (person who hires), to do a specified act for a stated period of time. An AGENT is one who acts for and with authority from another, called the principal.

Agents (brokers) usually select and control their own professional approach to selling a property. Sellers are responsible for their representations to the buyer. While brokers share this responsibility, they also have a responsibility for their individual representations. Agency is a fiduciary relationship based on trust. The agent representing the seller must disclose all pertinent facts to the seller and must not take advantage of, or gain from, this relationship in an unethical manner.

A "dual agent" is a broker acting as an agent for both the seller and the buyer in the same transaction, with the informed consent of both parties.

2. Principal

A *PRINCIPAL (CLIENT) is a person who hires or employs an agent to work for him or her.* If the principal is a buyer, the agent represents the buyer. On the other hand, if the principal is a seller, the agent represents the seller.

CHAPTER OUTLINE

3. Third Party

A **THIRD PARTY** *is the other person in a contractual negotiation, other than the principal and his or her agent.* If an agent works for the seller, the third party is the buyer. But if the agent works for the buyer, the third party is the seller. In effect, the agent is the second party to the transaction.

In the agency relationship, the broker and other salespeople are required to make certain disclosures about the property they are selling. They are expected to do what is necessary, proper, and usual to sell the real estate being offered. They must also make truthful representations to the buyer as to the condition of the property that may materially affect the value or desirability of the property and the terms of the sale. This is spelled out in the Disclosure Regarding Real Estate Agency Relationships Form (discussed later).

The broker, as agent of the seller, owes the buyer the duty of honest and fair dealing.

OSTENSIBLE *or* **IMPLIED AUTHORITY** *is the authority that a third person reasonably believes an agent possesses because of the acts or omissions of the principal.* This authority is conferred when a principal gives a third party reason to believe that another person is his or her agent. If the third party accepts this as true, the principal may well be bound by the acts of that person.

Example: As an owner, if you tell a prospective buyer to see Agent Ramos about seeing your property even though the listing has expired and Ramos sells the house, the buyer has every reason to believe that Miss Ramos had the authority as your agent to sell the home.

CHAPTER 4

AGENT, BROKER, SALESPERSON, ASSOCIATE
Who Holds a Real Estate License?

REAL ESTATE AGENT

A **REAL ESTATE AGENT** is a person licensed by the Department of Real Estate (DRE) who holds either a broker's or salesperson's license and negotiates sales for other people.

REAL ESTATE BROKER AND SALESPERSON

A **REAL ESTATE BROKER** is a broker's license holder (boss/owner) and therefore permitted by law to employ those individuals holding a salesperson's license (or another broker). A **REAL ESTATE SALESPERSON** is an individual holding a salesperson's license who must be employed by a real estate broker to perform any of the activities of a real estate broker.

REAL ESTATE ASSOCIATE

A **REAL ESTATE ASSOCIATE** or **ASSOCIATE LICENSEE** is another name for a real estate salesperson. An associate works for a broker as either an employee or an independent contractor.

An agent or licensee is either a broker or a salesperson who works for a broker.

DEPARTMENT OF REAL ESTATE (DRE)
Checking the Status of a Real Estate Salesperson or Broker

To check the status of a real estate salesperson or broker, access the following Department of Real Estate Internet address:

www.dre.ca.gov/licstats.htm
Department of Real Estate - Licensee Status Inquiries

Click on LICENSE RECORDS ON-LINE and enter the name or license number, and the DRE will do the rest.

An agency relationship may also come about by estoppel or ratification, although it is **not** advisable. *ESTOPPEL prohibits the principal from denying that a person is his or her agent if the principal has misled another to his prejudice into believing that person is the agent.* In the above example, you, the owner, would be "estopped" from denying that Miss Ramos was your agent, based on your past actions or words. *RATIFICATION is approval (confirmation) of a transaction which has already taken place.* For example, when you authorize a broker to have acted for you after he or she has already done so, the action is called ratification.

The best way to establish an agency relationship is through written agreement.

In California, most real estate transactions involve the use of a broker and his or her salespeople. To run a real estate office, a broker's license is required, and a licensed salesperson can only work for a licensed real estate broker (one broker at a time). In California, any person in real estate who is acting in return for compensation from others must have a Department of Real Estate license to:

1. Sell or offer to sell.
2. Buy or offer to buy.
3. Solicit prospective buyers or sellers.
4. Negotiate the purchase, sale, loan, or exchange of business opportunities or real estate.
5. Negotiate leases and collect rents.

Real estate license requirements are explained fully in Chapter 14.

B. LAW OF AGENCY

The Law of Agency is found in the Civil Code.

Real estate brokers are agents because they represent an interest other than their own (buyer's or seller's). A written agency contract (listing) exists, for which they may receive compensation if there is a sale. Whenever one person represents another in a business transaction, the "Law of Agency" applies.

An agency relationship requires the parties to be fiduciary and competent. It does NOT require "consideration."

Because the real estate broker is an agent, the California Civil Code, governing the Law of Agency, defines his or her duties and responsibilities. Further, since the broker is a licensed real estate agent, he or she must comply with the rules and regulations of the California Real Estate Commissioner, which are enforced by the Commissioner. Both codes and regulations can be enforced against all brokers and their salespeople. Throughout this chapter, when we speak of a broker we are also referring to any salesperson (or broker) who may be working for that company broker.

C. RESPONSIBILITIES OF AGENCY

In the California Civil Code, the law of agency boils down to three basic rules applying to licensed brokers and licensed salespeople:

1. The agent must inform the principal of all material facts pertaining to the handling of the principal's property. The agent must put client's interest above interest of self or others.

2. The agent may not gain any monetary interest in the property without the principal's prior consent.

3. An agent may not use the principal's property to his or her own advantage.

1. Fiduciary Relationship

A *FIDUCIARY is a person acting in a position of trust and confidence in a business relationship. A FIDUCIARY RELATIONSHIP requires the highest good faith from the agent to his or her principal.* An agent must act as though he or she is the principal and always seek to represent the principal's best interest. In this case, the agent takes on the responsibility of diligently finding a buyer or seller (see **Figure 4-1**).

Figure 4-1

BROKER'S DUTIES, RIGHTS, AND RESPONSIBILITIES	
FIDUCIARY RELATIONSHIP	**TRUTHFUL RELATIONSHIP**
PRINCIPAL	**THIRD PARTIES**
1. Honesty – Disclose Material Facts 2. Utmost Care 3. Integrity – Accounting for Actions 4. Loyalty 5. Obey – Lawful Instructions 6. No Secret Profits	1. Honesty – Disclose Material Facts 2. Reasonable Skill and Care 3. Fair Dealing 4. Good Faith

The broker (agent) works for the principal and forms a fiduciary relationship with him or her. The broker also must maintain an honest and truthful relationship with the third party (including full disclosure of material facts affecting value or desirability).

If the seller's agent informs the buyer that the seller will take less than the list price, the agent violates the fiduciary duty of loyalty to the seller.

An agent must exercise honesty, reasonable skill and care, fair dealing and good faith in dealing with a third party. An agent of the principal must disclose to the third party any facts known to the agent that could materially affect the value or desirability of the property.

> ## TOP AGENTS HIRE TOP ASSISTANTS
>
> It is estimated that 80 percent of the real estate business is handled by 10 percent of the agents. To handle the workload, more top agents are hiring personal assistants to take over the day-to-day brokerage chores, leaving the agents free to concentrate on sales. **PERSONAL ASSISTANTS** *handle such things as clerical tasks, paperwork, marketing, tickler files, and conduct computer research.* More and more real estate licensees are working as assistants.
>
> The growth in personal assistants is not without criticism. Among the complaints are that using assistants entrusts too many high-level tasks to unskilled employees and makes the agents inaccessible. It is important that the broker establish who is employing the assistants, and that unlicensed assistants do not act as agents. There is a wealth of educational materials available to improve the quality of real estate assistants.

D. LISTING AND SELLING AGENTS

When a salesperson obtains a listing agreement to sell a particular property, he or she is referred to as the "listing salesperson." That salesperson's broker is referred to as the "listing broker." A salesperson employed by a listing broker is an agent of the owner/seller. If a different brokerage company negotiates the sale, that agency is the "selling broker" and "selling salesperson." A broker or salesperson who both lists and sells the same property is referred to as the "listing and selling broker or salesperson."

II. Real Estate Agency Relationship Disclosure

The Real Estate Agency Relationship Disclosure Act (Civil Code) became law in 1988.

A. AGENCY DISCLOSURE LAW

According to the Disclosure Regarding Real Estate Agency Relationships form, the first thing the agent must do is establish if he or she is an agent for the seller, buyer, or both.

The three steps of agency disclosure are: disclose, elect, and confirm.

The Disclosure Regarding Real Estate Agency Relationships form states that both the listing broker and the selling broker must declare in writing, as soon as possible, whom they represent:

1. The seller/owner (seller's agency)
2. The buyer (buyer's agency) or
3. Both the seller and buyer (dual agency).

The only requirement is that the listing broker must at least represent the seller (owner). **This law applies to all sales of residential property of from one-to-four units.**

A real estate agency disclosure form must be given to all parties when the transaction involves the sale of a residential triplex.

> **WE LOVE BUYERS**
>
> ## THE GROWTH OF "BUYER BROKERAGES"
>
> A large number of brokers are responding to a need that a buyer be represented diligently by offering exclusive buyer's services. More than a fad, it is estimated that buyer's agents will represent 25% or more of the industry within the next ten years.
>
> It is believed that good buyer representation will cut down on disputes and lawsuits. In the future, the trend will be toward brokers working for either the seller or buyer, not just the seller. No longer do brokers have to exclude themselves from one entire side of the market.
>
> *In a "buyer's agency," the agent represents the buyer only.*

Figure 4-2 shows a Disclosure Regarding Real Estate Agency Relationships form used by the California Association of REALTORS® (CAR). Civil law requires that both parties to a transaction be informed of the various options they have regarding agency representation. Both the buyer and the seller must sign the lower part of this form as an acknowledgment that they understand their rights and have received a copy of this disclosure. In addition, agency disclosure must again be confirmed on the Residential Purchase Agreement (see Chapter 5). If it is not confirmed on the Residential Purchase Agreement, then it must be confirmed on a separate form. This confirmation will protect the licensee against any future charges of misrepresentation in the agency relationship. It should be completed as soon as possible.

The seller's agent cannot keep silent about any material facts that affect the value of the property (for example, the property is in an earthquake zone or backs up to a freeway or school).

But, the seller's agent cannot tell the buyer that the seller is insolvent because this would lower the offering price, violating the duty of loyalty in a fiduciary relationship.

Traditionally, the principal was usually a seller. Brokers are now free to represent the buyer, the seller, and sometimes both. **Figure 4-3** illustrates the agency options.

"Dual agency" occurs when a broker represents both the buyer and the seller in a real estate transaction.

Example: A broker holds a purchase-option on land owned by Nelson. When exercising the option to purchase, the broker must disclose to Seller Nelson that the broker is the principal.

As you can see from Figure 4-3, there may be several brokers involved in a single transaction. In California, the seller (owner) and the buyer are usually represented by different brokers. The listing broker always represents the seller but may represent both. Traditionally, the selling broker, who procures the buyer, customarily represents the buyer. In some other states, all the brokers and salespeople represent only the seller (owner).

If an agent does not disclose dual agency to both parties, he or she may be disciplined, not receive a commission, and it may be grounds for either party to rescind the contract.

Figure 4-2

CALIFORNIA
ASSOCIATION
OF REALTORS®

DISCLOSURE REGARDING
REAL ESTATE AGENCY RELATIONSHIPS
(As required by the Civil Code)
(C.A.R. Form AD, Revised 10/04)

When you enter into a discussion with a real estate agent regarding a real estate transaction, you should from the outset understand what type of agency relationship or representation you wish to have with the agent in the transaction.

SELLER'S AGENT

A Seller's agent under a listing agreement with the Seller acts as the agent for the Seller only. A Seller's agent or a subagent of that agent has the following affirmative obligations:

To the Seller:
A Fiduciary duty of utmost care, integrity, honesty, and loyalty in dealings with the Seller.

To the Buyer and the Seller:
(a) Diligent exercise of reasonable skill and care in performance of the agent's duties.
(b) A duty of honest and fair dealing and good faith.
(c) A duty to disclose all facts known to the agent materially affecting the value or desirability of the property that are not known to, or within the diligent attention and observation of, the parties.

An agent is not obligated to reveal to either party any confidential information obtained from the other party that does not involve the affirmative duties set forth above.

BUYER'S AGENT

A selling agent can, with a Buyer's consent, agree to act as agent for the Buyer only. In these situations, the agent is not the Seller's agent, even if by agreement the agent may receive compensation for services rendered, either in full or in part from the Seller. An agent acting only for a Buyer has the following affirmative obligations:

To the Buyer:
A fiduciary duty of utmost care, integrity, honesty, and loyalty in dealings with the Buyer.

To the Buyer and the Seller:
(a) Diligent exercise of reasonable skill and care in performance of the agent's duties.
(b) A duty of honest and fair dealing and good faith.
(c) A duty to disclose all facts known to the agent materially affecting the value or desirability of the property that are not known to, or within the diligent attention and observation of, the parties.

An agent is not obligated to reveal to either party any confidential information obtained from the other party that does not involve the affirmative duties set forth above.

AGENT REPRESENTING BOTH SELLER AND BUYER

A real estate agent, either acting directly or through one or more associate licensees, can legally be the agent of both the Seller and the Buyer in a transaction, but only with the knowledge and consent of both the Seller and the Buyer.

In a dual agency situation, the agent has the following affirmative obligations to both the Seller and the Buyer:
(a) A fiduciary duty of utmost care, integrity, honesty and loyalty in the dealings with either the Seller or the Buyer.
(b) Other duties to the Seller and the Buyer as stated above in their respective sections.

In representing both Seller and Buyer, the agent may not, without the express permission of the respective party, disclose to the other party that the Seller will accept a price less than the listing price or that the Buyer will pay a price greater than the price offered.

The above duties of the agent in a real estate transaction do not relieve a Seller or Buyer from the responsibility to protect his or her own interests. You should carefully read all agreements to assure that they adequately express your understanding of the transaction. A real estate agent is a person qualified to advise about real estate. If legal or tax advice is desired, consult a competent professional.

Throughout your real property transaction you may receive more than one disclosure form, depending upon the number of agents assisting in the transaction. The law requires each agent with whom you have more than a casual relationship to present you with this disclosure form. You should read its contents each time it is presented to you, considering the relationship between you and the real estate agent in your specific transaction.

This disclosure form includes the provisions of Sections 2079.13 to 2079.24, inclusive, of the Civil Code set forth on the reverse hereof. Read it carefully.

I/WE ACKNOWLEDGE RECEIPT OF A COPY OF THIS DISCLOSURE AND THE PORTIONS OF THE CIVIL CODE PRINTED ON THE BACK (OR A SEPARATE PAGE).

BUYER/SELLER _____ Date _____ Time _____ AM/PM

BUYER/SELLER _____ Date _____ Time _____ AM/PM

AGENT _____ By _____ Date _____
(Please Print)   (Associate-Licensee or Broker Signature)

THIS FORM SHALL BE PROVIDED AND ACKNOWLEDGED AS FOLLOWS (Civil Code § 2079.14):
- When the listing brokerage company also represents Buyer, the Listing Agent shall have one AD form signed by Seller and one signed by Buyer.
- When Buyer and Seller are represented by different brokerage companies, the Listing Agent shall have one AD form signed by Seller and the Buyer's Agent shall have one AD form signed by Buyer and one AD form signed by Seller.

The System for Success®

Published and Distributed by:
REAL ESTATE BUSINESS SERVICES, INC.
a subsidiary of the California Association of REALTORS®
525 South Virgil Avenue, Los Angeles, California 90020

Reviewed by _____ Date _____

EQUAL HOUSING
OPPORTUNITY

AD REVISED 10/04 (PAGE 1 OF 1)   PRINT DATE

DISCLOSURE REGARDING REAL ESTATE AGENCY RELATIONSHIPS (AD PAGE 1 OF 1)

CHAPTER 4

Figure 4-3

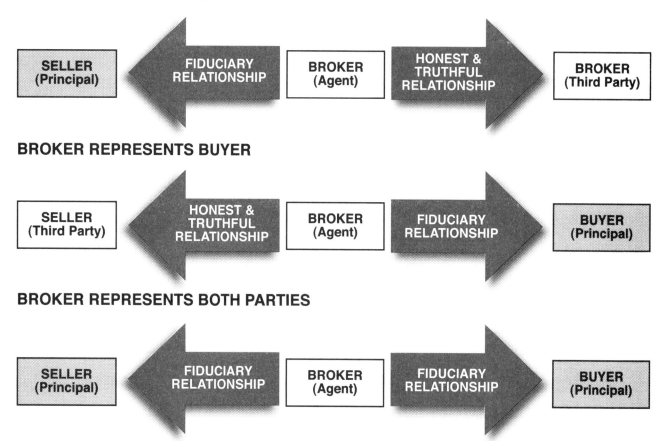

III. Listings and the Multiple Listing Service (MLS)

A. LISTING AGREEMENTS

The usual way to establish a broker's right to negotiate a sale of property is through a written contract, commonly called a listing. A *LISTING is a contract to employ a broker, legally referred to as an agent, to do certain things for the owner/seller. It is an employment contract for personal service.*

Listings are NOT assignable and death of the seller or broker cancels a listing, unless the seller is a corporation (which may live forever). There are six basic types of listings used in California. They are:

1. Open Listing (non-exclusive)
2. Exclusive Agency Listing
3. Exclusive Right to Sell Listing
4. Net Listing (rare)
5. Option Listing
6. Oral Listing (not discussed here)

80

The usual listing contract authorizes a broker to find a purchaser and accept a deposit with an offer to purchase.

You should also know: all real estate listing agreements or contracts should be in writing, and must be in writing to assure collection of a commission.

All listings are the property of the broker who employs him/her as a salesperson.

1. Open Listing (Unilateral, Non-Exclusive Contract)

An *OPEN LISTING is an authorization to sell a property. It may be given to several brokers or the property may be sold by the owner.* Only the agent who is the procuring cause earns the commission. If the owner sells the property, he or she is not required to pay a commission. Usually, no time limit is placed on an open listing. A description of the property is included in the agreement along with the selling price and other terms.

Open listings are the simplest form of broker authorization. They can be given to several brokers concurrently, and no notice of sale is required to terminate the listing. A broker should make sure an open listing is still valid before pursuing it. When an open listing is given to more than one broker, the first broker who finds a qualified buyer is entitled to the commission. On the other hand, if an owner finds his or her own buyer, that owner has no obligation to pay a commission to a broker.

Example: While prospecting, agent Roberts came upon a homeowner who said he would sell his home if he received the price he wanted. He did not want to list his property with agent Roberts, but said he would listen to any offers that might be presented and pay a commission if he accepted it. This type of listing is an open listing.

Few brokers use this type of listing because of its uncertainty and the expense of advertising when working an open listing.

2. Exclusive Agency Listing (No Commission if Owner Sells Privately)

The *EXCLUSIVE AGENCY LISTING is a listing providing that only one agent (the listing broker) has the right to be the only person, other than the owner, to sell the property during a specified period and earn a commission.* The owner, however, still has the right to independently sell the property without paying a commission to the listing broker. The drawback with this type of listing is that the broker is, or could be, in competition with the owner for the sale. These listings are entered into the MLS.

An exclusive agency listing and exclusive right to sell listing both require a definite termination date.

Example: A broker has listed a seller's home using an exclusive agency listing agreement. The exclusive agreement is for four months. During this time, the broker expends considerable time, effort, and money marketing and advertising on behalf of the seller. Ten days before the date the listing is to expire, the seller decides to sell his home to his next door neighbor. The seller now owes the broker no commission.

TECHNOLOGY AND THE BROKER

The evolution of the computer (both in the home and in the office) and the Internet has revolutionized the way brokers do business. The majority of the public may now transmit loan applications, check out credit histories and view color photos of properties, both in and out-of-state.

Customers must perceive that the REALTOR® utilizes the latest technological trends. Customers will not feel confident in using an agent who is not up to speed.

3. Exclusive Right to Sell Listing (Commission if Sold Within the Listing Period)

The most common type of listing is the exclusive right to sell listing. Only the *EXCLUSIVE RIGHT TO SELL LISTING entitles the listing broker named in the agency contract to a commission even if the owner sells the property.* **Figure 4-4** shows the CAR® Residential Listing Agreement - Exclusive (Exclusive Authorization and Right to Sell).

With an exclusive agency listing, the broker competes with the owner; with an exclusive right to sell listing, the broker is entitled to a commission even if the owner sells the property during the listing period. A seller may revoke an exclusive right to sell listing by sending a written letter to the broker.

This type of listing often contains a section referred to as a safety clause. A *SAFETY CLAUSE in a listing is a negotiated period (any agreed to time period) after the termination of a listing in which the listing broker may still be entitled to a commission.* To protect themselves, brokers must furnish the owner/seller with a written list of persons to whom they have shown the property during the listing period delivered no later than the listing termination date. If the owner or a new broker sells the property to someone on the list within the negotiated period, the original broker may be entitled to a commission. **If a seller signs, for example, a 90-day exclusive right to sell listing with one broker, cancels it two weeks later, and gives an open listing to another broker who brings in an offer that is accepted, both brokers are entitled to a full commission.**

An exclusive right to sell listing is a bilateral executory agreement when signed by both seller and broker.

4. Net Listing (Must Be Used With Other Listing – Seldom Used)

A *NET LISTING is an agreement providing that the agent agrees to sell the owner's property for a set minimum price, any amount over the minimum being retained by the agent as commission.* This authorization to sell must be used with one of the other three listings, taking the form of an open listing, an exclusive agency listing, or an exclusive right to sell listing.

With this type of listing it is imperative for the broker to explain, in writing, the exact meaning of a net listing so that there is no confusion about any earned compensation. Since this is a vague type of listing and the possibility of wide variations in commission, a net listing is seldom used in California.

5. Option Listing (Broker has a Reserved Right to Buy)

An *OPTION LISTING gives the listing broker the right to purchase the property.*

Figure 4-4

CALIFORNIA
ASSOCIATION
OF REALTORS®

RESIDENTIAL LISTING AGREEMENT
(Exclusive Authorization and Right to Sell)
(C.A.R. Form RLA, Revised 4/07)

a1. EXCLUSIVE RIGHT TO SELL: _____ ("Seller")
hereby employs and grants _____ ("Broker")
beginning (date) _____ and ending at 11:59 P.M. on (date) _____ ("Listing Period")
the exclusive and irrevocable right to sell or exchange the real property in the City of _____,
County of_____, Assessor's Parcel No. _____
California, described as: _____ ("Property").

2. ITEMS EXCLUDED AND INCLUDED: Unless otherwise specified in a real estate purchase agreement, all fixtures and fittings that are attached to the Property are included, and personal property items are excluded, from the purchase price.
ADDITIONAL ITEMS EXCLUDED: _____.
ADDITIONAL ITEMS INCLUDED: _____.
Seller intends that the above items be excluded or included in offering the Property for sale, but understands that: **(i)** the purchase agreement supersedes any intention expressed above and will ultimately determine which items are excluded and included in the sale; and **(ii)** Broker is not responsible for and does not guarantee that the above exclusions and/or inclusions will be in the purchase agreement.

3. LISTING PRICE AND TERMS:
    A. The listing price shall be: _____ Dollars ($ _____).
    B. Additional Terms: _____.

4. COMPENSATION TO BROKER:
Notice: The amount or rate of real estate commissions is not fixed by law. They are set by each Broker individually and may be negotiable between Seller and Broker (real estate commissions include all compensation and fees to Broker).
    A. Seller agrees to pay to Broker as compensation for services irrespective of agency relationship(s), either ☐ _____ percent of the listing price (or if a purchase agreement is entered into, of the purchase price), or ☐ $ _____, as follows:
    AND _____
        (1) If during the Listing Period, or any extension, Broker, Seller, cooperating broker, or any other person procures a buyer(s) who offers to purchase the Property on the above price and terms, or on any price and terms acceptable to Seller. (Broker is entitled to compensation whether any escrow resulting from such offer closes during or after the expiration of the Listing Period.)
    OR (2) If within _____ calendar days **(a)** after the end of the Listing Period or any extension; or **(b)** after any cancellation of this Agreement, unless otherwise agreed, Seller enters into a contract to sell, convey, lease or otherwise transfer the Property to anyone ("Prospective Buyer") or that person's related entity: **(i)** who physically entered and was shown the Property during the Listing Period or any extension by Broker or a cooperating broker; or **(ii)** for whom Broker or any cooperating broker submitted to Seller a signed, written offer to acquire, lease, exchange or obtain an option on the Property. Seller, however, shall have no obligation to Broker under paragraph 4A(2) unless, not later than **3 calendar days** after the end of the Listing Period or any extension or cancellation, Broker has given Seller a written notice of the names of such Prospective Buyers.
    OR (3) If, without Broker's prior written consent, the Property is withdrawn from sale, conveyed, leased, rented, otherwise transferred, or made unmarketable by a voluntary act of Seller during the Listing Period, or any extension.
    B. If completion of the sale is prevented by a party to the transaction other than Seller, then compensation due under paragraph 4A shall be payable only if and when Seller collects damages by suit, arbitration, settlement or otherwise, and then in an amount equal to the lesser of one-half of the damages recovered or the above compensation, after first deducting title and escrow expenses and the expenses of collection, if any.
    C. In addition, Seller agrees to pay Broker: _____.
    D. Seller has been advised of Broker's policy regarding cooperation with, and the amount of compensation offered to, other brokers.
        (1) Broker is authorized to cooperate with and compensate brokers participating through the multiple listing service(s) ("MLS") by offering MLS brokers either ☐ _____ percent of the purchase price, or ☐ $ _____.
        (2) Broker is authorized to cooperate with and compensate brokers operating outside the MLS as per Broker's policy.
    E. Seller hereby irrevocably assigns to Broker the above compensation from Seller's funds and proceeds in escrow. Broker may submit this Agreement, as instructions to compensate Broker pursuant to paragraph 4A, to any escrow regarding the Property involving Seller and a buyer, Prospective Buyer or other transferee.
    F. **(1)** Seller represents that Seller has not previously entered into a listing agreement with another broker regarding the Property, unless specified as follows: _____.
        (2) Seller warrants that Seller has no obligation to pay compensation to any other broker regarding the Property unless the Property is transferred to any of the following individuals or entities: _____.
        (3) If the Property is sold to anyone listed above during the time Seller is obligated to compensate another broker: **(i)** Broker is not entitled to compensation under this Agreement; and **(ii)** Broker is not obligated to represent Seller in such transaction.

Seller acknowledges receipt of a copy of this page.
Seller's Initials (_____)(_____)

EQUAL HOUSING OPPORTUNITY

Reviewed by _____ Date _____

RLA REVISED 4/07 (PAGE 1 OF 3) Print Date

RESIDENTIAL LISTING AGREEMENT - EXCLUSIVE (RLA PAGE 1 OF 3)

Property Address: _____ Date: _____

5. **OWNERSHIP, TITLE AND AUTHORITY:** Seller warrants that: **(i)** Seller is the owner of the Property; **(ii)** no other persons or entities have title to the Property; and **(iii)** Seller has the authority to both execute this Agreement and sell the Property. Exceptions to ownership, title and authority are as follows: _____

6. **MULTIPLE LISTING SERVICE:** All terms of the transaction, including financing, if applicable, will be provided to the selected MLS for publication, dissemination and use by persons and entities on terms approved by the MLS. Seller authorizes Broker to comply with all applicable MLS rules. MLS rules allow MLS data to be made available by the MLS to additional Internet sites unless Broker gives the MLS instructions to the contrary. MLS rules generally provide that residential real property and vacant lot listings be submitted to the MLS within 48 hours or some other period of time after all necessary signatures have been obtained on the listing agreement. However, Broker will not have to submit this listing to the MLS if, within that time, Broker submits to the MLS a form signed by Seller (C.A.R. Form SEL or the locally required form) instructing Broker to withhold the listing from the MLS. Information about this listing will be provided to the MLS of Broker's selection unless a form instructing Broker to withhold the listing from the MLS is attached to this listing Agreement.

7. **SELLER REPRESENTATIONS:** Seller represents that, unless otherwise specified in writing, Seller is unaware of: **(i)** any Notice of Default recorded against the Property; **(ii)** any delinquent amounts due under any loan secured by, or other obligation affecting, the Property; **(iii)** any bankruptcy, insolvency or similar proceeding affecting the Property; **(iv)** any litigation, arbitration, administrative action, government investigation or other pending or threatened action that affects or may affect the Property or Seller's ability to transfer it; and **(v)** any current, pending or proposed special assessments affecting the Property. Seller shall promptly notify Broker in writing if Seller becomes aware of any of these items during the Listing Period or any extension thereof.

8. **BROKER'S AND SELLER'S DUTIES:** Broker agrees to exercise reasonable effort and due diligence to achieve the purposes of this Agreement. Unless Seller gives Broker written instructions to the contrary, Broker is authorized to order reports and disclosures as appropriate or necessary and advertise and market the Property by any method and in any medium selected by Broker, including MLS and the Internet, and, to the extent permitted by these media, control the dissemination of the information submitted to any medium. Seller agrees to consider offers presented by Broker, and to act in good faith to accomplish the sale of the Property by, among other things, making the Property available for showing at reasonable times and referring to Broker all inquiries of any party interested in the Property. Seller is responsible for determining at what price to list and sell the Property. **Seller further agrees to indemnify, defend and hold Broker harmless from all claims, disputes, litigation, judgments and attorney fees arising from any incorrect information supplied by Seller, or from any material facts that Seller knows but fails to disclose.**

9. **DEPOSIT:** Broker is authorized to accept and hold on Seller's behalf any deposits to be applied toward the purchase price.

10. **AGENCY RELATIONSHIPS:**
   A. **Disclosure:** If the Property includes residential property with one-to-four dwelling units, Seller shall receive a "Disclosure Regarding Agency Relationships" form prior to entering into this Agreement.
   B. **Seller Representation:** Broker shall represent Seller in any resulting transaction, except as specified in paragraph 4F.
   C. **Possible Dual Agency With Buyer:** Depending upon the circumstances, it may be necessary or appropriate for Broker to act as an agent for both Seller and buyer, exchange party, or one or more additional parties ("Buyer"). Broker shall, as soon as practicable, disclose to Seller any election to act as a dual agent representing both Seller and Buyer. If a Buyer is procured directly by Broker or an associate-licensee in Broker's firm, Seller hereby consents to Broker acting as a dual agent for Seller and such Buyer. In the event of an exchange, Seller hereby consents to Broker collecting compensation from additional parties for services rendered, provided there is disclosure to all parties of such agency and compensation. Seller understands and agrees that: **(i)** Broker, without the prior written consent of Seller, will not disclose to Buyer that Seller is willing to sell the Property at a price less than the listing price; **(ii)** Broker, without the prior written consent of Buyer, will not disclose to Seller that Buyer is willing to pay a price greater than the offered price; and **(iii)** except for **(i)** and **(ii)** above, a dual agent is obligated to disclose known facts materially affecting the value or desirability of the Property to both parties.
   D. **Other Sellers:** Seller understands that Broker may have or obtain listings on other properties, and that potential buyers may consider, make offers on, or purchase through Broker, property the same as or similar to Seller's Property. Seller consents to Broker's representation of sellers and buyers of other properties before, during and after the end of this Agreement.
   E. **Confirmation:** If the Property includes residential property with one-to-four dwelling units, Broker shall confirm the agency relationship described above, or as modified, in writing, prior to or concurrent with Seller's execution of a purchase agreement.

11. **SECURITY AND INSURANCE:** Broker is not responsible for loss of or damage to personal or real property, or person, whether attributable to use of a keysafe/lockbox, a showing of the Property, or otherwise. Third parties, including, but not limited to, appraisers, inspectors, brokers and prospective buyers, may have access to, and take videos and photographs of, the interior of the Property. Seller agrees: **(i)** to take reasonable precautions to safeguard and protect valuables that might be accessible during showings of the Property; and **(ii)** to obtain insurance to protect against these risks. Broker does not maintain insurance to protect Seller.

12. **KEYSAFE/LOCKBOX:** A keysafe/lockbox is designed to hold a key to the Property to permit access to the Property by Broker, cooperating brokers, MLS participants, their authorized licensees and representatives, authorized inspectors, and accompanied prospective buyers. Broker, cooperating brokers, MLS and Associations/Boards of REALTORS® are **not** insurers against injury, theft, loss, vandalism or damage attributed to the use of a keysafe/lockbox. Seller does (or if checked ☐ does not) authorize Broker to install a keysafe/lockbox. If Seller does not occupy the Property, Seller shall be responsible for obtaining occupant(s)' written permission for use of a keysafe/lockbox.

13. **SIGN:** Seller does (or if checked ☐ does not) authorize Broker to install a FOR SALE/SOLD sign on the Property.

14. **EQUAL HOUSING OPPORTUNITY:** The Property is offered in compliance with federal, state and local anti-discrimination laws.

15. **ATTORNEY FEES:** In any action, proceeding or arbitration between Seller and Broker regarding the obligation to pay compensation under this Agreement, the prevailing Seller or Broker shall be entitled to reasonable attorney fees and costs from the non-prevailing Seller or Broker, except as provided in paragraph 19A.

16. **ADDITIONAL TERMS:** _____
_____
_____

Seller acknowledges receipt of a copy of this page.
Seller's Initials (_____)(_____)

RLA REVISED 4/07 (PAGE 2 OF 3)

Reviewed by _____ Date _____

EQUAL HOUSING OPPORTUNITY

RESIDENTIAL LISTING AGREEMENT - EXCLUSIVE (RLA PAGE 2 OF 3)

Property Address: _____ Date: _____

17. MANAGEMENT APPROVAL: If an associate-licensee in Broker's office (salesperson or broker-associate) enters into this Agreement on Broker's behalf, and Broker or Manager does not approve of its terms, Broker or Manager has the right to cancel this Agreement, in writing, within **5 Days** After its execution.

18. SUCCESSORS AND ASSIGNS: This Agreement shall be binding upon Seller and Seller's successors and assigns.

19. DISPUTE RESOLUTION:

A. MEDIATION: Seller and Broker agree to mediate any dispute or claim arising between them out of this Agreement, or any resulting transaction, before resorting to arbitration or court action, subject to paragraph 19B(2) below. Paragraph 19B(2) below applies whether or not the arbitration provision is initialed. Mediation fees, if any, shall be divided equally among the parties involved. If, for any dispute or claim to which this paragraph applies, any party commences an action without first attempting to resolve the matter through mediation, or refuses to mediate after a request has been made, then that party shall not be entitled to recover attorney fees, even if they would otherwise be available to that party in any such action. THIS MEDIATION PROVISION APPLIES WHETHER OR NOT THE ARBITRATION PROVISION IS INITIALED.

B. ARBITRATION OF DISPUTES: (1) Seller and Broker agree that any dispute or claim in law or equity arising between them regarding the obligation to pay compensation under this Agreement, which is not settled through mediation, shall be decided by neutral, binding arbitration, including and subject to paragraph 19B(2) below. The arbitrator shall be a retired judge or justice, or an attorney with at least 5 years of residential real estate law experience, unless the parties mutually agree to a different arbitrator, who shall render an award in accordance with substantive California law. The parties shall have the right to discovery in accordance with California Code of Civil Procedure §1283.05. In all other respects, the arbitration shall be conducted in accordance with Title 9 of Part III of the California Code of Civil Procedure. Judgment upon the award of the arbitrator(s) may be entered in any court having jurisdiction. Interpretation of this agreement to arbitrate shall be governed by the Federal Arbitration Act.

(2) EXCLUSIONS FROM MEDIATION AND ARBITRATION: The following matters are excluded from mediation and arbitration: (i) a judicial or non-judicial foreclosure or other action or proceeding to enforce a deed of trust, mortgage, or installment land sale contract as defined in California Civil Code §2985; (ii) an unlawful detainer action; (iii) the filing or enforcement of a mechanic's lien; and (iv) any matter that is within the jurisdiction of a probate, small claims, or bankruptcy court. The filing of a court action to enable the recording of a notice of pending action, for order of attachment, receivership, injunction, or other provisional remedies, shall not constitute a waiver of the mediation and arbitration provisions.

"NOTICE: BY INITIALING IN THE SPACE BELOW YOU ARE AGREEING TO HAVE ANY DISPUTE ARISING OUT OF THE MATTERS INCLUDED IN THE 'ARBITRATION OF DISPUTES' PROVISION DECIDED BY NEUTRAL ARBITRATION AS PROVIDED BY CALIFORNIA LAW AND YOU ARE GIVING UP ANY RIGHTS YOU MIGHT POSSESS TO HAVE THE DISPUTE LITIGATED IN A COURT OR JURY TRIAL. BY INITIALING IN THE SPACE BELOW YOU ARE GIVING UP YOUR JUDICIAL RIGHTS TO DISCOVERY AND APPEAL, UNLESS THOSE RIGHTS ARE SPECIFICALLY INCLUDED IN THE 'ARBITRATION OF DISPUTES' PROVISION. IF YOU REFUSE TO SUBMIT TO ARBITRATION AFTER AGREEING TO THIS PROVISION, YOU MAY BE COMPELLED TO ARBITRATE UNDER THE AUTHORITY OF THE CALIFORNIA CODE OF CIVIL PROCEDURE. YOUR AGREEMENT TO THIS ARBITRATION PROVISION IS VOLUNTARY."

"WE HAVE READ AND UNDERSTAND THE FOREGOING AND AGREE TO SUBMIT DISPUTES ARISING OUT OF THE MATTERS INCLUDED IN THE 'ARBITRATION OF DISPUTES' PROVISION TO NEUTRAL ARBITRATION."

Seller's Initials _____ / _____	Broker's Initials _____ / _____

20. ENTIRE AGREEMENT: All prior discussions, negotiations and agreements between the parties concerning the subject matter of this Agreement are superseded by this Agreement, which constitutes the entire contract and a complete and exclusive expression of their agreement, and may not be contradicted by evidence of any prior agreement or contemporaneous oral agreement. If any provision of this Agreement is held to be ineffective or invalid, the remaining provisions will nevertheless be given full force and effect. This Agreement and any supplement, addendum or modification, including any photocopy or facsimile, may be executed in counterparts.

By signing below, Seller acknowledges that Seller has read, understands, received a copy of and agrees to the terms of this Agreement.

Seller _____ Date _____
Address _____ City _____ State _____ Zip _____
Telephone _____ Fax _____ E-mail _____

Seller _____ Date _____
Address _____ City _____ State _____ Zip _____
Telephone _____ Fax _____ E-mail _____

Real Estate Broker (Firm) _____ DRE Lic. # _____
By (Agent) _____ DRE Lic. # _____ Date _____
Address _____ City _____ State _____ Zip _____
Telephone _____ Fax _____ E-mail _____

Published and Distributed by:
REAL ESTATE BUSINESS SERVICES, INC.
a subsidiary of the California Association of REALTORS®
525 South Virgil Avenue, Los Angeles, California 90020

Reviewed by _____ Date _____

RLA REVISED 4/07 (PAGE 3 OF 3)

RESIDENTIAL LISTING AGREEMENT - EXCLUSIVE (RLA PAGE 3 OF 3)

A broker with an option listing must disclose to prospective buyers that he/she is acting as a principal, and present all offers to the seller.

Prior to exercising an option, the broker must disclose any anticipated profit and get the written consent of the seller.

Example: Broker Able listed a property from Seller Baker, and reserved an option to purchase the property himself. If Broker Able exercises the option, he must obtain written consent from Seller Baker which discloses the amount of profit or anticipated profit he will receive.

B. LISTING AGREEMENT COPIES (Give Copy When Signed)

A copy of the listing agreement or any other real estate agreement, including the agency relationship form and the transfer disclosure statement, must be given to the signing party immediately after they are signed. This is a requirement of the Commissioner's Regulations, and a violation could result in license suspension or revocation.

C. MULTIPLE LISTING SERVICE (MLS) (Subagents and Cooperating Brokers)

A *MULTIPLE LISTING SERVICE (MLS) is an association of real estate brokers that provides a pooling of listings, recent sales, and the sharing of commissions on a specified basis.* The advantage to the seller is that his or her home or property will receive wider market exposure because it will be shown by other cooperating brokers.

A *MULTIPLE LISTING is a listing, usually an exclusive right to sell, taken by a member of a multiple listing service, with the provision that all members of the multiple listing service have the opportunity to find an interested buyer.* Sometimes in exclusive areas, sellers will request that their listing not be put into the multiple listing service. This would limit the number of people (looky-loos) who just look at their properties for curiosity's sake.

A "pocket listing" is the unethical practice of not giving a new listing to the MLS until the listing broker first tries to sell that listed property through only the other agents within the company.

An agent can delegate some authority to his or her salespeople or other brokers and their salespeople. This is known as subagency. A *SUBAGENT is a licensed broker or salesperson upon whom some of the powers of an agent have been conferred, not by the principal, but by the agent with the principal's authorization.* The agent can delegate purely mechanical acts such as typing to anyone, but a subagency can only be created with the principal's consent. The subagent has the same duties and responsibilities as the agent.

When a broker is acting as the subagent of the seller, the subagent is primarily responsible to the seller.

Example: Real estate broker Brown, acting as a subagent of the seller, has a fiduciary duty to the seller and the agent who appointed him as subagent.

A seller is bound by acts of the seller's broker, listing broker, and any subagent working under his broker. He is NOT bound by acts of the buyer's broker.

Generally, real estate agents will have to spend less time with clients who are better informed and have searched the Multiple Listing Services (MLSs).

The "Internet generation" will probably be searching MLSs on the Net for their "dream home" before they first see a real estate broker or his or her salespeople. Clients can click on **www. ca.realtor.com** or **www.realtor.com** to search through every multiple listing service and every listed property in California by region and zip code. Customers can now see on the Internet what agents used to have to wait a week to see when the MLS printed the books of the current listings. The following is only a partial list of MLS websites:

www.ca.realtor.com (California Living Network)
www.car.org (California Association of Realtors)
www.sucasa.net (Spanish Version)
www.realtor.com (NAR Home Finder Sites)

D. MULTIPLE LISTING SERVICES ON THE INTERNET

Internet Multiple Listing Services are here to stay. Some are independent but most are still controlled by the local Boards of REALTORS®. The California Association of REALTORS® has the most complete system linking the MLS services of the entire state into one Internet address. *WWW.CAR.ORG or WWW.CA.REALTOR.COM is a source of California Multiple Listing Services' databases that links and provides the largest directory of homes for sale in California.* This has become the main source of available California home listings on the Internet. It breaks down California by regions, maps, and counties in order to help locate the Multiple Listing Service that covers whatever geographical area the user wants. It is the gateway to real estate listing information.

E. COOPERATING BROKERS

A broker acting as a subagent for the seller has a fiduciary duty to both the seller and the listing broker.

A listing agreement usually authorizes the principal's agent to use cooperating brokers. A *COOPERATING BROKER is a non-listing broker who also works to sell the listed property.* The cooperating broker performs the same acts as the agent to find a buyer. Cooperating brokers and salespeople represent the buyer if it is disclosed to all parties.

A listing broker who appoints a subagent owes a fiduciary duty to the seller.

The purpose of a multiple listing service is to authorize and encourage cooperation within the real estate industry. Their members can act as cooperating brokers, thus sharing listings and commissions.

Agreements between brokers and salespeople must be in writing.

1. Selling in Other States

Since each state has its own licensing laws, how can a cooperating broker sell a property for a commission in another state? The answer is simple. Find a licensed, cooperating broker in that state.

"Comps" are the recent sales prices of similar properties in a neighborhood. It's the most important information a real estate salesperson can provide a buyer to pick a "realistic offering price" or a seller to "understand current market pricing."

A salesperson can quickly obtain a fairly accurate estimate of the probable selling price of a property to be listed or sold by knowing and comparing **recent selling prices (comps)**. Comps are proprietary information, the most comprehensive versions of which are given out only to members of the Multiple Listing Service (MLS) associations. As such, it can be difficult for buyers and sellers to access current comps—although similar information may be obtained by visiting the website listed below.

Because it can be so difficult to obtain accurate comps, buyers and sellers usually seek out the professional services of real estate salespeople.

Most sellers are not realistic about the "probable selling price" of their property. Sellers do not always realize that informed buyers will normally purchase only the lowest priced house among similarly priced homes. Comps are used by the buyers as a basis to determine a realistic offering price. Often a property owner mistakenly believes he or she can get 10% or more over what recent comps indicate a property is worth. Realistically, there is little chance a buyer will pay more than 3% over the probable selling price, the result of which is that the overpriced property is often overlooked by brokers and remains unsold for a long period of time.

While the MLS comps may be more accurate and detailed, surfing the Net can turn up alternative methods for finding similar information. The Internet company listed below can give a rough estimate of comps based on secondary sales information statistically averaged by recorded tracts or zip codes.

www.zillow.com
(Virtual comparables)

IV. Commissions (Negotiable)

A ***COMMISSION*** *in real estate is a fee paid, usually as a percentage of the selling price, to a broker/ agent as compensation for his or her services.* Traditionally, it is payment from the seller to the agent who finds a ready, willing, and able buyer to purchase the seller's property, according to the listing terms or any other terms acceptable to the seller.

A broker/agent can pay a finder's fee to an unlicensed individual only for introducing a client to the broker/agent.

A ***COMMISSION SPLIT*** *is a previously agreed split between a broker and his or her salesperson of a commission earned on a sale.* Commission rates vary by negotiation throughout California, but usually range from 3% to 10% of the selling price. The listing agreement states that a commission is to be paid only when all the terms of the listing or other acceptable terms of the sale are met.

An agent can accept a commission in the form of a note, cash, or personal check.

Photo Reality: Seeing is Believing

Imagine having an open house where clients can do a "walk through" without personally visiting the property. Streaming video tours on the Web allow your clients to see the listed properties anytime they want.

While "virtual tours" may never replace a good old fashion walk through, Internet screening may very well eliminate the real estate "drive-by" and "looky-loo" phenomenon. Potential homebuyers no longer need to drive-by a home to get a feel for such things as the neighborhood, condition of the house, curbside appeal, interior layout, spacial relationships, and kitchen design. Because of digital technology, a prospective buyer can zoom in and out, follow the camera to another room, check out the ceiling, and get a 360 degree view of a living room or bedroom. Once clients have seen a video of both the inside and outside of a home, they can decide if they're interested before contacting an agent.

"Streaming video tours" may encompass not only the house for sale, but also show the surrounding area, including schools, churches, shopping districts, and parks. If a picture is worth a thousand words, imagine how valuable a picture tour on a website could be. Picture tours are an effective means to attract both buyers and sellers.

You may want to lend a hand and prepare Web pictures for busy and non-computer oriented salespeople in your office, as it will benefit you and your company in the long run. In fact, many will be willing to pay you for this service. Because you offer picture tours on the Web, sellers will prefer to list properties with you. Not only will your listings increase, but they will also get more attention from buyers.

A real estate licensee who can provide photo or video services to real estate agents will always be in demand. He or she can take digital photos and videos of a property without the listing agent present and speed up the process of getting that property listed on the company's website tours. Panoramic videos are valuable visual aides for a buyer to see size and scale, and a walking video tour provides an unparalleled viewing experience for all to get the feel of space and flow.

SERVICES

www.ipix.com (Internet Pictures Corp.)
www.home-view.com/ (HomeView.com)
www.evox.com (eVox Productions)
www.virtualproperties.com (Virtual Tours)

SOFTWARE

www.enroute.com (Immersive Video)
www.smoothmove.com
(iMove Spherical Imaging Systems)
www.apple.com/quicktime/
(Quicktime)

When a broker lists a property for sale and a cooperating broker sells it, the commission is shared. Although the ratio for dividing the commission varies, it is often 50% to the listing broker, and 50% to the selling broker. If a salesperson is involved, he or she shares in the employing broker's part of the commission.

Salespeople only receive compensation for real estate transactions from their employing brokers. All persons performing real estate activities for compensation must hold a valid real estate license.

A commission can be earned even if the sale is not finalized. **The broker is entitled to a commission if all the "exact" terms of the listing agreement are met,** provided the buyer is ready, willing, and able to complete the transaction. This is true even if the seller changes his or her mind and refuses to sell. If there is a valid listing agreement and the exact terms are met, the seller is still responsible for the commission. See **Figure 4-5** for facts about commissions from auctions.

Example: Seller Able accepted an offer on his home presented by Broker Baker, and acceptance was communicated back to the buyer. Prior to opening escrow, however, Seller Able received an all cash offer to purchase the property. He decided to cancel the original contract and notified Broker Baker of his decision. Broker Baker has a good legal basis (excellent chance) to collect a commission.

A broker or his or her salesperson must be the procuring cause of a sale to earn a commission. *PROCURING CAUSE is defined as a series of unbroken events that lead to an acceptable agreement with the seller.* If there are several brokers trying to sell the same property, the one who is the procuring cause of the sale is entitled to the selling broker's portion of the commission.

A listing for a residential building containing 1-4 dwelling units must include a notice that the commission is negotiable.

V. Transfer Disclosure Statement

A. EASTON V. STRASSBURGER

A 1984 California Court of Appeals decision in the case of *Easton v. Strassburger* greatly extended the liability of brokers engaged in real estate sales. **Be warned:** Brokers are required to be aware (or should be aware) of all material facts negatively influencing the value or desirability of the property (**"red flags"**), discoverable by a reasonable visual inspection, and must disclose these facts to all prospective buyers.

Legally, the listing broker and the buyer's broker must conduct a reasonably competent, diligent, and visual inspection of accessible areas of the property and disclose to a prospective buyer all material facts affecting value and desirability.

B. TRANSFER DISCLOSURE STATEMENT (TDS)
(Seller and Selling Broker Must Provide This Form)

The law requires sellers of residential property of from one-to-four units (which includes triplexes) to provide prospective buyers with a Real Estate Transfer Disclosure Statement.

The *REAL ESTATE TRANSFER DISCLOSURE STATEMENT (TDS) identifies items of value attached to the structure or land and states whether these items are operational* (see **Figure 4-6**). It also asks the seller to identify any structural or material defects. This form provides an opportunity for the seller to completely disclose problems of any kind that might adversely affect the value of the property. The obligation to prepare and deliver the Transfer Disclosure Statement to the prospective buyer is imposed upon **the seller and the seller's broker** (see Civil Code Section 1102.6 for exemptions).

A buyer has two years to sue an agent for failure to make proper disclosures in the Transfer Disclosure Statement.

Figure 4-5

Real Estate Auction...
Another Way to Sell and Receive Commissions

A **REAL ESTATE AUCTION** *is a meeting where interested parties come together and continue to offer higher bids (purchase prices) until only one bidder is left, to whom the property is sold.* The person making the highest bid buys the property. The time and place are always stated on the announcement, but the amount of advertising depends on the type of auction. An **AUCTIONEER** *is a seller.* An auction is one of the quickest ways to unload a piece of property. Auctions are very popular with government agencies and builders in over-built or economically depressed communities. This can be a great way to pick up a real bargain property, as long as you bid using your head, not your heart. Auctions are emotional events where the excitement keeps rising until the property is sold. The best buys are at foreclosure sales, which are put on by public agencies, banks, or savings banks.

An **ABSOLUTE AUCTION** *is an auction where the property must be sold to the highest bidder no matter how low the final bid.* A **NO-SALE AUCTION** *is where there is a minimum bid underlying each property so that a certain price must be reached before the property will be sold.* In legitimate auctions, the starting bid is the minimum bid. But if that fact is not stated, make sure the minimum bid is stated clearly before the auction starts, or do not bid.

In an "auction without reserve," the auctioneer sets a minimum bid to begin an auction. If someone offers to buy at 10% more than the opening bid, this bid must be accepted, as an auctioneer is required to accept bids in an auction without reserve.

Do not attend a real property auction if you have not first seen the property and decided what you would be willing to pay for it. The broker auctioneers will be glad to give you maps or help you view the properties. Remember, don't get caught up in auction fever, because you should never go beyond your maximum bid price established well in advance of the auction.

An auction salesperson represents the seller and is required to have a real estate license.

 www.cwsmarketing.com (Online Auctions)
www.jpking.com (JP King Auction Company)

In New Zealand, auctions are the most common method of selling real estate!

Figure 4-6

CALIFORNIA
ASSOCIATION
OF REALTORS®

REAL ESTATE TRANSFER DISCLOSURE STATEMENT
(CALIFORNIA CIVIL CODE §1102, ET SEQ.)
(C.A.R. Form TDS, Revised 10/03)

THIS DISCLOSURE STATEMENT CONCERNS THE REAL PROPERTY SITUATED IN THE CITY OF _____
_____, **COUNTY OF** _____, **STATE OF CALIFORNIA,**
DESCRIBED AS _____.

THIS STATEMENT IS A DISCLOSURE OF THE CONDITION OF THE ABOVE DESCRIBED PROPERTY IN COMPLIANCE WITH SECTION 1102 OF THE CIVIL CODE AS OF (date) _____. **IT IS NOT A WARRANTY OF ANY KIND BY THE SELLER(S) OR ANY AGENT(S) REPRESENTING ANY PRINCIPAL(S) IN THIS TRANSACTION, AND IS NOT A SUBSTITUTE FOR ANY INSPECTIONS OR WARRANTIES THE PRINCIPAL(S) MAY WISH TO OBTAIN.**

I. COORDINATION WITH OTHER DISCLOSURE FORMS

This Real Estate Transfer Disclosure Statement is made pursuant to Section 1102 of the Civil Code. Other statutes require disclosures, depending upon the details of the particular real estate transaction (for example: special study zone and purchase-money liens on residential property).

Substituted Disclosures: The following disclosures and other disclosures required by law, including the Natural Hazard Disclosure Report/Statement that may include airport annoyances, earthquake, fire, flood, or special assessment information, have or will be made in connection with this real estate transfer, and are intended to satisfy the disclosure obligations on this form, where the subject matter is the same:

☐ Inspection reports completed pursuant to the contract of sale or receipt for deposit.
☐ Additional inspection reports or disclosures: _____
_____

II. SELLER'S INFORMATION

The Seller discloses the following information with the knowledge that even though this is not a warranty, prospective Buyers may rely on this information in deciding whether and on what terms to purchase the subject property. Seller hereby authorizes any agent(s) representing any principal(s) in this transaction to provide a copy of this statement to any person or entity in connection with any actual or anticipated sale of the property.

THE FOLLOWING ARE REPRESENTATIONS MADE BY THE SELLER(S) AND ARE NOT THE REPRESENTATIONS OF THE AGENT(S), IF ANY. THIS INFORMATION IS A DISCLOSURE AND IS NOT INTENDED TO BE PART OF ANY CONTRACT BETWEEN THE BUYER AND SELLER.

Seller ☐ is ☐ is not occupying the property.

A. The subject property has the items checked below (read across):

☐ Range	☐ Oven	☐ Microwave
☐ Dishwasher	☐ Trash Compactor	☐ Garbage Disposal
☐ Washer/Dryer Hookups		☐ Rain Gutters
☐ Burglar Alarms	☐ Smoke Detector(s)	☐ Fire Alarm
☐ TV Antenna	☐ Satellite Dish	☐ Intercom
☐ Central Heating	☐ Central Air Conditioning	☐ Evaporator Cooler(s)
☐ Wall/Window Air Conditioning	☐ Sprinklers	☐ Public Sewer System
☐ Septic Tank	☐ Sump Pump	☐ Water Softener
☐ Patio/Decking	☐ Built-in Barbecue	☐ Gazebo
☐ Sauna		
☐ Hot Tub	☐ Pool	☐ Spa
☐ Locking Safety Cover*	☐ Child Resistant Barrier*	☐ Locking Safety Cover*
☐ Security Gate(s)	☐ Automatic Garage Door Opener(s)*	☐ Number Remote Controls ____

Garage: ☐ Attached   ☐ Not Attached   ☐ Carport
Pool/Spa Heater: ☐ Gas   ☐ Solar   ☐ Electric
Water Heater: ☐ Gas   ☐ Water Heater Anchored, Braced, or Strapped*
Water Supply: ☐ City   ☐ Well   ☐ Private Utility or
Gas Supply: ☐ Utility   ☐ Bottled   Other _____
☐ Window Screens   ☐ Window Security Bars ☐ Quick Release Mechanism on Bedroom Windows*
Exhaust Fan(s) in _____ 220 Volt Wiring in _____ Fireplace(s) in _____
☐ Gas Starter _____ ☐ Roof(s): Type: _____ Age: _____ (approx.)
☐ Other: _____

Are there, to the best of your (Seller's) knowledge, any of the above that are not in operating condition? ☐ Yes ☐ No. If yes, then describe. (Attach additional sheets if necessary): _____

(*see footnote on page 2)

TDS REVISED 10/03 (PAGE 1 OF 3) Print Date

Buyer's Initials (_____)(_____)
Seller's Initials (_____)(_____)

Reviewed by _____ Date _____

EQUAL HOUSING
OPPORTUNITY

REAL ESTATE TRANSFER DISCLOSURE STATEMENT (TDS PAGE 1 OF 3)

Property Address: _____ Date: _____

B. Are you (Seller) aware of any significant defects/malfunctions in any of the following? ☐ Yes ☐ No. If yes, check appropriate space(s) below.

☐ Interior Walls ☐ Ceilings ☐ Floors ☐ Exterior Walls ☐ Insulation ☐ Roof(s) ☐ Windows ☐ Doors ☐ Foundation ☐ Slab(s) ☐ Driveways ☐ Sidewalks ☐ Walls/Fences ☐ Electrical Systems ☐ Plumbing/Sewers/Septics ☐ Other Structural Components

(Describe: _____
_____
_____
_____)

If any of the above is checked, explain. (Attach additional sheets if necessary.): _____
_____
_____
_____

*This garage door opener or child resistant pool barrier may not be in compliance with the safety standards relating to automatic reversing devices as set forth in Chapter 12.5 (commencing with Section 19890) of Part 3 of Division 13 of, or with the pool safety standards of Article 2.5 (commencing with Section 115920) of Chapter 5 of Part 10 of Division 104 of, the Health and Safety Code. The water heater may not be anchored, braced, or strapped in accordance with Section 19211 of the Health and Safety Code. Window security bars may not have quick release mechanisms in compliance with the 1995 edition of the California Building Standards Code.

C. Are you (Seller) aware of any of the following:

1. Substances, materials, or products which may be an environmental hazard such as, but not limited to, asbestos, formaldehyde, radon gas, lead-based paint, mold, fuel or chemical storage tanks, and contaminated soil or water on the subject property . . . . ☐ Yes ☐ No
2. Features of the property shared in common with adjoining landowners, such as walls, fences, and driveways, whose use or responsibility for maintenance may have an effect on the subject property . . . . ☐ Yes ☐ No
3. Any encroachments, easements or similar matters that may affect your interest in the subject property . . . . ☐ Yes ☐ No
4. Room additions, structural modifications, or other alterations or repairs made without necessary permits . . . . ☐ Yes ☐ No
5. Room additions, structural modifications, or other alterations or repairs not in compliance with building codes . . . ☐ Yes ☐ No
6. Fill (compacted or otherwise) on the property or any portion thereof . . . . ☐ Yes ☐ No
7. Any settling from any cause, or slippage, sliding, or other soil problems . . . . ☐ Yes ☐ No
8. Flooding, drainage or grading problems . . . . ☐ Yes ☐ No
9. Major damage to the property or any of the structures from fire, earthquake, floods, or landslides . . . . ☐ Yes ☐ No
10. Any zoning violations, nonconforming uses, violations of "setback" requirements . . . . ☐ Yes ☐ No
11. Neighborhood noise problems or other nuisances . . . . ☐ Yes ☐ No
12. CC&R's or other deed restrictions or obligations . . . . ☐ Yes ☐ No
13. Homeowners' Association which has any authority over the subject property . . . . ☐ Yes ☐ No
14. Any "common area" (facilities such as pools, tennis courts, walkways, or other areas co-owned in undivided interest with others) . . . . ☐ Yes ☐ No
15. Any notices of abatement or citations against the property . . . . ☐ Yes ☐ No
16. Any lawsuits by or against the Seller threatening to or affecting this real property, including any lawsuits alleging a defect or deficiency in this real property or "common areas" (facilities such as pools, tennis courts, walkways, or other areas co-owned in undivided interest with others) . . . . ☐ Yes ☐ No

If the answer to any of these is yes, explain. (Attach additional sheets if necessary.): _____
_____
_____
_____
_____

Seller certifies that the information herein is true and correct to the best of the Seller's knowledge as of the date signed by the Seller.

Seller_____ Date _____

Seller_____ Date _____

Buyer's Initials (_____)(_____)
Seller's Initials (_____)(_____)

Reviewed by _____ Date _____

TDS REVISED 10/03 (PAGE 2 OF 3)

EQUAL HOUSING OPPORTUNITY

REAL ESTATE TRANSFER DISCLOSURE STATEMENT (TDS PAGE 2 OF 3)

Property Address: _____ Date: _____

III. AGENT'S INSPECTION DISCLOSURE
(To be completed only if the Seller is represented by an agent in this transaction.)

THE UNDERSIGNED, BASED ON THE ABOVE INQUIRY OF THE SELLER(S) AS TO THE CONDITION OF THE PROPERTY AND BASED ON A REASONABLY COMPETENT AND DILIGENT VISUAL INSPECTION OF THE ACCESSIBLE AREAS OF THE PROPERTY IN CONJUNCTION WITH THAT INQUIRY, STATES THE FOLLOWING:

☐ Agent notes no items for disclosure.

☐ Agent notes the following items: _____

_____

_____

_____

_____

Agent (Broker Representing Seller) _____ By _____ Date _____
(Please Print)   (Associate Licensee or Broker Signature)

IV. AGENT'S INSPECTION DISCLOSURE
(To be completed only if the agent who has obtained the offer is other than the agent above.)

THE UNDERSIGNED, BASED ON A REASONABLY COMPETENT AND DILIGENT VISUAL INSPECTION OF THE ACCESSIBLE AREAS OF THE PROPERTY, STATES THE FOLLOWING:

☐ Agent notes no items for disclosure.

☐ Agent notes the following items: _____

_____

_____

_____

Agent (Broker Obtaining the Offer) _____ By _____ Date _____
(Please Print)   (Associate Licensee or Broker Signature)

V. BUYER(S) AND SELLER(S) MAY WISH TO OBTAIN PROFESSIONAL ADVICE AND/OR INSPECTIONS OF THE PROPERTY AND TO PROVIDE FOR APPROPRIATE PROVISIONS IN A CONTRACT BETWEEN BUYER AND SELLER(S) WITH RESPECT TO ANY ADVICE/INSPECTIONS/DEFECTS.

I/WE ACKNOWLEDGE RECEIPT OF A COPY OF THIS STATEMENT.

Seller _____ Date _____ Buyer _____ Date _____

Seller _____ Date _____ Buyer _____ Date _____

Agent (Broker Representing Seller) _____ By _____ Date _____
(Please Print)   (Associate Licensee or Broker Signature)

Agent (Broker Obtaining the Offer) _____ By _____ Date _____
(Please Print)   (Associate Licensee or Broker Signature)

SECTION 1102.3 OF THE CIVIL CODE PROVIDES A BUYER WITH THE RIGHT TO RESCIND A PURCHASE CONTRACT FOR AT LEAST THREE DAYS AFTER THE DELIVERY OF THIS DISCLOSURE IF DELIVERY OCCURS AFTER THE SIGNING OF AN OFFER TO PURCHASE. IF YOU WISH TO RESCIND THE CONTRACT, YOU MUST ACT WITHIN THE PRESCRIBED PERIOD.

A REAL ESTATE BROKER IS QUALIFIED TO ADVISE ON REAL ESTATE. IF YOU DESIRE LEGAL ADVICE, CONSULT YOUR ATTORNEY.

SURE TRAC
The System for Success™

Published by the
California Association of REALTORS®

TDS REVISED 10/03 (PAGE 3 OF 3)

Reviewed by _____ Date _____

EQUAL HOUSING OPPORTUNITY

REAL ESTATE TRANSFER DISCLOSURE STATEMENT (TDS PAGE 3 OF 3)

The following sequence of events may help explain how the four parties (seller, seller's agent, buyer, and buyer's agent) fill in and sign the Transfer Disclosure Statement form:

1. The Transfer Disclosure Statement form should be filled out and signed completely by the seller at the time of listing the property. Since the seller is the one most familiar with the property, he or she must be encouraged to be forthright and honest about all known defects.

2. The seller's agent makes a visual, diligent inspection of the property, fills out the appropriate section of the Transfer Disclosure Statement, and signs at the same time the seller lists the property for sale.

The listing agent can never legally complete the entire Real Property Transfer Disclosure Statement.

3. The buyer should receive a copy of the Transfer Disclosure Statement and sign that he or she has received it before making a written offer.

4. The buyer's agent must also visually inspect the property, fill out the appropriate section of the statement, and sign it.

5. If the buyer fails to receive the Transfer Disclosure Statement form prior to signing the contractual offer (purchase agreement), he or she has the right to cancel, after receipt of the Transfer Disclosure Statement, for any reason (three days if delivered by hand or five days if mailed). A written notice of termination must be delivered to the seller or to the seller's broker.

A "TDS" is required for an "as is" sale of a single-family residence by a private person.

VI. Broker's Responsibilities

A. TRUST ACCOUNTS (Other People's Money)

After reconciliation of a trust account, the client's liabilities should equal the trust account balance.

A broker accepting a money deposit (and instructions) is required to: 1) give it to the principal; 2) place it in a trust account; or 3) give it to an escrow company. **Deposits other than the initial deposit (usually around $200) to start the account are never the personal property of the broker**. Any moneys accepted should go, within three business days, into an independent bank trust account in the name of the broker as trustee. Most trust accounts are non-interest-bearing because all overages must be explained. Placing a buyer's cash or check in the broker's personal account is called commingling.

A broker can keep $200 of his/her personal funds in a trust account without being guilty of commingling.

COMMINGLING is the mixing together of the funds of a principal and a licensee. Commingling is a violation of the Commissioner's Regulations. Commingling is the opposite of segregating (keeping separate).

Commingling is the illegal practice of mixing a client's money with the agent's private funds. By law, each entry in the broker's trust fund account (bank) must be identified.

CHAPTER 4

CONVERSION is the unlawful misappropriation and use of a client's funds by a licensee. A broker, who upon receipt spends his or her principal's deposit without the principal's authorization, has not commingled funds with his or her own funds in a technical sense, but has converted them. This is a much more serious violation than commingling, with heavy criminal penalties.

An unlicensed employee of a broker who is authorized in writing can make withdrawals from the broker's trust account provided the employee is covered by a "fidelity bond" for at least the amount of funds to which the employee has access at any given time.

B. TRANSACTION FILE (Keep for Three Years)

A TRANSACTION FILE is the file or folder (all documents) kept for three years by the broker for each real estate transaction in which the broker or his or her salespeople participated.

The Commissioner of real estate has the right to inspect this file. Maintaining a complete, up-to-date transaction file is not only good business practice, **it is the law**.

A licensed broker must retain for three years copies of all listings, purchase agreements, canceled checks, trust fund records and other documents executed by the broker or obtained by him or her in connection with any real estate transaction. The retention period shall run from the date of the closing of the transaction or from the date of the listing, if the transaction is not consummated.

The Real Estate Commissioner requires that all records of a broker or salesperson be kept a minimum of three years.

Uniform Electronic Transactions Act (Record Retention)

A real estate broker who obtains documents in any transaction for which a real estate broker license is required, when such documents contain an electronic signature pursuant to the Uniform Electronic Transaction Act, must retain a copy of such documents by: 1) Causing a paper copy of the document to be made or 2) By using electronic image storing media. The broker may retain copies of such documents at a location other than the broker's place of business.

C. SALESPEOPLE MAY BE INDEPENDENT CONTRACTORS OR EMPLOYEES

A salesperson cannot act independently of a real estate broker.

In California, the Department of Real Estate considers a salesperson an employee of the broker for the purpose of the administration of the real estate broker law, even if he or she act as independent contractors for other purposes, such as income tax wage withholding, social security, or medicare coverage. **This makes the broker responsible for the real estate activities of the salesperson.**

An *INDEPENDENT CONTRACTOR sells results rather than time, and his or her physical conduct is not subject to the control of another. An EMPLOYEE, on the other hand, works under the direct control (designated hours and breaks) and supervision of the employer.*

A broker who hires an unlicensed person to practice real estate, as well as the unlicensed practitioner, may be fined up to $10,000 each. The county district attorney prosecutes law violations by unlicensed persons.

Most real estate licensees are considered independent contractors under Federal Income Tax Laws, but according to California Real Estate Law, and the Real Estate Commissioner, they are considered employees of the broker.

An unlicensed person (like a secretary or bookkeeper) cannot give information regarding a real estate transaction on the phone or in any way practice real estate for compensation. An unlicensed assistant who prepares an advertisement must have prior written approval by the employing broker.

In most real estate offices, the salespeople are treated as independent contractors. They come and go at will, working no fixed hours and paying their own payroll taxes (Federal and State Income Taxes, Social Security, Unemployment Insurance, and State Disability Insurance). More strictly supervised workers, such as secretaries, are generally considered employees. **The broker is required, however, to carry workers' compensation and public liability insurance for salespeople in the same way that they do for employees**.

Licenses do NOT have to be displayed, but must be kept at the employing broker's main office.

D. WRITTEN BROKER-ASSOCIATE CONTRACTS

As required by the Real Estate Commissioner's Regulations, **brokers must have a written contract with each licensed member of the sales staff**. The employment contract shall cover all material aspects of the relationship between the parties, including supervision of licensed activities, duties, and compensation. **A copy of this contract must be retained by all parties for three years from the date of termination**. This is also required of salespeople who are themselves brokers but are working under another broker's license. The agreement shall be dated and signed by the parties and shall cover material aspects of the relationship between the parties, including supervision of licensed activities, duties, and compensation.

"Broker-salesperson contracts" must be in writing. This contract is NOT required to be approved by the Department of Real Estate.

Figure 4-7 shows the three-page CAR® Independent Contractor Agreement (Between Broker and Associate-Licensee). It outlines the duties, responsibilities, and compensation to be provided and must be signed and dated by both the broker and the salesperson.

Other specific rules and policies for handling procedures at a specific brokerage firm are usually set down in the company POLICY MANUAL. This manual must be read by all salespeople.

E. DRE NOTIFICATION

When a salesperson chooses to leave the employ of a broker, that broker must notify the DRE within 10 days. When a salesperson transfers a license to a new broker, that broker must notify the DRE within 5 days of the new employment.

If a salesperson is fired for cause, the broker must notify the DRE in writing immediately.

Figure 4-7

CALIFORNIA
ASSOCIATION
OF REALTORS®

INDEPENDENT CONTRACTOR AGREEMENT
(Between Broker and Associate-Licensee)
(C.A.R. Form ICA, Revised 04/07)

This Agreement, dated _____, is made between _____
_____ ("Broker") and
_____ ("Associate-Licensee").
In consideration of the covenants and representations contained in this Agreement, Broker and Associate-Licensee agree as follows:
1. **BROKER:** Broker represents that Broker is duly licensed as a real estate broker by the State of California, ☐ doing business as
   _____ (firm name), ☐ a sole proprietorship, ☐ a partnership, or ☐ a corporation.
   Broker is a member of the _____
   Association(s) of REALTORS®, and a subscriber to the _____
   Multiple Listing Service(s). Broker shall keep Broker's license current during the term of this Agreement.
2. **ASSOCIATE-LICENSEE:** Associate-Licensee represents that: (i) he/she is duly licensed by the State of California as a ☐ real
   estate broker, ☐ real estate salesperson, and (ii) he/she has not used any other names within the past five years, except
   _____. Associate-Licensee shall
   keep his/her license current during the term of this Agreement, including satisfying all applicable continuing education and provisional
   license requirements.
3. **INDEPENDENT CONTRACTOR RELATIONSHIP:**
   A. Broker and Associate-Licensee intend that, to the maximum extent permissible by law: (i) This Agreement does not constitute an
   employment agreement by either party; (ii) Broker and Associate-Licensee are independent contracting parties with respect to all
   services rendered under this Agreement; and (iii) This Agreement shall not be construed as a partnership.
   B. Broker shall not: (i) restrict Associate-Licensee's activities to particular geographical areas, or (ii) dictate Associate-Licensee's
   activities with regard to hours, leads, open houses, opportunity or floor time, production, prospects, sales meetings, schedule,
   inventory, time off, vacation, or similar activities, except to the extent required by law.
   C. Associate-Licensee shall not be required to accept an assignment by Broker to service any particular current or prospective listing
   or parties.
   D. Except as required by law: (i) Associate-Licensee retains sole and absolute discretion and judgment in the methods, techniques,
   and procedures to be used in soliciting and obtaining listings, sales, exchanges, leases, rentals, or other transactions, and in
   carrying out Associate-Licensee's selling and soliciting activities; (ii) Associate-Licensee is under the control of Broker as to the
   results of Associate-Licensee's work only, and not as to the means by which those results are accomplished; (iii) Associate-
   Licensee has no authority to bind Broker by any promise or representation; and (iv) Broker shall not be liable for any obligation
   or liability incurred by Associate-Licensee.
   E. Associate-Licensee's only remuneration shall be the compensation specified in paragraph 8.
   F. Associate-Licensee who only performs as a real estate sales agent, shall not be treated as an employee for state and federal tax
   purposes. However, an Associate-Licencee who performs loan activity shall be treated as an employee for state and federal tax
   purposes unless the activity satisfies the legal requirements to establish an independant contractor relationship.
   G. The fact the Broker may carry workers' compensation insurance for Broker's own benefit and for the mutual benefit of Broker and
   licensees associated with Broker, including Associate-Licensee, shall not create an inference of employment.
   (Workers' Compensation Advisory: Even though Associate-Licensees may be treated as independent contractors for tax and other
   purposes, the California Labor and Workforce Development Agency considers them to be employees for workers' compensation
   purposes. According to the Agency: (i) Broker must obtain workers' compensation insurance for Associate-Licensees and (ii) Broker,
   not Associate-Licensees, must bear the cost of workers' compensation insurance. Penalties for failure to carry workers' compensation
   include, among others, the issuance of stop-work orders and fines of up to $1,000 per agent, not to exceed $100,000 per company.)
4. **LICENSED ACTIVITY:** All listings of property, and all agreements, acts or actions for performance of licensed acts, which are taken
   or performed in connection with this Agreement, shall be taken and performed in the name of Broker. Associate-Licensee agrees to
   and does hereby contribute all right and title to such listings to Broker for the benefit and use of Broker, Associate-Licensee, and
   other licensees associated with Broker. Broker shall make available to Associate-Licensee, equally with other licensees associated
   with Broker, all current listings in Broker's office, except any listing which Broker may choose to place in the exclusive servicing of
   Associate-Licensee or one or more other specific licensees associated with Broker. Associate-Licensee shall provide and pay for all
   professional licenses, supplies, services, and other items required in connection with Associate-Licensee's activities under this
   Agreement, or any listing or transaction, without reimbursement from Broker except as required by law. Associate-Licensee shall work
   diligently and with his/her best efforts to: (i) sell, exchange, lease, or rent properties listed with Broker or other cooperating Brokers;
   (ii) solicit additional listings, clients, and customers; and (iii) otherwise promote the business of serving the public in real estate
   transactions to the end that Broker and Associate-Licensee may derive the greatest benefit possible, in accordance with law.
   Associate-Licensee shall not commit any unlawful act under federal, state or local law or regulation while conducting licensed activity.
   Associate-Licensee shall at all times be familiar, and comply, with all applicable federal, state and local laws, including, but not limited
   to, anti-discrimination laws and restrictions against the giving or accepting a fee, or other thing of value, for the referral of business
   to title companies, escrow companies, home inspection companies, pest control companies and other settlement service providers
   pursuant to the California Business and Professions Code and the Real Estate Settlement Procedures Acts (RESPA). Broker shall
   make available for Associate-Licensee's use, along with other licensees associated with Broker, the facilities of the real estate office
   operated by Broker at _____
   and the facilities of any other office locations made available by Broker pursuant to this Agreement.

Broker's Initials (_____)(_____)
Associate-Licensee's Initials (_____)(_____)

Reviewed by _____ Date _____

EQUAL HOUSING
OPPORTUNITY

ICA REVISED 04/07 (PAGE 1 OF 3) Print Date

INDEPENDENT CONTRACTOR AGREEMENT (ICA PAGE 1 OF 3)

5. **PROPRIETARY INFORMATION AND FILES:** **(A)** All files and documents pertaining to listings, leads and transactions are the property of Broker and shall be delivered to Broker by Associate-Licensee immediately upon request or termination of this Agreement. **(B)** Associate- Licensee acknowledges that Broker's method of conducting business is a protected trade secret. **(C)** Associate-Licensee shall not use to his/her own advantage, or the advantage of any other person, business, or entity, except as specifically agreed in writing, either during Associate-Licensee's association with Broker, or thereafter, any information gained for or from the business, or files of Broker.

6. **SUPERVISION:** Associate-Licensee, within 24 hours (or ☐ _____) after preparing, signing, or receiving same, shall submit to Broker, or Broker's designated licensee: **(i)** all documents which may have a material effect upon the rights and duties of principals in a transaction, **(ii)** any documents or other items connected with a transaction pursuant to this Agreement in the possession of or available to Associate-Licensee; and **(iii)** all documents associated with any real estate transaction in which Associate-Licensee is a principal.

7. **TRUST FUNDS:** All trust funds shall be handled in compliance with the Business and Professions Code, and other applicable laws.

8. **COMPENSATION:**
   A. TO BROKER: Compensation shall be charged to parties who enter into listing or other agreements for services requiring a real estate license:
   ☐ as shown in "Exhibit A" attached, which is incorporated as a part of this Agreement by reference, or
   ☐ as follows: _____
   _____
   _____

   Any deviation which is not approved in writing in advance by Broker, shall be: **(1)** deducted from Associate-Licensee's compensation, if lower than the amount or rate approved above; and, **(2)** subject to Broker approval, if higher than the amount approved above. Any permanent change in commission schedule shall be disseminated by Broker to Associate-Licensee.

   B. TO ASSOCIATE-LICENSEE: Associate-Licensee shall receive a share of compensation actually collected by Broker, on listings or other agreements for services requiring a real estate license, which are solicited and obtained by Associate-Licensee, and on transactions of which Associate-Licensee's activities are the procuring cause, as follows:
   ☐ as shown in "Exhibit B" attached, which is incorporated as a part of this Agreement by reference, or
   ☐ other: _____
   _____

   C. PARTNERS, TEAMS, AND AGREEMENTS WITH OTHER ASSOCIATE-LICENSEES IN OFFICE: If Associate-Licensee and one or more other Associate-Licensees affiliated with Broker participate on the same side (either listing or selling) of a transaction, the commission allocated to their combined activities shall be divided by Broker and paid to them according to their written agreement. Broker shall have the right to withhold total compensation if there is a dispute between associate-licensees, or if there is no written agreement, or if no written agreement has been provided to Broker.

   D. EXPENSES AND OFFSETS: If Broker elects to advance funds to pay expenses or liabilities of Associate-Licensee, or for an advance payment of, or draw upon, future compensation, Broker may deduct the full amount advanced from compensation payable to Associate-Licensee on any transaction without notice. If Associate-Licensee's compensation is subject to a lien, garnishment or other restriction on payment, Broker shall charge Associate-Licensee a fee for complying with such restriction.

   E. PAYMENT: **(i)** All compensation collected by Broker and due to Associate-Licensee shall be paid to Associate-Licensee, after deduction of expenses and offsets, immediately or as soon thereafter as practicable, except as otherwise provided in this Agreement, or a separate written agreement between Broker and Associate-Licensee. **(ii)** Compensation shall not be paid to Associate-Licensee until both the transaction and file are complete. **(iii)** Broker is under no obligation to pursue collection of compensation from any person or entity responsible for payment. Associate-Licensee does not have the independent right to pursue collection of compensation for activities which require a real estate license which were done in the name of Broker. **(iv)** Expenses which are incurred in the attempt to collect compensation shall be paid by Broker and Associate-Licensee in the same proportion as set forth for the division of compensation (paragraph 8(B)). **(v)** If there is a known or pending claim against Broker or Associate-Licensee on transactions for which Associate-Licensee has not yet been paid, Broker may withhold from compensation due Associate-Licensee on that transaction amounts for which Associate-Licensee could be responsible under paragraph 14, until such claim is resolved. **(vi)** Associate-Licensee shall not be entitled to any advance payment from Broker upon future compensation.

   F. UPON OR AFTER TERMINATION: If this Agreement is terminated while Associate-Licensee has listings or pending transactions that require further work normally rendered by Associate-Licensee, Broker shall make arrangements with another associate-licensee to perform the required work, or Broker shall perform the work him/herself. The licensee performing the work shall be reasonably compensated for completing work on those listings or transactions, and such reasonable compensation shall be deducted from Associate-Licensee's share of compensation. Except for such offset, Associate-Licensee shall receive the compensation due as specified above.

9. **TERMINATION OF RELATIONSHIP:** Broker or Associate-Licensee may terminate their relationship under this Agreement at any time, with or without cause. After termination, Associate-Licensee shall not solicit: **(i)** prospective or existing clients or customers based upon company- generated leads obtained during the time Associate-Licensee was affiliated with Broker; **(ii)** any principal with existing contractual obligations to Broker; or **(iii)** any principal with a contractual transactional obligation for which Broker is entitled to be compensated. Even after termination, this Agreement shall govern all disputes and claims between Broker and Associate-Licensee connected with their relationship under this Agreement, including obligations and liabilities arising from existing and completed listings, transactions, and services.

Broker's Initials (_____)(_____)
Associate-Licensee's Initials (_____)(_____)

Reviewed by _____ Date _____

ICA REVISED 04/07 (PAGE 2 OF 3)

EQUAL HOUSING OPPORTUNITY

INDEPENDENT CONTRACTOR AGREEMENT (ICA PAGE 2 OF 3)

10. DISPUTE RESOLUTION:
   A. Mediation: Mediation is recommended as a method of resolving disputes arising out of this Agreement between Broker and Associate-Licensee.
   B. Arbitration: All disputes or claims between Associate-Licensee and other licensee(s) associated with Broker, or between Associate-Licensee and Broker, arising from or connected in any way with this Agreement, which cannot be adjusted between the parties involved, shall be submitted to the Association of REALTORS® of which all such disputing parties are members for arbitration pursuant to the provisions of its Bylaws, as may be amended from time to time, which are incorporated as a part of this Agreement by reference. If the Bylaws of the Association do not cover arbitration of the dispute, or if the Association declines jurisdiction over the dispute, then arbitration shall be pursuant to the rules of California law. The Federal Arbitration Act, Title 9, U.S. Code, Section 1, et seq., shall govern this Agreement.

11. AUTOMOBILE: Associate-Licensee shall maintain automobile insurance coverage for liability and property damage in the following amounts $_____/$_____. Broker shall be named as an additional insured party on Associate-Licensee's policies. A copy of the endorsement showing Broker as an additional insured shall be provided to Broker.

12. PERSONAL ASSISTANTS: Associate-Licensee may make use of a personal assistant, provided the following requirements are satisfied. Associate-Licensee shall have a written agreement with the personal assistant which establishes the terms and responsibilities of the parties to the employment agreement, including, but not limited to, compensation, supervision and compliance with applicable law. The agreement shall be subject to Broker's review and approval. Unless otherwise agreed, if the personal assistant has a real estate license, that license must be provided to the Broker. Both Associate-Licensee and personal assistant must sign any agreement that Broker has established for such purposes.

13. OFFICE POLICY MANUAL: If Broker's office policy manual, now or as modified in the future, conflicts with or differs from the terms of this Agreement, the terms of the office policy manual shall govern the relationship between Broker and Associate-Licensee.

14. INDEMNITY AND HOLD HARMLESS: Associate-Licensee agrees to indemnify, defend and hold Broker harmless from all claims, disputes, litigation, judgments, awards, costs and attorney's fees, arising from any action taken or omitted by Associate-Licensee, or others working through, or on behalf of Associate-Licensee in connection with services rendered or to be rendered pursuant to this Agreement. Any such claims or costs payable pursuant to this Agreement, are due as follows:
   ☐ Paid in full by Associate-Licensee, who hereby agrees to indemnify and hold harmless Broker for all such sums, or
   ☐ In the same ratio as the compensation split as it existed at the time the compensation was earned by Associate-Licensee
   ☐ Other: _____
   _____
   _____
   Payment from Associate-Licensee is due at the time Broker makes such payment and can be offset from any compensation due Associate-Licensee as above. Broker retains the authority to settle claims or disputes, whether or not Associate-Licensee consents to such settlement.

15. ADDITIONAL PROVISIONS: _____
   _____
   _____

16. DEFINITIONS: As used in this Agreement, the following terms have the meanings indicated:
   (A) "Listing" means an agreement with a property owner or other party to locate a buyer, exchange party, lessee, or other party to a transaction involving real property, a mobile home, or other property or transaction which may be brokered by a real estate licensee, or an agreement with a party to locate or negotiate for any such property or transaction.
   (B) "Compensation" means compensation for acts requiring a real estate license, regardless of whether calculated as a percentage of transaction price, flat fee, hourly rate, or in any other manner.
   (C) "Transaction" means a sale, exchange, lease, or rental of real property, a business opportunity, or a manufactured home, which may lawfully be brokered by a real estate licensee.

17. ATTORNEY FEES: In any action, proceeding, or arbitration between Broker and Associate-Licensee arising from or related to this Agreement, the prevailing Broker or Associate-Licensee shall be entitled to reasonable attorney fees and costs.

18. ENTIRE AGREEMENT: All prior agreements between the parties concerning their relationship as Broker and Associate-Licensee are incorporated in this Agreement, which constitutes the entire contract. Its terms are intended by the parties as a final and complete expression of their agreement with respect to its subject matter, and may not be contradicted by evidence of any prior agreement or contemporaneous oral agreement. This Agreement may not be amended, modified, altered, or changed except by a further agreement in writing executed by Broker and Associate-Licensee.

Broker:

_____
(Brokerage firm name)

By _____
Its Broker/Office manager (circle one)

_____
(Print name)

_____
(Address)

_____
(City, State, Zip)

_____
(Telephone)   (Fax)

Associate-Licensee:

_____
(Signature)

_____
(Print name)

_____
(Address)

_____
(City, State, Zip)

_____
(Telephone)   (Fax)

Published and Distributed by:
REAL ESTATE BUSINESS SERVICES, INC.
a subsidiary of the California Association of REALTORS®
525 South Virgil Avenue, Los Angeles, California 90020

ICA REVISED 04/07 (PAGE 3 OF 3)

Reviewed by _____ Date _____

EQUAL HOUSING OPPORTUNITY

INDEPENDENT CONTRACTOR AGREEMENT (ICA PAGE 3 OF 3)

F. AGENTS WHO BUY AND SELL FOR THEIR OWN ACCOUNT
(Disclose You Have a Real Estate License)

Many real estate professionals buy and sell property for themselves as part of their own personal investments (acting as a principal and not as an agent). The Real Estate Commissioner created a regulation requiring disclosure of license status (buyer and seller) which has the full force and effect of law. The commissioner has strongly suggested that it would be in the licensee's best interest to disclose this fact, in writing, as soon as possible. This protects the purchasers and others involved. Everyone should be aware that they are dealing with a person knowledgeable in real estate and that he or she is representing his or her own interests.

G. POWER OF ATTORNEY

A *POWER OF ATTORNEY is an acknowledged, written authorization of one person to act for another*. There are two categories of power of attorney: 1) a general power of attorney, and 2) a special power of attorney.

A *GENERAL POWER OF ATTORNEY allows the person so authorized to perform any act the principal could perform*. The person thus authorized to act on behalf of the principal is called the attorney in fact.

An *ATTORNEY IN FACT under a "general" power of attorney is a person who has been given the right to transact all of a principal's business*. The specific powers conferred must be set down in writing, duly acknowledged and recorded with the county recorder's office in the county where the property is located, in order for the agency to take effect. **Death of either party or an acknowledged declaration from the principal may revoke this power**. An attorney in fact cannot deed his client's property to himself.

A *SPECIAL POWER OF ATTORNEY allows the person so authorized to perform only a specific act (for example, sell your house)*. The *ATTORNEY IN FACT, under a "special" power of attorney, has the authorization to perform only a specific act*. A real estate agent under a special power of attorney is an "attorney in fact" who is usually authorized to find a ready, willing, and able buyer.

A listing agreement makes the broker a special agent to perform the authorized act of selling, exchanging, or otherwise transferring real property. Usually, an agent is given expressed authority, by written agreement (listing), to sell a home. If not otherwise expressed in writing, the agent is allowed to delegate parts of that authority under three circumstances:

1. If the act to be performed is purely mechanical, such as typing out a standard form.
2. If the agent is not legally qualified to do something, such as notarizing a document that requires a state license.
3. If it is customary to delegate authority for that task in that business or locality.

H. TORTS BY AN AGENT (Broker/Salesperson)

A *TORT is any civil injury or wrong committed upon a person or that person's property*. Fraud, misrepresentation, negligence, and secret profit all stem from a breach of an agent's duty. In some cases they can even be considered criminal acts. The broker and his or her salespeople,

as professionals, are expected to maintain a high standard of ethics. They are responsible for their own acts and representations even when following the seller's directions.

I. MISREPRESENTATION OF A MATERIAL FACT

A misrepresentation by a broker or salesperson may be material or immaterial. If the representation is slight, or would not have a measurable effect on the people relying on it, it is not a material fact. When a broker misrepresents his or her authority to act as an agent for someone else, he or she may be liable to the person who relies on the misrepresentation. A statement such as "I think this is the best house on the street" is a statement of opinion (puffing) and is not considered a misrepresentation.

"Puffing" is a statement of opinion (not fact) that exaggerates a property's benefits. It would only be a misrepresentation if a reasonable person would consider it a statement of fact.

The misrepresentation of a material fact can financially injure someone and may be punishable under the Civil Code or the Commissioner's Regulations. There are three types of misrepresentations:

1. Innocent Misrepresentations,
2. Negligent Misrepresentations, and
3. Fraudulent Misrepresentations (or nondisclosures).

The first misrepresentation usually has no broker liability. The second and third are subject to civil penalties and the Real Estate Commissioner's actions. **INNOCENT MISREPRESENTATIONS** *are false statements that are not known to be false at the time they are made.* These statements do not usually warrant legal liability for the broker but can cause a rescission of any contract. Everyone involved would then be reinstated to their original positions.

An agent who sells the wrong condo because a prankster switched the condo unit's number is an example of an innocent misrepresentation.

NEGLIGENT MISREPRESENTATIONS *are false statements believed to be true, but made without reasonable grounds for that belief.* This is breach of duty without fraudulent intent. The broker is liable for any negligent statements made to a buyer or seller. Such statements are in effect a form of deceit.

An agent mistakenly confirms that a property is within a particular school district without checking. This would be negligent misrepresentation.

FRAUDULENT MISREPRESENTATIONS *are statements made at a time when the broker knows the statement to be false, or statements in which the broker fails to disclose (conceals) material facts.* This is actual fraud. Any contract made under the influence of fraudulent information may become void, and the person making the fraudulent statements may be liable for civil or even criminal fraud.

"Intentional deceptions" or the "concealment of material facts" are fraudulent misrepresentations, which are immoral and unlawful.

Example: In July, Baker bought Able's home through Charlie, the listing broker. In November, when the first rain came, the tile roof leaked badly in many places. Baker sued Able and Charlie for the cost of the necessary new roof. Testimony in court showed that Able had mentioned the need of a new roof to Charlie, but Charlie had not mentioned it to Baker because "he had not asked about it." It is likely that Baker will recover damages from Able, who will, in turn, recover from Charlie.

J. SECRET PROFIT

An agent may not make any secret profit. This is a breach of the fiduciary relationship between the principal and the real estate agent. All financial offers, whether legitimate or not, must be presented to the seller. So, if a real estate agent is offered a secret profit, he or she has a duty to inform his or her principal of this. In addition, the broker may not allow others (friends and relatives) to make a secret profit with his or her knowledge.

Example: If a broker presented a full price offer to a seller, which the seller accepted, but the seller discovers during escrow that the buyer is the brother of the broker, the seller can cancel the transaction without any liability for the commission.

An unlicensed person may make a secret profit on the purchase of real property, but an agent may not.

K. WARRANTY OF AUTHORITY

The broker, as an agent, warrants that he or she has the authority to represent another person. *If there is a written listing between the seller and the broker, he or she has an express WARRANTY OF AUTHORITY to offer the property for sale.* The problem arises when the broker offers to sell a property, without the listing, to an unsuspecting buyer who relies on the fact that the agent has certain authority. In such cases, the broker could be liable for this untrue representation. A broker gives *IMPLIED WARRANTY OF AUTHORITY to act for a seller by the mere fact that he or she shows the seller's property.*

When a broker represents a seller, he or she does not warrant that the seller has the capacity to sell. If, in fact, the seller does not have the capacity to contract, then the broker is not liable, as long as he or she did not have knowledge of the fact. However, if the broker has knowledge that the seller could not contract, then the broker could be liable to the buyer.

The prosecution of an unlicensed salesperson, acting as a licensed salesperson, would be handled by the district attorney's office.

L. DISCLOSURE OF AIDS AND DEATH

An occupant's death from AIDS or AIDS-related illness, or any other contagious disease, is a highly emotional issue. Brokers must strive to balance the principle of full disclosure against the right to privacy of an AIDS victim. Disclosing casually that a tenant or former tenant (owner or occupant) died, or is dying, from AIDS might very well be in violation of that person's civil rights and might expose the broker to civil or criminal penalties. **By law, sellers, brokers, and landlords have no liability for failure to disclose a prior occupant's**

death or its cause after three years. On the other hand, intentional misrepresentation concerning an occupant's death on the property, in response to direct inquiry, is illegal.

VII. Required Disclosures – Agent Summary (One-to-Four Unit Residential Sales)

A. VISUAL INSPECTION

A listing and selling broker must each conduct a reasonably competent and diligent inspection of the property and disclose to the prospective buyer all material facts affecting the value, desirability, and intended use of the property. The real estate agent does not have to inspect: (a) areas not reasonably accessible; (b) areas off the site of the property; (c) public records or permits concerning the title or use of the property; or (d) in a common interest development where the seller or broker complies by furnishing controlling documents and a financial statement.

> **Example:** Agent Able notices a crack in the wall and the doors are not closing properly. Able should advise the buyer to get a soil report.

B. DISCLOSURE OF AGENCY RELATIONSHIP

As a real estate agent, you must disclose, in writing, the duties which arise from certain agency relationships, the broker's status as agent of the seller, agent of the buyer, or agent of both the seller and the buyer (dual agent).

C. DISCLOSURE OF THE NEGOTIABILITY OF REAL ESTATE COMMISSIONS

The listing or sales agreement must contain the following disclosure in not less than 10-point boldface: "**NOTICE:** The rate of real estate commissions is not fixed by law. They are set by each broker individually and may be negotiable between the seller and the broker" (see Chapter 1).

D. NO DISCLOSURE REQUIRED FOR MANNER/OCCURRENCE OF DEATH; AFFLICTION OF OCCUPANT WITH AIDS

Any death, which occurred within a 3-year period, should be disclosed if it is "material." If the death occurred more than 3 years before the date of the offer to buy, there is no liability for failing to disclose the fact of death. The seller and his/her agent need not voluntarily disclose affliction with AIDS or death from AIDS, but cannot make any misrepresentations to a direct question about death on the property.

VIII. Terminating an Agency Relationship

A. REASONS FOR TERMINATION OF AGENCY

An agency relationship between a seller and a real estate broker can be terminated by operation of law or by the acts of either the broker or the seller. **Figure 4-8** shows the seven subcategories of these methods.

Figure 4-8   **Termination of an Agency Relationship**

Operation of Law	Acts of the Seller or Broker
a. Expiration of the Agency (Listing) Agreement b. Destruction of the Property c. Death or Incapacity Broker or Seller (Listing Only)	a. Agreement by Both Broker and Seller b. Renouncement of Listing by the Broker c. Revocation of Listing by the Seller d. Close of Escrow

---

1. Operation of Law

a. Expiration of the Agency (Listing) Agreement

The Exclusive Agency Listing Agreement and the Exclusive Authorization and Right to Sell Listing Agreement have a definite termination date. These listings will end automatically on the stated date if not terminated in some other way before that date. The other type of listing, an open listing, does not require a termination date because it can be terminated at any time.

b. Destruction of the Property

A house burning down would terminate a listing agreement.

c. Death or Incapacity of the Broker or Seller (Listing Only)

If the broker in a large real estate office dies, all listings are automatically cancelled, and the new broker would need to re-list the properties.

2. Act of the Seller or Broker

a. Agreement by Both the Broker and Seller

If both parties to a contract want to end it, it may be terminated by mutual agreement.

b. Renouncement of the Listing Agreement by the Broker

The broker can refuse to fulfill the listing agreement, but may be subject to damages for breach of contract.

c. Revocation of the Listing Agreement by the Seller

The seller can refuse to sell the listed property, but may be liable for the commission if the broker has found a buyer who is ready, willing and able to purchase the property.

d. Close of Escrow

An agency relationship is terminated at the close of escrow.

A typical agency would be terminated by death of the principal, destruction of the subject property, or mutual consent of the principal and his/her agent. It would NOT be terminated by estoppel.

IX. A Brokerage Must be Run Like a Business

A "company dollar" is the dollar (income and commissions) a broker receives after all salespersons' commissions have been paid.

A **GROSS DOLLAR** is all the income that is received by the office before paying out commissions. A **COMPANY DOLLAR** is the amount left to management after payment of all commissions, including in-house salespeople and other multiple listings brokers and salespeople (see **Figure 4-9**). The concept of the company dollar allows the brokerage to examine and focus on how their after-commission income is spent.

Figure 4-9

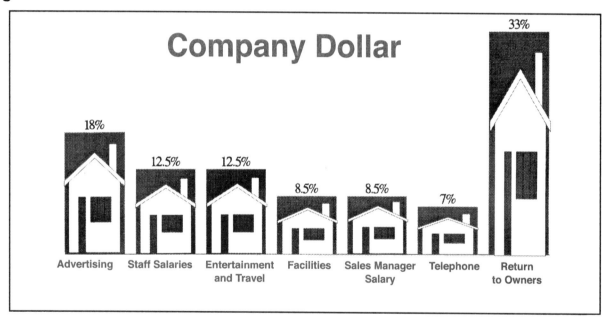

"**TOE**" is the acronym for Total Operating Expense.

T Total
O Operating
E Expense

The **DESK COST** *for a broker is the total operating expenses divided by the number of agents in the office.* The desk cost tells the broker the financial loss caused by an empty desk or an unproductive salesperson.

A. ONE-STOP SHOPPING

When the real estate market goes "soft," it means shrinking profit margins and fewer company dollars. Some brokerages respond to this by offering one-stop shopping. *ONE-*

STOP SHOPPING means the brokerage is involved in multiple facets of property transactions, including escrow and title services, property management, and mortgage brokerage.

X. CHAPTER SUMMARY

Agency is the relationship between a seller, broker (and his or her salespeople), and a buyer. A **principal** is the person who hires the agent. The agency of a real estate broker may be established by **express agreement, implied agreement, ratification,** or **estoppel.** The best evidence of an agency relationship is a **written agreement (listing).**

Agents can be identified as the **listing agents** or **selling agents.** A broker (agent) working for a principal owes him or her a **fiduciary duty,** including honesty, utmost care, integrity, accounting, disclosure, and loyalty. An agent owes a third party (the "other" party in a negotiation) an obligation of honesty and timely disclosure of material facts.

An agent can represent a seller, a buyer, or both **(dual agency),** if all parties consent to the transaction. The **Disclosure Regarding Real Estate Agency Relationships** Form states that the agency relationship must be disclosed as soon as practical. **Termination of agency** can be by **operation of law** or by **acts of the seller or broker,** but not by estoppel.

Salespeople can be **independent contractors** or **employees,** although the DRE considers them employees of the broker, making the broker responsible for their activities. A broker must immediately notify the DRE in writing of the hiring or firing of a salesperson. Signed **broker-salesperson contracts** must be kept for **three years** after termination of the contract (as well as all transactions files).

A **listing** is a personal service contract between an agent and a principal, creating an **agency relationship.** It may be for any period of time, but must have a definite, final termination date. An **open listing** may be given to several brokers, or the property may be sold by the owner without obligation to pay a commission. It is **unilateral,** because only the seller makes a promise, whereas an **exclusive agency listing** and **exclusive right to sell** are **bilateral** (a promise for a promise).

An **exclusive agency listing** entitles only the listing broker to a commission, unless the owner sells the property, in which case, no commission is owed. An **exclusive right to sell listing** entitles the listing broker to a commission during the listing period even if the owner sells the property.

The rarely used **net listing** sets the broker's commission at whatever amount a property sells for above the asking price set by the owner. A **multiple listing** is an exclusive right to sell held by all the members of a **Multiple Listing Service (MLS).**

A copy of the **listing agreement** (and any other real estate agreement) should be given to the buyer and seller immediately after signing. All listings belong to the broker, not the salesperson.

An agent can delegate authority to a **subagent** or to a **cooperating agent** or **broker**. While agreements between brokers don't need to be in writing, they must be in writing between brokers and salespeople.

Real estate commissions are negotiable. If an offer meets the exact terms of a listing, the agent has earned the commission even if the owner refuses to sell. The agent who is the **procuring cause** (series of unbroken events that lead to an acceptable agreement with the seller) is entitled to the commission.

The *Easton v. Strassburger* case extended the liabilities of brokers to include a duty to inspect and disclose any relevant facts that might materially affect the value or desirability of a property. The **Transfer Disclosure Statement** must be provided by both seller and broker and must be given to the prospective buyer as soon as practicable before or within three days after the **Purchase Agreement** is signed. A broker does not have to disclose a cause of death unless there is a direct inquiry, and no liability to disclose an occupant's cause of death after three years.

When a broker receives a buyer's money deposit, he or she must: 1) place the deposit in escrow, 2) give it to the principal, or 3) put it in the broker's trust fund account. All funds must be kept segregated, as **commingling**, or mixing the client's money with private funds, is illegal.

A real estate agent, under a **special power of attorney** is an **attorney in fact**, authorized to find a ready, willing, and able buyer. As an agent, the broker warrants that he or she has the authority to represent another person. He or she is obligated to maintain a high standard of ethics, and refrain from either material or immaterial misrepresentation. **Misrepresentations** can be innocent, negligent, or fraudulent. Intentional deceptions or concealment of material facts are examples of **fraudulent misrepresentations**. Agents are also prohibited from making **secret profits**.

A brokerage must be run like a business. A **gross dollar** is all the income received by the office, and the **company dollar** is all the money left after paying commissions. **"TOE"** is an easy way to remember **Total Operating Expense**.

XI. TERMINOLOGY

A. Agency
B. Agency Disclosure Form
C. Commingling
D. Conversion
E. Dual Agency
F. Easton v. Strassburger
G. Employee
H. Estoppel
I. Exclusive Agency Listing
J. Exclusive Right to Sell
Listing

K. Fiduciary Relationship
L. Fraudulent Misrepresentation
M. General Attorney in Fact
N. Independent Contractor
O. Innocent Misrepresentation
P. Multiple Listing Service (MLS)
Q. Negligent Misrepresentation
R. Net Listing
S. Open Listing
T. Policy Manual
U. Principal

V. Ratification
W. Secret Profit
X. Special Attorney in Fact
Y. Subagent
Z. Third Party
AA. Tort
BB. Transfer Disclosure
Statement

1.____ The mixing of funds held in trust with personal funds.

2.____ Authorization from a property owner giving a real estate agent the non-exclusive right to secure a purchaser. Other brokers, or the owners themselves, may also solicit a purchaser.

3.____ The unlawful taking and use of another's property placed in your trust, as an agent, by that person.

4.____ The person(s) who employs a real estate agent, usually through a listing agreement.

5.____ The relationship between the principal and the principal's agent that arises out of a contract, either expressed or implied, written or oral, wherein the agent is employed by the principal to do certain acts dealing with a third party.

6.____ A person upon whom the powers of an agent have been conferred, not by the principal, but by an agent authorized by the principal.

7.____ A civil wrong committed against a person or property, independent of any contractual agreement.

8.____ The theory of law that states a person cannot suddenly assert a legal right when that person has neglected to assert it previously. For example: If someone claims to be your agent and you know about it and don't stop that person, you can't later claim that person was not acting on your behalf.

9.____ A person who acts for another, selling final results and using his or her own judgment to achieve those results.

10.____ The approval of an act performed on behalf of a person without previous authorization, such as the approval by a principal of a previously unauthorized act of an agent.

11.____ An agency relationship in which the agent acts concurrently for both of the principals (buyer and seller), with their consent, in a transaction.

12.____ An association of real estate agents that provides a pooling of listings and the sharing of commissions.

13.____ Any party to a transaction other than the principal with whom you have an agency relationship.

14.____ One who is authorized to perform many acts for another under a power of attorney.

15.____ A listing agreement employing a broker as the sole agent for the seller of real property, under the terms of which the broker is entitled to a commission unless the homeowner sells the property.

16.____ A listing agreement employing a broker to act as an agent for the seller of real property. Under the terms of this agreement, the broker is entitled to a commission if the property is sold during the duration of the listing by the broker or by the owner without an agent.

17.____ A listing that provides for the agent to retain, as compensation for his or her services, all sums received over and above a net price to the owner.

18.____The major court decision which requires an agent to disclose any physical defects or evidence of defects that could affect the value of real property.

19.____An agent's making of additional money in a real estate transaction without disclosing it to the principal and third party.

20.____Knowingly making false and deceptive statements to help sell a property.

21.____Making false statements about a property, without realizing it.

22.____Making false statements regarding a property that could have been checked out or verified.

23.____A form that notifies buyers of any physical defects to a property and requires the seller and the agent to list any evidence of defects of which they are aware.

24.____A form presented to the principal(s) in a transaction stating exactly who the agent is working for: the buyer, the seller, or both.

25.____The relationship between the agent and the principal that requires the highest level of trust and good faith.

26.____One who works directly for another person, is told what to do, and is controlled in how they do it.

27.____A written book of procedures explaining how a broker expects the agents working under him or her to conduct business and handle routine problems.

28.____Someone authorized to represent a principal in a specific task, such as selling a property.

XII. CHAPTER QUIZ

1. When a seller grants the right to sell and the broker agrees to use diligence in obtaining a purchaser, this is called:

    a. attorney in fact.
    b. power of attorney.
    c. specific performance.
    d. agency.

2. The broker, as agent of the seller, owes the buyer:

    a. only a duty to disclose any item that relates directly to the sales price of the property.
    b. the same fiduciary obligations he or she owes to the seller.
    c. only the duty to answer questions honestly.
    d. the duty of honesty and fair dealing.

3. The best way to establish an agency relationship is through:

    a. written agreement.
    b. oral agreement.
    c. estoppel.
    d. consideration.

4. A salesperson's listings are the property of:

    a. the salesperson.
    b. the salesperson and his/her heirs.
    c. the broker who employs him/her as a salesperson.
    d. the MLS.

5. Seller Skinner signed a 90-day exclusive right to sell listing with Broker Bill. Two weeks later, Skinner cancelled the listing with Bill and gave an open listing to Broker Carl and another open listing to Broker Paul. Three weeks later, Paul presented an offer to Skinner that the seller accepted. Which of the following is most correct?

   a. Broker Bill only is entitled to a full commission
   b. A full commission will be divided equally between Bill, Carl, and Paul
   c. Broker Paul only is entitled to a full commission
   d. Paul is entitled to a full commission and Bill is entitled to a full commission as well

6. Seller signed a 90-day exclusive right to sell listing with Broker Able. When the listing expired, Seller gave an open listing to Broker Baker and Broker Charlie. Three weeks later, Broker Baker presented an offer to the seller which he accepted. Which of the following is most correct?

   a. Broker Able only is entitled to a full commission
   b. A full commission will be divided equally between Able, Baker, and Charlie
   c. Broker Charlie is entitled to a full commission
   d. Broker Baker is the procurring cause of the sale and is entitled to a full commission

7. When inspecting a seller's home the agent discovers several physical defects that the agent fails to disclose to the buyer. The buyer can file civil action against the agent for up to:

   a. 2 years.
   b. 3 years.
   c. 4 years.
   d. 5 years.

8. How much of a broker's personal funds can be kept in his or her trust account without being guilty of commingling?

   a. $100
   b. $200
   c. $400
   d. As much as he/she wants

9. Which of the following is most correct about "puffing?"

   a. It is legal, and proper business tactics
   b. It is usually unethical unless approved by the agent's broker
   c. It is only an "opinion of value" of a specific property as of a given date
   d. It may be misrepresentation if a reasonable person considers it a "statement of fact"

10. The broker in a large real estate office dies. All listings:

   a. usually belong to the subagents according to the terms of the broker/associate contract.
   b. are continued during probate, unless the subagent moves to another firm.
   c. are automatically cancelled and the new broker would need to re-list the properties.
   d. may be cancelled unilaterally by each principal with 24 hours written notice.

ANSWERS: 1. d.; 2. d.; 3. a.; 4. c.; 5. d.; 6. d.; 7. a.; 8. b.; 9. d.; 10. c

CHAPTER 5
Contracts

I. Contracts in General

Nothing is as important to the real estate broker and his/her salespeople than the law of contracts. Because every phase of a real estate transaction involves one or more contracts, it is important to understand the basic rules that govern the creation and life of a contract. This chapter will explain the elements of contracts and illustrate, in detail, the important parts of the Residential Purchase Agreement.

www.leginfo.ca.gov/calaw.html (California Law)
www.leginfo.ca.gov/statute.html (State Statutes)
www.courtinfo.ca.gov (California Courts)
www.ce9.uscourts.gov (9th Circuit Court)
www.calbar.org (State Bar of California)

A *CONTRACT is an agreement to do or not to do a certain act or service.* Every contract consists of a promise or a set of promises that are enforceable by law. These promises may be created in two ways, either in an express manner or in an implied manner.

An *EXPRESS CONTRACT describes a contract that is expressed in words, either oral or written.* Listings, purchase agreements, and leases are all express contracts.

On the other hand, an *IMPLIED CONTRACT is created when an agreement is made by acts and conduct (implication) rather than by words.* For example, suppose you entered a hardware store where you had an account, picked up an $8 paint brush, and waved it at the clerk as you departed. The clerk, judging from your conduct, would assume that you wanted the paint brush charged to your account and would bill you accordingly. An implied contract was formed. Implied contracts are not used in the practice of real estate.

A *BILATERAL CONTRACT is a promise made by one party in exchange for the promise of another party.* It is a promise for a promise. For instance, if a homeowner offers a painter $2,000 to paint his or her garage and the painter agrees to do it, a bilateral contract is formed: The painter promises to paint the garage, while the homeowner promises to give the painter $2,000. *When only one party makes a promise for an act of another, the agreement is called a UNILATERAL CONTRACT.* It is a promise for an act. If someone acts upon an offer, the one making the offer is obligated to complete his or her promise.

CHAPTER OUTLINE

Example: Mr. Bentley offers a reward to any person who can identify the arsonist who set his home on fire. Because this is a unilateral contract, Mr. Bentley is required to give the reward to any person who can fulfill the obligation.

A. CLASSIFICATION OF CONTRACTS

Some of the ways in which contracts may be classified include the following.

1. Valid

A fully operative contract that is binding and enforceable in a court of law is "valid." **If a buyer and seller signed a contract and the seller died, there is a valid contract.**

2. Voidable

A "voidable" contract can be affirmed or rejected at the option of a party. The victim can rescind, cancel, or annul. A voidable contract remains binding until it is rescinded.

3. Void

A "void" contract has no legal force or effect. It does not exist. It lacks one of the essential elements of a contract. A contract with an illegal purpose is void.

4. Unenforceable

An "unenforceable" contract is a valid contract that for some reason cannot be enforced in court (proved or sued upon).

B. LIFE OF A CONTRACT (Three Phases)

1. Phase 1 – Negotiation

During the **negotiation period**, the buyer and seller discuss the possibility of a contract. If there is mutual interest between the parties, then an offer, or perhaps several offers,

can be made. The offer becomes a contract when accepted, provided that all the other elements necessary for the creation of a contract are present.

2. Phase 2 – Performance

An **EXECUTORY CONTRACT** *is a legal agreement, the provisions of which have yet to be completely performed.* A purchase agreement is executory until payment is made and title is transferred. Then it becomes executed. A land contract might be executory for years.

An exclusive listing signed solely by an owner is an example of an express, bilateral, executory contract.

3. Phase 3 – Completion

This stage occurs after a contract has been completed. An **EXECUTED CONTRACT** *is one that has either been discharged or performed.* After a contract has been completed, there is the warranty that every aspect of the contract has been properly performed.

This term should not be confused with the execution of a contract. To **EXECUTE** *a contract is to sign a contract,* while the **EXECUTION** *of a contract is the act of performing or carrying out the contract.*

A contract to be performed is called "executory"; a completely performed contract has been "executed." The contract lives on until the time to bring legal action has expired. This is called the "statute of limitations."

II. Elements of a Contract

According to the California Civil Code, there must be four elements to any valid contract whether it involves real estate or not. However, in real estate, contracts generally must be in writing, which becomes a fifth element (see **Figure 5-1**).

These are the four elements of any contract: 1) capacity, 2) mutual consent, 3) legality, and 4) consideration. Often, in real estate, a proper writing is required, making this the fifth element.

The following are NOT essential elements of a valid contract: 1) money (can be other consideration), 2) writing (except for real estate contracts which frequently require it), and 3) performance.

A. CAPACITY

For a contract to be valid, there must be two or more parties who have the legal capacity to contract. Everyone is capable of contracting, except for the following persons: 1) minors, 2) incompetents, and 3) convicts.

1. Minor

A **MINOR** *is a person under the age of eighteen.* A minor cannot make contracts relating to real property or property not in his or her immediate possession or control, and

Figure 5-1

Elements of a Contract

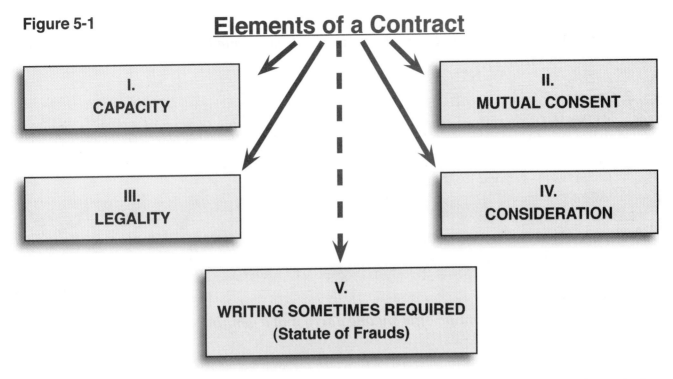

| I. CAPACITY | II. MUTUAL CONSENT |
| III. LEGALITY | IV. CONSIDERATION |

V. WRITING SOMETIMES REQUIRED (Statute of Frauds)

does not have the right to employ an agent, **unless the minor is emancipated**. An *EMANCIPATED MINOR is one who has the contractual rights of an adult.* The three ways that a minor becomes emancipated are:

1. through marriage,
2. as a member or former member of the armed forces, and
3. when declared to be self-supporting by the courts.

A minor who has been "emancipated" has legal capacity. Once emancipated, always emancipated. Otherwise, a contract or deed signed by a minor would be void. Any minor can acquire property by gift or inheritance.

A person under the age of 18 and divorced has the capacity to contract.

A contract with a minor is void because a minor cannot delegate authority. A guardian may, however, buy and sell real estate on behalf of a minor if the action is given court approval.

Both minors and incompetents may acquire real property by gift or inheritance.

2. Incompetent

An *INCOMPETENT is a person who is judged to be of unsound mind.* Such a person has no capacity (power) to contract; any contract made is void. In real estate transactions with incompetents, it is necessary to have the guardian's decision approved by the court. However, both minors and incompetents may acquire real property by gift or inheritance.

If a buyer and seller enter into a valid binding contract and one of the parties dies or becomes incompetent, the contract is valid if it was signed before the party died or became incompetent.

3. Convicts

CONVICTS are persons who have lost their civil rights during their imprisonment. Convicts are incapable of contracting, but they do not forfeit any property in their possession. They may acquire property by gift, inheritance, or will, but can only convey property if the action is ratified by the California Adult Authority.

ALIENS *are not citizens of the United States, but they have the right to own property in California.* This surprises some people, but it is true that any person, whether he or she is a U.S. citizen or not, may buy, hold or transfer real property.

B. MUTUAL CONSENT

"Mutual consent" is a genuine offer by one party and a genuine acceptance by the other party.

This acceptance need not be a true "meeting of the minds" of the parties because they are bound only by an objective standard (their apparent intentions as evidenced by words or acts). Since courts cannot read minds, any secret or unexpressed intentions are immaterial. The consent must be genuine and free from fraud or mistake, and there must be a true intention to be obligated, or it may be voidable by one or both of the parties.

Example: Two days after entering into a binding purchase contract, the buyer and seller decided to mutually surrender the contract. With respect to the deposit, the agent representing both parties must return the entire deposit to the buyer immediately.

1. The Offer

An *OFFER expresses a person's willingness to enter into a contract.* The *OFFEROR is the person (buyer) who has made the offer, and the OFFEREE is the person (seller) to whom the offer has been made.* The offer made by the offeror must be communicated to the offeree. Every offer must have contractual intent. *CONTRACTUAL INTENT exists when a party communicates an offer to another with the intention of forming a binding contract.* For example, a social invitation to attend a party is not meant to be a contract and, therefore, lacks contractual intent. Likewise, an advertisement in the newspaper is not an offer, but merely an invitation to deal.

A buyer can withdraw his or her offer at any time prior to receiving communication (in writing, personally, or by registered mail) of its acceptance and receive a refund of the money deposited.

Finally, offer terms must be definite and certain. *DEFINITE AND CERTAIN means that the precise acts to be performed must be clearly stated.* A court can neither create contracts for parties nor fix the terms and conditions of any contract. An *ILLUSORY CONTRACT is one in which the terms are not definite and certain, therefore the contract is unenforceable.*

2. Acceptance

ACCEPTANCE is the consent to the terms by the offeree. Acceptance of an offer must be in the manner specified in the offer, but if no particular manner of acceptance is specified, then acceptance may be made by any reasonable or usual mode.

On a purchase contract, the date of the contract is the date the seller's acceptance of the buyer's offer is communicated back to the buyer.

Silence cannot be interpreted as an acceptance of an offer because an acceptance must be communicated. One cannot say "If I do not hear from you in 10 days, the offer is considered accepted." There must be a communicated acceptance of an offer in writing.

A seller may accept a buyer's offer by fax (facsimile documents are legally binding).

The acceptance must be absolute and unqualified: If it modifies the terms of the offer, it becomes a counter offer. *A COUNTER OFFER is the rejection of an original offer and the proposal of a new offer.* The offeree rejects the offer, then becomes the offeror of the counter offer. **Once there is a counter offer, the previous offer is automatically terminated**. The counter offer is discussed later in the chapter (see Counter Offer form, **Figure 5-8**).

3. Termination of an Offer

The hope of the offeror is that the other party will accept and that a contract will be formed, but most initial offers are rejected. Here are six ways an offer can be terminated:

1. **Lapse of Time.** The offer is terminated if the offeree fails to accept within a prescribed period.
2. **Communication of Revocation.** An offer can be withdrawn any time before the other party has communicated his or her acceptance.
3. **Failure of Offeree to Fulfill a Condition.** A specified condition must be satisfied in a prescribed manner or the offer is terminated.
4. **Rejection.** If the offer is rejected, it is terminated.
5. **Death or Insanity of the Offeror or Offeree.** This voids the offer. The death of the offeror or offeree constitutes a revocation of the offer prior to acceptance—the offer died with the death of the offeror.
6. **Illegality of Purpose.** If the conditions or the purpose of a contract are illegal, then the contract is terminated.

4. Genuine Consent (Contract is Void or Voidable by Victim)

The final requirement for mutual consent is that the offer and acceptance must be real or genuine (freely given). If not, the contract is void or voidable by the victim. Genuine consent does not exist if any of the following conditions are present:

1. *FRAUD occurs when a person misrepresents a material fact, knowing it is not true, or is carelessly indifferent to the truth of the stated facts.* The contract is void or voidable, depending on the degree of fraud.

2. **MUTUAL MISTAKE** *exists when both parties are mistaken as to the matter of the agreement, or where the subject matter of the contract ceases to exist. A mistake is also void or voidable.*

> **Example:** A buyer made an offer to purchase a property through a real estate agent. The seller represented that the property was in a good school district. During escrow, the school district boundaries were changed and the seller's home became part of a poor school district. The buyer would probably be able to get out of the transaction because the contract between buyer and seller lacked mutual consent.

3. **DURESS** *is the unlawful detention of a person and/or that person's property.*
4. **MENACE** *is a threat to commit duress,* but it also can be a threat of unlawful violent injury to a person and/or his or her character as a party to the contract.
5. **UNDUE INFLUENCE** *occurs when a person in a position of authority uses that authority to an unfair advantage.* This is usually found in a confidential relationship.

If a contract was entered into under duress, it is voidable.

C. LEGALITY

A contract based on an unlawful consideration is void.

A contract must be legal in its formation and operation. **Both the consideration and its objective must also be lawful**. The objective refers to what the contract requires the parties to do or not to do. If the contract consists of a single objective that is unlawful in whole or in part, then the contract is void. If there are several objectives, the contract is normally valid as to those parts that are lawful.

The law will not enforce an illegal contract. If an illegal contract is not completed, the courts will not force its completion.

> **Example:** A contract to bribe a city building inspector to accept substandard work for $5,000 is illegal and void.

D. CONSIDERATION (Anything of Value)

VALUABLE CONSIDERATION *in a contract is anything of value given by one party to another party to make the agreement binding.* A valid contract must have sufficient consideration, which is any amount of valued consideration. Consideration need not be money. It may: (1) benefit the person making the contract or another person; (2) be a loss suffered or agreed to be suffered; or (3) be an agreement not to bring a legal suit. If the price paid is a promise, consideration may be a promise for a promise. The important point is that the consideration must be of some value.

Some rare types of contracts require that consideration be adequate. In such contracts the condition of adequate consideration must be met for those contracts to be enforceable. Other contracts, without such a condition, are enforceable no matter what the consideration is, as long as it is agreed on by all parties.

Payment of money is NOT needed as consideration. "Adequate, valuable, good, and sufficient" relate to consideration.

E. PROPER WRITING (Real Estate Contracts)

All contracts may be oral except those specifically required by the Statute of Frauds to be in writing. A contract for personal property can be oral or written, but the Statute of Frauds requires that most real estate contracts be in writing (see **Figure 5-2**).

A listing agreement must be in writing to enforce the payment of a commission. Oral agreements between brokers to share commissions are binding.

Personal property contracts, like rental agreements, for one year or less need not be in writing. Any contract that can't be performed within a year from the date of signing must be in writing.

1. Parol Evidence Rule

PAROL EVIDENCE refers to prior oral or written agreements of the parties, or even oral agreements made concurrently (contemporaneously) with a written contract. Under the "parol evidence rule," a contract expressed in writing is intended to be the complete and final expression of the rights and duties of the contracting parties. The parol evidence rule means that prior oral or written agreements of the parties cannot be introduced as evidence to contradict or modify the terms of the written contract. The courts, however, will permit such outside evidence to be introduced when the written contract is incomplete, ambiguous, or it is necessary to show that the contract is not enforceable because of mistake or fraud.

Rarely will the courts allow prior "oral parts or an entire oral contract" to be substituted for a later written contract. The courts would be jammed with people who wanted to rewrite their contracts. So do it properly. Make only written real estate contracts. Many real estate contracts contain preprinted clauses and spaces for which information is to be handwritten.

In a legal dispute, when there is a conflict between the preprinted clauses and the handwritten information in a real estate contract, the handwritten information takes precedence.

III. Performance, Discharge, and Breach of Contract

TIME IS OF THE ESSENCE refers to acts described in a contract that must be performed within time limits described in the contract. Most contracts are properly performed and discharged without any legal complications. If difficulties do arise, the parties, either by themselves or with the aid of legal counsel, usually work out an agreeable settlement. If there is no settlement, the courts are available for the resolution of any contractual conflicts.

The "time is of the essence" clause applies to the entire contract.

A. PERFORMANCE OF A CONTRACT

PERFORMANCE is the successful completion of a contractual duty, usually resulting in the performer's release from any past or future liability. Sometimes with performance of a contract, one of the parties would prefer to drop out of the picture without terminating the contract. He or she may, under proper circumstances, accomplish this by assignment.

Figure 5-2

STATUTE OF FRAUDS

Most contracts, which by statute are required to be in writing, are found under the Statute of Frauds. The Statute of Frauds was first adopted in England in 1677 and became part of English common law. Subsequently, it was introduced into this country and has become part of California's codified law. The main purpose of this law is to prevent forgery, perjury, and dishonest conduct by unscrupulous people, thus improving the existence and terms of certain important types of contracts.

The statute provides that certain contracts are invalid unless those contracts are in writing and signed by either the parties to be charged or their agents. Under California's Civil Code, the following contracts must be in writing:

1. Any agreement where the terms will not be performed within one year following the making of the contract.

2. A special promise to answer for the debt, default, or nonperformance of another, except in cases provided for by the Civil Code.

3. Agreement made upon the consideration of marriage, other than a mutual promise to marry.

4. An agreement for the leasing of real property for a period longer than one year (one year and one day), or for the sale of real property or of interest therein. It also applies to any agreement authorizing an agent to perform the above acts.

5. An agreement authorizing or employing an agent, broker, or any other person to purchase, sell, or lease real estate for more than one year. It is also an agreement to find a buyer, seller, or lessee for more than one year, in return for compensation.

6. An agreement, which by its terms is not to be performed during the lifetime of the promisor, or an agreement that devises or bequeaths any property, or makes provision for any reason by will.

7. An agreement by a purchaser of real estate to pay a debt secured by a trust deed or mortgage upon the property purchased, unless assumption of that debt by the purchaser is specifically provided for in the conveyance of such property.

The Statute of Frauds also applies to personal property. If the sales price of an item is more than $500, the contract must be in writing. Furthermore, if several items are purchased with the intent that the agreement be a single contract, the contract should be in writing if the total sales price is $500 or more.

An *ASSIGNMENT* is the transfer of a person's right in a contract to another party. An assignment happens when the *ASSIGNOR*, the party to the original contract, transfers his or her rights in the contract to another party, called an *ASSIGNEE*.

Any contract, unless it calls for some personal service, can be assigned if the contract does not state otherwise. For example, listings are not assignable because they are personal service contracts. If the assignee does not perform, the assignor remains liable (secondary liability) for the contract.

In some cases, the original contracting party may want to drop out of the contract completely. This can be done by novation. A **NOVATION** *is the substitution or exchange (by mutual agreement of the parties) of a new obligation or contract for an existing one with intent to cancel the old contract.*

Novation is the substitution, by agreement, of a new contract for an old one.

Time is often significant in a contract and is usually stated in the contract. By statute, if no time is specified for the performance of an act, a reasonable time is allowed. If an act, by its nature, can be done instantly (such as the payment of money) it must be done. If the last day for the performance of an act falls upon a holiday or weekend, the period is extended to include the next business day. **REVOCATION** *is the cancelling of an offer to contract by the the original offeror.*

B. DISCHARGE OF A CONTRACT

The **DISCHARGE OF A CONTRACT** *occurs when the contract has been terminated.* Contracts can be discharged in many ways, from the extreme of full performance (which is the usual pattern) to breach of contract (nonperformance). **Figure 5-3** illustrates these extremes and the variety of possibilities that may exist between them. A brief description of these possibilities follows.

Figure 5-3

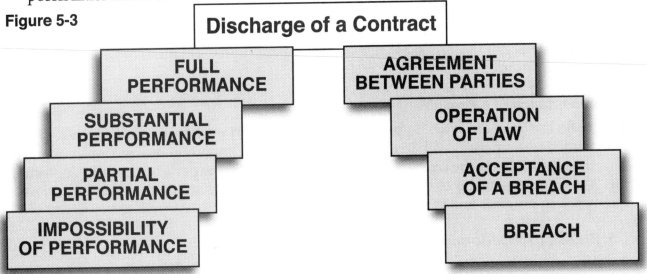

1. Full Performance

The contract is completed according to the terms specified in the original agreement.

2. Substantial Performance

Sometimes one party attempts to discharge a contract when the contract has almost, but not entirely, been completed. In certain cases the courts will accept this as a discharge of the contract. Otherwise, there are usually slight monetary charges for damages.

3. Partial Performance

If both parties agree to accept the value of the work partially completed, the contract is discharged. This agreement should be in writing. However, if a dispute arises, the courts will determine the obligations of the defaulting party. Damages are one of the hardest things to prove, and the courts usually lean towards the non-defaulting party. A judge will most likely award the non-defaulting party any amount necessary to complete the contract.

4. Impossibility of Performance

Under certain circumstances, the contract, for one reason or another, may be impossible to perform. An obvious example is where a painting contractor can no longer paint a house because it was destroyed by fire. In other cases, legality of the purpose may be challenged.

5. Agreement Between the Parties

If a contract is not completed, the usual way to discharge the contract is by mutual agreement (agree to disagree). A mutual agreement not to complete the contract is also a contract. Most knowledgeable contractors include ways for the contract to be discharged if one of the parties defaults on the original contract.

When a contract is mutually rescinded, the deposit must be returned to the buyer immediately.

6. Operation of Law (According to Statutes)

The law may excuse parties from contract performance because of: 1) illegality, 2) impossibility of performance, 3) rejection by bankruptcy, 4) failure of key contingency, and 5) statute of limitations.

7. Acceptance of a Breach

A **BREACH** *is the failure to perform a contract, in part or in whole, without legal excuse.* Sometimes a person will accept a breach. If time is important, the anxious party will usually discharge the contract and try to find a new party to perform the task. Contesting the contract sometimes only creates more problems, such as expensive interruption of work in progress and postponement of other contracts.

8. Breach (Nonperformance)

This is the nonperformance by one of the contracting parties. The performing party has his or her choice of several legal remedies.

The most common breaches, from the agent's point of view, are: (1) the buyer who decides not to buy after signing the purchase agreement or (2) the seller who decides not to sell after signing the listing and/or purchase agreement.

One week after entering into a legally binding purchase contract, the buyer backed out of the agreement. The seller can sue the buyer for money damages, must return the deposit to the buyer, and must attempt to resell the property to another buyer in an attempt to minimize damages.

a. Statute of Limitations (Time Limit for Civil Action)

According to the Statute of Limitations, a civil action for a breach of contract must be started within a certain period of time. If the civil action has not been started within that given time, no legal recourse will be possible. This policy of law states that a person who "sleeps upon his rights" may find himself barred from any legal action (see **Figure 5-5**).

IV. Remedies for Breach of a Contract

A breach of contract occurs when one party fails to perform his or her contractual obligations. By law, the party who has been wronged has only four choices. Action for dollar damages is the most common remedy for breach of a contract because most people prefer to receive money (cash) for their damages. **Figure 5-4** illustrates the four alternatives.

Figure 5-4

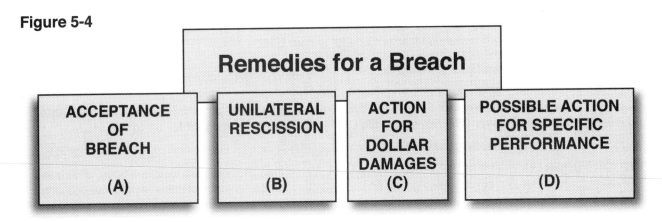

A. ACCEPTANCE OF BREACH

A discharge of a contract may be simply the acceptance of the breach. In an *ACCEPTANCE OF BREACH, the wronged party does not pursue legal action.* Sometimes he or she may feel that the damages recoverable are too limited to justify litigation. Perhaps the person considers the other party judgment-proof, which means that the other party does not have enough assets available to satisfy a judgment. Moreover, the legal cost of a lawsuit, the time, the effort, and the psychological effect may not be worth the possible outcome.

B. UNILATERAL RESCISSION

In a *UNILATERAL RESCISSION the wronged party (1) discloses the wrong and (2) restores everything of value to the offending party.* The legal grounds for a rescission are: fraud, mistake, duress, menace, undue influence, and faulty consideration. Rescission is possible when the contract is unlawful for causes not apparent on its face, when the parties are not equally at fault, or when the public interest would be hurt. Minors or incompetents may generally rescind their contracts.

Figure 5-5

STATUTE OF LIMITATIONS

Actions Which Must Be Brought Within 90 Days:

CIVIL ACTION FOR THE RECOVERY OF PERSONAL PROPERTY, such as trunks or baggage left in a hotel or other furnished establishment, must be started within 90 days after being left by the owner of the personal property.

Within Six Months:

AN ACTION AGAINST AN OFFICER TO RECOVER ANY GOODS, WAGES, MERCHANDISE, OR OTHER PROPERTY seized by any officer in his or her official capacity as tax collector must be started within six months.

Within One Year:

AN ACTION FOR LIBEL, SLANDER, INJURY, OR DEATH caused by the neglect of another or against a bank for the payment of a forged check must be started within one year of the alleged wrong.

Within Two Years:

ACTION MUST BE TAKEN WITHIN TWO YEARS UPON CONTRACTS OR OBLIGATIONS THAT WERE NOT MADE IN WRITING. Actions against contracts that have been founded on title insurance policies, certificates, or abstracts of title for real property must be made within two years from the date the cause of these actions is discovered. This does not include contracts made for accounts receivable.

Action for **misleading transfer disclosure statements** made by broker or agent must be taken within two years.

Example: When inspecting a seller's home, the agent discovers several physical defects which the agent fails to disclose to the buyer. The buyer can file civil action against the agent for up to two years.

Within Three Years (Attachments):

ACTIONS UPON LIABILITIES CREATED BY STATUTE (other than penalties) for trespass upon, or damage to, real property; for taking or damaging goods (including action for the recovery of specific personal property); and actions on the grounds of fraud or mistake caused before discovery by the injured party must be brought within three years.

Within Four Years (Listings and Purchase Agreements):

ACTIONS WHICH MUST BE MADE ON ANY WRITTEN CONTRACT WITHIN FOUR YEARS include most real estate contracts such as purchase agreements and listings, except for notes or obligations of publicly held corporations (where the limit is specified as being six years). Other exceptions exist when specific limitations are written into a contract. These exceptions include actions on a money judgment for the balance due upon a trust deed or mortgage, actions following the exercise of the power of sale (which may not be brought later than three months after the sale), and actions to recover upon accounts receivable.

Within Five Years:

ANY ACTION FOR INTERMEDIATE PROFITS OF REAL ESTATE from wrongful occupancy and any action for the recovery of real property may be started anytime within five years.

Within Ten Years (Judgments):

AN ACTION UPON A JUDGMENT OF ANY COURT OF THE UNITED STATES or of any state within the United States must be brought within ten years.

C. ACTION FOR DOLLAR DAMAGES

An *ACTION FOR DOLLAR DAMAGES occurs when a court suit for a breach requests payment of a fixed amount of money as compensation.* If a party to a contract causes you to lose money, it is only fair for you to receive compensation. In most purchase agreements (contract to purchase), there is usually a liquidated damages agreement. A *LIQUIDATED DAMAGES AGREEMENT sets, in advance, a specified amount of money as compensation if there is a breach.* This clause is used because it is usually impractical or difficult to determine the actual damages caused by a breach.

> **Example:** Seller Charlie sold his home through a real estate broker. The broker agreed verbally with Charlie that he would find him an acceptable place to live when the sale was completed. The home sold, but the broker does not keep his promise to the seller. Under these circumstances, the seller has the option of trying to recover damages in a court action against the broker.

The current award for liquidated damages on a purchase agreement form is a maximum of 3% (by law) of the home purchase price.

D. SPECIFIC PERFORMANCE

The final remedy for a breach of contract is specific performance. *SPECIFIC PERFORMANCE means that the party causing the breach is, through court action, forced to perform the terms of the contract.* For the most part, courts are skeptical of forcing a person to sell their real property and as a result this type of remedy is seldom used. Courts of equity will consider this action only if dollar damages cannot provide an adequate remedy. If specific performance is ordered, the remedy must be mutual. That is, neither party to a contract can be compelled specifically to perform unless the other party has performed or is also specifically compelled to perform.

To obtain specific performance, the plaintiff must show that the contract was just and reasonable. The contract must have been based on adequate consideration, meaning that the price received for the property must have been fair and reasonable. In addition, specific performance cannot be forced against a party if the contract was obtained by misrepresentation, concealment, circumvention, or any other unfair practice.

V. The Residential Purchase Agreement

A. THE OFFER AND ACCEPTANCE (With Deposit)

A promissory note secured by a deed of trust, a postdated check, or an unsecured promissory note could be used by a buyer as an earnest money deposit in purchasing real property.

The purchase agreement is the most important contract in the real estate field! Previously known as the **"Deposit Receipt,"** the *CALIFORNIA RESIDENTIAL PURCHASE AGREEMENT AND JOINT ESCROW INSTRUCTIONS is an offer and deposit to purchase a specific property on certain terms and conditions.* When acceptance is communicated to the buyer, this becomes a binding contract on the buyer and seller, and, generally, this becomes

the date of the purchase agreement. Acceptance is communicated in writing, in person, by mail, or by fax.

In addition, the purchase agreement discloses (as in the listing agreement) the percentage of commission to be paid to the brokers involved (see **Figure 5-6**, CAR® California Residential Purchase Agreement and Joint Escrow Instructions).

The purchase agreement is neater and more polished if it is typed, but there is nothing wrong with filling it in with a pen. Each form has three copies: a master copy, a buyer's copy, and a seller's copy.

NOTE: When using preprinted forms, the handwritten parts have control over the printed parts, and all corrections must be initialed by both parties.

B. THE DEPOSIT (Consideration for the Purchase Agreement)

The deposit is collected as consideration from a prospective buyer on behalf of the seller for the purchase agreement contract. Suppose the seller accepts the offer on the CAR® Purchase Agreement form and the buyer later defaults on the transaction. If the liquidated damages clause is initialed by both the buyer and seller, the seller may retain the deposit (up to three percent of the sale price). This would then be split 50-50 between the seller and the listing broker, unless otherwise stated in the purchase agreement.

If a seller rescinds a contract because a buyer defaults, the earnest money deposit must be returned to the buyer if the parties did NOT initial the liquidated damages clause in the purchase contract.

1. Covenants (A Promise in the Purchase Agreement)

COVENANTS are promises between the parties to a contract. Covenants represent promises, obligations and considerations exchanged to fulfill a contract.

Failure to perform a stipulated covenant does not release either party from his or her responsibility. The contract is still in effect, although the offended party may sue for damages.

2. Contingencies, Conditions, or Subject To (An "If" Clause in the Purchase Agreement)

CONTINGENCIES, CONDITIONS or SUBJECT TO are provisions by which all parties are released from any obligations of a contract if some stated condition occurs or fails to occur. For example, purchase offers may be made contingent upon the availability of financing, or subject to the successful sale of another property. If the contingency falls through, the contract is voidable by the buyer. Items that are usually found in contingency clauses include:

1. Obtaining financing at a certain interest rate or less.
2. Subject to the approval of my CPA and attorney within 20 days.
3. Conditional upon inspection and approval of each apartment.
4. Subject to property appraisal at no less than the specified price.

Figure 5-6

CALIFORNIA
ASSOCIATION
OF REALTORS ®

CALIFORNIA
RESIDENTIAL PURCHASE AGREEMENT
AND JOINT ESCROW INSTRUCTIONS
For Use With Single Family Residential Property — Attached or Detached
(C.A.R. Form RPA-CA, Revised 11/07)

Date _JUNE 14, 20XX_, at _COSTA MESA_, California.

1. **OFFER:**
   A. THIS IS AN OFFER FROM _WALTER AND DEBBIE BUYER_ ("Buyer").
   B. THE REAL PROPERTY TO BE ACQUIRED is described as _264 BEACH LANE_, Assessor's Parcel No. _____, situated in _COSTA MESA_, County of _ORANGE_, California, ("Property").
   C. THE PURCHASE PRICE offered is _EIGHT HUNDRED THOUSAND — NO/100_ Dollars $ _800,000_
   D. CLOSE OF ESCROW shall occur on _____(date)(or X _90_ Days After Acceptance).

2. **FINANCE TERMS:** Obtaining the loans below **is a contingency** of this Agreement unless: (i) either 2K or 2L is checked below; or (ii) otherwise agreed in writing. Buyer shall act diligently and in good faith to obtain the designated loans. Obtaining deposit, down payment and closing costs **is not a contingency.** Buyer represents that funds will be good when deposited with Escrow Holder.
   A. INITIAL DEPOSIT: Buyer has given a deposit in the amount of .... $ _10,000_
   to the agent submitting the offer (or to ☐ _____), by personal check (or _____), made payable to _ABC ESCROW_, which shall be held uncashed until Acceptance and then deposited within 3 business days after Acceptance (or ☐ _____), with Escrow Holder, (or ☐ into Broker's trust account).
   B. INCREASED DEPOSIT: Buyer shall deposit with Escrow Holder an increased deposit in the amount of ....$ _____ within _____ Days After Acceptance, or ☐ _____
   C. FIRST LOAN IN THE AMOUNT OF .... $ _640,000_
   (1) NEW First Deed of Trust in favor of lender, encumbering the Property, securing a note payable at maximum interest of _8_ % fixed rate, or _____ % initial adjustable rate with a maximum interest rate of _____ %, balance due in _____ years, amortized over _30_ years. Buyer shall pay loan fees/points not to exceed _2_. (These terms apply whether the designated loan is conventional, FHA or VA.)
   (2) ☐ FHA ☐ VA: (The following terms only apply to the FHA or VA loan that is checked.) Seller shall pay _____ % discount points. Seller shall pay other fees not allowed to be paid by Buyer, ☐ not to exceed $ _____. Seller shall pay the cost of lender required Repairs (including those for wood destroying pest) not otherwise provided for in this Agreement, ☐ not to exceed $ _____. (Actual loan amount may increase if mortgage insurance premiums, funding fees or closing costs are financed.)
   D. ADDITIONAL FINANCING TERMS: ☐ Seller financing, (C.A.R. Form SFA); ☐ secondary financing, ...$ _____ (C.A.R. Form PAA, paragraph 4A); ☐ assumed financing (C.A.R. Form PAA, paragraph 4B)
   E. BALANCE OF PURCHASE PRICE (not including costs of obtaining loans and other closing costs) in the amount of ... $ _150,000_ to be deposited with Escrow Holder within sufficient time to close escrow.
   F. PURCHASE PRICE (TOTAL): .... $ _800,000_
   G. LOAN APPLICATIONS: Within 7 (or ☐ _____) Days After Acceptance, Buyer shall provide Seller a letter from lender or mortgage loan broker stating that, based on a review of Buyer's written application and credit report, Buyer is prequalified or preapproved for the NEW loan specified in 2C above.
   H. VERIFICATION OF DOWN PAYMENT AND CLOSING COSTS: Buyer (or Buyer's lender or loan broker pursuant to 2G) shall, within 7 (or ☐ _____) Days After Acceptance, provide Seller written verification of Buyer's down payment and closing costs.
   I. LOAN CONTINGENCY REMOVAL: (i) Within 17 (or ☐ _____) Days After Acceptance, Buyer shall, as specified in paragraph 14, remove the loan contingency or cancel this Agreement; OR (ii) (if checked) ☐ the loan contingency shall remain in effect until the designated loans are funded.
   J. APPRAISAL CONTINGENCY AND REMOVAL: This Agreement is (OR, if checked, ☐ is NOT) contingent upon the Property appraising at no less than the specified purchase price. If there is a loan contingency, at the time the loan contingency is removed (or, if checked, ☐ within 17 (or _____) Days After Acceptance), Buyer shall, as specified in paragraph 14B(3), remove the appraisal contingency or cancel this Agreement. If there is no loan contingency, Buyer shall, as specified in paragraph 14B(3), remove the appraisal contingency within 17 (or _____) Days After Acceptance.
   K. ☐ NO LOAN CONTINGENCY (If checked): Obtaining any loan in paragraphs 2C, 2D or elsewhere in this Agreement is NOT a contingency of this Agreement. If Buyer does not obtain the loan and as a result Buyer does not purchase the Property, Seller may be entitled to Buyer's deposit or other legal remedies.
   L. ☐ ALL CASH OFFER (If checked): No loan is needed to purchase the Property. Buyer shall, within 7 (or ☐ _____) Days After Acceptance, provide Seller written verification of sufficient funds to close this transaction.

3. **CLOSING AND OCCUPANCY:**
   A. Buyer intends (or ☐ does not intend) to occupy the Property as Buyer's primary residence.
   B. Seller-occupied or vacant property: Occupancy shall be delivered to Buyer at _11_ ☐AM/PM, X on the date of Close Of Escrow; ☐ on _____; or ☐ no later than _____ Days After Close Of Escrow. (C.A.R. Form PAA, paragraph 2.) If transfer of title and occupancy do not occur at the same time, Buyer and Seller are advised to: (i) enter into a written occupancy agreement; and (ii) consult with their insurance and legal advisors.

Buyer's Initials (_WB_)(_da_)
Seller's Initials (_TA_)(_RfA_)

Reviewed by _JC_ Date _6/14/XX_

RPA-CA REVISED 11/07 (PAGE 1 OF 8) Print Date

EQUAL HOUSING OPPORTUNITY

CALIFORNIA RESIDENTIAL PURCHASE AGREEMENT (RPA-CA PAGE 1 OF 8)

Property Address: *264 BEACH LANE, COSTA MESA CA 92627*   Date: *JUNE 14, 20XX*

C. **Tenant-occupied property:** (i) Property shall be vacant at least 5 (or ☐ _____) Days Prior to Close Of Escrow, unless otherwise agreed in writing. **Note to Seller: If you are unable to deliver Property vacant in accordance with rent control and other applicable Law, you may be in breach of this Agreement.**

OR (ii) (if checked) ☐ **Tenant to remain in possession.** The attached addendum is incorporated into this Agreement (C.A.R. Form PAA, paragraph 3.);

OR (iii) (if checked) ☐ **This Agreement is contingent** upon Buyer and Seller entering into a written agreement regarding occupancy of the Property within the time specified in paragraph 14B(1). If no written agreement is reached within this time, either Buyer or Seller may cancel this Agreement in writing.

D. At Close Of Escrow, Seller assigns to Buyer any assignable warranty rights for items included in the sale and shall provide any available Copies of such warranties. Brokers cannot and will not determine the assignability of any warranties.

E. At Close Of Escrow, unless otherwise agreed in writing, Seller shall provide keys and/or means to operate all locks, mailboxes, security systems, alarms and garage door openers. If Property is a condominium or located in a common interest subdivision, Buyer may be required to pay a deposit to the Homeowners' Association ("HOA") to obtain keys to accessible HOA facilities.

4. **ALLOCATION OF COSTS (If checked):** Unless otherwise specified here, this paragraph only determines who is to pay for the report, inspection, test or service mentioned. If not specified here or elsewhere in this Agreement, the determination of who is to pay for any work recommended or identified by any such report, inspection, test or service shall be by the method specified in paragraph 14B(2).

   A. **WOOD DESTROYING PEST INSPECTION:**
   (1) ☐ Buyer ☒ Seller shall pay for an inspection and report for wood destroying pests and organisms ("Report") which shall be prepared by *BUG·B·GONE* _____, a registered structural pest control company. The Report shall cover the accessible areas of the main building and attached structures and, if checked: ☐ detached garages and carports, ☐ detached decks, ☐ the following other structures or areas _____. The Report shall not include roof coverings. If Property is a condominium or located in a common interest subdivision, the Report shall include only the separate interest and any exclusive-use areas being transferred and shall not include common areas, unless otherwise agreed. Water tests of shower pans on upper level units may not be performed without consent of the owners of property below the shower.

   OR (2) ☐ **(If checked)** The attached addendum (C.A.R. Form WPA) regarding wood destroying pest inspection and allocation of cost is incorporated into this Agreement.

   B. **OTHER INSPECTIONS AND REPORTS:**
   (1) ☐ Buyer ☐ Seller shall pay to have septic or private sewage disposal systems inspected _____.
   (2) ☐ Buyer ☐ Seller shall pay to have domestic wells tested for water potability and productivity _____.
   (3) ☐ Buyer ☐ Seller shall pay for a natural hazard zone disclosure report prepared by _____.
   (4) ☐ Buyer ☐ Seller shall pay for the following inspection or report _____.
   (5) ☐ Buyer ☐ Seller shall pay for the following inspection or report _____.

   C. **GOVERNMENT REQUIREMENTS AND RETROFIT:**
   (1) ☐ Buyer ☒ Seller shall pay for smoke detector installation and/or water heater bracing, if required by Law. Prior to Close Of Escrow, Seller shall provide Buyer a written statement of compliance in accordance with state and local Law, unless exempt.
   (2) ☐ Buyer ☐ Seller shall pay the cost of compliance with any other minimum mandatory government retrofit standards, inspections and reports if required as a condition of closing escrow under any Law. _____.

   D. **ESCROW AND TITLE:**
   (1) ☒ Buyer ☒ Seller shall pay escrow fee *50% / 50%* _____
   Escrow Holder shall be *ABC ESCROW* _____
   (2) ☒ Buyer ☐ Seller shall pay for **owner's** title insurance policy specified in paragraph 12E _____
   Owner's title policy to be issued by _____
   (Buyer shall pay for any title insurance policy insuring Buyer's **lender**, unless otherwise agreed in writing.)

   E. **OTHER COSTS:**
   (1) ☐ Buyer ☐ Seller shall pay County transfer tax or transfer fee _____.
   (2) ☐ Buyer ☐ Seller shall pay City transfer tax or transfer fee _____.
   (3) ☐ Buyer ☐ Seller shall pay HOA transfer fee _____.
   (4) ☐ Buyer ☐ Seller shall pay HOA document preparation fees _____.
   (5) ☐ Buyer ☐ Seller shall pay the cost, not to exceed $ _____, of a one-year home warranty plan, issued by _____
   with the following optional coverage: _____
   (6) ☐ Buyer ☐ Seller shall pay for _____.
   (7) ☐ Buyer ☐ Seller shall pay for _____.

5. **STATUTORY DISCLOSURES (INCLUDING LEAD-BASED PAINT HAZARD DISCLOSURES) AND CANCELLATION RIGHTS:**
   A. (1) Seller shall, within the time specified in paragraph 14A, deliver to Buyer, if required by Law: (i) Federal Lead-Based Paint Disclosures and pamphlet ("Lead Disclosures"); and (ii) disclosures or notices required by sections 1102 et. seq. and 1103 et. seq. of the California Civil Code ("Statutory Disclosures"). Statutory Disclosures include, but are not limited to, a Real Estate Transfer Disclosure Statement ("TDS"), Natural Hazard Disclosure Statement ("NHD"), notice or actual knowledge of release of illegal controlled substance, notice of special tax and/or assessments (or, if allowed, substantially equivalent notice regarding the Mello-Roos Community Facilities Act and Improvement Bond Act of 1915) and, if Seller has actual knowledge, of industrial use and military ordinance location disclosure (C.A.R. Form SSD).
   (2) Buyer shall, within the time specified in paragraph 14B(1), return Signed Copies of the Statutory and Lead Disclosures to Seller.
   (3) In the event Seller, prior to Close Of Escrow, becomes aware of adverse conditions materially affecting the Property, or any material inaccuracy in disclosures, information or representations previously provided to Buyer of which Buyer is otherwise unaware, Seller shall promptly provide a subsequent or amended disclosure or notice, in writing, covering those items. **However, a subsequent or amended disclosure shall not be required for conditions and material inaccuracies disclosed in reports ordered and paid for by Buyer.**

Buyer's Initials (*SB*)(*ab*)
Seller's Initials (*TA*)(*RL*)

Reviewed by *JR* Date *6/14/XX*

EQUAL HOUSING OPPORTUNITY

CALIFORNIA RESIDENTIAL PURCHASE AGREEMENT (RPA-CA PAGE 2 OF 8)

130

    (4) If any disclosure or notice specified in 5A(1), or subsequent or amended disclosure or notice is delivered to Buyer after the offer is Signed, Buyer shall have the right to cancel this Agreement within **3 Days** After delivery in person, or **5 Days** After delivery by deposit in the mail, by giving written notice of cancellation to Seller or Seller's agent. (Lead Disclosures sent by mail must be sent certified mail or better.)

    (5) **Note to Buyer and Seller: Waiver of Statutory and Lead Disclosures is prohibited by Law.**

  B. NATURAL AND ENVIRONMENTAL HAZARDS: Within the time specified in paragraph 14A, Seller shall, if required by Law: (i) deliver to Buyer earthquake guides (and questionnaire) and environmental hazards booklet; (ii) even if exempt from the obligation to provide a NHD, disclose if the Property is located in a Special Flood Hazard Area; Potential Flooding (Inundation) Area; Very High Fire Hazard Zone; State Fire Responsibility Area; Earthquake Fault Zone; Seismic Hazard Zone; and (iii) disclose any other zone as required by Law and provide any other information required for those zones.

  C. MEGAN'S LAW DATABASE DISCLOSURE: Notice: Pursuant to Section 290.46 of the Penal Code, information about specified registered sex offenders is made available to the public via an Internet Web site maintained by the Department of Justice at www.meganslaw.ca.gov. Depending on an offender's criminal history, this information will include either the address at which the offender resides or the community of residence and ZIP Code in which he or she resides. (Neither Seller nor Brokers are required to check this website. If Buyer wants further information, Broker recommends that Buyer obtain information from this website during Buyer's inspection contingency period. Brokers do not have expertise in this area.)

6. CONDOMINIUM/PLANNED UNIT DEVELOPMENT DISCLOSURES:

  A. SELLER HAS: 7 (or _____) Days After Acceptance to disclose to Buyer whether the Property is a condominium, or is located in a planned unit development or other common interest subdivision (C.A.R. Form SSD).

  B. If the Property is a condominium or is located in a planned unit development or other common interest subdivision, Seller has **3 (or ☐ _____) Days** After Acceptance to request from the HOA (C.A.R. Form HOA): (i) Copies of any documents required by Law; (ii) disclosure of any pending or anticipated claim or litigation by or against the HOA; (iii) a statement containing the location and number of designated parking and storage spaces; (iv) Copies of the most recent 12 months of HOA minutes for regular and special meetings; and (v) the names and contact information of all HOAs governing the Property (collectively, "CI Disclosures"). Seller shall itemize and deliver to Buyer all CI Disclosures received from the HOA and any CI Disclosures in Seller's possession. Buyer's approval of CI Disclosures is a contingency of this Agreement as specified in paragraph 14B(3).

7. CONDITIONS AFFECTING PROPERTY:

  A. Unless otherwise agreed: (i) the **Property is sold (a) in its PRESENT physical condition as of the date of Acceptance and (b) subject to Buyer's Investigation rights;** (ii) the Property, including pool, spa, landscaping and grounds, is to be maintained in substantially the same condition as on the date of Acceptance; and (iii) all debris and personal property not included in the sale shall be removed by Close Of Escrow.

  B. SELLER SHALL, within the time specified in paragraph 14A, DISCLOSE KNOWN MATERIAL FACTS AND DEFECTS affecting the Property, including known insurance claims within the past five years, **AND MAKE OTHER DISCLOSURES REQUIRED BY LAW** (C.A.R. Form SSD).

  C. NOTE TO BUYER: You are strongly advised to conduct investigations of the entire Property in order to determine its present condition since Seller may not be aware of all defects affecting the Property or other factors that you consider important. Property improvements may not be built according to code, in compliance with current Law, or have had permits issued.

  D. NOTE TO SELLER: Buyer has the right to inspect the Property and, as specified in paragraph 14B, based upon information discovered in those inspections: (i) cancel this Agreement; or (ii) request that you make Repairs or take other action.

8. ITEMS INCLUDED AND EXCLUDED:

  A. NOTE TO BUYER AND SELLER: Items listed as included or excluded in the MLS, flyers or marketing materials are not included in the purchase price or excluded from the sale unless specified in 8B or C.

  B. ITEMS INCLUDED IN SALE:

    (1) All EXISTING fixtures and fittings that are attached to the Property;

    (2) Existing electrical, mechanical, lighting, plumbing and heating fixtures, ceiling fans, fireplace inserts, gas logs and grates, solar systems, built-in appliances, window and door screens, awnings, shutters, window coverings, attached floor coverings, television antennas, satellite dishes, private integrated telephone systems, air coolers/conditioners, pool/spa equipment, garage door openers/remote controls, mailbox, in-ground landscaping, trees/shrubs, water softeners, water purifiers, security systems/alarms; and

    (3) The following items: _____

    (4) Seller represents that all items included in the purchase price, unless otherwise specified, are owned by Seller.

    (5) All items included shall be transferred free of liens and without Seller warranty.

  C. ITEMS EXCLUDED FROM SALE: _____

9. BUYER'S INVESTIGATION OF PROPERTY AND MATTERS AFFECTING PROPERTY:

  A. Buyer's acceptance of the condition of, and any other matter affecting the Property, is a contingency of this Agreement as specified in this paragraph and paragraph 14B. Within the time specified in paragraph 14B(1), Buyer shall have the right, at Buyer's expense unless otherwise agreed, to conduct inspections, investigations, tests, surveys and other studies ("Buyer Investigations"), including, but not limited to, the right to: (i) inspect for lead-based paint and other lead-based paint hazards; (ii) inspect for wood destroying pests and organisms; (iii) review the registered sex offender database; (iv) confirm the insurability of Buyer and the Property; and (v) satisfy Buyer as to any matter specified in the attached Buyer's Inspection Advisory (C.A.R. Form BIA). Without Seller's prior written consent, Buyer shall neither make nor cause to be made: (i) invasive or destructive Buyer Investigations; or (ii) inspections by any governmental building or zoning inspector or government employee, unless required by Law.

  B. Buyer shall complete Buyer Investigations and, as specified in paragraph 14B, remove the contingency or cancel this Agreement. Buyer shall give Seller, at no cost, complete Copies of all Buyer Investigation reports obtained by Buyer. Seller shall make the Property available for all Buyer Investigations. Seller shall have water, gas, electricity and all operable pilot lights on for Buyer's investigations and through the date possession is made available to Buyer.

Buyer's Initials (SHB)(db)
Seller's Initials (TA)(RVA)
Reviewed by ___ Date 6/14/XX

Property Address: 264 BEACH LANE, COST MESA, CA 92627   Date: JUNE 14, 20XX

10. **REPAIRS:** Repairs shall be completed prior to final verification of condition unless otherwise agreed in writing. Repairs to be performed at Seller's expense may be performed by Seller or through others, provided that the work complies with applicable Law, including governmental permit, inspection and approval requirements. Repairs shall be performed in a good, skillful manner with materials of quality and appearance comparable to existing materials. It is understood that exact restoration of appearance or cosmetic items following all Repairs may not be possible. Seller shall: (i) obtain receipts for Repairs performed by others; (ii) prepare a written statement indicating the Repairs performed by Seller and the date of such Repairs; and (iii) provide Copies of receipts and statements to Buyer prior to final verification of condition.

11. **BUYER INDEMNITY AND SELLER PROTECTION FOR ENTRY UPON PROPERTY:** Buyer shall: (i) keep the Property free and clear of liens; (ii) repair all damage arising from Buyer Investigations; and (iii) indemnify and hold Seller harmless from all resulting liability, claims, demands, damages and costs. Buyer shall carry, or Buyer shall require anyone acting on Buyer's behalf to carry, policies of liability, workers' compensation and other applicable insurance, defending and protecting Seller from liability for any injuries to persons or property occurring during any Buyer Investigations or work done on the Property at Buyer's direction prior to Close Of Escrow. Seller is advised that certain protections may be afforded Seller by recording a "Notice of Non-responsibility" (C.A.R. Form NNR) for Buyer Investigations and work done on the Property at Buyer's direction. Buyer's obligations under this paragraph shall survive the termination of this Agreement.

12. **TITLE AND VESTING:**
   A. Within the time specified in paragraph 14, Buyer shall be provided a current preliminary (title) report, which is only an offer by the title insurer to issue a policy of title insurance and may not contain every item affecting title. Buyer's review of the preliminary report and any other matters which may affect title are a contingency of this Agreement as specified in paragraph 14B.
   B. Title is taken in its present condition subject to all encumbrances, easements, covenants, conditions, restrictions, rights and other matters, whether of record or not, as of the date of Acceptance except: (i) monetary liens of record unless Buyer is assuming those obligations or taking the Property subject to those obligations; and (ii) those matters which Seller has agreed to remove in writing.
   C. Within the time specified in paragraph 14A, Seller has a duty to disclose to Buyer all matters known to Seller affecting title, whether of record or not.
   D. At Close Of Escrow, Buyer shall receive a grant deed conveying title (or, for stock cooperative or long-term lease, an assignment of stock certificate or of Seller's leasehold interest), including oil, mineral and water rights if currently owned by Seller. Title shall vest as designated in Buyer's supplemental escrow instructions. THE MANNER OF TAKING TITLE MAY HAVE SIGNIFICANT LEGAL AND TAX CONSEQUENCES. CONSULT AN APPROPRIATE PROFESSIONAL.
   E. Buyer shall receive a CLTA/ALTA Homeowner's Policy of Title Insurance. A title company, at Buyer's request, can provide information about the availability, desirability, coverage, and cost of various title insurance coverages and endorsements. If Buyer desires title coverage other than that required by this paragraph, Buyer shall instruct Escrow Holder in writing and pay any increase in cost.

13. **SALE OF BUYER'S PROPERTY:**
   A. This Agreement is NOT contingent upon the sale of any property owned by Buyer.
OR B. ☐ (If checked): The attached addendum (C.A.R. Form COP) regarding the contingency for the sale of property owned by Buyer is incorporated into this Agreement.

14. **TIME PERIODS; REMOVAL OF CONTINGENCIES; CANCELLATION RIGHTS:** The following time periods may only be extended, altered, modified or changed by mutual written agreement. Any removal of contingencies or cancellation under this paragraph must be in writing (C.A.R. Form CR).
   A. **SELLER HAS: 7 (or ☐ _____) Days** After Acceptance to deliver to Buyer all reports, disclosures and information for which Seller is responsible under paragraphs 4, 5A and B, 6A, 7B and 12.
   B. (1) **BUYER HAS: 17 (or ☐ _____) Days** After Acceptance, unless otherwise agreed in writing, to:
      (i) complete all Buyer Investigations; approve all disclosures, reports and other applicable information, which Buyer receives from Seller; and approve all matters affecting the Property (including lead-based paint and lead-based paint hazards as well as other information specified in paragraph 5 and insurability of Buyer and the Property); and
      (ii) return to Seller Signed Copies of Statutory and Lead Disclosures delivered by Seller in accordance with paragraph 5A.
      (2) Within the time specified in 14B(1), Buyer may request that Seller make repairs or take any other action regarding the Property (C.A.R. Form RR). Seller has no obligation to agree to or respond to Buyer's requests.
      (3) By the end of the time specified in 14B(1) (or 2i for loan contingency or 2J for appraisal contingency), Buyer shall, in writing, remove the applicable contingency (C.A.R. Form CR) or cancel this Agreement. However, if (i) government-mandated inspections/reports required as a condition of closing; or (ii) Common Interest Disclosures pursuant to paragraph 6B are not made within the time specified in 14A, then Buyer has 5 (or ☐ _____) Days After receipt of any such items, or the time specified in 14B(1), whichever is later, to remove the applicable contingency or cancel this Agreement in writing.
   C. **CONTINUATION OF CONTINGENCY OR CONTRACTUAL OBLIGATION; SELLER RIGHT TO CANCEL:**
      (1) **Seller right to Cancel; Buyer Contingencies:** Seller, after first giving Buyer a Notice to Buyer to Perform (as specified below), may cancel this Agreement in writing and authorize return of Buyer's deposit if, by the time specified in this Agreement, Buyer does not remove in writing the applicable contingency or cancel this Agreement. Once all contingencies have been removed, failure of either Buyer or Seller to close escrow on time may be a breach of this Agreement.
      (2) **Continuation of Contingency:** Even after the expiration of the time specified in 14B, Buyer retains the right to make requests to Seller, remove in writing the applicable contingency or cancel this Agreement until Seller cancels pursuant to 14C(1). Once Seller receives Buyer's written removal of all contingencies, Seller may not cancel this Agreement pursuant to 14C(1).
      (3) **Seller right to Cancel; Buyer Contract Obligations:** Seller, after first giving Buyer a Notice to Buyer to Perform (as specified below), may cancel this Agreement in writing and authorize return of Buyer's deposit for any of the following reasons: (i) if Buyer fails to deposit funds as required by 2A or 2B; (ii) if the funds deposited pursuant to 2A or 2B are not good when deposited; (iii) if Buyer fails to provide a letter as required by 2G; (iv) if Buyer fails to provide verification as required by 2H or 2L; (v) if Seller reasonably disapproves of the verification provided by 2H or 2L; (vi) if Buyer fails to return Statutory and Lead Disclosures as required by paragraph 5A(2); or (vii) if Buyer fails to sign or initial a separate liquidated damage form for an increased deposit as required by paragraph 16. **Seller is not required to give Buyer a Notice to Perform regarding Close of Escrow.**
      (4) **Notice To Buyer To Perform:** The Notice to Buyer to Perform (C.A.R. Form NBP) shall: (i) be in writing; (ii) be signed by Seller; and (iii) give Buyer at least **24 (or ☐ _____) hours** (or until the time specified in the applicable paragraph, whichever occurs last) to take the applicable action. A Notice to Buyer to Perform may not be given any earlier than **2 Days** Prior to the expiration of the applicable time for Buyer to remove a contingency or cancel this Agreement or meet a 14C(3) obligation.

Buyer's Initials (SVB)(ab)
Seller's Initials (TA)(RYL)
Reviewed by _____ Date 6/14/XX

RPA-CA REVISED 11/07 (PAGE 4 OF 8)

CALIFORNIA RESIDENTIAL PURCHASE AGREEMENT (RPA-CA PAGE 4 OF 8)

Property Address: _26d BEACH LANE, COSTA MESA, CA 92627_ Date: _JUNE 14, 20XX_

D. **EFFECT OF BUYER'S REMOVAL OF CONTINGENCIES :** If Buyer removes, in writing, any contingency or cancellation rights, unless otherwise specified in a separate written agreement between Buyer and Seller, Buyer shall conclusively be deemed to have: (i) completed all Buyer Investigations, and review of reports and other applicable information and disclosures pertaining to that contingency or cancellation right; (ii) elected to proceed with the transaction; and (iii) assumed all liability, responsibility and expense for Repairs or corrections pertaining to that contingency or cancellation right, or for inability to obtain financing.

E. **EFFECT OF CANCELLATION ON DEPOSITS:** If Buyer or Seller gives written notice of cancellation pursuant to rights duly exercised under the terms of this Agreement, Buyer and Seller agree to Sign mutual instructions to cancel the sale and escrow and release deposits to the party entitled to the funds, less fees and costs incurred by that party. Fees and costs may be payable to service providers and vendors for services and products provided during escrow. **Release of funds will require mutual Signed release instructions from Buyer and Seller, judicial decision or arbitration award. A party may be subject to a civil penalty of up to $1,000 for refusal to sign such instructions if no good faith dispute exists as to who is entitled to the deposited funds (Civil Code §1057.3).**

15. **FINAL VERIFICATION OF CONDITION:** Buyer shall have the right to make a final inspection of the Property within 5 (or _____) Days Prior to Close Of Escrow, NOT AS A CONTINGENCY OF THE SALE, but solely to confirm: (i) the Property is maintained pursuant to paragraph 7A; (ii) Repairs have been completed as agreed; and (iii) Seller has complied with Seller's other obligations under this Agreement.

16. **LIQUIDATED DAMAGES:** If Buyer fails to complete this purchase because of Buyer's default, Seller shall retain, as liquidated damages, the deposit actually paid. If the Property is a dwelling with no more than four units, one of which Buyer intends to occupy, then the amount retained shall be no more than 3% of the purchase price. Any excess shall be returned to Buyer. Release of funds will require mutual, Signed release instructions from both Buyer and Seller, judicial decision or arbitration award.
BUYER AND SELLER SHALL SIGN A SEPARATE LIQUIDATED DAMAGES PROVISION FOR ANY INCREASED DEPOSIT. (C.A.R. FORM RID)

Buyer's Initials _JB_, _db_	Seller's Initials _TA_ / _RJA_

17. **DISPUTE RESOLUTION:**

A. **MEDIATION:** Buyer and Seller agree to mediate any dispute or claim arising between them out of this Agreement, or any resulting transaction, before resorting to arbitration or court action. Paragraphs 17B(2) and (3) below apply to mediation whether or not the Arbitration provision is initialed. Mediation fees, if any, shall be divided equally among the parties involved. If, for any dispute or claim to which this paragraph applies, any party commences an action without first attempting to resolve the matter through mediation, or refuses to mediate after a request has been made, then that party shall not be entitled to recover attorney fees, even if they would otherwise be available to that party in any such action. THIS MEDIATION PROVISION APPLIES WHETHER OR NOT THE ARBITRATION PROVISION IS INITIALED.

B. **ARBITRATION OF DISPUTES: (1)** Buyer and Seller agree that any dispute or claim in Law or equity arising between them out of this Agreement or any resulting transaction, which is not settled through mediation, shall be decided by neutral, binding arbitration, including and subject to paragraphs 17B(2) and (3) below. The arbitrator shall be a retired judge or justice, or an attorney with at least 5 years of residential real estate Law experience, unless the parties mutually agree to a different arbitrator, who shall render an award in accordance with substantive California Law. The parties shall have the right to discovery in accordance with California Code of Civil Procedure §1283.05. In all other respects, the arbitration shall be conducted in accordance with Title 9 of Part III of the California Code of Civil Procedure. Judgment upon the award of the arbitrator(s) may be entered into any court having jurisdiction. Interpretation of this agreement to arbitrate shall be governed by the Federal Arbitration Act.
(2) EXCLUSIONS FROM MEDIATION AND ARBITRATION: The following matters are excluded from mediation and arbitration: (i) a judicial or non-judicial foreclosure or other action or proceeding to enforce a deed of trust, mortgage or installment land sale contract as defined in California Civil Code §2985; (ii) an unlawful detainer action; (iii) the filing or enforcement of a mechanic's lien; and (iv) any matter that is within the jurisdiction of a probate, small claims or bankruptcy court. The filing of a court action to enable the recording of a notice of pending action, for order of attachment, receivership, injunction, or other provisional remedies, shall not constitute a waiver of the mediation and arbitration provisions.
(3) BROKERS: Buyer and Seller agree to mediate and arbitrate disputes or claims involving either or both Brokers, consistent with 17A and B, provided either or both Brokers shall have agreed to such mediation or arbitration prior to, or within a reasonable time after, the dispute or claim is presented to Brokers. Any election by either or both Brokers to participate in mediation or arbitration shall not result in Brokers being deemed parties to the Agreement.
"**NOTICE: BY INITIALING IN THE SPACE BELOW YOU ARE AGREEING TO HAVE ANY DISPUTE ARISING OUT OF THE MATTERS INCLUDED IN THE 'ARBITRATION OF DISPUTES' PROVISION DECIDED BY NEUTRAL ARBITRATION AS PROVIDED BY CALIFORNIA LAW AND YOU ARE GIVING UP ANY RIGHTS YOU MIGHT POSSESS TO HAVE THE DISPUTE LITIGATED IN A COURT OR JURY TRIAL. BY INITIALING IN THE SPACE BELOW YOU ARE GIVING UP YOUR JUDICIAL RIGHTS TO DISCOVERY AND APPEAL, UNLESS THOSE RIGHTS ARE SPECIFICALLY INCLUDED IN THE 'ARBITRATION OF DISPUTES' PROVISION. IF YOU REFUSE TO SUBMIT TO ARBITRATION AFTER AGREEING TO THIS PROVISION, YOU MAY BE COMPELLED TO ARBITRATE UNDER THE AUTHORITY OF THE CALIFORNIA CODE OF CIVIL PROCEDURE. YOUR AGREEMENT TO THIS ARBITRATION PROVISION IS VOLUNTARY.**"
"**WE HAVE READ AND UNDERSTAND THE FOREGOING AND AGREE TO SUBMIT DISPUTES ARISING OUT OF THE MATTERS INCLUDED IN THE 'ARBITRATION OF DISPUTES' PROVISION TO NEUTRAL ARBITRATION.**"

Buyer's Initials _JB_, _db_	Seller's Initials _TA_ / _RJA_

Buyer's Initials (_JB_)(_db_)
Seller's Initials (_TA_)(_RJA_)
Reviewed by _JR_ Date _6/14/XX_

RPA-CA REVISED 11/07 (PAGE 5 OF 8)

CALIFORNIA RESIDENTIAL PURCHASE AGREEMENT (RPA-CA PAGE 5 OF 8)

Property Address: 264 BEACH LANE, COSTA MESA, CA 92627 Date: JUNE 14, 20XX

18. **PRORATIONS OF PROPERTY TAXES AND OTHER ITEMS:** Unless otherwise agreed in writing, the following items shall be PAID CURRENT and prorated between Buyer and Seller as of Close Of Escrow: real property taxes and assessments, interest, rents, HOA regular, special, and emergency dues and assessments imposed prior to Close Of Escrow, premiums on insurance assumed by Buyer, payments on bonds and assessments assumed by Buyer, and payments on Mello-Roos and other Special Assessment District bonds and assessments that are now a lien. The following items shall be assumed by Buyer WITHOUT CREDIT toward the purchase price: prorated payments on Mello-Roos and other Special Assessment District bonds and assessments and HOA special assessments that are now a lien but not yet due. Property will be reassessed upon change of ownership. Any supplemental tax bills shall be paid as follows: **(i)** for periods after Close Of Escrow, by Buyer; and **(ii)** for periods prior to Close Of Escrow, by Seller. TAX BILLS ISSUED AFTER CLOSE OF ESCROW SHALL BE HANDLED DIRECTLY BETWEEN BUYER AND SELLER. Prorations shall be made based on a 30-day month.

19. **WITHHOLDING TAXES:** Seller and Buyer agree to execute any instrument, affidavit, statement or instruction reasonably necessary to comply with federal (FIRPTA) and California withholding Law, if required (C.A.R. Forms AS and AB).

20. **MULTIPLE LISTING SERVICE ("MLS"):** Brokers are authorized to report to the MLS a pending sale and, upon Close Of Escrow, the terms of this transaction to be published and disseminated to persons and entities authorized to use the information on terms approved by the MLS.

21. **EQUAL HOUSING OPPORTUNITY:** The Property is sold in compliance with federal, state and local anti-discrimination Laws.

22. **ATTORNEY FEES:** In any action, proceeding, or arbitration between Buyer and Seller arising out of this Agreement, the prevailing Buyer or Seller shall be entitled to reasonable attorney fees and costs from the non-prevailing Buyer or Seller, except as provided in paragraph 17A.

23. **SELECTION OF SERVICE PROVIDERS:** If Brokers refer Buyer or Seller to persons, vendors, or service or product providers ("Providers"), Brokers do not guarantee the performance of any Providers. Buyer and Seller may select ANY Providers of their own choosing.

24. **TIME OF ESSENCE; ENTIRE CONTRACT; CHANGES:** Time is of the essence. All understandings between the parties are incorporated in this Agreement. Its terms are intended by the parties as a final, complete and exclusive expression of their Agreement with respect to its subject matter, and may not be contradicted by evidence of any prior agreement or contemporaneous oral agreement. If any provision of this Agreement is held to be ineffective or invalid, the remaining provisions will nevertheless be given full force and effect. **Neither this Agreement nor any provision in it may be extended, amended, modified, altered or changed, except in writing Signed by Buyer and Seller.**

25. **OTHER TERMS AND CONDITIONS,** including attached supplements:
    A. ✓ Buyer's Inspection Advisory (C.A.R. Form BIA)
    B. ✓ Purchase Agreement Addendum (C.A.R. Form PAA paragraph numbers:)
    C. ✓ Statewide Buyer and Seller Advisory (C.A.R. Form SBSA)
    D. ✓ Seller shall provide Buyer with a completed Seller Property Questionnaire (C.A.R. form SPQ) within the time specified in paragraph 14A
    E. _____

26. **DEFINITIONS:** As used in this Agreement:
    A. **"Acceptance"** means the time the offer or final counter offer is accepted in writing by a party and is delivered to and personally received by the other party or that party's authorized agent in accordance with the terms of this offer or a final counter offer.
    B. **"Agreement"** means the terms and conditions of this accepted California Residential Purchase Agreement and any accepted counter offers and addenda.
    C. **"C.A.R. Form"** means the specific form referenced or another comparable form agreed to by the parties.
    D. **"Close Of Escrow"** means the date the grant deed, or other evidence of transfer of title, is recorded. If the scheduled close of escrow falls on a Saturday, Sunday or legal holiday, then close of escrow shall be the next business day after the scheduled close of escrow date.
    E. **"Copy"** means copy by any means including photocopy, NCR, facsimile and electronic.
    F. **"Days"** means calendar days, unless otherwise required by Law.
    G. **"Days After"** means the specified number of calendar days after the occurrence of the event specified, not counting the calendar date on which the specified event occurs, and ending at 11:59PM on the final day.
    H. **"Days Prior"** means the specified number of calendar days before the occurrence of the event specified, not counting the calendar date on which the specified event is scheduled to occur.
    I. **"Electronic Copy"** or **"Electronic Signature"** means, as applicable, an electronic copy or signature complying with California Law. Buyer and Seller agree that electronic means will not be used by either party to modify or alter the content or integrity of this Agreement without the knowledge and consent of the other.
    J. **"Law"** means any law, code, statute, ordinance, regulation, rule or order, which is adopted by a controlling city, county, state or federal legislative, judicial or executive body or agency.
    K. **"Notice to Buyer to Perform"** means a document (C.A.R. Form NBP), which shall be in writing and Signed by Seller and shall give Buyer at least 24 hours **(or as otherwise specified in paragraph 14C(4))** to remove a contingency or perform as applicable.
    L. **"Repairs"** means any repairs (including pest control), alterations, replacements, modifications or retrofitting of the Property provided for under this Agreement.
    M. **"Signed"** means either a handwritten or electronic signature on an original document, Copy or any counterpart.
    N. **Singular and Plural** terms each include the other, when appropriate.

Buyer's Initials (JB)(db)
Seller's Initials (TA)(RGL)

RPA-CA REVISED 11/07 (PAGE 6 OF 8)

Reviewed by _____ Date 6/14/XX

CALIFORNIA RESIDENTIAL PURCHASE AGREEMENT (RPA-CA PAGE 6 OF 8)

Property Address: *264 BEACH LANE, COSTA MESA, CA 92627* Date: *JUNE 14, 20XX*

27. AGENCY:

    A. DISCLOSURE: Buyer and Seller each acknowledge prior receipt of C.A.R. Form AD "Disclosure Regarding Real Estate Agency Relationships."

    B. POTENTIALLY COMPETING BUYERS AND SELLERS: Buyer and Seller each acknowledge receipt of a disclosure of the possibility of multiple representation by the Broker representing that principal. This disclosure may be part of a listing agreement, buyer-broker agreement or separate document (C.A.R. Form DA). Buyer understands that Broker representing Buyer may also represent other potential buyers, who may consider, make offers on or ultimately acquire the Property. Seller understands that Broker representing Seller may also represent other sellers with competing properties of interest to this Buyer.

    C. CONFIRMATION: The following agency relationships are hereby confirmed for this transaction:
Listing Agent *SAIL REALTY* _____ (Print Firm Name) is the agent of (check one): ☒ the Seller exclusively; or ☐ both the Buyer and Seller.
Selling Agent *RAMOS REALTY* _____ (Print Firm Name) (if not same as Listing Agent) is the agent of (check one): ☒ the Buyer exclusively; or ☐ the Seller exclusively; or ☐ both the Buyer and Seller. Real Estate Brokers are not parties to the Agreement between Buyer and Seller.

28. JOINT ESCROW INSTRUCTIONS TO ESCROW HOLDER:

    A. The following paragraphs, or applicable portions thereof, of this Agreement constitute the joint escrow instructions of Buyer and Seller to Escrow Holder, which Escrow Holder is to use along with any related counter offers and addenda, and any additional mutual instructions to close the escrow: 1, 2, 4, 12, 13B, 14E, 18, 19, 24, 25B and 25D, 26, 28, 29, 32A, 33 and paragraph D of the section titled Real Estate Brokers on page 8. If a Copy of the separate compensation agreement(s) provided for in paragraph 29 or 32A, or paragraph D of the section titled Real Estate Brokers on page 8 is deposited with Escrow Holder by Broker, Escrow Holder shall accept such agreement(s) and pay out from Buyer's or Seller's funds, or both, as applicable, the Broker's compensation provided for in such agreement(s). The terms and conditions of this Agreement not set forth in the specified paragraphs are additional matters for the information of Escrow Holder, but about which Escrow Holder need not be concerned. Buyer and Seller will receive Escrow Holder's general provisions directly from Escrow Holder and will execute such provisions upon Escrow Holder's request. To the extent the general provisions are inconsistent or conflict with this Agreement, the general provisions will control as to the duties and obligations of Escrow Holder only. Buyer and Seller will execute additional instructions, documents and forms provided by Escrow Holder that are reasonably necessary to close the escrow.

    B. A Copy of this Agreement shall be delivered to Escrow Holder within **3** business days after Acceptance (or ☐ _____). Buyer and Seller authorize Escrow Holder to accept and rely on Copies and Signatures as defined in this Agreement as originals, to open escrow and for other purposes of escrow. The validity of this Agreement as between Buyer and Seller is not affected by whether or when Escrow Holder Signs this Agreement.

    C. Brokers are a party to the escrow for the sole purpose of compensation pursuant to paragraphs 29, 32A and paragraph D of the section titled Real Estate Brokers on page 8. Buyer and Seller irrevocably assign to Brokers compensation specified in paragraphs 29 and 32A, respectively, and irrevocably instruct Escrow Holder to disburse those funds to Brokers at Close Of Escrow or pursuant to any other mutually executed cancellation agreement. Compensation instructions can be amended or revoked only with the written consent of Brokers. Escrow Holder shall immediately notify Brokers: **(i)** if Buyer's initial or any additional deposit is not made pursuant to this Agreement, or is not good at time of deposit with Escrow Holder; or **(ii)** if Buyer and Seller instruct Escrow Holder to cancel escrow.

    D. A Copy of any amendment that affects any paragraph of this Agreement for which Escrow Holder is responsible shall be delivered to Escrow Holder within **2** business days after mutual execution of the amendment.

29. BROKER COMPENSATION FROM BUYER: If applicable, upon Close Of Escrow, **Buyer** agrees to pay compensation to Broker as specified in a separate written agreement between Buyer and Broker.

30. TERMS AND CONDITIONS OF OFFER:

This is an offer to purchase the Property on the above terms and conditions. All paragraphs with spaces for initials by Buyer and Seller are incorporated in this Agreement only if initialed by all parties. If at least one but not all parties initial, a counter offer is required until agreement is reached. Seller has the right to continue to offer the Property for sale and to accept any other offer at any time prior to notification of Acceptance. Buyer has read and acknowledges receipt of a Copy of the offer and agrees to the above confirmation of agency relationships. If this offer is accepted and Buyer subsequently defaults, Buyer may be responsible for payment of Brokers' compensation. This Agreement and any supplement, addendum or modification, including any Copy, may be Signed in two or more counterparts, all of which shall constitute one and the same writing.

Buyer's Initials (*JVB*)(*dh*)
Seller's Initials (*TA*)(*RSH*)

Reviewed by ___ Date *6/14/XX*

CALIFORNIA RESIDENTIAL PURCHASE AGREEMENT (RPA-CA PAGE 7 OF 8)

Property Address: _264 BEACH LANE, COSTA MESA CA 92627_ Date: _JUNE 14, 20XX_

31. EXPIRATION OF OFFER: This offer shall be deemed revoked and the deposit shall be returned unless the offer is Signed by Seller and a Copy of the Signed offer is personally received by Buyer, or by _____, who is authorized to receive it by 5:00 PM on the third Day after this offer is signed by Buyer (or, if checked, ☐ by _____ (date), at _____ AM/PM).

Date _JUNE 14, 20XX_   Date _JUNE 14, 20XX_
BUYER _Walter Buyer_   BUYER _Debbie Buyer_
WALTER BUYER   _DEBBIE BUYER_
(Print name)   (Print name)
100 BOAT AVENUE, MARINA DEL REY, CA 90292
(Address)

32. BROKER COMPENSATION FROM SELLER:
　　A. Upon Close Of Escrow, **Seller** agrees to pay compensation to Broker as specified in a separate written agreement between Seller and Broker.
　　B. If escrow does not close, compensation is payable as specified in that separate written agreement.

33. ACCEPTANCE OF OFFER: Seller warrants that Seller is the owner of the Property, or has the authority to execute this Agreement. Seller accepts the above offer, agrees to sell the Property on the above terms and conditions, and agrees to the above confirmation of agency relationships. Seller has read and acknowledges receipt of a Copy of this Agreement, and authorizes Broker to deliver a Signed Copy to Buyer.
　　☐ (If checked) **SUBJECT TO ATTACHED COUNTER OFFER, DATED** _____

Date _JUNE 15, 20XX_   Date _JUNE 15, 20XX_
SELLER _Tony Seller_   SELLER _Ramona J Seller_
TONY SELLER   _RAMONA J SELLER_
(Print name)   (Print name)
264 BEACH LANE, COSTA MESA, CA 92627
(Address)

_TB db_   **CONFIRMATION OF ACCEPTANCE:** A Copy of Signed Acceptance was personally received by Buyer or Buyer's authorized
(Initials)   agent on (date) _6/15/20XX_ at _____ AM/PM. A binding Agreement is created when a Copy of Signed Acceptance is personally received by Buyer or Buyer's authorized agent whether or not confirmed in this document. Completion of this confirmation is not legally required in order to create a binding Agreement; it is solely intended to evidence the date that Confirmation of Acceptance has occurred.

REAL ESTATE BROKERS:
A. Real Estate Brokers are not parties to the Agreement between Buyer and Seller.
B. Agency relationships are confirmed as stated in paragraph 27.
C. If specified in paragraph 2A, Agent who submitted the offer for Buyer acknowledges receipt of deposit.
D. **COOPERATING BROKER COMPENSATION:** Listing Broker agrees to pay Cooperating Broker (**Selling Firm**) and Cooperating Broker agrees to accept, out of Listing Broker's proceeds in escrow: **(i)** the amount specified in the MLS, provided Cooperating Broker is a Participant of the MLS in which the Property is offered for sale or a reciprocal MLS; or **(ii)** ☐ (if checked) the amount specified in a separate written agreement (C.A.R. Form CBC) between Listing Broker and Cooperating Broker.

Real Estate Broker (Selling Firm) _RAMOS REALTY_ _____ DRE Lic. # _00 000 000_
By _Joseph Ramos_ DRE Lic. # _00 000 000_ Date _6/14/20XX_
Address _777 NEWPORT BLVD_ City _NEWPORT BEACH_ State _CA_ Zip _92663_
Telephone _714.647.0000_ Fax _714.647.0001_ E-mail _JR@ramosrealty.com_

Real Estate Broker (Listing Firm) _SAIL REALTY_ _____ License # _00 000 000_
By _Carmen Caro_ License # _00 000 000_ Date _6/15/20XX_
Address _227 HARBOR BLVD_ City _COSTA MESA_ State _CA_ Zip _92627_
Telephone _714.626.2828_ Fax _714.626.2829_ E-mail _carmen@sailreal.com_

ESCROW HOLDER ACKNOWLEDGMENT:
Escrow Holder acknowledges receipt of a Copy of this Agreement, (if checked, ☐ a deposit in the amount of $_____),
counter offer numbers _____ and _____, and agrees to act as Escrow Holder subject to paragraph 28 of this Agreement, any supplemental escrow instructions and the terms of Escrow Holder's general provisions.

Escrow Holder is advised that the date of Confirmation of Acceptance of the Agreement as between Buyer and Seller is _____

Escrow Holder _____   Escrow # _____
By _____   Date _____
Address _____
Phone/Fax/E-mail _____
Escrow Holder is licensed by the California Department of ☐ Corporations, ☐ Insurance, ☐ Real Estate. License # _____

(___ / ___)   **REJECTION OF OFFER:** No counter offer is being made. This offer was reviewed and rejected by Seller on _____
(Seller's Initials) _____ (Date)

THIS FORM HAS BEEN APPROVED BY THE CALIFORNIA ASSOCIATION OF REALTORS® (C.A.R.). NO REPRESENTATION IS MADE AS TO THE LEGAL VALIDITY OR ADEQUACY OF ANY PROVISION IN ANY SPECIFIC TRANSACTION. A REAL ESTATE BROKER IS THE PERSON QUALIFIED TO ADVISE ON REAL ESTATE TRANSACTIONS. IF YOU DESIRE LEGAL OR TAX ADVICE, CONSULT AN APPROPRIATE PROFESSIONAL.
This form is available for use by the entire real estate industry. It is not intended to identify the user as a REALTOR®. REALTOR® is a registered collective membership mark which may be used only by members of the NATIONAL ASSOCIATION OF REALTORS® who subscribe to its Code of Ethics.

Published and Distributed by:
REAL ESTATE BUSINESS SERVICES, INC.
a subsidiary of the California Association of REALTORS®
525 South Virgil Avenue, Los Angeles, California 90020

Reviewed by _JR_ Date _6/14/XX_

RPA-CA REVISED 11/07 (PAGE 8 OF 8)

CALIFORNIA RESIDENTIAL PURCHASE AGREEMENT (RPA-CA PAGE 8 OF 8)

California Residential Purchase Agreement and Joint Escrow Instructions – Highlights

1. Includes fixed times for delivery of disclosures and removal of contingencies.
2. Allows Buyer to cancel within a set time without first requesting Seller to make repairs.
3. Requires written removal of contingencies.
4. Requires Seller to give Notice to Buyer to Perform before Seller may cancel.
5. Gives Seller a cancellation right if Buyer does not meet certain contractual obligations.
6. Refers to separate agreement for broker compensation.
7. No pre-allocation of costs to cure problems with wood destroying pests.
8. Use of addendum required to accommodate pre-allocation requests.

Example: An offer made by a prospective buyer was contingent on the sale of the buyer's current residence. Seller Billings made a counter offer accepting the offer provided the seller could continue to market the home in an attempt to obtain a better offer while granting the buyer a "first right of refusal" to remove the sale contingency if another offer was presented. The buyer accepted the terms and immediately listed his current residence for sale. One week later, Billings notified the buyer that a better offer with no contingencies was "on the table." The agent representing the buyer should advise the buyer about the advantages and disadvantages of removing the contingency feature at this time.

C. THE PURCHASE AGREEMENT ADDENDUM

The *PURCHASE AGREEMENT ADDENDUM form is used as an addendum to either the Residential Purchase Agreement, another offer form, or the counter offer form.* Only the paragraphs that are checked are included as part of the contract. The CAR® two-page addendum (see **Figure 5-7**) covers six separate topics that are occasionally relevant to a transaction:

1. The cancellation of prior sale; back-up offers.
2. Seller to remain in possession after close of escrow.
3. Tenant to remain in possession.
4. Junior or assumed financing.
5. Short pay.
6. Court confirmation.

ERRORS AND OMISSIONS INSURANCE is the liability insurance that brokers and salespeople should carry in order to pay for any costly lawsuits.

D. THE COUNTER OFFER (Replaces Original Offer with Changes in Terms)

A counter offer automatically cancels the original offer if terms of the new offer vary from the original.

Figure 5-7

PURCHASE AGREEMENT ADDENDUM No. _____

May Also Be Used With Counter Offer

(C.A.R. Form PAA, Revised 4/06)

This is an addendum to the ☐ California Residential Purchase Agreement, ☐ Counter Offer No._____, ☐ Other _____
_____, ("Agreement"), dated _____,
on property known as _____ ("Property"),
between _____ ("Buyer"),
and _____ ("Seller").
(The definitions in the California Residential Purchase Agreement are applicable to this Purchase Agreement Addendum.)

1. ☐ **CANCELLATION OF PRIOR SALE; BACK-UP OFFER** (If checked): This Agreement is in back-up position number
_____, and is contingent upon written cancellation of any prior contracts and related escrows ("Prior Contracts") between
Seller and other buyers. Seller and other buyers may mutually agree to modify or amend the terms of Prior Contracts.
Buyer may cancel this Agreement in writing at any time before Seller provides Buyer Copies of written cancellations of
Prior Contracts Signed by all parties to those contracts. If Seller is unable to provide such written Signed cancellations to
Buyer by _____ (date), then either Buyer or Seller may cancel the Agreement in writing.

    A. BUYER'S DEPOSIT CHECK shall be: **(i)** held uncashed until Copies of the written cancellations Signed by all parties
to the Prior Contracts are provided to Buyer; OR **(ii)** (if checked) ☐ immediately handled as provided in the Agreement.

    B. TIME PERIODS in the Agreement for Investigations, contingencies, covenants and other obligations **(i)** shall begin on
the Day After Seller provides Buyer Copies of Signed cancellations of Prior Contracts; OR **(ii)** (if checked) ☐ all time
periods shall begin as provided in this Agreement. However, if the date for Close Of Escrow is a specific calendar date,
that date shall NOT be extended, unless agreed to in writing by Buyer and Seller.

2. ☐ **SELLER TO REMAIN IN POSSESSION AFTER CLOSE OF ESCROW** (If checked): This provision is intended for short-
term occupancy (i.e. less than 30 Days). If occupancy is intended to be for 30 Days or longer, use Residential Lease After
Sale (C.A.R. Form RLAS). **Note: Local rent control or other Law regarding tenant's rights may impact Buyer's and Seller's
rights and obligations.**

    A. TERM: Seller to remain in possession of Property for _____ **Days** After Close Of Escrow (or ☐ _____).
Seller has no right to remain in possession beyond this term and may be responsible for court awarded damages if seller
does remain.

    B. COMPENSATION: Seller agrees to pay Buyer (i) For the term specified in 2A, $_____ per Day (or ☐
_____), and (ii) a security deposit in the amount of $_____. Seller shall deposit such
funds with escrow holder prior to Close Of Escrow or such funds shall be withheld from Seller's proceeds. At Close Of
Escrow, security deposit will be released to Buyer (or ☐ held in escrow).

    C. LATE CHARGE/NSF CHECKS: If any payment from Seller to Buyer is required outside of escrow, and any such payment
is not received by Buyer within **5 (or ☐ _____) Days** After date due, Seller shall pay to Buyer an additional sum of
$_____ as a Late Charge. If a check is returned for non-sufficient funds ("NSF"), Seller shall pay to Buyer
$25.00 as an NSF charge. Seller and Buyer agree that these charges represent a fair and reasonable estimate of the
costs Buyer may incur by reason of Seller's late or NSF payment. Buyer's acceptance of any Late Charge or NSF fee
shall not constitute a waiver as to any default by Seller.

    D. UTILITIES: Seller agrees to pay for all utilities and services, and the following charges: _____
_____ except _____, which shall be paid for by Buyer.

    E. ENTRY: Seller shall make Property available to Buyer for the purpose of entering to make necessary or agreed repairs,
or to supply necessary or agreed services, or to show Property to prospective or actual purchasers, tenants, mortgagees,
lenders, appraisers or contractors. Buyer and Seller agree that 24 hours notice (oral or written) shall be reasonable and
sufficient notice. In an emergency, Buyer may enter Property at any time without prior notice.

    F. MAINTENANCE: Seller shall maintain the Property, including pool, spa, landscaping and grounds, and all personal property
included in the sale in substantially the same condition as on the date of Acceptance of the Agreement. Except as provided
in the Agreement, Seller shall not make alterations to the Property without Buyer's written consent.

    G. ASSIGNMENT; SUBLETTING: Seller shall not assign or sublet all or any part of the Property, or assign or transfer the right to
occupy the Property. Any assignment, subletting or transfer of the Property by voluntary act of Seller, by operation of Law or
otherwise, without Buyer's prior written consent shall give Buyer the right to terminate Seller's right to possession.

    H. SELLER'S OBLIGATIONS UPON DELIVERY OF POSSESSION: Upon delivery of possession to Buyer, Seller shall deliver the
Property in the condition and on the terms provided in the Agreement.

    I. INSURANCE: Seller's personal property (including vehicles) is not insured by Buyer, and, if applicable, owner's association, against
loss or damage due to fire, theft, vandalism, rain, water, criminal or negligent acts of others, or any other cause. Seller is to carry
Seller's own insurance to protect Seller from such loss.

    J. WAIVER: The waiver of any breach shall not be construed as a continuing waiver of the same or any subsequent breach.

    K. OTHER TERMS AND CONDITIONS/SUPPLEMENTS: _____
_____
_____

Buyer's Initials (_____)(_____)
Seller's Initials (_____)(_____)

PAA REVISED 4/06 (PAGE 1 OF 2) Print Date

Reviewed by _____ Date _____

EQUAL HOUSING OPPORTUNITY

PURCHASE AGREEMENT ADDENDUM (PAA PAGE 1 OF 2)

Property Address: _____ Date: _____

3. ☐ **TENANT TO REMAIN IN POSSESSION** (If checked): Buyer shall take Property subject to the rights of existing tenants. Seller shall, within **7 (or ☐ _____) Days** After Acceptance, deliver to Buyer Copies of all: estoppel certificates sent to and received back from tenants; leases; rental agreements; and current income and expense statements ("Rental Documents"). Seller shall give Buyer written notice of any changes to existing leases or tenancies or new agreements to lease or rent ("Proposed Changes") at least **7 (or ☐ _____) Days** prior to any Proposed Changes. Buyer's approval of the Rental Documents and Proposed Changes is a contingency of the Agreement. Buyer shall, within **5 (or ☐ _____) Days** After receipt of Rental Documents or Proposed Changes remove the applicable contingency or cancel the Agreement. Seller shall transfer to Buyer, through escrow, all unused tenant deposits. No warranty is made concerning compliance with governmental restrictions, if any, limiting the amount of rent that can lawfully be charged, and/or the maximum number of persons who can lawfully occupy the Property, unless otherwise agreed in writing.

4. ☐ **SECONDARY OR ASSUMED LOAN** (If checked): Obtaining the secondary loan or assumption below and approval of such financing is a contingency of this Agreement. Buyer shall act diligently and in good faith to obtain the designated financing.

    A. ☐ **SECONDARY LOAN:**

        (1) New second deed of trust in favor of LENDER encumbering the Property, securing a note payable at maximum interest of _____% fixed rate or _____% initial adjustable rate, with a maximum interest rate of _____%, balance due in _____ years. Buyer shall pay loan fees/points not to exceed _____. (These terms apply whether the designated loan is conventional, FHA or VA.)

        (2) Within **17 (or ☐ _____) Days)** After Acceptance, Buyer shall, as specified in the Agreement, remove this contingency or cancel this Agreement; OR (if checked) ☐ secondary loan contingency shall remain in effect until the loan is funded.

    B. ☐ **ASSUMPTION OF EXISTING LOAN:**

        (1) Assumption of existing deed of trust encumbering the Property, securing a note payable at maximum interest of _____% fixed rate or _____% initial adjustable rate, with a maximum interest rate of _____%, balance due in _____ years. Buyer shall pay loan fees/points not to exceed _____. Seller shall, within **5 (or ☐ _____) Days** After Acceptance, request from Lender, and upon receipt provide to Buyer, Copies of all applicable notes and deeds of trust, loan balances and current interest rates. Differences between estimated and actual loan balances shall be adjusted at Close Of Escrow by cash down payment. Impound accounts, if any, shall be assigned and charged to Buyer and credited to Seller. If this is an assumption of a VA Loan, the sale is contingent upon Seller being provided a release of liability and substitution of eligibility, unless otherwise agreed in writing.

        (2) Within **17 (or ☐ _____ Days)** After Acceptance, Buyer shall, as specified in the Agreement, remove this contingency or cancel this Agreement. However, if the assumed loan documents are not provided to Buyer within **7 Days After Acceptance,** Buyer has **5 (or ☐ _____) Days** After receipt of these documents, or the fixed time specified in 4B(2), whichever occurs last, to remove this contingency or cancel the Agreement; OR (if checked) ☐ assumed loan contingency shall remain in effect until the assumption is approved.

5. ☐ **SHORT PAY** (If checked): This Agreement is contingent upon Seller's receipt of written consent from all existing secured lenders and lienholders ("Short-Pay Lenders"), no later than 5:00 P.M. on _____ (date) ("Short-Pay Contingency Date"), to reduce their respective loan balances by an amount sufficient to permit the proceeds from the sale of the Property, without additional funds from Seller, to pay the existing balances on loans, real property taxes, brokerage commissions, closing costs, and other monetary obligations the Agreement requires Seller to pay at Close Of Escrow (including, but not limited to, escrow charges, title charges, documentary transfer taxes, prorations, retrofit costs and Repairs). If Seller fails to give Buyer written notice of all existing Short-Pay Lenders' consent by the Short-Pay Contingency Date, either Seller or Buyer may cancel the Agreement in writing. Seller shall reasonably cooperate with existing Short-Pay Lenders in the short-payoff process. Buyer and Seller understand that Lenders are not obligated to accept a short-payoff and may accept other offers, and that Seller, Buyer and Brokers do not have control over whether Short-Pay Lenders will consent to a short-payoff, or any act, omission, or decision by any Short-Pay Lender in the short-payoff process. Seller is informed that a short-pay may create credit or legal problems or may result in taxable income to Seller. Seller may present to Short-Pay Lender any additional offers that are received on the Property. **Seller is advised to seek advice from an attorney, certified public accountant or other expert regarding such potential consequences of a short-payoff.**

6. ☐ **COURT CONFIRMATION** (If checked): This Agreement is contingent upon court confirmation on or before _____ (date). If court confirmation is not obtained by that date, Buyer may cancel this Agreement in writing. Court confirmation may be required in probate, conservatorship, guardianship, receivership, bankruptcy or other proceedings. The court may allow open, competitive bidding, resulting in Property being sold to the highest bidder. Broker recommends that Buyer appear at the court confirmation hearing. Buyer understands that **(i)** Broker and others may continue to market the Property and **(ii)** Broker may represent other competitive bidders prior to and at the court confirmation.

By signing below Buyer and Seller acknowledge that each has read, understands, received a copy of and agrees to the terms of this Purchase Agreement Addendum.

Date _____   Date _____

Buyer _____   Seller _____

Buyer _____   Seller _____

Published and Distributed by:
REAL ESTATE BUSINESS SERVICES, INC.
a subsidiary of the California Association of REALTORS®
525 South Virgil Avenue, Los Angeles, California 90020

SURE TRAC
The System for Success®

PAA REVISED 4/06 (PAGE 2 OF 2)

Reviewed by _____ Date _____

EQUAL HOUSING OPPORTUNITY

PURCHASE AGREEMENT ADDENDUM (PAA PAGE 2 OF 2)

Rather than preparing a whole new purchase agreement when presenting a counter offer, most sellers prefer to use a standard counter offer form like the sample CAR® form shown in **Figure 5-8**. This form is used to change some of the terms of the original purchase agreement and allows the seller and buyer to accept the remaining agreed-to terms and conditions of the original agreement. Plenty of blank space is provided to list these exceptions that formally amend the purchase agreement without the necessity of completing an entirely new purchase agreement.

In a counter offer, the offeree becomes the offeror.

If there is only a minor change in a term (like sale's price), the counter offer can be written on the back of the original purchase agreement and signed by the buyer and seller. **The seller can never change the purchase agreement on its face by crossing out sections or adding new information**. The counter offer must contain a clause stating that all of the conditions of the original purchase agreement are acceptable except for the listed new terms. If there are major changes, the formal counter offer form may be required. Finally, if there are significant changes it is better to start the process again by filling out a new purchase agreement.

> **Example:** A buyer made an offer to purchase a property and placed $5,000 as an earnest money deposit. The seller amended the offer with some terms of her own and did not change the amount of the earnest money deposit. The buyer then changed the amount of the earnest money deposit to $1,000. The buyer's change is considered a counter offer, a contract has not been formed, and the seller must accept the buyer's change in the amount of the earnest money deposit.

When accepting an offer on her home, the seller changed one of the terms of the buyer's offer. This is best described as a counter offer.

E. INSPECTION ADVISORY FOR BUYERS

Property inspection is important. The physical condition of the land and improvements being purchased are not guaranteed by either sellers or brokers, except as specifically set forth in the purchase agreement. For this reason, most salespeople are required by their brokers to "advise" buyers of their right to have a personal and professional inspection of the property they are purchasing. Furthermore, brokers have been advised by their attorneys to have potential buyers sign the Buyer's Inspection Advisory Form to protect the salesperson and broker. This form expressly states in bold print:

"YOU ARE STRONGLY ADVISED TO INVESTIGATE THE CONDITION AND SUITABILITY OF ALL ASPECTS OF THE PROPERTY. IF YOU DO NOT DO SO, YOU ARE ACTING AGAINST THE ADVICE OF BROKERS."

As professionals, we have a duty to advise buyers to exercise reasonable care to protect themselves. The buyer acknowledges receipt of a copy of the Buyer's Inspection Advisory CAR® form by signing a copy (see **Figure 5-9**).

If an agent fails to disclose known defects in a property to the buyer, the buyer can file civil action against the agent within two years.

Figure 5-8

CALIFORNIA
ASSOCIATION
OF REALTORS®

COUNTER OFFER   No. _____
For use by Seller or Buyer. May be used for Multiple Counter Offer.
(C.A.R. Form CO, Revised 10/04)

Date _____, at _____, California.
This is a counter offer to the: ☐ California Residential Purchase Agreement, ☐ Counter Offer, or ☐ Other _____ ("Offer"),
dated _____, on property known as _____ ("Property"),
between _____ ("Buyer") and _____ ("Seller").

1. **TERMS:** The terms and conditions of the above referenced document are **accepted subject to the following:**
   A. Paragraphs in the Offer that require initials by all parties, but are not initialed by all parties, are excluded from the final agreement unless specifically referenced for inclusion in paragraph 1C of this or another Counter Offer.
   B. Unless otherwise agreed in writing, down payment and loan amount(s) will be adjusted in the same proportion as in the original Offer.
   C. _____
      _____
      _____
      _____
      _____
      _____
      _____
   D. The following attached supplements are incorporated into this Counter Offer: ☐ Addendum No. _____
      ☐ _____   ☐ _____

2. **RIGHT TO ACCEPT OTHER OFFERS:** Seller has the right to continue to offer the Property for sale or for other transaction, and to accept any other offer at any time prior to notification of acceptance, as described in paragraph 3. If this is a Seller Counter Offer, Seller's acceptance of another offer prior to Buyer's acceptance and communication of notification of this Counter Offer, shall revoke this Counter Offer.

3. **EXPIRATION:** This Counter Offer shall be deemed revoked and the deposits, if any, shall be returned unless this Counter Offer is signed by the Buyer or Seller to whom it is sent and a Copy of the signed Counter Offer is personally received by the person making this Counter Offer or _____,
   who is authorized to receive it, by 5:00PM on the third day after this Counter Offer is made or, (if checked)
   by ☐ _____ (date), at _____ AM/PM. This Counter Offer may be executed in counterparts.

4. ☐ **(If checked:) MULTIPLE COUNTER OFFER:** Seller is making a Counter Offer(s) to another prospective buyer(s) on terms that may or may not be the same as in this Counter Offer. Acceptance of this Counter Offer by Buyer shall **not** be binding unless and until it is subsequently re-Signed by Seller in paragraph 7 below and a Copy of the Counter Offer Signed in paragraph 7 is personally received by Buyer or by _____, who is authorized to receive it, by 5:00 PM on the third Day After this Counter Offer is made or, (if checked) by ☐ _____ (date), at _____ AM/PM. Prior to the completion of all of these events, Buyer and Seller shall have no duties or obligations for the purchase or sale of the Property.

5. **OFFER:** BUYER OR SELLER MAKES THIS COUNTER OFFER ON THE TERMS ABOVE AND ACKNOWLEDGES RECEIPT OF A COPY.
   _____ Date _____
   _____ Date _____

6. **ACCEPTANCE: I/WE** accept the above Counter Offer (**If checked** ☐ **SUBJECT TO THE ATTACHED COUNTER OFFER**) and acknowledge receipt of a Copy.
   _____ Date _____ Time _____ AM/PM
   _____ Date _____ Time _____ AM/PM

7. **MULTIPLE COUNTER OFFER SIGNATURE LINE:** By signing below, Seller accepts this Multiple Counter Offer. NOTE TO SELLER: Do NOT sign in this box until after Buyer signs in paragraph 6. (Paragraph 7 applies only if paragraph 4 is checked.)
   _____ Date _____ Time _____ AM/PM
   _____ Date _____ Time _____ AM/PM

8. (_____/_____) (Initials) **Confirmation of Acceptance:** A Copy of Signed Acceptance was personally received by the maker of the Counter Offer, or that person's authorized agent as specified in paragraph 3 (or, if this is a Multiple Counter Offer, the Buyer or Buyer's authorized agent as specified in paragraph 4) on (date) _____, at _____ AM/PM. **A binding Agreement is created when a Copy of Signed Acceptance is personally received by the the maker of the Counter Offer, or that person's authorized agent (or, if this is a Multiple Counter Offer, the Buyer or Buyer's authorized agent) whether or not confirmed in this document.** Completion of this confirmation is not legally required in order to create a binding Agreement; it is solely intended to evidence the date that Confirmation of Acceptance has occurred.

Published and Distributed by:
REAL ESTATE BUSINESS SERVICES, INC.
a subsidiary of the California Association of REALTORS®
525 South Virgil Avenue, Los Angeles, California 90020

SURE TRAC
The System for Success®

Reviewed by _____ Date _____

EQUAL HOUSING OPPORTUNITY

CO REVISED 10/04 (PAGE 1 OF 1)   Print Date

COUNTER OFFER (CO PAGE 1 OF 1)

Figure 5-9

CALIFORNIA
ASSOCIATION
OF REALTORS®

BUYER'S INSPECTION ADVISORY

(C.A.R. Form BIA, Revised 10/02)

Property Address: _264 BEACH LANE   COSTA MESA, CA 92627_ ("Property").

A. IMPORTANCE OF PROPERTY INVESTIGATION: The physical condition of the land and improvements being purchased is not guaranteed by either Seller or Brokers. For this reason, you should conduct thorough investigations of the Property personally and with professionals who should provide written reports of their investigations. A general physical inspection typically does not cover all aspects of the Property nor items affecting the Property that are not physically located on the Property. If the professionals recommend further investigations, including a recommendation by a pest control operator to inspect inaccessible areas of the Property, you should contact qualified experts to conduct such additional investigations.

B. BUYER RIGHTS AND DUTIES: You have an affirmative duty to exercise reasonable care to protect yourself, including discovery of the legal, practical and technical implications of disclosed facts, and the investigation and verification of information and facts that you know or that are within your diligent attention and observation. The purchase agreement gives you the right to investigate the Property. If you exercise this right, and you should, you must do so in accordance with the terms of that agreement. This is the best way for you to protect yourself. It is extremely important for you to read all written reports provided by professionals and to discuss the results of inspections with the professional who conducted the inspection. You have the right to request that Seller make repairs, corrections or take other action based upon items discovered in your investigations or disclosed by Seller. If Seller is unwilling or unable to satisfy your requests, or you do not want to purchase the Property in its disclosed and discovered condition, you have the right to cancel the agreement if you act within specific time periods. If you do not cancel the agreement in a timely and proper manner, you may be in breach of contract.

C. SELLER RIGHTS AND DUTIES: Seller is required to disclose to you material facts known to him/her that affect the value or desirability of the Property. However, Seller may not be aware of some Property defects or conditions. Seller does not have an obligation to inspect the Property for your benefit nor is Seller obligated to repair, correct or otherwise cure known defects that are disclosed to you or previously unknown defects that are discovered by you or your inspectors during escrow. The purchase agreement obligates Seller to make the Property available to you for investigations.

D. BROKER OBLIGATIONS: Brokers do not have expertise in all areas and therefore cannot advise you on many items, such as soil stability, geologic or environmental conditions, hazardous or illegal controlled substances, structural conditions of the foundation or other improvements, or the condition of the roof, plumbing, heating, air conditioning, electrical, sewer, septic, waste disposal, or other system. The only way to accurately determine the condition of the Property is through an inspection by an appropriate professional selected by you. If Broker gives you referrals to such professionals, Broker does not guarantee their performance. You may select any professional of your choosing. In sales involving residential dwellings with no more than four units, Brokers have a duty to make a diligent visual inspection of the accessible areas of the Property and to disclose the results of that inspection. However, as some Property defects or conditions may not be discoverable from a visual inspection, it is possible Brokers are not aware of them. If you have entered into a written agreement with a Broker, the specific terms of that agreement will determine the nature and extent of that Broker's duty to you. **YOU ARE STRONGLY ADVISED TO INVESTIGATE THE CONDITION AND SUITABILITY OF ALL ASPECTS OF THE PROPERTY. IF YOU DO NOT DO SO, YOU ARE ACTING AGAINST THE ADVICE OF BROKERS.**

E. YOU ARE ADVISED TO CONDUCT INVESTIGATIONS OF THE ENTIRE PROPERTY, INCLUDING, BUT NOT LIMITED TO THE FOLLOWING:
1. **GENERAL CONDITION OF THE PROPERTY, ITS SYSTEMS AND COMPONENTS:** Foundation, roof, plumbing, heating, air conditioning, electrical, mechanical, security, pool/spa, other structural and non-structural systems and components, fixtures, built-in appliances, any personal property included in the sale, and energy efficiency of the Property. (Structural engineers are best suited to determine possible design or construction defects, and whether improvements are structurally sound.)
2. **SQUARE FOOTAGE, AGE, BOUNDARIES:** Square footage, room dimensions, lot size, age of improvements and boundaries. Any numerical statements regarding these items are APPROXIMATIONS ONLY and have not been verified by Seller and cannot be verified by Brokers. Fences, hedges, walls, retaining walls and other natural or constructed barriers or markers do not necessarily identify true Property boundaries. (Professionals such as appraisers, architects, surveyors and civil engineers are best suited to determine square footage, dimensions and boundaries of the Property.)
3. **WOOD DESTROYING PESTS:** Presence of, or conditions likely to lead to the presence of wood destroying pests and organisms and other infestation or infection. Inspection reports covering these items can be separated into two sections: Section 1 identifies areas where infestation or infection is evident. Section 2 identifies areas where there are conditions likely to lead to infestation or infection. A registered structural pest control company is best suited to perform these inspections.
4. **SOIL STABILITY:** Existence of fill or compacted soil, expansive or contracting soil, susceptibility to slippage, settling or movement, and the adequacy of drainage. (Geotechnical engineers are best suited to determine such conditions, causes and remedies.)

BIA REVISED 10/02 (PAGE 1 OF 2) Print Date

Buyer's Initials (_WB_)(_db_)
Seller's Initials (_TS_)(_RJS_)

Reviewed by _SR_ Date _4/14/xx_

EQUAL HOUSING
OPPORTUNITY

BUYER'S INSPECTION ADVISORY (BIA PAGE 1 OF 2)

Property Address: 264 BEACH LANE, COSTA MESA CA 92627   Date: 6/14/xx

5. **ROOF:** Present condition, age, leaks, and remaining useful life. (Roofing contractors are best suited to determine these conditions.)
6. **POOL/SPA:** Cracks, leaks or operational problems. (Pool contractors are best suited to determine these conditions.)
7. **WASTE DISPOSAL:** Type, size, adequacy, capacity and condition of sewer and septic systems and components, connection to sewer, and applicable fees.
8. **WATER AND UTILITIES; WELL SYSTEMS AND COMPONENTS:** Water and utility availability, use restrictions and costs. Water quality, adequacy, condition, and performance of well systems and components.
9. **ENVIRONMENTAL HAZARDS:** Potential environmental hazards, including, but not limited to, asbestos, lead-based paint and other lead contamination, radon, methane, other gases, fuel oil or chemical storage tanks, contaminated soil or water, hazardous waste, waste disposal sites, electromagnetic fields, nuclear sources, and other substances, materials, products, or conditions (including mold (airborne, toxic or otherwise), fungus or similar contaminants). (For more information on these items, you may consult an appropriate professional or read the booklets "Environmental Hazards: A Guide for Homeowners, Buyers, Landlords and Tenants," "Protect Your Family From Lead in Your Home" or both.)
10. **EARTHQUAKES AND FLOODING:** Susceptibility of the Property to earthquake/seismic hazards and propensity of the Property to flood. (A Geologist or Geotechnical Engineer is best suited to provide information on these conditions.)
11. **FIRE, HAZARD AND OTHER INSURANCE:** The availability and cost of necessary or desired insurance may vary. The location of the Property in a seismic, flood or fire hazard zone, and other conditions, such as the age of the Property and the claims history of the Property and Buyer, may affect the availability and need for certain types of insurance. Buyer should explore insurance options early as this information may affect other decisions, including the removal of loan and inspection contingencies. (An insurance agent is best suited to provide information on these conditions.)
12. **BUILDING PERMITS, ZONING AND GOVERNMENTAL REQUIREMENTS:** Permits, inspections, certificates, zoning, other governmental limitations, restrictions, and requirements affecting the current or future use of the Property, its development or size. (Such information is available from appropriate governmental agencies and private information providers. Brokers are not qualified to review or interpret any such information.)
13. **RENTAL PROPERTY RESTRICTIONS:** Some cities and counties impose restrictions that limit the amount of rent that can be charged, the maximum number of occupants, and the right of a landlord to terminate a tenancy. Deadbolt or other locks and security systems for doors and windows, including window bars, should be examined to determine whether they satisfy legal requirements. (Government agencies can provide information about these restrictions and other requirements.)
14. **SECURITY AND SAFETY:** State and local Law may require the installation of barriers, access alarms, self-latching mechanisms and/or other measures to decrease the risk to children and other persons of existing swimming pools and hot tubs, as well as various fire safety and other measures concerning other features of the Property. Compliance requirements differ from city to city and county to county. Unless specifically agreed, the Property may not be in compliance with these requirements. (Local government agencies can provide information about these restrictions and other requirements.)
15. **NEIGHBORHOOD, AREA, SUBDIVISION CONDITIONS; PERSONAL FACTORS:** Neighborhood or area conditions, including schools, proximity and adequacy of law enforcement, crime statistics, the proximity of registered felons or offenders, fire protection, other government services, availability, adequacy and cost of any speed-wired, wireless internet connections or other telecommunications or other technology services and installations, proximity to commercial, industrial or agricultural activities, existing and proposed transportation, construction and development that may affect noise, view, or traffic, airport noise, noise or odor from any source, wild and domestic animals, other nuisances, hazards, or circumstances, protected species, wetland properties, botanical diseases, historic or other governmentally protected sites or improvements, cemeteries, facilities and condition of common areas of common interest subdivisions, and possible lack of compliance with any governing documents or Homeowners' Association requirements, conditions and influences of significance to certain cultures and/or religions, and personal needs, requirements and preferences of Buyer.

Buyer and Seller acknowledge and agree that Broker: **(i)** Does not decide what price Buyer should pay or Seller should accept; **(ii)** Does not guarantee the condition of the Property; **(iii)** Does not guarantee the performance, adequacy or completeness of inspections, services, products or repairs provided or made by Seller or others; **(iv)** Does not have an obligation to conduct an inspection of common areas or areas off the site of the Property; **(v)** Shall not be responsible for identifying defects on the Property, in common areas, or offsite unless such defects are visually observable by an inspection of reasonably accessible areas of the Property or are known to Broker; **(vi)** Shall not be responsible for inspecting public records or permits concerning the title or use of Property; **(vii)** Shall not be responsible for identifying the location of boundary lines or other items affecting title; **(viii)** Shall not be responsible for verifying square footage, representations of others or information contained in Investigation reports, Multiple Listing Service, advertisements, flyers or other promotional material; **(ix)** Shall not be responsible for providing legal or tax advice regarding any aspect of a transaction entered into by Buyer or Seller; and **(x)** Shall not be responsible for providing other advice or information that exceeds the knowledge, education and experience required to perform real estate licensed activity. Buyer and Seller agree to seek legal, tax, insurance, title and other desired assistance from appropriate professionals.

By signing below, Buyer and Seller each acknowledge that they have read, understand, accept and have received a Copy of this Advisory. Buyer is encouraged to read it carefully.

Walter Buyer ____ 6/14/xx   _Debbie Buyer_ ____ 6/14/xx
Buyer Signature ____ Date   Buyer Signature ____ Date

Tony Seller ____ 6/15/xx   _Ramona J Seller_ ____ 6/15/xx
Seller Signature ____ Date   Seller Signature ____ Date

Published and Distributed by:
REAL ESTATE BUSINESS SERVICES, INC
a subsidiary of the California Association of REALTORS®
525 South Virgil Avenue, Los Angeles, California 90020

Reviewed by _____ Date 6/15/xx

BIA REVISED 10/02 (PAGE 2 OF 2)

BUYER'S INSPECTION ADVISORY (BIA PAGE 2 OF 2)

VI. Seller/Agent Required Disclosures

The Transfer Disclosure Statement (TDS) requires the disclosure of the known presence of mold, drug lab use, military ordnance, and Mello-Roos bonds and taxes. Additional disclosures may be needed to further detail this information.

The following is an alphabetical list of the disclosure forms that may typically be required in a residential real estate transaction:

Agent's Inspection Disclosure – Designed for use by agents on properties that are exempt from California Civil Code § 1102.6 (TDS) requirements.

Buyer's Affidavit (FIRPTA Compliance) – Documents whether or not federal Foreign Investment in Real Property Tax Act (FIRPTA) withholding is required. Explains the criteria buyer and property must meet.

Confirmation: Real Estate Agency Relationships – Used to comply with California Civil Code requirements to confirm agency relationships in a transaction. This clause is preprinted in CAR® Purchase Contracts.

Data Base Disclosure (Regarding Registered Sex Offenders) – Complies with requirement that certain printed information regarding registered sex offenders be part of residential real estate contracts and leases.

Disclosure and Consent For Representation Of More Than One Buyer Or Seller – This form is used to disclose that a real estate brokerage may represent a buyer or seller that is competing with the broker's principal. It also discloses the possibility that the same real estate brokerage company may represent both buyer and seller in the same transaction.

Disclosure Regarding Real Estate Agency Relationships – Used to comply with California Civil Code. Explains types of agency relationships.

Homeowner's Guide to Earthquake Safety – The **Alquist-Priolo Earthquake Fault Zoning Act** requires the seller and agent to disclose to the buyer that the property is or may be situated in an earthquake fault zone. (See chapter 12 for more details.)

Lead-Based Paint and Lead-Based Paint Hazards Disclosure, Acknowledgment, and Addendum for Pre-1978 Housing – Used to comply with federal requirements for disclosure of any known lead-based paint or lead-based paint hazards on any housing constructed prior to 1978. From seller to buyer or from owner or landlord to tenant.

Manufactured Home and Mobilehome: Transfer Disclosure Statement – This is a statutory form required in the sales of manufactured homes.

The seller is primarily responsible for disclosing the presence of Mello-Roos tax liens or other assessments.

Methamphetamine Contamination Notice – This form is used by a landlord or property owner to notify a tenant or purchaser that the property has been identified as being contaminated by methamphetamine (drug lab).

Mortgage Loan Disclosure Statement (Borrower) – Complies with DRE regulations requiring disclosure when a broker is acting as an arranger of credit. Outlines loan terms, costs and expenses.

Natural Hazard Disclosure Statement – Used to comply with State requirements when a substituted Zone Disclosure Report is not used.

The Natural Hazard Disclosure Statement covers six zones: Seismic Hazard Zone, Earthquake Fault Zone, Wildland Fire Zone, State Responsibility Area, Flood Zone, and Dam Inundation Zone.

Pest Control Inspection and Certification Report – Identifies any wood destroying pests (termites) or conditions likely to cause pest infestation. (See Chapter 7 for more details.)

The Structural Pest Control Board collects termite reports, copies of which can be obtained by anyone upon request for a fee.

Radon Gas and Mold Notice and Release Agreement – As required by HUD, this form gives Buyers of HUD-owned property notice that no representation is made regarding radon gas or mold. In addition, Buyer releases HUD and its agents from any liability associated with either of these substances. The form also advises Buyer to contact a lawyer and have an inspection. (A **spectrometer** is used to measure radon.)

Real Estate Transfer Disclosure Statement (TDS) – The property disclosure statement required by law in most residential sales transactions in California. It includes Seller's mandatory disclosure of specified items and any known adverse material conditions, as well as sections for seller's and buyer's agents to comply with diligent visual inspection requirements.

In addition to disclosing any known environmental hazards on the TDS, the seller and his/her agent should provide the buyer with the pamphlet entitled "Environmental Hazards: a Guide for Homeowners, Buyers, Landlords, and Tenants," which includes sections on asbestos, lead, mold, formaldehyde, and radon. The Environmental Hazards Guide does NOT include fire, flood, or earthquake information.

Seller Financing Addendum and Disclosure – Designed to be used with the financing paragraph of the RPA-CA or RIPA. Contains terms of seller financing and the legally required disclosures. It also grants seller the right to obtain and review buyer's credit report, and requires buyer to complete a loan application.

Seller's Affidavit of Nonforeign Status and/or California Withholding Exemption – Used to comply with federal Foreign Investment in Real Property Tax Act (FIRPTA) and California nonresident withholding laws. Documents whether tax withholding is required. Requirements are listed on the reverse. One form is used for each person or entity on title.

Smoke Detector Statement of Compliance – Seller uses this form to certify that smoke detectors are properly installed in compliance with state and local laws.

Statewide Buyer and Seller Advisory – This document advises both Buyer and Seller of various factors that may affect the decision to buy, different types of inspections that can be obtained and questions to ask about or research and information to be disclosed.

Supplemental Statutory and Contractual Disclosures – Provides for delivery and confirmation of receipt of statutory disclosures and contractual disclosures (such as insurance claims affecting the Property) not provided for in the Real Estate Transfer Disclosure Statement (TDS).

Water Heater Statement of Compliance – Used by Seller to certify that water heaters are properly installed in compliance with state and local laws.

VII. Purchase Options

A. OPTIONS (A Unilateral Contract)

An **OPTION** *is a right to purchase a property upon specified terms within a specific time period, which is granted in exchange for money* (see **Figure 5-10** for the CAR® three-page Option Agreement). An option is normally purchased to take a property off the open market. The prospective purchaser holds an exclusive right to buy during the option period.

The optionee owns the option.

An **OPTIONOR** *is a property owner who gives an interested buyer an exclusive right to purchase a property.* An **OPTIONEE** *is a potential buyer who purchases an agreed-to amount of time to buy a specific property upon set terms.* The optionee does not have to go through with the purchase.

It is a good practice to obtain a preliminary title report or otherwise verify that the owner will be able to convey marketable title.

If the optionee decides to buy the property during his or her option period, the optionor must sell. In this case, the option will become a sales contract and both parties are bound by its terms.

A salesperson who has a listing and an option to purchase a property, from the seller, must, at the same time, disclose all offers, material information, and obtain consent from the seller of any anticipated profits from the seller before exercising the option to purchase.

The optionee may also secure another buyer for the property (sell his or her option to another party) during its term. Thus, all rights and interests may be transferred without the consent of the optionor, unless stated otherwise.

If an optionee has, for example, a one-year recorded option and, after six months decides not to exercise his or her option, the property owner should see to it that a quitclaim deed is recorded so that the option might be removed from the records.

It's always advisable to seek the services of a real estate attorney who is knowledgeable in lease options.

Due to the 2007-2009 credit crunch/slump, option agreements, which can be used with a purchase agreement or a lease, are becoming more popular.

Figure 5-10

CALIFORNIA
ASSOCIATION
OF REALTORS®

OPTION AGREEMENT

To be used with a purchase agreement. May also be used with a lease.

(C.A.R. Form OA, Revised 10/05)

Date_____, at _____, California
_____ ("Optionor"), grants to
_____ ("Optionee"),
on the following terms and conditions, an option ("Option") to purchase the real property and improvements situated in
(City) _____, County of _____,
California, described as _____ ("Property") on the terms and
conditions specified in the attached: ☐ Real Estate Purchase Agreement ☐ Other_____,
which is incorporated by reference as a part of this Option.

1. **OPTION CONSIDERATION:**
   A. _____ Dollars ($_____),
   _____,
   payable upon acceptance of this Option, or, if checked, ☐ _____,
   by ☐ cash, ☐ cashier's check, ☐ personal check, or ☐ _____
   made payable to _____.
   OR B. ☐ (If checked) Mutual execution of the attached lease specified in paragraph 2A.
   OR C. ☐ (If checked) Both 1A and 1B.

2. ☐ **LEASE (If checked):**
   A. The attached lease agreement, dated _____, between Optionee as Tenant and Optionor as Landlord, is incorporated by reference as part of this Option.
   B. If the Option is exercised, the lease shall terminate on the earliest of (i) the date scheduled for close of escrow under the purchase agreement, or as extended in writing, (ii) the close of escrow of the purchase agreement, or (iii) mutual cancellation of the purchase agreement.

3. **OPTION PERIOD:** The Option shall begin on (date) _____, and shall end at 11:59 p.m.
   (or at ☐ _____), on (date) _____.

4. **MANNER OF EXERCISE:** Optionee may exercise the Option **only** by delivering a written unconditional notice of exercise, signed by Optionee, to Optionor, or _____, who is authorized to receive it.
   A copy of the unconditional notice of exercise shall be delivered to the Brokers identified in this Agreement.

5. **NON-EXERCISE:** If the Option is not exercised in the manner specified, within the option period or any written extension thereof, or if it is terminated under any provision of this Option, then:
   A. The Option and all rights of Optionee to purchase the Property shall immediately terminate without notice; and
   B. All Option Consideration paid, rent paid, services rendered to Optionor, and improvements made to the Property, if any, by Optionee, shall be retained by Optionor in consideration of the granting of the Option; and
   C. Optionee shall execute, acknowledge, and deliver to Optionor, within **5 (or ☐ _____) calendar Days** of Optionor's request, a release, quitclaim deed, or any other document reasonably required by Optionor or a title insurance company to verify the termination of the Option.

6. **EFFECT OF DEFAULT ON OPTION:**
   A. Optionee shall have no right to exercise this Option if Optionee has not performed any obligation imposed by, or is in default of, any obligation of this Option, any addenda, or any document incorporated by reference.
   B. In addition, if a lease is incorporated by reference in paragraph 2A, Optionee shall have no right to exercise this Option if Optionor, as landlord, has given to Optionee, as tenant, two or more notices to cure any default or non-performance under that lease.

7. **OPTIONOR DISCLOSURE:**
   A. Unless exempt, if the Property contains one-to-four residential dwelling units, Optionor shall provide to Optionee (i) a Real Estate Transfer Disclosure Statement , a Natural Hazard Disclosure Statement and other disclosures required by Civil Code §§1102 and 1103 et seq., (ii) ☐ a preliminary title report, and (iii) ☐ _____.
   B. If any disclosure or notice specified in 7A is delivered to Optionee after the Option is Signed, Optionee shall have the right to cancel this Option within **3 Days After** delivery in person or **5 Days After** delivery by deposit in the mail by giving written notice of cancellation to Optionor or Optionor's agent.

Optionee and Optionor acknowledge receipt of copy of this page, which constitutes Page 1 of _____ Pages.
Optionee's Initials (_____) (_____)   Optionor's Initials (_____) (_____)

Reviewed by _____ Date _____

OA REVISED 10/05 (PAGE 1 OF 3) Print Date

OPTION AGREEMENT (OA PAGE 1 OF 3)

Property Address: _____ Date: _____

8. **PURCHASE AGREEMENT:**
   A. All of the time limits contained in the attached purchase agreement, which begin on the date of Acceptance of the purchase agreement, shall instead begin to run on the date the Option is exercised.
   B. If this Option is exercised and Optionee cancels pursuant to any contingency in the attached purchase agreement, including but not limited to any right of inspection or financing provision, all option consideration paid, rent paid, services rendered to Optionor, and improvements to the Property, if any, by Optionee, shall be retained by Optionor in consideration of the granting of the Option.
   C. If this Option is exercised, upon close of escrow of the attached purchase agreement, ☐ all, or ☐ $_____, of the Option Consideration, and ☐ (if checked) $_____ per month of rent actually paid by Optionee, shall be applied toward Optionee's down payment obligations under that agreement. Optionee is advised that the full amount of the option consideration applied toward any down payment may not be counted by a lender for financing purposes.

9. **DISPUTE RESOLUTION:** Optionee and Optionor agree that any dispute or claim arising between them out of this Agreement shall be decided by the same method agreed to for resolving disputes in the attached purchase agreement.

10. **DAMAGE OR DESTRUCTION:** If, prior to exercise of this Option, by no fault of Optionee, the Property is totally or partially damaged or destroyed by fire, earthquake, accident or other casualty, Optionee may cancel this Agreement by giving written notice to Optionor, and is entitled to the return of all Option Consideration paid. However, if, prior to Optionee giving notice of cancellation to Optionor, the Property has been repaired or replaced so that it is in substantially the same condition as of the date of acceptance of this Agreement, Optionee shall not have the right to cancel this Agreement.

11. **OPTIONEE INSPECTION:** Optionee ☐ has, ☐ has not conducted inspections, investigations, tests, surveys and other studies of the Property prior to entering into this Option.

12. **RECORDING:** Optionor or Optionee shall, upon request, execute, acknowledge, and deliver to the other a memorandum of this Option for recording purposes. All resulting fees and taxes shall be paid by the party requesting recordation.

13. **OTHER TERMS AND CONDITIONS,** including attached supplements: _____
_____
_____
_____
_____
_____
_____
_____
_____
_____

14. **ATTORNEY FEES:** In any action, proceeding, or arbitration between Optionee and Optionor arising out of this Agreement, the prevailing Optionee or Optionor shall be entitled to reasonable attorney fees and costs from the non-prevailing Optionee or Optionor.

15. **BROKER COMPENSATION FROM OPTIONEE:** If applicable, Optionee agrees to pay compensation to Broker as specified in a separate written agreement between Optionee and Broker.

16. **TIME OF ESSENCE; ENTIRE CONTRACT; CHANGES:** Time is of the essence. All understandings between the parties are incorporated in this Option. Its terms are intended by the parties as a final, complete, and exclusive expression of their agreement with respect to its subject matter, and may not be contradicted by evidence of any prior agreement or contemporaneous oral agreement. **This Agreement may not be extended, amended, modified, altered, or changed, except in writing signed by Optionee and Optionor.**

17. **TERMS AND CONDITIONS OF OFFER:** This is an offer for an option to purchase Property on the above terms and conditions. This Option and any supplement, addendum, or modification, including any photocopy or facsimile, may be signed in two or more counterparts, all of which shall constitute one and the same writing. Optionee has read and acknowledges receipt of a copy of this offer.

Optionee and Optionor acknowledge receipt of copy of this page, which constitutes Page 2 of _____ Pages.
Optionee's Initials (_____) (_____)   Optionor's Initials (_____) (_____)

OA REVISED 10/05 (PAGE 2 OF 3)

Reviewed by _____ Date _____

EQUAL HOUSING OPPORTUNITY

OPTION AGREEMENT (OA PAGE 2 OF 3)

Property Address: _____ Date: _____

18. EXPIRATION OF OFFER: Unless Acceptance of Offer is signed by Optionor, and a signed copy delivered in person, by mail, or facsimile, and personally received by Optionee, or by _____, who is authorized to receive it, by (date) _____, at _____ AM/PM, the offer shall be deemed revoked.

OPTIONEE _____

OPTIONEE _____
Address _____

Telephone _____ Fax _____

19. BROKER COMPENSATION FROM OPTIONOR: If applicable, Optionor agrees to pay compensation to Broker as specified in a separate written agreement between Optionor and Broker.

20. ACCEPTANCE OF OPTION: Optionor warrants that Optionor is the owner of the Property or has the authority to execute this Agreement. Optionor accepts and agrees to grant an Option to purchase the Property on the above terms and conditions.

If checked: ☐ SUBJECT TO ATTACHED COUNTER OFFER, DATED _____.

OPTIONOR _____

OPTIONOR _____
Address _____

Telephone _____ Fax _____

REAL ESTATE BROKERS:
A. Real Estate Brokers are not parties to the Agreement between Optionee and Optionor.
B. COOPERATING BROKER COMPENSATION: Listing Broker agrees to pay Cooperating Broker and Cooperating Broker agrees to accept, (i) the amount specified in the MLS, provided Cooperating Broker is a Participant of the MLS in which the Property is offered for Option or a reciprocal MLS; or (ii) ☐ (If checked) the amount specified in a separate written agreement (C.A.R. Form CBC) between Listing Broker and Cooperating Broker.

Broker _____ By _____ Date _____
Address _____

Telephone _____ Fax _____

Broker _____ By _____ Date _____
Address _____

Telephone _____ Fax _____

Published and Distributed by:
REAL ESTATE BUSINESS SERVICES, INC.
a subsidiary of the California Association of REALTORS®
525 South Virgil Avenue, Los Angeles, California 90020

Reviewed by _____ Date _____

OA REVISED 10/05 (PAGE 3 OF 3)

OPTION AGREEMENT (OA PAGE 3 OF 3)

VIII. CHAPTER SUMMARY

A **contract** is an agreement to perform or not perform a certain act or service. It can be **express** (verbal or written) or **implied** (by actions). A **bilateral contract** obligates two people, whereas a **unilateral contract** only obligates one party. A **valid contract** is binding and enforceable, but a **voidable contract** can be disavowed. A contract can also be **void** (no contract exists) and **unenforceable** if, for example, it's now against the law.

A contract has three phases: **negotiation**, **performance**, and **completion**. If some provision of a contract is not yet fulfilled, it's called an **executory contract**. If it has been discharged or performed, it's considered an **executed contract**.

The **four elements of any contract** are 1) **capacity**, 2) **mutual consent**, 3) **legality**, and 4) **consideration**. (Money, writing, and performance are NOT necessary for a contract to be valid.) Real estate contracts, however, are required to be in **writing**, making that a **fifth element**. Every offer must be made with **contractual intent**, although a buyer can withdraw an offer before acceptance. If the offer is rejected and a new offer is proposed, it's known as a **counter offer**, and automatically terminates the previous offer. The **offeree** becomes the **offeror** in a counter offer. If any of the following conditions exist, a contract is void or voidable: **fraud, misrepresentation, mistake, duress, menace**, or **undue influence**.

A contract for personal property can be oral or written but the **Statute of Frauds** requires that real estate contracts be in **writing**. Any contract that can't be performed **within a year** from the date of signing must also be in writing.

A contract can be discharged by **performance** (full, substantial, and partial), **impossibility of performance**, **agreement between parties**, **operation of law**, **acceptance of breach**, or **breach**. The remedies for a breach of contract include **acceptance of breach, unilateral rescission, action for money damages**, and **specific performance**. (The current **liquidated damages** on a CAR purchase agreement form is a maximum of 3% of the home purchase price.) Remedies for a breach must be sought within a certain period of time called the **Statute of Limitations**.

The **California Residential Purchase Agreement and Joint Escrow Instructions** is a contract, and is also called the **"purchase agreement"** or **"purchase contract."** A deposit of money or items of value (always the property of the seller, not the buyer) must accompany a purchase agreement to be a valid offer. The term "deposit receipt" is an outdated reference to the Purchase Agreement, and no longer appropriate in California real estate transactions.

A **covenant** in a purchase agreement is a promise between the parties to contract. A **contingency** clause is an "if" situation, also referred to as **conditions** or **"subject to"** provisions that, if not met, can make the contract voidable.

An **option** allows a prospective purchaser to hold the exclusive right to buy during a specified period, in exchange for money. It cannot be revoked by the **optionor** (seller) who could be forced to sell the property by specific performance to the **optionee** (buyer). To avoid a conflict of interest, an agent with a listing and an option to purchase must disclose all offers, any material information, and obtain consent of any anticipated profits from the seller before exercising the option.

IX. TERMINOLOGY

A. Acceptance
B. Assignee
C. Assignment
D. Assignor
E. Bilateral Contract
F. Breach
G. Capacity of Parties
H. Consideration
I. Contingencies
J. Contract
K. Counter Offer
L. Covenant
M. Definite and Certain

N. Dollar Damages
O. Execute
P. Executory Contract
Q. Expressed Contract
R. Fraud, Duress, Menace
S. Implied Contract
T. Incompetent
U. Liquidated Damages
V. Minors
W. Mutual Consent
X. Novation
Y. Offer
Z. Offeree

AA. Offeror
BB. Option
CC. Optionee
DD. Optionor
EE. Pest Control Report
FF. Purchase Agreement
GG. Rescission
HH. Specific Performance
II. Undue Influence
JJ. Unilateral Contract
KK. Valid Contract
LL. Void, Voidable,
    Unenforceable

1.____ A court action to compel the performance of an agreement, e.g., sale of land.
2.____ Anything given or promised by a party to induce another to enter into a contract.
3.____ A contract in which something remains to be done by one or both the parties.
4.____ A right given, for consideration, to purchase a property upon specified terms within a specified time period, without obligating the party to purchase the property.
5.____ A written offer to purchase real property upon stated terms and conditions, accompanied by a deposit toward the purchase price, which becomes the contract for the sale of the property upon acceptance.
6.____ All persons under 18 years of age.
7.____ The act of agreeing or consenting to the terms of an offer, thereby establishing "the meeting of the minds" that is an essential element of a contract; genuine assent from both parties.
8.____ One who assigns his or her right in a contract.
9.____ A person to whom property or interests therein shall have been assigned.
10.____ One who is mentally incapable of managing or taking care of self or property and therefore cannot enter into a contract without a guardian.
11.____ A promise to do or not to do a particular act.
12.____ The substitution or exchange of a new contract for an old one by the mutual agreement of the parties.
13.____ A transfer by a person of that person's rights under a contract.
14.____ An agreement to do or not to do a certain thing. It must have four essential elements: parties capable of contracting, consent of the parties, a lawful object, and consideration.
15.____ The terms and provisions of a contract, which are clear, definite, and set forth.
16.____ A binding contract created by the actions of the principals rather than by written or oral agreement.
17.____ A contract under which the parties enter into mutual promises, such as sales contracts.
18.____ A contract under which only one party expressly makes a promise.
19.____ Having no legal force or binding effect, or cannot be enforced for one reason or another.
20.____ One making an offer.
21.____ One to whom an offer is made.
22.____ A proposal for acceptance, in order to form a contract. It must be definite as to price and terms.
23.____ Voluntarily agreeing to the price and terms of an offer. Offer and acceptance create a contract.
24.____ An offer in response to an offer.
25.____ Failure to perform a contract, in whole or part, without legal excuse.
26.____ Annulling a contract and placing the parties to it in a position as if there had not been a contract.

CHAPTER 5

27.____ A definite amount of damage, set forth in a contract, to be paid by the party breaching the contract. A predetermined estimate of actual damages from a breach.

28.____ An inspection report required, in the sale of property, to determine if termites are present within a building.

29.____ One who, for consideration, receives an option.

30.____ One who, for consideration, gives an option.

31.____ A contract under which the parties expressly enter into mutual promises.

32.____ The dependence upon a stated event before a contract becomes binding.

33.____ An action that abandons all other remedies and simply asks for money.

34.____ Influence used to destroy the will of another so that any decision is not his or her free act.

35.____ To complete a contract by signing it.

36.____ Legally binding, the terms of which can be sued for in a court of law.

37.____ Deceptive statements or acts used to wrongfully obtain money or property.

38.____ Individuals who have a legal capacity to contract, as opposed to minors, convicts and incompetents.

X. CHAPTER QUIZ

1. The term "express contract" describes a contract which is expressed:

    a. only orally.

    b. only in writing.

    c. in words, either oral or written.

    d. none of the above.

2. If a buyer and seller enter into a valid binding contract and one of the parties dies or becomes incompetent, the contract is:

    a. void by statute.

    b. valid, if it was signed before the party died or became incompetent.

    c. voidable by one of the parties.

    d. valid.

3. A contract based on an unlawful consideration is:

    a. valid, until voided.

    b. void.

    c. legal.

    d. enforceable, if in writing.

4. Novation is:

    a. realization of an unexpected profit.

    b. creation of an existing agreement.

    c. substitution of a new contract for an old one.

    d. modification of a contract.

5. The following could be used by a buyer as earnest money deposit in purchasing real property:

    a. a promissory note secured by a deed of trust.

    b. a postdated check.

    c. an unsecured promissory note.

    d. all of the above.

6. An offer made by a prospective buyer was contingent on the sale of the buyer's current residence. Seller Billings made a counter offer accepting the offer provided the seller could continue to market the home in an attempt to obtain a better offer while granting the buyer a "first right of refusal" to remove the sale contingency if another offer was presented. The buyer accepted the terms and immediately listed his current residence for sale. One week later, Billings notified the buyer that a better offer with no contingencies was "on the table." The agent representing the buyer should:

    a. advise the buyer to immediately remove the sale contingency.

    b. advise the buyer to obtain a bridge loan in order to assure that the escrow will be completed without the need of the contingency.

    c. advise the buyer about the advantages and disadvantages of removing the contingency feature at this time.

    d. under no circumstances give advice about the contingency feature. The buyer must consult an attorney.

7. When accepting an offer on his home, Seller Thomas changed one of the terms of the buyer's offer. This is best described as:

    a. a modification or amendment.

    b. a purchase contract.

    c. an alteration.

    d. a counter offer.

8. The primary responsibility for disclosing any Mello-Roos bonds or assessments to a buyer when a home is sold lies with:

    a. the seller.

    b. the seller's agent.

    c. the buyer's agent.

    d. all of the above.

9. What state agency would a consumer contact in order to obtain a written report disclosing the presence of wood destroying organisms?

    a. Department of Real Estate

    b. Department of Corporations

    c. Structural Pest Control Board

    d. Department of Housing and Community Development

10. In an option agreement, the owner of the option is the:

    a. optionor.

    b. optionee.

    c. property owner.

    d. lender.

ANSWERS: *1. c; 2. b; 3. b; 4. c; 5. d; 6. c; 7. d; 8. a; 9. c; 10. b*

CHAPTER 6
Landlord and Tenant (Lessor and Lessee)

I. Landlord and Tenant – An Overview

A landlord and tenant relationship is created when the owner gives the possession and use of his or her property to another for rent or other consideration. The *LANDLORD (LESSOR) is the owner of the property being rented or leased.* The landlord, or his or her agent, may lease only the land, the land and buildings, or only the buildings or parts of the buildings. The *TENANT (LESSEE) is the person or persons renting or leasing the property.*

A *LEASE is a contract for a set time, typically one year or longer.* A *RENTAL AGREEMENT is different in that it is usually made on a monthly basis and is renewable at the end of each period (week-to-week, month-to-month, or any period-to-period up to one year).* Because a rental agreement is a type of lease, the principles are the same as those of the lease, except for the time periods involved.

II. Leasehold Estates (Less-Than-Freehold)

A. TYPES OF LEASEHOLD ESTATES (Tenancies)

A leasehold is a personal property right in real property.

As discussed before, with less-than-freehold estates, there is no direct ownership of real estate. They are chattel real estates. A *CHATTEL REAL is a personal property estate, such as a lease.* We call this type of interest in a property a lease or leasehold. A *LEASEHOLD is an exclusive right to occupy and use the property on a temporary basis.* There are no ownership rights in real property. The owner has *REVERSIONARY INTEREST, which means that he or she can regain possession at the end of the leasehold period.* **Figure 6-1** shows the four types of leasehold estates.

1. Estate For Years (A Lease for a Predetermined Amount of Time)

A conveyance of an estate in real property, such as a lease, to someone for a certain length of time is called a DEMISE. An ESTATE FOR YEARS is an agreement, in advance, between a lessee and a lessor for use of a property for a fixed (predetermined) period of time. As stated earlier, a lease is a contractual agreement to possess and use a property for an agreed to (predetermined) period of time. If the lease period is longer than one year from the date of the signing, it must be in writing and signed by the lessor. The *LESSOR is the owner, sometimes referred to as the landlord, and the LESSEE is the tenant.*

CHAPTER OUTLINE

Figure 6-1

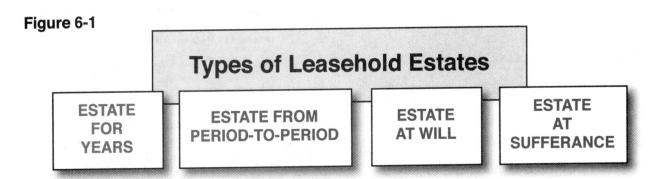

Types of Leasehold Estates

| ESTATE FOR YEARS | ESTATE FROM PERIOD-TO-PERIOD | ESTATE AT WILL | ESTATE AT SUFFERANCE |

2. Estate From Period-To-Period (Periodic Tenancy – Renewable Each Period)

An *ESTATE FROM PERIOD-TO-PERIOD is periodic tenancy that continues from year-to-year, month-to-month, week-to-week, or from any other designated period-to-period.* This period-to-period tenancy, which is automatically renewable, is called a rental agreement. As previously stated, a rental agreement is an agreement between a tenant and landlord for continuing periods of time, usually from month-to-month. Rental agreements do not expire; notice must be given by one of the parties.

Written rental agreements have become the most commonly used real estate agreements in the United States. They are used frequently when renting apartments, duplexes, houses, condominiums, and other types of residential property. The California Association of REALTORS® (CAR) has a Residential Lease or Month-To-Month Rental Agreement form that covers all the basic conditions desired in such a contract (see **Figure 6-2**). **Figure 6-3** is an Application To Rent, Receipt For Deposit/Screening Fee form to be filled out by the prospective tenant.

A landlord holds a reversionary right to the property. A *REVERSIONARY RIGHT means the landlord grants the tenant the right to occupy (possess) the property, but retains the right to retake possession after the lease or rental term has expired.* Periodic tenancy is usually terminated when the appropriate party gives a 30- or 60-day notice, because most rental agreements are month-to-month. If the rental period is less than one month, then only one period (that is, agreed length of the tenancy) notice is required. For example, if tenancy was from week-to-week, only seven days notice would be necessary.

3. Estate At Will (Tenancy at Will – Uncommon)

An *ESTATE AT WILL can be terminated at the will of either the lessor or the lessee, and has no fixed duration period.* By California statute, 1) the parties involved must give a notice of termination and 2) since a periodic tenancy is automatically created when a landlord accepts rent, there is no true estate at will in California.

An estate at will can be terminated by either the lessor or lessee.

4. Estate At Sufferance (Tenancy at Sufferance)

An *ESTATE AT SUFFERANCE occurs when a lessee, who has rightfully come into possession of the land, retains possession after the expiration of his or her term.* (In other words, the tenant does not leave after expiration of the lease.) An estate at sufferance does not require a notice of termination because the expiration of the lease is an automatic termination. If the landlord accepts any payment of rent, the lease reverts to periodic tenancy.

Figure 6-2

CALIFORNIA
ASSOCIATION
OF REALTORS®

**RESIDENTIAL LEASE OR
MONTH-TO-MONTH RENTAL AGREEMENT**
(C.A.R. Form LR, Revised 10/04)

_____ ("Landlord") and
_____ ("Tenant") agree as follows:

1. **PROPERTY:**
   A. Landlord rents to Tenant and Tenant rents from Landlord, the real property and improvements described as: _____
      _____ ("Premises").
   B. The Premises are for the sole use as a personal residence by the following named person(s) **only:** _____
      _____
   C. The following personal property, maintained pursuant to paragraph 11, is included: _____
      _____ or □ (if checked) the personal property on the attached addendum.

2. **TERM:** The term begins on (date) _____ ("Commencement Date"), **(Check A or B):**
   □ A. **Month-to-Month:** and continues as a month-to-month tenancy. Tenant may terminate the tenancy by giving written notice
     at least 30 days prior to the intended termination date. Landlord may terminate the tenancy by giving written notice as
     provided by law. Such notices may be given on any date.
   □ B. **Lease:** and shall terminate on (date) _____ at _____ □ AM/□ PM.
     Tenant shall vacate the Premises upon termination of the Agreement, unless: **(i)** Landlord and Tenant have extended this
     agreement in writing or signed a new agreement; **(ii)** mandated by local rent control law; or **(iii)** Landlord accepts Rent from
     Tenant (other than past due Rent), in which case a month-to-month tenancy shall be created which either party may
     terminate as specified in paragraph 2A. Rent shall be at a rate agreed to by Landlord and Tenant, or as allowed by law. All
     other terms and conditions of this Agreement shall remain in full force and effect.

3. **RENT:** "Rent" shall mean all monetary obligations of Tenant to Landlord under the terms of the Agreement, except security deposit.
   A. Tenant agrees to pay $ _____ per month for the term of the Agreement.
   B. Rent is payable in advance on the **1st (or** □ _____**) day** of each calendar month, and is delinquent on the next day.
   C. If Commencement Date falls on any day other than the day Rent is payable under paragraph 3B, and Tenant has paid one full
      month's Rent in advance of Commencement Date, Rent for the second calendar month shall be prorated based on a 30-day
      period.
   D. **PAYMENT:** Rent shall be paid by □ personal check, □ money order, □ cashier's check, or □ other _____, to (name)
      _____ (phone) _____ at (address)
      _____, (or at any other location
      subsequently specified by Landlord in writing to Tenant) between the hours of _____ and _____ on the following days
      _____. If any payment is returned for non-sufficient funds ("NSF") or
      because tenant stops payment, then, after that: **(i)** Landlord may, in writing, require Tenant to pay Rent in cash for three months
      and **(ii)** all future Rent shall be paid by □ money order, or □ cashier's check.

4. **SECURITY DEPOSIT:**
   A. Tenant agrees to pay $ _____ as a security deposit. Security deposit will be
      □ transferred to and held by the Owner of the Premises, or □ held in Owner's Broker's trust account.
   B. All or any portion of the security deposit may be used, as reasonably necessary, to: **(i)** cure Tenant's default in payment of Rent (which
      includes Late Charges, NSF fees or other sums due); **(ii)** repair damage, excluding ordinary wear and tear, caused by Tenant or by a
      guest or licensee of Tenant; **(iii)** clean Premises, if necessary, upon termination of the tenancy; and **(iv)** replace or return personal
      property or appurtenances. **SECURITY DEPOSIT SHALL NOT BE USED BY TENANT IN LIEU OF PAYMENT OF LAST
      MONTH'S RENT.** If all or any portion of the security deposit is used during the tenancy, Tenant agrees to reinstate the total security
      deposit within five days after written notice is delivered to Tenant. Within 21 days after Tenant vacates the Premises, Landlord shall:
      (1) furnish Tenant an itemized statement indicating the amount of any security deposit received and the basis for its
      disposition and supporting documentation as required by California Civil Code § 1950.5(g); and **(2)** return any remaining
      portion of the security deposit to Tenant.
   C. **Security deposit will not be returned until all Tenants have vacated the Premises. Any security deposit returned by
      check shall be made out to all Tenants named on this Agreement, or as subsequently modified.**
   D. No interest will be paid on security deposit unless required by local law.
   E. If the security deposit is held by Owner, Tenant agrees not to hold Broker responsible for its return. If the security deposit is held
      in Owner's Broker's trust account, **and** Broker's authority is terminated before expiration of this Agreement, **and** security deposit
      is released to someone other than Tenant, **then** Broker shall notify Tenant, in writing, where and to whom security deposit has
      been released. Once Tenant has been provided such notice, Tenant agrees not to hold Broker responsible for the security
      deposit.

5. **MOVE-IN COSTS RECEIVED/DUE:** Move-in funds made payable to _____
   shall be paid by □ personal check, □ money order, or □ cashier's check.

Category	Total Due	Payment Received	Balance Due	Date Due
Rent from _____ to _____ (date)				
*Security Deposit				
Other _____				
Other _____				
Total				

*The maximum amount Landlord may receive as security deposit, however designated, cannot exceed two months' Rent for
unfurnished premises, or three months' Rent for furnished premises.

LR REVISED 10/04 (PAGE 1 OF 6) Print Date

Tenant's Initials (_____)(_____)
Landlord's Initials (_____)(_____)

Reviewed by _____ Date _____

EQUAL HOUSING
OPPORTUNITY

RESIDENTIAL LEASE OR MONTH-TO-MONTH RENTAL AGREEMENT (LR PAGE 1 OF 6)

Premises: .... Date: ....

6. **LATE CHARGE; RETURNED CHECKS:**
   A. Tenant acknowledges either late payment of Rent or issuance of a returned check may cause Landlord to incur costs and expenses, the exact amounts of which are extremely difficult and impractical to determine. These costs may include, but are not limited to, processing, enforcement and accounting expenses, and late charges imposed on Landlord. If any installment of Rent due from Tenant is not received by Landlord within 5 (or ☐ ....) **calendar days** after the date due, or if a check is returned, Tenant shall pay to Landlord, respectively, an additional sum of $ ____________ or ______% of the Rent due as a Late Charge and $25.00 as a NSF fee for the first returned check and $35.00 as a NSF fee for each additional returned check, either or both of which shall be deemed additional Rent.
   B. Landlord and Tenant agree that these charges represent a fair and reasonable estimate of the costs Landlord may incur by reason of Tenant's late or NSF payment. Any Late Charge or NSF fee due shall be paid with the current installment of Rent. Landlord's acceptance of any Late Charge or NSF fee shall not constitute a waiver as to any default of Tenant. Landlord's right to collect a Late Charge or NSF fee shall not be deemed an extension of the date Rent is due under paragraph 3 or prevent Landlord from exercising any other rights and remedies under this Agreement and as provided by law.
7. **PARKING: (Check A or B)**
   ☐ A. Parking is permitted as follows: ....
   The right to parking ☐ is ☐ is not included in the Rent charged pursuant to paragraph 3. If not included in the Rent, the parking rental fee shall be an additional $ ______________ per month. Parking space(s) are to be used for parking properly licensed and operable motor vehicles, except for trailers, boats, campers, buses or trucks (other than pick-up trucks). Tenant shall park in assigned space(s) only. Parking space(s) are to be kept clean. Vehicles leaking oil, gas or other motor vehicle fluids shall not be parked on the Premises. Mechanical work or storage of inoperable vehicles is not permitted in parking space(s) or elsewhere on the Premises.

   OR ☐ B. Parking is not permitted on the Premises.
8. **STORAGE: (Check A or B)**
   ☐ A. Storage is permitted as follows: ....
   The right to storage space ☐ is, ☐ is not, included in the Rent charged pursuant to paragraph 3. If not included in the Rent, storage space fee shall be an additional $ ______________ per month. Tenant shall store only personal property Tenant owns, and shall not store property claimed by another or in which another has any right, title or interest. Tenant shall not store any improperly packaged food or perishable goods, flammable materials, explosives, hazardous waste or other inherently dangerous material, or illegal substances.

   OR ☐ B. Storage is not permitted on the Premises.
9. **UTILITIES:** Tenant agrees to pay for all utilities and services, and the following charges: ______________ except ______________, which shall be paid for by Landlord. If any utilities are not separately metered, Tenant shall pay Tenant's proportional share, as reasonably determined and directed by Landlord. If utilities are separately metered, Tenant shall place utilities in Tenant's name as of the Commencement Date. Landlord is only responsible for installing and maintaining one usable telephone jack and one telephone line to the Premises. Tenant shall pay any cost for conversion from existing utilities service provider.
10. **CONDITION OF PREMISES:** Tenant has examined Premises and, if any, all furniture, furnishings, appliances, landscaping and fixtures, including smoke detector(s).
   (Check all that apply:)
   ☐ A. Tenant acknowledges these items are clean and in operable condition, with the following exceptions: ______________
   ☐ B. Tenant's acknowledgment of the condition of these items is contained in an attached statement of condition (C.A.R. Form MIMO).
   ☐ C. Tenant will provide Landlord a list of items that are damaged or not in operable condition within 3 (or ☐ ....) **days** after Commencement Date, not as a contingency of this Agreement but rather as an acknowledgment of the condition of the Premises.
   ☐ D. Other: ______________
11. **MAINTENANCE:**
   A. Tenant shall properly use, operate and safeguard Premises, including if applicable, any landscaping, furniture, furnishings and appliances, and all mechanical, electrical, gas and plumbing fixtures, and keep them and the Premises clean, sanitary and well ventilated. Tenant shall be responsible for checking and maintaining all smoke detectors and any additional phone lines beyond the one line and jack that Landlord shall provide and maintain. Tenant shall immediately notify Landlord, in writing, of any problem, malfunction or damage. Tenant shall be charged for all repairs or replacements caused by Tenant, pets, guests or licensees of Tenant, excluding ordinary wear and tear. Tenant shall be charged for all damage to Premises as a result of failure to report a problem in a timely manner. Tenant shall be charged for repair of drain blockages or stoppages, unless caused by defective plumbing parts or tree roots invading sewer lines.
   B. ☐ Landlord ☐ Tenant shall water the garden, landscaping, trees and shrubs, except: ______________
   C. ☐ Landlord ☐ Tenant shall maintain the garden, landscaping, trees and shrubs, except: ______________
   D. ☐ Landlord ☐ Tenant shall maintain ______________
   E. Tenant's failure to maintain any item for which Tenant is responsible shall give Landlord the right to hire someone to perform such maintenance and charge Tenant to cover the cost of such maintenance.
   F. The following items of personal property are included in the Premises without warranty and Landlord will not maintain, repair or replace them: ______________

Tenant's Initials (..........)(..........)
Landlord's Initials (..........)(..........)

LR REVISED 10/04 (PAGE 2 OF 6)

Reviewed by .... Date ....

EQUAL HOUSING OPPORTUNITY

RESIDENTIAL LEASE OR MONTH-TO-MONTH RENTAL AGREEMENT (LR PAGE 2 OF 6)

Premises: .... Date: ....

12. **NEIGHBORHOOD CONDITIONS:** Tenant is advised to satisfy him or herself as to neighborhood or area conditions, including schools, proximity and adequacy of law enforcement, crime statistics, proximity of registered felons or offenders, fire protection, other governmental services, availability, adequacy and cost of any speed-wired, wireless internet connections or other telecommunications or other technology services and installations, proximity to commercial, industrial or agricultural activities, existing and proposed transportation, construction and development that may affect noise, view, or traffic, airport noise, noise or odor from any source, wild and domestic animals, other nuisances, hazards, or circumstances, cemeteries, facilities and condition of common areas, conditions and influences of significance to certain cultures and/or religions, and personal needs, requirements and preferences of Tenant.
13. **PETS:** Unless otherwise provided in California Civil Code § 54.2, no animal or pet shall be kept on or about the Premises without Landlord's prior written consent, except: ______________
14. **RULES/REGULATIONS:**
   A. Tenant agrees to comply with all Landlord rules and regulations that are at any time posted on the Premises or delivered to Tenant. Tenant shall not, and shall ensure that guests and licensees of Tenant shall not, disturb, annoy, endanger or interfere with other tenants of the building or neighbors, or use the Premises for any unlawful purposes, including, but not limited to, using, manufacturing, selling, storing or transporting illicit drugs or other contraband, or violate any law or ordinance, or commit a waste or nuisance on or about the Premises.
   B. **(If applicable, check one)**
   ☐ 1. Landlord shall provide Tenant with a copy of the rules and regulations within .... days or ______________.
   OR ☐ 2. Tenant has been provided with, and acknowledges receipt of, a copy of the rules and regulations.
15. ☐ (If checked) **CONDOMINIUM; PLANNED UNIT DEVELOPMENT:**
   A. The Premises is a unit in a condominium, planned unit development, common interest subdivision or other development governed by a homeowners' association ("HOA"). The name of the HOA is ______________. Tenant agrees to comply with all HOA covenants, conditions and restrictions, bylaws, rules and regulations and decisions. Landlord shall provide Tenant copies of rules and regulations, if any. Tenant shall reimburse Landlord for any fines or charges imposed by HOA or other authorities, due to any violation by Tenant, or the guests or licensees of Tenant
   B. **(Check one)**
   ☐ 1. Landlord shall provide Tenant with a copy of the HOA rules and regulations within ______________ days or ______________.
   OR ☐ 2. Tenant has been provided with, and acknowledges receipt of, a copy of the HOA rules and regulations.
16. **ALTERATIONS; REPAIRS:** Unless otherwise specified by law or paragraph 27C, without Landlord's prior written consent, (i) Tenant shall not make any repairs, alterations or improvements in or about the Premises including: painting, wallpapering, adding or changing locks, installing antenna or satellite dish(es), placing signs, displays or exhibits, or using screws, fastening devices, large nails or adhesive materials; (ii) Landlord shall not be responsible for the costs of alterations or repairs made by Tenant; (iii) Tenant shall not deduct from Rent the costs of any repairs, alterations or improvements; and (iv) any deduction made by Tenant shall be considered unpaid Rent.
17. **KEYS; LOCKS:**
   A. Tenant acknowledges receipt of (or Tenant will receive ☐ prior to the Commencement Date, or ☐ ....):
   ☐ ________ key(s) to Premises, ☐ ________ remote control device(s) for garage door/gate opener(s),
   ☐ ________ key(s) to mailbox, ☐ ______________,
   ☐ ________ key(s) to common area(s), ☐ ______________.
   B. Tenant acknowledges that locks to the Premises ☐ have, ☐ have not, been re-keyed.
   C. If Tenant re-keys existing locks or opening devices, Tenant shall immediately deliver copies of all keys to Landlord. Tenant shall pay all costs and charges related to loss of any keys or opening devices. Tenant may not remove locks, even if installed by Tenant.
18. **ENTRY:**
   A. Tenant shall make Premises available to Landlord or Landlord's representative for the purpose of entering to make necessary or agreed repairs, decorations, alterations, or improvements, or to supply necessary or agreed services, or to show Premises to prospective or actual purchasers, tenants, mortgagees, lenders, appraisers, or contractors.
   B. Landlord and Tenant agree that 24-hour written notice shall be reasonable and sufficient notice, except as follows. 48-hour written notice is required to conduct an inspection of the Premises prior to the Tenant moving out, unless the Tenant waives the right to such notice. Notice may be given orally to show the Premises to actual or prospective purchasers provided Tenant has been notified in writing within 120 days preceding the oral notice that the Premises are for sale and that oral notice may be given to show the Premises. No notice is required: (i) to enter in case of an emergency; (ii) if the Tenant is present and consents at the time of entry or (iii) if the Tenant has abandoned or surrendered the Premises. No written notice is required if Landlord and Tenant orally agree to an entry for agreed services or repairs if the date and time of entry are within one week of the oral agreement.
   C. ☐ (If checked) Tenant authorizes the use of a keysafe/lockbox to allow entry into the Premises and agrees to sign a keysafe/lockbox addendum (C.A.R. Form KLA).
19. **SIGNS:** Tenant authorizes Landlord to place FOR SALE/LEASE signs on the Premises.
20. **ASSIGNMENT; SUBLETTING:** Tenant shall not sublet all or any part of Premises, or assign or transfer this Agreement or any interest in it, without Landlord's prior written consent. Unless such consent is obtained, any assignment, transfer or subletting of Premises or this Agreement or tenancy, by voluntary act of Tenant, operation of law or otherwise, shall, at the option of Landlord, terminate this Agreement. Any proposed assignee, transferee or sublessee shall submit to Landlord an application and credit information for Landlord's approval and, if approved, sign a separate written agreement with Landlord and Tenant. Landlord's consent to any one assignment, transfer or sublease, shall not be construed as consent to any subsequent assignment, transfer or sublease and does not release Tenant of Tenant's obligations under this Agreement.
21. **JOINT AND INDIVIDUAL OBLIGATIONS:** If there is more than one Tenant, each one shall be individually and completely responsible for the performance of all obligations of Tenant under this Agreement, jointly with every other Tenant, and individually, whether or not in possession.

Tenant's Initials (..........)(..........)
Landlord's Initials (..........)(..........)

LR REVISED 10/04 (PAGE 3 OF 6)

Reviewed by ______ Date ______

EQUAL HOUSING OPPORTUNITY

RESIDENTIAL LEASE OR MONTH-TO-MONTH RENTAL AGREEMENT (LR PAGE 3 OF 6)

Premises: ______________________________ Date: ____________

22. ☐ **LEAD-BASED PAINT (If checked):** Premises was constructed prior to 1978. In accordance with federal law, Landlord gives and Tenant acknowledges receipt of the disclosures on the attached form (C.A.R. Form FLD) and a federally approved lead pamphlet.

23. ☐ **MILITARY ORDNANCE DISCLOSURE:** (If applicable and known to Landlord) Premises is located within one mile of an area once used for military training, and may contain potentially explosive munitions.

24. ☐ **PERIODIC PEST CONTROL:** Landlord has entered into a contract for periodic pest control treatment of the Premises and shall give Tenant a copy of the notice originally given to Landlord by the pest control company.

25. **DATABASE DISCLOSURE:** NOTICE: The California Department of Justice, sheriff's departments, police departments serving jurisdictions of 200,000 or more, and many other local law enforcement authorities maintain for public access a database of the locations of persons required to register pursuant to paragraph (1) of subdivision (a) of Section 290.4 of the Penal Code. The data base is updated on a quarterly basis and a source of information about the presence of these individuals in any neighborhood. The Department of Justice also maintains a Sex Offender Identification Line through which inquiries about individuals may be made. This is a "900" telephone service. Callers must have specific information about individuals they are checking. Information regarding neighborhoods is not available through the "900" telephone service.

26. **POSSESSION:**

A. Tenant is not in possession of the premises. If Landlord is unable to deliver possession of Premises on Commencement Date, such Date shall be extended to the date on which possession is made available to Tenant. If Landlord is unable to deliver possession within 5 (or ☐ ______) **calendar days** after agreed Commencement Date, Tenant may terminate this Agreement by giving written notice to Landlord, and shall be refunded all Rent and security deposit paid. Possession is deemed terminated when Tenant has returned all keys to the Premises to Landlord.

B. ☐ Tenant is already in possession of the Premises.

27. **TENANT'S OBLIGATIONS UPON VACATING PREMISES:**

A. Upon termination of the Agreement, Tenant shall: **(i)** give Landlord all copies of all keys or opening devices to Premises, including any common areas; **(ii)** vacate and surrender Premises to Landlord, empty of all persons; **(iii)** vacate any/all parking and/or storage space; **(iv)** clean and deliver Premises, as specified in paragraph C below, to Landlord in the same condition as referenced in paragraph 10; **(v)** remove all debris; **(vi)** give written notice to Landlord of Tenant's forwarding address; and **(vii)** ______________________________.

B. All alterations/improvements made by or caused to be made by Tenant, with or without Landlord's consent, become the property of Landlord upon termination. Landlord may charge Tenant for restoration of the Premises to the condition it was in prior to any alterations/improvements.

C. **Right to Pre-Move-Out Inspection and Repairs as follows: (i)** After giving or receiving notice of termination of a tenancy (C.A.R. Form NTT), or before the end of a lease, Tenant has the right to request that an inspection of the Premises take place prior to termination of the lease or rental (C.A.R. Form NRI). If Tenant requests such an inspection, Tenant shall be given an opportunity to remedy identified deficiencies prior to termination, consistent with the terms of this Agreement. **(ii)** Any repairs or alterations made to the Premises as a result of this inspection (collectively, "Repairs") shall be made at Tenant's expense. Repairs may be performed by Tenant or through others, who have adequate insurance and licenses and are approved by Landlord. The work shall comply with applicable law, including governmental permit, inspection and approval requirements. Repairs shall be performed in a good, skillful manner with materials of quality and appearance comparable to existing materials. It is understood that exact restoration of appearance or cosmetic items following all Repairs may not be possible. **(iii)** Tenant shall: **(a)** obtain receipts for Repairs performed by others; **(b)** prepare a written statement indicating the Repairs performed by Tenant and the date of such Repairs; and **(c)** provide copies of receipts and statements to Landlord prior to termination. Paragraph 27C does not apply when the tenancy is terminated pursuant to California Code of Civil Procedure § 1161(2), (3) or (4).

28. **BREACH OF CONTRACT; EARLY TERMINATION:** In addition to any obligations established by paragraph 27, in the event of termination by Tenant prior to completion of the original term of the Agreement, Tenant shall also be responsible for lost Rent, rental commissions, advertising expenses and painting costs necessary to ready Premises for re-rental. Landlord may withhold any such amounts from Tenant's security deposit.

29. **TEMPORARY RELOCATION:** Subject to local law, Tenant agrees, upon demand of Landlord, to temporarily vacate Premises for a reasonable period, to allow for fumigation (or other methods) to control wood destroying pests or organisms, or other repairs to Premises. Tenant agrees to comply with all instructions and requirements necessary to prepare Premises to accommodate pest control, fumigation or other work, including bagging or storage of food and medicine, and removal of perishables and valuables. Tenant shall only be entitled to a credit of Rent equal to the per diem Rent for the period of time Tenant is required to vacate Premises.

30. **DAMAGE TO PREMISES:** If, by no fault of Tenant, Premises are totally or partially damaged or destroyed by fire, earthquake, accident or other casualty that render Premises totally or partially uninhabitable, either Landlord or Tenant may terminate this Agreement by giving the other written notice. Rent shall be abated as of the date Premises become totally or partially uninhabitable. The abated amount shall be the current monthly Rent prorated on a 30-day period. If the Agreement is not terminated, Landlord shall promptly repair the damage, and Rent shall be reduced based on the extent to which the damage interferes with Tenant's reasonable use of Premises. If damage occurs as a result of an act of Tenant or Tenant's guests, only Landlord shall have the right of termination, and no reduction in Rent shall be made.

31. **INSURANCE:** Tenant's or guest's personal property and vehicles are not insured by Landlord, manager or, if applicable, HOA, against loss or damage due to fire, theft, vandalism, rain, water, criminal or negligent acts of others, or any other cause. **Tenant is advised to carry Tenant's own insurance (renter's insurance) to protect Tenant from any such loss or damage.** Tenant shall comply with any requirement imposed on Tenant by Landlord's insurer to avoid: (i) an increase in Landlord's insurance premium (or Tenant shall pay for the increase in premium); or (ii) loss of insurance.

32. **WATERBEDS:** Tenant shall not use or have waterbeds on the Premises unless: **(i)** Tenant obtains a valid waterbed insurance policy; **(ii)** Tenant increases the security deposit in an amount equal to one-half of one month's Rent; and **(iii)** the bed conforms to the floor load capacity of Premises.

Tenant's Initials (________)(________)
Landlord's Initials (________)(________)
Reviewed by ______ Date ______

Copyright © 1994-2004, CALIFORNIA ASSOCIATION OF REALTORS®, INC.
LR REVISED 10/04 (PAGE 4 OF 6)

RESIDENTIAL LEASE OR MONTH-TO-MONTH RENTAL AGREEMENT (LR PAGE 4 OF 6)

Premises: ______________________________ Date: ____________

33. **WAIVER:** The waiver of any breach shall not be construed as a continuing waiver of the same or any subsequent breach.

34. **NOTICE:** Notices may be served at the following address, or at any other location subsequently designated.

Landlord: ______________________ Tenant: ______________________

35. **TENANT ESTOPPEL CERTIFICATE:** Tenant shall execute and return a tenant estoppel certificate delivered to Tenant by Landlord or Landlord's agent within 3 days after its receipt. Failure to comply with this requirement shall be deemed Tenant's acknowledgment that the tenant estoppel certificate is true and correct, and may be relied upon by a lender or purchaser.

36. **TENANT REPRESENTATIONS; CREDIT:** Tenant warrants that all statements in Tenant's rental application are accurate. Tenant authorizes Landlord and Broker(s) to obtain Tenant's credit report periodically during the tenancy in connection with the modification or enforcement of this Agreement. Landlord may cancel this Agreement: **(i)** before occupancy begins; **(ii)** upon disapproval of the credit report(s); or **(iii)** at any time, upon discovering that information in Tenant's application is false. A negative credit report reflecting on Tenant's record may be submitted to a credit reporting agency if Tenant fails to fulfill the terms of payment and other obligations under this Agreement.

37. **MEDIATION:**

A. Consistent with paragraphs B and C below, Landlord and Tenant agree to mediate any dispute or claim arising between them out of this Agreement, or any resulting transaction, before resorting to court action. Mediation fees, if any, shall be divided equally among the parties involved. If, for any dispute or claim to which this paragraph applies, any party commences an action without first attempting to resolve the matter through mediation, or refuses to mediate after a request has been made, then that party shall not be entitled to recover attorney fees, even if they would otherwise be available to that party in any such action.

B. The following matters are excluded from mediation: **(i)** an unlawful detainer action; **(ii)** the filing or enforcement of a mechanic's lien; and **(iii)** any matter within the jurisdiction of a probate, small claims or bankruptcy court. The filing of a court action to enable the recording of a notice of pending action, for order of attachment, receivership, injunction, or other provisional remedies, shall not constitute a waiver of the mediation provision.

C. Landlord and Tenant agree to mediate disputes or claims involving Listing Agent, Leasing Agent or property manager ("Broker"), provided Broker shall have agreed to such mediation prior to, or within a reasonable time after, the dispute or claim is presented to such Broker. Any election by Broker to participate in mediation shall not result in Broker being deemed a party to this Agreement.

38. **ATTORNEY FEES:** In any action or proceeding arising out of this Agreement, the prevailing party between Landlord and Tenant shall be entitled to reasonable attorney fees and costs, except as provided in paragraph 37A.

39. **C.A.R. FORM:** C.A.R. Form means the specific form referenced or another comparable from agreed to by the parties.

40. **OTHER TERMS AND CONDITIONS;SUPPLEMENTS:** ______________________________

The following ATTACHED supplements are incorporated in this Agreement: ☐ Keysafe/Lockbox Addendum (C.A.R. Form KLA); ☐ Interpreter/Translator Agreement (C.A.R. Form ITA); ☐ Lead-Based Paint and Lead-Based Paint Hazards Disclosure (C.A.R. Form FLD)

41. **TIME OF ESSENCE; ENTIRE CONTRACT; CHANGES:** Time is of the essence. All understandings between the parties are incorporated in this Agreement. Its terms are intended by the parties as a final, complete and exclusive expression of their Agreement with respect to its subject matter, and may not be contradicted by evidence of any prior agreement or contemporaneous oral agreement. If any provision of this Agreement is held to be ineffective or invalid, the remaining provisions will nevertheless be given full force and effect. Neither this Agreement nor any provision in it may be extended, amended, modified, altered or changed except in writing. This Agreement is subject to California landlord-tenant law and shall incorporate all changes required by amendment or successors to such law. This Agreement and any supplement, addendum or modification, including any copy, may be signed in two or more counterparts, all of which shall constitute one and the same writing.

42. **AGENCY:**

A. **CONFIRMATION:** The following agency relationship(s) are hereby confirmed for this transaction:
Listing Agent: (Print firm name) ______________________________ is the agent of (check one): ☐ the Landlord exclusively; or ☐ both the Landlord and Tenant.
Leasing Agent: (Print firm name) ______________________________ (if not same as Listing Agent) is the agent of (check one): ☐ the Tenant exclusively; or ☐ the Landlord exclusively; or ☐ both the Tenant and Landlord.

B. **DISCLOSURE:** ☐ (If checked): The term of this lease exceeds one year. A disclosure regarding real estate agency relationships (C.A.R. Form AD) has been provided to Landlord and Tenant, who each acknowledge its receipt.

43. ☐ **TENANT COMPENSATION TO BROKER:** Upon execution of this Agreement, Tenant agrees to pay compensation to Broker as specified in a separate written agreement between Tenant and Broker.

44. ☐ **INTERPRETER/TRANSLATOR:** The terms of this Agreement have been interpreted for Tenant into the following language: ______________________________. Landlord and Tenant acknowledge receipt of the attached interpretor/translator agreement (C.A.R. Form ITA).

45. **FOREIGN LANGUAGE NEGOTIATION:** If this Agreement has been negotiated by Landlord and Tenant primarily in Spanish, Chinese, Tagalog, Korean or Vietnamese. Pursuant to the California Civil Code Tenant shall be provided a translation of this Agreement inthe language used for the negotiation.

Tenant's Initials (________)(________)
Landlord's Initials (________)(________)
Reviewed by ______ Date ______

Copyright © 1994-2004, CALIFORNIA ASSOCIATION OF REALTORS®, INC.
LR REVISED 10/04 (PAGE 5 OF 6)

RESIDENTIAL LEASE OR MONTH-TO-MONTH RENTAL AGREEMENT (LR PAGE 5 OF 6)

Premises: _____ Date: _____

Landlord and Tenant acknowledge and agree Brokers: **(a)** do not guarantee the condition of the Premises; **(b)** cannot verify representations made by others; **(c)** cannot provide legal or tax advice; **(d)** will not provide other advice or information that exceeds the knowledge, education or experience required to obtain a real estate license. Furthermore, if Brokers are not also acting as Landlord in this Agreement, Brokers: **(e)** do not decide what rental rate a Tenant should pay or Landlord should accept; and **(f)** do not decide upon the length or other terms of tenancy. Landlord and Tenant agree that they will seek legal, tax, insurance and other desired assistance from appropriate professionals.

Tenant   Date
Address _____ City _____ State _____ Zip _____
Telephone _____ Fax _____ E-mail_____
Tenant _____ Date _____
Address _____ City _____ State _____ Zip _____
Telephone _____ Fax _____ E-mail_____

46. ☐ **GUARANTEE:** In consideration of the execution of the Agreement by and between Landlord and Tenant and for valuable consideration, receipt of which is hereby acknowledged, the undersigned ("Guarantor") does hereby: **(i)** guarantee unconditionally to Landlord and Landlord's agents, successors and assigns, the prompt payment of Rent or other sums that become due pursuant to this Agreement, including any and all court costs and attorney fees included in enforcing the Agreement; **(ii)** consent to any changes, modifications or alterations of any term in this Agreement agreed to by Landlord and Tenant; and **(iii)** waive any right to require Landlord and/or Landlord's agents to proceed against Tenant for any default occurring under this Agreement before seeking to enforce this Guarantee.

Guarantor (Print Name) _____
Guarantor _____ Date _____
Address _____ City _____ State _____ Zip _____
Telephone _____ Fax _____ E-mail_____

47. OWNER COMPENSATION TO BROKER: Upon execution of this Agreement, Owner agrees to pay compensation to Broker as specified in a separate written agreement between Owner and Broker (C.A.R. Form LCA).

48. RECEIPT: If specified in paragraph 5, Landlord or Broker, acknowledges receipt of move-in funds.

Landlord _____ Date _____
(Owner or Agent with authority to enter into this Agreement)
Landlord _____ Date _____
(Owner or Agent with authority to enter into this Agreement)
Landlord Address _____ City _____ State _____ Zip _____
Telephone _____ Fax _____ E-mail_____

REAL ESTATE BROKERS:
A. Real estate brokers who are not also Landlord under the Agreement are not parties to the Agreement between Landlord and Tenant.
B. Agency relationships are confirmed in paragraph 42.
C. **COOPERATING BROKER COMPENSATION:** Listing Broker agrees to pay Cooperating Broker (Leasing Firm) and Cooperating Broker agrees to accept: **(i)** the amount specified in the MLS, provided Cooperating Broker is a Participant of the MLS in which the Property is offered for sale or a reciprocal MLS; or **(ii)** ☐ (if checked) the amount specified in a separate written agreement between Listing Broker and Cooperating Broker.

Real Estate Broker (Leasing Firm) _____
By (Agent) _____ Date _____
Address _____ City _____ State
Zip _____
Telephone _____ Fax _____ E-mail_____

Real Estate Broker (Leasing Firm) _____
By (Agent) _____ Date _____
Address _____ City _____ State _____ Zip _____
Telephone _____ Fax _____ E-mail_____

SURE TRAC
The System for Success®
Published and Distributed by:
REAL ESTATE BUSINESS SERVICES, INC.
a subsidiary of the California Association of REALTORS®
525 South Virgil Avenue, Los Angeles, California 90020

Reviewed by _____ Date _____

EQUAL HOUSING OPPORTUNITY

LR REVISED 10/04 (PAGE 6 OF 6)

RESIDENTIAL LEASE OR MONTH-TO-MONTH RENTAL AGREEMENT (LR PAGE 6 OF 6)

Figure 6-3

CALIFORNIA
ASSOCIATION
OF REALTORS®

APPLICATION TO RENT/SCREENING FEE
(C.A.R. Form LRA, Revised 4/03)

I. APPLICATION TO RENT

THIS SECTION TO BE COMPLETED BY APPLICANT. A SEPARATE APPLICATION TO RENT IS REQUIRED FOR EACH OCCUPANT 18 YEARS OF AGE OR OVER, OR AN EMANCIPATED MINOR.

Applicant is completing Application as a (check one) ☐ tenant, ☐ tenant with co-tenant(s) or ☐ guarantor/co-signor.
Total number of applicants _____.

PREMISES INFORMATION

Application to rent property at _____ ("Premises")
Rent: $ _____ per _____ Proposed move-in date _____

PERSONAL INFORMATION

FULL NAME OF APPLICANT _____
Social security No. _____ Driver's license No. _____ State _____ Expires _____
Phone number: Home _____ Work _____ Other _____
Email _____
Name(s) of all other proposed occupant(s) and relationship to applicant _____

Pet(s) or service animals (number and type) _____
Auto: Make _____ Model _____ Year _____ License No. _____ State _____ Color _____
Other vehicle(s): _____
In case of emergency, person to notify _____ Relationship _____
Address _____ Phone _____
Does applicant or any proposed occupant plan to use liquid-filled furniture? ☐ No ☐ Yes Type _____
Has applicant been a party to an unlawful detainer action or filed bankruptcy within the last seven years? ☐ No ☐ Yes
If yes, explain _____
Has applicant or any proposed occupant ever been convicted of or pleaded no contest to a felony? ☐ No ☐ Yes
If yes, explain _____
Has applicant or any proposed occupant ever been asked to move out of a residence? ☐ No ☐ Yes
If yes, explain _____

RESIDENCE HISTORY

Current address _____	Previous address _____
City/State/Zip _____	City/State/Zip _____
From _____ to _____	From _____ to _____
Name of Landlord/Manager _____	Name of Landlord/Manager _____
Landlord/Manager's phone _____	Landlord/Manager's phone _____
Do you own this property? ☐ No ☐ Yes	Did you own this property? ☐ No ☐ Yes
Reason for leaving current address _____	Reason for leaving this address _____

EMPLOYMENT AND INCOME HISTORY

Current employer _____	Supervisor _____ From _____ To _____
Employer's address _____	Supervisor's phone _____
Position or title _____	Phone number to verify employment _____
Employment gross income $ _____ per _____	Other $ _____ per _____ Source _____
Previous employer _____	Supervisor _____ From _____ To _____
Employer's address _____	Supervisor's phone _____
Position or title _____	Employment gross income $ _____ per _____

LRA REVISED 4/03 (PAGE 1 OF 2) Print Date

Applicant's Initials (_____)(_____)
Reviewed by _____ Date _____

EQUAL HOUSING OPPORTUNITY

APPLICATION TO RENT/SCREENING FEE (LRA PAGE 1 OF 2)

162

Property Address: _____   Date: _____

CREDIT INFORMATION

Name of creditor	Account number	Monthly payment	Balance due

Name of bank/branch	Account number	Type of account	Account balance

PERSONAL REFERENCES

Name _____ Address _____
Phone _____ Length of acquaintance _____ Occupation _____
Name _____ Address _____
Phone _____ Length of acquaintance _____ Occupation _____

NEAREST RELATIVE(S)

Name _____ Address _____
Phone _____ Relationship _____
Name _____ Address _____
Phone _____ Relationship _____

Applicant understands and agrees: **(i)** this is an application to rent only and does not guarantee that applicant will be offered the Premises; and **(ii)** Landlord or Manager or Agent may accept more than one application for the Premises and, at using their sole discretion, will select the best qualified applicant.

Applicant represents the above information to be true and complete, and hereby authorizes Landlord or Manager or Agent to: **(i)** verify the information provided; and **(ii)** obtain credit report on applicant.

If application is not fully completed, or received without the screening fee: (i) the application will not be processed, and (ii) the application and any screening fee will be returned.

Applicant _____ Date _____ Time _____

Return your completed application and any applicable fee not already paid to: _____
Address _____ City _____ State _____ Zip _____

II. SCREENING FEE

THIS SECTION TO BE COMPLETED BY LANDLORD, MANAGER OR AGENT.
Applicant has paid a **nonrefundable** screening fee of $ _____, applied as follows: (The screening fee may not exceed $30.00 (adjusted annually from 1-1-98 commensurate with the increase in the Consumer Price Index).)

$ _____ for credit reports prepared by _____;
$ _____ for _____ (other out-of-pocket expenses); and
$ _____ for processing.
The undersigned has read the foregoing and acknowledges receipt of a copy.

_____   Date _____
Applicant Signature

The undersigned has received the screening fee indicated above.

_____   Date _____
Landlord or Manager or Agent Signature

SURE TRAC
The System for Success™
Published by the
California Association of REALTORS®

LRA REVISED 4/03 (PAGE 2 OF 2)

Reviewed by _____ Date _____

EQUAL HOUSING OPPORTUNITY

APPLICATION TO RENT/SCREENING FEE (LRA PAGE 2 OF 2)

CHAPTER 6

B. MINIMUM REQUIREMENTS OF A LEASE (or Rental Agreement)

As long as there is intent to rent property, the creation of a lease requires no particular language and can be either a written or an oral agreement. A lease or rental agreement must, at a minimum, include these four items:

1. **L**ength or duration of the lease.
2. **A**mount of rent.   Think of
3. **N**ames of parties.   **L.A.N.D.** !
4. **D**escription of property.

Leases for one year or less do not need to be in writing, but it makes good business sense to have all real estate agreements in writing. Under the Statute of Frauds, any lease lasting longer than one year from the date of signing must be in writing. California courts have held that in the event the lease is written, it must be signed by the lessor. It is not necessary for the lessee to sign if the lease has been delivered to, and accepted by, the lessee. The payment of rent and possession of the property is sufficient acceptance. Hotels, motels, and other types of lodging fall into the category of leases, even though the duration of use may be for a much shorter time and eviction or termination is handled differently for these daily or weekly rentals.

A lease for more than one year must be in writing and signed by the lessor; but if the lessee does not sign, moves in and pays rent, he or she is bound to the terms of the lease.

C. RIGHTS AND OBLIGATIONS OF THE PARTIES

In addition to the minimum requirements, a number of contractual matters between a landlord and tenant should be considered before entering into a lease. The importance of these factors increases as the time period covered by the contract increases. Certain points that should be covered are:

1. **duration of lease;**
2. **amount of rent and manner of payment;**
3. **security deposits;**
4. **assignment and subleasing provisions;**
5. **liabilities for injuries and repairs;**
6. **conditions and provisions of a lease;**
7. **termination of a lease or rental agreement, and**
8. **renewal or extension provisions in bold type.**

1. Duration of Lease

There are certain statutory restrictions on the terms of certain leases:

1. Agricultural lands cannot be leased for more than 51 years.
2. Property situated in a city or town cannot be leased for more than 99 years.
3. A mineral, oil, or gas lease cannot be longer than 99 years after work begins.
4. A minor or incompetent can possess property only for the time a court has approved.

164

2. Amount of Rent

RENT is the amount of money paid for the use of a property. It is important to state both the specific amount of rent and when the rent is to be paid to the landlord. With a periodic tenancy, if the rent is to be paid in advance, or any time other than the end of the term, it should be stated in the agreement. **By law, rent becomes due only at the end of the term, unless the lease agreement states otherwise.** Preprinted lease forms normally specify that rent is due on the first day of each calendar month.

The actual amount of rent to be paid is called contract rent. *CONTRACT RENT is the payment designated in a lease contract, at the time the lease is signed, for the use of the property.* This amount must be distinguished from the economic rent. *ECONOMIC RENT is the amount of rent a property might be expected to yield if it were available for lease in the current market.* The economic rent and contract rent of a given property might differ if the lessor is receiving more or less rent than the property should reasonably yield.

Rents are prorated in escrow.

For income tax purposes, the amount of rent paid in advance must be included in the landlord's income for that year. If the landlord collects both the first month's and the last month's rent, both are considered current year income.

3. Security Deposits (Refundable)

A *SECURITY DEPOSIT provides the landlord with funds to pay for damages or unpaid rent when the tenant vacates.* It is in the landlord's and tenant's best interests to have an inspection of the premises before the tenant moves in and before the tenant moves out.

A *STATEMENT OF PROPERTY CONDITION is a report filled out by the landlord, in the presence of the tenant, that states the condition of the premises on moving in and moving out.* If both parties to a lease or rental agreement complete this form together, the chances of any disputes arising with regard to damages and the security deposit are greatly reduced.

The maximum rental agreement security deposits for a residential property (in addition to first month's rent) is 2 months' rent for an unfurnished property and 3 months' rent for a furnished property.

Security (and "cleaning") deposits for residential leases in California must be refunded, in full, within twenty-one days of the tenant vacating the premises unless there is damage to the property or required cleaning. If part (or all) of the security deposit is to be withheld from the tenant, the landlord must furnish the tenant an itemized, written statement within the same twenty-one day period. There are a limited number of areas in California that require a minimal amount of interest to be paid on deposits.

4. Assignment and Subleasing Provisions

A sublease is a transfer of less than the entire leasehold estate to the sublessee.

The tenant, without a clause to the contrary in the lease, may assign or sublease the property. An *ASSIGNMENT of a lease is a transfer of the entire lease*, whereas a *SUBLEASE is a transfer of less than the entire time or space of the lease.* For example, if there is a two-year lease, then an assignment could be for those two years, or a sublease could be for one year of the two-year lease, as long as it's not forbidden in the lease contract.

Example: A tenant signed a written lease for two years on a home. The lease made no mention of assignments and/or subleasing. The tenant may assign or sublease the home since the lease did not address those items.

In a sublease, the lessee is still obligated for the original lease, whereas in an assignment, all the rights and obligations are transferred to the new tenant (assignee). When a tenant signs an assignment, the assignee who acquired the leasehold estate becomes the tenant.

When a lessee or sublessee subleases a property, he or she holds a sandwich lease. A *SANDWICH LEASE is a leasehold interest in a property that lies between the primary (ownership) interest and the operating (tenancy) interest.*

The lessee or sublessee with a sandwich lease is both a tenant and landlord to the same property.

5. Liabilities for Injuries and Repairs

Generally, when the entire property is leased, the landlord is not liable for injuries to the tenant or any guests that resulted from a defective condition on the premises. This is true even if reasonable care would have disclosed the defects. In apartments or situations where the tenant does not lease the entire property, the liability for injury in the common areas belongs to the landlord. Therefore, it is the landlord's responsibility to either repair defective conditions in the common areas or be liable for injuries resulting from them. If a landlord has knowledge of such defects or disrepair but conceals the fact from the tenant, the landlord is liable for any resulting injuries.

It's easy to see why landlords should carry a large amount of liability insurance. Building defects may cause serious injury that could result in a lawsuit against the landlord. The tenant may also carry a renter's liability policy to protect against injuries sustained by others while visiting his or her apartment. This type of protection is usually contained in a "renter's" or "content's" policy, which protects the tenants from most losses, including liability and personal property damages.

6. Conditions and Provisions of a Lease

The California State Bar Association, in conjunction with CAR, has developed a standard combination lease and rental agreement form (refer back to Figure 6-2). This lease contains a number of conditions and provisions that both groups believe provide a good lease contract. As well as explaining who is responsible for any breach, this lease covers most of the common problems that may arise.

If a real estate broker sells a property where the buyer will take possession prior to transferring title, the document he/she would have the buyer and seller execute is called an "interim occupancy agreement."

III. Termination of a Lease (or Rental Agreement)

A lease or rental agreement can be terminated for a variety of reasons. **Figure 6-4** lists the seven most common reasons for termination. A lease ends at the expiration of the term and without

Figure 6-4

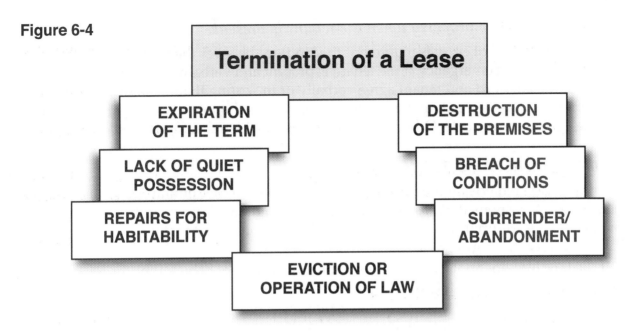

notice. Rental agreements terminate by a written notice that must be at least one rental period in length. For example, if a tenancy is on a two-week basis, and the rent is paid for that period, then two week's notice is required.

A. TERMINATION: EXPIRATION OF THE TERM (Most Common Reason)

A lease ends, without notice, at the expiration of the term. Rental agreements are usually terminated by either party with a 30-day written notice, unless a longer period is agreed to by both parties. As stated before, if the rental period is less than a month, only that much time is required. "Tenancies at will" require no less than a 30-day written "notice to vacate" to be served upon the tenant, or a 30-day notice given to the landlord by a vacating tenant. The 30-day notice may be made at any time during the rental period, with the balance of the rent due prorated. **Any condition in a rental agreement may be changed with a 30-day written notice.**

B. TERMINATION: LACK OF QUIET POSSESSION

A tenant is entitled to the quiet possession and enjoyment of the premises without interference. The lease or rental agreement is made with the assumption that the tenant will have use of the premises and enjoy a quiet, uninterrupted stay. The landlord has the responsibility to maintain reasonable quiet on the premises for his or her tenants, and must not harass them unduly. Failure in either responsibility can give a tenant grounds for terminating a lease.

The California Civil Code permits the landlord to enter a tenant's unit under the following conditions:

1. Emergencies
2. Necessary repairs
3. To show premises to prospective tenants, buyers, or appraisers
4. If the tenant has abandoned the premises
5. With a court order to enter

A landlord can enter the property when the tenant is present.

No written notice of entry is required if the landlord believes the tenant has abandoned the premises, it is an emergency, if the tenant is present and verbally consents at the time of entry, or if the landlord and tenant agree verbally or in writing that the landlord will enter the property to make agreed upon repairs or supply agreed upon services within one week after the agreement is made. Otherwise, 24 hours is considered sufficient notice.

C. TERMINATION: REPAIRS FOR HABITABILITY

The landlord of a rented home, whether the home is a house, a condominium or an apartment, has the implied responsibility to keep the premises maintained in a condition that meets at least bare living requirements: Hazardous conditions cannot exist that threaten the tenant's health or safety (see **Figure 6-5**).

If the landlord does not live up to this implied warranty of habitability, the tenant is not obligated to pay all the rent. However, a tenant must give notice of any necessary repairs to the landlord. The landlord has a reasonable amount of time to make any necessary repairs. A "reasonable amount of time" is determined by the type of repair needed. If the landlord, after a reasonable amount of time, has failed to make the necessary repairs, the tenant has two methods of recourse:

1. Spend up to (maximum) one month's rent in repairs, up to twice in a twelve consecutive month period. (A tenant cannot charge for his or her labor.)
2. Abandon the premises, which terminates the lease or rental agreement.

D. TERMINATION: EVICTION OR OPERATION OF LAW

If a tenant does not pay the rent, or the tenant performs illegal acts on the premises, legal action is available to the landlord. *EVICTION is the legal process of removing a tenant because there is a breach of the lease or rental agreement.* **Figure 6-6** shows the life of an eviction process. An alternative would be for the landlord to sue for each payment (installment) as it becomes due. This is true whether the tenant remains in possession or abandons the premises. But at this point most landlords elect to evict the lessee. If the tenant moves and the landlord leases the property, the landlord can only sue for the rent lost while the property was vacant. A *RETALIATORY EVICTION is the process whereby a landlord evicts a tenant in response to a complaint lodged, or a repair deducted from rent, by the tenant.*

When the tenant refuses to give up possession but does not pay the rent, the landlord normally serves a "three-day notice to pay rent or quit" and, if necessary, files an "unlawful detainer" action. A *THREE-DAY NOTICE TO PAY RENT OR QUIT (Eviction Notice) is a legal document that informs the tenant that he/she has three straight days (excluding weekend days and holidays) to pay all past due rent, vacate the premises, or face an unlawful detainer court action* (see **Figure 6-7**). For example, a notice served on Monday expires at midnight on Thursday, but a notice served on Wednesday does not expire until the following Monday at midnight, unless Monday is a holiday.

An *UNLAWFUL DETAINER is a legal action in which a complaint is filed with the court asserting charges against the tenant.* After it is served, the tenant has five days to surrender possession or answer the complaint, and is no longer entitled to a pre-move out inspection.

Figure 6-5

Habitability Obligations
(Civil Code Section 1941.1)

LANDLORD'S LEGAL MINIMUM OBLIGATIONS

The landlord's minimum habitability obligations are:

1. Effective waterproofing of roof and exterior walls, including unbroken windows and doors.
2. Plumbing and gas facilities installation maintained in good working order.
3. A water supply capable of hot and cold running water, fixtures, and connection to a sewage disposal system.
4. Heating facilities maintained in good working order.
5. Electrical lighting maintained in good working order.
6. Building and grounds kept clean and sanitary, free from all accumulations of debris, filth, rubbish, garbage, and rodents.
7. An adequate number of rubbish receptacles.
8. Floors, stairways, and railings maintained in good repair.

If property is declared "untenable" for 35 days, the landlord can be fined $5,000 if he or she attempts to collect rent, issues a three-day notice to quit, or a notice to increase rent.

TENANT'S LEGAL OBLIGATIONS

Tenant's Legal Obligations for Care of Premises. A tenant's affirmative obligations to a landlord for reasonable care and habitability are:

1. Keep his or her part of the premises as clean and sanitary as possible.
2. Dispose of garbage and trash in a clean and sanitary manner.
3. Properly use the plumbing, electrical, and gas fixtures and keep them as clean as their condition permits.
4. Not permit any person on the premises to willfully destroy, deface, damage, impair, or remove any part of the structure, facilities, or equipment.
5. Occupy the premises for sleeping, cooking, dining, or other purposes for which they were designed or intended.

Figure 6-6

Life of an Eviction Process

3 Days	5 Days	5 Days
Three-Day Notice to Pay Rent or Quit	Unlawful Detainer	Writ of Possession

Minimum Time Span

Along with the unlawful detainer, many landlords caused to be served upon the tenants a *PREJUDGMENT CLAIM OF RIGHT OF POSSESSION, which covers any persons who appear to be or who may claim to have occupied the premises at the time of the filing of the action, even if their names do not appear on the lease (rental) agreement.*

If the tenant loses or does not answer the unlawful detainer complaint (defaults), the clerk of the court may issue a writ of possession. A **WRIT OF POSSESSION** *is a court order directing the sheriff to remove the tenant from the premises within five days of eviction notice.* Often, the landlord will have to account for the storage of the tenant's personal property. This can be complicated, so a landlord should consult an attorney before obtaining an unlawful detainer or writ of possession. Although an entire eviction process could take only thirteen days, it will most likely take a longer period of time. If the tenant answers the complaint, the matter could take several months.

E. TERMINATION: SURRENDER/ABANDONMENT

When a tenant voluntarily gives up a lease before the expiration of its term, it is known as **SURRENDER.** If the tenant gives up the right of possession and surrenders the property back to the landlord, and the landlord accepts the surrender, the tenant is no longer liable for rent. Leases may be surrendered either by mutual agreement of the parties or through operation of law.

If a tenant just moves out or vacates the premises without a formal surrender and never returns, it is called "abandonment."

If a tenant abandons a property without cause, he or she has, by "operation of law," surrendered the property back to the landlord. Any cost for legal action by the landlord, plus the cost of any rental loss, may be charged to the tenant. The losses will be minimized if the landlord recovers possession and re-leases the premises quickly. A landlord can bring a lawsuit against the tenant for the lost rents, advertising expenses, and repairs or cleaning.

If a tenant's rent is 14 days delinquent and the landlord has reasonable cause to believe that the lessee has abandoned the premises, the lessor may bring action to reclaim the property. The lease is terminated 15 days after a **Notice of Belief of Abandonment** was personally served or posted in a conspicuous place (door, window) on the premises or 18 days after the notice was deposited in the mail. This will occur unless the lessee pays the rent or notifies the landlord that the premises has not been abandoned and he or she does not wish to surrender the leasehold estate.

Figure 6-7

3-DAY NOTICE TO PAY RENT OR QUIT

	Owner(s)
Plaintiff(s) VS.	Tenant(s)
Defendant(s) and Does 1 to 10 inclusive	

TO the above named TENANTS/RESIDENTS AND ALL OTHERS IN POSSESSION. PLEASE TAKE NOTICE, that you are justly indebted to the owner of the herein described premises; and notice is hereby given that pursuant to the lease and/or rental agreement under which you hold possession there is now due, unpaid and delinquent rent.

The total amount owing represents rent due for the following period(s).

Due from _____ , 20____ thru _____ , 20____ $ _____

Due from _____ , 20____ thru _____ , 20____ $ _____

Due from _____ , 20____ thru _____ , 20____ $ _____

Due from _____ , 20____ thru _____ , 20____ $ _____

Total Rent Now Due $ _____

WITHIN THREE (3) DAYS after service on you of this notice, you are hereby required to pay the amount of the above stated rent in full OR quit the subject premises, move out, and deliver up possession to the owner and/or his authorized agent. **No personal checks will be accepted.**

PLEASE TAKE FURTHER NOTICE that unless you pay the rent in full OR vacate the premises WITHIN THREE (3) DAYS as required by this notice, that the undersigned does hereby elect to declare forfeiture of your lease or rental agreement and institute legal proceedings for an unlawful detainer against you to recover possession of the premises plus court costs, attorney fees, and THREE TIMES THE AMOUNT OF RENT AND DAMAGES due as provided for by California law.

The premises herein referred to which you hold and/or occupied by you are:

Address: _____ Apartment or Suite No.: _____

City: _____ State: _____ Zip: _____

County of: _____

Location to pay rent:
Name _____
Address _____
City, State, Zip _____
Usual Days **M-F** Usual Hours **9AM TO 4PM**
Phone Number _____

_____
PERSON AUTHORIZED TO GIVE NOTICE

PROOF OF SERVICE

I, the undersigned, being at least 18 years of age, declare under penalty of perjury that I served the above notice, of which this is a true copy, on the following tenant(s) in possession in the manner(s) indicated below:

☐ On _____ , I handed the notice to the tenant(s) personally.

☐ On _____ , after attempting personal service, I handed the notice to a person of suitable age and discretion at the residence/business of the tenant(s), AND I deposited a true copy in the U.S. Mail, in a sealed envelope with postage fully prepaid, addressed to the tenant(s) at his/her/their place of residence (date mailed, if different _____).

☐ On _____ , after attempting service in both manners indicated previously, I posted the notice in a conspicuous place at the residence of the tenant(s), AND I deposited a true copy in the U.S. Mail, in a sealed envelope with postage fully prepaid, addressed to the tenant(s) at his/her/their place of residence (date mailed, if different _____).

Executed on _____ Served by _____

F. TERMINATION: BREACH OF CONDITIONS

The violation of any conditions of the lease is a breach of contract and may terminate the agreement. Both the lessee and lessor have the responsibility of being informed of all contractual conditions and understand that violation of the conditions may cause termination.

G. TERMINATION: DESTRUCTION OF THE PREMISES

If a structure is destroyed, there is usually a clause in the contract that automatically terminates the lease. If the damage is light, the tenant may stay while the landlord makes repairs. The lessee has the right to vacate the lease if the property is condemned.

Selling an apartment building does NOT terminate the leases of the tenants in possession.

IV. Special Purpose Leases

In this section we will cover unique types of leases designed to meet specific needs.

A. SALE-LEASEBACK

A *SALE-LEASEBACK occurs when an owner sells his or her property to another party and leases it back for a stated period of time; the original owner becomes the lessee.* This is also a financing device, but it is used mostly for commercial buildings where large business concerns are involved. The main reason for this type of lease is that a large company usually builds structures to its specifications. A large amount of money is required, therefore the company sells the building to get back most of its invested capital. By doing this, the company increases its working capital.

The original owner of property in a sale-leaseback becomes the lessee.

Large investors, such as insurance companies and pension funds, will purchase or build such a property, provided they get a well written, long-term lease. Of course the credit rating and financial position of the lessee must be outstanding. This is one device that nets a high rental income to the investor and allows the business a better cash flow. Chain stores, such as department stores and discount stores, use this device frequently.

A single line of retail stores located along a major transportation corridor in a commercially zoned area is known as a "strip commercial development."

B. LEASE-PURCHASE OPTION

A *LEASE-PURCHASE OPTION exists only when a tenant leases a property with the option to purchase it at some later date.* See Chapter 5 for mor details.

> **Example:** Able holds a two-year lease with an option to purchase and assigns it to Baker. Baker would now hold the option, even if it is not stated in the assignment of the lease.

The credit crunch/slump in making lease-purchase options more popular as alternative financing methods.

C. GROUND LEASE

A *GROUND LEASE is for the exclusive use and possession of a specific parcel of land.*

D. GRADUATED LEASE

A *GRADUATED LEASE provides for a varying rental rate. It is often based upon future determination, such as periodic appraisals.* (Also called a "stair-step" lease.)

E. GROSS LEASE (Income Property)

With a GROSS LEASE, the lessee pays only a rental fee for the use of the property.

F. NET LEASE (Income Property)

A *NET LEASE is one where the lessee pays the property taxes, insurance, and other operating costs in addition to rental payments and is commonly used for stores.* The lessor receives only a net amount and does not pay the other related property expenses. Sometimes the net lease is referred to as a **"triple net lease"** because the lessee pays for (1) property taxes, (2) fire and hazard insurance, and (3) assessments or other operating expenses.

The lessor benefits from a net lease because it generates a fixed income.

G. PERCENTAGE LEASE (Retail Sales Property)

A *PERCENTAGE LEASE is a commercial (retail sales) lease in which the lessee pays, or may pay, a certain percentage of the monthly gross sales to the lessor.* The idea is that if the lessee has a good or excellent location, the lessor will also benefit. Most percentage leases are written for a base rental amount, paid in advance, with an additional amount due if a predetermined percentage of the gross income receipts exceeds the base rental amount.

Percentage lease payments are based upon monthly gross income receipts (with a fixed minimum rental).

V. Other Lease/Property Issues

A. CONSUMER PRICE INDEX (CPI)

The *CONSUMER PRICE INDEX (CPI) is a government indicator (also called the "cost of living index") that shows changes in the cost of living from period-to-period.* As one of the largest expenses for consumers, **housing expenses are one of the largest denominators used when calculating the CPI.** Leases are often tied to the CPI, so that rents will adjust to give the lessor the same relative purchasing power from rents during a period of inflation. Long-term commercial leases generally include an *ESCALATOR CLAUSE whereby rents increase with inflation.*

The most frequently used standard (index) for making commercial lease adjustments for inflation is the "Consumer Price Index for Wage Earners and Clerical Workers (CPI-W)."

B. LICENSE

A *LICENSE is a personal nonownership right to use personal or real property for a specific period of time.* It is nontransferable and can be **revoked.** Think of it as a ticket to a movie.

CHAPTER 6

VI. Property Management (Real Estate License Required)

In ever growing numbers, real estate brokers are now functioning as real property managers. A *PROPERTY MANAGER is a licensed real estate person who is paid to oversee the proper management and operations of rental and commercial property*. A property management company in California must be run by a licensed real estate broker and may include licensed salespeople working as property managers. Property managers include, for example, those who only engage in the management of one- and two-family homes as well as agents who oversee large projects such as office and industrial complexes, apartment buildings, and condominiums.

The ultimate responsibility for the maintenance of an apartment building rests with the owner.

Property managers must also be familiar with rent control laws in their city. *RENT CONTROL is government regulation of the amount of rent a landlord may charge tenants*. It is usually in the form of restrictions, by percentage, of annual increases in rental payments. Commercial, industrial, and luxury rentals are generally exempt from rent control.

"Maturity" in property management means income has stabilized.

A. MANAGEMENT CONTRACT

It is good business practice for a property manager, managing properties for an owner, to have a well written contract with the property owner that sets forth the responsibilities of both parties (see **Figure 6-8** for the **CAR Property Management Agreement** form). This should include the terms and period of the contract, policies pertaining to the management of the premises, management fees, and the powers granted the agent by the owner.

Property management contracts usually provide for the property manager to be compensated through a flat fee plus a percentage of the gross income.

B. RESIDENTIAL MANAGER

California law requires that rental unit buildings of 16 units or more must have an on-site resident manager in the employ of the owner or property management company living on the premises. *RESIDENTIAL MANAGERS are tenants of the property who rent units, handle tenants' complaints, and maintain the premises*. They are not required to have a real estate license.

An on-site residential manager does NOT need a real estate license to manage a property where he/she is living, but does need a license to manage other properties.

VII. Professional Associations

A. INSTITUTE OF REAL ESTATE MANAGEMENT® (IREM)

The Institute of Real Estate Management® (IREM), created by the National Association of REALTORS® (NAR) bolsters professionalism within the industry by offering qualified candidates the designations of Certified Property Manager® (CPM), Accredited

174

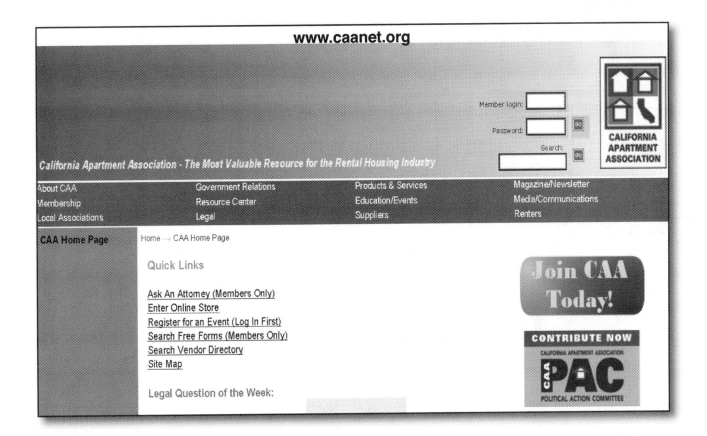

Management Organization® (AMO), and Accredited Resident Managers® (ARM) designation.

www.irem.org
Institute of Real Estate Management

B. CALIFORNIA APARTMENT ASSOCIATION® (CAA)

The California Apartment Association® (CAA) has many local associations to assist property owners with forms and credit checks. Their professional designation for resident managers is Certified Apartment Manager® (CAM) for on-site managers.

www.caanet.org/AM/Template.cfm
California Apartment Association

The 2007-2009 slowdown allows salespeople to earn commissions by leasing homes and condos.

Figure 6-8

CALIFORNIA
ASSOCIATION
OF REALTORS®

PROPERTY MANAGEMENT AGREEMENT
(C.A.R. Form PMA, Revised 4/03)

_____ ("Owner"), and
_____ ("Broker"), agree as follows:

1. **APPOINTMENT OF BROKER:** Owner hereby appoints and grants Broker the exclusive right to rent, lease, operate and manage the property(ies) known as _____
_____
_____ and any additional property that may later be added to this Agreement ("Property"), upon the terms below, for the period beginning (date) _____ and ending (date) _____, at 11:59 PM.
(If checked:) ☐ Either party may terminate this Property Management Agreement ("Agreement") on at least 30 days written notice _____ months after the original commencement date of this Agreement. After the exclusive term expires, this Agreement shall continue as a non-exclusive agreement that either party may terminate by giving at least 30 days written notice to the other.

2. **BROKER ACCEPTANCE:** Broker accepts the appointment and grant, and agrees to:
   A. Use due diligence in the performance of this Agreement.
   B. Furnish the services of its firm for the rental, leasing, operation and management of the Property.

3. **AUTHORITY AND POWERS:** Owner grants Broker the authority and power, at Owner's expense, to:
   A. **ADVERTISING:** Display FOR RENT/LEASE and similar signs on the Property and advertise the availability of the Property, or any part thereof, for rental or lease.
   B. **RENTAL;LEASING:** Initiate, sign, renew, modify or cancel rental agreements and leases for the Property, or any part thereof; collect and give receipts for rents, other fees, charges and security deposits. Any lease or rental agreement executed by Broker for Owner shall not exceed _____ year(s) or ☐ shall be month-to-month. Unless Owner authorizes a lower amount, rent shall be: ☐ at market rate; OR ☐ a minimum of $ _____ per _____; OR ☐ see attachment.
   C. **TENANCY TERMINATION:** Sign and serve in Owner's name notices that are required or appropriate; commence and prosecute actions to evict tenants; recover possession of the Property in Owner's name; recover rents and other sums due; and, when expedient, settle, compromise and release claims, actions and suits and/or reinstate tenancies.
   D. **REPAIR;MAINTENANCE:** Make, cause to be made, and/or supervise repairs, improvements, alterations and decorations to the Property; purchase, and pay bills for, services and supplies. Broker shall obtain prior approval of Owner for all expenditures over $ _____ for any one item. Prior approval shall not be required for monthly or recurring operating charges or, if in Broker's opinion, emergency expenditures over the maximum are needed to protect the Property or other property(ies) from damage, prevent injury to persons, avoid suspension of necessary services, avoid penalties or fines, or suspension of services to tenants required by a lease or rental agreement or by law, including, but not limited to, maintaining the Property in a condition fit for human habitation as required by Civil Code §§ 1941 and 1941.1 and Health and Safety Code §§ 17920.3 and 17920.10.
   E. **REPORTS, NOTICES AND SIGNS:** Comply with federal, state or local law requiring delivery of reports or notices and/or posting of signs or notices.
   F. **CONTRACTS;SERVICES:** Contract, hire, supervise and/or discharge firms and persons, including utilities, required for the operation and maintenance of the Property. Broker may perform any of Broker's duties through attorneys, agents, employees, or independent contractors and, except for persons working in Broker's firm, shall not be responsible for their acts, omissions, defaults, negligence and/or costs of same.
   G. **EXPENSE PAYMENTS:** Pay expenses and costs for the Property from Owner's funds held by Broker, unless otherwise directed by Owner. Expenses and costs may include, but are not limited to, property management compensation, fees and charges, expenses for goods and services, property taxes and other taxes, Owner's Association dues, assessments, loan payments and insurance premiums.
   H. **SECURITY DEPOSITS:** Receive security deposits from tenants, which deposits shall be ☐ given to Owner, or ☐ placed in Broker's trust account and, if held in Broker's trust account, pay from Owner's funds all interest on tenants' security deposits if required by local law or ordinance. Owner shall be responsible to tenants for return of security deposits and all interest due on security deposits held by Owner.
   I. **TRUST FUNDS:** Deposit all receipts collected for Owner, less any sums properly deducted or disbursed, in a financial institution whose deposits are insured by an agency of the United States government. The funds shall be held in a trust account separate from Broker's personal accounts. Broker shall not be liable in event of bankruptcy or failure of a financial institution.
   J. **RESERVES:** Maintain a reserve in Broker's trust account of $_____.
   K. **DISBURSEMENTS:** Disburse Owner's funds held in Broker's trust account in the following order:
      (1) Compensation due Broker under paragraph 6.
      (2) All other operating expenses, costs and disbursements payable from Owner's funds held by Broker.
      (3) Reserves and security deposits held by Broker.
      (4) Balance to Owner.
   L. **OWNER DISTRIBUTION:** Remit funds, if any are available, monthly (or ☐ _____), to Owner.
   M. **OWNER STATEMENTS:** Render monthly (or ☐ _____), statements of receipts, expenses and charges for each Property.
   N. **BROKER FUNDS:** Broker shall not advance Broker's own funds in connection with the Property or this Agreement.
   O. ☐ (If checked) Owner authorizes the use of a keysafe/lockbox to allow entry into the Property and agrees to sign a keysafe/lockbox addendum (C.A.R. Form KLA).

Owner's Initials (_____)(_____)
Broker's Initials (_____)(_____)

Reviewed by _____ Date _____

EQUAL HOUSING OPPORTUNITY

PROPERTY MANAGEMENT AGREEMENT (PMA PAGE 1 OF 3)

Owner Name: _____ Date: _____

4. **OWNER RESPONSIBILITIES:** Owner shall:
   A. Provide all documentation, records and disclosures as required by law or required by Broker to manage and operate the Property, and immediately notify Broker if Owner becomes aware of any change in such documentation, records or disclosures, or any matter affecting the habitability of the Property.
   B. Indemnify, defend and hold harmless Broker, and all persons in Broker's firm, regardless of responsibility, from all costs, expenses, suits, liabilities, damages, attorney fees and claims of every type, including but not limited to those arising out of injury or death of any person, or damage to any real or personal property of any person, including Owner, for: **(i)** any repairs performed by Owner or by others hired directly by Owner; or **(ii)** those relating to the management, leasing, rental, security deposits, or operation of the Property by Broker, or any person in Broker's firm, or the performance or exercise of any of the duties, powers or authorities granted to Broker.
   C. Maintain the Property in a condition fit for human habitation as required by Civil Code §§ 1941 and 1941.1 and Health and Safety Code §§ 17920.3 and 17920.10 and other applicable law.
   D. Pay all interest on tenants' security deposits if required by local law or ordinance.
   E. Carry and pay for: **(i)** public and premises liability insurance in an amount of no less than $1,000,000; and **(ii)** property damage and worker's compensation insurance adequate to protect the interests of Owner and Broker. Broker shall be, and Owner authorizes Broker to be, named as an additional insured party on Owner's policies.
   F. Pay any late charges, penalties and/or interest imposed by lenders or other parties for failure to make payment to those parties, if the failure is due to insufficient funds in Broker's trust account available for such payment.
   G. Immediately replace any funds required if there are insufficient funds in Broker's trust account to cover Owner's responsibilities.

5. **LEAD-BASED PAINT DISCLOSURE:**
   A. ☐ The Property was constructed on or after January 1, 1978.
   OR B. ☐ The Property was constructed prior to 1978.
      (1) Owner has no knowledge of lead-based paint or lead-based paint hazards in the housing except: _____
         _____
      (2) Owner has no reports or records pertaining to lead-based paint or lead-based paint hazards in the housing, except the following, which Owner shall provide to Broker: _____

6. **COMPENSATION:**
   A. Owner agrees to pay Broker fees in the amounts indicated below for:
      (1) Management: _____
      (2) Renting or Leasing: _____
      (3) Evictions: _____
      (4) Preparing Property for rental or lease: _____
      (5) Managing Property during extended periods of vacancy: _____
      (6) An overhead and service fee added to the cost of all work performed by, or at the direction of, Broker: _____
      (7) Other: _____
   B. This Agreement does not include providing on-site management services, property sales, refinancing, preparing Property for sale or refinancing, modernization, fire or major damage restoration, rehabilitation, obtaining income tax, accounting or legal advice, representation before public agencies, advising on proposed new construction, debt collection, counseling, attending Owner's Association meetings or _____
      _____

      If Owner requests Broker to perform services not included in this Agreement, a fee shall be agreed upon before these services are performed.
   C. Broker may divide compensation, fees and charges due under this Agreement in any manner acceptable to Broker.
   D. Owner further agrees that:
      (1) Broker may receive and keep fees and charges from tenants for: **(i)** requesting an assignment of lease or sublease of the Property; **(ii)** processing credit applications; **(iii)** any returned checks and/or (☐ if checked) late payments; and **(iv)** any other services that are not in conflict with this Agreement.
      (2) Broker may perform any of Broker's duties, and obtain necessary products and services, through affiliated companies or organizations in which Broker may own an interest. Broker may receive fees, commissions and/or profits from these affiliated companies or organizations. Broker has an ownership interest in the following affiliated companies or organizations: _____

         Broker shall disclose to Owner any other such relationships as they occur. Broker shall not receive any fees, commissions or profits from unaffiliated companies or organizations in the performance of this Agreement, without prior disclosure to Owner.
      (3) Other: _____

7. **AGENCY RELATIONSHIPS:** Broker shall act, and Owner hereby consents to Broker acting, as dual agent for Owner and tenant(s) in any resulting transaction. If the Property includes residential property with one-to-four dwelling units and this Agreement permits a tenancy in excess of one year, Owner acknowledges receipt of the "Disclosure Regarding Agency Relationships" (C.A.R. Form AD). Owner understands that Broker may have or obtain property management agreements on other property, and that potential tenants may consider, make offers on, or lease through Broker, property the same as or similar to Owner's Property. Owner consents to Broker's representation of other owners' properties before, during and after the expiration of this Agreement.

8. **NOTICES:** Any written notice to Owner or Broker required under this Agreement shall be served by sending such notice by first class mail or other agreed-to delivery method to that party at the address below, or at any different address the parties may later designate for this purpose. Notice shall be deemed received three (3) calendar days after deposit into the United States mail OR ☐ _____

Owner's Initials (_____)(_____)
Broker's Initials (_____)(_____)

PMA REVISED 4/03 (PAGE 2 OF 3)

Reviewed by _____ Date _____

EQUAL HOUSING OPPORTUNITY

PROPERTY MANAGEMENT AGREEMENT (PMA PAGE 2 OF 3)

Owner Name: _____ Date: _____

9. **DISPUTE RESOLUTION**

    A. **MEDIATION:** Owner and Broker agree to mediate any dispute or claim arising between them out of this Agreement, or any resulting transaction before resorting to arbitration or court action, subject to paragraph 9B(2) below. Paragraph 9B(2) below applies whether or not the arbitration provision is initialed. Mediation fees, if any, shall be divided equally among the parties involved. If, for any dispute or claim to which this paragraph applies, any party commences an action based on a dispute or claim to which this paragraph applies, without first attempting to resolve the matter through mediation, or refuses to mediate after a request has been made, then that party shall not be entitled to recover attorney fees, even if they would otherwise be available to that party in any such action. THIS MEDIATION PROVISION APPLIES WHETHER OR NOT THE ARBITRATION PROVISION IS INITIALED.

    B. **ARBITRATION OF DISPUTES: (1) Owner and Broker agree that any dispute or claim in law or equity arising between them regarding the obligation to pay compensation under this agreement, which is not settled through mediation, shall be decided by neutral, binding arbitration, including and subject to paragraph 9B(2) below. The arbitrator shall be a retired judge or justice, or an attorney with at least 5 years of residential real estate law experience, unless the parties mutually agree to a different arbitrator, who shall render an award in accordance with substantive California Law. The parties shall have the right to discovery in accordance with Code of Civil Procedure § 1283.05. In all other respects, the arbitration shall be conducted in accordance with Title 9 of Part III of the California Code of Civil Procedure. Judgment upon the award of the arbitrator(s) may be entered in any court having jurisdiction. Interpretation of this agreement to arbitrate shall be governed by the Federal Arbitration Act.**
    (2) EXCLUSIONS FROM MEDIATION AND ARBITRATION: The following matters are excluded from mediation and arbitration hereunder: **(i)** a judicial or non-judicial foreclosure or other action or proceeding to enforce a deed of trust, mortgage, or installment land sale contract as defined in Civil Code § 2985; **(ii)** an unlawful detainer action; **(iii)** the filing or enforcement of a mechanic's lien; and **(iv)** any matter that is within the jurisdiction of a probate, small claims, or bankruptcy court. The filing of a court action to enable the recording of a notice of pending action, for order of attachment, receivership, injunction, or other provisional remedies, shall not constitute a waiver of the mediation and arbitration provisions.

    "NOTICE: BY INITIALING IN THE SPACE BELOW YOU ARE AGREEING TO HAVE ANY DISPUTE ARISING OUT OF THE MATTERS INCLUDED IN THE 'ARBITRATION OF DISPUTES' PROVISION DECIDED BY NEUTRAL ARBITRATION AS PROVIDED BY CALIFORNIA LAW AND YOU ARE GIVING UP ANY RIGHTS YOU MIGHT POSSESS TO HAVE THE DISPUTE LITIGATED IN A COURT OR JURY TRIAL. BY INITIALING IN THE SPACE BELOW YOU ARE GIVING UP YOUR JUDICIAL RIGHTS TO DISCOVERY AND APPEAL, UNLESS THOSE RIGHTS ARE SPECIFICALLY INCLUDED IN THE 'ARBITRATION OF DISPUTES' PROVISION. IF YOU REFUSE TO SUBMIT TO ARBITRATION AFTER AGREEING TO THIS PROVISION, YOU MAY BE COMPELLED TO ARBITRATE UNDER THE AUTHORITY OF THE CALIFORNIA CODE OF CIVIL PROCEDURE. YOUR AGREEMENT TO THIS ARBITRATION PROVISION IS VOLUNTARY."

    "WE HAVE READ AND UNDERSTAND THE FOREGOING AND AGREE TO SUBMIT DISPUTES ARISING OUT OF THE MATTERS INCLUDED IN THE 'ARBITRATION OF DISPUTES' PROVISION TO NEUTRAL ARBITRATION."

Owner's Initials _____ / _____	**Broker's Initials** _____ / _____

10. **EQUAL HOUSING OPPORTUNITY:** The Property is offered in compliance with federal, state and local anti-discrimination laws.

11. **ATTORNEY FEES:** In any action, proceeding or arbitration between Owner and Broker regarding the obligation to pay compensation under this Agreement, the prevailing Owner or Broker shall be entitled to reasonable attorney fees and costs from the non-prevailing Owner or Broker, except as provided in paragraph 9A.

12. **ADDITIONAL TERMS:** ☐ Keysafe/Lockbox Addendum (C.A.R. Form KLA); ☐ Lead-Based Paint and Lead-Based Paint Hazards Disclosure (C.A.R. Form FLD)
_____

13. **TIME OF ESSENCE; ENTIRE CONTRACT; CHANGES:** Time is of the essence. All understandings between the parties are incorporated in this Agreement. Its terms are intended by the parties as a final, complete and exclusive expression of their Agreement with respect to its subject matter, and may not be contradicted by evidence of any prior agreement or contemporaneous oral agreement. If any provision of this Agreement is held to be ineffective or invalid, the remaining provisions will nevertheless be given full force and effect. Neither this Agreement nor any provision in it may be extended, amended, modified, altered or changed except in writing. This Agreement and any supplement, addendum or modification, including any copy, may be signed in two or more counterparts, all of which shall constitute one and the same writing.

Owner warrants that Owner is the owner of the Property or has the authority to execute this contract. Owner acknowledges Owner has read, understands, accepts and has received a copy of the Agreement.

Owner _____ Date _____
Owner _____
     Print Name
Address _____ City _____ Social Security/Tax ID # (for tax reporting purposes
                                                State _____ Zip _____
Telephone _____ Fax _____ E-mail _____

Owner _____ Date _____
Owner _____
     Print Name
Address _____ City _____ Social Security/Tax ID # (for tax reporting purposes
                                                State _____ Zip _____
Telephone _____ Fax _____ E-mail _____

Real Estate Broker (Firm) _____ Date _____
By (Agent) _____
Address _____ City _____ State _____ Zip _____
Telephone _____ Fax _____ E-mail _____

SURE TRAC
The System for Success™
Published by the
California Association of REALTORS®

PMA REVISED 4/03 (PAGE 3 OF 3)

Reviewed by _____ Date _____

PROPERTY MANAGEMENT AGREEMENT (PMA PAGE 3 OF 3)

VIII. CHAPTER SUMMARY

A **less-than-freehold** (chattel) estate is a **personal property** estate in real property, with no ownership rights, such as a lease or leasehold. A **leasehold** is an exclusive right to occupy and use a property on a temporary basis. The types of leasehold estates include: 1) an **estate for years**; 2) an **estate from period-to-period**; 3) an **estate at will**; and 4) an **estate at sufferance**.

The minimum requirements of a lease (or rental agreement) can be remembered by the acronym **LAND**, for: 1) **length** of time or duration of lease; 2) **amount** of rent; 3) **names** of parties; and 4) **descriptions** of property.

Contract rent is actual rent, whereas **economic rent** is the amount a property might get if it were for lease in the current market. **Rent control** is a governmental regulation of the amount of rent a landlord may charge tenants.

A tenant may be required to pay a **security deposit** of two months' rent for an unfurnished property (three months for furnished) to cover any damage repair necessary when he or she moves out. A **statement of property** condition ensures that both parties are aware of the condition of the premises before the tenant moves in.

Without a clause disallowing it, a tenant may **assign** (transfer entire lease) or **sublease** (for less than the entire time or space) to another. If the tenant (**assignor**) signs a new valid lease with an **assignee**, the assignee is the tenant. An owner who is a landlord and a tenant (like a developer who rents out his apartment complex) has a **sandwich lease**. **Possessory rights** belong to the lessee, **reversionary rights** to the lessor.

A lease or rental agreement can be terminated by: 1) **expiration of the term**; 2) **lack of quiet possession**; 3) **repairs for habitability**; 4) **eviction** or **operation of law**; 5) **destruction of the premises**; 6) **breach of conditions**; or 7) **surrender/abandonment**. A landlord has a legal minimum obligation to maintain habitability, and a tenant has a legal obligation to care for the premises. Selling an apartment does not terminate a lease.

In the case of **eviction**, it is unlawful for a landlord to lock out tenants, take their property, remove doors, shut off utilities, or trespass. First, the landlord must give a **3-Day Notice to Pay or Quit** (eviction notice), then file an **unlawful detainer** with the court, who issues a **writ of possession**, directing the sheriff to remove the tenant in five days.

Sale-leasebacks, lease-purchase options, ground leases, graduated leases, gross leases, net leases, and **percentage leases** are all specialty leases.

A **property manager** is a licensed real estate person paid to oversee the proper management and operations of rental and commercial property. A **residential manager** is a tenant of the property, and as an **on-site manager**, does not need to have a real estate license. The **Institute of Real Estate Management (IREM)** offers the designation of **Certified Property Manager (CPM), Accredited Management Organization (AMO)**, and **Accredited Resident Manager (ARM)**.

CHAPTER 6

IX. TERMINOLOGY

A. Assignment
B. Contract Rent
C. Economic Rent
D. Estate at Sufferance
E. Estate at Will
F. Estate for Years
G. Estate From Period-to-Period
H. Eviction Process
I. Ground Lease

J. Landlord
K. Lease
L. Lease-Purchase Option
M. Lessee
N. Lessor
O. Net Lease
P. Percentage Lease
Q. Rent
R. Rent Control

S. Rental Agreement
T. Sale-Leaseback
U. Sandwich Lease
V. Sublease
W. Surrender
X. Tenant
Y. Unlawful Detainer or Notice to Quit
Z. Writ of Possession

1.____ A financial arrangement in which, at the time of sale, the seller retains occupancy by concurrently agreeing to lease the property back from the purchaser.
2.____ One who pays rent under a lease agreement.
3.____ Lease on the property, the rental payment for which is determined by a percentage of gross receipts from the business.
4.____ The amount of rent expected if the property were currently available for renting.
5.____ One who rents his or her property to another under a lease or rental agreement.
6.____ An owner who enters into a lease agreement with a tenant.
7.____ A lease requiring a lessee to pay charges against the property, such as taxes, insurance, and maintenance costs, in addition to rental payments.
8.____ The party who pays rent for a lease or rental agreement.
9.____ An agreement for the use of the land only.
10.____ The occupation of property by a tenant for an indefinite period, terminable by one or both parties (not common in California).
11.____ The general name of the process, from beginning to end, that serves to remove a person from the possession of real property.
12.____ A lease given by a lessee.
13.____ A leasehold interest that lies between the primary lease and the operating lease.
14.____ The concept of possessing an interest in real property by virtue of a contract for a fixed and definite period of time.
15.____ A transfer of a person's entire rights under a contract.
16.____ An estate contract between owner and tenant, setting forth conditions of a period-to-period tenancy.
17.____ A contract between an owner and tenant, setting forth conditions of tenancy for a fixed period of time.
18.____ An estate arising when the tenant wrongfully holds over after the expiration of the term.
19.____ A contract for the monthly rental of residential property.
20.____ Consideration paid for the occupancy and use of real property.
21.____ Rent paid under a lease; the actual rent as opposed to the market rental value of the property.
22.____ The name of the legal process to initiate the removal of a tenant.
23.____ The giving up of an estate, such as a lease. A contractual agreement, having the consent of both parties, such as lessor and lessee, as opposed to abandonment.
24.____ A legal maximum on rental price.
25.____ The court order physically expelling a tenant.
26.____ A lease that includes the right to purchase later.

X. CHAPTER QUIZ

1. An estate at will can be ended by:

   a. the buyer.

   b. the seller.

   c. the lessor or lessee.

   d. only the lessee.

2. If a real estate broker sells a property where the buyer will take possession prior to transferring title, the document he would have the buyer and seller execute is called:

   a. an option.

   b. an interim occupancy agreement.

   c. a quitclaim deed.

   d. a land contract of sale.

3. Which of the following is usually prorated in escrow?

   a. Purchase price

   b. Rents

   c. Documentary transfer tax

   d. City transfer tax

4. The maximum deposit that can be collected and held for an unfurnished apartment is:

   a. 2 months.

   b. 3 months.

   c. 1 month.

   d. 4 months.

5. The maximum deposit that can be collected and held for a furnished apartment is:

   a. 2 months.

   b. 3 months.

   c. 1 month.

   d. 4 months.

6. A tenant signed a written lease for two years on a home. The lease made no mention of assignments and/or subleasing. The tenant may:

   a. assign or sublease the home since the lease did not address those items.

   b. not assign or sublease the home to another tenant.

   c. only assign or sublease the home with the landlord's prior written approval.

   d. assign the lease to an assignee, but cannot sublease the home to another tenant.

7. Able holds a two-year lease with an option to purchase and assigns it to Baker. Which of the following is correct?

    a. Baker would not hold the option.
    b. Able would continue to hold the option.
    c. This is not permissible.
    d. Baker would now hold the option.

8. Which of the following is a benefit of a net lease?

    a. Lessee receives net income
    b. Lessee does not have to pay taxes, maintenance, and insurance
    c. Lessor receives net income
    d. Lessor pays taxes, maintenance, and insurance

9. A single line of retail stores located along a major transportation corridor in a commercially zoned area would be known as a:

    a. street commercial zone development.
    b. commercial cluster center.
    c. strip commercial development.
    d. commercial redevelopment zone.

10. Which of the following is often used when a commercial lease contains an escalator clause to adjust the rental amount periodically (usually annually) for inflation?

    a. Average commercial rental rates in an area
    b. The Consumer Price Index (CPI)
    c. General economic indicators averaged over the past 12 months
    d. Standard and Poor's statistics of 500 individuals

ANSWERS: 1. c; 2. b; 3. b; 4. a; 5. b; 6. a; 7. d; 8. c; 9. c; 10. b

CHAPTER 7
Escrows and Title Insurance

I. Escrows in General

The purpose of an escrow is to ensure that the terms of the transaction are met.

An *ESCROW* is created when a separate written agreement instructs a neutral third party to hold funds and only proceed when all the agreed to conditions have been performed. In California, an escrow is usually a requirement for the sale of a home or any other real estate. Although it is not always required by law, it is an indispensable process by which an independent third party handles the legal paperwork of a real estate sale. An escrow is not only an effective tool for handling normal real estate transactions like sales or refinancing, but is also for the sale of trust deeds, exchanges, and transfer of liquor licenses, businesses, securities, and court-required transfers. The legally required and recommended uses of an escrow are illustrated in **Figure 7-1**.

Figure 7-1

Highly Recommended	Required by Law
1. Sales of Real Property	1. Liquor License Transfers
2. Loans	2. Security Sales (Impound Accounts)
3. Exchanges	3. Court-Ordered Transfers (Probate Sales)

A. REQUIREMENTS FOR A VALID ESCROW

The Escrow Act is found in the Financial Code.

The three requirements for a valid escrow are:

1. Signed escrow instructions, forming a binding contract between two or more parties (usually a buyer and seller).

2. A neutral party, which is the escrow company, acting as a dual agent of the buyer and seller.

185

CHAPTER 7

CHAPTER OUTLINE

3. Conditional delivery of funds and documents when all the conditions in the escrow are met.

When escrow closes, dual agency (representing both parties, usually buyers and sellers, at once) changes to separate agency (handling each party's separate paperwork requirements).

An escrow may be initiated with a written contract, such as a purchase agreement, or through oral instructions. It is important to have agreed upon the written instructions drawn by the escrow company. Since this may be a new experience for most people, the escrow agent will, when necessary, explain each step to a buyer or seller. **A helpful escrow officer can point out possible problems, suggest alternatives, but cannot give legal advice.**

B. ESCROW OFFICER

An escrow holder can be: 1) a corporation, 2) an attorney, or 3) a real estate broker who acts as a real estate agent in the transaction.

A *NEUTRAL DEPOSITORY is an escrow business conducted by a licensed escrow holder.* An *ESCROW OFFICER, HOLDER, or AGENT, though not licensed by the state, is an employee of a escrow company who acts as the agent.* Escrow law is found in the California Financial Code. An independent escrow corporation must be licensed by the Department of Corporations to handle escrows. Corporations that are exempt from the escrow law but can handle escrows include: banks, savings banks, and title insurance companies, because they are under the supervision of their respective authorizing agencies.

There are two other types of escrow holders: attorneys who perform escrow duties as a part of their practice, and real estate brokers who handle their own escrows (must be the broker in the transaction). Regardless of the type of escrow company, each performs three essential duties (diagrammed in **Figure 7-2**).

Figure 7-2

Conditional	Confidentiality	Deposit Holder
Delivery of all funds and documents when the conditions of the escrow have been met.	All escrow instructions are confidential, and disclosure can be authorized only by the buyer or seller.	The escrow company can disburse funds and documents only when all conditions have been met and both parties have reached an agreement.

The complete sequence of events in an escrow is:

1. Preliminary title search and report
2. Lender's demand (amount owed, pay-off statement)
3. Request for new loan documents
4. Completion of conditions and depositing of funds
5. Adjustments and prorations

6. Transfer of existing fire policies or creation of new ones
7. Recording and issuing of title policy
8. Disbursement of funds
9. Escrow statement sent to each party

After these steps have been completed and all other escrow conditions have been met, the closing of an escrow is usually routine (see **Figure 7-3**). The escrow agent is authorized to call for a buyer's documents and funds.

C. REAL ESTATE BROKERS CAN CONDUCT ESCROWS

As a licensed broker, you can handle an escrow for a fee if you are acting as a broker in that real estate transaction.

This is your personal right, and you shall not delegate any duties other than escrow duties normally performed under the direct supervision of the broker.

All written escrow instructions executed by a buyer or seller must contain a statement, in not less than 10-point type, that includes the licensee's name and the fact that he or she is licensed by the Department of Real Estate.

If a problem arose during escrow, a broker would file an interpleader action.

II. How Escrows Work

Escrow amendments must be signed by the parties to change the escrow.

A. ESCROW RULES

Once the escrow instructions have been drawn from the original contract (purchase agreement) and signed by each party, neither party may change the escrow instructions without the written agreement of the other. (All time frames commence from the time the contract became binding; usually the purchase agreement has a provision for escrow to acknowledge receipt of this document.) The escrow is complete when: 1) all conditions of the escrow have been met; 2) all conditions of the parties have been met; and 3) the parties have received an accounting of the procedure. If both parties mutually agree to change the instructions, the change can be put into effect at any time. However, if a dispute should arise, the escrow company will not proceed until both parties come to terms. If the parties cannot agree to terms, an escrow company will bring an interpleader action (court action) to determine where the money or consideration goes. **Figure 7-4** illustrates the three ways in which an escrow can be terminated.

If there is a disagreement between buyer and seller during escrow, the escrow officer may disburse funds as a result of a judgment between buyer and seller, if the parties to the escrow agree, and if a binding arbitrator settles the matter.

B. WHO SELECTS THE ESCROW COMPANY?

Selection of an escrow company and an escrow officer are part of the negotiation between buyer and seller. Like any other item in a real estate transaction, it is part of the negotiated agreement. Either one of the parties may choose the escrow company, which should be

Figure 7-3

California Customs (North vs. South) for Escrow Services and Title Insurance

When are signed escrow instructions delivered?

Customarily, in Southern California, the (bilateral) escrow instructions are signed by both the buyer and seller just after the **start of escrow**.

Customarily, in Northern California, the (unilateral) escrow instructions are given to the escrow officer just before the **close of escrow**.

Who performs the escrow services?

Escrow services in Southern California are traditionally performed by **independent escrow companies (corporations)** or **financial institutions**.

Escrow services in Northern California are traditionally performed by **title insurance companies**.

Who pays the escrow fees?

Escrow service fees in Southern California are usually **split 50-50 between the buyer and the seller**.

Escrow service fees in Northern California are usually **paid for by the buyer**.

Who traditionally pays title insurance fees?

Customarily in Southern California, the **seller pays for the California Land Title Association (CLTA) policy (standard policy)**.

Customarily in Northern California, the **buyer pays for the California Land Title Association (CLTA) policy (standard policy)**.

In both the North and the South, the buyers pay for any coverage **above** the California Land Title Insurance (CLTA) policy.

explained when completing the purchase agreement. The salesperson may certainly make suggestions as to a preferred escrow company for both the buyer and seller. When the escrow company is named in the listing agreement, the real estate listing agent cannot change the escrow company without the consent of the seller or the seller's agent. If the buyer and seller each desire a different escrow company, then the salesperson must work for a mutual agreement before there can be an offer and acceptance of the sale.

Figure 7-4

It is imperative that you, as the salesperson, disclose in writing any shared interest that you or your broker have with the selected escrow company. This disclosure must be made either at the time of listing or whenever the escrow company is selected. Disciplinary action will be taken against any salesperson or broker who, in bad faith and against the wishes of the buyer and seller, attempts to force the use of a particular escrow company.

A real estate licensee is prohibited by law from receiving any "kickback" for solicitation of escrow business.

C. ESCROW INSTRUCTIONS

ESCROW INSTRUCTIONS are formal instructions drawn from the information contained in the original agreement, usually the signed purchase agreement. When these instructions are drawn and signed, they become an enforceable contract binding on all parties.

Since the escrow instructions supplement the original contract, both are interpreted together whenever possible. If a conflict should arise between the content of the instructions and the original contract, the instructions will usually prevail. **Therefore, all parties to the escrow should read the escrow instructions very carefully, and sign them only after every detail is absolutely correct and the terms meet with their approval.**

D. FINANCING IS AN IMPORTANT ASPECT OF THE ESCROW

Most escrows for the sale of a home include obtaining a new loan and the payoff or assumption of an old loan. The brokers and their salespeople can be helpful to the buyer obtaining new financing by providing the necessary loan documentation to the escrow company in a timely manner. Keeping the buyer and seller informed about the progress of the financing and escrow helps to maintain good client-agent communication and trust.

The *PAYOFF DEMAND STATEMENT is a formal demand statement from the lender that details the amounts owed, as calculated by the lender, for the purpose of **paying off the loan in full**.* The failure to obtain a payoff or beneficiary statement in a timely manner could hold up the escrow. A payoff demand statement is different from a beneficiary's statement. A *BENIFICIARY'S (LENDER'S) STATEMENT is a demand statement by a lender, under a deed of trust, that provides information, such as the unpaid balance, monthly payment, and interest rate, necessary **if the loan is to be assumed**.* The lender may charge up to $100 for furnishing the payoff or beneficiary statement, except when the loan is insured by the FHA or guaranteed by the VA.

E. ESCROW EXAMPLE

To help illustrate the closing statements used in a simple escrow, we'll assume the following facts.

Figure 7-5 illustrates the buyer's escrow statement, and **Figure 7-6** illustrates the seller's statement. These statements include many other miscellaneous costs that are a usual part of the escrow.

An Escrow Example

BUYER	John Buyer and Jane Buyer	
SELLER	John Seller and Jane Seller	
SALES PRICE		$800,000
1ST TRUST DEED		$640,000
2ND TRUST DEED		$80,000
DOWN PAYMENT		$80,000
BROKER	J.Q. Smart	$48,000
EXISTING LIENS		
1) 1ST TRUST DEED		$290,000
2) STREET ASSESSMENT BOND		$1,300
CLTA TITLE POLICY PAID BY SELLER		$2,165
Date of Closing is June 1, 2020		

(Next Page)

F. CLOSING DATE IS THE DATE OF RECORDATION

The *CLOSING DATE is the date that the documents are recorded*. Escrow usually approximates the closing date, but the actual date is when all the conditions of the escrow have been completed, the buyer's remaining money (cashier's checks) is received, and when all the documents are recorded. Most escrows are for handling the paperwork of property sale and loan financing, but escrows can be for almost any purpose.

In closing statements, the buyer's and seller's totals are usually different. However, each closing statement must balance within itself. In the buyer's closing statement, the purchase price is debited.

III. Proration

Property taxes, interest, fire insurance, and rents are prorated. Title insurance would NOT be prorated in escrow.

PRORATION is the process of proportionately dividing expenses or income to the precise date that escrow closes, or any other date previously agreed upon. It enables the buyer and seller to pay or receive their proportionate share of expenses or income. Items that are commonly prorated include:

1. property taxes,
2. fire insurance,
3. interest, and
4. rents.

Figure 7-5

601 East Glenoaks Blvd. Suite 210
Glendale, CA 91207
P.O. Box 433 Glendale, CA 91209-0433
Tel: (818) 500-1633
Fax: (818) 500-0862

BUYER FINAL SETTLEMENT STATEMENT

PROPERTY: 123 Purchase Lane   CLOSING DATE: 06/01/20
           Glendale, CA   ESCROW NO.:   1-10533
BUYER: John Buyer and Jane Buyer

	DEBITS	CREDITS
FINANCIAL		
Total Consideration	$ 800,000.00	$
Cash Deposit		5,000.00
Cash Deposit		86,000.00
New 1st Trust Deed		640,000.00
New 2nd Trust Deed		80,000.00
PRORATIONS AND ADJUSTMENTS		
Taxes at 4000.00/6 mo. from 06/01/20 to 07/01/20	666.67	
OTHER DISBURSEMENTS		
Property Insurance, Inc. for Fire Insurance	1,000.00	
TITLE CHARGES TO AMERICAN COAST TITLE		
Title Policy Premium	628.50	
Sub Escrow Fee	75.00	
Recording Grant Deed	8.00	
Recording Trust Deed(s)	20.00	
Title Endorsement Fee(s)	50.00	
ESCROW CHARGES TO COLONIAL ESCROW, INC.		
Escrow Fee	900.00	
Messenger Fee	50.00	
Loan Tie In Fee	125.00	
NEW 1ST TRUST DEED TO GET SMART SAVINGS AND LOAN		
Loan Fees	6,400.00	
Credit Report	45.00	
Appraisal	350.00	
Tax Service	89.00	
Document Fee	250.00	
Interest at 7.5000% from 05/31/20 to 06/01/20	131.51	
REFUND		211.32
TOTALS	811,000.00	811,000.00

SAVE FOR INCOME TAX PURPOSES

Figure 7-6

601 East Glenoaks Blvd. Suite 210
Glendale, CA 91207
P.O. Box 433 Glendale, CA 91209-0433
Tel: (818) 500-1633
Fax: (818) 500-0862

SELLER FINAL SETTLEMENT STATEMENT

PROPERTY: 123 Purchase Lane
           Glendale, CA

CLOSING DATE: 06/01/20
ESCROW NO.: 1-10533

SELLER: John Seller and Jane Seller

	DEBITS	CREDITS
FINANCIAL		
Total Consideration	$	$ 800,000.00
New 2nd Trust Deed	80,000.00	
PRORATIONS AND ADJUSTMENTS		
Taxes at 4000.00/6 mo. from 06/01/20 to 07/01/20		666.67
PAYOFF CHARGES TO MOST SUPERIOR		
SAVINGS AND LOAN		
Principal Balance	490,000.00	
Interest on Principal Balance at 10.0000% from 05/01/20 to 06/01/20	4,161.64	
Forwarding Fee	50.00	
Reconveyance Fee	60.00	
OTHER DISBURSEMENTS		
Pest Control, Inc. for Termite Report/Work	1,000.00	
Home Warranty, Inc. for Home Protection Policy	400.00	
COMMISSION		
Listing Broker: J. Q. Smart	48,000.00	
TITLE CHARGES TO AMERICAN COAST		
TITLE		
Title Policy Premium	2,165.00	
Sub Escrow Fee	75.00	
Documentary Transfer Tax	880.00	
Recording Reconveyance	5.00	
Street Assessment Bond	1,300.00	
ESCROW CHARGES TO COLONIAL ESCROW, INC.		
Escrow Fee	900.00	
Processing Demands	35.00	
Document Fee	85.00	
NET PROCEEDS	171,550.03	
TOTALS	800,666.67	800,666.67

SAVE FOR INCOME TAX PURPOSES

193

Proration of prepaid taxes is a credit to the seller.

A. 30 DAYS IS THE BASIS FOR PRORATION

All escrow companies use 30 days as a base month. For example, if an escrow closes on the 10th day of the month, all prepaid rents for that month would constitute 9/30 of the rent left for the seller, and 21/30 of the rent would go to the buyer. If the rent is $2,000, the seller's portion would be 9/30 of $2,000, or $600, and the buyer's portion would be 21/30 of $2,000, or $1,400. (Rents belong to the buyer as of the closing date.)

Property tax prorations are based on the amount of tax the seller is paying. Escrow uses the old assessed valuation when prorating.

The date used in calculating proration is usually assumed to be the date of closing, but any date may be used if agreed upon by all parties. This is the case when the possession date differs from the closing date.

Taxes are prorated either from July 1, which marks the beginning of the county fiscal year, or January 1, the middle of the fiscal year. If the property taxes on a home, amounting to $2,400 per year, have been paid up to July 1, what is the proration if escrow is to be closed on June 1? In this case, the buyer would reimburse the seller for one month's taxes (or $2,400 divided by twelve months, equaling $200 per month). The seller would then be credited for the $200 in property taxes that he or she had already paid in advance.

Escrow Company Reports Information to the I.R.S.

All real estate transactions must be reported to the Internal Revenue Service. This is done by the escrow company or whoever handles the closing. A 1099 Form is required for any sale or exchange.

Escrow reports real estate transactions to the I.R.S. using the seller's social security number.

IV. Termites and Other Problems

A. STRUCTURAL PEST CONTROL CERTIFICATION REPORT *(Report and Clearance)*

Pest control inspection reports are not required by law in California, but many lenders will require this report. A *STRUCTURAL PEST CONTROL CERTIFICATION REPORT is a written report given by a licensed pest control company identifying any wood-destroying pests or conditions likely to cause pest infestation. The report states the condition and correction cost of any pest, dry rot, excessive moisture, earth-wood contacts, or fungus damage in accessible areas of a structure.* Who pays for the (1) pest control inspection report and (2) any required or recommended repair work is up to the buyer and seller, although they are usually paid for by the seller. There may sometimes be a local custom that dictates who will pay, while in other instances financial institutions or financing agencies will decide which one of the parties will pay.

The escrow officer accepts and holds the pest control report and awaits further instructions from both parties.

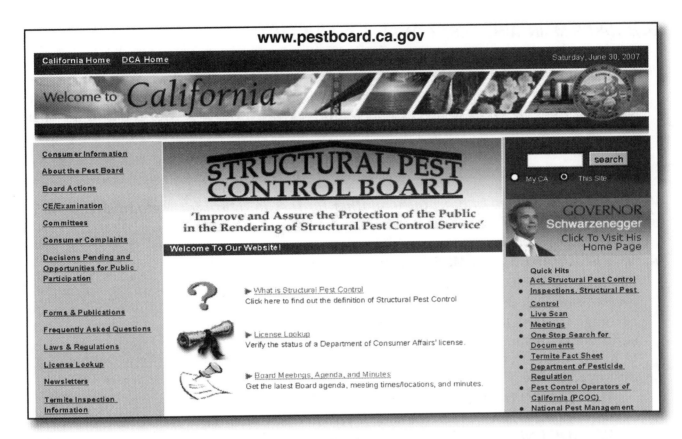

If there is Section I infestation damage (required work), it is usually paid for by the seller. If there is only Section II potential for infestation damage (recommended work), the extent of repairs is up to the parties.

Most lenders require a pest control inspection report before making a loan, and every VA and FHA loan application requires an inspection report. The usual cost for an inspection report is about $65. The cost, in some areas, may be as high as $175 to $195.

If escrow holds two pest control reports, escrow will notify the broker and get instructions from both buyer and seller.

The question of which party pays for any necessary repairs to obtain a "Notice of Work Completed" report is also a matter of local custom. In most areas the seller usually pays. However, FHA and VA termite certificates and repairs are always paid for by the seller. The seller is allowed to include a clause stating what the maximum cost of repairs will be as a condition of the sale.

The best time for a seller to have a termite report issued is before putting the home on the market.

When a structural pest control company is hired, it is accountable to both the buyer and seller, regardless of who pays for the inspection. It is required to furnish the person who ordered the inspection with a copy of the report within ten business days. For a few dollars, any person may request certified copies of any certificate inspection report, filed during the preceding two years, from the State Structural Pest Control Board.

B. BROKER MAINTAINS PEST CONTROL DOCUMENTATION

The Civil Code requires that the broker shall deliver a copy of the Structural Pest Control Certification Report and Notice of Work Completed to the buyer, if such a report is a condition of the purchase agreement or is a requirement imposed as a condition of financing. If more than one broker is acting as an agent in the transaction, the broker who obtained the offer (selling broker) made by the buyer shall deliver the required documents to the buyer.

V. Fire Insurance

When one party agrees to indemnify another for loss in return for periodic premium payments, it is called "insurance."

A. FIRE INSURANCE . . . A MUST!

Fire insurance is very inexpensive compared to the possible dollar loss due to fire, and all property owners should have this financial protection. A lending institution will require coverage for the amount of its loan. However, it is in the owner's best interest to carry sufficient fire insurance to replace the structure if it is totally destroyed. It is only necessary to insure the current replacement value of the dwelling, since the land itself cannot be destroyed by fire.

The **CALIFORNIA STANDARD FORM FIRE INSURANCE POLICY** *insures the dwelling against (1) fire and (2) lightning.* If you so desire, you may procure an **EXTENDED COVERAGE ENDORSEMENT** *that will insure you against the additional perils of windstorm, explosion, hail, aircraft, smoke, riot, and vehicles not attributed to a strike or civil commotion.* Other types of endorsements may insure you against vandalism, malicious mischief, floods, and other damage. Coverage depends on your needs and the perils common to your area.

B. FIRE INSURANCE PRORATION

Fire insurance coverage protects an owner of real property. When filing a claim, he or she will neither gain nor lose.

When purchasing property, a buyer usually obtains a new policy. **If the seller/owner has filed an insurance claim during the previous three years, he or she must disclose this to the buyer in writing.** This may cause some hardship to the new owner/buyer in obtaining his or her own insurance. Cancellation of the seller's insurance must be initiated by the seller after close of escrow, with any unused premium to be prorated and reimbursed to the seller. It is always the buyer's choice to select his or her own house insurance. Condo insurance is chosen by the association.

An insurance company may short-rate fire insurance. A *SHORT RATE CANCELLATION FEE is a fee/penalty charged to the seller who cancels the policy before it expires.* The money returned is the unused premium minus administrative expenses.

C. COINSURANCE CLAUSE

A *COINSURANCE CLAUSE is a provision in an insurance policy requiring a property owner to carry separate insurance up to an amount stated in the policy to qualify for full coverage. That amount is usually 80% of the value of the dwelling in order to receive full insurance benefits.* The percentage paid represents the actual percentage of insurance carried (up to 80%), which is then divided by the required 80% (see **Figure 7-7**).

Figure 7-7

HOW NONRESIDENTIAL COINSURANCE WORKS

1. Actual value of your improvements	=	$200,000
2. 80% coinsurance clause requires you to carry fire insurance on 80% of the actual value of the dwelling. (80% of $200,000)	=	$160,000
3. Amount of fire insurance carried (Face amount on your policy)	=	**$120,000**
4. Ratio of loss payment $120,000 (actual amount) $160,000 (required amount)	=	75%
5. If your actual fire loss is	=	$80,000
6. Your insurance would pay 75% of actual loss (75% of $80,000)	=	$60,000
7. Your out-of-pocket cost would be the loss less insurance payments ($80,000 - $60,000)	=	**$20,000**

VI. Title Insurance

A. CHAIN OF TITLE (Recorded Public History)

Every recorded change of ownership and/or claim of ownership on a property is in the abstract of title.

If one person sells a property to another person, *a recorded public history of a specific property called the CHAIN OF TITLE* is compiled. These public records include files at the county recorder's office, various tax agencies, federal court clerk, and the Secretary of State. *All such information about people and their real property is stored in computers (within a grantor-grantee index) and is referred to as a TITLE PLANT.*

A title insurance company is primarily concerned with a search of the public records, which includes: the Federal Court Clerk, the County Clerk's Office, the County Recorder's Office, and other sources. This search establishes what is called the "chain of title."

B. TITLE INSURANCE (Has Four Functions)

Title insurance companies are regulated by the California Insurance Commissioner. Fee schedules must be available to the general public upon request. To guarantee solvency, each title insurance company must set aside reserves.

TITLE INSURANCE insures a lender (and property owner for an additional fee) against losses that result from imperfections in title. Title insurance companies examine the records documenting chain of title, review any risks that might not be found in the public records, interpret legality, help the seller correct any defects, and insure marketable title to the property. Title insurance is only paid once, unlike auto or fire insurance, which must be paid annually. **Figure 7-8** emphasizes the four most important functions of title insurance.

Figure 7-8

C. PRELIMINARY TITLE REPORT (Ordered First)

The first step in a title search is for the escrow officer to order the preliminary title report. After the buyer or borrower completes a **Statement of Information**, a title search can begin (see **Figure 7-9**). A *PRELIMINARY TITLE REPORT is a report showing the condition of title before a sale or loan transaction.* After completion of the transaction, a title insurance policy is issued. The preliminary title report consists of the following items:

1. The name of the owner and a description of the property.
2. A list of any outstanding taxes, bonds, or other assessments.
3. The identity of any covenants, conditions or restrictions.
4. Any recorded liens or other encumbrances must be eliminated before any loan is made.

VII. Types of Title Insurance Policies

A. CALIFORNIA LAND TITLE ASSOCIATION (CLTA)
(Standard Coverage Policy)

In California, the standard title insurance policy is the CLTA. The *CALIFORNIA LAND TITLE ASSOCIATION (CLTA) policy is the basic title insurance policy.* It may be issued to insure a lender only, or an owner only, or it may insure both the lender and the owner (a joint-protection standard coverage policy). This standard policy insures the lender only, unless the owner requests and pays for owner coverage.

Figure 7-10 is a sample of a standard CLTA policy form.

The standard coverage CLTA title insurance policy is most often used.

Besides insuring against all items of record, the CLTA policy offers protection against many off-record risks. Some of these off-record risks include forgeries, acts of minors and incompetents, acts of an agent whose authority has terminated, invalid deed delivery, unrecorded federal estate tax liens, undisclosed rights of husband and wife when the chain of title states "unmarried," and the expenses (including attorneys' fees) incurred in defending title.

Figure 7-9

NORTH AMERICAN TITLE COMPANY

Complete, Sign and Return

STATEMENT OF INFORMATION

Order No. 5278

To expedite the completion of your escrow, please fill out and return this form at your earliest convenience. This information is for confidential use by North American Title Company in searching the land records in connection with the order number shown above. Further explanation of the need for this information is printed on the reverse side of this form.

Please Print all information

PERSONAL IDENTIFICATION

Name _____

FIRST NAME   FULL MIDDLE NAME—IF NONE, INDICATE   LAST NAME

Year of Birth _____ Birthplace _____ Social Security No. _____

Full name of Wife Husband _____

FIRST NAME   FULL MIDDLE NAME—IF NONE, INDICATE   LAST NAME

Year of Birth _____ Birthplace _____ Social Security No. _____

We were married on _____ at _____

DATE   CITY AND STATE

Wife's maiden name _____

RESIDENCES DURING PAST 10 YEARS

NUMBER AND STREET	CITY	FROM (DATE)	TO (DATE)
NUMBER AND STREET	CITY	FROM (DATE)	TO (DATE)
NUMBER AND STREET	CITY	FROM (DATE)	TO (DATE)

(If more space is needed, use reverse side of form)

OCCUPATIONS DURING PAST 10 YEARS

Husband's

OCCUPATION	FIRM NAME	STREET AND CITY	FROM (DATE) TO (DATE)
OCCUPATION	FIRM NAME	STREET AND CITY	FROM (DATE) TO (DATE)
OCCUPATION	FIRM NAME	STREET AND CITY	FROM (DATE) TO (DATE)

Wife's

OCCUPATION	FIRM NAME	STREET AND CITY	FROM (DATE) TO (DATE)
OCCUPATION	FIRM NAME	STREET AND CITY	FROM (DATE) TO (DATE)

(If more space is needed, use reverse side of form)

FORMER MARRIAGE(S), IF ANY

If no former marriages, write "None" _____ Otherwise, please complete the following:

Name of former wife _____

Deceased ☐   Divorced ☐   When _____ Where _____

Name of former husband _____

Deceased ☐   Divorced ☐   When _____ Where _____

(If more space is needed, use reverse side of form)

Buyer intends to reside on the property in this transaction   Yes ☐   No ☐

THIS PORTION IS TO BE COMPLETED BY THE SELLER

The Street Address of the property in this transaction is _____ (LEAVE BLANK IF NONE)

The land is unimproved ☐ or improved with a structure of the following type;

IMPROVEMENTS: ☐ SINGLE RESIDENCE OR 1–4 FAMILY   ☐ MULTIPLE RESIDENCE   ☐ COMMERCIAL

OCCUPIED BY: ☐ OWNER   ☐ LESSEE   ☐ TENANTS

ANY PORTION OF NEW LOAN FUNDS TO BE USED FOR CONSTRUCTION

IMPROVEMENTS, REMODELING OR REPAIRS TO THIS PROPERTY HAVE BEEN MADE WITHIN THE PAST SIX MONTHS ☐ YES ☐ NO

IF YES,

HAVE ALL COSTS FOR LABOR AND MATERIALS ARISING IN CONNECTION THEREWITH BEEN PAID IN FULL? ☐ YES ☐ NO

The undersigned declare, under penalty of perjury, that the foregoing is true and correct.

DATE _____

HOME PHONE _____ BUSINESS PHONE _____

(IF MARRIED, BOTH HUSBAND AND WIFE SHOULD SIGN)

NAT 44 (5/88)

www.clta.org

California Land Title Association

CLTA

PO Box 13968, Sacramento CA 95853-3968
1215 K Street, #1816, Sacramento CA 95814-3905
tel: 916-444-2647 * fax: 916-444-2851
web: www.clta.org * email: mail.clta.org

SINCE 1907

Insuring the American Dream

| About CLTA |
| Calendar of Events |
| Consumer Information |
| Directory of Members |
| Education |
| E-Commerce |
| Industry Links |
| Industry News |
| Legal Developments |
| Legislative |
| Legislative Bill Tracking |
| Media Kit |

Recent News

February 21, 2007 - <u>Office of Administrative Law Rejects Department of Insurance Regulations</u> (News Express) California Land Title Association (CLTA) Executive Vice President Craig Page today released the following statement upon notification that the Office of Administrative Law rejected rate setting regulations submitted by the California Department of Insurance. ...

January 8, 2007 - <u>California Department of Insurance Submits Proposed Regulations to the Office of Administrative Law</u> *(News Express)* The CLTA has confirmed with the California Office of Administrative Law that the Department of Insurance submitted their proposed regulations on Friday, January 5, 2007.

It is very important to note those items NOT included in the standard policy. The items not included are:

1. Easements, encumbrances, and liens that are not shown by the public record. (CLTA, no – ALTA, yes)

2. Rights or claims of persons in physical possession of the land. (CLTA, no – ALTA, yes)

3. Unrecorded claims not shown by the public record that could be ascertained by physical inspection or correct survey. ((CLTA, no – ALTA, yes)

4. Mining claims, reservations in patents, water rights, and government actions, such as zoning ordinances. (CLTA, no – ALTA, yes)

Standard title insurance (CLTA) does NOT insure against undisclosed liens placed on a property by a grantor (although it is warranted in a grant deed). NO title insurance policy covers everything.

A warranty found in a grant deed, which is not covered by a CLTA standard coverage title policy, is there are no undisclosed encumbrances on the property.

B. AMERICAN LAND TITLE ASSOCIATION (ALTA)
(Extended Coverage Policy - Survey Included)

The *AMERICAN LAND TITLE ASSOCIATION (ALTA) policy is an extended coverage policy that insures against many exclusions of the standard coverage (CLTA) policy.* The ALTA policy (which includes a competent survey or physical inspection) is usually required by California lenders and by out-of-state lenders who are not able to make a personal physical inspection of the property.

Figure 7-10

POLICY OF TITLE INSURANCE

ISSUED BY

NORTH AMERICAN TITLE INSURANCE COMPANY

SUBJECT TO THE EXCLUSIONS FROM COVERAGE, THE EXCEPTIONS FROM COVERAGE CONTAINED IN SCHEDULE B AND THE CONDITIONS AND STIPULATIONS, NORTH AMERICAN TITLE INSURANCE COMPANY, a California corporation, herein called the Company, insures, as of Date of Policy shown in Schedule A, against loss or damage, not exceeding the Amount of Insurance stated in Schedule A, sustained or incurred by the insured by reason of:

1. Title to the estate or interest described in Schedule A being vested otherwise than as stated therein;
2. Any defect in or lien or encumbrance on such title;
3. Unmarketability of the title;
4. Lack of a right of access to and from the land;
5. The invalidity or unenforceability of the lien of the insured mortgage upon the title;
6. The priority of any lien or encumbrance over the lien of the insured mortgage;
7. Lack of priority of the lien of the insured mortgage over any statutory lien for services, labor or material:
    (a) arising from an improvement or work related to the land which is contracted for or commenced prior to Date of Policy; or
    (b) arising from an improvement or work related to the land which is contracted for or commenced subsequent to Date of Policy and which is financed in whole or in part by proceeds of the indebtedness secured by the insured mortgage which at Date of Policy the insured has advanced or is obligated to advance.
8. Any assessments for street improvements under construction or completed at Date of Policy which now have gained or hereafter may gain priority over the insured mortgage; or
9. The invalidity or unenforceability of any assignment of the insured mortgage, provided the assignment is shown in Schedule A, or the failure of the assignment shown in Schedule A to vest title to the insured mortgage in the named insured assignee free and clear of all liens.

The Company will also pay the costs, attorneys' fees and expenses incurred in defense of the title or the lien of the insured mortgage, as insured, but only to the extent provided in the Conditions and Stipulations.

NORTH AMERICAN TITLE INSURANCE COMPANY

BY _Gerald B. Beery_ PRESIDENT

ATTEST _____ SECRETARY

NORTH AMERICAN TITLE INSURANCE COMPANY
INCORPORATED
— • —
SEPT 18, 1958
★ CALIFORNIA ★

SCHEDULE A

POLICY NO. 116823   FILE NO.: 14-15360-63

AMOUNT OF INSURANCE: $296,800.00   PREMIUM: $1,161.75

DATE OF POLICY: JULY 22, 1992 AT 8:00 A.M.

1. **NAME OF INSURED:**

SYCAMORE FINANCIAL GROUP, INC., A CALIFORNIA CORPORATION

2. **THE ESTATE OR INTEREST IN THE LAND WHICH IS ENCUMBERED BY THE INSURED MORTGAGE IS:**

A CONDOMINIUM, AS DEFINED IN SECTION 783 OF THE CALIFORNIA CIVIL CODE, IN FEE

3. **TITLE TO THE ESTATE OR INTEREST IN THE LAND IS VESTED IN:**

WALTER ROY HUBER AND DEBBIE R. HUBER, HUSBAND AND WIFE AS COMMUNITY PROPERTY

4. **THE INSURED MORTGAGE AND ASSIGNMENTS THEREOF, IF ANY, ARE DESCRIBED AS FOLLOWS:**

A DEED OF TRUST TO SECURE AN INDEBTEDNESS IN THE AMOUNT SHOWN BELOW AND ANY OTHER OBLIGATIONS SECURED THEREBY:

RECORDED: JULY 22, 1992 AS INSTRUMENT NO. 92-1329290 OF OFFICIAL RECORDS
AMOUNT: $296,800.00
DATED: JULY 13, 1992
TRUSTOR: WALTER ROY HUBER AND DEBBIE R. HUBER, HUSBAND AND WIFE AS COMMUNITY PROPERTY
TRUSTEE: UTICA ESCROW INC., A CALIFORNIA CORPORATION
BENEFICIARY: SYCAMORE FINANCIAL GROUP, INC., A CALIFORNIA CORPORATION

5. **THE LAND REFERRED TO IN THIS POLICY IS DESCRIBED AS FOLLOWS:**

PARCEL 1:

THAT PORTION OF PARCEL A OF PARCEL MAP L.A. NO. 3111, IN THE CITY OF LOS ANGELES, COUNTY OF LOS ANGELES, STATE OF CALIFORNIA, AS PER MAP FILED IN BOOK 72 PAGE 26 OF PARCEL MAPS, IN THE OFFICE OF THE COUNTY RECORDER OF SAID COUNTY, SHOWN AND DEFINED AS UNIT 1 AND AIR SPACE A ON THE CONDOMINIUM PLAN, RECORDED DECEMBER 17, 1976 AS INSTRUMENT NO. 5334, OF OFFICIAL RECORDS OF SAID COUNTY.

PARCEL 2:

AN UNDIVIDED 1/4 INTEREST IN AND TO PARCEL A OF SAID PARCEL MAP LOS ANGELES NO. 3111.

EXCEPT THEREFROM THOSE PORTIONS SHOWN AND DEFINED AS UNITS 1 TO 4 AND AIR SPACE A AND B ON SAID CONDOMINIUM PLAN.

EXCLUSIONS FROM COVERAGE

The following matters are expressly excluded from the coverage of this policy and the Company will not pay loss or damage, costs, attorneys' fees or expenses which arise by reason of:

1. (a) Any law, ordinance or governmental regulation (including but not limited to building and zoning laws, ordinances, or regulations) restricting, regulating, prohibiting or relating to (i) the occupancy, use, or enjoyment of the land; (ii) the character, dimensions or location of any improvement now or hereafter erected on the land; (iii) a separation in ownership or a change in the dimensions or area of the land or any parcel of which the land is or was a part; or (iv) environmental protection, or the effect of any violation of these laws, ordinances or governmental regulations, except to the extent that a notice of the enforcement thereof or a notice of a defect, lien or encumbrance resulting from a violation or alleged violation affecting the land has been recorded in the public records at Date of Policy.

   (b) Any governmental police power not excluded by (a) above, except to the extent that a notice of the exercise thereof or a notice of a defect, lien or encumbrance resulting from a violation or alleged violation affecting the land has been recorded in the public records at Date of Policy.

2. Rights of eminent domain unless notice of the exercise thereof has been recorded in the public records at Date of Policy, but not excluding from coverage any taking which has occurred prior to Date of Policy which would be binding on the rights of a purchaser for value without knowledge.

3. Defects, liens, encumbrances, adverse claims or other matters:

   (a) created, suffered, assumed or agreed to by the insured claimant;

   (b) not known to the Company, not recorded in the public records at Date of Policy, but known to the insured claimant and not disclosed in writing to the Company by the insured claimant prior to the date the insured claimant became an insured under this policy;

   (c) resulting in no loss or damage to the insured claimant;

   (d) attaching or created subsequent to Date of Policy (except to the extent that this policy insures the priority of the lien of the insured mortgage over any statutory lien for services, labor or material or the extent insurance is afforded herein as to assessments for street improvements under construction or completed at Date of Policy); or

   (e) resulting in loss or damage which would not have been sustained if the insured claimant had paid value for the insured mortgage.

4. Unenforceability of the lien of the insured mortgage because of the inability or failure of the insured at Date of Policy, or the inability or failure of any subsequent owner of the indebtedness, to comply with applicable doing business laws of the state in which the land is situated.

5. Invalidity or unenforceability of the lien of the insured mortgage, or claim thereof, which arises out of the transaction evidenced by the insured mortgage and is based upon usury or any consumer credit protection or truth in lending law.

6. Any statutory lien for services, labor or materials (or the claim of priority of any statutory lien for services, labor or materials over the lien of the insured mortgage) arising from an improvement or work related to the land which is contracted for and commenced subsequent to Date of Policy and is not financed in whole or in part by proceeds of the indebtedness secured by the insured mortgage which at Date of Policy the insured has advanced or is obligated to advance.

7. Any claim, which arises out of the transaction creating the interest of the mortgagee insured by this policy, by reason of the operation of federal bankruptcy, state insolvency, or similar creditors' rights laws.

CONDITIONS AND STIPULATIONS

1. DEFINITION OF TERMS.

The following terms when used in this policy mean:

(a) "insured": the insured named in Schedule A. The term "insured" also includes

(i) the owner of the indebtedness secured by the insured mortgage and each successor in ownership of the indebtedness except a successor who is an obligor under the provisions of Section 12(c) of these Conditions and Stipulations (reserving, however, all rights and defenses as to any successor that the Company would have had against any predecessor insured, unless the successor acquired the indebtedness as a purchaser for value without knowledge of the asserted defect, lien, encumbrance, adverse claim or other matter insured against by this policy as affecting title to the estate or interest in the land);

(ii) any governmental agency or governmental instrumentality which is an insurer or guarantor under an insurance contract or guaranty insuring or guaranteeing the indebtedness secured by the insured mortgage, or any part thereof, whether named as an insured herein or not;

(iii) the parties designated in Section 2(a) of these Conditions and Stipulations.

(b) "insured claimant": an insured claiming loss or damage.

(c) "knowledge" or "known": actual knowledge, not constructive knowledge or notice which may be imputed to an insured by reason of the public records as defined in this policy or any other records which impart constructive notice of matters affecting the land.

(d) "land": the land described or referred to in Schedule (A), and improvements affixed thereto which by law constitute real property. The term "land" does not include any property beyond the lines of the area described or referred to in Schedule (A), nor any right, title, interest, estate or easement in abutting streets, roads, avenues, alleys, lanes, ways or waterways, but nothing herein shall modify or limit the extent to which a right of access to and from the land is insured by this policy.

(e) "mortgage": mortgage, deed of trust, trust deed, or other security instrument.

(f) "public records": records established under state statutes at Date of Policy for the purpose of imparting constructive notice of matters relating to real property to purchasers for value and without knowledge. With respect to Section 1(a)(iv) of the Exclusions From Coverage, "public records" shall also include environmental protection liens filed in the records of the clerk of the United States district court for the district in which the land is located.

(g) "unmarketability of the title": an alleged or apparent matter affecting the title to the land, not excluded or excepted from coverage, which would entitle a purchaser of the estate or interest described in Schedule A or the insured mortgage to be released from the obligation to purchase by virtue of a contractual condition requiring the delivery of marketable title.

2. CONTINUATION OF INSURANCE.

(a) After Acquisition of Title. The coverage of this policy shall continue in force as of Date of Policy in favor of (i) an insured who acquires all or any part of the estate or interest in the land by foreclosure, trustee's sale, conveyance in lieu of foreclosure, or other legal manner which discharges the lien of the insured mortgage; (ii) a transferee of the estate or interest so acquired from an insured corporation, provided the transferee is the parent or wholly-owned subsidiary of the insured corporation, and their corporate successors by operation of law and not by purchase, subject to any rights or defenses the Company may have against any predecessor insureds; and (iii) any governmental agency or governmental instrumentality which acquires all or any part of the estate or interest pursuant to a contract of insurance or guaranty insuring or guaranteeing the indebtedness secured by the insured mortgage.

settlement, and (ii) in any other lawful act which in the opinion of the Company may be necessary or desirable to establish the title to the estate or interest or the lien of the insured mortgage, as insured. If the Company is prejudiced by the failure of the insured to furnish the required cooperation, the Company's obligations to the insured under the policy shall terminate, including any liability or obligation to defend, prosecute, or continue any litigation, with regard to the matter or matters requiring such cooperation.

5. PROOF OF LOSS OR DAMAGE.

In addition to and after the notices required under Section 3 of these Conditions and Stipulations have been provided the Company, a proof of loss or damage signed and sworn to by the insured claimant shall be furnished to the Company within 90 days after the insured claimant shall ascertain the facts giving rise to the loss or damage. The proof of loss or damage shall describe the defect in, or lien or encumbrance on the title, or other matter insured against by this policy which constitutes the basis of loss or damage and shall state, to the extent possible, the basis of calculating the amount of the loss or damage. If the Company is prejudiced by the failure of the insured claimant to provide the required proof of loss or damage, the Company's obligations to the insured under the policy shall terminate, including any liability or obligation to defend, prosecute, or continue any litigation, with regard to the matter or matters requiring such proof of loss or damage.

In addition, the insured claimant may reasonably be required to submit to examination under oath by any authorized representative of the Company and shall produce for examination, inspection and copying, at such reasonable times and places as may be designated by any authorized representative of the Company, all records, books, ledgers, checks, correspondence and memoranda, whether bearing a date before or after Date of Policy, which reasonably pertain to the loss or damage. Further, if requested by any authorized representative of the Company, the insured claimant shall grant its permission, in writing, for any authorized representative of the Company to examine, inspect and copy all records, books, ledgers, checks, correspondence and memoranda in the custody or control of a third party, which reasonably pertain to the loss or damage. All information designated as confidential by the insured claimant provided to the Company pursuant to this Section shall not be disclosed to others unless, in the reasonable judgment of the Company, it is necessary in the administration of the claim. Failure of the insured claimant to submit for examination under oath, produce other reasonably requested information or grant permission to secure reasonably necessary information from third parties as required in this paragraph, unless prohibited by law or governmental regulation, shall terminate any liability of the Company under this policy as to that claim.

the insured was and continued to be obligated to advance at and after Date of Policy.

9. REDUCTION OF INSURANCE; REDUCTION OR TERMINATION OF LIABILITY.

(a) All payments under this policy, except payments made for costs, attorneys' fees and expenses, shall reduce the amount of the insurance pro tanto. However, any payments made prior to the acquisition of title to the estate or interest as provided in Section 2(a) of these Conditions and Stipulations shall not reduce pro tanto the amount of the insurance afforded under this policy except to the extent that the payments reduce the amount of the indebtedness secured by the insured mortgage.

(b) Payment in part by any person of the principal of the indebtedness, or any other obligation secured by the insured mortgage, or any voluntary partial satisfaction or release of the insured mortgage, to the extent of the payment, satisfaction or release, shall reduce the amount of insurance pro tanto. The amount of insurance may thereafter be increased by accruing interest and advances made to protect the lien of the insured mortgage and secured thereby, with interest thereon, provided in no event shall the amount of insurance be greater than the amount of insurance stated in Schedule A.

(c) Payment in full by any person or the voluntary satisfaction or release of the insured mortgage shall terminate all liability of the Company except as provided in Section 2(a) of these Conditions and Stipulations.

10. LIABILITY NONCUMULATIVE.

If the insured acquires title to the estate or interest in satisfaction of the indebtedness secured by the insured mortgage, or any part thereof, it is expressly understood that the amount of insurance under this policy shall be reduced by any amount the Company may pay under any policy insuring a mortgage to which exception is taken in Schedule B or to which the insured has agreed, assumed, or taken subject, or which is hereafter executed by an insured and which is a charge or lien on the estate or interest described or referred to in Schedule A, and the amount so paid shall be deemed a payment under this policy.

11. PAYMENT OF LOSS.

(a) No payment shall be made without producing this policy for endorsement of the payment unless the policy has been lost or destroyed, in which case proof of loss or destruction shall be furnished to the satisfaction of the Company.

(b) When liability and the extent of loss or damage has been definitely fixed in accordance with these Conditions and Stipulations, the loss or damage shall be payable within 30 days thereafter.

(b) **After Conveyance of Title.** The coverage of this policy shall continue in force as of Date of Policy in favor of an insured only so long as the insured retains an estate or interest in the land, or holds an indebtedness secured by a purchase money mortgage given by a purchaser from the insured, or only so long as the insured shall have liability by reason of covenants of warranty made by the insured in any transfer or conveyance of the estate or interest. This policy shall not continue in force in favor of any purchaser from the insured of either (i) an estate or interest in the land, or (ii) an indebtedness secured by a purchase money mortgage given to the insured.

(c) **Amount of Insurance.** The amount of insurance after the acquisition or after the conveyance shall in neither event exceed the least of:

(i) the amount of insurance stated in Schedule A;

(ii) the amount of the principal of the indebtedness secured by the insured mortgage as of Date of Policy, interest thereon, expenses of foreclosure, amounts advanced pursuant to the insured mortgage to assure compliance with laws or to protect the lien of the insured mortgage prior to the time of acquisition of the estate or interest in the land and secured thereby and reasonable amounts expended to prevent deterioration of improvements, but reduced by the amount of all payments made; or

(iii) the amount paid by any governmental agency or governmental instrumentality, if the agency or instrumentality is the insured claimant, in the acquisition of the estate or interest in satisfaction of its insurance contract or guaranty.

3. NOTICE OF CLAIM TO BE GIVEN BY INSURED CLAIMANT.

The insured shall notify the Company promptly in writing (i) in case of any litigation as set forth in Section 4(a) below, (ii) in case knowledge shall come to an insured hereunder of any claim of title or interest which is adverse to the title to the estate or interest or the lien of the insured mortgage, as insured, and which might cause loss or damage for which the Company may be liable by virtue of this policy, or (iii) if title to the estate or interest or the lien of the insured mortgage, as insured, is rejected as unmarketable. If prompt notice shall not be given to the Company, then as to the insured all liability of the Company shall terminate with regard to the matter or matters for which prompt notice is required; provided, however, that failure to notify the Company shall in no case prejudice the rights of any insured under this policy unless the Company shall be prejudiced by the failure and then only to the extent of the prejudice.

4. DEFENSE AND PROSECUTION OF ACTIONS; DUTY OF INSURED CLAIMANT TO COOPERATE.

(a) Upon written request by the insured and subject to the options contained in Section 6 of these Conditions and Stipulations, the Company, at its own cost and without unreasonable delay, shall provide for the defense of an insured in litigation in which any third party asserts a claim adverse to the title or interest as insured, but only as to those stated causes of action alleging a defect, lien or encumbrance or other matter insured against by this policy. The Company shall have the right to select counsel of its choice (subject to the right of the insured to object for reasonable cause) to represent the insured as to those stated causes of action and shall not be liable for and will not pay the fees of any other counsel. The Company will not pay any fees, costs or expenses incurred by the insured in the defense of those causes of action which allege matters not insured against by this policy.

(b) The Company shall have the right, at its own cost, to institute and prosecute any action or proceeding or to do any other act which in its opinion may be necessary or desirable to establish the title to the estate or interest or the lien of the insured mortgage, as insured, or to prevent or reduce loss or damage to the insured. The Company may take any appropriate action under the terms of this policy, whether or not it shall be liable hereunder, and shall not thereby concede liability or waive any provision of this policy. If the Company shall exercise its rights under this paragraph, it shall do so diligently.

(c) Whenever the Company shall have brought an action or interposed a defense as required or permitted by the provisions of this policy, the Company may pursue any litigation to final determination by a court of competent jurisdiction and expressly reserves the right, in its sole discretion, to appeal from any adverse judgment or order.

(d) In all cases where this policy permits or requires the Company to prosecute or provide for the defense of any action or proceeding, the insured shall secure to the Company the right to so prosecute or provide defense in the action or proceeding, and all appeals therein, and permit the Company to use, at its option, the name of the insured for this purpose. Whenever requested by the Company, the insured, at the Company's expense, shall give the Company all reasonable aid (i) in any action or proceeding, securing evidence, obtaining witnesses, prosecuting or defending the action or proceeding, or effecting

6. OPTIONS TO PAY OR OTHERWISE SETTLE CLAIMS; TERMINATION OF LIABILITY.

In case of a claim under this policy, the Company shall have the following options:

(a) To Pay or Tender Payment of the Amount of Insurance or to Purchase the Indebtedness.

(i) to pay or tender payment of the amount of insurance under this policy together with any costs, attorneys' fees and expenses incurred by the insured claimant, which were authorized by the Company, up to the time of payment or tender of payment and which the Company is obligated to pay; or

(ii) to purchase the indebtedness secured by the insured mortgage for the amount owing thereon together with any costs, attorneys' fees and expenses incurred by the insured claimant which were authorized by the Company up to the time of purchase and which the Company is obligated to pay.

If the Company offers to purchase the indebtedness as herein provided, the owner of the indebtedness shall transfer, assign, and convey the indebtedness and the insured mortgage, together with any collateral security, to the Company upon payment therefor.

Upon the exercise by the Company of either of the options provided for in paragraphs a(i) or (ii), all liability and obligations to the insured under this policy, other than to make the payment required in those paragraphs, shall terminate, including any liability or obligation to defend, prosecute, or continue any litigation, and the policy shall be surrendered to the Company for cancellation.

(b) To Pay or Otherwise Settle With Parties Other than the Insured or With the Insured Claimant.

(i) to pay or otherwise settle with other parties for or in the name of an insured claimant any claim insured against under this policy, together with any costs, attorneys' fees and expenses incurred by the insured claimant which were authorized by the Company up to the time of payment and which the Company is obligated to pay; or

(ii) to pay or otherwise settle with the insured claimant the loss or damage provided for under this policy, together with any costs, attorneys' fees and expenses incurred by the insured claimant which were authorized by the Company up to the time of payment and which the Company is obligated to pay.

Upon the exercise by the Company of either of the options provided for in paragraphs b(i) or (ii), the Company's obligations to the insured under this policy for the claimed loss or damage, other than the payments required to be made, shall terminate, including any liability or obligation to defend, prosecute or continue any litigation.

7. DETERMINATION AND EXTENT OF LIABILITY.

This policy is a contract of indemnity against actual monetary loss or damage sustained or incurred by the insured claimant who has suffered loss or damage by reason of matters insured against by this policy and only to the extent herein described.

(a) The liability of the Company under this policy shall not exceed the least of:

(i) the amount of insurance stated in Schedule A, or, if applicable, the amount of insurance as defined in Section 2 (c) of these Conditions and Stipulations;

(ii) the amount of the unpaid principal indebtedness secured by the insured mortgage as limited or provided under Section 8 of these Conditions and Stipulations or as reduced under Section 9 of these Conditions and Stipulations, at the time the loss or damage insured against by this policy occurs, together with interest thereon; or

(iii) the difference between the value of the insured estate or interest as insured and the value of the insured estate or interest subject to the defect, lien or encumbrance insured against by this policy.

(b) In the event the insured has acquired the estate or interest in the manner described in Section 2(a) of these Conditions and Stipulations or has conveyed the title, then the liability of the Company shall continue as set forth in Section 7(a) of these Conditions and Stipulations.

(c) The Company will pay only those costs, attorneys' fees and expenses incurred in accordance with Section 4 of these Conditions and Stipulations.

8. LIMITATION OF LIABILITY.

(a) If the Company establishes the title, or removes the alleged defect, lien or encumbrance, or cures the lack of a right of access to or from the land, or cures the claim of unmarketability of title, or otherwise establishes the lien of the insured mortgage, all as insured, in a reasonably diligent manner by any method, including litigation and the completion of any appeals therefrom, it shall have fully performed its obligations with respect to that matter and shall not be liable for any loss or damage caused thereby.

(b) In the event of any litigation, including litigation by the Company or with the Company's consent, the Company shall have no liability for loss or damage until there has been a final determination by a court of competent jurisdiction, and disposition of all appeals therefrom, adverse to the title or to the lien of the insured mortgage, as insured.

(c) The Company shall not be liable for loss or damage to any insured for liability voluntarily assumed by the insured in settling any claim or suit without the prior written consent of the Company.

(d) The Company shall not be liable for:

(i) any indebtedness created subsequent to Date of Policy except for advances made to protect the lien of the insured mortgage and secured thereby and reasonable amounts expended to prevent deterioration of improvements; or

(ii) construction loan advances made subsequent to Date of Policy, except construction loan advances made subsequent to Date of Policy for the purpose of financing in whole or in part the construction of an improvement to the land which at Date of Policy were secured by the insured mortgage and which

12. SUBROGATION UPON PAYMENT OR SETTLEMENT.

(a) **The Company's Right of Subrogation.**

Whenever the Company shall have settled and paid a claim under this policy, all right of subrogation shall vest in the Company unaffected by any act of the insured claimant.

The Company shall be subrogated to and be entitled to all rights and remedies which the insured claimant would have had against any person or property in respect to the claim had this policy not been issued. If requested by the Company, the insured claimant shall transfer to the Company all rights and remedies against any person or property necessary in order to perfect this right of subrogation. The insured claimant shall permit the Company to sue, compromise or settle in the name of the insured claimant and to use the name of the insured claimant in any transaction or litigation involving these rights or remedies.

If a payment on account of a claim does not fully cover the loss of the insured claimant, the Company shall be subrogated to all rights and remedies of the insured claimant after the insured claimant shall have recovered its principal, interest, and costs of collection.

(b) **The Insured's Rights and Limitations.**

Notwithstanding the foregoing, the owner of the indebtedness secured by the insured mortgage, provided the priority of the lien of the insured mortgage or its enforceability is not affected, may release or substitute the personal liability of any debtor or guarantor, or extend or otherwise modify the terms of payment, or release a portion of the estate or interest from the lien of the insured mortgage, or release any collateral security for the indebtedness.

When the permitted acts of the insured claimant occur and the insured has knowledge of any claim of title or interest adverse to the title to the estate or interest or the priority or enforceability of the lien of the insured mortgage, as insured, the Company shall be required to pay only that part of any losses insured against by this policy which shall exceed the amount, if any, lost to the Company by reason of the impairment by the insured claimant of the Company's right of subrogation.

(c) **The Company's Rights Against Non-insured Obligors.**

The Company's right of subrogation against non-insured obligors shall exist and shall include, without limitation, the rights of the insured to indemnities, guaranties, other policies of insurance or bonds, notwithstanding any terms or conditions contained in those instruments which provide for subrogation rights by reason of this policy.

The Company's right of subrogation shall not be avoided by acquisition of the insured mortgage by an obligor (except an obligor described in Section 1(a)(ii) of these Conditions and Stipulations) who acquires the insured mortgage as a result of an indemnity, guarantee, other policy of insurance, or bond and the obligor will not be an insured under this policy, notwithstanding Section 1(a)(i) of these Conditions and Stipulations

13. ARBITRATION.

Unless prohibited by applicable law, either the Company or the insured may demand arbitration pursuant to the Title Insurance Arbitration Rules of the American Arbitration Association. Arbitrable matters may include, but are not limited to, any controversy or claim between the Company and the insured arising out of or relating to this policy, any service of the Company in connection with its issuance or the breach of a policy provision or other obligation. All arbitrable matters when the Amount of Insurance is $1,000,000 or less shall be arbitrated at the option of either the Company or the insured. All arbitrable matters when the Amount of Insurance is in excess of $1,000,000 shall be arbitrated only when agreed to by both the Company and the insured. Arbitration pursuant to this policy and under the Rules in effect on the date the demand for arbitration is made or, at the option of the insured, the Rules in effect at Date of Policy shall be binding upon the parties. The award may include attorneys' fees only if the laws of the state in which the land is located permit a court to award attorneys' fees to a prevailing party. Judgment upon the award rendered by the Arbitrator(s) may be entered in any court having jurisdiction thereof.

The law of the situs of the land shall apply to an arbitration under the Title Insurance Arbitration Rules.

A copy of the Rules may be obtained from the Company upon request.

14. LIABILITY LIMITED TO THIS POLICY; POLICY ENTIRE CONTRACT.

(a) This policy together with all endorsements, if any, attached hereto by the Company is the entire policy and contract between the insured and the Company. In interpreting any provision of this policy, this policy shall be construed as a whole.

(b) Any claim of loss or damage, whether or not based on negligence, and which arises out of the status of the lien of the insured mortgage or of the title to the estate or interest covered hereby or by any action asserting such claim, shall be restricted to this policy.

(c) No amendment of or endorsement to this policy can be made except by a writing endorsed hereon or attached hereto signed by either the President, a Vice President, the Secretary, an Assistant Secretary, or validating officer or authorized signatory of the Company.

15. SEVERABILITY.

In the event any provision of this policy is held invalid or unenforceable under applicable law, the policy shall be deemed not to include that provision and all other provisions shall remain in full force and effect.

16. NOTICES, WHERE SENT.

All notices required to be given the Company and any statement in writing required to be furnished the Company shall include the number of this policy and shall be addressed to the Company at 114 East Fifth Street, Santa Ana, California 92701, or to the office which issued this policy.

Purchasers should note that there are still certain exceptions to the CLTA standard policy and even to the ALTA extended policy. There is no insurance coverage for the following:

1. Defects known to the insured at the time the policy was issued, but not designated in writing, and
2. Government regulations regarding occupancy and use (zoning).

A CLTA standard title insurance policy does NOT require an on-site inspection, but an ALTA extended policy does.

C. ALTA-R (One-to-Four Residential Units)

The *ALTA-R POLICY is recommended by title companies for one-to-four unit owner-occupied residential dwellings.* It doesn't include a survey because the property lines are already established by a recorded subdivision map. Since the title company does not have to do a survey, it gives the buyer more coverage for the same price. The CAR® California Residential Purchase Agreement and Joint Escrow Instructions form includes the ALTA-R as the preferred residential title policy choice.

D. WHO PAYS TITLE INSURANCE FEES?

Title insurance fees are a part of the escrow closing costs. Title insurance companies are required to publish rate schedules and charge according to the published rates. Who assumes payment of the fees, however, varies depending upon the area in which one lives.

In Southern California it is customary for the seller to pay the title fees, whereas in Northern California it is usually the buyer who assumes the cost. Because there is no law determining who must pay, it should be stated in the purchase agreement to prevent any

misunderstanding. This, however, covers only the standard CLTA policy. The additional cost of the ALTA extended policy is usually charged to the party purchasing the property (the buyer).

E. TITLE INSURANCE DISCLOSURE

In any escrow transaction for the purchase or exchange of real property where a title insurance policy will not be issued to the buyer (or exchanger), the buyer (or exchanger) must sign and acknowledge a disclosure statement stating that it may be advisable to obtain title insurance.

VIII. Real Estate Settlement Procedures Act (RESPA)

RESPA (enforced by HUD) allows borrowers to shop for settlement services. The law covers first loans on one-to-four unit residential dwellings.

The *REAL ESTATE SETTLEMENT PROCEDURES ACT (RESPA) is a law for the sale or transfer of one-to-four residential units requiring: 1) specific procedures and 2) forms for settlements (closing costs) involving most home loans from financial institutions with federally insured deposits, including FHA and VA loans.*

This law, although amended several times, states that the closing settlement cost of a real estate transaction must be made known to the borrower, on or before the settlement date, although, at the buyer's request, it must be provided one business day before escrow closes. Before this law was passed, buyers were unaware of the exact amount needed until the actual escrow closing day. Sometimes the buyers were surprised to find that more money than expected was needed to complete the procedure. The current law alleviates this problem.

Under RESPA, a lender has three business days from the date the lender receives the borrower's loan application to provide a booklet entitled "Settlement Costs and You."

Other provisions required by the Real Estate Settlement Procedures Act include the following:

1. At the time of loan application, or within three business days, the lender must give a good faith estimate of the total closing charges to the borrower.

2. At the same time, the lender must furnish the buyer with an information booklet.

3. The escrow agent must give a uniform settlement statement to the borrower, the seller, and the lender. **Figure 7-11** illustrates the settlement statement. It must be furnished by the time of settlement, except when the borrower waives it, or in areas where the HUD (Department of Housing and Urban Development) permits a later date for supplying it.

The Uniform Settlement Statement must be delivered or mailed to the borrower on or before the date of settlement, at no charge. The buyer can request it one business day before closing.

4. Individuals are prohibited from receiving kickbacks and unearned fees. Payments to cooperating brokerages and referral agreements between brokers are exempt.

Figure 7-11

A. U.S. DEPARTMENT OF HOUSING AND URBAN DEVELOPMENT	B. TYPE OF LOAN
	1. [ ] FHA 2. [ ] FmHA 3. [X] Conv. unis
SETTLEMENT STATEMENT	4. [ ] VA 5. [ ] Conv. ins
	6. ESCROW NUMBER: 1-10533 7. LOAN NUMBER:
	8. MORTGAGE INSURANCE NUMBER:

THIS NOTE IS FURNISHED TO GIVE YOU A STATEMENT OF THE ACTUAL SETTLEMENT COSTS. AMOUNTS PAID TO AND BY THE SETTLEMENT AGENT ARE SHOWN. ITEMS MARKED "(P.O.C.)" WERE PAID OUTSIDE OF THE CLOSING; THEY ARE SHOWN HERE FOR INFORMATIONAL PURPOSES AND ARE NOT INCLUDED IN THE TOTALS.

D. NAME OF BORROWER:	E. NAME OF SELLER:	F. NAME OF LENDER:
JOHN BUYER	JOHN SELLER	GET SMART SAVINGS AND LOAN
JANE BUYER	JANE SELLER	123 Lending Lane
123 Purchase Lane		Beverly Hills, CA 91020
Glendale, CA		

G. PROPERTY LOCATION:	H. SETTLEMENT AGENT: COLONIAL ESCROW, INC.	I. SETTLEMENT DATE:
123 PURCHASE LANE	PLACE OF SETTLEMENT:	
GLENDALE, CA	601 EAST GLENOAKS BLVD. SUITE 210	06/01/20
	GLENDALE, CA 91207	
	P.O. BOX 433 GLENDALE, CA 91209-0433	

J. SUMMARY OF BORROWER'S TRANSACTIONS		K. SUMMARY OF SELLER'S TRANSACTIONS	
100. GROSS AMOUNT DUE FROM BORROWER		**400. GROSS AMOUNT DUE TO SELLER**	
101. CONTRACT SALES PRICE	800,000.00	401. CONTRACT SALES PRICE	800,000.00
102. PERSONAL PROPERTY		402. PERSONAL PROPERTY	
103. SETTL. CHRGS. TO BORROWER (LINE 1400)	10,122.01	403. DEPOSITS	
104.		404.	
105.		405.	
Adjustments: items paid by seller in advance		Adjustments: items paid by seller in advance	
106. CITY/TOWN TAXES		406. CITY/TOWN TAXES	
107. COUNTY TAXES		407. COUNTY TAXES	
108. ASSESSMENTS		408. ASSESSMENTS	
109. TAXES : 06/01/20 TO 07/01/20	666.67	409. TAXES : 06/01/20 TO 07/01/20	666.67
110.		410.	
111.		411.	
112.		412.	
120. GROSS AMOUNT DUE FROM BORROWER	810,788.68	420. GROSS AMOUNT DUE TO SELLER	800,666.67
200. AMOUNTS PAID BY OR IN BEHALF OF BORROWER		**500. REDUCTIONS IN AMOUNT DUE TO SELLER**	
201. DEPOSITS	91,000.00	501. EXCESS DEPOSIT	
202. PRINCIPAL AMOUNT OF NEW LOAN(S)	640,000.00	502. SETTL. CHRGS. TO SELLER (LINE 1400)	54,845.00
203. EXISTING LOAN(S) TAKEN SUBJECT TO		503. EXISTING LOAN(S) TAKEN SUBJECT TO	
204. NEW 2ND TRUST DEED	80,000.00	504. PAYOFF TO MOST SUPERIOR SAVINGS AND L	490,000.00
205.		505. INTEREST FROM 05/01/20 TO 06/01/20	4,161.64
206.		506. FORWARDING FEE	50.00
207.		507. RECONVEYANCE FEE	60.00
208.		508. NEW 2ND TRUST DEED	80,000.00
209.		509.	
Adjustments: Items unpaid by seller		Adjustments: Items unpaid by seller	
210. CITY/TOWN TAXES		510. CITY/TOWN TAXES	
211. COUNTY TAXES		511. COUNTY TAXES	
212. ASSESSMENTS		512. ASSESSMENTS	
213.		513.	
214.		514.	
215.		515.	
216.		516.	
217.		517.	
218.		518.	
219.		519.	
220. TOTAL PAID BY/FOR BORROWER	811,000.00	520. TOTAL REDUCTION AMOUNT DUE SELLER	629,116.64
300. CASH AT SETTLEMENT FROM/TO BORROWER		**600. CASH AT SETTLEMENT TO/FROM SELLER**	
301. Gross amounts due from borrower (line 120)	810,788.68	601. Gross amount due to seller (line 420)	800,666.67
302. Less amounts paid by/for borrower (line 220)	811,000.00	602. Less reductions in amount due seller (line 520)	629,116.64
303. CASH FROM[ ] TO[X] BORROWER	211.32	603. CASH FROM[ ] TO[X] SELLER	171,550.03

L. SETTLEMENT STATEMENT

	PAID FROM BORROWER'S FUNDS AT SETTLEMENT	PAID FROM SELLER'S FUNDS AT SETTLEMENT
700. TOTAL SALES/BROKER'S COMMISSION		
BASED ON PRICE $ 800,000.00 @ 6.00%		
701. BROKER: J. Q. SMART 48,000.00		
702.		
703.		
704. COMMISSIONS PAID AT SETTLEMENT		48,000.00
800. ITEMS PAYABLE IN CONNECTION WITH LOAN		
801. LOAN FEE	6,400.00	
802. LOAN DISCOUNT		
803. APPRAISAL	350.00	
804. CREDIT REPORT	45.00	
805. LENDER'S INSPECTION FEE		
806. MORTGAGE INSURANCE APPLICATION FEE		
807. ASSUMPTION FEE		
808. TAX SERVICE	89.00	
809. DOCUMENT FEE	250.00	
810.		
811.		
900. ITEMS REQUIRED BY LENDER TO BE PAID IN ADVANCE		
901. INTEREST AT 7.5000% FROM 05/31/20 TO 06/01/20	131.51	
902. MORTGAGE INSURANCE		
903. PROPERTY INSURANCE, INC. FOR FIRE INSURANCE	1,000.00	
904.		
905.		
1000. RESERVES DEPOSITED WITH LENDER		
1001. HAZARD INSURANCE		
1002. MORTGAGE INSURANCE		
1003. CITY PROPERTY TAXES		
1004. COUNTY PROPERTY TAXES		
1005. ANNUAL ASSESSMENTS		
1006.		
1007.		
1008.		
1100. ESCROW AND TITLE CHARGES		
1101. ESCROW FEE TO COLONIAL ESCROW, INC.	900.00	900.00
1102. ABSTRACT OR TITLE SEARCH		
1103. TITLE EXAMINATION		
1104. TITLE INSURANCE BINDER		
1105. DOCUMENT PREPARATION TO COLONIAL ESCROW, INC.		
1106. MESSENGER FEE TO COLONIAL ESCROW, INC.	50.00	
1107. ATTORNEY'S FEES		
1108. TITLE POLICY TO AMERICAN COAST TITLE	628.50	2,165.00
1109. LENDERS COVERAGE $ 640,000.00		
1110. OWNERS COVERAGE $ 800,000.00		
1111. PROCESSING DEMANDS TO COLONIAL ESCROW, INC.		35.00
1112. DOCUMENT FEE TO COLONIAL ESCROW, INC.		85.00
1113. LOAN TIE IN FEE TO COLONIAL ESCROW, INC.	125.00	
1200. GOVERNMENT RECORDING AND TRANSFER CHARGES		
1201. RECORDING FEES: DEED $8.00; MORTGAGE $20.00; RELEASES $5.00	28.00	5.00
1202. DOCUMENTARY TRANSFER TAX		880.00
1203. STATE TAX/STAMPS		
1204.		
1205.		
1300. ADDITIONAL SETTLEMENT CHARGES		
1301. SURVEY		
1302. PEST CONTROL, INC. FOR TERMITE REPORT/WORK		1,000.00
1303. SUB ESCROW FEE TO AMERICAN COAST TITLE	75.00	75.00
1304. TITLE ENDORSEMENT FEE(S) TO AMERICAN COAST TITLE	50.00	
1305. STREET ASSESSMENT BOND TO AMERICAN COAST TITLE		1,300.00
1306. HOME WARRANTY, INC. FOR HOME PROTECTION POLICY		400.00
1307.		
1400. TOTAL SETTLEMENT CHARGES		
(ENTER ON LINES 103 SECTION J AND 501 SECTION K)	10,122.01	54,845.00

5. No seller may require a buyer to purchase title insurance from any particular company as a condition of sale.

There are penalties for "kickbacks" and unearned fees. The seller may request a specific title insurer, but only the buyer can require a specific insurance company.

It is not permissible for a title company to accept or pay referral fees to or from an agent.

It is permissible for a title company to refer clients to a real estate broker.

IX. California Escrow Association

The California Escrow Association has developed a statewide program to promote professional service and educational opportunities for its members. Many community colleges have also adopted certificate courses for escrow personnel and real estate brokers to provide a better understanding of the highly technical escrow field.

X. CHAPTER SUMMARY

An **escrow** is created when a written agreement (usually from a **Purchase Agreement**) instructs a **neutral third party** to hold funds and proceed only when all the agreed to conditions have been completed. An escrow is strongly recommended in connection with real estate sales, loan agreements, or exchanges made in California. But escrows are required for liquor license transfers, security sales, and court ordered transfers (**probate sales**).

A valid escrow requires: 1) signed escrow instructions (a written escrow contract) between the buying and selling parties; 2) a neutral escrow company acting as a dual agent for the buyer and the seller; and 3) conditional delivery of funds until the escrow conditions are completed.

An **escrow holder** can be a corporation, an attorney, or a real estate broker acting as a real estate agent in the transaction. An escrow officer, holder, or agent, though not licensed by the state, must be an employee of a licensed escrow company acting as agent. The **duties of an escrow company** include **conditional delivery of funds** until escrow conditions are met, **confidentiality of escrow instructions**, and **acting as a deposit holder** until funds are disbursed when escrow closes.

A real estate broker can handle escrow for a fee, but only if the broker acts as a real estate agent in that transaction, or if the broker is a principal (buyer or seller).

The escrow is complete when: 1) all escrow conditions of the parties have been met and 2) the parties have received an accounting of the procedure. Escrows can be terminated in three ways: by **completion**, **mutual agreement**, or court action **interpleader**.

Amendments changing escrow instructions must be signed by both parties. The seller cannot rescind escrow without consent of the buyer. **Selection of an escrow company and officer is negotiated between buyer and seller, but the salesperson may recommend an escrow company**. It is illegal for a real estate licensee to receive a **kickback** for solicitation of escrow business.

Escrow instructions for the sale of a house are formal instructions drawn from the information contained in the purchase agreement. Most escrows for home sales include getting a new loan and the payoff or assumption of an old one. The **payoff demand statement** details the lender's calculations of the amounts owed for the purpose of paying off the loan in full. If a loan is to be assumed, a **beneficiary's (lender's) statement** under a deed of trust provides information, such as the unpaid balance, monthly payment, and interest rate.

Closing escrow is the process of signing various documents, transfer of documents, recordation of deed and trust deeds, and distribution of funds. The **closing date** is the date that the documents are recorded.

Proration is the process of dividing expenses or income proportionately between buyer and seller to the precise date that escrow closes, or an agreed date. Items commonly prorated include: **property taxes (credit to seller)**, **fire insurance**, **interest**, and **rents (debit to seller)**. All escrow companies use **30 days as a "base month."** The two important dates in determining proration amounts are the dates escrow closes and when the item is paid.

A **Structural Pest Control Report** (termite report) is usually a condition of the escrow. This report is given by a licensed pest control company to identify any wood-destroying pests or conditions likely to cause pest infestation. It also states the conditions and correction costs of any pest, dry rot, excessive moisture, earth-wood contacts, or fungus damage in accessible areas of a structure. Payment for the report is negotiated between parties, but is usually made by the seller, as indicated in the allocation of costs signed by both parties. **Required repairs** are usually paid for by the seller, then a notice of work completed is obtained. But **recommended repairs** are negotiated between the parties.

Most lenders require a pest control inspection before making a loan. Every VA and FHA loan application requires one. A copy of the pest control report and **notice of work completed** must be delivered to the buyer if it's a condition of the purchase agreement or financing.

Fire insurance is a necessity. A lending institution requires fire coverage for the amount of its loan. **California Standard Form Fire Insurance Policy** insures the dwelling **only against fire and lightning**. An **Extended Coverage Endorsement** insures against windstorms, explosions, hail, aircraft, smoke, riot, and vehicles not attributed to a strike or civil commotion. Buyers usually obtain new fire insurance policies. A **coinsurance clause** in a policy requires that 80% of the value of a commercial dwelling be insured or only a percentage of the insurance value will be payable.

Chain of title is the recorded public history of a specific property. Information about people and their real property is stored in computers in a grantor-grantee index and referred to as a **title plant**. Title insurance companies examine chain of title records, review any risks not found in public records, seek legal interpretation of deeds or other real estate documents, help the seller correct any defects, and insure marketable title to the property.

A **preliminary title report** is the first step in a title search. It shows the condition of title before a sale or loan transaction.

Title insurance policies in California include the **California Land Title Association (CLTA) Policy**, the more comprehensive **American Land Title Association (ALTA) Policy**, or the **ALTA-R Policy**.

The **CLTA policy** is the most common and basic title insurance policy. The standard CLTA policy insures only the lender, unless the owner pays for "owner" coverage. It protects against lack of capacity of a party in the chain of title, deeds not properly delivered, and forgery.

The **ATLA policy** is an extended coverage policy that insures against many exclusions in the standard coverage (CTLA) policy. The ALTA policy (which includes a competent survey or physical inspection) is usually required by California lenders and out of state lenders unable to make personal inspections of the property. Neither ALTA nor CTLA covers unwritten **title defects known** to the insured at the time of policy issuance or **zoning changes**.

The **ALTA-R policy** is recommended by title companies for one-to-four owner-occupied residential dwellings. It offers more coverage for the same money because no survey is necessary.

Payment for the CTLA policy insurance fees is negotiable, but the purchase agreement must state who pays the insurance fees to prevent any misunderstanding. In Southern California, the seller customarily pays for the CTLA policy. In Northern California, the buyer pays. The fees to upgrade the coverage from a CTLA to an ALTA policy are paid by the buyer in either part of the state.

Escrow service fees are usually split 50-50 in Southern California. The buyer usually pays in Northern California.

The **Real Estate Settlement Procedures Act (RESPA)** involves most federally insured home loans. It is a federal law relating to the sale or transfer of one-to-four residential units requiring specific procedures and forms for settlements closing costs. All settlement closing costs must be disclosed to the borrower one business day before escrow closes.

XI. TERMINOLOGY

A. ALTA
B. Chain of Title
C. CLTA
D. Coinsurance
E. Date of Closing

F. Escrow
G. Escrow Instructions
H. Escrow Officer
I. Payoff Demand Statement
J. Pest Control Report

K. Preliminary Title Report
L. Proration
M. RESPA
N. Title Insurance
O. Title Plant

1.____ Insurance to protect a real property owner or lender up to a specified amount against certain types of loss; e.g., defective or unmarketable title.
2.____ The process of depositing instruments, funds, and instructions, with a third neutral party who finalizes the transaction.
3.____ A history of conveyances and encumbrances affecting the title from the time the original patent was granted, or as far back as records are available, used to determine how title came to be vested in current owner.
4.____ Adjustments of interest, taxes, and insurance, etc., on a prorated basis as of the closing or agreed upon date.
5.____ The person at the escrow company who handles the paperwork of the escrow.
6.____ The written instructions of the escrow, prepared by the escrow officer and approved by both the buyer and the seller.
7.____ The most all inclusive title insurance policy; it requires a property survey and is usually required by most lenders.
8.____ The minimum standard title insurance policy in California that does NOT require a property survey.
9.____ The requirement by a lender that a property be insured up to its full value, or only a proportion of any loss will be reimbursed.
10.____ A report from a structural pest control company stating the termite or other type of pest damage found and the cost of repairing it.
11.____ The date documents are recorded and title insurance is written.
12.____ A federal statute requiring disclosure of certain costs in the sale of residential property.
13.____ A report showing the condition of title before a sale or loan transaction.
14.____ Written instructions by a lender stating and demanding the amount necessary to pay off a loan.
15.____ A filing of all recorded information to real property.

XII. CHAPTER QUIZ

1. The Escrow Act is found in the:

    a. Business Code.
    b. Civil Code.
    c. Administrative Code.
    d. Financial Code.

2. An interpleader action is:

    a. a court action.
    b. a formal written protest to the seller.
    c. a formal written apology to the buyer.
    d. none of the above.

3. If there is a disagreement between the buyer and seller during escrow, the escrow officer may disburse funds:

    a. as a result of a judgment between the buyer and seller.
    b. if the parties to the escrow agree.
    c. if a binding arbitrator settles the matter.
    d. all of the above would allow the escrow officer to disburse funds.

4. Which of the following would not be prorated in escrow?

    a. Rents
    b. Impounds
    c. Title insurance premium
    d. Property taxes

5. A premium refund on fire insurance is called:

    a. a short rate.
    b. an impound.
    c. title insurance.
    d. all of the above.

6. Every recorded change of ownership and/or claim of ownership on a property is in the:

    a. grant deed.
    b. abstract of title.
    c. title insurance policy.
    d. preliminary title report.

7. What type of title insurance policy is most often used?

    a. State coverage
    b. Standard coverage (CLTA)
    c. ALTA
    d. Extended-coverage

8. A loan officer gives a broker a small referral fee in return for his referral of a client looking to purchase a single-family home. Under RESPA:

    a. this is legal, if disclosures are made to all parties.
    b. this is forbidden.
    c. this is illegal if this fact is not disclosed to the buyer.
    d. this is legal.

9. Under RESPA, a lender cannot charge for:

    a. appraisal fees.
    b. loan documents.
    c. credit reports.
    d. uniform settlements statements (HUD-1).

10. RESPA requires that the Uniform Settlement Statement be delivered or mailed to the borrower no later than:

    a. at or before the date of settlement.
    b. 3 days after signing the loan application.
    c. at the time the mortgage loan disclosure statement is signed.
    d. at the time the loan application is made.

ANSWERS: 1. d; 2. a; 3. d; 4. c; 5. a; 6. b; 7. b; 8. b; 9. d; 10. a

CHAPTER 8
Real Estate Finance

The 2007-2009 credit crunch was caused by lax loan standards.

Real estate is expensive compared to most other possessions. A person or business seldom has enough cash to buy the real estate outright, and therefore must borrow the necessary money to help finance the transaction. If a buyer makes a cash down payment of 20% for example, he or she must then obtain a loan for the remaining 80% of the purchase price. Most buyers must finance at least part of the purchase, so a good rule to remember is, "If you can't finance a property, you probably can't sell it later." If a property can't be easily financed, don't waste time with it: find another, more easily financed property.

To utilize the "principle of leverage,"an investor would use the maximum amount of borrowed money.

Even buyers with large amounts of cash rarely purchase real estate outright. An investment principle known as "leverage" favors buying real estate using borrowed funds. *LEVERAGE is the practice of purchasing real estate using a small amount of your own money and a larger proportion of borrowed funds.* The more money borrowed to buy a property, the greater the leverage.

Employing leverage makes it possible for real estate investors to reap the same profits as those buying entirely with their own funds without having to tie up as much cash. This chapter explores the different ways in which real estate can be financed. Each type of financing instrument will be discussed, including the many clauses in the note and trust deed.

I. Hypothecation (Property as Collateral)

Real estate finance is based on the principle of hypothecation. To *HYPOTHECATE is to provide title to a property as security for a loan without giving up possession.* Although one can hypothecate or "pledge" stocks as security for a bank loan, most real property buyers hypothecate their property as security for a real estate loan. In neither case does the person surrender the use or possession of the property. The hypothecation principle is fundamental to the major instruments of real estate finance: the trust deed in California and the less common mortgage. Each of these instruments uses the promissory note as the primary evidence of debt, which creates a lien on the property.

California's housing slump will increase the use of sellers "carrying back" second trust deeds.

CHAPTER OUTLINE

II. The Promissory Note

A *PROMISSORY NOTE is the basic instrument used to **evidence** the obligation or debt.* It is an unconditional promise in writing by one person to another to pay on demand, or over a fixed determinable time, a certain sum of money. Borrowers hypothecate real property as security for payment of the promissory note. The trust deed or mortgage is used with the promissory note to hypothecate the property as security for the note.

A loan payment on a note is made up of principal and interest. *PRINCIPAL is the dollar amount of the loan.* Commonly we call it the amount of money remaining to be paid off on a promissory note (the loan balance). *INTEREST is the rent charged for the use of money.*

Interest on most real estate loans is "simple interest," paid only on the principal amount owed.

Figure 8-1 illustrates the three basic kinds of promissory notes that affect real estate financing.

Figure 8-1

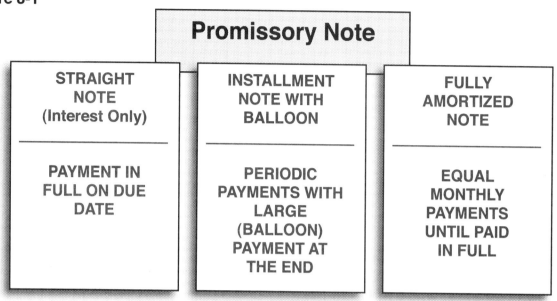

A. STRAIGHT NOTE (Interest Only)

A *STRAIGHT NOTE is a promissory note in which a borrower repays the principal in one lump sum, at maturity, while interest is paid in installments or at maturity.* The parties could agree that interest be paid monthly, quarterly, annually, or any agreed-to term, but the principal is a lump sum payment. In real estate, this type of note is usually for relatively small amounts of money being borrowed for a short time.

B. INSTALLMENT NOTE WITH A BALLOON PAYMENT

An *INSTALLMENT NOTE WITH A BALLOON PAYMENT (PARTIALLY AMORTIZED NOTE) is a promissory note with periodic payments of principal and interest and a large payment at the end (maturity date or due date).* This type of note and the straight note are usually in the form of secondary financing (second trust deeds). See **Figure 8-2**.

C. FULLY AMORTIZED INSTALLMENT NOTE
(Level Payment – Most Common)

A *FULLY AMORTIZED INSTALLMENT NOTE is a promissory note for which both the principal and interest are paid in equal installments until the debt is paid in full.* Installments make it easy to pay off a note, and there is no balloon payment at the end of the loan period.

For real estate financing in California, the fully amortized installment note is the most commonly used type of note. Loan payments are either fixed or adjustable.

A fully amortized loan has equal monthly payments except for the last payment, which is slightly higher or lower. With *EQUAL MONTHLY PAYMENTS, the monthly payment amount, including principal and interest, is constant, but as the loan is paid off, the amount of the payment attributed to interest decreases and the amount attributed to principal increases.*

A "promotional note" is a short-term note of up to and including a term of 36 months. A "seasoned note" is longer than 36 months.

Figure 8-2   **Installment Note with a Balloon Payment**

$_____ _____, California_____, 20_____

In installments as herein stated, for value received, I promise to pay to_____

_____, or order,

at_____

the sum of _____ DOLLARS,

with interest from_____ on unpaid principal at the

rate of_____per cent per annum; principal and interest payable in installments of

_____ Dollars

or more on the_____day of each _____month, beginning

on the_____day of _____, 20 _____ . _____

_____

_____

_____

_____ and continuing until said principal and interest have been paid.

Each payment shall be credited first on interest then due and the remainder on principal; and interest shall thereupon cease upon the principal so credited. Should default be made in payment of any installment when due the whole sum of principal and interest shall become immediately due at the option of the holder of this note. Principal and interest payable in lawful money of the United States. If action be instituted on this note I promise to pay such sum as the Court may fix as attorney's fees. I promise to pay Servicing Agent a late payment charge of $5 or 10% of installment due of principal and interest, whichever is greater. For First Trust Deed loans of $16,000 or more; and for Junior Lien loans of $8,000 or more, the following clause governs: $5 or 6% of installment due of principal and interest, whichever is greater. For all loans, regardless of principal amount, no late payment charge will be made if the installment is paid or tendered in full within 10 days after its scheduled

due date. This note is secured by a DEED OF TRUST to _____

_____   _____

_____   _____

DEED OF TRUST NOTE-INSTALLMENT NOTE-WOLCOTTS FORM 1456 REV.

III. Negotiable Instruments

A. PROMISSORY NOTES, CHECKS, OTHERS

A *NEGOTIABLE INSTRUMENT is any financial document (promissory note, check or other) that can be passed easily from one person to another, if it meets certain legal requirements.* Any promissory note may be a negotiable instrument that is freely transferable. A negotiable instrument must be:

1. an unconditional promise,
2. in writing,
3. made by one person to another,
4. signed by the maker,
5. payable on demand or on a set date,
6. for a set amount of money.

Promissory notes are negotiable instruments, and easily transferable. The most common example is a personal check.

B. HOLDER IN DUE COURSE (No Knowledge of Defect)

A *HOLDER IN DUE COURSE is one who has taken a negotiable instrument from another, in good faith, without knowledge of defect.*

IV. Important Clauses in Financial Instruments

The following financial instrument clauses are the most commonly used terms, and they have definite meanings that affect the financial obligations of both a lender and borrower.

A. ACCELERATION CLAUSE (Entire Amount Due)

In an *ACCELERATION CLAUSE, upon the occurrence of a specific event, the lender has the right to demand immediate payment of the entire note.* An acceleration clause is used to demand immediate payment in full because of a default in loan payments, property taxes, fire insurance, or upon the transfer of property. The main purpose of an acceleration clause is to make the entire balance of the loan due and payable at once. A *LATE PAYMENT is a payment that is, unless otherwise stated, more than ten days past due.*

An "acceleration clause" is always found in a trust deed.

B. ALIENATION CLAUSE (Due on Sale)

An *ALIENATION CLAUSE is a form of the acceleration clause, stating that the entire loan becomes due and payable when the property is sold, assigned, transferred, or otherwise alienated.* The lender, whether a financial institution or a private party, is given the right to full payment when the original borrower transfers the property. This is also commonly referred to as a **"due on sale"** clause.

An "alienation (due on sale) clause" is enforceable and benefits the lender.

C. ASSUMPTION

If a buyer *ASSUMES a loan on a property that is already encumbered, he or she accepts responsibility, with the lender's consent, for the full payment of the loan.* The name on the loan is changed to that of the buyer. With a true assumption, the seller has **secondary responsibility**. To end his or her liability and put the loan in the name of the buyer, the seller files a Substitution of Liability form.

Taking title *SUBJECT TO a prior loan constitutes an agreement to take over and make the payments or lose the property.* The current seller (the buyer to whom the loan was originally made) remains legally responsible for the note, but the new buyer makes the payments.

A seller is protected from liability for payments on an existing loan when the buyer "assumes" the trust deed (and note liability). In a "subject to" loan takeover, the seller remains liable.

D. SUBORDINATION CLAUSE (Current Loan Stands Still; New Loan Moves Ahead)

A *SUBORDINATION CLAUSE is part of a trust deed or mortgage that allows for a future change in the priority of financial liens.* It is used when the buyer wants future financial liens to have priority over a lien he or she is now acquiring. The seller of vacant land will sometimes lend money to the buyer as part of the transaction and will allow the subordination of that loan to any new construction loans.

The subordination clause is used to change the priority on one or more financial liens, but the terms of a subordination clause must be clear and definite. The courts are skeptical about loosely written subordination clauses. Subordination clauses are not used that often, but a salesperson must know and understand them.

E. PREPAYMENT PENALTIES (Fee for Early Payment)

A *PREPAYMENT PENALTY is a charge to the borrower for paying off all or part of a loan balance before the due date.*

Most financial institutions use a prepayment penalty clause on fixed rate loans, but they are rarely employed with the adjustable rate loans. A prepayment penalty is only enforceable during the first five years of a (one-to-four unit) home loan. The penalty is usually six months' interest on the amount prepaid (each year) that exceeds 20% of the original principal amount of the loan. However, penalties do vary among lenders. **After negotiating, a lender may sometimes waive the prepayment penalty if the borrower obtains a new loan from that institution, or if the money market is tight and the lender needs to use the money to lend out at a higher interest rate**.

According to the Business and Professions Code, a prepayment penalty is only enforceable during the first five years of a one-to-four unit home loan.

F. IMPOUND ACCOUNTS (Reserves)

IMPOUND ACCOUNTS (RESERVES) are moneys collected in advance from borrowers to assure the payment of recurring costs, such as property taxes and fire insurance. Some lenders require impound accounts. Impound accounts are especially appropriate when there is a relatively low down payment.

G. ASSIGNMENT OF RENTS (Take Possession)

An *ASSIGNMENT OF RENTS CLAUSE allows a lender, upon default of the borrower, to take possession of the property, collect rents, and pay expenses.* It benefits the lender.

V. Interest and Types of Loans

A. INTEREST (Simple Interest)

INTEREST is the charge for borrowing money. In real estate we use simple interest, not compound interest. Interest can be thought of as a rental charge for the use of money.

The *NOMINAL INTEREST RATE is the rate stated in the note.* The *EFFECTIVE INTEREST RATE is the rate the borrower is actually paying (including interest, points, and loan fees).*

The formula for calculating interest is:

$$I = P \times R \times T$$
or
Interest = Principal x Rate x Time

To find the interest on an $80,000 loan at 12 percent interest for 3 years, we would make the following calculation:

$$I = P \times R \times T$$
$$\$28,800 = \$80,000 \times .12 \times 3 \text{ years}$$

(See Chapter 15 for a more detailed discussion of interest calculations.)

B. FIXED INTEREST RATES (Fixed Rate)

A *FIXED INTEREST RATE LOAN is a loan for which the payments are the same each month for the life of the loan.* The equal monthly payment includes both the principal and the interest. A loan with this kind of fixed rate of interest is said to be a "fully amortized fixed rate loan."

C. AMORTIZATION PAYMENTS

AMORTIZATION is the repaying of a loan (principal and interest), in regular payments, over the term of the loan. This repayment is usually in monthly payments but can be paid quarterly or semi-annually. Amortization is the liquidation of a note including principal and interest.

NEGATIVE AMORTIZATION means the interest rate charges are higher than the monthly payment. Negative amortization means that the loan payment does not cover the interest charges, and the amount of unpaid interest is added to the unpaid loan balance.

Real estate salespeople should always have amortization books handy so that they can figure out the monthly payment on any loan. The *AMORTIZATION (SCHEDULE) BOOK shows the monthly payments necessary to amortize a loan, over a given number of years, at different interest rates and for different loan amounts.* This amortization table book is usually given free, upon request, to salespeople by title insurance companies or financial institutions. Salespeople can also use specially programmed, hand-held calculators to instantly determine the monthly payment amount.

Figure 8-3 is an example of an amortization table at 7% interest per annum for 20, 25, 30, and 40 years at different loan amounts. The loan amounts range from $100 to $100,000, but any loan amount can be obtained by adding the necessary increments. If, for example, we want to determine the monthly payments for a $155,000 loan at 7% interest for 30 years, this is what we would do:

1. Check the 30 years' column for the monthly payment on $100,000.

2. Next, determine the monthly payment for $50,000 and $5,000 using the same method.

3. Lastly, add the monthly payment amounts together.

Amount	Payment
$100,000.00	$665.30
50,000.00	332.65
5,000.00	33.27

TOTAL LOAN $155,000.00   **$1,031.22 Monthly Payment**

Lenders determine monthly payments by using amortization tables and charts.

Figure 8-3

Monthly Payments Necessary to Amortize a Loan

7%

TERM AMOUNT	20 YEARS	25 YEARS	30 YEARS	40 YEARS
$100	0.78	0.71	0.67	0.62
200	1.55	1.41	1.33	1.24
300	2.33	2.12	2.00	1.86
400	3.10	2.83	2.66	2.49
500	3.88	3.53	3.33	3.11
600	4.65	4.24	3.99	3.73
700	5.43	4.95	4.66	4.35
800	6.20	5.65	5.32	4.97
900	6.98	6.36	5.99	5.59
1,000	7.75	7.07	6.65	6.21
2,000	15.51	14.14	13.31	12.43
3,000	23.26	21.20	19.96	18.64
4,000	31.01	28.27	26.61	24.86
5,000	38.76	35.34	33.27	31.07
6,000	46.52	42.41	39.92	37.29
7,000	54.27	49.47	46.57	43.50
8,000	62.02	56.54	53.22	49.71
9,000	69.78	63.61	59.88	55.93
10,000	77.53	70.68	66.53	62.14
20,000	155.06	141.36	133.06	124.29
30,000	232.59	212.03	199.59	186.43
40,000	310.12	282.71	266.12	248.57
50,000	387.65	353.39	332.65	310.72
100,000	775.30	706.78	665.30	621.43

www.bankrate.com/gookeyword/mortgage-calculator.asp
Bankrate.com Mortgage calculator
www.interest.com/hugh/calc/
Hugh's Mortgage and Financial Calculators

D. ADJUSTABLE RATE MORTGAGE (ARM)

Many lenders will allow the borrower a choice of either 1) a fixed interest rate loan or 2) an adjustable rate mortgage (ARM) loan. An ARM allows the interest rate to fluctuate (go up or down) depending on money market conditions. Rather than making equal monthly payments as with a fixed rate loan, the ARM payments will vary over the term of the loan.

An *ADJUSTABLE RATE MORTGAGE "ARM" (OR TRUST DEED) is a loan in which the interest rate fluctuates periodically, based on a specific index, which makes the payment amount*

also change. Each lending institution has its own ARM terms and provisions. **Figure 8-4** illustrates how an adjustable rate mortgage (ARM) works. The interest rate, and therefore

---

Figure 8-4

How ARMs Work

THE INDEX

The **INDEX** *is the starting interest rate used as the indicator so that changes from it can be calculated.* If the index rises 1%, the ARM interest rate you pay goes up 1%. The index must be: 1) beyond the control of the lender, and 2) available and verifiable by the public. Examples of indexes used are the Cost of Living Index, the 11th District Cost of Funds Index, the One Year T-Bill, and the London Interbank Offered Rate (LIBOR).

THE ADJUSTABLE INTERVAL

The **ADJUSTABLE INTERVAL** *is the frequency with which interest rates are reset.* This period can be monthly, quarterly, every six months, or even once a year. If the index has risen .3% by the end of the interval period, the interest rate you pay goes up .3%.

THE CAP

The **CAP** *is a percentage rate ceiling or restriction on the 1) periodic (adjustable) interval; and 2) lifetime change in interest rates or payments.* An adjustable interval cap limits the percentage of change upward or downward to, for example, 1/2% every quarter. The lifetime cap is often around a maximum of 5% above or below the initial agreed-to contract rate.

THE MARGIN

The **MARGIN** *is the spread between the index rate and the initial contract rate from which the lender will make a profit and cover its costs.* It is the agreed to, in advance, amount of profit for the lender. If the index rate is 4% and the margin is 3%, then the current interest rate paid by the borrower is 7%. Even if the index rate moves up to 5%, the margin will always remain at 3% and the new interest rate will be 8%. Some adjustables have **teaser rates** that are even below the starting rate to entice the borrower into the transaction. The borrower is qualified based on the teaser rate, which only lasts for a short period of time and then goes up to the agreed upon rate.

ADVANTAGES OF ARMs

The main advantage of an ARM is a lower interest rate than can be found with a fixed rate loan because the lender is protected if interest rates rise over the loan period. This makes an ARM more affordable, thus more people can qualify for it. Generally there are no prepayment penalties, and an assumption is usually permitted if the new buyer meets credit standards. ARMs benefit first-time buyers and short-term investors who just want a lower interest rate, because interest rates are initially lower.

---

the payments, will change often over the term of the loan. ARM lenders attempt to make this type of loan attractive to a potential borrower by starting it out at a low **teaser rate**. The following are helpful nonprofit debt counselors who can negotiate with home lenders:

1. **Acorn Housing:** 888-409-3557
2. **Homeownership Preservation:** 888-995-4673
3. **HUD:** www.hud.gov

E. SOME SPECIAL PURPOSE TYPES OF LOANS

1. Graduated Payment Mortgage (For First Time Buyers)

A *GRADUATED PAYMENT MORTGAGE (TRUST DEED) is a type of fixed interest rate loan for which the monthly payments start out lower and then gradually increase (for example, after five years the payments will be higher for the remainder of the loan payment).* Although the final level of payments is higher than the payments would have been had the loan been fully amortized, the initial payments are much lower than the fully amortized rate.

2. Biweekly Mortgage (26 Payments)

A *BIWEEKLY mortgage (trust deed) is a fixed interest rate loan for which the payments are made every two weeks, but each payment is one-half the amount of a regular monthly payment.* Since there are 52 weeks in a year, the borrower pays a total of 26 payments.

3. 15-Year Fixed and Adjustable Rate Loans

Fifteen-year fixed-rate loans are gaining in popularity because, for a slight increase in the monthly payment, the loan can be paid off in only 15 years, usually at a lower interest rate than 30-year loans.

4. Reverse Annuity Loans (Seniors Who Need Income)

REVERSE ANNUITY LOANS are loans in which the lender pays the borrower a fixed monthly payment based on the value of the property. The loan is not repaid until the last owner dies or the property is sold, at which time it is paid back through probate. This type of loan is good for senior citizens who need a monthly income and have a large amount of equity in their homes. The senior citizens can pay off the FHA-backed loans earlier if they so desire.

VI. Points, Loan Fees, and Usury

A. POINTS (1 Point = 1% of the Loan Amount)

A *POINT is an origination fee of 1% of the amount borrowed, charged by the lender.* Most financial institutions charge the borrower points when he or she obtains a new loan. Points vary, but generally range from 1% to 7% of the loan amount. They are usually paid by the buyer but, if so negotiated, the seller may also pay.

If you purchase a home for $150,000 and obtain a loan for $120,000 plus two points, the loan points will cost you $2,400 ($120,000 x .02). These points are an additional cost and are

added to the down payment and other closing costs required to complete the transaction at the time of purchase.

Points paid are usually adjustments to the interest rate. If the interest rate quoted is lower than what is currently being charged, more points are charged to make up the difference, which is paid to the lender. If a savings bank wants to quote a lower interest rate, the borrower can expect a larger point charge.

B. LOAN FEES

There is usually a loan fee in addition to points. A *LOAN FEE is the fee charged by the lender in order to apply for a loan*. This charge usually runs about $250 to $400. Other charges may include the appraisal and credit report.

The FHA charges a 1 percent loan fee, which is usually paid by the seller.

C. USURY

USURY is charging more than the legally allowed percentage of interest. In California, the maximum interest rate charged for various loans is set by law. Anyone charging more than the designated rate is committing usury and is breaking the law. In determining whether an interest charge is usurious or not, all loan fees and points are added to the interest rate. Prepayment penalties are not included in the usury law test.

The constitutional usury rate in California is ten percent, or five percent above the discount rate charged by the Federal Reserve Bank of San Francisco, whichever is higher. This limit only applies to lenders who are not exempt from the law. Nearly every conventional source of real estate financing, however, has been exempted from the usury limit. Banks, savings banks, and other institutional lenders are all exempt. Sellers carrying back a purchase money trust deed as part of their equity in a real estate sale are exempt. **Any transaction made through a licensed broker is also exempt from usury laws.** The problem arises when a private individual lends money to another private individual. Check with an attorney first.

www.frbsf.org (Federal Reserve Bank of San Francisco, 12th District)
www.fdic.gov (Federal Deposit Insurance Corporation - FDIC)

VII. Security Devices

SECURITY DEVICES (FINANCIAL INSTRUMENTS) are written documents that pledge real property as security for a promissory note.

The three financial instruments (security devices to collateralize real property) used in California are: mortgages, trust deeds, and land contracts.

In California we have three common types of security devices (financing instruments). See **Figure 8-5**. Any of the three previously mentioned notes may be used in conjunction with these financial instruments.

Figure 8-5

Financial Instruments

| MORTGAGES (Rare) | TRUST DEEDS (1st and 2nd) | LAND CONTRACTS (Not Common) |

A. MORTGAGES

A *MORTGAGE is a financial instrument in the form of a lien that secures a property for payment of a promissory note.* It is not common in California. The *MORTGAGOR is the buyer/owner who is borrowing*, and the *MORTGAGEE is the lender*.

Mortgage: A General Term

Although mortgages are rarely used in California, the term "mortgage" is so ingrained in the tradition of lending that often trust deeds and other loans are referred to as "mortgages." Adjustable Rate Mortgages and Fixed Rate Mortgages, for example, are deeds of trust. We will use the general words mortgage and deed of trust interchangeably, but mortgagee or mortgagor refer only to mortgages and trustee, trustor, and beneficiary refer only to trust deeds.

If the mortgagor defaults in his or her payments, a foreclosure action may be started. After the foreclosure sale, the borrower has one year to redeem (buy back) the property, pay all the accumulated charges, or pay the mortgagee rent. **Figure 8-6** is a two-page comparison of the differences between mortgages and trust deeds.

1. Power of Sale Clause

Some mortgages have a power of sale clause. A *POWER OF SALE CLAUSE allows the mortgagee to sell the property without a court proceeding (much like a trustee's sale) if the mortgagor is in default.* But it still requires a lengthy proceeding. If there is no power of sale clause, court (judicial) action is required for a foreclosure.

In a trust deed, the "power of sale" clause is given from the trustor to the trustee.

2. Mortgages Compared to Trust Deeds

a. Parties

In a mortgage there are two parties: the mortgagor (borrower) and the mortgagee (lender). The deed of trust has three: trustor (borrower), trustee (third party), and beneficiary (lender).

b. Title

A mortgage does not convey title; it creates a lien. In a deed of trust the title is conveyed to a trustee (third party) for the benefit of the lender (beneficiary) and is in effect a lien.

Figure 8-6

Trust Deed

1. Parties:

    a. Trustor – Borrower who conveys title to trustee who holds as security for debt.

    b. Trustee – Receiver of naked legal title who will reconvey it when debt is paid or will sell if foreclosure necessary (must be a corporation or division of an escrow company).

    c. Beneficiary – Lender who holds note and trust deed.

2. Legal Title – Conveyed to trustee with trustor retaining possession of the property.

3. Statute of Limitations – Since security for the debt (title) is held by trustee, rights of creditor are not ended when statute has run out on note.

4. Remedy for Default – Foreclosure can be instituted through:

    a. Trustee's Sale, or

    b. Court Foreclosure.

5. Right of Redemption – When title has been sold by trustee at Trustee's Sale, no right of redemption previously existed, but in rare cases the courts now say it does.

6. Satisfaction – Trustor has beneficiary send original note and trust deed to trustee with request for full reconveyance. Upon payment of fees, trustee issues reconveyance deed, which must be recorded.

7. Foreclosure by Trustee's Sale:

    a. Beneficiary notifies trustee of default, who in turn notifies trustor and also records notice. Anyone with recorded "Request for Notice of Default" must also be notified.

    b. Trustee waits at least three months. During three-month period, trustor can reinstate loan.

    c. Trustee advertises "Notice of Sale" once a week for three weeks and posts notice on property.

    d. Trustee conducts sale and issues Trustee's Deed to highest bidder.

8. Deficiency Judgment – No judgment available:

    a. if foreclosure by Trustee's Sale.

    b. on purchase money trust deeds, even if by court foreclosure. (Deficiency judgments may be obtained on FHA and VA first purchase money trust deeds.)

(continued)

Mortgage

1. Parties:

    a. Mortgagor – Borrower who retains title but gives lender a lien on the property as the security for debt.

    b. Mortgagee – Lender who holds the mortgage.

2. Title – Retained by mortgagor together with possession.

3. Statute of Limitations – Foreclosure is barred if no action is taken within four years of delinquency. Mortgage is said to have "outlawed."

4. Remedy for Default – Court foreclosure is usually the only remedy.

5. Right of Redemption – Mortgagor has one year to redeem following court foreclosure; called "Equity of Redemption."

6. Satisfaction of Mortgage – Upon final payment and on demand, mortgagee signs certificate that debt is satisfied. Certificate or release is recorded.

7. Foreclosure by Court:

    a. Court action commenced by mortgagee. Court issues decree of foreclosure and order of sale.

    b. Commissioner appointed by court sells to highest bidder after publication and posting of sale notice.

    c. Certificate of Sale issued by Commissioner. Mortgagor has one year to redeem property and to remain in possession.

    d. Sheriff's Deed issued after one year.

8. Deficiency Judgment – Available in court foreclosure unless mortgage was purchase money mortgage as noted below.

Note: Purchase money is defined as:

    1. Mortgage or trust deed or real property sales contract given to seller as part of purchase price, or

    2. Mortgage or trust deed given to lender to finance purchase of owner-occupied dwelling of four or fewer units.

c. Statute of Limitations

In a mortgage, an action to foreclose is subject to the statute of limitations. Since it is a promissory note, the mortgagee has four years from the date of the last payment to start foreclosure. With a trust deed, there is no time limit because the third party (trustee) has title and power of sale.

d. Remedy for Default

In a mortgage, the only remedy of the mortgagee (lender) is judicial (court) foreclosure, unless the mortgage contains a power of sale clause. Although the actual mortgage foreclosure takes a short period of time, the redemption period is very long (1 year). The **REDEMPTION PERIOD** *is the legally acceptable time period for buying back one's property after a judicial sale.* In a deed of trust the entire process, including any redemption or sale, requires a short period of time (4 months).

3. Trust Deeds are Preferred to Mortgages

In California, the trust deed is preferred to the mortgage as the usual financing device. The lender has fewer restrictions when using a trust deed. There is: 1) A short period to reinstate prior to the sale and the fact that the sale, once made, is usually absolute. The purchaser can take possession at once, which is not true for a mortgage; 2) The ease and convenience, without having to resort to court action, with which the property may be sold to satisfy the debt if the borrower defaults. California laws favor lenders who use the trust deed, which allows them more freedom in granting loans to deserving buyers.

B. TRUST DEEDS

1. Trust Deeds are Used in California

Trust deeds (deeds of trust loans) are personal property.

In California the trust deed, sometimes called a deed of trust, is the usual financing instrument. The **TRUST DEED** *is a security device that makes the real property collateral for the promissory note.* **Figure 8-7** shows a copy of a trust deed.

A trust deed needs a note for security, but a note does NOT need a trust deed. A trust deed is not a negotiable instrument; the note is. If the conditions of a note and the trust deed are in conflict, the note prevails.

2. Parties to a Trust Deed

In a trust deed there are three parties. The **TRUSTOR** *is usually the party that is borrowing the money.* This is often the buyer, but may also be the owner if the property is being refinanced. The **BENEFICIARY** *is the lender who is lending money for the purchase of real property.* Home lenders in California are usually savings banks, but may also be commercial banks. The **TRUSTEE** *is the third, disinterested party (usually a corporation) who holds naked legal title to the property, but only in so far as the trustee may have to sell the property for the beneficiary, should the trustor default.* This is normally a title insurance company. **Figure 8-8** illustrates this three-party relationship.

Figure 8-7

RECORDING REQUESTED BY

ORDER #
APN

WHEN RECORDED MAIL TO

Name
Street
Address
City &
State

——— SPACE ABOVE THIS LINE FOR RECORDER'S USE ———

SHORT FORM DEED OF TRUST AND ASSIGNMENT OF RENTS

ALL | PTN.

This Deed of Trust, made this _____ day of _____ , between

_____ , herein called TRUSTOR,

whose address is _____
(number and street)   (city)   (state)   (zip)

OLD REPUBLIC TITLE COMPANY, a California corporation, herein called TRUSTEE, and

_____ , herein called BENEFICIARY,

Witnesseth: That Trustor IRREVOCABLY GRANTS, TRANSFERS AND ASSIGNS TO TRUSTEE IN TRUST, WITH POWER OF SALE, that property in _____ County, California, described as:

TOGETHER WITH the rents, issues and profits thereof, SUBJECT, HOWEVER, to the right, power and authority given to and conferred upon Beneficiary by paragraph (10) of the provisions incorporated herein by reference to collect and apply such rents, issues and profits.

For the Purpose of Securing: 1. Performance of each agreement of Trustor incorporated by reference or contained herein. 2. Payment of the indebtedness evidenced by one promissory note of even date herewith, and any extension or renewal thereof, in the principal sum of $_____ executed by Trustor in favor of Beneficiary or order. 3. Payment of such further sums as the then record owner of said property hereafter may borrow from Beneficiary, when evidenced by another note (or notes) reciting it is so secured.

To Protect the Security of This Deed of Trust, Trustor Agrees: By the execution and delivery of this Deed of Trust and the note secured hereby, that provisions (1) to (14), inclusive, of the fictitious deed of trust recorded in Santa Barbara County and Sonoma County October 18, 1961, and in all other counties October 23, 1961, in the book and at the page of Official Records in the office of the county recorder of the county where said property is located, noted below opposite the name of such county, viz:

COUNTY	BOOK	PAGE	COUNTY	BOOK	PAGE	COUNTY	BOOK	PAGE	COUNTY	BOOK	PAGE
Alameda	435	684	Kings	792	833	Placer	895	301	Sierra	29	335
Alpine	1	250	Lake	362	39	Plumas	151	5	Siskiyou	468	181
Amador	104	348	Lassen	171	471	Riverside	3005	523	Solano	1105	182
Butte	1145	1	Los Angeles	T2055	899	Sacramento	4331	62	Sonoma	1851	689
Calaveras	145	152	Madera	810	170	San Benito	271	383	Stanislaus	1715	456
Colusa	296	617	Marin	1508	339	San Bernardino	5567	61	Sutter	572	297
Contra Costa	3978	47	Mariposa	77	292	San Francisco	A332	905	Tehama	401	289
Del Norte	78	414	Mendocino	579	530	San Joaquin	2470	311	Trinity	93	366
El Dorado	568	456	Merced	1547	538	San Luis Obispo	1151	12	Tulare	2294	275
Fresno	4626	572	Modoc	184	851	San Mateo	4078	420	Tuolumne	135	47
Glenn	422	184	Mono	52	429	Santa Barbara	1878	860	Ventura	2062	386
Humboldt	657	527	Monterey	2194	538	Santa Clara	5336	341	Yolo	653	245
Imperial	1091	501	Napa	639	86	Santa Cruz	1431	494	Yuba	334	486
Inyo	147	598	Nevada	305	320	Shasta	684	528			
Kern	3427	60	Orange	5889	611	San Diego	Series 2	Book 1961,	Page 183887		

(which provisions, identical in all counties, are printed on the reverse hereof) hereby are adopted and incorporated herein and made a part hereof as fully as though set forth herein at length; that he will observe and perform said provisions; and that the references to property, obligations, and parties in said provisions shall be construed to refer to the property, obligations, and parties set forth in this Deed of Trust.

The undersigned Trustor requests that a copy of any Notice of Default and of any Notice of Sale hereunder be mailed to him at his address hereinbefore set forth.

STATE OF CALIFORNIA } SS.
COUNTY OF _____

On _____ before me, the undersigned, a Notary Public in and for said State, personally appeared _____

_____,

personally known to me (or proved to me on the basis of satisfactory evidence) to be the person(s) whose name(s) is/are subscribed to the within instrument and acknowledged to me that he/she/they executed the same in his/her/their authorized capacity(ies), and that by his/her/their signature(s) on the instrument the person(s), or the entity upon behalf of which the person(s) acted, executed the instrument.

WITNESS my hand and official seal.

Signature _____

_____
Name (Typed or Printed)

(Seal)

ORT 100

OLD REPUBLIC
TITLE COMPANY

SHORT FORM
DEED OF TRUST AND
ASSIGNMENT OF RENTS

234

Figure 8-8

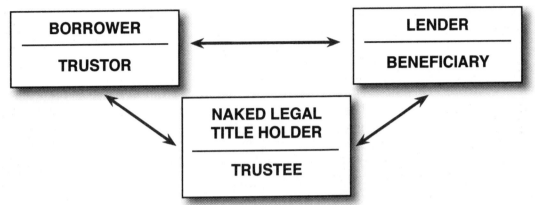

The trustor (borrower) signs the promissory note and trust deed, as he or she owes the debt. The lender is also known as the beneficiary.

A trust deed conveys bare (or naked) legal title (but not possession) of a property to a trustee as security for a loan. **A trust deed differs from other deeds in that the legal title only is thus conveyed**. A trust deed is a security device in the nature of a lien and differs in one respect from other deeds in that the trust deed and the promissory note for which it was given may be assigned.

When a real estate broker negotiates a loan on real property and creates a new trust deed, he/she must record the trust deed within 10 days.

A trust deed must have all three parties: trustor, trustee, and beneficiary. The trust deed and note form the lien, which conveys the "bare" or "naked" legal title of the property to the trustee, to be held until the trust deed is paid in full, at which time the title is reconveyed to the trustor through a reconveyance. If the trustor defaults in payments, the beneficiary will instruct the trustee to start the default period, which could ultimately lead to a trustee foreclosure sale.

EQUITABLE TITLE is held by a trustor while he or she is repaying a trust deed and note. It is **true ownership** in that the trustor may enjoy all customary rights of title and possession.

LEGAL TITLE, "Bare or Naked Legal Title," is held by a trustee until the terms of a trust deed and note have been fulfilled. When the trustor has paid the note in full, the trustee will reconvey the naked legal title.

3. Deed of Reconveyance (Proof of Payment in Full)

A *DEED OF RECONVEYANCE (Full Reconveyance) provides proof that a promissory note and the accompanying trust deed have been paid in full.* When the note has been paid in full, the beneficiary requests the trustee to grant a full reconveyance, which makes the trustor's legal title a part of the public record and gives evidence that the debt has been paid off. A full reconveyance must be recorded to give public notice, in the county records, that it has been paid. The reconveyance is paid for by the trustor.

When a debt has been paid in full, the trustee will record a deed of reconveyance to remove the lien of a trust deed from the public record.

See **Figure 8-9** for more information about a deed of reconveyance and **Figure 8-10** for an example.

Figure 8-9 **Full Reconveyance**

A full reconveyance is a simple written document that offers proof that a loan on real property has been paid off in full. If a trust deed (loan on real property) is to be paid off in full, a request for full reconveyance is to be signed by the beneficiary and sent to the trustee for recording.

The trustor (borrower), who is in the process of paying off a loan secured by a note and deed of trust on a certain piece of real property, wants the following:

1. The return of the original note,
2. The return of the original trust deed, and
3. A "Reconveyance deed" should be recorded in the county recorder's office where the deed of trust is recorded.

When the trustor originally borrowed the money to purchase property or later obtained a loan secured by the property, he or she signed a promissory note and a trust deed. This trust deed, when recorded, became a specific lien. If the trustor tries to sell or refinance the property, this lien will show up on all title searches or title reports until the deed of trust has been "reconveyed."

So it is extremely important for the trustor to have the deed of trust and note returned along with having the beneficiary sign a "Request for Full Reconveyance." Under California Civil Code Section 2941, the beneficiary must forward a deed of reconveyance, within 90 days of receiving the "Request for Full Reconveyance," to the trustee. Violation of this law is a misdemeanor punishable by a $300 fine, plus damages, and/or six months in jail.

VIII. Default and Foreclosure of a Trust Deed

A. DEFAULT ON A TRUST DEED

In California, the procedure and remedy for nonpayment of a trust deed is well established by law. The trust deed is a lien on the property involved. The lender has the legal right to receive the trust deed payment on time. By law the lender can start default action after the 10- to 15-day grace period. A *GRACE PERIOD is a set number of days in which a lender will allow a payment to be late without any penalty.* The lender, at any time after the grace period, may start default action/foreclosure against the trustor. **Figure 8-11** shows the sequence of events that will follow if the trustor does not make the trust deed payments.

When a borrower defaults on his or her payments under the trust deed and note, the beneficiary's remedy is to start default action. The beneficiary notifies the trustee of the trustor's failure to make the payments. **The trustee then records a notice of default, which will start the foreclosure action.**

When the trustee is notified by the lender (beneficiary) of the trustor's nonpayment, the trustee records a "notice of default" (see **Figure 8-12**). This notice contains all the pertinent

Figure 8-10

RECORDING REQUESTED BY

AND WHEN RECORDED MAIL TO

_____SPACE ABOVE THIS LINE FOR RECORDER'S USE_____

TITLE ORDER NO.   TRUSTEE SALE NO.   COMPUTER NO.

FULL RECONVEYANCE

now duly appointed Trustee under Deed of Trust

EXECUTED BY:

TRUSTOR(S)
TRUSTEE

TO:

Recorded on   as Document no.   Book   Page
of Official Records in the office of the Recorder of   County,
California, having been requested in writing, by the holder of the obligation secured by said deed of trust, to reconvey the
estate granted to trustee under said deed of trust, DOES HEREBY RECONVEY to the person or persons legally entitled
thereto, without warranty, all the estate, title, and interest acquired by trustee under said deed of trust.
Brief description of property:

DATE:

BY: _____
                    Assistant Secretary

STATE OF CALIFORNIA   } SS.

COUNTY OF _____
On this the_____ day of_____ 19____,
before me the, the undersigned, a Notary Public in and for
said County and State, personally appeared _____

_____
personally known to me or proved to me on the basis of
satisfactory evidence to be the person who executed the within
instrument as an Assistant Secretary, on behalf of the corporation therein named, and acknowledged to me that such
corporation executed the within instrument pursuant to its bylaws or a resolution of its board of directors.

_____
Notary's Signature
SAFECO Stock No. **CA-BNL-0110**

Full Reconveyance

CHAPTER 8

Figure 8-11

PAYMENT PAST DUE	3 MONTHS MINIMUM	21 DAYS MINIMUM	1 DAY
NOTICE OF DEFAULT RECORDED	REINSTATEMENT PERIOD (up to 5 days before sale)	PUBLISHING PERIOD (3 weeks)	TRUSTEE'S SALE

information about the default. Within 10 days after the recording, the borrower (trustor) and all people who have filed a "request for notice," such as junior lienholders, will receive (by certified or registered mail) notification from the trustee of the default. In addition, the notice of default must be published in a newspaper of general circulation once a week for three weeks.

A seller who agrees to carry back a second trust deed has a "request for notice of default" recorded to protect his or her interests as a beneficiary of the second trust deed.

B. TRUSTOR'S RIGHT OF REINSTATEMENT

1. Reinstatement Period (Three Months)

During the three-month reinstatement period after the "notice of default" is filed, the trustor may reinstate the loan. The *REINSTATEMENT PERIOD is the time within which the trustor may pay all past due payments.* To do this, the trustor must pay the beneficiary the following:

1. All past due payments, penalties, taxes, and interest.
2. Any other costs to the beneficiary.
3. All costs and fees owed to the trustee.

The trustor can reinstate a loan up until five days prior to foreclosure (the trustee's sale). If reinstated, it is again in good standing.

If the trustor does not pay the past due payments, taxes, interest, and other charges within the three-month reinstatement period, the reinstatement rights are lost. This reinstatement period runs until five days before the date of sale. Sometimes in special circumstances, and always at the discretion of the lender, the trustor may still be allowed to reinstate the loan after this period. If the beneficiary decides to foreclose, however, he or she will start the process by recording a "notice of sale."

2. Notice Of Sale (21 Days)

After recording a "notice of default," a trustee must wait three months (90 days) before publishing a "notice of sale."

The *NOTICE OF SALE is a recorded notice stating the time, place, property description, and type of sale.* See Figure 8-12, the notice of default. It also serves as the notice of sale. **The notice must be published in a newspaper of general circulation once a week during the 21-day publishing period.** A copy of the notice must also be posted on the property

238

Figure 8-12

RECORDING REQUESTED BY

WHEN RECORDED MAIL TO

_____
_____
_____

SPACE ABOVE THIS LINE FOR RECORDER'S USE

TRUST ORDER NO.

Notice of Default and Election to Sell Under Deed of Trust

NOTICE IS HEREBY GIVEN: That _____, a corporation, is Trustee, or successor Trustee, or substituted Trustee under a deed of trust dated_____, executed by_____ as Trustor,

to secure certain obligations in favor of _____

as Beneficiary, recorded_____, in Book_____, Page_____, of Official Records in the office of the Recorder of _____ County, California, describing land therein as:

said obligations including_____note_____for the_____ sum of $_____,

That the beneficial interest under such deed and the obligations secured thereby have been transferred to the undersigned;
That a breach of, and default in, the obligations for which such deed is security has occurred in that payment has not been made of:

That by reason thereof, the undersigned, present beneficiary under such deed, has executed and delivered to said Trustee, or successor Trustee, or substituted Trustee a written Declaration of Default and Demand for sale, and has deposited with said Trustee, or successor Trustee, or substituted Trustee such deed and all documents evidencing obligations secured thereby, and has declared and does hereby declare all sums secured thereby immediately due and payable and has elected and does hereby elect to cause the trust property to be sold to satisfy the obligations secured thereby.

Dated _____

STATE OF CALIFORNIA
COUNTY OF _____ } ss.
On _____
before me, the undersigned, a Notary Public in and for said County and State, personally appeared

known to me to be the person___ whose name___
subscribed to the within instrument and acknowledged that_____
executed the same.
WITNESS my hand and official seal.

(Seal) _____
Notary Public in and for said County and State
NOTARY—PLEASE PRINT OR TYPE YOUR NAME BELOW SIGNATURE

THIS NOTICE MUST BE RECORDED BY ←

TRUST ORDER NO._____

239

and in a public place, such as the city hall. Most title insurance companies also post a copy if they are acting as trustee.

3. The Trustee's Sale (Foreclosure Sale)

The trustee's sale is held at the time and place stated in the notice of sale. At the public sale, the trustee states the purpose of the sale and describes the property to be sold. All bids must be in the form of cash or cashier's checks.

The first deed holder may bid up to the total amount of the debt without cash. Because it costs the first trust deed holder nothing more than what he or she is already owed, that person will usually make the first bid. The highest bidder obtains the property and will be issued a trustee's deed. Any money more than the amount owed is reimbursed to the trustor. The new owner is entitled to immediate possession.

A trustee's sale is a nonjudicial foreclosure under the "power of sale" clause in the deed of trust and promissory note.

4. Judicial Court Foreclosure for a Trust Deed (Rare)

In rare cases, a beneficiary (lender) in California may want to foreclose by court action instead of the simpler trustee's sale. The reason would be to obtain a **deficiency judgment** if it was not a purchase money trust deed. See the purchase money section below.

5. Deed in Lieu of Foreclosure

A DEED IN LIEU OF FORECLOSURE is a deed given by an owner (borrower) to a lender to prevent the lender from bringing foreclosure proceedings. **The lender (beneficiary) becomes the new owner of the property and takes responsibility for any junior liens (loans) on the property.** It is up to the lender to accept or reject such an offer. This could save the borrower's credit in some circumstances.

6. Short Sale (Increasing Foreclosure Alternative Due to 2007-2009 Credit Crunch)

A SHORT SALE is when a lender will accept less than the amount owed on a debt if the property is sold. This arrangement must be approved by the lender who knows the borrower has financial problems (see **Figure 8-13**, CAR Short Sale Listing Addendum).

If you convince your lender to mark a short sale as paid, it may not affect your credit as badly as a foreclosure. See an attorney for advice.

C. LIENS NOT ELIMINATED BY FORECLOSURE SALE

Most junior liens are eliminated by foreclosure. The following liens might not be eliminated:

1. Federal tax liens
2. State, county, and city taxes or assessments
3. Mechanic's liens for work begun before the trust deed was recorded

D. PURCHASE MONEY TRUST DEED OR MORTGAGE

A PURCHASE MONEY INSTRUMENT is a trust deed or mortgage obtained during the purchase of a home (1-to-4 units, owner-occupied). It is called a purchase money instrument **only when**

Figure 8-13

CALIFORNIA
ASSOCIATION
OF REALTORS®

SHORT SALE LISTING ADDENDUM
(C.A.R. Form SSL, 8/07)

This is an addendum to the ☐ Residential Listing Agreement, ☐ Other _____ ,
("Agreement"), dated _____ on property known as _123 WinSail,_ _____
_____ ("Property"), between
_____ ("Seller"),
_____ ("Broker").
and _____

1. **SHORT SALE LISTING:** Broker has advised Seller that the amount of money necessary to pay in full all loans and other debt or obligations that are secured by a lien(s), including any IRS liens, on the Property (Loans/Liens) as well as Broker commissions and other costs of sale may exceed the current market value of the Property. Accordingly, in order to sell the Property, Seller may be required to: (1) deposit his/her own funds into escrow, (2) obtain the agreement of secured lender(s) or creditor(s) (Lender) to accept, as payment in full, less money than they are owed (Short Sale), and/or (3) pay back some or all of the shortage after the sale is complete. Broker has advised Seller that other options, such as, but not limited to, negotiating a modification of existing Loans/Liens, refinancing, bankruptcy, foreclosure, or deed in lieu of foreclosure may be more appropriate for Seller. Any sale of the Property will be contingent on Lender approval (C.A.R. Form PAA, # 5).
2. **TAX CONSEQUENCES:** Broker has advised Seller that if Lender agrees to accept less than full payment, the difference may result in taxable income to Seller even though Seller does not receive any cash proceeds from the sale. Seller may also be taxed on the gain in value of the Property from the date of Seller's purchase to the date of sale, regardless of the amount of any existing Loans/Liens.
3. **CREDIT CONSEQUENCES:** A Short Sale may have a negative impact on Seller's credit rating even if a foreclosure process has not officially begun or once begun, is not completed.
4. **LENDER CONSIDERATIONS:** Seller acknowledges that a Short Sale is subject to Lender approval. Lender is not obligated to accept a Short Sale. Lender may impose conditions prior to consideration or approval of a Short Sale, such as obtaining a new appraisal, or requiring Seller to demonstrate hardship or provide copies of tax returns, pay stubs, assets, or other financial information. Lender may inform the IRS or credit reporting companies of the payment shortage. Broker has no control over Lender's decisions. Accordingly, Seller agrees to hold Broker harmless for acts or omissions of Lender.
5. **BROKER AUTHORITY:** Seller authorizes Broker to: (1) market the Property for sale, (2) contact Lender concerning Lender's approval of a Short Sale (C.A.R. Form ARC) and Seller agrees to give Broker any necessary information to negotiate with Lender, and (3) advertise in the MLS and other advertising medium that the Property transfer, sales price and payment of commissions are subject to Lender approval. If Lender will not cooperate, Broker may cancel this listing agreement.
6. **TAX AND LEGAL ADVICE:** Broker has advised Seller to consult with legal and tax counsel, prior to signing this listing, regarding the decision to seek a Short Sale. Broker cannot give legal or tax advice.

By signing below, Seller acknowledges that Seller has read, understands and received a copy of this Short Sale Listing Addendum. Seller is encouraged to read it carefully.

Date _____   Date _____

SELLER _____   SELLER _____

_____   _____
(Print name)   (Print name)

_____
(Address)

Real Estate Broker (Listing Firm) _____ DRE Lic. # _____

By _____ DRE Lic. # _____ Date _____

Address _____ City _____ State _____ Zip _____

Telephone _____ Fax _____ E-mail _____

Published and Distributed by:
REAL ESTATE BUSINESS SERVICES, INC.
a subsidiary of the CALIFORNIA ASSOCIATION OF REALTORS®
525 South Virgil Avenue, Los Angeles, California 90020

Reviewed by _____ Date _____

SSL 8/07 (PAGE 1 OF 1)   **SHORT SALE LISTING ADDENDUM (SSL PAGE 1 OF 1)**

WALT HUBER, REALTOR   123 Winsail   , MARINA DEL REY   CA 90292
Phone: Fax: Walt Huber   123 WindSail.z

it is obtained at the time of purchase, **not on a refinanced loan**. It is an automatic protection given to homeowners (nothing is signed and nothing is mentioned). This is important because if the property is forced into foreclosure, a purchase money trust deed holder, or mortgage lender, cannot obtain a deficiency judgment. (Deficiency judgments may be obtained on **FHA and VA home loans** because federal law supercedes state law.)

A *DEFICIENCY JUDGMENT is given when the security pledged for a loan does not satisfy the debt upon its default.* If a home was sold at a court foreclosure sale for $217,000 and $240,000 was owed on the property, a lender would have a $23,000 deficiency judgment against the borrower. If it were a purchase money instrument, however, there would be no deficiency judgment.

The purchase money instrument only protects owners of residential dwellings of 1-to-4 units where the owner lives in one unit. Owners of properties having more than four units or properties that do not have a purchase money instrument are not protected against possible deficiency judgments. **Remember:** deficiency judgments can be obtained only if the owner doesn't have a purchase money instrument and is foreclosed upon in a court foreclosure sale.

IX. Second Trust Deeds (Junior TDs)

Due to the tight financial market of 2007-2009, a seller may have to take back a second trust deed as part of his or her equity in order to make the sale.

Even if a buyer qualifies for a loan to cover 80% of the cost of a home, he or she may still have a difficult time scraping together the 20% needed for the down payment. **When a buyer does not have enough cash to cover the gap between the sales price and the loan amount, another loan, or "second" trust deed, is sometimes obtained (often from the seller) and the interest charged the buyer is not governed by the usury law (10% is common).**

A. JUNIOR LIENS ("Private Parties")

Besides seconds, it is also possible for borrowers who qualify to obtain "third" or "fourth" trust deeds, but they are all commonly referred to as second trust deeds or junior liens. They all may be called second trust deeds but their priority is determined by the order in which they were recorded. *Any loan on real property obtained after the first trust deed and secured by a second, third, or subsequent trust deed, is known as a JUNIOR LIEN.* The most senior lien, on the other hand, is the first trust deed.

> **Example:** Smith is buying a house with a sale's price of $250,000. She assumes the seller's loan on the property of $200,000. She applies to her company credit union and is given a second trust deed of $30,000, so all she needs is a cash down payment of $20,000, plus closing costs, to complete the transaction.

B. HOMEOWNER EQUITY LOANS

Second trust deeds are not only obtainable as part of the financing package when a property is first being purchased. Seconds and other junior liens may be arranged any time a qualified borrower wants to borrow money, for whatever reason, as long as there is sufficient equity and enough ready income to support the payments. *EQUITY is the fair market value of a property, minus the amount of money owed to lenders and all other lienholders.* **HOMEOWNER EQUITY LOANS** *are loans based on the homeowner's increase in equity caused by inflation, rising property values, and the reduction, by payments, of the existing loan balance.*

Let's suppose Smith, who purchased that new home for $250,000, finds herself in need of money after a few years. Fortunately, her property has increased in market value and is now worth more than $300,000. Even though Smith is already mortgaged up to her ears, she can borrow on her equity; the difference between what she owes and what her property is worth.

Homeowner equity loans are generally secured by second (junior) trust deeds. They are available from institutional lenders, small finance companies, and individuals who specialize in this area. Lenders will charge a higher interest rate on seconds and other junior trust deeds because they are less secure than primary financing.

C. HOLDER OF A SECOND TRUST DEED (Lender)

Sometimes when purchasing a property, additional funds will be required beyond the cash down payment and the first trust deed. As a result, the seller may loan the buyer more money through the use of a second trust deed. Usually the second trust deed has a higher rate of interest and a shorter payoff period because of the higher risk involved. The usual monthly payment is one percent of the loan.

Second trust deeds often require a balloon payment at the end of the term because they are not fully amortized. The holder of a second trust deed or any junior trust deed has the same rights as does the holder of the first deed of trust. He or she is entitled to his or her payment each month, as is the first trust deed holder. If the trustor defaults on the second, the second trust deed holder, just like the first trust deed holder, can start default action. In addition, if the trustor defaults on the first trust deed, the second trust deed holder can reinstate the first trust deed and start default action against the trustor. If the property's market value is higher than the total amount owed on the first trust deed, it is a wise move for the second trust deed holder to start his or her own default and sale action.

D. REQUEST FOR NOTICE

When a **REQUEST FOR NOTICE** *is recorded, the trustee is required to notify all persons who request notice if a "notice of default" is recorded on a particular property* (see **Figure 8-14**). Any person who has an interest in a particular trust deed, usually a second or third trust deed holder, should want to be informed if the buyer is not paying on the first deed of trust. This information not only informs the junior deed holders of nonpayment on the first trust deed, but it also allows them time to prepare to purchase the trust deed at the forthcoming trustee's sale. It will also give them time to start default actions on their own junior trust deeds.

This request for notice is recorded in the county recorder's office where the property is located. If a seller takes back a second or even a third trust deed, thereby becoming a junior trust deed holder on the property that person has just sold, that person would be wise to record a request for notice. Some request for notice forms are incorporated into the trust deed form, so the request for notice is automatically filed.

Figure 8-14

RECORDING REQUESTED BY

AND WHEN RECORDED MAIL TO

NAME
ADDRESS
CITY &
    STATE

————— SPACE ABOVE THIS LINE FOR RECORDER'S USE —————

REQUEST FOR NOTICE

In accordance with section 2924b, Civil Code, request is hereby made that a copy of any notice of default

and a copy of any notice of sale under the deed of trust recorded   19

in Book   page   of official records of   County, (or filed for record

with recorder's serial No.

                          County) California, executed by

as trustor in which

is named as beneficiary and

as trustee be mailed to   whose

address is

                          Signature ....

FOR NOTARY SEAL OR STAMP

STATE OF CALIFORNIA

COUNTY OF   SS.

On this the   day of   19   . before me.
the undersigned. a Notary Public in and for said County and State.
personally appeared

_____ . personally known
to me or proved to me on the basis of satisfactory evidence to be the
person   whose name   subscribed to the within
instrument and acknowledged that
executed the same.

NOTARY SIGNATURE

STATE OF CALIFORNIA
COUNTY OF_____

On this the_____ day of _____19_____ before
me, the undersigned, a Notary Public in and for said County and State.
personally appeared_____

_____ , personally
known to me or proved to me on the basis of satisfactory evidence to
be the_____ President, and_____

_____ , personally
known to me or proved to me on the basis of satisfactory evidence to
be _____ Secretary of the corporation that executed the
within instrument on behalf of the corporation therein named, and
acknowledged to me that such corporation executed the within instrument pursuant to its by-laws or a resolution of its board of directors.

_____
NOTARY SIGNATURE

Title Order No.   Escrow No.

SAFECO Stock No. **CAL-0038**

244

E. WRAPAROUND – ALL INCLUSIVE TRUST DEEDS (AITD)

An *ALL INCLUSIVE TRUST DEED (WRAPAROUND) is a second trust deed with a face value of both the new amount it secures and the balance due under the first trust deed.* A wraparound trust deed can take the form of a land contract or a deed of trust. The wraparound is seldom used except when a property is difficult to sell or credit is tight (high interest rates). This form of security may be used to increase the lender's (seller's) yield upon the sale of property and to provide easy financing for the buyer. Rather than having a new buyer assume an existing loan, the seller carries back a wraparound trust deed at a higher rate of interest (if the loan is assumable). The seller continues to pay off the old trust deed out of the payment received from the buyer. Since these payments are larger, the seller gets a margin of profit. The buyer, in turn, gets easy financing and avoids the new loan fees charged by institutional lenders. As always, an attorney should be consulted because wraparound contracts may require special handling and will not be available with all loans.

X. Land Contract
(Conditional Installment Sales Contract)

A buyer purchasing a home under a valid land sales contact holds equitable title, and is entitled to full use and enjoyment of the property.

The *LAND CONTRACT is an instrument of finance in which the seller retains legal ownership of the property until the buyer has made the last payment.* It is usually called a land contract in California, but may also be referred to as a "contract of sale," "agreement of sale," "conditional sales contract," or an "installment sales contract." Since this is a contract between the buyer and seller, the requirements as to the down payment and other conditions of the land contract are negotiable.

A vendee (buyer) under a land contract should record the land contract for his/her protection.

When financing is hard to obtain, this can be an alternative to the usual financing methods. Although it is not widely used, it is a valid financing device (see **Figure 8-15**).

With a land contract, the seller keeps legal title to the property until the last payment is made. This is a 2007-2009 credit crunch/slump alternative financing method!

An owner selling under a land contract is known as a **VENDOR**. A **VENDEE** is a buyer using a land contract. A vendor can sell his or her store (real property) and store fixtures (personal property) to a vendee by use of a land contract. A land contract is a common way to sell a business.

With a land contract the buyer holds **equitable title**, like a borrower purchasing under a trust deed. He or she is entitled, though, to the full use and enjoyment of the property. Legal title is held by the seller until the land contract terms have been completely fulfilled. A grant deed to the property is given only when the land contract is paid off in full.

Land contracts should be recorded. If the buyer were to default, his or her interest would show as a cloud on the title. To protect his or her interests, the vendee (buyer) should record the land contract. This alternative financing method increased (2007-2009).

If a buyer (vendee) defaults on a recorded land contract, the seller (vendor) should file a "quiet title action" to remove the "cloud on title."

Figure 8-15

RECORDING REQUESTED BY

AND WHEN RECORDED MAIL TO

Name
Street
Address
City &
State

━━━━━━━━━━ SPACE ABOVE THIS LINE FOR RECORDER'S USE ━━━━━━━━━━

FORM 1   LONG FORM SECURITY (INSTALLMENT) LAND CONTRACT WITH POWER OF SALE   D-120

THIS AGREEMENT, made and entered into .his _____ day of _____ , 19 ____ , by and
between _____ (Vendor's name),
whose address is
(hereinafter sometimes referred to as "Vendor"), and
_____ (Vendee's name), whose address is
_____ (hereinafter sometimes referred to as "Vendee"); and
STEWART TITLE, (hereinafter sometimes referred to as "Trustee.")
W I T N E S S E T H :
WHEREAS, Vendor is now the owner of certain real property situated in the County of
State of California, commonly known as
_____ (property street address), and described as follows:

WHEREAS, Vendor has agreed to sell, and Vendee has agreed to buy said real property on the terms and conditions hereinafter set
forth;
WHEREAS, Vendor shall retain legal title as a security interest in said real property until the payment of the balance of the purchase
price has been paid by Vendee to Vendor as set forth below.
NOW, THEREFORE, THE PARTIES HERETO DO HEREBY AGREE AS FOLLOWS:
PURCHASE PRICE
1. Vendor agrees to sell, and Vendee agrees to buy all of the aforedescribed real property for the sum of
_____ (Total purchase price) ($_____),
lawful money of the United States, as hereinafter more fully set forth.

REQUEST FOR NOTICE OF DEFAULT
2. In accordance with Section 2924b, Civil Code, request is hereby made by the undersigned Vendor and
Vendee that a copy of any Notice of Default and a copy of any Notice of Sale under Deed of Trust re-
corded_____ in Book_____ , Page_____ , Official Records of
_____ County, California, as affecting above described property, executed by
_____ as Trustor in which_____
is named as beneficiary, and_____ as Trustee, be mailed to Vendor
and Vendee at address in paragraph 3 below.
NOTICES AND REQUEST FOR NOTICE
3. Notices required or permitted under this agreement shall be binding if delivered personally to party
sought to be served or if mailed by registered or certified mail, postage prepaid in the United States mail
to the following:
Vendor: _____
_____
_____   Trustee: Stewart Title
Vendee: _____   505 North Brand, 12th Floor
_____   Glendale, California 91203
_____
Vendor and Vendee hereby request that notice of default and notice of sale hereunder be mailed to them at the above address.

PAYMENT OF PURCHASE PRICE
4. Vendee shall pay said purchase price of $_____ as follows:
   (a) Vendee shall pay to Vendor the sum of $_____ (Down Payment) as and for a down payment.
   (b) Vendee shall take subject to and pay the balance due on that certain note secured by a first trust deed on the above mentioned real property, the principal balance of which is $_____ , together with interest thereon at the rate of
percent per annum, payable in installments of
$_____ , (monthly payments amount; add "or more" if applicable) per month on the _____ day of each and
every month with the whole of the then outstanding balance thereof due on the _____ day of
19 ____ . Each such payment includes payment of the following items under the terms of said note and trust deed:
        (1)   Principal and interest;
        (2)   Impounds for taxes;   (Strike out
        (3)   Impounds for fire insurance;   inapplicable
                                                     items.)
        (4)   Impounds for _____
Payments shall be made by Vendee directly to beneficiary of said first trust deed at the following address:
_____
_____
                    (If a second trust deed exists, complete (c) below)
   (c) Vendee shall take subject to and pay the balance due on that certain note secured by a second trust deed on the above
mentioned real property, principal balance of which is $_____ together with interest thereon at the rate of
percent per annum, payable in installments of $_____ (monthly payment amount, add "or more"

Land contracts are legal documents that should be drawn by and discussed with an attorney before use. Legal problems associated with a land contract are: obtaining marketable title, non-recorded status, intervening liens, foreclosure, and quiet title action. As you can see, legal advice is necessary.

XI. Truth in Lending Act (Regulation Z) and Other Acts

Regulation Z applies to 1-4 residential units, NOT to agricultural, business, or commercial loans.

A. TRUTH IN LENDING

The **TRUTH IN LENDING ACT**, *known as Regulation Z, was enacted to protect the consumer by requiring that the lender (creditor) tell the borrower how much he or she is paying for credit.* This enables the consumer to make comparisons between various credit sources. Regulation Z also states that the lender (creditor) must express all related financing costs as a percentage, known as the annual percentage rate (APR).

Regulation Z is enforced by the Federal Trade Commission (FTC). The CAR® 3-page Mortgage Loan Disclosure Statement is used to implement Regulation Z (see **Figure 8-16**). See **Figure 8-17** for an example of the CAR® Seller Financing Addendum and Disclosure form.

A low down payment and a long-term loan will increase the total financing cost.

1. Annual Percentage Rate (APR)

APR is the measure or "relative cost of credit" expressed as an annual rate. If the APR appears in an advertisement, NO other disclosure of terms need be stated because it includes all credit costs.

The **ANNUAL PERCENTAGE RATE (APR)** *represents the relationship between the total of the finance charges (interest rate, points, and the loan fee) and the total amount financed, expressed as a percentage.* It must be computed to the nearest one-quarter of one percent and must be printed on the loan form more conspicuously than the rest of the printed material.

Interest rates can be calculated by many different methods that can be very confusing to the borrower. The APR standardizes these figures, calculating all rates by the same formula. Borrowers should look for the APR figure (usually in a box) to compare and find the best APR available.

According to the Federal Truth in Lending Act, the lender must disclose the annual percentage rate of a loan, which is the cost of credit, including interest and other financing costs, expressed as an annual rate.

2. Advertising Terms May Require Additional Disclosures

Anyone placing an advertisement for consumer credit must comply with the advertising requirements of the Truth in Lending Act. Disclosures must be made "clearly and conspicuously." If **only the annual percentage (APR) rate is disclosed, additional**

Figure 8-16

CALIFORNIA
ASSOCIATION
OF REALTORS®

**MORTGAGE LOAN DISCLOSURE STATEMENT
(BORROWER)**

(As required by the Business and Professions Code §10241
and Title 10, California Administrative Code, §2840)

_____
(Name of Broker/Arranger of Credit)

_____
(Business Address of Broker)

I. SUMMARY OF LOAN TERMS
  A. PRINCIPAL AMOUNT . . . . $ _____
  B. ESTIMATED DEDUCTIONS FROM PRINCIPAL AMOUNT
    1. Costs and Expenses (See Paragraph III-A) . . . . $ _____
    *2. Broker Commission/Organization Fee (See Paragraph III-B) . . . . $ _____
    3. Lender Origination Fee/Discounts (See Paragraph III-B) . . . . $ _____
    4. Additional compensation will/may be received from lender not deducted from loan proceeds.
       ☐ YES $ _____ (if known) or ☐ NO
    5. Amount to be Paid on Authorization of Borrower (See Paragraph III) . . . . $ _____
  C. ESTIMATED CASH PAYABLE TO BORROWER (A less B) . . . . $ _____
II. GENERAL INFORMATION ABOUT LOAN
  A. If this loan is made, Borrower will be required to pay the principal and interest at _____% per year, payable
     as follows: _____ _____ payments of $ _____
                  (number of payments)   (monthly/quarterly/annually)
     and a **FINAL/BALLOON** payment of $ _____ to pay off the loan in full.

  **NOTICE TO BORROWER: IF YOU DO NOT HAVE THE FUNDS TO PAY THE BALLOON PAYMENT WHEN IT
  COMES DUE, YOU MAY HAVE TO OBTAIN A NEW LOAN AGAINST YOUR PROPERTY TO MAKE THE
  BALLOON PAYMENT. IN THAT CASE, YOU MAY AGAIN HAVE TO PAY COMMISSIONS, FEES AND EXPENSES
  FOR THE ARRANGING OF THE NEW LOAN. IN ADDITION, IF YOU ARE UNABLE TO MAKE THE MONTHLY
  PAYMENTS OR THE BALLOON PAYMENT, YOU MAY LOSE THE PROPERTY AND ALL OF YOUR EQUITY
  THROUGH FORECLOSURE. KEEP THIS IN MIND IN DECIDING UPON THE AMOUNT AND TERMS OF THIS LOAN.**

  B. This loan will be evidenced by a promissory note and secured by a deed of trust on property identified as (street
     address or legal description):
     _____
     _____

  C. 1. Liens presently against this property (do not include loan being applied for):
        Nature of Lien   Priority   Lienholder's Name   Amount Owing
        _____   _____   _____   _____
        _____   _____   _____   _____

     2. Liens that will remain against this property after the loan being applied for is made or arranged (include loan
        being applied for):
        Nature of Lien   Priority   Lienholder's Name   Amount Owing
        _____   _____   _____   _____
        _____   _____   _____   _____

  NOTICE TO BORROWER: Be sure that you state the amount of all liens as accurately as possible. If you contract
  with the broker to arrange this loan, but it cannot be arranged because you did not state these liens correctly, you
  may be liable to pay commissions, fees and expenses even though you do not obtain the loan.

Borrower acknowledges receipt of copy of this page.

Borrower's Initials (_____)(_____)

MS REVISED 10/2000 (PAGE 1 OF 3) Print Date

Reviewed by _____ Date _____

EQUAL HOUSING
OPPORTUNITY

MORTGAGE LOAN DISCLOSURE STATEMENT (MS PAGE 1 OF 3)

Property Address: _____ Date: _____

D. If Borrower pays all or part of the loan principal before it is due, a PREPAYMENT PENALTY computed as follows may be charged:

_____

_____

_____

E. Late Charges: ☐ YES, see loan documents or ☐ NO
F. The purchase of credit life or credit disability insurance by a borrower is not required as a condition of making this loan.
G. Is the real property which will secure the requested loan an "owner-occupied dwelling?" ☐ YES____ or ☐ NO____
   (Borrower initial opposite YES or NO)

An "owner-occupied dwelling" means a single dwelling unit in a condominium or cooperative or residential building of four or fewer separate dwelling units, one of which will be owned and occupied by a signatory to the mortgage or deed of trust for this loan within 90 days of the signing of the mortgage or deed of trust.

III. DEDUCTIONS FROM LOAN PROCEEDS

A. Estimated Maximum Costs and Expenses of Arranging the Loan to be Paid Out of Loan Principal:

	PAYABLE TO	
	Broker	**Others**
1. Appraisal fee	_____	_____
2. Escrow fee	_____	_____
3. Title insurance policy	_____	_____
4. Notary fees	_____	_____
5. Recording fees	_____	_____
6. Credit investigation fees	_____	_____
7. Other costs and expenses:		
_____	_____	_____
_____	_____	_____
Total Costs and Expenses	$ _____	

*B. Compensation .... | $ _____
   1. Brokerage Commission/Origination Fee .... | $ _____
   2. Lender Origination Fee/Discounts .... | $ _____

C. Estimated Payment to be Made out of Loan Principal on Authorization of Borrower

	PAYABLE TO	
	Broker	**Others**
1. Fire or other hazard insurance premiums	_____	_____
2. Credit life or disability insurance premiums (see Paragraph II-F)	_____	_____
3. Beneficiary statement fees	_____	_____
4. Reconveyance and similar fees	_____	_____
5. Discharge of existing liens against property:		
_____	_____	_____
_____	_____	_____
6. Other:		
_____	_____	_____
_____	_____	_____
Total to be Paid on Authorization of Borrower	$ _____	

If this loan is secured by a first deed of trust on dwellings in a principal amount of less than $30,000 or secured by a junior lien on dwellings in a principal amount of less than $20,000, the undersigned licensee certifies that the loan will be made in compliance with Article 7 of Chapter 3 of the Real Estate Law.

*This loan **may / will / will not** (delete two) be made wholly or in part from broker-controlled funds as defined in Section 10241(j) of the Business and Professions Code.

MS REVISED 10/2000 (PAGE 2 OF 3) Print Date

Borrower acknowledges receipt of copy of this page.

Borrower's Initials (_____)(_____)

| Reviewed by _____ Date _____ |

EQUAL HOUSING OPPORTUNITY

MORTGAGE LOAN DISCLOSURE STATEMENT (MS PAGE 2 OF 3)

Property Address: _____ Date: _____

*NOTICE TO BORROWER: This disclosure statement may be used if the Broker is acting as an agent in arranging the loan by a third person or if the loan will be made with funds owned or controlled by the broker. If the Broker indicates in the above statement that the loan "may" be made out of Broker-controlled funds, the Broker must notify the borrower prior to the close of escrow if the funds to be received by the Borrower are in fact Broker-controlled funds.

_____   _____
Name of Broker   Broker Representative

_____   _____
License Number   License Number

_____ OR _____
Signature of Broker   Signature

The Department of Real Estate License Information phone number is _____.

NOTICE TO BORROWER:

DO NOT SIGN THIS STATEMENT UNTIL YOU HAVE READ AND UNDERSTAND ALL OF THE INFORMATION IN IT. ALL PARTS OF THE FORM MUST BE COMPLETED BEFORE YOU SIGN.

Borrower hereby acknowledges the receipt of a copy of this statement.

DATED _____   _____
                                                                                       (Borrower)

                                                                 _____
                                                                                       (Borrower)

Broker Review: Signature of Real Estate Broker after review of this statement.

DATED _____

                                                                 Real Estate Broker or Assistant Pursuant to Section 2725

SURE TRAC
The System for Success®

Published and Distributed by:
REAL ESTATE BUSINESS SERVICES, INC.
a subsidiary of the California Association of REALTORS®
525 South Virgil Avenue, Los Angeles, California 90020

MS REVISED 10/2000 (PAGE 3 OF 3) Print Date

Reviewed by _____ Date _____

EQUAL HOUSING OPPORTUNITY

MORTGAGE LOAN DISCLOSURE STATEMENT (MS PAGE 3 OF 3)

Figure 8-17

CALIFORNIA
ASSOCIATION
OF REALTORS®

SELLER FINANCING ADDENDUM AND DISCLOSURE
(California Civil Code §§2956-2967)
(C.A.R. Form SFA, Revised 10/02)

This is an addendum to the ☐ Residential Purchase Agreement, ☐ Counter Offer, or ☐ Other _____
_____, ("Agreement"), dated _____
On property known as _____ ("Property"),
between _____ ("Buyer"),
and _____ ("Seller").
Seller agrees to extend credit to Buyer as follows:

1. **PRINCIPAL; INTEREST; PAYMENT; MATURITY TERMS:** ☐ Principal amount $ _____, interest at _____%
   per annum, payable at approximately $ _____ per ☐ month, ☐ year, or ☐ other _____,
   remaining principal balance due in _____ years.
2. **LOAN APPLICATION; CREDIT REPORT:** Within **5 (or ☐ _____) Days** After Acceptance: **(a)** Buyer shall provide Seller a completed
   loan application on a form acceptable to Seller (such as a FNMA/FHLMC Uniform Residential Loan Application for residential one to four
   unit properties); and **(b)** Buyer authorizes Seller and/or Agent to obtain, at Buyer's expense, a copy of Buyer's credit report. Buyer shall
   provide any supporting documentation reasonably requested by Seller. Seller may cancel this Agreement in writing if Buyer fails to
   provide such documents within that time, or if Seller disapproves any above item within **5 (or ☐ _____) Days** After receipt of each item.
3. **CREDIT DOCUMENTS:** This extension of credit by Seller will be evidenced by: ☐ Note and deed of trust; ☐ All-inclusive
   note and deed of trust; ☐ Installment land sale contract; ☐ Lease/option (when parties intend transfer of equitable title);
   OR ☐ Other (specify) _____

**THE FOLLOWING TERMS APPLY ONLY IF CHECKED. SELLER IS ADVISED TO READ ALL TERMS, EVEN THOSE NOT
CHECKED, TO UNDERSTAND WHAT IS OR IS NOT INCLUDED, AND, IF NOT INCLUDED, THE CONSEQUENCES THEREOF.**

4. ☐ **LATE CHARGE:** If any payment is not made within _____ **Days** After it is due, a late charge of either $ _____,
   or ____% of the installment due, may be charged to Buyer. **NOTE:** On single family residences that Buyer intends to occupy,
   California Civil Code §2954.4(a) limits the late charge to no more than 6% of the total monthly payment due and requires a grace
   period of no less than 10 days.
5. ☐ **BALLOON PAYMENT:** The extension of credit will provide for a balloon payment, in the amount of $ _____,
   plus any accrued interest, which is due on _____ (date).
6. ☐ **PREPAYMENT:** If all or part of this extension of credit is paid early, Seller may charge a prepayment penalty as follows (if
   applicable): _____. Caution: California Civil Code
   §2954.9 contains limitations on prepayment penalties for residential one-to-four unit properties.
7. ☐ **DUE ON SALE:** If any interest in the Property is sold or otherwise transferred, Seller has the option to require immediate
   payment of the entire unpaid principal balance, plus any accrued interest.
8.* ☐ **REQUEST FOR COPY OF NOTICE OF DEFAULT:** A request for a copy of Notice of Default as defined in California Civil
   Code §2924b will be recorded. **If Not**, Seller is advised to consider recording a Request for Notice of Default.
9.* ☐ **REQUEST FOR NOTICE OF DELINQUENCY:** A request for Notice of Delinquency, as defined in California Civil Code §2924e,
   to be signed and paid for by Buyer, will be made to senior lienholders. **If not**, Seller is advised to consider making a Request for
   Notice of Delinquency. Seller is advised to check with senior lienholders to verify whether they will honor this request.
10.*☐ **TAX SERVICE:**
   A. If property taxes on the Property become delinquent, tax service will be arranged to report to Seller. **If not**, Seller is
   advised to consider retaining a tax service, or to otherwise determine that property taxes are paid.
   B. ☐ Buyer, ☐ Seller, shall be responsible for the initial and continued retention of, and payment for, such tax service.
11. ☐ **TITLE INSURANCE:** Title insurance coverage will be provided to **both** Seller and Buyer, insuring their respective interests
   in the Property. **If not**, Buyer and Seller are advised to consider securing such title insurance coverage.
12. ☐ **HAZARD INSURANCE:**
   A. The parties' escrow holder or insurance carrier will be directed to include a loss payee endorsement, adding Seller to
   the Property insurance policy. **If not**, Seller is advised to secure such an endorsement, or acquire a separate
   insurance policy.
   B. Property insurance **does not** include earthquake or flood insurance coverage, unless checked:
   ☐ Earthquake insurance will be obtained; ☐ Flood insurance will be obtained.
13. ☐ **PROCEEDS TO BUYER:** Buyer will receive cash proceeds at the close of the sale transaction. The amount received will be
   approximately $ _____, from _____ (indicate source of
   proceeds). Buyer represents that the purpose of such disbursement is as follows: _____.
14. ☐ **NEGATIVE AMORTIZATION; DEFERRED INTEREST:** Negative amortization results when Buyer's periodic payments are
   less than the amount of interest earned on the obligation. Deferred interest also results when the obligation does not
   require periodic payments for a period of time. In either case, interest is not payable as it accrues. This accrued interest
   will have to be paid by Buyer at a later time, and may result in Buyer owing more on the obligation than at its origination.
   The credit being extended to Buyer by Seller will provide for negative amortization or deferred interest as indicated below.
   (Check A, B, or C. CHECK ONE ONLY.)
   ☐ **A.** All negative amortization or deferred interest shall be added to the principal _____
        (e.g., annually, monthly, etc.), and thereafter shall bear interest at the rate specified in the credit documents (compound interest);
   OR ☐ **B.** All deferred interest shall be due and payable, along with principal, at maturity; _____
   OR ☐ **C.** Other _____

   *(For Paragraphs 8-10) In order to receive timely and continued notification, Seller is advised to record appropriate notices and/or to
   notify appropriate parties of any change in Seller's address.

Buyer's Initials (_____)(_____)
Seller's Initials (_____)(_____)

Reviewed by _____ Date _____

EQUAL HOUSING
OPPORTUNITY

SELLER FINANCING ADDENDUM AND DISCLOSURE (SFA PAGE 1 OF 3)

Property Address: _____ Date: _____

15. ☐ **ALL-INCLUSIVE DEED OF TRUST; INSTALLMENT LAND SALE CONTRACT:** This transaction involves the use of an all-inclusive (or wraparound) deed of trust or an installment land sale contract. That deed of trust or contract shall provide as follows:
    A. In the event of an acceleration of any senior encumbrance, the responsibility for payment, or for legal defense is: _____ _____ ; OR ☐ **Is not** specified in the credit or security documents.
    B. In the event of the prepayment of a senior encumbrance, the responsibilities and rights of Buyer and Seller regarding refinancing, prepayment penalties, and any prepayment discounts are: _____ ; OR ☐ **Are not** specified in the documents evidencing credit.
    C. Buyer will make periodic payments to _____ (Seller, collection agent, or any neutral third party), who will be responsible for disbursing payments to the payee(s) on the senior encumbrance(s) and to Seller. **NOTE:** The Parties are advised to designate a neutral third party for these purposes.

16. ☐ **TAX IDENTIFICATION NUMBERS:** Buyer and Seller shall each provide to each other their Social Security Numbers or Taxpayer Identification Numbers.

17. ☐ **OTHER CREDIT TERMS** _____
_____

18. ☐ **RECORDING:** The documents evidencing credit (paragraph 3) will be recorded with the county recorder where the Property is located. **If not,** Buyer and Seller are advised that their respective interests in the Property may be jeopardized by intervening liens, judgments, encumbrances, or subsequent transfers.

19. ☐ **JUNIOR FINANCING:** There will be additional financing, secured by the Property, junior to this Seller financing. Explain: _____

20. SENIOR LOANS AND ENCUMBRANCES: The following information is provided on loans and/or encumbrances that will be **senior** to Seller financing. **NOTE:** The following are estimates, unless otherwise marked with an asterisk (*). If checked: ☐ A separate sheet with information on additional senior loans/encumbrances is attached

	1st	2nd
A. Original Balance	$ _____	$ _____
B. Current Balance	$ _____	$ _____
C. Periodic Payment (e.g. $100/month)	$ _____	$ _____ / _____
Including Impounds of:	$ _____	$ _____ / _____
D. Interest Rate (per annum)	_____ %	_____ %
E. Fixed or Variable Rate:	_____	_____
If Variable Rate: Lifetime Cap (Ceiling)	_____	_____
Indicator (Underlying Index)	_____	_____
Margins	_____	_____
F. Maturity Date	_____	_____
G. Amount of Balloon Payment	$ _____	$ _____
H. Date Balloon Payment Due	_____	_____
I. Potential for Negative Amortization? (Yes, No, or Unknown)	_____	_____
J. Due on Sale? (Yes, No, or Unknown)	_____	_____
K. Pre-payment penalty? (Yes, No, or Unknown)	_____	_____
L. Are payments current? (Yes, No, or Unknown)	_____	_____

21. BUYER'S CREDITWORTHINESS: (CHECK EITHER A OR B. Do not check both.) In addition to the loan application, credit report and other information requested under paragraph 2:
    A. ☐ No other disclosure concerning Buyer's creditworthiness has been made to Seller;
OR B. ☐ The following representations concerning Buyer's creditworthiness are made by Buyer(s) to Seller:

Borrower _____	**Co-Borrower** _____
1. Occupation _____	1. Occupation _____
2. Employer _____	2. Employer _____
3. Length of Employment _____	3. Length of Employment _____
4. Monthly Gross Income _____	4. Monthly Gross Income _____
5. Other _____	5. Other _____

22. ADDED, DELETED OR SUBSTITUTED BUYERS: The addition, deletion or substitution of any person or entity under this Agreement or to title prior to close of escrow shall require Seller's written consent. Seller may grant or withhold consent in Seller's sole discretion. Any additional or substituted person or entity shall, if requested by Seller, submit to Seller the same documentation as required for the original named Buyer. Seller and/or Brokers may obtain a credit report, at Buyer's expense, on any such person or entity.

SFA REVISED 10/02 (PAGE 2 OF 3)

Buyer's Initials (_____)(_____)
Seller's Initials (_____)(_____)

Reviewed by _____ Date _____

EQUAL HOUSING OPPORTUNITY

SELLER FINANCING ADDENDUM AND DISCLOSURE (SFA PAGE 2 OF 3)

Property Address: _____ Date: _____

23. CAUTION:
  A. If the Seller financing requires a balloon payment, Seller shall give Buyer written notice, according to the terms of Civil Code §2966, at least 90 and not more than 150 days before the balloon payment is due if the transaction is for the purchase of a dwelling for not more than four families.
  B. If **any** obligation secured by the Property calls for a balloon payment, Seller and Buyer are aware that refinancing of the balloon payment at maturity may be difficult or impossible, depending on conditions in the conventional mortgage marketplace at that time. There are no assurances that new financing or a loan extension will be available when the balloon prepayment, or any prepayment, is due.
  C. If **any** of the existing or proposed loans or extensions of credit would require refinancing as a result of a lack of full amortization, such refinancing might be difficult or impossible in the conventional mortgage marketplace.
  D. In the event of default by Buyer: (1) Seller may have to reinstate and/or make monthly payments on any and all senior encumbrances (including real property taxes) in order to protect Seller's secured interest; (2) Seller's rights are generally limited to foreclosure on the Property, pursuant to California Code of Civil Procedure §580b; and (3) the Property may lack sufficient equity to protect Seller's interests if the Property decreases in value.

If this three-page Addendum and Disclosure is used in a transaction for the purchase of a dwelling for not more than four families, it shall be prepared by an Arranger of Credit as defined in California Civil Code §2957(a). (The Arranger of Credit is usually the agent who obtained the offer.)

Arranger of Credit - (Print Firm Name) _____ By _____ Date _____

Address _____ City _____ State _____ Zip _____

Phone _____ Fax _____

BUYER AND SELLER ACKNOWLEDGE AND AGREE THAT BROKERS: (A) WILL NOT PROVIDE LEGAL OR TAX ADVICE; (B) WILL NOT PROVIDE OTHER ADVICE OR INFORMATION THAT EXCEEDS THE KNOWLEDGE, EDUCATION AND EXPERIENCE REQUIRED TO OBTAIN A REAL ESTATE LICENSE; OR (C) HAVE NOT AND WILL NOT VERIFY ANY INFORMATION PROVIDED BY EITHER BUYER OR SELLER. BUYER AND SELLER AGREE THAT THEY WILL SEEK LEGAL, TAX AND OTHER DESIRED ASSISTANCE FROM APPROPRIATE PROFESSIONALS. BUYER AND SELLER ACKNOWLEDGE THAT THE INFORMATION EACH HAS PROVIDED TO THE ARRANGER OF CREDIT FOR INCLUSION IN THIS DISCLOSURE FORM IS ACCURATE. BUYER AND SELLER FURTHER ACKNOWLEDGE THAT EACH HAS RECEIVED A COMPLETED COPY OF THIS DISCLOSURE FORM.

Buyer _____ Date _____
 (signature)

Address _____ City _____ State _____ Zip _____

Phone _____ Fax _____ E-mail _____

Buyer _____ Date _____
 (signature)

Address _____ City _____ State _____ Zip _____

Phone _____ Fax _____ E-mail _____

Seller _____ Date _____
 (signature)

Address _____ City _____ State _____ Zip _____

Phone _____ Fax _____ E-mail _____

Seller _____ Date _____
 (signature)

Address _____ City _____ State _____ Zip _____

Phone _____ Fax _____ E-mail _____

THIS FORM HAS BEEN APPROVED BY THE CALIFORNIA ASSOCIATION OF REALTORS® (C.A.R.). NO REPRESENTATION IS MADE AS TO THE LEGAL VALIDITY OR ADEQUACY OF ANY PROVISION IN ANY SPECIFIC TRANSACTION. A REAL ESTATE BROKER IS THE PERSON QUALIFIED TO ADVISE ON REAL ESTATE TRANSACTIONS. IF YOU DESIRE LEGAL OR TAX ADVICE, CONSULT AN APPROPRIATE PROFESSIONAL.

This form is available for use by the entire real estate industry. It is not intended to identify the user as a REALTOR®. REALTOR® is a registered collective membership mark which may be used only by members of the NATIONAL ASSOCIATION OF REALTORS® who subscribe to its Code of Ethics.

SURE TRAC
The System for Success™

Published by the
California Association of REALTORS®

Reviewed by _____ Date _____

EQUAL HOUSING OPPORTUNITY

SFA REVISED 10/02 (PAGE 3 OF 3)

SELLER FINANCING ADDENDUM AND DISCLOSURE (SFA PAGE 3 OF 3)

CHAPTER 8

disclosures are not required. If, however, an advertisement contains any one of the following terms, then the ad must also disclose other credit terms:

1. The amount or percentage of any down payment
2. The number of payments or period of repayment
3. The amount of any payment
4. The amount of any finance charge

When advertising a graduated payment loan, differences in monthly payments must be disclosed.

B. RIGHT TO CANCEL (Federal Notice of Right to Cancel)

Loans subsequent (future loans) have a 3-day right of rescission by the borrower (not original first trust deeds).

The **RIGHT TO CANCEL** *is the federal law that gives a borrower the right to rescind (cancel) any loan transaction only if it is a business loan or a second trust deed secured by the borrower's home.*

The right to rescind lasts for three business days from the last of the following events: 1) delivery of the notice of right to rescind; 2) signing of the transaction; or 3) delivery of the truth in lending disclosure.

A first trust deed loan to finance the purchase of the borrower's home carries no right of rescission. However, a first loan secured on the borrower's home for any other purpose, including refinancing, or a **second loan on the same home, may be cancelled within 3 business days** (see **Figure 8-18**).

The borrower has the right to rescind when a loan is secured by a junior trust deed on an owner-occupied single-family residence already owned by the borrower (refinancing).

C. EQUAL CREDIT OPPORTUNITY ACT

The **EQUAL CREDIT OPPORTUNITY ACT** *is a federal law prohibiting those who lend money from discriminating against borrowers based on their race, sex, color, religion, national origin, age, or marital status.* It is specifically designed to come to the aid of low income group members (who receive income from public assistance programs), women, and the elderly. This law limits the lender's access to personal information regarding:

1. marriage and divorce,
2. receipt of alimony and child support, and
3. birth control and child bearing.

It can also require lenders to consider individuals on the merits of their personal credit, as distinct from the bad credit history of a joint account. It also insists that lenders respond quickly to loan applications and be prepared to explain any loan refusal.

Figure 8-18

NOTICE OF RIGHT TO CANCEL
CALIFORNIA ASSOCIATION OF REALTORS® (CAR) STANDARD FORM

Name(s) of Customer(s)_____

Type of Loan _____

Amount of Loan _____ $_____

   You have entered into a transaction which will result in a deed of trust or mortgage on your home. You

have a legal right under federal law to cancel this transaction, without cost, within three business days from

whichever of the following occurs last:

(1)   the date of the transaction, which is _____ : or

(2)   the date you received your Tru___ ___ding disclosures; or

(3)   the date you received this ___otic___ ___f y___ ___ right to cancel.

   If you cancel the transaction, ___ ___ed of trust or mortgage is also cancelled. Within 20 calendar days

after we receive your notice, we must ___ ___s necessary to reflect the fact that the deed of trust or

mortgage on your home has been cance___ ___d we must return to you any money or property you have

given to us or to anyone else in connecti___ ___ith thi___ ___saction.

   You may keep any money or property ___ ___av ___given you until we have done the things mentioned

above, but you must then offer to return the mon___ ___ ___ If it is impractical or unfair for you to return the

property you must offer its reasonable value. You ___ ___offer t___ ___eturn the property at your home or at the

location of the property. Money must be returned to th___ ___ess ___low. If we do not take possession of the

money or property within 20 calendar days of your offer, y___ ___ ___eep it without further obligation.

ACKNOWLEDGEMENT OF R___ ___ ___T

   I hereby acknowledge receipt of TWO copies of the f___ ___ ___oing Notice of Right to Cancel.

_____ , 19_____   _____
              (Date)   ___er's Signature)

                                              _____
                                              (Al___ ___nt o___ ___ers must sign)

HOW TO CANCEL

   If you decide to cancel this transaction, you may do so by notifyin___ ___s in writing, at the following address:

_____
              (Creditor's Name)

_____
              (Address)

_____
              (City, State, Zip Code)

   You may use any written statement that is signed and dated by you and states your intention to cancel,

or you may use this notice by dating and signing below. Keep one copy of this notice because it contains

important information about your rights.

   If you cancel by mail or telegram, you must send the notice no later than midnight of _____

_____ (or midnight of the third business day following
                         (date)

the latest of the three events listed above). If you send your written notice to cancel some other way, it must

be delivered to the above address no later than that time.

_____ , 19_____   _____
              (Date)   (Customer's Signature)

--- OFFICE USE ONLY ---
Reviewed by Broker or Designee _____
Date _____

SF-Apr-90

FORM NRC 14

255

CHAPTER 8

D. SERVICE MEMBERS CIVIL RELIEF ACT OF 2003

The *SERVICE MEMBERS CIVIL RELIEF ACT OF 2003 is a law that was passed by Congress to protect persons serving in the military, and their dependents, from loss of real property through foreclosure.*

In general, the law prohibits the sale or foreclosure of real estate owned by a military person without his or her expressed approval or a court order. It also extends foreclosure proceedings and the mortgage redemption period. Career soldiers are exempt.

XII. CHAPTER SUMMARY

Leverage is the practice of purchasing real estate using a small amount of your own money and a larger proportion of borrowed funds. Buyers generally **hypothecate** their property as security for a real estate loan, meaning they provide title as security for the loan, without giving up possession.

A **promissory note** is the basic instrument used to evidence the obligation or debt and can be a **straight note**, an **installment note with a balloon payment**, or the most commonly used in California, a **fully amortized note**.

With the proper requirements, a promissory note can be a **fully negotiable instrument**, like a check, easily transferred to an innocent third party known as a **holder in due course**.

An **acceleration clause** speeds up the balance due based on the occurrence of a specific event. A buyer can assume a loan on a property by accepting responsibility (with the lender's consent) for the full payment of the loan, but cannot assume an existing loan that contains an **alienation clause** (where the entire balance becomes due when the property is sold, assigned, or transferred). A **subordination clause** allows a borrower to obtain additional loans on the property that have a higher priority. A **prepayment penalty** may only be charged during the first five years of a one-to-four unit home loan.

Real estate loans involve **simple interest**. The **nominal interest rate** is stated in the note, whereas the **effective interest rate** includes interest, points, and loan fees. The formula for finding interest is:

$$\text{Interest} = \text{Principal} \times \text{Rate} \times \text{Time}$$

With a **fixed interest rate loan**, the payments are the same for the life of the loan. **Amortization** is the repaying of a loan (principal and interest), in regular payments over the term of the loan. If the interest rate charges are higher than the monthly payment, it's called **negative amortization**. An **adjustable rate mortgage ("ARM" or trust deed)** has a fluctuating interest rate based on a specific index, meaning the payment amounts may also change.

A **point** equals 1% of the loan amount. **Usury** is charging more than the legally allowed percentage of interest.

The **three financial instruments (security devices)** used in California are: 1) **mortgages** (rare), 2) **trust deeds** (1st and 2nds are common), and 3) **land contracts** (uncommon). In California, the terms mortgage and trust deed are often used interchangeably, but in reality we are usually referring to trust deeds.

A **trust deed** (deed of trust loan) is personal property, and needs a **note** for security. It is not a negotiable instrument, but the note is. The **trustor** borrows the money from the **beneficiary**, who is the lender. A **trustee** is the third, disinterested party (usually a corporation) who holds title to the property on the condition it may have to be sold for the beneficiary if the trustor defaults. **Equitable title** is held by the trustor while repaying the trust deed and note in full, at which time he or she receives the **"bare"** or **"naked"** legal title. A full reconveyance provides proof that a promissory note and trust deed have been paid in full.

If a borrower defaults on a trust deed and note, the remedy is to start a **default action** (after a 10-15 day grace period). The sequence of events includes: 1) the recording of the default, 2) a 3-month minimum reinstatement period, 3) a three consecutive week minimum publishing period, and 4) a one-day trustee's sale (**foreclosure**).

Any loan on real property secured by a second, third, or subsequent trust deed is known as a **junior lien**. The best sources for junior liens are **private lenders**.

Homeowner equity loans are based on the increase in equity caused by inflation, rising property values, and the reduction, by payments, of the existing loan balance. They are generally secured by second (junior) trust deeds.

A **land contract** is also called a real property sales contract, an agreement of sale, an agreement to purchase, or an installment sales contract. It is an instrument of finance in which the **vendor** (seller) retains legal ownership of property until the **vendee** (buyer) has made the last payment. A **wraparound**, or all **inclusive trust deed (AITD)**, is a second trust deed with a face value of both the new amount it secures and the balance due under the first trust deed.

The **Truth in Lending Act (Regulation Z)** requires lenders to disclose the costs of credit terms to borrowers within three business days of receiving a loan application. The two most important terms are the **Annual Percentage Rate (APR)** and amount financed. APR is the "cost of credit" expressed in percentage terms.

A borrower has the right to rescind within three days when a loan is secured by a second trust deed and on an owner-occupied, single-family residence already owned by the borrower.

The **Equal Credit Opportunity Act** is a federal law prohibiting money lenders from discriminating against borrowers based on race, sex, color, religion, national origin, age, or marital status. The **Service Members Civil Relief Act of 2003** protects military personnel and their dependents from foreclosure.

XIII. TERMINOLOGY

A. Acceleration Clause
B. Adjustable Rate Mortgage
C. Alienation Clause
D. Amortization
E. Amortization Chart
F. Annual Percentage Rate
G. Assumption
H. Beneficiary
I. Default
J. Deficiency Judgment
K. Equal Credit Opportunity
L. Equitable Title
M. Equity
N. Grace Period
O. Graduated Payment Mortgage

P. Holder in Due Course
Q. Hypothecation
R. Interest
S. Junior Lien or Second Trust Deed
T. Land Contract
U. Legal Title
V. Leverage
W. Point
X. Prepayment Penalty
Y. Promissory Note
Z. Purchase Money Instrument
AA. Reconveyance Deed
BB. Reinstatement Period
CC. Request for Notice of Default

DD. Right to Cancel
EE. Straight Note
FF. Subordination Clause
GG. Trust Deed
HH. Trustee
II. Trustee's Sale
JJ. Trustor
KK. Truth in Lending Act
LL. Usury
MM. Vendee
NN. Vendor
OO. Wraparound Trust Deed

1.____ An instrument used to transfer title back from a trustee to the equitable owner of real estate.

2.____ A second trust deed for which the monthly payment includes the amount of monthly payment on the existing first trust deed.

3.____ Federal law granting women financial independence and preventing lenders from considering such negative credit aspects as the possibility of a woman having children and dropping out of the labor market.

4.____ A mortgage or deed of trust for which the payments increase over the term of the loan. The payments may increase as the buyer's earnings increase.

5.____ The amount for which the borrower is personally liable on a note and mortgage if the foreclosure sale does not bring enough to cover the debt.

6.____ A penalty under a note, mortgage, or deed of trust imposed when the loan is paid before it is due.

7.____ The total cost of financing expressed as one simple annual percentage rate. This rate must be clearly expressed on any loan agreement.

8.____ A promise in writing to pay a specified amount during a limited time, or on demand, to a named person.

9.____ Clause used in a deed of trust that gives the lender the right to demand payment in full upon the happening of a certain event.

10.____ Ownership by one who does not have legal title, such as a vendee under a land contract or, technically, a trustor under a deed of trust.

11.____ A sale at auction by a trustee under a deed of trust, pursuant to foreclosure proceedings.

12.____ A type of lien that is subordinate to a prior lien.

13.____ An instrument used in place of a mortgage in most western states that is based on the Spanish legal tradition. Property is transferred to a trustee by the borrower (trustor) in favor of the lender (beneficiary) and reconveyed upon payment in full.

14.____ A type of acceleration clause, calling for a debt under a mortgage or deed of trust, to be due in its entirety upon transfer of ownership.

15.____ The use of financing to allow a small amount of cash to purchase and control a large property investment.

16.____ A period of time past the due date for a payment (mortgage, insurance, etc.) during which a payment may be made and not considered delinquent.

17. ____ Purchaser or buyer, especially on a land contract.
18. ____ A nonamortized note for which the principal is due in a lump sum upon maturity.
19. ____ Charging an illegal rate or amount of interest on a loan.
20. ____ Payment of debt in regular, periodic installments of principal and interest, as opposed to interest-only payments.
21. ____ The seller of property under a land contract.
22. ____ The kind of title held by the vendor under a land contract and the trustee under a deed of trust. They are still owed money by the buyer.
23. ____ An installment contract for the sale of land. The seller (vendor) has legal title until paid in full. The buyer (vendee) has equitable title during the contract term.
24. ____ A financing charge equal to one percent of the amount of the loan.
25. ____ Money charged for the use of money.
26. ____ A failure to perform the financial obligation to pay under a loan.
27. ____ A holder of a check or note who takes the note in good faith, on the assumption it is valid.
28. ____ The borrower under a deed of trust.
29. ____ In a deed of trust, the person who acts as an intermediary between the trustor and the beneficiary.
30. ____ A lender for whose benefit a trust is created in those states where trust deeds are commonly used instead of mortgages.
31. ____ The ownership interest in real property; it is the market value minus any unpaid loan amount.
32. ____ Agreement by the buyer to take over the financial responsibility for real property under the existing note and trust deed.
33. ____ An agreement by which a lender substitutes a junior loan position for a senior loan position.
34. ____ A schedule of monthly payments that varies according to interest rates and number of monthly payments.
35. ____ Mortgage loans on which the interest rate is periodically adjusted to more closely coincide with current rates.
36. ____ Regulation Z under the Federal Reserve regulations that requires a credit purchaser be advised, in writing, of all costs connected with the credit portion of their purchase.
37. ____ The principle of using real property as security for a debt while the borrower retains possession.
38. ____ A recorded form requiring the trustee to notify other creditors in the event of a default on the deed of trust to a property.
39. ____ A limited amount of time during which the trustor has the right to pay all past due payments and charges due on a loan to bring it current.
40. ____ Part of the Truth in Lending Law that allows a borrower to rescind a loan transaction until midnight of the third business day, on business loans and second trust deeds secured by a borrower's residence.
41. ____ The original loan taken out when purchasing a property, not a refinanced or junior loan.

CHAPTER 8

XIV. CHAPTER QUIZ

1. Amortization tables are used to calculate:
    a. the annual payment.
    b. the monthly payment.
    c. only interest due with each payment.
    d. the amount of a straight loan.

2. The 1% loan fee on FHA loans is usually paid by the:
    a. borrower.
    b. seller.
    c. lender.
    d. PMI.

3. In a deed of trust, the power of sale in event of foreclosure is given from the:
    a. trustee to the trustor.
    b. beneficiary to the trustor.
    c. trustor to the trustee.
    d. trustee to the beneficiary.

4. Which of the following is a true statement regarding recording a trust deed?
    a. A trust deed conveys bare legal title (but not possession) of a property to a trustee (third party) as security for a loan.
    b. A trust deed differs from other deeds in that the legal title only is thus conveyed.
    c. A trust deed is a security device in the nature of a lien and differs in one respect from other deeds in that the trust deed and the promissory note for which it was given may be assigned.
    d. All of the above.

5. A request for notice of default is recorded to protect:
    a. the beneficiary on the first loan.
    b. the beneficiary on the second loan/trust deed.
    c. trustor on the first loan.
    d. trustor on the second loan.

6. If a lender accepts a deed in lieu of foreclosure:
    a. the trustor under certain circumstances assumes the deed and any liens.
    b. the beneficiary may assume any junior loans/liens on the property.
    c. the trustee will assume any junior liens on the property.
    d. any of the three parties depending on the value of the property and the amount of any liens on the property may assume any junior encumbrance on the property.

7. A vendee (buyer) under a land contract should:
  a. record the land contract for his/her protection.
  b. hold legal title in a safe deposit box.
  c. obtain a CLTA title insurance policy to assure that the vendor cannot encumber the property.
  d. have a reconveyance deed held in escrow.

8. According to Federal Truth in Lending, the lender must disclose the annual percentage rate of a loan, which is:
  a. the nominal interest rate.
  b. the cost of credit, including interest and other financing costs, expressed as an annual rate.
  c. the yearly compounded interest rate.
  d. none of the above.

9. The right to rescind lasts for 3 days from the last of these events to occur:
  a. delivery of the notice of right to rescind.
  b. signing of the transaction.
  c. delivery of the truth in lending disclosure.
  d. all of the above.

10. A lender would not be exempt from the requirement of providing the borrower with a Federal Right to Rescind Notice when the:
  a. loan is for more than $25,000 and is not secured by the borrower's personal residence.
  b. security for the loan is commercial property.
  c. loan is for business expansion.
  d. borrower is refinancing his personal residence.

ANSWERS: 1. b; 2. b; 3. c; 4. d; 5. b; 6. b; 7. a; 8. b; 9. d; 10. d

261

CHAPTER 9
Financial Institutions

www.bankofamerica.com
Bank of America
www.wellsfargo.com
Wells Fargo

The credit crunch of 2007-2009 has profoundly impacted the home loan business.

The real estate money market, like any other commodity market, changes constantly. Money for financing real estate may be plentiful in one month or quarter, then scarce and expensive in the next. The money market is no longer national, it has become a global market. A broker must be able to finance real estate transactions every month if he or she expects to remain in business. Because of this, a broker must be able to use all the standard financing methods and any unconventional methods that may fit the time and situation.

Before you advertise a property or present it to a prospect, try to visualize all the ways the property may be financed. The more alternatives available, the more likely you are to negotiate a sale. Real estate finance continues to become more variable and more complex as time goes on. This chapter will explain the sources of funds available from financial institutions, the government's role, and other creative prospects and information that will assist you when offering financing.

I. Our Ever Changing Economy (Economic Cycles)

With regard to inflation, market value increases and sales price increases. When the general level of prices decreases, the value of money increases.

Because our government's spending and taxing policies shift with every new election, our economy is in a constant state of transition. From month-to-month, it is difficult to predict what amount of financing money will be available and what rate of interest will be charged. These influences, multiplied over a period of years, make it nearly impossible to accurately project long-term trends in the money supply.

INFLATION *is the result of too much money chasing too few goods.* When the economy is going very well, most people are making more money and spending it too freely, thereby driving up the price of real estate and other goods. The Fed, sensing that inflation is out of control, starts applying the brakes and starts restricting the amount of money available. This and higher interest rates decrease borrowing. If the Fed is forced to apply the brakes hard, deflation will occur. ***DEFLATION*** *is when prices of real estate, goods, and services go down.*

CHAPTER 9

CHAPTER OUTLINE

A "seller's market" is when prices rise due to shortages of available properties, and a "buyer's market" is when prices fall.

It is a **BUYER'S MARKET** *when the prices of real estate are down; terms are easy and there is usually a great deal of real estate listed for sale or rent.* Buyers have a choice; there is more to pick and choose from, at lower prices. In a **SELLER'S MARKET**, *the prices of real estate are up and there is less real estate listed for sale or rent.* This is due to increased demand and lagging supplies.

A. THE FEDERAL RESERVE BANKING SYSTEM ("Fed")

The Federal Reserve Banking System is the single greatest influence on the cost and supply of money for real estate loans. It is the link between America's private financial institutions and the taxing and spending policies of the federal government. The **FEDERAL RESERVE BANKING SYSTEM (The "Fed")** *is the nation's central banking authority.* If the Fed makes money tight, thus restricting the amount of available loan funds, demand for the available funds increases, pushing interest rates higher. Conversely, if the Fed increases the amount of money in circulation, interest rates go down. In this way they keep centralized control over the interest rates for not only banks, but for all lending institutions.

When the federal reserve wants to create a tight money market, it raises the discount rate and sells government bonds. When the federal reserve wants a "loose" money market, it buys back bonds and lowers reserve requirements of banks.

These operations and the other important functions of the Federal Reserve System are supervised by the Federal Reserve Board. The *FEDERAL RESERVE BOARD is a committee appointed by the President, but is politically independent.* In regulating the amount and flow of loan money available to banks, the board has indirect but far-reaching influence over all lending institutions and the economy as a whole. The Federal Reserve's monetary policies influence the supply of money by:

1. buying and selling government T-bonds and T-securities;
2. raising and lowering the reserve requirement;
3. raising and lowering the discount rate to member banks; and
4. margin requirements (percentage loaned on stocks and bonds).

www.federalreserve.gov/sitemap.htm (Federal Reserve Board)
www.ustreas.gov (U.S. Treasury)
www.occ.treas.gov (Office of the Comptroller of the Currency)
www.frbsf.org (Federal Reserve Bank of San Francisco - 12th District)

B. GROSS DOMESTIC PRODUCT (Measures Economic Activity)

We can monitor growth in our economy and the influence of the Fed by watching closely any changes in the gross domestic product. The *GROSS DOMESTIC PRODUCT (GDP) is the total value of all goods and services produced by an economy during a specific period of time.* It serves as a kind of monetary barometer that shows us the rate and areas of greatest growth.

Depression, recession, expansion, and prosperity represent four phases of the business cycle.

C. CHANGING INTEREST RATES (Affect Real Estate)

The economy goes in cycles. Interest rates go up and down. When interest rates go down, people will buy more homes. When interest rates go up, people will buy fewer homes, and have a harder time selling their homes. When interest rates go down, homes become more affordable.

If a homeowner has a high interest rate and the rate goes down, he or she may choose to refinance. *REFINANCING is the process of obtaining a new loan to pay off the old loan.* If interest rates fall dramatically, it is wise to consider refinancing.

In a tight money market, lenders may waive prepayment penalty clauses in order to lend out that money at a higher rate than old loans.

II. Shopping for a Loan

All the variables of our changing economy come home in a very personal way when a borrower goes out to look for a loan. For the average person, borrowing the money necessary to buy a house is the largest financial obligation he or she is likely to assume in his or her lifetime. It's an extremely important decision, second only to the selection of the property itself. The salesperson should advise caution and careful consideration before a promissory note is signed. Shopping around for a loan from several different loan sources is an excellent idea. Even if the borrower has found financing that he or she feels is acceptable, talking to other lenders should never be discouraged. **Figure 9-1** provides a detailed discussion of the steps in obtaining a loan.

A. LOAN TO VALUE (Percent of Appraised Value Lender Will Loan)

LOAN TO VALUE is the percentage of appraised value the lender will loan to the borrower to purchase the property. It is abbreviated as L-T-V or L to V. The lower the L to V, the higher the down payment has to be. The lower the L to V, the more equity is required.

B. ESTIMATE OF SETTLEMENT COSTS (RESPA)

The lender must give the applicant the HUD booklet that explains closing costs and has until **three business days after receipt of a loan application** to provide a good faith estimate of the actual settlement costs to the borrower. The Real Estate Settlement Procedures Act (RESPA) disclosure must include:

1. the rate of interest;
2. points to be charged;
3. any additional loan fees and charges, and
4. escrow, title, and other allowable costs, which could add up to $1,000 or more above lender's estimates.

The idea is to alert the borrower, at the beginning of the loan process, to how much cash besides the down payment will be needed to close escrow. Usually the lender will provide the complete estimated settlement cost form along with the loan application.

C. CREDIT SCORING (Access to Credit Profile)

CREDIT SCORING gives lenders a fast, objective measurement of your ability to repay a loan or make timely credit payments. It is based solely on information in consumer credit reports maintained at one of the credit reporting agencies. Factors comprising a credit score include:

1. **Payment History** – What is your track record?
2. **Amounts Owed** – How much is too much?
3. **Length of Credit History** – How established is yours?
4. **New Credit** – Are you taking on more debt?
5. **Types of Credit Use** – Is it a "healthy" mix?

The most widely used credit bureau scores are developed by Fair, Isaac and Company. These are known as FICO SCORES. See **Figure 9-2** for a fuller description of credit scoring, which is often difficult to explain.

If a credit agency refuses to provide a copy of a credit report to an applicant who is denied credit, the applicant can:

1. *file civil action against the credit agency;*
2. *negotiate a settlement, or*
3. *require the credit agency to pay all legal fees.*

Figure 9-1

Steps in Obtaining a Loan

1. Application

After deciding that a real estate loan is necessary, the first step in obtaining the loan is filling out a loan application. It would be a good idea to shop around and check for the best rate and terms at various savings institutions before applying because, despite what many people suspect, every lender is different. Finding the right loan is as important as finding the right piece of real estate. The application will request detailed information regarding both the property and the borrower.

2. Analysis

The application generally receives a preliminary screening to determine if there are any obvious and glaring reasons why either the prospective borrower or the property could not qualify for a loan. This process is accomplished by credit scoring. This analysis is followed by a professional appraisal of the property and an in-depth investigation into the credit background of the applicant (in addition to credit scoring). The lender wants to know how likely the borrower is to meet monthly payments and pay back the loan. This is analyzed with reference to the borrower's "capacity" and "desire" to pay.

CAPACITY is determined based upon a borrower's savings, valuable property, and income, and is evaluated in terms of the reliability of these assets. Excellent evidence of capacity would be good collateral. COLLATERAL is valuable property pledged as a guarantee for payment of a loan. DESIRE (to pay) is demonstrated by a good credit history reflecting the discipline to make monthly payments on time. A background of late payments and loan defaults would make it difficult to get loan approval.

3. Processing

If loan analysis proves favorable and financing terms are acceptable to all parties, it is then time to get the terms of the agreement down on paper. Processing involves typing up the loan documents, preparing necessary disclosure statements, and issuing instructions to the escrow holder.

4. Escrow

All the paperwork of the loan transaction ends up in escrow along with all the other contracts involved in the purchase of real property. The trust deed and promissory note are signed and passed along to the escrow company where the deal is closed.

5. Servicing

Loan servicing involves mailing monthly loan statements, collecting payments, and seeing to it that all records are kept up to date. Some lenders service their own loans while others hire independent mortgage companies to handle the paperwork for them. Loan servicing also involves all correspondence for late and delinquent payments.

(continued)

Qualifying for a Loan

All lenders set their own standards for evaluating who qualifies and who does not qualify for loan money. These standards are reflected in the interest rates charged. Some lenders have very strict requirements, while others will take a greater risk but charge a higher rate of interest—especially on second trust deeds. Real estate agents can obtain more specific guidelines simply by contacting local lenders.

Traditionally, lending institutions decided whether or not a borrower was qualified based upon a simple formula: the property should not cost more than two-and-a-half times the borrower's annual income. Today, however, many lenders recognize that this method can be very inadequate. It fails to take into account other debts that the borrower might be paying off and doesn't give the middle income property buyer, or those entering the housing market for the first time, much of a chance with today's high-cost real estate.

New rules of thumb consider a borrower's other debts along with the housing payments. Long term debts are added to these payments, and the sum is referred to as the borrower's total monthly expenses.

One standard rule was that a borrower's monthly expenses should be no more than 25 percent of all total monthly income. Now, in California, it is closer to 3½ to 1 ratio. Another rule, which is applied to borrowers who are not heavily in debt elsewhere, requires that their annual income be approximately 30 percent of the cost of the property. This is a variation on the traditional formula reflecting a more realistic attitude on the part of lenders.

Appraisal of the Property

Just as the borrower is evaluated during the loan process, lenders evaluate the property being purchased. They want to be certain that the price being paid reflects a fair market value. If a property is overpriced and the borrower defaults, it might be difficult for the lender to recoup the amount of the loan. This process of determining a property's fair market value is known as appraisal and is discussed in detail in Chapters 10 and 11.

Institutional lenders are not likely to lend the entire amount needed for the purchase of a property. Most often they will determine the fair market value and lend a set percentage of that amount. This "loan to value ratio" (L-T-V) is generally 80 percent to 90 percent at banks and savings banks and 70 percent if the loan comes from an insurance company. Collateral is required but most often the property itself (including any structures) is used as security for the loan.

The lower the L-T-V, the greater the down payment required.

Figure 9-2

Credit Scoring

A credit score is a three-digit number assigned to consumers based on credit history that is used by lenders to determine the level of risk they maybe taking if they lend to someone. The system awards points based on information in the credit report, and compared to others with similar profiles, lenders can use this information to predict how likely someone is to repay a loan and make payments on time – and therefore decide whether or not to make a loan and at what interest rate.

Credit scores are often referred to as FICO scores due to the fact that Fair Isaac and Company was the first company to develop a mathematical credit scoring model based on selected criteria in a credit report. The following are the systems now used:

Experian – Experian/Fair Isaac system
TransUnion – Empirica system
Equifax – Beacon system

FICO scores, which still dominate the industry, range from 300 to 850. Any score under 620 is considered high risk, and subject to higher interest rates, and anything over 720 qualifies for the best interest rate.

Loan applicants are entitled to know the specific credit scores and the "reason codes" used in determining their scores. Reason codes may include too high a debt-to-credit limit ratio, late payments, or too short a credit history.

In addition to a consumer's right to receive a free credit report from each of the three national credit reporting agencies once a year, by law, credit reporting agencies are required to correct inaccurate information in a timely manner, and are subject to legal recourse if inaccurate information continues to be reported once they are made aware of mistakes.

www.experian.com/consumer/index.html
Experian
www.transunion.com
TransUnion
www.equifax.com
Equifax

Once popular ALT-A programs (where applicants with good credit couldn't document their income) used only the last 12 to 24 months' personal bank statements to support the income stated on the loan application.

SUBPRIME LOANS *are generally made to borrowers with less than excellent credit scores.* Due to higher risk, they are generally charged higher interest rates, points, fees, and prepayment penalties. After initial ***TEASER RATES,*** *where low ARM loan interest rates accelerate after two years*, many subprime borrowers are now faced with difficulty making much higher payments and face foreclosure.

D. THE LOAN APPLICATION

The lender needs a loan application from the borrower so that the borrower's financial condition can be analyzed. **Figure 9-3** shows two pages of the FHLMC/FNMA application form that is used by most financial institutions. The application provides the lender with the following:

1. Information about property being financed
2. Information about borrower (and co-borrower, if any)
3. Sources of income and analysis
4. Monthly housing expenses (present and proposed)
5. Balance sheet
6. Other information relevant to the borrower's financial status

If a loan application section requests information regarding marital status or race, the applicant can refuse to complete this section.

E. EQUITY (Market Value Less Debt)

When shopping for a loan, the lender wants to determine your worth, or equity, so they will require you to fill out an accounting balance sheet as part of the application. *EQUITY is your net worth; it is the amount that is left after subtracting all that you owe (debt) from what you own (assets).* Lenders want to see your equity on paper. Equity shows them your ability to make the down payment and meet other expenses. It is common practice to ask buyers what the equity is in their current home in order to determine if they financially qualify for the price of a new home.

Equity in real property is the difference between mortgage indebtedness and market value of the property.

F. LIQUIDITY (Convert Assets into Cash)

LIQUIDITY is the ease and rate with which an asset can be converted into a medium of exchange (like cash). It is not enough to make money; there also must be the ability to pay bills on time. Real estate has very little liquidity. Depending on market conditions, it could take a very long time to sell a piece of real estate. On the other hand, income property may bring in more cash monthly than goes out for expenditures.

G. OPPORTUNITY COST (Cost of Non-Liquidity)

OPPORTUNITY COST is the lost profit one could have made by the alternative investment action not taken. It is the cost of non-liquidity. If you own a home, the lost return on that equity is referred to as opportunity cost.

III. Sources of Real Estate Funds

The remainder of this chapter will deal with the different institutions that lend money to finance the purchase of real property. Details concerning the types of lenders and how they make loans will be explained and different kinds of government loan participation are compared and discussed. In addition, the responsibilities of a broker acting as a loan agent or security dealer are outlined.

271

Figure 9-3

Uniform Residential Loan Application

This application is designed to be completed by the applicant(s) with the lender's assistance. Applicants should complete this form as "Borrower" or "Co Borrower", as applicable. Co-Borrower information must also be provided (and the appropriate box checked) when ☐ the income or assets of a person other than the "Borrower" (including the Borrower's spouse) will be used as a basis for loan qualification or ☐ the income or assets of the Borrower's spouse will not be used as a basis for loan qualification, but his or her liabilities must be considered because the Borrower resides in a community property state, the security property is located in a community property state, or the Borrower is relying on other property located in a community property state as a basis for repayment of the loan.

I. TYPE OF MORTGAGE AND TERMS OF LOAN

Mortgage Applied for:	☐ VA ☐ FHA	☐ Conventional ☐ FmHA	☐ Other:	Agency Case Number		Lender Case No.
Amount $	Interest Rate %	No. of Months	Amortization Type	☐ Fixed Rate ☐ GPM	☐ Other (explain): ☐ ARM (type):	

II. PROPERTY INFORMATION AND PURPOSE OF LOAN

Subject Property Address (street, city, state, & ZIP) — No. of Units

Legal Description of Subject Property (attach description if necessary) — Year Built

Purpose of Loan	☐ Purchase ☐ Refinance	☐ Construction ☐ Construction-Permanent	☐ Other (explain):	Property will be: ☐ Primary Residence ☐ Secondary Residence ☐ Investment

Complete this line if construction or construction-permanent loan.

Year Lot Acquired	Original Cost $	Amount Existing Liens $	(a) Present Value of Lot $	(b) Cost of Improvements $	Total (a + b) $

Complete this line if this is a refinance loan.

Year Acquired	Original Cost $	Amount Existing Liens $	Purpose of Refinance	Describe Improvements ☐ made ☐ to be made Cost: $

Title will be held in what Name(s)	Manner in which Title will be held	Estate will be held in: ☐ Fee Simple ☐ Leasehold (show expiration date)

Source of Down Payment, Settlement Charges and/or Subordinate Financing (explain)

III. BORROWER INFORMATION

	Borrower		Co Borrower

Borrower's Name (include Jr. or Sr. if applicable)		Co-Borrower's Name (include Jr. or Sr. if applicable)

Social Security Number	Home Phone (incl. area code)	Age	Yrs. School	Social Security Number	Home Phone (incl. area code)	Age	Yrs. School

☐ Married ☐ Separated	☐ Unmarried (include single, divorced, widowed)	Dependents (not listed by Co-Borrower) no. ages	☐ Married ☐ Separated	☐ Unmarried (include single, divorced, widowed)	Dependents (not listed by Borrower) no. ages

Present Address (street, city, state, ZIP) ☐ Own ☐ Rent No. Yrs.	Present Address (street, city, state, ZIP) ☐ Own ☐ Rent No. Yrs.

If residing at present address for less than two years, complete the following:

Former Address (street, city, state, ZIP) ☐ Own ☐ Rent No. Yrs.	Former Address (street, city, state, ZIP) ☐ Own ☐ Rent No. Yrs.

Former Address (street, city, state, ZIP) ☐ Own ☐ Rent No. Yrs.	Former Address (street, city, state, ZIP) ☐ Own ☐ Rent No. Yrs.

IV. EMPLOYMENT INFORMATION

	Borrower		Co Borrower

Name & Address of Employer ☐ Self Employed	Yrs. on this job	Name & Address of Employer ☐ Self Employed	Yrs. on this job
	Yrs. employed in this line of work/profession		Yrs. employed in this line of work/profession

Position/Title/Type of Business	Business Phone (incl. area code)	Position/Title/Type of Business	Business Phone (incl. area code)

If employed in current position for less than two years or if currently employed in more than one position, complete the following:

Name & Address of Employer ☐ Self Employed	Dates (from - to)	Name & Address of Employer ☐ Self Employed	Dates (from - to)
	Monthly Income $		Monthly Income $

Position/Title/Type of Business	Business Phone (incl. area code)	Position/Title/Type of Business	Business Phone (incl. area code)

Name & Address of Employer ☐ Self Employed	Dates (from - to)	Name & Address of Employer ☐ Self Employed	Dates (from - to)
	Monthly Income $		Monthly Income $

Position/Title/Type of Business	Business Phone (incl. area code)	Position/Title/Type of Business	Business Phone (incl. area code)

Freddie Mac Form 65

Fannie Mae Form 1003

V. MONTHLY INCOME AND COMBINED HOUSING EXPENSE INFORMATION

Gross Monthly Income	Borrower	Co-Borrower	Total	Combined Monthly Housing Expense	Present	Proposed
Base Empl. Income *	$	$	$	Rent	$	
Overtime				First Mortgage (P&I)		$
Bonuses				Other Financing (P&I)		
Commissions				Hazard Insurance		
Dividends/Interest				Real Estate Taxes		
Net Rental Income				Mortgage Insurance		
Other (before completing, see the notice in "describe other income," below)				Homeowner Assn. Dues		
				Other:		
Total	$	$	$	Total	$	$

* Self Employed Borrower(s) may be required to provide additional documentation such as tax returns and financial statements.

Describe Other Income *Notice:* Alimony, child support, or separate maintenance income need not be revealed if the Borrower (B) or Co-Borrower (C) does not choose to have it considered for repaying this loan.

B/C		Monthly Amount
		$

VI. ASSETS AND LIABILITIES

This Statement and any applicable supporting schedules may be completed jointly by both married and unmarried Co-Borrowers if their assets and liabilities are sufficiently joined so that the Statement can be meaningfully and fairly presented on a combined basis; otherwise separate Statements and Schedules are required. If the Co-Borrower section was completed about a spouse, this Statement and supporting schedules must be completed about that spouse also.

Completed ☐ Jointly ☐ Not Jointly

ASSETS Description	Cash or Market Value	Liabilities and Pledged Assets. List the creditor's name, address and account number for all outstanding debts, including automobile loans, revolving charge accounts, real estate loans, alimony, child support, stock pledges, etc. Use continuation sheet, if necessary. Indicate by (*) those liabilities which will be satisfied upon sale of real estate owned or upon refinancing of the subject property.	Monthly Payt. & Mos. Left to Pay	Unpaid Balance
Cash deposit toward purchase held by:	$	**LIABILITIES**		
		Name and address of Company	$ Payt./Mos.	$
List checking and savings accounts below				
Name and address of Bank, S&L, or Credit Union				
		Acct. no.		
		Name and address of Company	$ Payt./Mos.	$
Acct. no.	$			
Name and address of Bank, S&L, or Credit Union				
		Acct. no.		
		Name and address of Company	$ Payt./Mos.	$
Acct. no.	$			
Name and address of Bank, S&L, or Credit Union				
		Acct. no.		
		Name and address of Company	$ Payt./Mos.	$
Acct. no.	$			
Name and address of Bank, S&L, or Credit Union				
		Acct. no.		
		Name and address of Company	$ Payt./Mos.	$
Acct. no.	$			
Stocks & Bonds (Company name/number & description)	$			
		Acct. no.		
		Name and address of Company	$ Payt./Mos.	$
Life insurance net cash value	$			
Face amount: $				
Subtotal Liquid Assets	$			
Real estate owned (enter market value from schedule of real estate owned)	$			
		Acct. no.		
Vested interest in retirement fund	$	Name and address of Company	$ Payt./Mos.	$
Net worth of business(es) owned (attach financial statement)	$			
Automobiles owned (make and year)	$			
		Acct. no.		
		Alimony/Child Support/Separate Maintenance Payments Owed to:	$	
Other Assets (itemize)	$	Job Related Expense (child care, union dues, etc.)	$	
		Total Monthly Payments	$	
Total Assets a.	$	Net Worth (a minus b) ▶ $	Total Liabilities b.	$

Freddie Mac Form 65

Fannie Mae Form 1003

10-03

The three areas of demand for borrowing money are:

1. *Construction funds to build*
2. *Financing a purchase*
3. *Refinancing*

IV. Institutional Lenders

INSTITUTIONAL LENDERS *are very large corporations that lend the money of their depositors to finance real estate transactions.* Their principal function is to act as financial intermediaries; to transfer money from those who have funds to those who wish to borrow. **Figure 9-4** illustrates which groups are institutional and which are noninstitutional lenders.

Figure 9-4

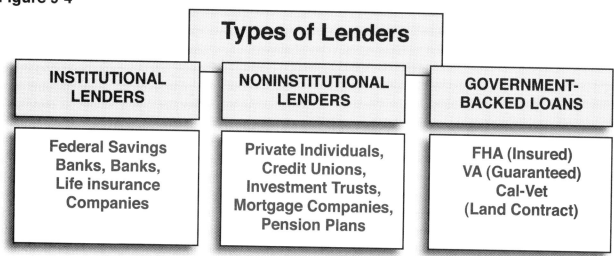

A. FEDERAL DEPOSIT INSURANCE CORPORATION (FDIC)

The **FEDERAL DEPOSIT INSURANCE CORPORATION (FDIC)** *is a government corporation that, for a fee, insures each account of a depositor up to $100,000.* All the deposits in savings banks and banks in California are insured by the FDIC because they pay for the premiums. If a depositor has more than the insured $100,000 in any one account, then he or she may lose that amount in excess of $100,000 if there is a savings bank or bank failure. It would be wise to put any excess in a different account or financial institution.

www.fdic.gov
Federal Deposit Insurance Corp.

B. FEDERAL SAVINGS BANKS (Greatest Source of Money for Home Loans)

In California, most of the home purchases are financed by federal savings banks. They make more real estate loans than any other financial institution. This is because until recently all the money that savings banks lent out was in the form of real estate loans. Even with current changes in the banking industry, savings banks are still the primary home mortgage lenders. Savings banks are either federally or state licensed.

How Financial Institutions Determine Interest Rates

Financial institutions obtain funds from their depositors and pay a modest return in the form of interest or dividends to keep their depositors money invested with them. In order to make money, the spread that a financial institution must make between the interest rate it charges on loans and the interest rate paid to its depositors must be at least 2%. So if a bank pays 7% to depositors, it must make loans at 9% or higher in order to stay in business.

This is a brief description of how a federal savings bank works: A person wishing to deposit funds in exchange for interest would open an account (i.e., savings, money market, or checking) at a federal savings bank. These funds would then be invested in real estate loans, which yield higher rates of interest for the institution than is being paid out to depositors. This system allows savers to obtain interest from federal savings bank accounts and at the same time provide a source of loan funds to home buyers. All federal savings banks can make 80% loans on any amount that is acceptable to them. Federal savings banks will occasionally make 90 and 95 percent (loan-to-value) loans if the loans are covered by private mortgage insurance.

Federal savings banks primarily make loans on single-family homes or condos that are owner-occupied. They will also make loans on apartment buildings and manufactured homes. Larger federal savings banks will often make construction loans for a tract and then supply each owner with permanent, long-term financing.

Federal savings banks, like banks and insurance companies, charge points and loan fees. Points will range from one to five percent (points) of the total loan amount. Loan fees are usually $300 to $500 while appraisal costs start at $200, but vary depending on the property. All institutional lenders tend to charge comparable points and fees according to economic conditions in the market place.

Federal savings banks are primary sources for residential loans because they invest most of their money in home loans.

Institutions that specialize in making home loans obtain their funds mainly from individual savings.

Figure 9-5 compares the lending priorities of federal savings banks with banks and life insurance companies.

C. BANKS

Banks are *GENERAL PURPOSE LENDERS*, *which means they lend money for anything from real estate to sailboats.* Even so, they are the second largest lenders for real estate in California. All national banks are required to be members of the Federal Reserve System, while a state bank may be a member by choice. There is no great difference between real estate loans that a state bank makes and loans that the federal banks make. Interest rates and other loan terms are comparable to those offered by mutual savings banks.

Any commercial bank may lend money on real property if it is a first loan on that property. In general, there are four types of real estate financing:

1. **First Trust Deed Loans** – The bank finances long-term loans for existing land and the buildings.

Figure 9-5

Priorities of Institutional Lenders

Federal Savings Banks (Residential Lenders)	Banks (General Purpose Lenders)	Life Insurance Companies (Big Money Lenders)
1. Single-family homes and condos	1. Business and auto loans	1. Large shopping centers and office buildings
2. Apartment buildings	2. Conventional home loans	2. Hotels and industrial properties
3. Home improvement loans	3. Government-backed FHA and VA home loans	3. FHA and VA home loans through mortgage companies (Government-backed loans)
4. Manufactured homes	4. Credit cards	
	5. Construction loans	

2. **Construction Loans (or Interim Loans)** – Money is provided for the construction of a building, to be repaid when the construction is complete.

Construction loan and interim loan are synonymous.

3. **Take-Out Loans (Repayment of Interim Loan)** – Permanent long-term loans are made to pay off the interim lender upon completion of construction of commercial or apartment projects and are called "takeout loans" because they take out the interim lender.

4. **Home Improvement Loans** – This type of loan is for repairing and modernizing existing buildings.

D. LIFE INSURANCE COMPANIES

Life insurance companies have more money to lend than either a bank or a savings bank. They are more conservative lenders and specialize in large loans for commercial projects, but they also make conventional loans on residential property. These companies supply most of the loan funds for properties where a great deal of capital is required (such as high-rise office buildings, shopping centers, industrial properties, and hotels).

Life insurance companies also invest large amounts of money in trust deeds that are either insured by the FHA or guaranteed by the VA. Mortgage companies make such loans for insurance companies. Quite often, these mortgage companies, in return for a servicing fee, collect the loan payments for the insurance company.

An insurance company is the least likely source to refinance an existing home loan.

Truth in Savings Act

"Annual Percentage Yield" defined as APY

The Truth in Savings Act requires depository institutions to furnish "clear, complete, and uniform disclosures" of the terms of their savings and checking deposit accounts. It also requires institutions to pay interest on the consumer's daily balance. Certain practices are no longer permitted, such as advertising "Free Accounts" and then charging maintenance or per-check fees, or requiring minimum balances.

This Act introduces a standard method of expressing interest paid to depositors called "Annual Percentage Yield" or APY. This new method takes into account the interest rate and also the compounding. So if the APY is 4.46 percent, a hundred dollars will earn $4.46 in one year. The higher the APY, the more interest is paid.

Life insurance companies are governed by the laws of the state in which they are incorporated, as well as the laws of the states in which they do business. There is no state restriction concerning the number of years for which a loan can be made. However, company policy usually restricts the term to no more than 30 years and requires a loan to be amortized.

When making loans, life insurance companies in California are restricted to a 75 percent maximum of market value of any given property. This is not a requirement if the loan is insured by the Federal Housing Administration (FHA) or guaranteed by the Veterans Administration (VA).

V. Noninstitutional Lenders

Noninstitutional lenders are smaller lenders, including: credit unions, investment trusts, pension plans, and mortgage companies.

NONINSTITUTIONAL LENDERS *are individuals and organizations that lend on a private or individual basis.* Both institutional and noninstitutional lenders make loans that may be or may not be backed by one of the government loan programs.

CONVENTIONAL LOANS *are loans that are not insured or guaranteed by the United States government.*

A. PRIVATE INDIVIDUALS

Any real estate loan by an individual is considered a private individual loan. Most individuals who lend money on real estate are sellers who take back a second trust deed as part of the real estate transaction. The seller will be a likely lender when the buyer needs a little more money to purchase a property. Most second trust deed loans are of this type and are the most important type of secondary financing in California.

When the current money market is tight, it often means that a seller will have to take back a second trust deed as part of the equity in his/her home. Many second loans on real estate, called junior loans (second trust deeds), are obtained from private parties.

Common second trust deed terms are:

1. The loan amount is usually relatively small (under $50,000).
2. There is a relatively high interest rate (8% to 15%).
3. The loan term is usually from 3 to 7 years, with payments on a monthly basis.
4. Loan payments are usually 1% of the original loan, and there is usually a balloon payment at the end of the term (if more than six years).
5. There is usually an acceleration clause that makes the entire loan due if any payment is missed or the property is transferred.

B. CREDIT UNIONS

A **CREDIT UNION** *is a co-operative association organized to promote thrift among its members and provide them with a source of credit.*

Under the Federal Credit Union Act of 1934, a credit union charter may be given to any group having a common bond of association or occupation—a factory, store, office, church, trade group, club, or fraternal organization.

Although there are thousands of credit unions across the country, they play a much smaller role than banks, savings banks, and insurance companies in financing real estate. The typical credit union is smaller than the average commercial bank or savings bank.

Most credit unions are incorporated and accumulate funds by selling shares to members. From this pool of funds, loans are made at an interest rate equal to or below the current market rate. Low interest rate loans to members are a big plus for credit unions.

The modern credit union offers savings plans, credit cards, ATM cards, travelers' checks, vehicle loans, signature loans, and real estate loans. All deposit accounts have FDIC insurance up to $100,000.

Recent changes in the law have enabled credit unions to make not only second trust deed loans, but also first trust deed loans. This source of real estate funding is expected to grow and expand in coming years.

C. REAL ESTATE INVESTMENT TRUST (REIT)

A **REAL ESTATE INVESTMENT TRUST (REIT)** *is a type of company that sells securities to invest in real estate properties.* If the company distributes 95 percent or more of its income to its shareholders, it does not pay federal income taxes on that distribution. Because of these formalities, a real estate investment trust is taxed like any other real estate investment.

An **EQUITY TRUST** *is a company that invests in real estate itself or several real estate projects.* The **MORTGAGE TRUST** *is a company that invests in mortgages and other types of real estate loans or obligations.* Now there are even combination trusts that invest in real estate and lend money in the form of real estate mortgages.

D. PENSION PLANS

A **PENSION PLAN** *is an investment organization that obtains funds from people before they retire and invests this money for their clients' retirement.* Company pension plans have become a popular source of real estate funds and are expected to grow even larger in the future.

Enormous amounts of money, gathered through deductions from each pay period, are held by these plans. Those who administer pension money are becoming more and more inclined to invest it directly in large real estate projects rather than investing in the stock market or simply investing in savings institutions and insurance companies.

E. MORTGAGE BANKERS (COMPANIES) – Secondary Mortgage Market

MORTGAGE BANKERS (COMPANIES) usually lend their own money or roll it over so they can originate, finance, and close first trust deeds or mortgages secured by real estate. They then sell the loans to institutional investors and service the loans through a contractual relationship with the investors.

Mortgage loan brokers (correspondents) are licensed by the DRE as real estate brokers and/or by the Department of Corporations as Residential Mortgage Lenders (RML) or California Finance Lenders (CFL).

In California, the brokerage function is one of the prime sources for loans on homes and income property, and they are the largest originator of FHA and VA trust deeds or mortgages. Sometimes private mortgage insurance is necessary to make a loan.

"Warehousing" is the action of a mortgage banker collecting loans in a package prior to sale.

F. PRIVATE MORTGAGE INSURANCE (PMI)

PRIVATE MORTGAGE INSURANCE is a guarantee to lenders that the upper portion of a conventional loan will be repaid if a borrower defaults and a deficiency occurs at the foreclosure sale.

Example: Smith is buying a property for $300,000 but he has only $15,000 for a down payment. He approaches lender Jones for financing. Lender Jones is eager to see this sale go through but he does not feel entirely comfortable putting up $285,000 when normally he would limit the loan to 80%, or $240,000. He is uncomfortable lending Smith the extra $45,000. He agrees to make the loan if Smith will pay for private mortgage insurance to cover the upper portion ($45,000) of the $285,000 loan.

Private mortgage insurance is obtainable on properties with one-to-four units and generally covers the top 20% of the loan amount. The borrower generally pays an initial premium or an annual fee of one-half of one percent on the remaining principal balance.

VI. Government-Backed Loans

The government is very involved in helping people obtain homes. The three programs we will discuss have already helped millions to enjoy "owning a home," the American dream. FHA insurance (part of Housing and Urban Development – HUD) and VA guarantees are federal programs. They approve loans made by private lenders, but lend no actual money. The CalVet program makes direct loans to qualified borrowers from the state of California (see **Figure 9-6** and the chart in **Figure 9-7**).

Figure 9-6

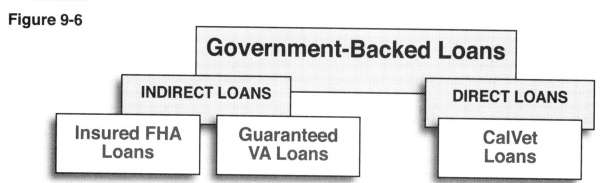

A. FHA INSURED LOANS (A Division of HUD)

Unlike conventional lenders, the Federal Housing Administration (FHA) does not make loans, but insures them.

The FHA has two main programs that affect California homeowners and buyers: 1) Title I home improvement loans, and 2) Title II (Section 203b) purchase and construction loans. There are other types of FHA financing available. For information, contact a lender who specializes in FHA loans (see Figure 9-7).

www.hud.gov
Housing and Urban Development
www.hud.gov/oig/oigindex.html
Office of The Inspector General - OIG

The main purpose of FHA is to promote home ownership by insuring loans made by approved lenders.

1. FHA Title I: Home Improvement Loans

The FHA can make home improvement loans to a maximum of $25,000. The funds can be used only for home improvement purposes.

2. FHA Title II: Home Purchase or Build Loans

The maximum FHA loan amount varies from area-to-area in California and could change each year if median home prices change or Federal National Mortgage Association (FNMA) loan amounts change. The maximum loan amount is determined as follows:

1. On homes sold at over $125,000, the maximum loan-to-value ratio is 97.15%.
2. On homes from $50,000 to $125,000, the maximum loan-to-value ratio is 97.65%.
3. On homes below $50,000, the maximum loan-to-value ratio is 98.75%.

Obviously, different geographical areas warrant different maximum loans based on the median home values. Accessing the HUD's website at www.hud.gov will give the agent the latest quotes for the various counties.

www.comerica.com
Independent FHA Lender

Minimum Property Requirements (MPRs)

All of these government-backed finance programs have increased the number of houses and condominiums that people in California can afford to buy. They also have an indirect influence on the quality of homes constructed because they require that the home involved meet minimum property requirements as a prerequisite to financing. Minimum Property Requirements (MPRs) are set standards of materials and construction required for FHA and VA loans. These requirements are often more restrictive than the building codes. As a real estate licensee, you should be familiar with the basic financing programs and qualification requirements. In addition, most mortgage companies will help you qualify the buyer and complete the necessary forms for FHA and VA loans.

Minimum Property Requirements (or MPRs) are minimum quality standards established by the FHA and VA.

www.fix.net/~chase/fha.html
Independent FHA lender

All FHA home buyers must obtain loans at an approved lender's office. The approved local lender (such as banks, insurance companies, and mortgage companies) will make the loan if the FHA qualifies the buyer. The FHA has many requirements for its different loan programs. Both the borrower and the property must meet these criteria. If either the borrower or the property does not meet the minimum standards, it would probably be better to look for a lender who deals in conventional rather than FHA loans.

The FHA does not lend the money. It only insures the approved lender against foreclosure loss. The FHA collects a percentage of the loan for this insurance called the mortgage insurance premium. The *MORTGAGE INSURANCE PREMIUM (MIP) is the protection for the FHA that insures the lender for any loss if there is a foreclosure.* It is an up-front fee (paid by the borrower) in cash, or through insurance as part of the loan. If there is a foreclosure, FHA will take over the property and reimburse the lender for the cost of default.

An *FHA MORTGAGE LOAN CORRESPONDENT is a mortgagee approved by the Secretary of the Department Housing and Urban Development.* The loan correspondent has as his or her principal activity either 1) the origination of mortgages for sale or transfer to a sponsor or sponsors, or 2) satisfies the definition of a supervised mortgagee contained in the regulations of the Secretary of the Department of Housing and Urban Development.

3. Advantages and Disadvantages of FHA Financing

The advantages and disadvantages of FHA financing includethe following.

a. Advantages

1. Low down payment compared to conventional loans.
2. Loans are assumable. Loans require approval of the FHA and non-owner-occupied are permitted under some circumstances.

Figure 9-7

Federal Housing Administration
(FHA 203b "basic")

ELIGIBILITY	Anyone residing in the United States
SOURCE OF FUNDS	Approved Lenders
LOAN INSTRUMENT	**Trust Deed or Mortgage**
TERM	30 years
INTEREST RATE	Current interest rates plus mortgage insurance premiums paid up front, prior to close of escrow
MAXIMUM PURCHASE	**No Maximum**
MAXIMUM LOAN AMOUNTS (For high cost areas) (Alaska & Hawaii up to 150% higher)	97% of the maximum for the county average: house-condo $290,319; duplex $371,621; tri-plex $449,181, and 4-unit $558,236
DOWN PAYMENT	3% minimum cash investment; 100% over appraisal
SECONDARY FINANCING	**Allowed**
PREPAYMENT PENALTY	None (30-days' notice)
ASSUMABLE	After 2 years, if owner occupant
POINTS PAID BY	**Buyer or Seller**
BORROWER'S MONTHLY PAYMENT	Monthly principal and interest 29% to 41% of annual gross income
MONTHLY SALARY (AFTER FEDERAL TAXES)	Approximately 3 times total monthly payment

Department of Veterans Affairs VA	State of California CalVet
W.W. II, Korean Conflict, Vietnam Era, Persian Gulf War, or continuous active duty for 90 days (181 days peacetime)	90 day's active duty and received a discharge classified as Honorable or Under Honorable Conditions
Approved Lenders	California Bond Issues
Trust Deed or Mortgage	**Conditional Sales Contract**
30-year maximum	30-year maximum
Set by VA	Set by California, but may increase later
No Maximum by VA (Restricted by Guarantee)	**None**
1-to-4 units, owner occupied, up to CRV. No loan maximum, but usually under $240,000; Guaranty Maximum is $60,000	Mauufactured Home – $125,000 (in Mobile Park) (on owned lot – $250,000) House – $521,250
None required, lender may require down payment	Manufactured Home – 3% to 20% House – 3% to 20%
Only up to amount of CRV	
None	None
Subject to VA approval of assumer's credit	To a CalVet, YES
Buyer or Seller	**Buyer**
Monthly principal and interest 29% to 41% of annual gross income	Monthly principal and interest 28% to 50% of annual gross income
Approximately 3 times total monthly payment	Approximately 2 times total monthly payment

3. No prepayment penalty is allowed by the FHA.

4. Minimum property requirements (MPRs) give the buyer a quality home.

5. A seller receives all cash because of the high loan-to-value ratio.

FHA-backed loans generally have lower interest rates than conventional loans. There are NO prepayment penalties on FHA loans.

b. Disadvantages

1. Lots of processing time and red tape.

2. Existing properties may require repairs necessary to meet minimum property requirements.

B. DEPARTMENT OF VETERANS AFFAIRS (VA)

1. VA Loans (Loan Guarantees to Approved Lenders)

The Congress of the United States has passed legislation to assist veterans in obtaining housing. A *VA LOAN is not a loan, but rather a guarantee to an approved institutional lender.*

a. Veteran's Eligibility

Veterans are eligible for a Department of Veterans Affairs (VA) loan guarantee if they served on active duty for 90 days or more (181 days during certain peacetime periods) and were honorably discharged.

American citizens who served in the armed forces of our Allies in World War II may also apply. Widows or widowers of service people or veterans who were eligible at the time of death, but did not use their benefits, may apply to use their husbands' or wives' benefits. Also, the VA Adjudication Board, at its discretion, may give eligibility to any veteran who received other than an honorable discharge.

b. Veterans May be Entitled to More Than One Loan

A veteran may restore his or her eligibility and apply for an additional loan if the previous home was sold and its loan paid in full. Other veterans who are eligible for a new VA loan program may apply even if they have a prior VA loan, if the prior loan is not in default and if the veteran no longer owns the property. The previous VA loan need not be paid off. The veteran who purchased a home under a previous program may be eligible again under a new program.

2. Certificate of Reasonable Value (CRV)

A *CERTIFICATE OF REASONABLE VALUE (CRV) is an appraisal of the property to be purchased by the veteran.* The property is appraised by an independent fee appraiser who is appointed by the Department of Veterans Affairs. Although the appraisal may be paid for by the veteran, it may also be paid for by the seller. The CRV appraisal expires after six months.

The amount of down payment required for a VA loan is determined by the CRV.

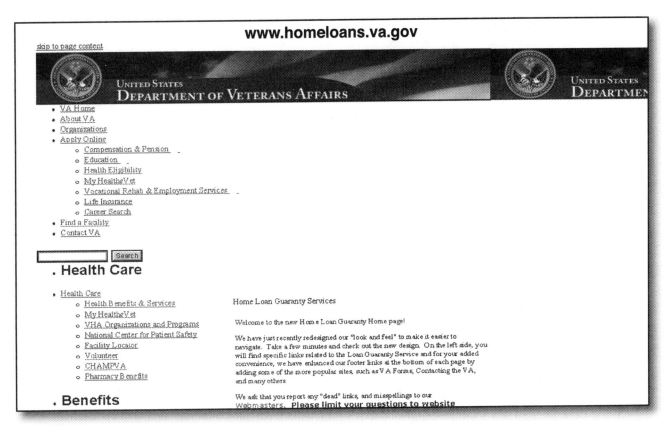

3. VA Loan Provisions

VA loans require NO down payment (100% financing), and NO prepayment penalties.

No down payment VA loans can be for any amount, but California lenders will only make a loan up to $240,000.

The veteran has the choice of several types of VA loans. They include fixed-rate mortgages, graduated payment mortgages, growing equity mortgages, and buy-down loans. The duration of a VA loan is generally 30 years. Discount points charged sellers and interest rates vary according to the current economic conditions. **The main advantage to the veteran is that no down payment is needed**, unless the property's price exceeds the VA's appraisal. This "no money down" feature is unique among government programs. Loans can be above the $240,000 guaranteed maximum loan amount, but require that the difference between the $240,000 maximum and the actual loan be in the form of a cash down payment.

4. Advantages and Disadvantages of VA Financing

The advantages and disadvantages of VA financing include the following.

a. Advantages

1. **No down payment**, but a funding fee is paid by the veteran.

2. **Low interest rate** because of the VA loan guarantee.

3. **No prepayment penalty** is allowed by the VA.

b. Disadvantages

1. Buyer's creditworthiness is a requirement for assumption; VA must approve credit and a fee of up to $500 is required; assumption only after one year if owner-occupied or after two years if investor owned.

2. Buyer or seller can pay discount points.

3. Lengthy processing time and red tape.

C. CALIFORNIA DEPARTMENT OF VETERAN'S AFFAIRS (CalVet)

1. CalVet (Land Contract – Direct Loans)

Land contracts (contracts of sale or real property sales contracts) are used by the California Department of Veterans Affairs, who retains legal title until the loan is paid in full.

The **CALVET** *loan program is administered by the California Department of Veterans Affairs.* As part of its comprehensive veterans program, the State of California has developed and operates a program to assist its veterans in purchasing a farm, home, or manufactured home. Home property must be a single-family dwelling, condominium unit or apartment townhouse.

CalVet will NOT loan on rental property purchases, but FHA-backed lenders will.

Funds for the CalVet loans come from the sale of Veterans Bonds, voted into law by the people of California. All money lent to veterans is repaid through installments (including principal, property taxes, insurance, and interest) at a rate to cover all operating costs. The bonds are retired at maturity from veterans' loan payments without cost to the State of California.

Funds may not be immediately available for loans to all applicants. The availability of these funds is limited, therefore wartime veterans (especially those disabled with war-connected injuries) may be given higher priority when applying for these loans.

A veteran who intends to obtain a CalVet loan should contact a representative of the Department of Veterans Affairs for complete California Farm and Home Purchase Plan information before committing to purchase a property. To apply for a loan, he or she should obtain the necessary information and forms from one of the California Department of Veterans Affairs offices throughout the state.

The CalVet maximum for the purchase of a home is $521,250 and up to $625,500 for a farm. A farm loan, however, may not exceed 95 percent of the CalVet appraisal. The veteran must pay to the seller the difference between the sales price and the CalVet loan.

The loan term is determined by the amount of the loan and the age and income of each applicant. Most loans are for 30 years. New loan interest rates are usually lower than current market rates, but may vary according to economic conditions during the life of the loan.

A loan may be paid in full at any time. A CalVet loan can be obtained for a manufactured home if the ownership of the land is included. The maximum manufactured home loan is $125,000 in a park and $250,000 on a single-family lot.

CalVet has NO points and no prepayment penalties.

a. Eligibility

There is no residency requirement. All veterans are eligible for the CalVet program.

To qualify, a California veteran must have served a minimum of 90 days active duty (not including active duty for training purposed only), and received a discharge classified as Honorable or Under Honorable Conditions. Recent changes in the Military and Veterans Code and CalVet Home Loan funding policies have made most veterans eligible under state law, including those whose entire active service was during peacetime.

There are exceptions to the 90 days service requirement for veterans who:

1. were discharged sooner due to a service-connected disability; or

2. are eligible to receive a U.S. campaign or expeditionary medal, or

3. were called to active duty from the Reserves or National Guard due to a Presidential Executive Order.

Current members of the California National Guard or the U.S. Military Reserves who have served a minimum of one year of a six-year obligation are also eligible provided they qualify as first time home buyers or purchase properties located in certain Targeted Areas.

A qualified veteran must apply for a CalVet loan within 30 years following release from active military duty. However, those who were wounded or disabled during war or who were prisoners of war have an indefinite period in which to apply.

D. CALIFORNIA HOUSING FINANCE AGENCY (Cal HFA)

CALIFORNIA HOUSING FINANCE AGENCY (Cal HFA) is a state agency that sells bonds so that it can provide funds for low-income family housing on a project or individual home basis. It is self-supporting and has political support across party lines. **Figure 9-8** explains Cal HFA in detail.

VII. Lending Corporations and the Secondary Mortgage Market

A. PRIVATE AND QUASI-GOVERNMENTAL CORPORATIONS

There were once three federal corporations that used cash to buy and sell trust deeds between financial institutions. These corporations are now either private or quasi-governmental and provide stability and flexibility for real estate financing in the United States. Each has different programs and areas of focus, but all work together to keep sufficient financing money available at lending institutions so they can make home loans.

B. SECONDARY MORTGAGE (TRUST DEED) MARKET

Lenders in the secondary market are concerned with the "liquidity and marketability" of loans.

The **SECONDARY MORTGAGE (TRUST DEED) MARKET** *provides an opportunity for financial institutions to buy from, and sell first mortgages (trust deeds) to, other financial institutions.* California has a growing real estate market that will pay higher interest rates than other parts of the country. Therefore, California's financial institutions will make trust deed loans and sell them to other institutions for a profit. The secondary mortgage market enables lenders to keep an adequate supply of money for new loans.

The secondary mortgage market provides additional funds to mortgage lenders.

1. Federal National Mortgage Association (Fannie Mae – Private)

Fannie Mae is not a demand source to borrow money.

The Federal National Mortgage Association (FNMA), which is commonly referred to as Fannie Mae, dominates the secondary mortgage market. Originally it bought and sold only FHA and VA trust deeds. In 1968 it became a private corporation and now sells securities over the stock exchange to get money so that it can buy and sell conventional loans in addition to government-backed notes. **It is not a demand source**.

Fannie Mae is the largest investor in the secondary market. It was created to increase the amount of money available for credit financing of houses.

www.fanniemaefoundation.org
Fannie Mae

2. Government National Mortgage Association (Ginnie Mae)

The Government National Mortgage Association (GNMA) is a government corporation referred to as Ginnie Mae. It sells secondary mortgages to the public and provides the federal government with cash. These trust deeds are grouped together in pools, and

Figure 9-8

Cal HFA
California Housing Finance Agency

Cal HFA

1121 "L" STREET 7TH FLOOR · SACRAMENTO, CA 95814 · (916) 322-3991

The **California Housing Finance Agency** is an exciting program providing real estate funds for low-income families, encouraging homeownership over a wider spectrum than has been possible in recent years. This plan is being hailed as a boon from all quarters because it provides a desperately needed funding source and helps stimulate the real estate industry. At the same time, it is entirely self-supporting.

Bonds Issued

Seb Sterpa, past president of CAR, is credited with originating the idea for this program and promoting it to the governor and house speaker. The money for these loans is provided by the issuance of tax-free bonds by the state. These bonds sell quickly at a very favorable rate. Because this rate is below the current level, it enables approved lenders to provide loans with affordable rates of interest and still make a reasonable return.

Entirely Self-Supporting

Everyone benefits from this program. Housing in California has become more accessible to buyers with restricted resources. Young couples starting out are now able to enter the housing market. The market is stimulated by the influx of new participants. Investors who purchase the bonds enjoy this profitable form of investment. No tax money is involved and the program is entirely self-supporting.

Support Across Party Lines

Because of the universal benefits, this program claims support across traditional party lines. Democrats favor this program because of the opportunity it offers to the economically disadvantaged. Many Republicans in the state are delighted because of the boost these loans bring to the real estate industry and the state economy in general.

 www.calhfa.ca.gov

shares are sold on the stock market exchange. All shares are federally guaranteed, making this one of the safest investments available.

www.ginniemae.gov
Ginnie Mae

3. Federal Home Loan Mortgage Corporation (Freddie Mac)

The Federal Home Loan Mortgage Corporation (FHLMC), commonly known as Freddie Mac, is a government corporation that issues preferred stock to the public. It is supervised by the Federal Home Loan Bank Board. It helps savings banks maintain a stable and adequate money supply by purchasing their home loan mortgages and repackaging them for sale to investors. The savings banks use the money obtained to make new loans available for home buyers.

The Federal Home Loan Mortgage Corporation, commonly called "Freddie Mac," increases the availability of funds through its involvement in the maintenance of the secondary mortgage market.

www.freddiemac.com
Freddie Mac

C. FINAL WORD ON CONVENTIONAL LOANS
(Risk – Loans Without Government Backing)

Since conventional loans are loans made without government backing or guarantees, they are riskier. Even if conventional loans have lower loan-to-value (LTV) ratios, which make them safer, government-backed loans are the safest. Because the government will pay off if there is a foreclosure, Fannie Mae and Freddie Mac currently have loan limits of $417,000 (expected to increase) for a single-family house or condo. *If the requested loan amount is higher than the Fannie Mae and Freddie Mac loan limit, it is called a JUMBO LOAN.*

VIII. Real Estate Broker Can Make Loans

The broker or salesperson, as part of most real estate transactions, may help the buyer fill out a loan application for a financial institution or arrange financing for the buyer. In either case, there are certain restrictions that apply to a real estate licensee acting as a loan broker in buying, selling, or exchanging loans. Most of these loans are in the form of a trust deed since it is the usual financing instrument in California.

Advertising criteria (pertinent information) ensures that advertisements are not misleading.

The "Mortgage Loan Broker Law," sections 10240-10248 of Article 7 of the Business and Professions Code, requires loan brokers to give a Mortgage Loan Disclosure Statement to all borrowers before they become obligated for the loan.

A. MORTGAGE LOAN DISCLOSURE STATEMENT
(Keep on File for Three Years)

A real estate licensee negotiating a loan for a prospective borrower must present to that person a completed loan disclosure statement. This statement must be given to the borrower prior to his or her signing the loan documents. It is usually referred to as the Mortgage Loan Disclosure Statement.

A **MORTGAGE LOAN DISCLOSURE STATEMENT** is a form that completely and clearly states all the information and charges connected with a particular loan. Nontraditional mortgage product information must be disclosed to the borrower. It must be kept on file for three years (see **Figure 9-10**). Expect more changes to this form.

Besides providing the borrower with the disclosure statement, the broker is prohibited from doing certain things and is restricted as to the amount of commission that he or she may charge the borrower. The broker's (fiduciary) obligation is to fully explain the terms of a loan to the borrower.

Anyone negotiating real estate loans (fiduciary relationship) must be a real estate licensee. If you make collections on real estate loans and you make more than ten a year, or collect more than $40,000, you must also be a licensed real estate broker. Many brokers establish a regular, ongoing business relationship with individuals or financial institutions that will loan money to prospective buyers.

www.calbankers.com
California Bankers association

B. BUSINESS AND PROFESSIONS CODE – Division 4 – Real Estate
(Commissions and Other Requirements)

1. Article 7 – Loan Broker Laws ($20,000 – $30,000)

Brokers negotiating trust deed loans are subject to certain limitations regarding commissions and expenses and must meet other requirements set out by the real estate commissioner (see **Figure 9-9**). Legislation also requires that brokers provide both the borrower and the lender, on property for first trust deed loans under $30,000 and seconds under $20,000, with copies of the appraisal report.

Anyone performing these services, whether soliciting borrowers or lenders in home loans secured by real property must have a real estate license. This restriction applies even if no advance fee is paid.

Loans on owner-occupied homes negotiated by brokers for a term of six years or less may not have a balloon payment. If a home is nonowner occupied, loans are exempt from balloon payments when the term is less than three years. Neither of these restrictions apply to transactions where the seller extends credit to the buyer. When such transactions have balloon payments, the seller is obligated to notify the buyer 60 to 150 days before the payment is due. Also, the broker is obligated to inform the buyer regarding the likelihood of obtaining new financing.

CHAPTER 9

Figure 9-9

Loan Broker Commission Limits

	Loans for Less Than 2 Years	Loans for 2 Years and Less Than 3 Years	Loans for 3 Years and Over	Transactions That are Exempt (No Limit on Commission)
First Trust Deeds	5%	5%	10%	Loans of $30,000 and over
Junior Trust Deeds	5%	10%	15%	Loans of $20,000 and over

a. Threshold Reporting (Big Lending – $2,000,000)

THRESHOLD REPORTING is the requirement of reporting annual and quarterly loan activity (review of trust fund) to the Department of Real Estate if, within the past 12 months, the broker has negotiated any combination of 20 or more loans to a subdivision or a total of more than $2,000,000 in loans. In addition, advertising must be submitted to the DRE for review. This regulation is intended to protect the public by overseeing the loan activity of big lenders who are using their real estate broker's licenses.

2. Article 5 – Broker Restrictions

The licensee is prohibited from pooling funds. A broker may not accept funds except for a specifically identified loan transaction. Before accepting a lender's money, the broker must:

1. Own the loan or have an unconditional written contract to purchase a specific note.

2. Have the authorization from a prospective borrower to negotiate a secured loan.

3. Article 6 – Real Property Securities Dealer

A DRE broker's license and endorsement are required: A $100 fee plus a $10,000 surety bond. DRE permit is required to sell specific security.

No real estate investment type security shall be sold to the public without first obtaining a permit from the Commissioner. A *COMMISSIONER'S PERMIT is the approval of the proposed real property security and plan of distribution.* If, in the commissioner's opinion, the security and proposed plan of distribution is fair, just, and equitable, he or she will authorize the sale, subject to any limiting conditions. A permit is not an endorsement or recommendation of the security; it is only a permit to sell. The application for the permit is extensive and may require supplementary filings. The duration of the permit is one year, and the permit may not be used in advertising unless it is used in its entirety. **A Commissioner's permit requires a $10,000 surety bond.**

Figure 9-10

CALIFORNIA
ASSOCIATION
OF REALTORS®

MORTGAGE LOAN DISCLOSURE STATEMENT
(BORROWER)

(As required by the Business and Professions Code §10241
and Title 10, California Administrative Code, §2840)

_____
(Name of Broker/Arranger of Credit)

_____
(Business Address of Broker)

I. SUMMARY OF LOAN TERMS
  A. PRINCIPAL AMOUNT . . . . $ _____
  B. ESTIMATED DEDUCTIONS FROM PRINCIPAL AMOUNT
    1. Costs and Expenses (See Paragraph III-A) . . . . $ _____
    *2. Broker Commission/Organization Fee (See Paragraph III-B) . . . . $ _____
    3. Lender Origination Fee/Discounts (See Paragraph III-B) . . . . $ _____
    4. Additional compensation will/may be received from lender not deducted from loan proceeds.
      ☐ YES $ _____ (if known) or ☐ NO
    5. Amount to be Paid on Authorization of Borrower (See Paragraph III) . . . . $ _____
  C. ESTIMATED CASH PAYABLE TO BORROWER (A less B) . . . . $ _____

II. GENERAL INFORMATION ABOUT LOAN
  A. If this loan is made, Borrower will be required to pay the principal and interest at _____% per year, payable
  as follows: _____ payments of $ _____
      (number of payments)   (monthly/quarterly/annually)
  and a **FINAL/BALLOON** payment of $ _____ to pay off the loan in full.

  NOTICE TO BORROWER: IF YOU DO NOT HAVE THE FUNDS TO PAY THE BALLOON PAYMENT WHEN IT COMES DUE, YOU MAY HAVE TO OBTAIN A NEW LOAN AGAINST YOUR PROPERTY TO MAKE THE BALLOON PAYMENT. IN THAT CASE, YOU MAY AGAIN HAVE TO PAY COMMISSIONS, FEES AND EXPENSES FOR THE ARRANGING OF THE NEW LOAN. IN ADDITION, IF YOU ARE UNABLE TO MAKE THE MONTHLY PAYMENTS OR THE BALLOON PAYMENT, YOU MAY LOSE THE PROPERTY AND ALL OF YOUR EQUITY THROUGH FORECLOSURE. KEEP THIS IN MIND IN DECIDING UPON THE AMOUNT AND TERMS OF THIS LOAN.

  B. This loan will be evidenced by a promissory note and secured by a deed of trust on property identified as (street
  address or legal description):
  _____
  _____

  C. 1. Liens presently against this property (do not include loan being applied for):

Nature of Lien	Priority	Lienholder's Name	Amount Owing
_____	_____	_____	_____
_____	_____	_____	_____
_____	_____	_____	_____

    2. Liens that will remain against this property after the loan being applied for is made or arranged (include loan
    being applied for):

Nature of Lien	Priority	Lienholder's Name	Amount Owing
_____	_____	_____	_____
_____	_____	_____	_____
_____	_____	_____	_____

  NOTICE TO BORROWER: Be sure that you state the amount of all liens as accurately as possible. If you contract with the broker to arrange this loan, but it cannot be arranged because you did not state these liens correctly, you may be liable to pay commissions, fees and expenses even though you do not obtain the loan.

MS REVISED 10/2000 (PAGE 1 OF 3) Print Date

Borrower acknowledges receipt of copy of this page.
  Borrower's Initials (_____)(_____)

Reviewed by _____ Date _____

EQUAL HOUSING OPPORTUNITY

MORTGAGE LOAN DISCLOSURE STATEMENT (MS PAGE 1 OF 3)

Property Address: _____ Date: _____

D. If Borrower pays all or part of the loan principal before it is due, a PREPAYMENT PENALTY computed as follows may be charged:

_____
_____
_____

E. Late Charges: ☐ YES, see loan documents or ☐ NO

F. The purchase of credit life or credit disability insurance by a borrower is not required as a condition of making this loan.

G. Is the real property which will secure the requested loan an "owner-occupied dwelling?" ☐ YES____ or ☐ NO____
(Borrower initial opposite YES or NO)

An "owner-occupied dwelling" means a single dwelling unit in a condominium or cooperative or residential building of four or fewer separate dwelling units, one of which will be owned and occupied by a signatory to the mortgage or deed of trust for this loan within 90 days of the signing of the mortgage or deed of trust.

III. DEDUCTIONS FROM LOAN PROCEEDS

A. Estimated Maximum Costs and Expenses of Arranging the Loan to be Paid Out of Loan Principal:

PAYABLE TO

	Broker	Others
1. Appraisal fee	_____	_____
2. Escrow fee	_____	_____
3. Title insurance policy	_____	_____
4. Notary fees	_____	_____
5. Recording fees	_____	_____
6. Credit investigation fees	_____	_____
7. Other costs and expenses:		

_____
_____

Total Costs and Expenses .... $ _____

*B. Compensation .... $ _____
  1. Brokerage Commission/Origination Fee .... $ _____
  2. Lender Origination Fee/Discounts .... $ _____

C. Estimated Payment to be Made out of Loan Principal on Authorization of Borrower

PAYABLE TO

	Broker	Others
1. Fire or other hazard insurance premiums	_____	_____
2. Credit life or disability insurance premiums (see Paragraph II-F)	_____	_____
3. Beneficiary statement fees	_____	_____
4. Reconveyance and similar fees	_____	_____
5. Discharge of existing liens against property:		

_____
_____

6. Other:

_____
_____

Total to be Paid on Authorization of Borrower .... $ _____

If this loan is secured by a first deed of trust on dwellings in a principal amount of less than $30,000 or secured by a junior lien on dwellings in a principal amount of less than $20,000, the undersigned licensee certifies that the loan will be made in compliance with Article 7 of Chapter 3 of the Real Estate Law.

*This loan **may / will / will not** (delete two) be made wholly or in part from broker-controlled funds as defined in Section 10241(j) of the Business and Professions Code.

MS REVISED 10/2000 (PAGE 2 OF 3) Print Date

Borrower acknowledges receipt of copy of this page.
Borrower's Initials (_____)(_____)

Reviewed by _____ Date _____

MORTGAGE LOAN DISCLOSURE STATEMENT (MS PAGE 2 OF 3)

Property Address: _____ Date: _____

*NOTICE TO BORROWER: This disclosure statement may be used if the Broker is acting as an agent in arranging the loan by a third person or if the loan will be made with funds owned or controlled by the broker. If the Broker indicates in the above statement that the loan "may" be made out of Broker-controlled funds, the Broker must notify the borrower prior to the close of escrow if the funds to be received by the Borrower are in fact Broker-controlled funds.

_____   _____
Name of Broker   Broker Representative

_____   _____
License Number   OR   License Number

_____   _____
Signature of Broker   Signature

The Department of Real Estate License Information phone number is _____.

NOTICE TO BORROWER:

DO NOT SIGN THIS STATEMENT UNTIL YOU HAVE READ AND UNDERSTAND ALL OF THE INFORMATION IN IT. ALL PARTS OF THE FORM MUST BE COMPLETED BEFORE YOU SIGN.

Borrower hereby acknowledges the receipt of a copy of this statement.

DATED _____   _____
                                                                                      (Borrower)

                                                                        _____
                                                                                      (Borrower)

Broker Review: Signature of Real Estate Broker after review of this statement.

DATED _____   _____
                                                                        Real Estate Broker or Assistant Pursuant to Section 2725

SURE TRAC
The System for Success®

Published and Distributed by:
REAL ESTATE BUSINESS SERVICES, INC.
a subsidiary of the California Association of REALTORS®
525 South Virgil Avenue, Los Angeles, California 90020

MS REVISED 10/2000 (PAGE 3 OF 3) Print Date

Reviewed by _____ Date _____

EQUAL HOUSING OPPORTUNITY

MORTGAGE LOAN DISCLOSURE STATEMENT (MS PAGE 3 OF 3)

a. Real Property Securities Dealer Endorsement

A *REAL PROPERTY SECURITIES DEALER (RPSD) is any person acting as principal or agent who engages in the business of selling real property securities (such as promissory notes or sales contracts)*. These dealers also accept or offer to accept funds for reinvestment in real property securities or for placement in an account. Before a licensed real estate broker may act in this capacity, he or she must obtain an RPSD endorsement on his or her broker's license. To obtain an RPSD endorsement on a broker's license, submit the appropriate endorsement fee ($100) along with proof of a properly executed $10,000 surety bond. (For information on Real Property Securities, call the DRE.)

"Equity Sharing"

A Different Financing and Ownership Idea

EQUITY SHARING (SHARED EQUITY FINANCING) is a contractual arrangement whereby an investor shares any equity gain with a homeowner. Since California has high housing costs that require a large down payment, many potential homeowners cannot qualify or do not have the cash for a down payment. The concept is that an investor puts up most of the down payment, and receives no interest deductions but shares in any equity gain when the property is sold. The homeowner gets his or her home quickly with a minimum down payment, with relaxed credit, and with full income tax write-offs. Consult an attorney or CPA before investing.

IX. CHAPTER SUMMARY

Inflation (when prices appreciate) protects both lender and trustor because there will be more equity protecting the lender in the case of a default. When prices decrease, the value of money increases and vice versa. In a **seller's market**, prices rise due to a shortage of properties available, whereas in a **buyer's market**, prices fall, terms are easy and properties plentiful.

The **Federal Reserve (Fed)** is the nation's central banking authority and controls the availability of loan funds, but has nothing to do with raising or lowering interest rates. The Fed's influence on the economy is evidenced by changes in the **Gross Domestic Product (GDP)**.

The three areas of demand for borrowing money are: construction funds, financing a purchase, and refinancing. Most lenders request an 80% **L-T-V (loan to value) ratio**. The lower the L-T-V, the greater the down payment.

The primary purpose of **RESPA** is to require lenders to make special disclosures, without cost to the borrower, for loans involving the sale or transfer of one-to-four residential dwellings.

Large **institutional lenders** who pool funds to lend to individual borrowers, include: **insurance companies, savings banks,** and **banks**. Depositor's accounts in savings banks and banks are insured up to $100,000 by the **Federal Deposit Insurance Corporation (FDIC)**. Savings banks have the highest percentage of funds invested in real estate loans, followed by banks, which are **general purpose lenders**.

Smaller, **noninstitutional lenders** include: private lenders, mortgage companies, investment trusts, pension plans and credit unions. Private investors make many of the **second (junior) loans** on real estate. **Real estate investment trusts (REITs)** sell securities specializing in real estate ventures, and are of two types, 1) **equity trust** and 2) **mortgage trust**.

Mortgage bankers (companies) like to make loans that can be sold easily on the **secondary mortgage market**, which is a resale marketplace for smaller lenders to sell their loans to larger lenders. Buyers may be required to obtain **private mortgage insurance (PMI)** to protect the lender in case of default.

The **Federal Housing Administration (FHA)** is a division of **HUD** that **insures loans** but does not make them. **FHA Title 1** involves home improvement loans and **FHA Title II** insures home loan purchase or building loans. The **Mortgage Insurance Premium (MIP)** is the FHA insurance protection against owner default (also called mutual mortgage insurance).

Veterans may qualify for a **Department of Veterans Affairs (VA) Loan**, which is not really a loan, but a **loan guarantee** to approved institutional lenders. The amount of down payment on a VA loan is determined by the **Certificate of Reasonable Value (CRV)**. Vets may be required to pay origination fees and discount points. On the state level, **CalVet**, administered by the California Department of Veteran Affairs, will purchase a **land contract (contract of sale or real property sales contract)** and hold legal title to a property until the veteran pays off the loan in full.

The **secondary mortgage (trust deed) market** is the market where lenders buy and sell mortgages. **Fannie Mae (FNMA)** buys and sells conventional loans. It helps set loan standards and maintain the secondary market, but is not a demand source to borrow money. **Freddie Mac (FHLMC)** purchases home loan mortgages and repackages them for sale to investors, freeing up savings banks to make new loans. Conventional loans are riskier than FHA loans; the higher the risk the higher the interest rates.

Ginnie Mae (GNMA) sells secondary mortgages to the public and provides the federal government cash.

A loan broker must provide a borrower with a **Mortgage Loan Disclosure Statement**, clearly stating all information and charges connected with a loan, and keep it on file for three years. Brokers negotiating trust deed loans (fiduciary relationship) may charge whatever commission the buyer will pay on loans of $30,000+ for first trust deeds and $20,000+ for junior deeds of trust.

A broker must make a **threshold report** if he or she negotiates more than $2 million in loans or 20+ subdivision loans. Other broker restrictions are covered by **Article 5**.

A **real property securities dealer (RPSD)** acts as a principal or agent engaged in the business of selling real property securities such as promissory notes or sales contracts. A DRE broker's license and endorsement are required including a $10,000 surety bond.

X. TERMINOLOGY

A. Buyer's Market
B. California Housing Financing Agency (Cal HFA)
C. CalVet Loans
D. Certificate of Reasonable Value (CRV)
E. Collateral
F. Conventional Loans
G. Credit Union
H. Equity Investment Trust
I. Fannie Mae

J. FDIC
K. Federal Reserve Board
L. Federal Reserve System (The "Fed")
M. Freddie Mac
N. Ginnie Mae
O. Gross Domestic Product (GDP)
P. Institutional Lender
Q. Minimum Property Requirements (MPRs)
R. Mortgage Banker

S. Mortgage Company
T. Mortgage Investment Trust
U. Mortgage Loan Disclosure Statement
V. Noninstitutional Lender
W. Private Mortgage Insurance (PMI)
X. Seller's Market
Y. Soft Money Financing
Z. VA Loans

1.____A company providing mortgage financing with its own funds rather than simply bringing together lender and borrower, as does a mortgage broker. The mortgages are sold to investors within a short time.

2.____(FHLMC) Federal Home Loan Mortgage Corporation. A federal agency purchasing first mortgages, both conventional and federally insured, from savings banks.

3.____A company authorized to service real estate loans, charging a fee for this service.

4.____The federal corporation that insures against loss of deposits in banks, up to a maximum amount (currently $100,000).

5.____Insurance issued by a private insurance company against a loss by a lender in the event of default by a borrower (mortgagor). The premium is paid by the borrower and is included in the mortgage payment.

6.____Loans made under a land contract directly from the California Department of Veterans Affairs, which has its own specific qualifications.

7.____A mortgage or deed of trust not obtained under a government insured or guaranteed program.

8.____The money value of all goods and services produced by a nation's economy for a given period of time.

9.____Government National Mortgage Association: A federal corporation, working with the FHA, which offers special assistance in obtaining mortgages and purchases mortgages in the secondary market.

10.____Banks, savings banks, loan associations, and other businesses that make loans to the public in the ordinary course of business, rather than individuals, or companies that may make loans to employees.

11.____ Housing loans to veterans by banks, savings banks, or other lenders that are guaranteed by the Veteran's Administration, enabling veterans to buy a residence with little or no down payment.

12.____ A private corporation that acts as a secondary market for the purchase of existing first mortgages, at a discount.

13.____ The central banking system that controls the amount of money and the rate of interest in the United States.

14.____ The powerful nine-member banking panel which controls the destiny of the United State's monetary system. Along with the President of the United States, the Chairman is one of the most powerful positions in the country.

15.____ A form that California law requires be given to the borrower, breaking down all the costs and fees of securing a loan.

16.____ An agency, sponsored by the state of California, which sponsors special housing projects and certain types of loans.

17.____ The real estate pledged to back up a loan. The value of the real estate should be worth substantially more than the loan amount.

18.____ Smaller lenders such as sellers, credit unions, and pension plans that lend money on real estate.

19.____ An appraisal document stating the fair market value of real estate under a VA loan.

20.____ The minimal property standards for a property to qualify for an FHA loan.

21.____ A loan made by the seller to the buyer as part of the purchase transaction.

22.____ A market condition favoring the seller, when fewer homes are for sale than there are interested buyers.

23.____ A trust company specializing in making mortgages as an investment.

24.____ A trust company that specializes in taking an ownership position in other projects.

25.____ A market condition favoring the buyer, when more homes are for sale than there are interested buyers.

26.____ An organization whose members often have a common bond of occupation. Considered a growing source of real estate funds.

CHAPTER 9

XI. CHAPTER QUIZ

1. With regard to inflation:

    a. market value increases and sales price increases.
    b. sales price increases and market value decreases.
    c. market value decreases and sale price decreases.
    d. sale price decreases and market value increases.

2. When the general level of prices decreases:

    a. the value of money decreases.
    b. the value of money increases.
    c. inflation increases.
    d. the GNP increases/market value increases.

3. When the federal reserve wants a "loose" money market:

    a. the fed buys back bonds and lowers reserve requirements of banks.
    b. the fed sells bonds and increases the reserve requirements of banks.
    c. the fed sells bonds and keeps the reserve requirements the same.
    d. none of the above.

4. Depression, recession, expansion, and prosperity represent four phases of:

    a. the elements of value.
    b. the right of survivorship.
    c. joint tenancy.
    d. the business cycle.

5. If a loan application includes a section requesting information about marital status and race, an applicant may:

    a. sue the lender for fraud.
    b. file a complaint under The Housing Financial Discrimination Act of 1977.
    c. refuse to complete this section of the application.
    d. all of the above.

6. For financing the purchase of residential properties, the principal lender of money is:

    a. Federal National Mortgage Association.
    b. federal savings banks.
    c. insurance companies.
    d. commercial banks.

7. Institutions that specialize in making home loans most commonly get their funds from:

    a. mortgage bankers.
    b. mortgage brokers.
    c. individual savings.
    d. Federal Reserve.

8. Which of the following are synonymous?

    a. Interim loan/take out loan
    b. Take out loan/construction loan
    c. Construction loan/interim loan
    d. None of the above

9. For which of the following is an FHA loan available, but not a Cal-Vet loan?

    a. A loan to purchase a single-family dwelling to be rented to a tenant
    b. A loan to purchase a business opportunity
    c. A loan to purchase agricultural land
    d. A loan to purchase farm equipment

10. Many lenders consider the liquidity and marketability of loans to be very important when they make a loan secured by a mortgage. The importance of liquidity and marketability relates to:

    a. activities of the secondary mortgage markets.
    b. desirability of fixed rate loans over adjustable rate loans.
    c. ability to resell homes.
    d. the mix of loans made by banks only.

ANSWERS: 1. a; 2. b; 3. a; 4. d; 5. c; 6. b; 7. c; 8. c; 9. a; 10. a

CHAPTER 10
Appraisal Basics

I. What is an Appraisal?

An *APPRAISAL is an opinion as to the monetary value of a particular property at a given date.* One of the most important factors for you to consider in deciding whether to sell or buy a home or any specific piece of real estate is its selling price. Each parcel of land (and the buildings on it) is unique. No two are exactly alike, so prices vary. The *MARKET PRICE (SELLING PRICE) is the total price, including down payment and financing, that a property actually brought when sold.* Market price is what it sold for, whereas market value is what it should have sold for in a competitive market.

The market value is what the property is actually worth. *MARKET VALUE is the price that a willing buyer will pay and a willing seller accept, both being fully informed and with the sale property exposed for a reasonable period.* The courtroom definition is even more technical:

> *"The highest price, estimated in terms of money, that a property will bring if it is exposed for sale in the open market, allowing a reasonable length of time to find a buyer who buys with full knowledge of all the uses to which it is adapted and for which the property is capable of being used."*

Appraisers are required to consider the impact of financing terms and creative financing when determining price or value. *The more favorable the financing terms, the better the appraised value*

IMPROVED VALUE OF LAND *is the market value of the land and any improvements.*

In comparing real property price to value, a change in financing terms will affect price, but NOT value.

Current market value is not affected in any way by the original cost of the property. The market value of a particular property is an opinion of value, by an appraiser, based on analysis of actual and relevant data, as of a given date. Appraisers must have the required experience, education, and have passed one of the three California State Appraisal Exams (see end of Chapter 11).

Market value is primarily based upon the "willing buyer and willing seller" concept.

A. FOUR ESSENTIAL ELEMENTS OF VALUE

VALUE is a relationship between the thing desired and a potential purchaser. Four elements must be present to create and maintain value. The four essential elements of value are:

CHAPTER 10

CHAPTER OUTLINE

D **1. Demand** – the desire, need, and ability to purchase
U **2. Utility** – usefulness; ability to instill a desire for possession
S **3. Scarcity** – in short supply, usually more expensive
T **4. Transferability** – can change ownership, as with a deed.

Elements of value include demand, utility, scarcity, and transferability (DUST). Neither cost nor expectation is an element of value.

II. The Appraisal Process (Four Logical Steps)

An appraisal is the solution to the problem of determining value. To solve this problem, an orderly procedure has been developed; it is called the appraisal process. The *APPRAISAL PROCESS is an orderly program by which the problem is defined, the work is planned, and the data is gathered, analyzed, and correlated to estimate the value.* Although the characteristics of real property differ, this is an orderly procedure for solving any appraisal problem (see **Figure 10-1**). The appraisal process consists of four logical steps:

1. Defining and clarifying the problem (Chapter 10)
2. Gathering the data (Chapter 10)
3. Performing the three appraisal methods (Chapter 11)
4. Correlating the three methods and determining the final opinion of value. (Chapter 11)

Figure 10-1

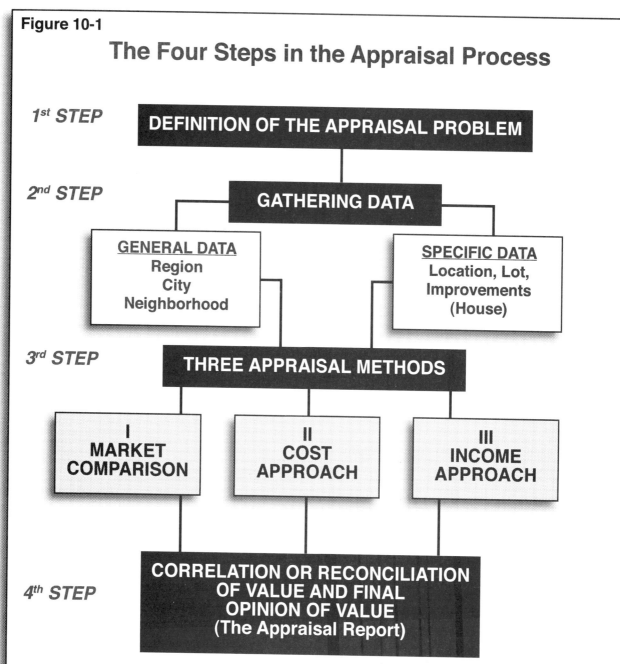

The Four Steps in the Appraisal Process

1st STEP — DEFINITION OF THE APPRAISAL PROBLEM

2nd STEP — GATHERING DATA

GENERAL DATA
Region
City
Neighborhood

SPECIFIC DATA
Location, Lot,
Improvements
(House)

3rd STEP — THREE APPRAISAL METHODS

I
MARKET
COMPARISON

II
COST
APPROACH

III
INCOME
APPROACH

4th STEP — CORRELATION OR RECONCILIATION OF VALUE AND FINAL OPINION OF VALUE
(The Appraisal Report)

This correlation or reconciliation is never an averaging of the three approaches. For instance, in a single-family residential appraisal, the Income Approach is not as valuable as the Market Comparison Approach. This is one of the reasons why the experience and knowledge of the appraiser is so important in any appraisal.

A. DEFINITION OF THE APPRAISAL PROBLEM (1st Step in the Appraisal Process)

The first step in the appraisal process must include a definition of what questions are to be answered during the appraisal. To begin with, the precise location of the property must be established. Next, the extent of ownership (fee simple or partial) to be appraised must be identified. The date and purpose of the appraisal (usually to establish market value) is then determined. Any limiting conditions (facts unknown to the appraiser) must be clarified. Finally, the appraiser will determine the fee for his or her services.

1. Purpose of an Appraisal

An appraisal can serve several purposes. Here is a partial list of the kinds of appraisals that you, as an owner or a potential owner (or as a broker representing an owner or potential owner), may need:

1. Market Value
2. Insurance Value
3. Loan Value
4. Tax Assessment Value
5. Rental Value
6. Value for certain Internal Revenue Service Purposes
7. Settlements
8. Salvage Value
9. Other

2. Highest and Best Use

The primary purpose of a site analysis by an appraiser is to determine highest and best use. Land is always appraised separately as if vacant and available for highest and best use.

Before we can properly appraise a property, we must determine its highest and best use. ***HIGHEST AND BEST USE*** *is the use that will produce the maximum amount of profit or net return.* For example, should we build a house or an apartment on an available piece of land? From the standpoint of economics, it would be best to build that which brings the highest net return.

When the current use is expected to soon change to the property's highest and best use, the current use is called the "interim use."

B. GATHERING DATA (2nd Step in the Appraisal Process)

There are logical reasons why one home is worth more than another that appears comparable and why the choice of a neighborhood is as important, or even more important, than the house itself. There are also differences in location within a neighborhood that must be taken into account. Differences in the actual building construction must also be considered. The background information needed for real estate appraisal is very broad, but there is a simple, sensible way to make a wise decision about buying a home or investment property. Start with the largest aspects and work toward the details. Look at:

CHAPTER 10

1. GENERAL DATA

    a. Region
    b. City
    c. Neighborhood

2. SPECIFIC DATA (Site Analysis)

    a. Location
    b. Lot
    c. Improvements (House)

1. General Data (Region, City, Neighborhood)

The gathering of general data (regional, city or county, and neighborhood information) allows us to understand whether the area is prospering, holding its own, or declining and, if so, why.

a. Region (State is Divided into Regions)

The condition of the nation's economy can be reflected in the California real estate market and can affect the ease with which financing is available. But real estate markets are essentially regional and local. If the regional or local economy is expanding, people are working and can afford to buy homes because lending institutions are eager to grant loans. In a recession, jobs are less secure, confidence is low, and financing may not be as easy to obtain. So, the economic mood of the nation as a whole can indirectly affect the economic mood in California, but it is the local and regional economy that directly affects the mood in a particular real estate market.

A regional economy is affected by upturns and also downtrends. Not only do large areas reflect the national picture, but they also respond to more localized forces, such as the rapid growth of large cities and industrial complexes and the downsizing of defense-related industries or even the weather in agricultural areas. California is divided into north and south regions and many subregions and cities.

California, like most large states, is a very geographically diverse state. Geographical considerations can easily affect an entire region. For example, if an area has snow for eight months of the year, the value of the property may be reduced when compared to regions that have year-round moderate or sunny climates.

b. City (or County)

A desirable city or county is a growing area where people can get good jobs and where people want to live. If the city is undesirable or even unsafe, people want to leave. Features to look for in cities, besides the availability of work and safety, are good public facilities, parks, good school systems, and active citizens who care and take part in the city's affairs.

c. Neighborhood

A residential **NEIGHBORHOOD** *is normally a limited area where the homes are physically similar and where the occupants have a certain degree of social and economic* *background in common.* It may cover a few square miles or it may be only one block square. Boundaries may be defined by physical, social, or economic differences. The important thing is that your neighborhood is the environment in which you live day-in and day-out. **The neighborhood in which you live is usually a more important factor than the house itself!** This is because the surroundings of a house influence the property value even more than the house itself does.

Neighborhoods influence homeowners' location decisions more than renters'. The reason is that many people rent apartments in neighborhoods in which they would never think of buying, because they plan to stay there for only a short time. Renters may rent in a less desirable area, but when they buy they will select a neighborhood they like.

Owner-occupied homes lend economic stability to a neighborhood, as owners tend to take better care of property than renters. The most important factor influencing value is location, location, location.

The selection or acceptance of a neighborhood should come before the actual decision of whether to buy a particular house or not. The four primary forces that affect value of a neighborhood are shown in **Figure 10-2**.

Neighborhoods are always changing, sometimes at a fast pace, but usually at a slow, steady pace. The four considerations discussed in Figure 10-2 can change a prestigious area to a shabby neighborhood or vice versa. Each consideration can change the outlook for any neighborhood.

Social forces, economic influences, and political influences are all forces affecting value. Private deed restrictions may be (in an appraiser's opinion) a force affecting value.

2. Specific Data (Property Itself)

There is plenty of land in the world, but the exact location of each parcel makes it unlike any other on earth. Its location is the major factor that determines its value.

a. Location

A *SITE is a particular parcel within a neighborhood.* Since each parcel is unique, the individual site that one selects for a home should be chosen with care. There are several site selection factors that affect the value of the home, but the personal needs and objectives of the buyer should be of the utmost concern.

Site: the location of a plot of ground for a building.

b. Lot (Types)

There are six major types of lots (see **Figure 10-3**):

1. Cul-de-sac (**Lot A**)
2. Corner (**Lot B**)
3. Key (**Lot C**)
4. T-Intersection (**Lot D**)
5. Interior (**Lot E**)
6. Flag (**Lot F**)

Figure 10-2

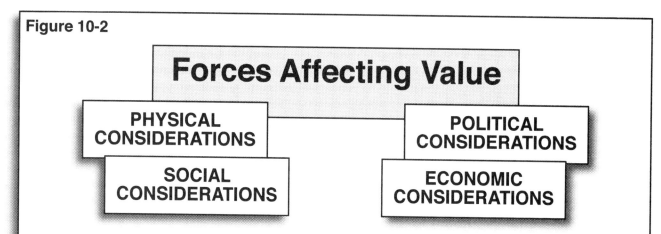

Forces Affecting Value

| PHYSICAL CONSIDERATIONS | POLITICAL CONSIDERATIONS |
| SOCIAL CONSIDERATIONS | ECONOMIC CONSIDERATIONS |

PHYSICAL CONSIDERATIONS

A neighborhood that is close to a commercial area is generally highly desirable. Being close to downtown areas, employment centers, and major shopping areas only adds to this desirability, as long as an owner is not located right next to such a facility. If the street patterns are curved and there are wide boulevards, the neighborhood also looks more attractive.

Access to transportation is necessary. The availability of freeways, transit systems, and convenient parking is an important consideration in making comparisons between various areas. However, this factor is less important in high-value suburban areas where estate living is desirable.

Balanced Land Use

The best efficiency and highest value come when there is a balance between different types of use. A city is a naturally attractive environment when it has a proper balance between residential, commercial, industrial, and recreational space.

Families are attracted to a neighborhood with good schools. Certain private or parochial schools may create a demand for homes in that area. Churches are also a definite benefit. Other institutions such as libraries, colleges, and universities may also enhance a community.

The first trip into a neighborhood may be impressive, or, on the other hand, it may be depressing. First impressions are important: the landscaping, architectural style, and the streets can create either impression. Well-maintained buildings create enhanced marketability.

Physical conditions such as lakes, beaches, rivers, or hilly areas may be either advantageous or disadvantageous depending on where they are. A feature such as a wooded hillside or lake front property would probably enhance a neighborhood, but a river that frequently floods the surrounding area is a disadvantage.

(continued)

Invasion of a residential area by commercial or industrial usage around it is usually a disadvantage, especially if the neighborhood is exposed to noise or odors. A bar located across from a home is usually a devaluing factor. Some areas may be hazardous because of landslides or simply from heavy truck and auto traffic.

SOCIAL CONSIDERATIONS

Neighborhoods often consist of persons of similar income, education, cultural background and lifestyle. As such, the neighborhood may or may not appeal to certain individual buyers. Could a change in the social makeup of a neighborhood affect values? Whether or not such a change has any influence either positive or negative and the effect of any change is a field of inquiry that must be left to sociologists. Appraisers, lenders, and real estate agents are forbidden by both federal and state law to consider race, religion, sex, ethnicity, or lifestyle as factors of value. Only economic factors may be considered by real estate professionals.

BLIGHT occurs as a result of a lack of property maintenance in a neighborhood. This is generally due to an economic inability to provide maintenance on the part of the owners. The result is lowered property values.

GENTRIFICATION is the rehabilitation of a blighted neighborhood. It is generally a result of low property values attracting buyers who are economically able to upgrade and maintain the properties in the neighborhood.

POLITICAL CONSIDERATIONS

Property tax rates vary from area to area. Wealthy, more stable economic areas usually have a slightly higher tax rate because the residents are willing and have the ability to pay for more public services. In areas where the taxes are very high, potential buyers are often scared off. Special assessments for lighting, sewers, and street improvements may temporarily turn some people away, but they generally add to the property's total value.

Some cities use **zoning** and **building codes** as devices to ensure the continued stability of a neighborhood. If the desirability of the neighborhood warrants such regulation, then the city will continue to be a growing one. In the end, most city leaders politically control changes in their cities by enacting zoning and building codes.

ECONOMIC CONSIDERATIONS

Population growth is an indication of the economic health of a neighborhood. If more people want to live in an area, then it must be desirable: an economically alive neighborhood has well-maintained lawns and buildings, whereas in a deteriorating neighborhood the lack of maintenance is obvious and so is the lowered value of the homes.

The rents charged and income levels of the people indicate a community's prestige (or lack of it). **The larger the percentage of home ownership versus those renting, the more economically stable the area is**. If many rentals are vacant, you can surmise that renters are not interested in the area. New construction, on the other hand, indicates that the area is growing and its value is increasing.

1. Cul-De-Sac Lot

The *CUL-DE-SAC LOT is a lot facing the turnaround portion of a dead-end street.* Figure 10-3 shows that Lot A is a cul-de-sac. The main advantage of a cul-de-sac lot is privacy and lack of traffic one gets by living on a "not a through" street. Due to its pie-shaped design, it has the disadvantage of a small front yard, but this is offset by generally having a large backyard. The design makes it more secluded and limits through traffic from both autos and pedestrians. Limited parking and front yard space does not stop it from rivaling the corner lot as one of the most desirable types of lots. A cul-de-sac lot's desirability may vary due to view, size, area, and family characteristics. **Figure 10-3, Lot A, Cul-de-sac.**

Figure 10-3

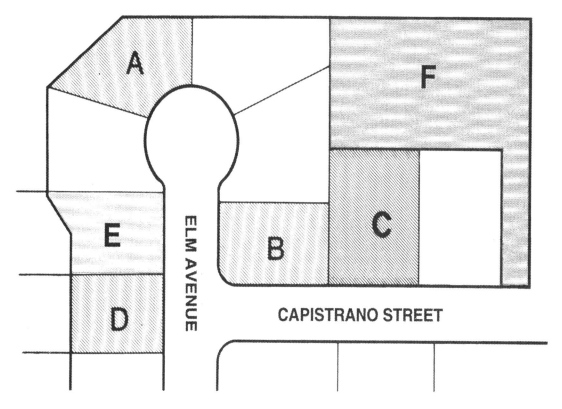

2. Corner Lot

The *CORNER LOT is a lot that is located at the intersection of two streets.* A corner site frequently has a higher value than a lot fronting only on one street. The appraiser must be careful to look at the local market in determining the actual effects of a corner influence on the surrounding lots. *CORNER INFLUENCE is the theory that a variety of forces affect corner lots (and also lots located near a corner) to a greater degree than most other lots.* A corner lot is generally more desirable for commercial use and undesirable, because of noise and set backs, for residential use. Other people like it because there is more light, fresh air, and also more lot area for gardens and other types of landscaping.

The main disadvantage of a corner lot is the loss of privacy and higher cost, since both sides of the lot require off-site improvements, such as streets, curbs, gutters, and sidewalks. Also, zoning setbacks may reduce the buildable lot space. Usually commercial corner lots benefit because of easy access and added traffic exposure. **Figure 10-3, Lot B, Corner**.

3. Key Lot

A *KEY LOT is a lot that is bordered on the side by the back of other lots that front on another street*. Key lots are the least desirable lots because of the lack of privacy caused by the close proximity of several neighbors abutting the side of the property. **Figure 10-3, Lot C, Key**.

4. T-Intersection Lot

The *T-INTERSECTION LOT is an interior lot that is faced head-on by a street; it is the lot at the end of a dead-end street*. The streets form a "T" shape. It is an interior lot with one advantage and two disadvantages. The advantage is a clear view down the street, which gives a more spacious feeling. Intersection noise and annoying headlights at night are its disadvantages. **Figure 10-3, Lot D, T-Intersection**.

5. Interior Lot

An *INTERIOR LOT is a lot generally surrounded by other lots on three sides*. It is usually in the shape of a rectangle, but can be almost any shape. It is the most common type of lot and it is preferred by most people. Interior lots have larger backyards than corner lots, which make them much better for recreational purposes. Since the front yards are smaller than those found on corner lots, they require less yard maintenance and benefit from less intersection noise. Because of typical long block design, interior lots are by far the most numerous. The disadvantages are limited backyard access and three or more adjoining neighbors. **Figure 10-3, Lot E, Interior**.

6. Flag Lot

A *FLAG LOT is a rear lot, in back of other lots, with a long, narrow access driveway*. This type of lot takes on the shape a flag. The flag lot's shape allows for a maximum of privacy and can be easily gated. In hilly areas, flag lots have some of the better views, while others can be pushed up against a steep mountain side. The value of a flag lot verses other types of lots depends on the circumstances. The same can be said about all other types of lots: their value depends on the specifics of each lot and the local market conditions. But it is up to the salesperson to gain a working knowledge of lot shapes and the pluses and minuses attributed to each type of lot. **Figure 10-3, Lot F, Flag**.

c. Physical Aspects of a Lot

The major physical aspects of the actual site are:

1. Size and shape
2. Slope, drainage, and soil (lot design layouts)

3. View, exposure to sun, and weather

4. Improvements (on-site and off-site)

1. Size and Shape of Lot

Lots or parcels can be subdivided into almost any shape imaginable, but most lots are rectangular and front onto a street. Any lot is valuable if it offers enough area to build a house that is compatible with the surroundings. In general, the more land or frontage on the street, the higher the value of the land. An example of a depth table will explain this concept. A *DEPTH TABLE is a percentage table that illustrates how the highest value is located in the front part of a lot.* **Figure 10-4** is an example of the "4-3-2-1" depth table. The "4-3-2-1 rule" is best used by appraisers to determine the value of commercial properties on which the lots vary in depth.

Figure 10-4

The "4-3-2-1" Depth Table

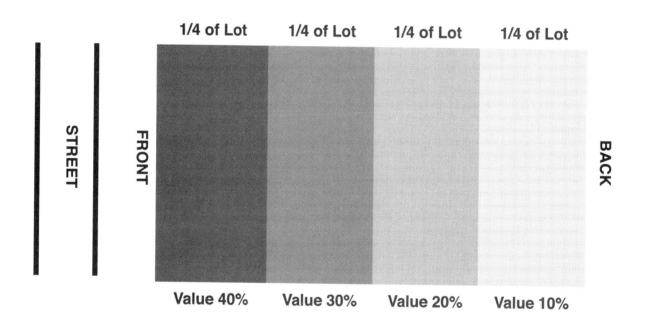

The percentage of value for each ¼ or 25% section of the lot varies: 40%, 30%, 20%, to 10% in value for each quarter back from the front.

In Figure 10-4, the highest value is in the front portion of the lot. For example, a small backyard will not affect the value of the property as much as a small front yard. This is especially true with commercial property such as shopping centers where there is plenty of parking in the back, but most people prefer to park in the front. Remember, though, that the percentage and values of a depth table vary from property to property.

Since the front portion of the lot has the most value, the more frontage there is, the better. *FRONT FOOTAGE is the width of the property in the front, along the street.* Generally speaking, we can say that a house with a large front yard is worth more than the same house with a large backyard. But people do have different preferences, such as large backyards for swimming pools, tennis courts, or other recreational activities.

When two or more contiguous properties are joined to make one property, and become more valuable than the sum of the properties separately, it is called "plottage."

2. Lot Design Layouts

There are several ways to lay out lots in a parcel of land being subdivided. Zoning regulations usually state the minimum amount of square feet a lot can have, but a developer can get better prices if he or she divides the land wisely. **Figure 10-5** shows the same parcel of land twice. **Plan 1** is a good design, giving a variety of desirable lots. **Plan 2** is a poor design, giving too little variation, too little front area and too much depth.

The layout of lots in a large subdivision is illustrated in **Figure 10-6**. Often a subdivision tract with fewer, well-planned lots will bring a higher total sales price than a poorly designed tract with more lots. The best tract layout is the one that considers all the costs involved and the marketability of all the lots. This kind of planning is not easy and requires the services of a specialist.

3. Slope, Drainage, and Soil

The slope of a lot will lower its value if it will be costly to improve. A lot that is higher or lower in relation to the street level may be costly to improve because of possible slope and drainage problems. Erosion may also be a part of slope or drainage problems. These problems, however, can be easily offset by an excellent view or location.

The soil composition of a lot may or may not be of any great concern. There are certain types of soil, however, that may create a problem depending on your lifestyle or possible construction needs. In some regions there are certain peat moss areas that must be corrected before a foundation can be poured. In other areas the soil content can destroy a pipeline within 10 years. If you like gardens and plant life, it is wise to see how the plants are growing in the surrounding lots. Some hillside tracts are built on bedrock covered by a thin layer of topsoil; to dig a swimming pool might even require blasting with dynamite, which is very costly.

4. View, Exposure to Sun, and Weather (Orientation)

The south and west sides of streets are preferred by merchants: pedestrians seek the shady side and displayed merchandise is not damaged by the sun. The northeast corner is the least desirable.

Most people appreciate a good view from their homes; it is pleasant to sit back and enjoy the beautiful surroundings. In a new tract of homes, the lots with the best views usually sell first and apartments with views rent for more. Places like Nob Hill (in San Francisco), Lake Tahoe, and La Jolla are examples of areas that are expensive because of their beautiful views.

CHAPTER 10

Figure 10-5

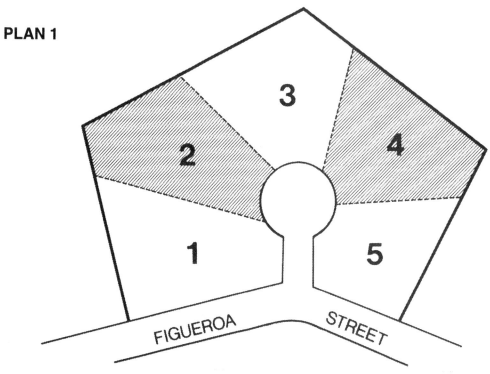

GOOD LAYOUT – LOTS ARE WELL DESIGNED

PLAN 1

POOR LAYOUT – LOTS ARE TOO DEEP

PLAN 2

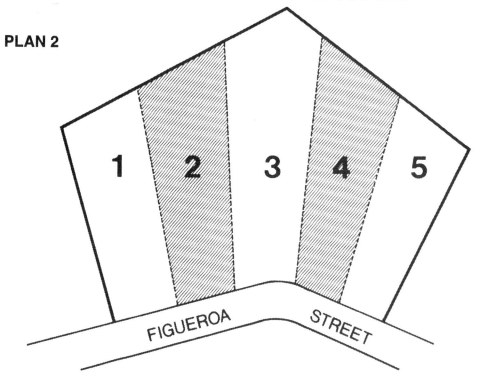

Figure 10-6

TENTATIVE SUBDIVISION MAP

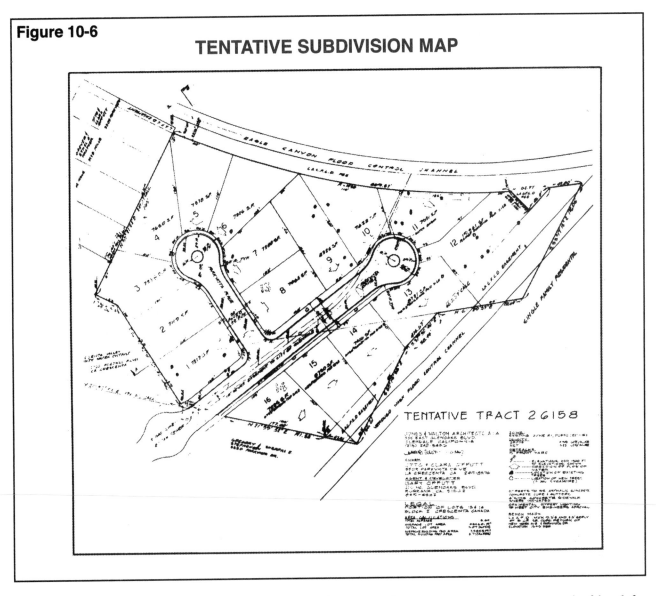

ORIENTATION *is planning the most advantageous place on a parcel of land for an improvement to be located.* The exposure of a house to the sun and weather elements may influence a person's decision to buy a house. If the wind usually blows from the northwest, it is best for the house to face the northwest. In this case the house can be a shield for backyard entertaining. The exposure to the sun is a different matter. Most people prefer the sun to shine on their backyard, so the backyard should face the south or the west. In this way the backyard receives the best exposure throughout the day. In windy areas on the coast, sheltered patios, away from cold sea breezes, are desirable.

A map showing the house and its location relating to other plants, buildings, and streets is an example of "orientation."

AMENITIES *are those improvements or views that increase the desirability or enjoyment rather than the necessities of the residents.* For example, a view of the

ocean, mountains, or city lights at night increase the value of a home. Amenity improvements would include jacuzzis, swimming pools, and tennis courts.

Amenity properties are usually single-family residences.

III. Improvements

Real estate is logically divided into land (site) and improvements. *IMPROVEMENTS are any buildings, walkways, pools, and other structures. CAPITAL IMPROVEMENTS are permanent improvements made to increase the useful life of the property or increase the property's value. They stay with the property.* These include off-site improvements (streets and utilities) and on-site improvements (buildings). *OFF-SITE IMPROVEMENTS are the improvements made to areas adjoining the parcel that add to the parcel's usefulness and sometimes its value.* Examples of off-site improvements are: streets, street lights, sewers, sidewalks, curbs, and gutters. These items generally add value to urban property but may be of little value in rural areas. Off-site improvements are usually paid for by the homeowners through the levying of special assessments. On the other hand, *ON-SITE IMPROVEMENTS are structures erected permanently for use on a site, such as buildings and fences.*

The three steps or phases in construction of a home are land acquisition, development, and construction.

A. HOUSE STRUCTURE ILLUSTRATED

This section identifies different parts of a house. Figure **10-7** shows roof types. **Figure 10-8** is a diagram of a house that illustrates the 20 most used construction terms. Each part is labeled and defined so that it can be identified. **Figure 10-9** lists construction and other terms.

B. HOME WARRANTY PLANS

A *WARRANTY PLAN is an insurance plan that provides financial protection against defects in any major home construction.* There are a growing number of such warranty plans in California. These warranty plans insure the new owner of an existing home against such things as malfunction of built-in appliances and defects in major systems such as structure, roof, heating, plumbing, and electrical wiring. For this protection, the previous owner or the buyer pays a fee that varies according to the type of coverage received. Some companies inspect the property (thereby giving notice of any existing defects). The CAR® purchase agreement informs buyers and sellers that there are warranty plans available. But this item, along with who pays for the warranty plan, is negotiable. **Note: All new homes automatically carry a one-year warranty, from the contractor, against labor or material defects**.

IV. Basic Appraisal Principles

There are several "principles of appraisal." These principles are valid economic concepts that are applied to the appraisal of real estate. A few of the basic principles are explained so that you can understand the logic and reasons why a particular home is worth more than another. **Figure 10-10** shows you seven of the basic appraisal principles.

Figure 10-7

ROOF TYPES

Before purchasing a house, a potential buyer should carefully evaluate the structure, checking to see that its style of architecture is compatible with that of the surrounding neighborhood. This should also be an element of consideration when building a new house or remodeling.

Examining the type of roof, the way it is framed and finished, is one of the simplest ways to assess the architectural compatibility of a given house.

Pictured below are several of the most common roof types. One is likely to see examples of flat, gable, hip, gambrel, mansard, and pyramid roofs throughout California.

A roof sloping on all four sides is called a "hip roof."

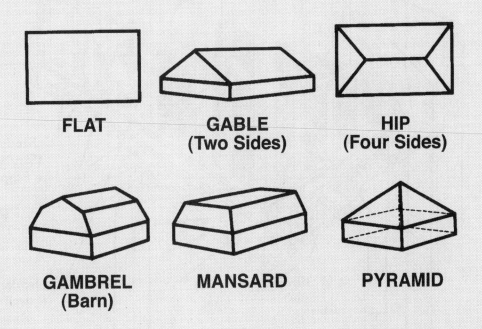

| FLAT | GABLE (Two Sides) | HIP (Four Sides) |
| GAMBREL (Barn) | MANSARD | PYRAMID |

Figure 10-8

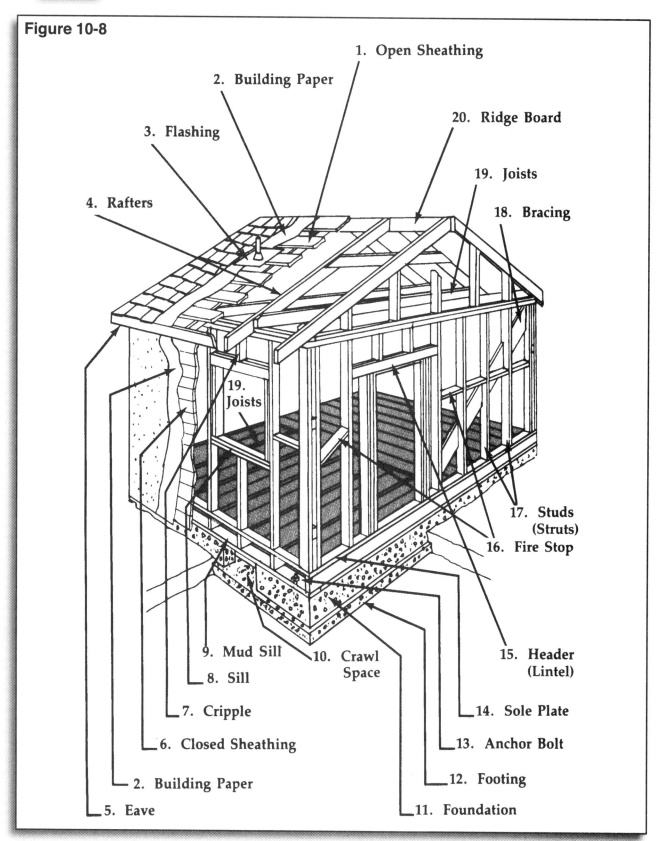

1. Open Sheathing
2. Building Paper
3. Flashing
4. Rafters
20. Ridge Board
19. Joists
18. Bracing
19. Joists
17. Studs (Struts)
16. Fire Stop
15. Header (Lintel)
14. Sole Plate
13. Anchor Bolt
12. Footing
11. Foundation
9. Mud Sill
10. Crawl Space
8. Sill
7. Cripple
6. Closed Sheathing
2. Building Paper
5. Eave

EXPLANATION OF DIAGRAM DETAILS

1. **Open Sheathing** — Boards nailed to rafters as foundation for the roof covering. Open sheathing is used with wood shingles.

2. **Building Paper** — Heavy waterproof paper used between sheathing and roof covering or siding.

3. **Flashing** — Sheet metal used to protect a roof from seepage.

4. **Rafters** — Sloping members of a roof used to support the roof boards and shingles (Maximum 24" apart).

5. **Eave** — Protruding underpart of roof overhanging exterior walls.

6. **Closed Sheathing** — Boards nailed to studding as foundation for exterior siding. "Closed" means butted together.

7. **Cripple** — Stud above or below a window opening or above a doorway.

8. **Sill** — Bottom portion lining doorway or window.

9. **Mud Sill** — Treated lumber (or redwood) bolted to the foundation.

10. **Crawl Space** — Unexcavated area under the house (**Minimum 18″**).

11. **Foundation** — Concrete base of house.

12. **Footing** — The spreading element that supports a pier, column, wall, or foundation. (**Can be located in the interior of a house**.)

13. **Anchor Bolt** — Large bolt used for fastening mud sill to foundation. Bolt is anchored into concrete foundation.

14. **Sole Plate** — Support on which the studs rest.

15. **Header (Lintel)** — The beam over a doorway or window.

16. **Fire Stop** — Blocking used to restrict flames from spreading to attic. May be placed horizontally or diagonally.

17. **Studs (Struts)** — Vertical 2″ x 4″ framework in the walls **spaced 16″ on center**.

18. **Bracing** — Board running diagonally across the wall framing to prevent sway.

19. **Joists** — Structural parts supporting floor or ceiling loads. A beam which supports them would be called a girder.

20. **Ridge Board** — Highest point of construction in a frame building.

Figure 10-9

Construction and Other Terms

Backfill – The replacement of excavated earth against a structure (wall). If a property is backfilled, it will fill in around piers, columns, and footings.

A contractor/builder who buys a large quantity of backfill is probably using it to fill in space around the foundation, retaining wall, or other excavations.

Bearing Wall – A strong wall supporting any vertical load in addition to its own weight, usually a roof or floor above.

Boardfoot – 1 board foot = 6 inches x 12 inches x 2 inches. Any 144 cu. ins. of lumber.

BTU (British Thermal Unit) – A unit of measurement used to calculate heat - the quantity of heat required to raise one pound of water one degree Fahrenheit.

Capital Assets – Expenditures of a permanent nature that increase property values. Examples: buildings and street improvements.

Cash Flow – In investment property, the actual cash the investor will receive after deduction of operating expenses and debt servicing (loan payment) from his or her gross income.

Conduit – A flexible metal pipe used to protect the electrical wiring inside.

Dry Wall – Also known as wallboard or plasterboard; comes in dry sheets (usually 4′ x 8′) of varying thickness: 1/2″ is standard for most interior walls.

EER (Energy Efficiency Ratio) – A measure of energy efficiency; when an air conditioning unit has a higher energy efficiency ratio, the unit is more efficient.

Elevation Sheet – A rendering which shows the front and side views of a building; it shows the exterior views.

Foundation Plan – A plan that refers to piers, columns, footings, and subfloor.

H2O Pressure – Testing water pressure by turning on all faucets and flushing all toilets.

HVAC – Heating, ventilation, and air conditioning systems in commercial buildings.

Hoskold Tables – Concept of a "sinking fund" as a compound interest-bearing account, into which the portion of the investment returned each year is reinvested immediately.

(continued)

Construction and Other Terms

Inwood Tables – Concept of using present value of income in a perpetuity table to help appraisers.

Joists – Parallel wooden members used to support floor and ceiling loads.

Kiosk – An information booth.

Local Building Inspector – Person who enforces construction standards.

Over-Improvement – An expenditure to a property that doesn't improve its value.

Percolation Test – A test to determine how well water is absorbed by the soil. (Used when installing a sewage system.)

Plot Plan – The placement of improvements (buildings) on a lot.

Potable Water – Drinkable water.

Property Residual, Building Residual, and Land Residual – All are methods of working backwards to find the unknown variable when appraising property.

R-Value – A measure used to calculate the heat resistance of insulation (the higher the better). Insulation is considered adequate if the temperature on the inside of an exterior wall is the same as the temperature on an interior wall.

Rehabilitation – The restoration of a property to a satisfactory condition without changing the interior or exterior design.

Soil Pipe – A pipe used to carry waste and sewage from a property.

Toxic Waste Report – A report evaluating how harmful the dangerous material is on a property.

Turnkey Property – A single-family home ready to move into.

Unearned Increment – An increase in value of real estate due to no effort on the part of the owner; often caused by population increase.

Wainscoting – The wood lining of the lower portion of an interior wall with the upper portion wallpapered or covered with another material different from the lower portion.

Figure 10-10

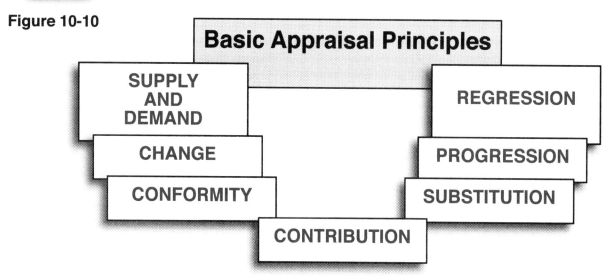

Basic Appraisal Principles

SUPPLY AND DEMAND

CHANGE

CONFORMITY

REGRESSION

PROGRESSION

SUBSTITUTION

CONTRIBUTION

A. PRINCIPLE OF SUPPLY AND DEMAND

The principle of supply and demand shows why "location" is important. The *PRINCIPLE OF SUPPLY AND DEMAND states that as the supply of land decreases, the value of land increases, because more people are competing for the desirable land.* Living next to the Pacific Ocean is expensive because the land is scarce. Even small lots bring very high selling prices in these areas. To beach lovers, these are the most desirable neighborhoods because there are only so many ocean view lots. In areas where there are many lots available, like the desert, the supply is large and the price of a lot can be very low. Downtown high-rise commercial locations in cities like San Francisco, Los Angeles, and San Diego are scarce and therefore expensive.

B. PRINCIPLE OF CHANGE

The *PRINCIPLE OF CHANGE is that real property is constantly changing.* Value is influenced by changes in such things as: population size, shopping centers, schools and colleges, freeways, economic and social trends. It is hard to see change on a day-to-day basis, but if you go back to the area where you grew up, the change is apparent.

The real property life cycle goes through three stages: development, maturity, and decline, which are illustrated in **Figure 10-11**.

1. Development (Integration)

This is the stage when the land is subdivided into lots, the streets are paved, and street lights are installed. Soon, homes are built and the community starts. As new people move in, landscaping and fences improve the homes.

The three steps in construction of a home are land acquistion, development, and construction.

2. Maturity (Equilibrium)

The maturity stage starts when the homes become older and the children grow up and move away. Most of the residents are long-time homeowners and the community has a solid, well-established look.

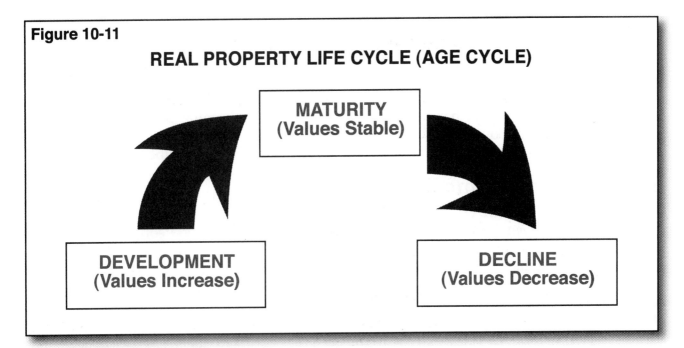

Figure 10-11

REAL PROPERTY LIFE CYCLE (AGE CYCLE)

MATURITY
(Values Stable)

DEVELOPMENT
(Values Increase)

DECLINE
(Values Decrease)

3. Decline (Disintegration)

In this stage, the buildings show some wear and tear and the oldest buildings are starting to deteriorate. As the useful life of the property declines, lower social or economic groups move into the area. Large homes may be converted into multiple family use.

The life cycle of real property may take a few years, such as that of a mining town going "bust," or may span a century, such as that of a community that constantly revitalizes itself.

C. PRINCIPLE OF CONFORMITY

The *PRINCIPLE OF CONFORMITY states that the maximum value is obtained when a reasonable degree of building similarity is maintained in the neighborhood.* So, if all the homes in an area are similar (not identical), the maximum value of real property is created. The word "similar" is the key. If all the tract homes are identical, as if they were all made with the same cookie cutter, the maximum value is not present.

When a residential neighborhood is composed mostly of owner-occupied residential properties, it tends to stabilize values.

The principle of conformity is one of the primary reasons for zoning regulations (discussed in Chapter 12). They protect the neighborhood from other nonconforming uses and from infiltration of incompatible structures. An attractive neighborhood would quickly decline in value if zoning did not help protect its conformity.

D. PRINCIPLE OF CONTRIBUTION

The *PRINCIPLE OF CONTRIBUTION states that the value of a particular component is measured in terms of its contribution to the value of the whole property.* Consequently, cost does not necessarily equal value. It either adds more or less to the value of real property.

CHAPTER 10

Example: If an apartment building produces a 10% return to investors, a $50,000 investment in a swimming pool, without an equal ($50,000 x 10%) $5,000 or higher increase in rents, would not be a good idea.

Thus, in some cases, a property's market value may not increase even if it has had additions, alterations, or has been rehabilitated. If the swimming pool were added, the property would be considered "over-built." The principle of contribution is also referred to as increasing and (decreasing) "diminishing returns" in economic textbooks.

E. PRINCIPLE OF SUBSTITUTION

Under the *PRINCIPLE OF SUBSTITUTION, a buyer will not pay more for a particular property if it costs less to buy a similar property of equal utility and desirability.* People prefer the less expensive price if all other things are considered equal. When appraisers use the principle of substitution, they compare properties to adjust for differences. The maximum value of a property tends to be set by the cost of acquiring an equally desirable substitute property.

F. PRINCIPLE OF REGRESSION (Value Goes Down)

When a house of greater value is adversely affected by houses of comparably lesser value, it is called the PRINCIPLE OF REGRESSION. For example, if a house that would easily be worth $790,000 in a neighborhood of similar homes was to be built in a neighborhood of $210,000 homes, it would not sell for $790,000. Anyone in the market for a $790,000 house would not want to live in a tract where the average price of a house was $210,000. Because of its superior quality or size, the house would undoubtedly sell for more than the average house in the tract, but it would not approach $790,000.

The same principle applies to the over-improved home. When owners invest very large sums in major additions, lavish landscaping, and swimming pools, and the other residents do not improve their homes, the house is no longer similar to the others. The owners of the over-built house will not receive the full value for the cost of improvements they have made.

When the best property in the neighborhood is adversely affected by the presence of a substandard property, it is called regression.

G. PRINCIPLE OF PROGRESSION (Value Goes Up)

In the *PRINCIPLE OF PROGRESSION, the value of a lesser residence is increased in value by its location in a neighborhood of better homes.* This is the opposite of the principle of regression. A smaller, unattractive, and poorly maintained home in an exclusive area will sell for much more than if it were located in a comparable neighborhood. People who wish to live in an exclusive area would think of the smaller home as a bargain.

V. CHAPTER SUMMARY

An **appraisal** is an opinion of value based on judgment and professional experience for a **specific property as of a certain date**. Appraisers, who must be licensed in California, want "open market results," not prudent values or prices. The **value** of a property is determined by the elements of **demand**, **utility**, **scarcity**, and **transferability**. Cost and/or expectation are never one of these elements.

The **appraisal process** consists of four steps: 1) **defining the problem**, 2) **gathering the data**, 3) **performing the three appraisal methods**, and 4) **determining the final opinion of value**. Whether the reason for the appraisal is transfer of ownership, obtaining a loan, condemnation, or insurance, the first step is to do a **site analysis** to determine **highest and best use**.

The second step involves gathering data, including **general data** (region, city, and neighborhood) and **specific data** (location, lot, and improvements). The **neighborhood** is the most important general data. The **four forces** affecting value are: **physical**, **social**, **economic**, and **political considerations**. The most important economic characteristic is area preference (**location**).

Front footage is a pricing tool often used to sell commercial property and a **4-3-2-1 depth table** is used when the lots vary in depth. **Plottage** (assemblage) refers to separately owned, contiguous lots brought under single ownership resulting in increased value. The **shady south and west sides of streets** are preferred by merchants with the northeast corner being the least desirable.

There are several principles of appraisal, including **supply and demand**, and the **principle of change**, which is evident in the **real estate life cycle of development**, **maturity**, and **decline**. The **principle of conformity** states that the maximum value is obtained when building similarity is maintained in the neighborhood, and is one of the major reasons for **zoning regulations**.

The **principle of contribution** (or diminishing returns) states that the value of a particular component is measured in terms of its contribution to the value of the whole property. The **principle of substitution** states that a buyer will not pay more for a particular property if it costs less to buy a similar property of equal utility and desirability.

The **principle of regression** states that between properties in the same neighborhood, the value of the best property will be negatively affected by the value of the other properties. The opposite of regression is the **principle of progression**, where a lesser residence increases in value by its location in a neighborhood of better homes.

VI. TERMINOLOGY

A. Appraisal	**I.** Frontage	**Q.** Progression Principle
B. Appraisal Process	**J.** Highest and Best Use	**R.** Regression Principle
C. Change	**K.** Interior Lot	**S.** Site
D. Conformity	**L.** Key Lot	**T.** Supply and Demand
E. Corner Lot	**M.** Market Price	**U.** T-Intersection Lot
F. Cul-de-Sac	**N.** Market Value	**V.** Warranty Plan
G. Depth Table	**O.** Neighborhood	
H. Flag Lot	**P.** Off-Site Improvements	

1.____ The appraisal principle that maintains the maximum value of a property is realized when a reasonable degree of similarity is present in the area where the property is located.

2.____ The least desirable type of lot because the back ends of other lots face one of its sides.

3.____ A general term describing people living or working together in an area of similar properties with similar social, economic, and political backgrounds.

4.____ The highest price a willing buyer would pay and a willing seller accept, both being fully informed, and the property exposed for a reasonable period of time. This value may be different from the price a property can actually be sold for at a given time.

5.____ Not a corner lot, but an inside lot; the most common type of lot.

6.____ Development of large parcels into smaller lots suitable for construction. This includes sidewalks, curbs, streets, sewers, streetlights, etc.

7.____ A lot at the U-shaped end of a street. Even though they are narrower in the front and wider in the back, these lots are popular because the street itself makes the area exclusive.

8.____ An opinion of real property value based upon a factual analysis by a qualified (licensed) person with education and experience.

9.____ The use of land that will bring the greatest economic return over a given time.

10.____ The price a property sells for, which may be higher or lower than its actual market value.

11.____ The orderly process of determining the fair market value of real property by: 1) defining the problem, 2) gathering the data, 3) applying the three methods of appraisal (cost approach, market comparison approach, income approach), and 4) correlating the information for a final estimate of value.

12.____ A general term for a lot or plot of land.

13.____ A lot with both the front and side facing different streets. Such a residential lot is generally more desirable because of its increased exposure to light and fresh air. A commercial lot benefits from better street access and exposure to traffic patterns.

14.____ An interior lot facing down a street into traffic. Such a lot benefits from the view down the open street but suffers from additional traffic noise and on-coming headlights at night.

15.____ A lot with a long, narrow entrance, forming the shape of a flag. While it has limited frontage, such a lot can be very desirable if the odd shape is accompanied by a spectacular view in the back.

16.____ A chart illustrating the principle that the greatest value exists in the front portion of the lot, and the value of the land decreases the further back from the street you go.

17.____ The linear measure of the front portion of a parcel facing a major street, walkway, lake, or ocean.

18.____ An insurance plan covering the major systems of a home such as electrical, heating, plumbing, and major appliances.

19.____ A principle of real estate appraisal suggesting that the value of property increases when there is more demand and a short supply in an area. Conversely, the value decreases when there is an abundant supply and less demand.

20.____ The concept that although changes may be imperceptible, neighborhoods are constantly changing. Population shifts and economic changes, along with many other variables, will constantly work to alter the value of property.

21.____ The real estate principle that a smaller, low-quality home will gain value if larger, nicer homes are being built in the neighborhood.

22.____ The real estate principle that a larger, nicer home will not enjoy its full value if it is located in a neighborhood of smaller, low-quality homes.

VII. CHAPTER QUIZ

1. In comparing real property price to value, a change in creative financing terms will affect:

    a. value and price.
    b. value.
    c. price.
    d. neither price nor value.

2. The primary purpose of a site analysis by an appraiser is to determine the:

    a. applicable zoning laws.
    b. highest and best use.
    c. soil conditions.
    d. available amenities.

3. When the highest and best use of a property is expected to change, the current use is called:

    a. the interim use.
    b. the temporary use.
    c. the transitional use.
    d. the possible use.

4. When two properties are joined to make one property, and becomes more valuable than the sum of the properties separately, it is called:

    a. leverage.
    b. inflation.
    c. plottage.
    d. subdividing.

5. A map shows the house and its location relating to other plants, buildings, and streets. This is an example of:

    a. plottage.
    b. orientation.
    c. elevation.
    d. topography.

6. Which of the following is one board foot?

    a. Six inches x twelve inches x one foot

    b. Six inches x twelve inches x two inches

    c. Six inches x six inches x two inches

    d. Six inches x twelve inches x one inch

7. When an air conditioning unit has a higher energy efficiency ratio (EER), the:

    a. unit needs more watts of electricity.

    b. unit is more efficient.

    c. unit is less efficient.

    d. BTUs are larger.

8. "HVAC" refers to:

    a. heating, ventilation, and air conditioning systems in commercial buildings.

    b. Home Value After Correlation.

    c. Highest Value Appraising Consideration.

    d. House Vitality Area Consultants.

9. When a residential neighborhood is composed mostly of owner-occupied residential properties it tends to:

    a. attract commercial shopping centers to the neighborhood.

    b. stabilize values.

    c. deteriorate faster than areas with many rental properties.

    d. lower property values.

10. When a house of greater value is adversely affected by houses of comparably lesser value, it is called:

    a. anticipation.

    b. regression.

    c. contribution.

    d. balance.

ANSWERS: 1. a; 2. b; 3. a; 4. c; 5. b; 6. b; 7. b; 8. a; 9. b; 10. b

CHAPTER 11
Appraisal Methods

Real estate salespeople need to know enough about appraisal techniques and practices so that they can determine, in advance, the approximate selling price of a property. Salespeople have the advantage of determining the "probable" sales price of a property quickly because they see what similar properties in their area sell for each day. They can be on top of the market because of their multiple listing service and close contact with other knowledgeable agents. They are constantly being updated as to the current listing and selling prices.

By completing a **Comparative Market Analysis (CMA)** form and presenting it to a seller, the seller can see at a glance the selling prices of other houses or condos in his/her neighborhood. This enables the sellers to "price their listings" close to a realistic selling price.

An agent can download comparable sales information ("comps") in a variety of forms by accessing an MLS website.

www.appraisalfoundation.org
Appraisal Foundation
www.asfmra.org/
American Society of Farm Managers and Rural Appraisers (ASFMRA)
http://aicanada.org
The Appraisal Institute of Canada

A state licensed (expert) appraiser will use all three of the valuation approaches to determine the value of a property, but will emphasize only one to establish the final value. These approaches are:

   I. COMPARATIVE APPROACH (MARKET DATA METHOD)
   II. COST (REPLACEMENT) APPROACH
   III. CAPITALIZATION (INCOME) APPROACH

The appraisal is also an opinion of a value "range." Let us assume that a range of $450,000 to $500,000 is established from the three appraisal approaches mentioned above. By correlating the economic information from the three approaches, an experienced appraiser can estimate a more precise value. The results of the three approaches can be weighed and it can then be determined which method has provided the best information about the property. In this case, let's say that the appraiser felt he or she should emphasize the market comparison approach

CHAPTER 11

that was $490,000. The appraiser would state that, in his or her opinion, the property was worth $490,000; but the value "ranged" from $450,000 to $500,000.

I. Comparative Approach (Market Data Method)

Of the three approaches previously mentioned, the market comparison method is the one most frequently used. It is easy for an alert student to master this technique within a short time, and it is the most logical way to appraise a house.

The market data method uses the "principle of substitution" to compare similar properties. **A person will not pay more for a property if he/she can buy something similar for less.**

The *MARKET DATA METHOD is a method of appraising real property by comparing the current selling prices of recently sold similar properties and adjusting those prices for any differences.* The comparative (market data method) approach uses the principle of substitution; a person will not pay more for a property if he or she can buy something similar for less.

Simply adjust the value of the comparable sales price. If a house is comparable except that it has a pool, sells for $640,000 and the value of the $40,000 pool is subtracted, the house we are appraising is valued at $600,000.

A. HOW TO ADJUST FOR A COMPARABLE SALE (Comps)

The market data method is basically common sense. If your neighbor has a similar house to yours that he just sold for $400,000, then yours is worth about $400,000. The only problem is that adjustments must be made for any differences between the houses. For example, if a similar $400,000 house had a fireplace worth $8,000 and yours did not, then your house would be worth $392,000 ($400,000 - $8,000). Adjustments should be made to the selling price of the comparable house for any differences between the properties. **The usual adjustments are made for differences in location, age, lot size, building size, condition of the property, and any time difference between the sales**.

Subtract or add from or to the selling price of the comparable property to adjust for differences.

If the comparable property has an item not present in the subject property, the appraiser subtracts the value of the item from the comparable property's selling price. Likewise, if the subject property has an item not present in the comparable property, the appraiser adds the value of the item to the comparable property's selling price. After all these adjustments are made to the comparable selling price, the resulting figure gives the appraiser the subject property's value.

By comparing recent selling prices of properties in the same area, it is easy to see the trends in selling prices and why certain properties sell for more than others. The more comparable sales you gather, the more reliable the results. Real estate salespeople often refer to comparable sales as "comps."

An appraiser using the market data approach would be most interested in the date that the price was agreed upon.

Unsold properties are important when using the market data method. If a property has been listed "for sale" for a long time, it is usually overpriced. Such comparable "unsold

properties" suggest an upper limit of value. Unsold listings can therefore help establish the highest comparable price. An experienced appraiser can easily estimate the amount of an adjustment. The adjustment is an estimate or opinion determined solely by the appraiser, and reflects his or her broad experience and education.

Comparable sales information can be obtained from many different sources. Brokers and salespeople are familiar with property sales prices in their area, so naturally they are a good source for appraisal data. In addition, most brokers are members of the local multiple listing service and have access to past sales information. Other people in the real estate field, such as loan officers, title insurance agents, and escrow officers can also supply comparable sales information.

It is essential that: 1) the information is from a reliable source; 2) there is an adequate number of comparable sales, and 3) the comparable sales are truly comparable.

The market data method is the most common approach for houses and condominiums. It is also the best method for appraising lots and vacant land (unimproved property).

Figure 11-1 shows the first three pages of the Uniform Residential Appraisal Report (URAR) that is accepted by Fannie Mae and Freddie Mac.

B. ADVANTAGES OF THE MARKET DATA METHOD

This method is excellent for appraising single family homes. Here are the reasons why:

1. The market data method is easy to learn, and with a little experience it is easy to apply.
2. Since there are usually many recent comparable sales, the required information is readily available.
3. This method is used mostly for houses or condos, which makes this method the most relevant to us as homeowners, salespeople, or investors.

The most difficult part of the market data method is to adjust similar properties for differences. The market data method is limited when market conditions are rapidly changing.

Marketability and acceptability of a property are the primary concerns when appraising a residential property. Marketability is the ultimate test of functional utility.

C. DISADVANTAGES OF THE MARKET DATA METHOD

The disadvantages of using the market data method are concentrated into several areas which are listed below:

1. This method requires many recent comparable sales of similar properties.
2. **This method is least reliable when there are rapid economic changes**. If market prices are increasing rapidly, the comparables, which are based on past sales prices, lag behind. If prices are decreasing rapidly, the comparables, which are based on past sales prices, still remain high.
3. The market data method is less valid with certain income properties because a separate analysis of the income is required.

336

Figure 11-1

Uniform Residential Appraisal Report
File #

The purpose of this summary appraisal report is to provide the lender/client with an accurate, and adequately supported, opinion of the market value of the subject property.

SUBJECT

Property Address		City		State	Zip Code
Borrower	Owner of Public Record			County	

Legal Description

Assessor's Parcel #   Tax Year   R.E. Taxes $

Neighborhood Name   Map Reference   Census Tract

Occupant ☐ Owner ☐ Tenant ☐ Vacant   Special Assessments $ ☐ PUD   HOA $ ☐ per year ☐ per month

Property Rights Appraised ☐ Fee Simple ☐ Leasehold ☐ Other (describe)

Assignment Type ☐ Purchase Transaction ☐ Refinance Transaction ☐ Other (describe)

Lender/Client   Address

Is the subject property currently offered for sale or has it been offered for sale in the twelve months prior to the effective date of this appraisal? ☐ Yes ☐ No

Report data source(s) used, offering price(s), and date(s).

CONTRACT

I ☐ did ☐ did not analyze the contract for sale for the subject purchase transaction. Explain the results of the analysis of the contract for sale or why the analysis was not performed.

Contract Price $ Date of Contract   Is the property seller the owner of public record? ☐ Yes ☐ No   Data Source(s)

Is there any financial assistance (loan charges, sale concessions, gift or downpayment assistance, etc.) to be paid by any party on behalf of the borrower? ☐ Yes ☐ No
If Yes, report the total dollar amount and describe the items to be paid.

NEIGHBORHOOD

Note: Race and the racial composition of the neighborhood are not appraisal factors.

Neighborhood Characteristics	One-Unit Housing Trends	One-Unit Housing	Present Land Use %
Location ☐ Urban ☐ Suburban ☐ Rural	Property Values ☐ Increasing ☐ Stable ☐ Declining	PRICE AGE	One-Unit %
Built-Up ☐ Over 75% ☐ 25–75% ☐ Under 25%	Demand/Supply ☐ Shortage ☐ In Balance ☐ Over Supply	$ (000) (yrs)	2-4 Unit %
Growth ☐ Rapid ☐ Stable ☐ Slow	Marketing Time ☐ Under 3 mths ☐ 3–6 mths ☐ Over 6 mths	Low	Multi-Family %
Neighborhood Boundaries		High	Commercial %
		Pred.	Other %

Neighborhood Description

Market Conditions (including support for the above conclusions)

SITE

Dimensions	Area	Shape	View

Specific Zoning Classification   Zoning Description

Zoning Compliance ☐ Legal ☐ Legal Nonconforming (Grandfathered Use) ☐ No Zoning ☐ Illegal (describe)

Is the highest and best use of the subject property as improved (or as proposed per plans and specifications) the present use? ☐ Yes ☐ No If No, describe

Utilities	Public	Other (describe)		Public	Other (describe)	Off-site Improvements—Type	Public	Private
Electricity	☐	☐	Water	☐	☐	Street	☐	☐
Gas	☐	☐	Sanitary Sewer	☐	☐	Alley	☐	☐

FEMA Special Flood Hazard Area ☐ Yes ☐ No   FEMA Flood Zone   FEMA Map #   FEMA Map Date

Are the utilities and off-site improvements typical for the market area? ☐ Yes ☐ No If No, describe

Are there any adverse site conditions or external factors (easements, encroachments, environmental conditions, land uses, etc.)? ☐ Yes ☐ No If Yes, describe

IMPROVEMENTS

General Description	Foundation	Exterior Description materials/condition	Interior materials/condition
Units ☐ One ☐ One with Accessory Unit	☐ Concrete Slab ☐ Crawl Space	Foundation Walls	Floors
# of Stories	☐ Full Basement ☐ Partial Basement	Exterior Walls	Walls
Type ☐ Det. ☐ Att. ☐ S-Det./End Unit	Basement Area sq. ft.	Roof Surface	Trim/Finish
☐ Existing ☐ Proposed ☐ Under Const.	Basement Finish %	Gutters & Downspouts	Bath Floor
Design (Style)	☐ Outside Entry/Exit ☐ Sump Pump	Window Type	Bath Wainscot
Year Built	Evidence of ☐ Infestation	Storm Sash/Insulated	Car Storage ☐ None
Effective Age (Yrs)	☐ Dampness ☐ Settlement	Screens	☐ Driveway # of Cars
Attic ☐ None	Heating ☐ FWA ☐ HWBB ☐ Radiant	Amenities ☐ Woodstove(s) #	Driveway Surface
☐ Drop Stair ☐ Stairs	☐ Other Fuel	☐ Fireplace(s) # ☐ Fence	☐ Garage # of Cars
☐ Floor ☐ Scuttle	Cooling ☐ Central Air Conditioning	☐ Patio/Deck ☐ Porch	☐ Carport # of Cars
☐ Finished ☐ Heated	☐ Individual ☐ Other	☐ Pool ☐ Other	☐ Att. ☐ Det. ☐ Built-in

Appliances ☐ Refrigerator ☐ Range/Oven ☐ Dishwasher ☐ Disposal ☐ Microwave ☐ Washer/Dryer ☐ Other (describe)

Finished area **above** grade contains: Rooms   Bedrooms   Bath(s)   Square Feet of Gross Living Area Above Grade

Additional features (special energy efficient items, etc.)

Describe the condition of the property (including needed repairs, deterioration, renovations, remodeling, etc.).

Are there any physical deficiencies or adverse conditions that affect the livability, soundness, or structural integrity of the property? ☐ Yes ☐ No If Yes, describe

Does the property generally conform to the neighborhood (functional utility, style, condition, use, construction, etc.)? ☐ Yes ☐ No If No, describe

Freddie Mac Form 70 March 2005   Page 1 of 6   Fannie Mae Form 1004 March 2005

Uniform Residential Appraisal Report

There are _____ comparable properties currently offered for sale in the subject neighborhood ranging in price from $ _____ to $ _____
There are _____ comparable sales in the subject neighborhood within the past twelve months ranging in sale price from $ _____ to $ _____

FEATURE	SUBJECT	COMPARABLE SALE # 1	COMPARABLE SALE # 2	COMPARABLE SALE # 3
Address				
Proximity to Subject				
Sale Price	$	$	$	$
Sale Price/Gross Liv. Area	$ sq. ft.	$ sq. ft.	$ sq. ft.	$ sq. ft.
Data Source(s)				
Verification Source(s)				
VALUE ADJUSTMENTS	DESCRIPTION	DESCRIPTION +(-) $ Adjustment	DESCRIPTION +(-) $ Adjustment	DESCRIPTION +(-) $ Adjustment
Sale or Financing Concessions				
Date of Sale/Time				
Location				
Leasehold/Fee Simple				
Site				
View				
Design (Style)				
Quality of Construction				
Actual Age				
Condition				
Above Grade	Total	Bdrms	Baths	Total	Bdrms	Baths	Total	Bdrms	Baths	Total	Bdrms	Baths
Room Count				
Gross Living Area	sq. ft.	sq. ft.	sq. ft.	sq. ft.
Basement & Finished Rooms Below Grade				
Functional Utility				
Heating/Cooling				
Energy Efficient Items				
Garage/Carport				
Porch/Patio/Deck				
Net Adjustment (Total)		+ - $	+ - $	+ - $
Adjusted Sale Price of Comparables		Net Adj. % / Gross Adj. % $	Net Adj. % / Gross Adj. % $	Net Adj. % / Gross Adj. % $

I [ ] did [ ] did not research the sale or transfer history of the subject property and comparable sales. If not, explain

My research [ ] did [ ] did not reveal any prior sales or transfers of the subject property for the three years prior to the effective date of this appraisal.
Data source(s)
My research [ ] did [ ] did not reveal any prior sales or transfers of the comparable sales for the year prior to the date of sale of the comparable sale.
Data source(s)
Report the results of the research and analysis of the prior sale or transfer history of the subject property and comparable sales (report additional prior sales on page 3).

ITEM	SUBJECT	COMPARABLE SALE # 1	COMPARABLE SALE # 2	COMPARABLE SALE # 3
Date of Prior Sale/Transfer				
Price of Prior Sale/Transfer				
Data Source(s)				
Effective Date of Data Source(s)				

Analysis of prior sale or transfer history of the subject property and comparable sales

Summary of Sales Comparison Approach

Indicated Value by Sales Comparison Approach $

Indicated Value by: Sales Comparison Approach $ _____ Cost Approach (if developed) $ _____ Income Approach (if developed) $ _____

This appraisal is made [ ] "as is", [ ] subject to completion per plans and specifications on the basis of a hypothetical condition that the improvements have been completed, [ ] subject to the following repairs or alterations on the basis of a hypothetical condition that the repairs or alterations have been completed, or [ ] subject to the following required inspection based on the extraordinary assumption that the condition or deficiency does not require alteration or repair:

Based on a complete visual inspection of the interior and exterior areas of the subject property, defined scope of work, statement of assumptions and limiting conditions, and appraiser's certification, my (our) opinion of the market value, as defined, of the real property that is the subject of this report is $ _____ , as of _____ , which is the date of inspection and the effective date of this appraisal.

COST APPROACH TO VALUE (not required by Fannie Mae)

Provide adequate information for the lender/client to replicate the below cost figures and calculations.
Support for the opinion of site value (summary of comparable land sales or other methods for estimating site value)

ESTIMATED [ ] REPRODUCTION OR [ ] REPLACEMENT COST NEW	OPINION OF SITE VALUE	= $
Source of cost data	Dwelling Sq. Ft. @ $	= $
Quality rating from cost service Effective date of cost data		= $
Comments on Cost Approach (gross living area calculations, depreciation, etc.)	Garage/Carport Sq. Ft. @ $	= $
	Total Estimate of Cost-New	= $
	Less Physical	Functional	External	
	Depreciation	= $( )
	Depreciated Cost of Improvements	= $
	"As-is" Value of Site Improvements	= $
Estimated Remaining Economic Life (HUD and VA only) _____ Years	Indicated Value By Cost Approach	= $

INCOME APPROACH TO VALUE (not required by Fannie Mae)

Estimated Monthly Market Rent $ _____ X Gross Rent Multiplier _____ = $ _____ Indicated Value by Income Approach
Summary of Income Approach (including support for market rent and GRM)

PROJECT INFORMATION FOR PUDs (if applicable)

Is the developer/builder in control of the Homeowners' Association (HOA)? [ ] Yes [ ] No   Unit type(s) [ ] Detached [ ] Attached
Provide the following information for PUDs ONLY if the developer/builder is in control of the HOA and the subject property is an attached dwelling unit.
Legal name of project
Total number of phases _____   Total number of units _____   Total number of units sold _____
Total number of units rented _____   Total number of units for sale _____   Data source(s) _____
Was the project created by the conversion of an existing building(s) into a PUD? [ ] Yes [ ] No   If Yes, date of conversion
Does the project contain any multi-dwelling units? [ ] Yes [ ] No   Data source(s)
Are the units, common elements, and recreation facilities complete? [ ] Yes [ ] No   If No, describe the status of completion.
Are the common elements leased to or by the Homeowners' Association? [ ] Yes [ ] No   If Yes, describe the rental terms and options.

Describe common elements and recreational facilities

338

The effectiveness of the market data approach is limited by economic conditions that change rapidly.

II. Cost Approach (Replacement Cost Method)

The *COST APPROACH is the process of calculating the cost of the land and buildings (as if they were new today) and then subtracting the accrued depreciation to arrive at the current value of the property.* To use the cost approach, the appraiser must be able to determine the new construction cost of replacing the building today using current construction methods. Depreciation is estimated by the appraiser and is then subtracted from the estimated cost of the new building. The value of the lot and depreciated building is then added to find the market value.

The cost approach objective is to determine the land value plus the cost to replace the improvements new (minus depreciation) while maintaining the same utility value.

Of the three approaches, the cost approach tends to set what the appraisers call an "upper limit of value." Most home buyers or investors prefer a newer building over an older one if the price is about the same. The cost approach therefore tends to set the highest price that a knowledgeable person will pay for a property. Why not build if the construction cost of a newer building is close to the sales price of an older building?

The cost approach is most useful when appraising: 1) new buildings and 2) special purpose or unique structures. Estimating depreciation is critical in this approach. As a building gets older, the depreciation becomes more difficult to estimate, eventually making the cost approach impractical. Since newer structures have little depreciation, the cost approach is the most suitable. The cost approach may also be preferred for special purpose or unique structures as they have few, if any, market comparable sales. Special purpose structures, such as an airplane factory, a city hall, or a church, are best appraised by the cost approach.

The cost approach is more appropriate for new buildings because there is almost no depreciation.

It is limited in its effectiveness for appraising old buildings because determining depreciation is the most difficult part of the cost approach for the appraiser.

Some properties **require** the use of the cost approach. If, for example, there have been no recent sales in an area, the market comparison approach cannot be used effectively. Furthermore, if there is no income (as for example, from government-owned properties), the appraiser must rely solely on the cost approach.

A. COSTS ARE BOTH DIRECT AND INDIRECT

Any method used for estimating cost requires the calculation of direct (hard) or indirect (soft) costs. Both types of costs are equally necessary for construction and must be measured accurately.

DIRECT COSTS are expenditures for labor and materials used in the construction of the improvement(s). A contractor's overhead and profit are generally treated as direct costs.

INDIRECT COSTS are expenditures other than material and labor costs. Examples are administrative costs, professional fees, financing costs, insurance, and taxes. Indirect costs are usually calculated separately from direct costs.

339

B. STEPS IN THE COST APPROACH

The steps used in the cost approach are easy to follow, but studying **Figure 11-2** will help to explain each step.

1. Estimate the value of the land (use the market comparison approach).
2. Estimate the replacement cost of the building as if it were new.
3. Deduct estimated depreciation from the replacement cost of the building.
4. Add the value of the lot (Step 1) and the depreciated cost of the building Steps 2 & 3) to find the total value (Step 4).

Figure 11-2

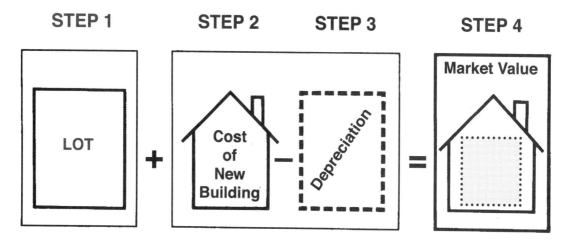

1. Step 1 – Appraise the Land (Lot) Separately

Appraise the land (lot) separately. The value of the vacant land is determined by comparing the lot of the property to be appraised with similar lots that have just been sold. The market comparison approach is used by the appraiser to estimate the lot value of the appraised property.

The cost approach requires the appraiser to identify land values separately by the use of the market data approach.

2. Step 2 – Estimate Replacement Cost

Estimate the replacement cost of the improvements to the land. This includes all the buildings and the landscaping improvements.

"Replacement cost" is the present cost to build a building having the same amount of utility.

a. Replacement Cost

REPLACEMENT COST is the cost of building a similar new structure today (of equal utility) using modern construction methods. These methods may differ from the original building techniques, but are becoming an important factor due to the ever increasing costs of new construction. As construction costs increase for new homes, the replacement cost of existing homes also increases. Therefore, well-located older homes will keep rising in value year after year, no matter how old they are, because the newer substitutes are so costly. This is not necessarily because of excellent upkeep, but because it is becoming impossible to find a newer home with the same features at a reasonable price. *REPRODUCTION or REPLICATION COST is the cost of reproducing a structure (usually destroyed) at current prices using identical (older) style materials and methods as used in the original structure.* This method is rarely used, but it is the type, for example, used by Disneyland to recreate its historical Main Street.

b. Three Replacement Methods

The *COMPARATIVE-UNIT METHOD is used to derive a cost estimate in terms of dollars per square foot or per cubic foot, based on known costs of similar structures and adjusted for time and physical differences.* The comparative-unit method represents a relatively uncomplicated, practical approach to a cost estimate and is widely used.

The *UNIT-IN-PLACE METHOD employs unit costs for the various building components such as foundations, floors, walls, windows, and roofs as installed and uses square foot, linear foot, or other appropriate units of measurement to estimate each component part.* These estimates include labor and overhead. To use this method, the appraiser must have specialized construction knowledge.

The *QUANTITY SURVEY METHOD involves detailed estimates of the quantities of raw materials used, such as brick, lumber, cement, the price of such materials, and the labor costs.* It is the most comprehensive and accurate method of cost estimating, but too complicated to fully explain here.

Although there are several ways to determine replacement cost, the simplest way is to *measure the outside of the building to determine **SQUARE FOOTAGE**.* After you determine the square footage, multiply it by the current cost of construction, per square foot, to get the value (as if it were new) of the building.

To determine square feet, use the formula: **LENGTH x WIDTH**

The square foot cost for a smaller house is higher than the square foot cost for a larger house. If other factors are equal, including square footage, the cost of building a two-story house is up to 50% cheaper than a one-story house. A two-story house utilizes 50% less land (foot print).

The cubic foot method is used to appraise warehouses. To determine cubic feet, use the formula: **LENGTH x WIDTH x HEIGHT**

A warehouse building is appraised by the cubic foot but is usually rented by the square foot. **Caution: the industrial land the warehouse is on is appraised by the square foot.**

As construction costs vary from city-to-city and from builder-to-builder, many appraisers use cost engineers to help them determine the square foot cost of different types of construction. One of the most popular building cost information services is Marshall and Swift.

They compile a residential cost handbook that details the current cost of most types of residential construction in California. This is published quarterly.

3. Step 3 – Estimate and Deduct Depreciation

DEPRECIATION is a reduction in the value of a property due to any cause. The difference between replacement cost of a property and its market value is depreciation.

Loss of value from any cause is called depreciation.

Estimate and deduct the depreciation from the replacement cost of the building being appraised. This accumulated depreciation is sometimes called accrued depreciation. Accrued depreciation (observed) is the loss in value of improvements from any cause at the date of the appraisal. Accrued depreciation is what has happened in the past, whereas the accrual for depreciation is the amount of future depreciation. There are five methods of estimating accrued depreciation:

1. Capitalized Income
2. Market
3. Straight-line (Most common and explained below)
4. Engineering
5. Breakdown

The straight-line method is explained here. For information on the other methods, please see Educational Textbook Company's *Real Estate Appraisal – Principles and Procedures*, by Walt Huber, Levin P. Messick, IFAC, and William Pivar (see **Order Form** at back of this book). The *STRAIGHT-LINE METHOD (AGE LIFE) assumes the value declines in equal amounts of depreciation each year, until it reaches zero.* A building with an economic life of 50 years would depreciate 2 percent (100 percent ÷ 50 years = 2 percent) in value each year. Actual age is the current (real) age of the building. When using the age life method, an appraiser will use an age other than the actual age of the building. This is known as the effective age. *EFFECTIVE AGE is determined by the condition of the building rather than the actual age.* If a building has been maintained, its effective age may be less than the actual age; if there has been inadequate maintenance, it may be greater. *ECONOMIC LIFE is the estimated number of years of anticipated usefulness of the improvements.*

"Effective age" is determined by the condition and usefulness of the property, not the actual age. The economic life of an improvement is usually shorter than its estimated physical life.

ACCRUAL FOR DEPRECIATION is the concept of estimating the amount of depreciation there will be in the future. The accrual for depreciation is used in the income approach, discussed in the next section.

Example: A 19-year-old home looks like it is only 6 years old because it has been well maintained. The estimated life of the home is 40 years. Using the cost approach to appraise the home, the appraiser most likely would use the effective age of the improvements.

To accurately estimate accrued depreciation, the appraiser must have experience, skill, and good judgment. He or she must not only estimate the physical wear and tear on the building, but also the losses in value due to outmoded styles, poor design, and

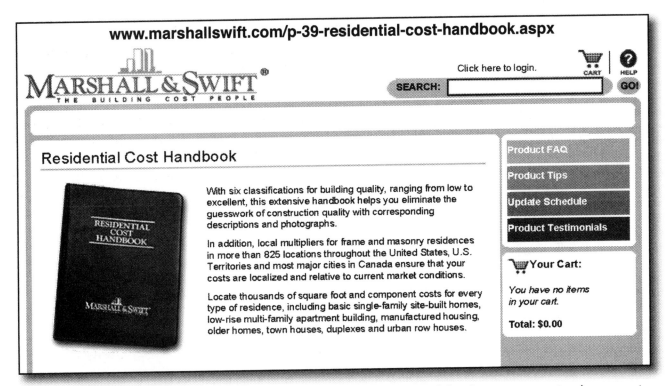

www.marshallswift.com/p-39-residential-cost-handbook.aspx

neighborhood changes that tend to reduce the value of the improvements. A property can lose value through three different types of depreciation.

The three types of depreciation causes are: 1) physical deterioration, 2) functional obsolescence, and 3) economic obsolescence.

a. Physical Deterioration (Curable or Incurable)

PHYSICAL DETERIORATION is the loss in value due to wear and tear. As a building gets older, its age will start to show visibly. Since most types of physical deterioration (like a deteriorated driveway) can be repaired, we usually think of it as curable depreciation. On the other hand, severe structural deterioration may not be curable. So physical deterioration can be either curable or incurable. *CURABLE DEPRECIATION are repairs that add more to a building's value than they cost. INCURABLE DEPRECIATION refers to repairs that would be so expensive they are not economically feasible.* Examples of physical deterioration (curable or incurable) are:

1. all forms of wear and tear;
2. damage from dry rot and termites;
3. negligent care (deferred maintenance); and
4. depreciation that has already occurred.

Obsolescence is not a method of calculating depreciation, but is a term meaning a "major cause" of depreciation.

b. Functional Obsolescence (Curable or Incurable)

FUNCTIONAL OBSOLESCENCE is the loss in value due to outmoded style or non-usable space. Examples of functional obsolescence would be a bedroom that can be

reached only by walking through another bedroom. By modern standards this is very inconvenient and reduces the value of the second bedroom. **Another devaluing factor is a home with a single-car garage**. Functional depreciation is hard to cure. If the cost of curing the defect adds at least the same amount to the property's value, then it is worth the investment.

A one-car garage is an example of functional obsolescence.

Types of functional obsolescence (curable or incurable) are:

1. an outdated kitchen;
2. antique fixtures;
3. a four-bedroom, one-bath home;
4. a one-car garage, and
5. massive cornices.

c. Economic Obsolescence (Incurable)

An appraiser is trying to determine the amount of economic obsolescence when appraising a commercial property. He probably wonders, "Are the tenants in the neighborhood prospering?"

> **ECONOMIC OBSOLESCENCE (also referred to as SOCIAL OBSOLESCENCE)** *is the loss in value due to changes in the neighborhood and is external to the property itself.* It is always incurable. If a freeway is built next to your property, your home will decrease in value because of the noise and nuisance factor. On the other hand, if the freeway is three blocks away, your house will increase in value because of improved freeway access. If social or economic factors (such as loss of jobs) cause a neighborhood to become shabby and rundown, the value of your property will decrease accordingly.

Since economic obsolescence results from "off the property" causes, it is always incurable. Economic (profitable) life remaining is the main concern when purchasing an older property.

> **Example:** Average priced homes coming into an area of expensive priced homes would cause real estate values to become unstable.

> **Example:** An airport flight pattern is changed and causes the affected homes to decrease in value due to economic obsolescence.

> **Example:** A zoning change would be considered economic obsolescence.

Types of economic obsolescence (incurable) are:

1. an oversupply of similar or competitive units;
2. beyond the confines of the property;
3. aircraft noise;
4. adverse zoning and legislative acts;
5. economic recession;
6. departure of major industries from the area, and
7. number of rental units increases.

4. Step 4 – Value of the Property

The last step in the cost approach is to add the depreciated value of any improvements to the value of the land. This figure is the market value of the property using the cost approach.

C. ADVANTAGES OF THE COST APPROACH

The main advantages of the cost approach is that it can be used on: 1) newly constructed buildings; 2) unique structures; and 3) public buildings.

Since there is little depreciation, if any, to calculate on newer buildings and there is available construction cost data, the value can be easily determined using the cost approach. Unique structures, public buildings, and one-of-a-kind structures have no comparables, so the cost approach may be the only logical way to appraise them.

D. DISADVANTAGES OF THE COST APPROACH

The disadvantages of using the cost approach are:

1. There must be an accurate value of the site (land).
2. Since determining depreciation is more difficult as buildings age, the reliability of the depreciation estimate may be questioned.
3. This approach may be difficult to apply to condos or planned unit developments because the land, improvements and marketing costs are not always easy to determine just for appraising one unit.

Economic obsolescence is the hardest or most difficult to change.

III. Capitalization Approach (Income Approach)

The income approach determines the "present worth of future benefits." Capitalization is the process of converting income into value.

The **INCOME APPROACH** *is the process of analyzing the future net income from a property to determine its current market value.* Another word for this process is capitalization. The appraiser, when using the income approach, is determining the present property value based upon the information he or she has on future income and expenses of that given property.

The actual process of capitalization is simple. Divide a capitalization rate into the yearly net income; the answer you obtain is the value of the property.

$$\frac{\text{NET INCOME}}{\text{CAPITALIZATION RATE}} = \text{VALUE OF PROPERTY}$$

$$\frac{\$110,000}{10\%} = \$1,100,000$$

Rent producing (income) properties such as apartments, offices, warehouses, and manufacturing concerns can best be appraised by the income approach. This is because the people who invest in such projects are primarily interested in the income that they will receive. It is only natural that an investor would choose the property producing the highest return. The income approach allows a comparison of different types of income producing real estate and, at the same time, analyzes each as to the return of income to be received from that investment in the future.

A. STEPS IN THE INCOME APPROACH

There are five basic steps to establish value using the income approach:

1. Calculate the annual effective gross income.
2. Complete an operating expense statement.
3. Deduct related operating expenses from gross income to get net income.
4. Divide net income by the appropriate capitalization rate.
5. Result of dividing net income by capitalization rate.

Figure 11-3 illustrates the five steps.

Figure 11-3

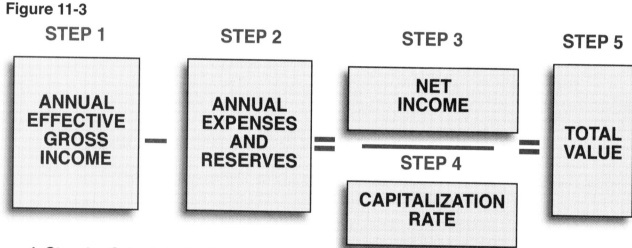

1. Step 1 – Calculate the Annual Effective Gross Income

Calculate the annual effective gross income from the investment property. *EFFECTIVE GROSS INCOME is the gross income minus any vacancies or rental losses.* In the case of rental properties, the annual gross rental income will be the annual rent that an owner receives if he or she charges the going rental rates with no vacancies. Sometimes managers charge rents that are below the market level, resulting in a very low number of vacancies. On the other hand, rents that are set too high usually yield a higher vacancy rate. The *VACANCY FACTOR is the loss in rents due to any cause.* This is commonly expressed as a percentage. The vacancy factor increases while trying to find a new tenant or because of cleaning, repairs, or non-paying renters.

2. Step 2 – Complete an Operating Expense Statement

Complete an operating expense statement. All of the following would be considered operating expenses when appraising an apartment building:

1. Property taxes
2. Insurance and licenses
3. Manager fees
4. Utilities
5. Maintenance, repairs, and services (i.e., gardeners)
6. Replacement reserves

Cost of capital (mortgage payments of principal or interest) is NOT an operating expense.

The expenses listed in the operating statement should represent the actual cost of each item. Though costs may vary, it is the appraiser's responsibility to determine what actual costs are on an annual basis.

An item that may need explanation is the replacement reserve. A *REPLACEMENT RESERVE consists of funds set aside for the purpose of replacing items in the future.* An example of a replacement reserve cost would be a $2,000 water heater with a life expectancy of five years. The replacement reserve for this item would be $400 per year ($2,000 ÷ 5).

Management fees and replacement reserves must always be included in the basic operating expenses.

VARIABLE COSTS are operating expenses that can vary (utilities and repairs). FIXED COSTS remain constant, such as property taxes and fire insurance.

3. Step 3 – Deduct Related Operating Expenses From Gross Income to Get Net Income

To determine net income, simply deduct the related operating expenses (Step 2) from the annual effective gross income (Step 1).

4. Step 4 – Divide Net Income by the Appropriate Capitalization Rate

Divide the net income by the appropriate capitalization rate. Selection of a capitalization rate can be a delicate task. A one percent change in the capitalization rate, for example, can alter the estimated value of a property by up to ten percent or more. The capitalization rate is composed of an interest rate return to the investor "on" his or her original investment and "of" the return of the original investment. The higher the rate, the greater the perceived risk is to the investor/owner.

Example: An owner of a vacant building is trying to decide whether to lease her building to a hardware store or to a post office. The owner would likely prefer the post office because the post office would probably have a lower risk than the hardware store. Thus, a lower rate would be acceptable.

There are several ways to select the proper capitalization rate. One way of selecting the appropriate capitalization rate is to sample similar recent apartment sales. Simply divide the net income by the sales price to obtain the capitalization rate used in that particular area.

CHAPTER 11

The capitalization rate is composed of two parts: (1) a rate of return "on" the money invested and (2) a return "of" the original investment of money. This latter item is commonly referred to as the recapture rate (see **Figure 11-4**).

Figure 11-4

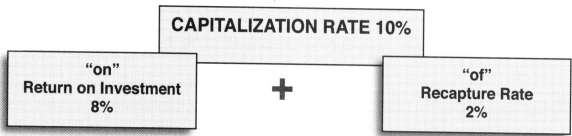

The capitalization rate is composed of two parts: the rate "on" the money invested (expected investor's return) and the annual rate "of" (recapture) of the investment.

A capitalization rate can be determined by band of investment theory, market data/comparison, or summation.

5. Step 5 – Result of Dividing Net Income by Capitalization Rate

This is the easiest and final step in the income approach. It is simply the result of dividing net income by the capitalization rate.

Net Income divided by Capitalization Rate = Market Value

$$\frac{I}{R} = V$$

$$\frac{\text{Net income \$65,000}}{\text{Capitalization Rate 10\% (.10)}} = \text{\$650,000 Estimated Market Value}$$

THE MARKET VALUE USING THE INCOME APPROACH IS \$650,000

The best appraisal approach to use on a shopping center would be the cost-income method.

B. GROSS RENT MULTIPLIER – GRM (Rule of Thumb)

GROSS RENT MULTIPLIER (GRM) is a multiplication rule of thumb used to convert the rental income into market value. If we use a gross rent multiplier of 125 times the monthly rent of \$1,000, the property is worth approximately \$125,000 (125 x \$1,000). See **Figure 11-5** for more details. This is definitely not an accurate way to appraise a property, but it does give a quick estimate of value. Many professional investors use it as a screening device to eliminate undesirable investment opportunities. This monthly gross multiplier is often used for single-family homes and small apartment buildings.

The *GROSS (RENT) is the money received from a property before any expenses are deducted.* It can be expressed as monthly or annual income, as long as it is applied consistently.

Example: A desert cabin which rents for $600 per month just sold for $96,000. A similar property rents for $660 per month, so the market value is most likely to be near $105,600.

In the real estate investment field (commercial and industrial), it is common knowledge that the annual gross income multiplier of "x 6.2" is a good "rule of thumb" for an investment. For example, if the annual gross income from an apartment project is $40,000, its value should be approximately $248,000 ($40,000 x 6.2). The annual gross income multiplier varies from "x 5" to "x 12," depending upon the location of the property and the condition of the individual buildings. Remember: this is an approximation device and should be used only as a quick estimate—not in place of an actual appraisal.

Gross income changed to value in one operation describes a rent multiplier.

C. ADVANTAGES OF THE INCOME APPROACH

The advantage of the income approach method is that no other method focuses solely on determining the present value of the future income stream from the subject property. It is a little different than the other two methods of determining value in that "If the purpose of the property is to generate income, use the income approach." For example a house that is zoned for commercial use may be valued at a much higher amount when used as an insurance office rather than as a house. The location may bring in a great deal of income; as a house the market value is low, but as an income-producing property the market value may be very high.

The "present worth of future benefits" is what the income approach is all about.

It is most often used for multi-family residential income property but could be used on any type of property that generates income.

D. DISADVANTAGES OF THE INCOME APPROACH

The disadvantage of the income approach is that it may be difficult to determine the proper capitalization rate. For example, it may be impossible to ascertain the cap-rate for a theme park or alligator farm. These other items used in the income approach may also be difficult to estimate: vacancy rate, economic rent, operation expenses, and reserve requirements.

IV. Correlation of Value (Bracketing)

The last and most important part of the appraisal process is the correlation (sometimes referred to as reconciliation) of the three approaches to value. *CORRELATION is the process of selecting the most appropriate approach for the particular appraisal job and giving it the most consideration in pinpointing the final value.* Although all three methods are used in appraisal, one is usually most appropriate for a specific appraisal problem.

In general, the "market comparison approach" is best for single-family homes or lots; the "cost approach" is best for new, unique or unusual structures; and the "income approach" is best for properties that can be used to generate income.

Figure 11-5

Gross Rent Multiplier

The **GROSS RENT MULTIPLIER (GRM)** *is a rough, quick way of converting gross monthly rent into market value.* To obtain the gross rent multiplier, divide the "sales" price by the monthly rent. It is not a very accurate method, but it is a good estimator because it is so easy. The gross rent multiplier is best used for single or small multi-family residential properties.

$$\frac{\text{SALES PRICE}}{\text{RENT}} = \text{GROSS RENT MULTIPLIER}$$

TYPICAL PROBLEMS:

If a house that rented for $600 a month sold for $78,000, what is the gross rent multiplier?

$$\frac{\$78,000\ \text{Sales price}}{\text{Monthly Rent }\$600} = 130\ \text{(Gross Rent Multiplier)}$$

If a similar house down the street is renting for $690, what would the selling price be?

Monthly Rent $690 x 130 (Gross Rent Multiplier) = $89,700

CAN ANNUAL RENTS BE USED?

The gross rent multiplier is not a percentage, so it can be expressed as either a monthly or annual figure. If the above problem were expressed as an annual rent figure, the gross rent multiplier would have to be divided by 12. The annual gross rent multiplier is 10.83 (130 ÷ 12).

If a house that rents for $72,000 a year sold for $780,000, what is the annual gross multiplier?

$$\frac{\$780,000\ \text{Sales Price}}{\text{Annual Rent }\$72,000} = 10.83\ \text{Annual Gross Rent Multiplier}$$

NOTE: Sometimes a different multiplier is used, the Gross Income Multiplier (GIM), when the revenues being considered are not just from rental income (like coin-operated washers and dryers). The GIM is preferred for commercial and income properties.

V. Final Estimate of Value (Appraisal Report)

After the appraiser has collected all the data and applied the appropriate appraisal method(s), the next step in the appraisal process is to reconcile or correlate the adjusted sales price of the comparables.

The *APPRAISAL REPORT is the documentation of the appraiser's findings.* It can be a prepared fill-in form. However, if it is complicated or subject to close interpretation, the report should be written in a narrative form with supporting data contained in supplemental exhibits. **In practice, most appraisal reports are written.** There are two main types of written appraisal reports:

1. **Short form** (a form with checks and explanations, often used by lenders)

A short form appraisal report is called a short form, form report, or summary report.

2. **Narrative report** (most complete and extensive)

A narrative appraisal report is the most comprehensive and complete and typically contains the headings "Introduction," "Site and Improvement," "Property Description," "Supporting Data," and "Final Value Estimate."

Whether the report is a simple one-page report or an extensive volume, the following information should be presented:

1. An adequate description for the property that is being appraised.
2. A statement as to the purpose and scope of the appraisal.
3. An adequate description of the neighborhood.
4. The date on which the value is estimated.

An appraiser's "effective date" is usually the date of the inspection of the property.

5. The qualifying conditions and assumptions.
6. The factual data, maps, and photos with their analysis and interpretations.
7. The processing of the data by one or more of the three approaches to value (correlation).

An appraiser's "date signed" is the date of final writing or delivery of the appraisal report.

8. The estimate of value.
9. The name, address, type of license (and any certifications), and signature of the appraiser.

A. COST OF AN APPRAISAL

Appraisal costs can vary from relatively small amounts to thousands of dollars. The cost of an appraisal may be affected by its purpose, the qualifications of the appraiser, and how detailed the appraisal. An appraisal used to document a court case could cost several thousand dollars.

It would be impractical to spend thousands of dollars for a home appraisal just to determine a selling price. If you are thinking about selling your home, your local real estate broker will probably do this at no cost. Local brokers are familiar with your area and are knowledgeable about current sales prices of similar homes in your neighborhood. On the other hand, appraisal

of large parcels, commercial buildings, and apartment houses, or appraisals to be used in court, may require the services of a highly skilled appraiser. Although the fees are higher, they reflect the experience and ability of the appraiser. The appraisal fee and an outline of what is to be accomplished in the appraisal should be set in advance. It is unethical to set an appraisal fee as a percentage of the determined value. This may influence the appraiser to increase the value.

Appraisal Report Copies

A lender must provide a notice to a loan applicant stating that the applicant is entitled to a consumer information copy of the appraisal report if the applicant requests and pays for the report.

The notice must be provided on any loan secured by residential property and on purchase money financing (or refinancing of purchase money debt) on nonresidential property.

VI. Licensing, Fee Appraisers, and Appraisal Organizations

A. APPRAISAL LICENSE AND CERTIFICATION (California)

All California appraisers are required to be licensed or certified (see **Figure 11-6**). The license/certification categories are:

1. TRAINEE APPRAISER
2. RESIDENTIAL APPRAISER
3. CERTIFIED RESIDENTIAL APPRAISER
4. CERTIFIED GENERAL APPRAISER

A Certified General License would be needed to appraise a strip mall valued at approximately $540,000.

B. FEE APPRAISERS

While the Standards permit an appraiser to appraise a property in which he or she has an interest, as long as the fact is disclosed to the lender/client in writing, it would be highly unusual for it to be accepted by any lender/client.

A *FEE APPRAISER is an independent, self-employed appraiser; he or she appraises for a fee or charge.* In California a license or certification is required to appraise real estate as a profession. Other appraisers are dependent on large corporations or organizations for their employment. Gas, electric, telephone, and other utility companies have appraisal departments. Banks, savings banks, mortgage companies, and other lenders often have in-house appraisal staffs. Most cities and counties have large appraisal staffs in their assessors' offices. There are also various state agencies, such as Cal-Trans, that maintain appraisal staffs.

A fee appraiser is self-employed; he/she appraises for a fee or charge. Remember: both appraisers and real estate agents are concerned with the marketability of residential properties.

Figure 11-6

CALIFORNIA OFFICE OF REAL ESTATE APPRAISERS (OREA)
EDUCATION REQUIREMENTS

TRAINEE LICENSE AND RESIDENTIAL LICENSE

150 hours of education. Qualifying Education hours must include instruction in the following modules:

30 hours	**Basic Appraisal Principles**
30 hours	**Basic Appraisal Procedures**
15 hours	**The 15-hour National USPAP Course**
15 hours	**Residential Market Analysis and Highest and Best Use**
15 hours	**Residential Appraiser Site Valuation and Cost Approach**
30 hours	**Residential Sales Comparison and Income Approaches**
15 hours	**Residential Report Writing and Case Studies**

Note: *Course work for the Trainee License cannot be taken more than 5 years prior to the application date.*

CERTIFIED RESIDENTIAL LICENSE

200 hours of education and an Associate Degree from a Regionally Accredited College. Qualifying Education hours must include instruction in the following modules:

30 hours	Basic Appraisal Principles
30 hours	Basic Appraisal Procedures
15 hours	The 15-hour National USPAP Course
15 hours	Residential Market Analysis and Highest and Best Use
15 hours	Residential Appraiser Site Valuation and Cost Approach
30 hours	Residential Sales Comparison and Income Approaches
15 hours	Residential Report Writing and Case Studies
15 hours	Statistics, Modeling and Finance
15 hours	Advanced Residential Applications and Case Studies
20 hours	Appraisal Subject Matter Electives. May include hours over the minimum requirement in the above modules or in modules not listed above.

* In lieu of the Associate Degree, an applicant can complete 21 college semester credits in courses covering specific subject matters: English Composition; Principles of Economics (Micro or Macro); Finance; Algebra, Geometry or higher mathematics; Statistics; Introduction to Computers; and Business or Real Estate Law.

CERTIFIED GENERAL LICENSE

300 hours of education and a Bachelors Degree from a Regionally Accredited College or University. Qualifying Education hours must include instruction in the following modules:

30 hours	Basic Appraisal Principles
30 hours	Basic Appraisal Procedures
15 hours	The 15-hour National USPAP Course
30 hours	General Appraiser Market Analysis and Highest and Best Use
15 hours	Statistics, Modeling and Finance
30 hours	General Appraiser Sales Comparison Approach
30 hours	General Appraiser Site Valuation and Cost Approach
60 hours	General Appraiser Income Approach
30 hours	General Appraiser Report Writing and Case Studies
30 hours	Appraisal Subject Matter Electives. May include hours over the minimum requirement in the above modules or in modules not listed above.

** In lieu of the Bachelors Degree, an applicant can complete 30 college semester credits in courses covering specific subject matters: English Composition; Micro Economics; Macro Economics; Finance; Algebra, Geometry or higher mathematics; Statistics; Introduction to Computers; and Business or Real Estate Law; and two elective courses in accounting, geography, ag-economics, business management, or real estate.

CHAPTER 11

Many community colleges and universities offer courses in appraisal or investment properties to acquaint you with the techniques involved in the income approach.

www.cccco.edu/
Information on the California Community Colleges

C. PROFESSIONAL APPRAISAL ASSOCIATIONS

American Society of Appraisers (ASA)
555 Herndon Parkway, Suite 125
Herndon, VA 20170
www.appraisers.org

American Society of Farm Managers and Rural Appraisers (ASFMRA)
950 Cherry Street, Suite 508
Denver, CO 80246-2664
www.asfmra.org

Appraisal Institute (AI)
550 West Van Buren Street, Suite 1000
Chicago, IL 60607
www.appraisalinstitute.org

Appraisal Institute of Canada (AIC)
403-200 Catherine Street
Ottawa ON K2P 2K9 Canada
www.aicanada.org

International Association of Assessing Officers (IAAO)
314 West 10th Street
Kansas City, MO 64105-1616
www.iaao.org

International Right of Way Association (IRWA)
19750 South Vermont Avenue, Suite 220
Torrance, CA 90502-1144
www.irwaonline.org

National Association of Independent Fee Appraisers (NAIFA)
401 North Michigan Avenue, Suite 2200
Chicago, IL 60611
www.naifa.com

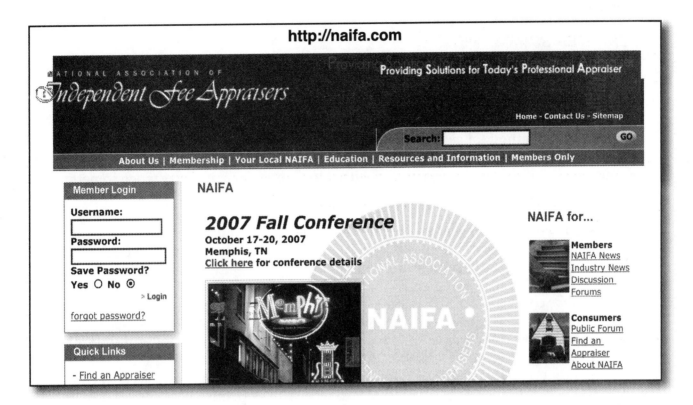

National Association of Master Appraisers (NAMA)
303 West Cypress Street
San Antonio, TX 78212-0617
www.masterappraisers.org

VII. CHAPTER SUMMARY

A **licensed appraiser** will use three different approaches to establish **final value**. These include the: 1) **comparative (market data) approach**; 2) **cost (replacement) approach**; and 3) **capitalization (income) approach**.

The **market data method** (or **sales comparison approach**) takes the current selling prices of similar or comparable properties (comps) and adjusts for any differences. The **principle of substitution** is applied, assuming a person will not pay more for a property when something similar is available for less.

The **cost approach** (or **replacement cost method**) determines the current market value of a property by adding the value of the land plus (+) replacement or reproduction cost of buildings today, minus (-) depreciation, maintaining the same amount of utility.

In step one of the cost approach, the appraiser finds the **value of the land** using the market data approach. In step two, the **reproduction** or **replacement cost** is calculated. The three replacement methods include the **comparative-unit method** (most commonly used), the **unit-in-place method**, and the **quantity survey method**. In step three, **depreciation** is factored in. The three types of depreciation are: 1) **physical**, 2) **functional**, and 3) **economic**, and can be either **curable** (profitable to repair) or **incurable** (unprofitable to repair). In step four the depreciated value of improvements is added to the value of the land to find the **market value** of the property.

The **capitalization** (or **income**) **approach** is concerned with the present worth of future benefits. The basic formula to determine total value is: **Annual effective gross income minus (-) annual expenses and reserves equals (=) net income**. Then **divide the net income by the capitalization rate to find (=) market value**. The **cap rate** is the percentage rate that an investor expects to earn "on" a real estate investment. A quick rule of thumb to convert gross income into approximate value is to use the **gross rent multiplier**, which is based on monthly rent and is used for residential properties. The **gross income multiplier** is based on annual rents and is used for commercial properties.

Correlation (or **reconciliation**) is the process of selecting the most appropriate approach for the appraisal job. Generally, the market comparison approach is best for single-family homes or lots; the cost approach is best for new, unique or unusual structures; and the income approach is best for properties that can be used to generate income. The **final estimate of value** (or **appraisal report**) is then generated, the **narrative report** being the most comprehensive and complete.

The **cost of an appraisal** can be effected by its purpose, how detailed it is, and the experience of the appraiser. All appraisers must be licensed or certified, the categories being **trainee license**, **residential license**, **certified residential license**, and **certified general license**. A **fee appraiser** is self employed, and charges a fee for his or her services. Although highly unusual, it is technically permissible for a fee appraiser to appraise a property in which he or she owns an interest as long as it is disclosed in writing. It is the **marketability of real property** that concerns appraisers and real estate agents.

VIII. TERMINOLOGY

A. Accrual for Depreciation
B. Accrued Depreciation
C. Actual Age
D. Correlation
E. Cost Approach
F. Curable Depreciation
G. Depreciation
H. Direct Cost

I. Economic Life
J. Economic Obsolescence
K. Effective Age
L. Effective Gross Income
M. Functional Obsolescence
N. Gross Rent Multiplier
O. Income Approach
P. Incurable Depreciation

Q. Indirect Costs
R. Market Comparison
S. Physical Deterioration
T. Replacement
U. Replacement Reserve
V. Reproduction Cost
W. Square Footage
X. Vacancy Factor

1.____ The estimated percentage of vacancies in a rental property, such as in an apartment building.
2.____ The use of different appraisal methods to reach an estimate of the value of a property. The methods must be weighed as to which is most appropriate for the type of property being appraised.
3.____ The theoretical cost of replacing a building with one of equivalent usefulness.
4.____ A simple method of using gross monthly or yearly rents to obtain an approximate value of an income property.
5.____ The need to replace part of a structure because new improvements have come along that make the older structure inefficient by comparison. For example, a one-bathroom, eight-bedroom house.
6.____ An appraisal method, estimating the replacement cost of a structure, less depreciation, plus land value.
7.____ Loss of desirability and useful life of a property through economic forces, such as zoning changes, traffic pattern changes, etc., rather than wear and tear.
8.____ A decrease in the value of real property improvements for any reason.
9.____ An appraisal method to determine the present value today of rental property by estimating the income it will generate over the life of the structure.
10.____ A way of measuring real property in 1 ft. by 1 ft. segments.
11.____ The method of estimating the value of real property by adjusting the sales price of comparable properties for differences.
12.____ Gradual physical wear and tear on a structure that decreases its value.
13.____ Periodically setting money aside to replace systems and appliances in a building. For example, a landlord putting aside a portion of monthly rents toward a new roof or water heater.
14.____ The chronological age of a structure as opposed to its effective or economic life.
15.____ Accumulation of depreciation.
16.____ Construction costs (material and labor).
17.____ The cost of reproducing a property (usually one that has been destroyed) at current prices using the same materials.
18.____ Repairs that would be so expensive they are not economically feasible.
19.____ Age of a structure as estimated by its condition rather than its actual age.
20.____ Repairs that are economically logical to do.
21.____ Costs other than labor and materials.
22.____ Amount of depreciation in the future, not past.
23.____ The "profitable" life of an improvement. Generally shorter than the physical life.
24.____ Gross income of a building if fully rented, less an allowance for estimated vacancies.

CHAPTER 11

IX. CHAPTER QUIZ

1. An appraiser using the market data approach in appraising would be most interested in the date that:

    a. the offer was written.
    b. the buyer moved into the property.
    c. recording occurred.
    d. the price was agreed upon.

2. The ultimate test of functional utility is:

    a. marketability.
    b. cost of the item.
    c. market cost.
    d. All of the above.

3. A 19 year-old home looks like it is only 6 years old because it has been well maintained. The estimated life of the home is 40 years. Using the cost approach to appraise the home, the appraiser most likely would use the:

    a. effective age of the improvements.
    b. economic age of the improvements.
    c. physical age of the improvements.
    d. chronological age of the improvements.

4. Which of the following would be an example of functional obsolescence?

    a. New zoning laws
    b. Incompatible land use in the neighborhood
    c. A deteriorated driveway
    d. A one-car garage

5. An airport flight pattern is changed and causes the affected homes to decrease in value due to:

    a. economic obsolescence.
    b. aviation obsolescence.
    c. political obsolescence.
    d. functional obsolescence.

6. An appraiser is using the replacement cost approach to appraise a building built in 1901. The appraiser would:

    a. determine the labor cost in 1901 adjusted for inflation based on the consumer price index (CPI) since 1901.
    b. use the cost to build the building in 1901 if the data is available. Otherwise, use the available data from the closest year to 1901.
    c. use the current cost to build the building today and deduct the depreciation over the economic life of the building.
    d. utilize the average labor costs over the building's economic life.

7. When appropriate, an appraiser would use the cost approach to determine the value of:

    a. special purpose property or service buildings.

    b. vacant land.

    c. an expensive family home.

    d. constructing a building.

8. An owner of a vacant building is trying to decide whether to lease his building to a hardware store or to a post office. The owner would likely prefer the post office because the post office would probably:

    a. have a higher capitalization rate than that of the hardware store.

    b. have a lower capitalization rate than that of the hardware store.

    c. provide a higher return for the owner than the hardware store.

    d. sign a longer lease if unemployment rises in the area.

9. A capitalization rate can be determined by:

    a. summation.

    b. band of investment theory.

    c. market data (comparison).

    d. all of the above.

10. Which appraisal report would typically contain the headings, "Introduction," "Site and Improvement," "Property Description," "Supporting Data," and "Final Value Estimate?"

    a. The letter form report

    b. The short form report

    c. The narrative report

    d. The certified general report

ANSWERS: 1. c; 2. a; 3. a; 4. d; 5. a; 6. c; 7. a; 8. b; 9. d; 10. c

CHAPTER 12
Subdivisions and Government Control

I. Doctrine of Police Power

There are currently over 35 million people in California and we are adding over 1,700 new residents each day.

With a population of more than thirty-five million people, California has more people than any other state. That means we have approximately 12.5% of the United States population. Since we are such a fast growing and mobile state, the problems encountered can be tremendous. The state and local governments have the responsibility (under the doctrine of police power) to enact and enforce legislative acts to protect the general public. This public protection in the real estate area prevents fraud, misrepresentation, and deceit.

A. POLICE POWER

Police power is the right of public officials to control the use of private property for the health, safety, and general welfare of the public.

> *POLICE POWER is the power to make rulings to control the "use and taking of private property" for the protection of the public's health, safety, and welfare.* Police power allows the state, county, or city to protect its citizens by controlling how land is being used.
>
> Police power provides for the regulation of lot design and physical improvements for the orderly and proper development of the community, the construction of streets, highways and parking facilities adequate for our car-oriented society, and the certainty of an adequate water supply. It ensures the protection of life and property by police and firemen, the maintenance of the purity of air we breathe, the control of noise, the disposal of sewage and waste, and the provision under public or private regulation for essential utility services. **Figure 12-1** shows seven basic areas of government control at either the state or local level.

Zoning, planning, and governmental land use are important examples of the exercise of police power.

II. The Basic Subdivision Laws

A SUBDIVISION is a parcel of land divided into smaller parcels with the intent to sell, lease, or finance them now or in the future. It can also be some form of common or mutual ownership rights in

CHAPTER 12

Figure 12-1

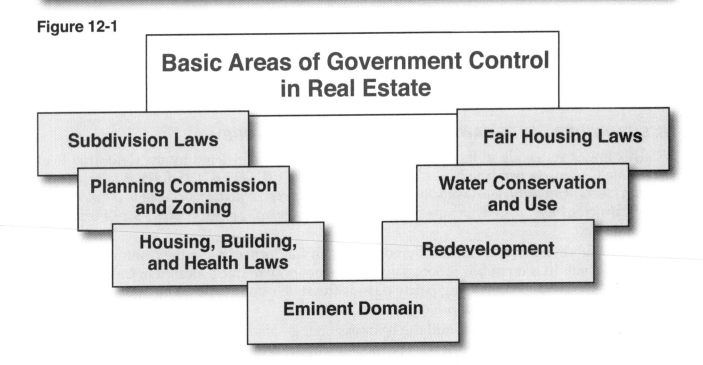

one parcel. A **condominium** is sometimes referred to as a "one lot subdivision." There are two basic laws under which subdivisions are controlled in California:

   A. Subdivision Map Act (City or County) – Two or more parcels or lots
   B. Subdivided Lands Law (Department of Real Estate) – Five or more parcels or lots

These two laws were enacted for different purposes, and were adopted to achieve the objective for which each was designed.

A. SUBDIVISION MAP ACT (Enforced by Local City or County)

*The primary objective of the **SUBDIVISION MAP ACT** is to provide an outline of the methods for the subdivision filing procedure at the city or county level and to make sure subdividers comply with* *the city's or county's master plan*. This law permits the local government of the city or county to enact subdivision ordinances. Thus, the direct control of the kind and type of subdivision for each community, and the public physical improvements to be installed, is left to the local city (if incorporated) or county (if unincorporated). This act has two major objectives:

1. To coordinate the subdivision plans including lot design, street patterns, drainage, and sewers with the community pattern (master plan) as laid out by the local planning authorities.

2. To ensure, by the filing of the subdivision maps, that parts of the subdivision area will be dedicated to the city or county for public purposes. These dedications include public streets and other public areas, dedicated by the subdivision so that they will not be an unmanageable future burden upon the taxpayers of the community.

State law now requires that each community (city or county government) shall enact local subdivision ordinances. Before the Department of Real Estate will approve the subdivision, a tentative subdivision map must be approved by the local government.

The Subdivision Map Act (for two or more parcels or lots) gives local government entities (planning commissions) control over the physical design of a subdivision.

B. SUBDIVIDED LANDS LAW (State Law Enforced by the DRE)

This law is statewide in its operation and is directly administered by the California Real Estate Commissioner. The *basic objective of the SUBDIVIDED LANDS LAW is to protect the purchasers of property in new subdivisions from fraud, misrepresentation, or deceit in the marketing of subdivided lots, parcels, condominiums, or other undivided property interests in the state of California.*

No subdivision unit can be offered for sale in California unless the commissioner has issued a subdivision public report. This applies not only to tracts located in California, but also to subdivided lands lying partly outside the state's boundaries. The public report is a factual account of the subdivided property.

The report is not issued until the commissioner is satisfied that the subdivider has met all the statutory requirements, with particular emphasis on the establishment and facilities included in the offering, and demonstrates that the lots or parcels can be used for the purpose for which they are being offered.

The Subdivided Lands Law (public report) requirements apply when a parcel is divided into five or more lots (units).

III. Public Report (Consumer Information)

The public report (issued by the Department of Real Estate) is required reading by any purchaser.

As provided by the Subdivided Lands Law, purchasers of a home in a new subdivision must receive a Public Report from the California Real Estate Commissioner's office. A *PUBLIC REPORT is a formal disclosure report of the important facts regarding a subdivision*. It is, in a sense, a developer's "permit" to sell. It is not, however, a recommendation pro or con. The report

makes clear the physical characteristics of the land, so that the buyer can know exactly what he or she is buying. The buyer is told the size, arrangement, and location of the lot and exactly what off-site improvements and recreation facilities to expect.

A subdivider must give a copy of the Commissioner's Public Report to anyone who requests it orally or in writing.

There may be two public reports. The optional preliminary report may be submitted to the Department of Real Estate for tentative approval. The required final report must be issued and given to the buyer. The *PRELIMINARY PUBLIC REPORT (PINK) is a tentative public report that must be given to each prospective purchaser*. The report is printed on pink paper, making it easily recognizable. It is given to a buyer when he or she makes a reservation to purchase or lease a lot, unit, or parcel in a subdivision.

Preliminary reports allow subdividers to obtain reservations only. They cannot sell and the deposit is fully refundable. Any preliminary report issued will expire when the final report is published or after one year passes, whichever is first.

A prospective purchaser must be given a copy of the preliminary report and sign a receipt to that effect. A copy of the reservation agreement is signed by the prospective buyer and the money deposited with a neutral escrow company. **The reservation to buy or lease must contain a clause allowing the buyer the option to cancel his or her reservation at any time and immediately have the deposit returned**. Any preliminary report issued will expire when the final report is published or after one year passes, whichever occurs first. The subdivider must keep receipts taken for any public report on file for three years.

A "Desist and Refrain Order" is issued by the Real Estate Commissioner to stop sales for violations.

The *FINAL PUBLIC REPORT (WHITE)*, *"Real Estate Commissioner's Final Subdivision Public Report,"* is the official report that must be given to the buyer. The buyer must receive a copy of the final public report even if he or she has a preliminary public report. After having enough time to read it, the buyer must sign a receipt stating that the report has been received. There is a five-year time limit on the report, and it can be updated and renewed.

Note – The public report process only applies to the first sale of each lot. Later resales are exempt.

A. PUBLIC REPORT RECEIPTS

The subdivider must keep a receipt of the public report for a three-year period.

The receipt stating that the buyer has received a copy of any public report, and had the opportunity to read it, must be kept on file by the owner, his or her agent, or the subdivider. Receipts for any public reports are subject to inspection by the commissioner for a three-year period. An approved reservation agreement form is furnished by the Department of Real Estate (see **Figure 12-2**). This form, or a form similar to it, is to be used when taking reservations and deposits under a preliminary public report or deposits under the final public report.

If there is a discrepancy between local and state building codes, the highest standard of safety will prevail. A developer is responsible for streets, curbs, and utilities in a new subdivision.

B. MATERIAL CHANGES (Notify Commissioner)

Change in price is NOT a material fact.

Any material change in the subdivision or its handling after the filing is made, or the public report is issued, must be reported to the Commissioner of Real Estate. This not only includes physical changes, such as changes in the lot or street lines, but any new condition or development that may affect the value of the subdivision or the terms of how it is offered to the public.

The owner of a standard type subdivision or planned development must report to the commissioner the sale of five or more parcels. The sale to a single purchaser of two or more units in a community apartment, condominium, or stock cooperative project must also be reported. Failure to report material changes not only violates the law, but may furnish a basis for rescission, by court action, of purchases.

If a person purchases, or has an option to purchase, five or more lots in a subdivision, whether contiguous or not, the subdivider must immediately notify the Department of Real Estate with the name and address. The reason for this is that another subdivision has been created within the original subdivision, so a new Final Public Report will be required.

IV. Subdivision Defined by Law

Although the definitions of the Subdivided Lands Law and the Subdivision Map Act are in many ways similar, there are some differences. Both define a subdivision as **improved or unimproved land divided for the purpose of sale, leasehold, or financing into several parcels.** They are applied not only to residential land, but include lands used for any purpose, including business, industry, recreation, or agriculture.

Figure 12-2

REGULATION 2795.1

REQUIRED RECEIPT FOR PUBLIC REPORT

The following form shall be duplicated and used by the owner, subdivider or agent as the prospective purchaser's receipt for the copy of the Public Report which was given to said prospective purchaser.

It shall also be used pertinent to all prospective purchasers who sign a reservation agreement under the authority of a Preliminary Public Report or a Short Form Preliminary Public Report.

The receipt is to be kept on file by the subdivider or his/her representative/agent for three years

---

RECEIPT FOR PUBLIC REPORT

The Laws and Regulations of the Real Estate Commissioner require that you as a prospective purchaser or lessee be afforded an opportunity to read the public report for this subdivision before you make any written offer to purchase or lease a subdivision interest or before any money or other consideration toward purchase or lease of a subdivision interest is accepted from you.

In the case of a preliminary subdivision public report, you must be afforded an opportunity to read the report before a written reservation or any deposit in connection therewith is accepted from you.

DO NOT SIGN THIS RECEIPT UNTIL YOU HAVE RECEIVED A COPY OF THE REPORT AND HAVE READ IT.

I have read the Commissioner's Public Report on

"CENTURY PARK PLACE"

054916LA-A04	37164, Phase 4, Lot 1
(File No.)	(Tract No. or Name)

I understand the report is not a recommendation or endorsement of the subdivision, but is for information only.

The date of the public report which is received and read is: _6/7/XX_ .

Vic Lester
Name

1207 Arden Street
Address

_6/7/XX_
Date

There are several differences between the two Acts. In general, the Subdivided Lands Law applies to five or more units while the Subdivision Map Act applies to two or more units.

Full compliance with all the provisions of the Subdivision Map Act and the Subdivided Lands Law is required by law. Subdividers and their professional consultants should be thoroughly familiar with the provisions of the state laws and with the specific city and county provisions that affect the particular community in question. Many variations are found in local subdivision ordinances due to the great diversity of communities and conditions throughout the state (see **Figure 12-3** for a summary of subdivision laws).

Figure 12-3

Subdivision Laws Summarized

SUBDIVISION MAP ACT	SUBDIVIDED LANDS LAW
Two or more lots or parcels	Five or more lots or parcels
Land must be contiguous units	No contiguity requirement
No exemption for 160 acres and larger	160 and larger parcels are exempt
Administered by local officials	Administered by the California Real Estate Commissioner
No public report required	Public report required

A. LAND PROJECTS (State Law)

In recent years, lots in some subdivisions located in sparsely populated areas have been sold by intensive promotional efforts that tend to obscure the gamble involved in such speculations. Such subdivisions are referred to as land projects. A *LAND PROJECT is a remote subdivision of 50 or more vacant lots in a rural area (having fewer than 1,500 registered voters within two miles).*

Certain laws have been established to protect the public from these risky ventures. By law, any contract to buy or lease in a land project may be rescinded without cause, by written notice, before midnight on the fourteenth day after the sales contract is signed.

B. OUT-OF-STATE BUYERS (Federal Law)

Subdividers of large subdivisions to be sold interstate are registered with HUD.

Under the Federal Interstate Land Sales Full Disclosure Act, such sales are subject to special registration and control. A contract for the purchase or lease of a lot of this kind is voidable at the option of the buyer if the contract is made without prior inspection of the site. The buyer has seven days after receiving the public report to rescind the contract.

V. Common Interest Development (CID)

A *COMMON INTEREST DEVELOPMENT (CID) is a project where there are common areas used by all—excepting separate interests for the use of individual living units and managed by a nonprofit association*. The four basic types of common interest ownership, which are defined as subdivisions, include:

A. **Planned Development (PD)**
B. **Community Apartment Project**
C. **Condominiums (including Timesharing)**
D. **Stock Cooperative**

To be defined as subdivisions by the Department of Real Estate as part of the Subdivided Lands Law, a planned unit development must have five or more lots, but all the other types only need two units.

A. PLANNED DEVELOPMENT (PD)

A *PLANNED DEVELOPMENT (PD), sometimes referred to as a planned unit development (PUD), is a subdivision where lots are owned separately, but certain areas are owned in common by all owners.* Generally, an owner's association is elected by all the owners to manage and maintain the common areas.

The *COMMON AREA is that part of a lot or unit in a subdivision that is shared equally by all owners (undivided interest).* An ***UNDIVIDED INTEREST*** *is the right of any owner to use any part of the project.*

An example of a PD (or PUD) is a subdivided tract of homes, each on its own lot, that share a swimming pool on a separate lot, which is owned in common by all the tract owners.

B. COMMUNITY APARTMENT PROJECTS

COMMUNITY APARTMENT PROJECTS are two or more apartments, defined as a subdivision, where the operation, maintenance, and control is usually exercised by a governing board elected by the owners of the fractional interests. An owner receives an undivided interest in the land together with an exclusive leasehold right to occupy a unit. There is only one property tax bill for the entire project.

Purchasers receive only a right to occupy (leasehold interest) in an apartment unit, while a condo purchaser gets a deed (fee interest) to a unit.

C. CONDOMINIUM (Most Common Type)

A condominium owner gets a deed (fee interest) to a unit and a separate tax bill.

A *CONDOMINIUM is the ownership of the land and buildings in common with other owners plus the individual ownership of specific air spaces.* A "condominium" is a type of ownership; a "townhouse" is a type of architecture. In a PD, the property owner owns the living unit as well as the lot. Condominiums may be used for residential, industrial, or commercial purposes, although the residential type is most commonly seen in California. Condominium projects having two or more units are defined as subdivisions.

A condominium is the ownership of unit (airspace) and shared ownership of the land and all improvements. Each "condo" has a separate grant deed, trust deed, and tax bill. You "own what you see"; the airspace between the paint on one wall to the paint on the other wall.

In effect, a condominium buyer owns, in fee simple, the air space in which his or her particular unit is situated. He or she receives a separate tax bill for private airspace and percentage share of the common area. Each airspace unit is given a grant deed, and the owner can acquire a title insurance policy. The common area is managed by an elected governing board.

A copy of the CC&Rs, a copy of the bylaws, and a copy of the most recent financial statement of the condo association must be given to every buyer of a condominium unit.

1. Timesharing

TIMESHARING *is a form of ownership where each investor holds a share in a specific unit or home and possesses the right to occupy that home for a specified period each year* (see **Figure 12-4**).

Fifty-two owners (usually less because of downtime for maintenance) may each own a specific one-week share in one unit at a resort property.

Example: A timeshare company advertises the sale of timeshares on a billboard or the world wide web. If the billboard does not disclose the requirement to listen to a sales presentation in order to receive the promised prize, this is illegal, because the broker did not disclose the requirement to listen to a sales presentation.

D. STOCK COOPERATIVE (Corporation is the Owner)

A **STOCK COOPERATIVE** *is a corporation that is formed to own the land and improved real property.* A stock cooperative either owns or leases real property. The buyer does not receive a grant deed but owns a share of the corporation and the right to occupy a certain unit. The right to occupy can be transferred only with the share of stock in the corporation.

VI. Subdivision Advertising

Guidelines for subdividers in advertising and promotions have been developed by the Department of Real Estate. The pamphlet contains filing procedures, requirements and prohibitions on advertising. Since misleading advertising is watched very carefully, it is now a requirement that the public report must be given to each advertising media selected by the subdivider. In addition, a true copy of any advertising proposed for use in connection with a land project offering must be submitted as part of the documentation required prior to the issuance of the public report.

VII. Environmental Laws

In recent years there has been increasing attention focused on the problems of our environment. These problems include energy, water pollution, air pollution, population growth, preservation of wild life, waste disposal and the quality of life in general. In response, the federal, state and local governments have passed laws and made regulations to help protect us and our environment.

An **ENVIRONMENTAL IMPACT REPORT (EIR)** *is a study of how a subdivision will affect the ecology of a subdivision's surroundings.* An EIR may be required by either city or county authorities prior to their approval of the subdivision map, but some projects may be exempt. In rare cases, the responsibility for the preparation of the EIR will belong to the Department of Real Estate.

Figure 12-4

TIMESHARING:

Pro or Con? — You Decide! A chalet at Lake Tahoe...a condo in Palm Springs...beachfront property in La Jolla...

TIMESHARING is a form of ownership where each investor holds a share in a specific unit or home and possesses the right to occupy that home for a specified period each year. For instance, fifty-two owners may each own a one-week share in the property. Each is given a grant deed and each has the right to sell his or her share, rent out the week, or stay there for one seven-day period every year. The ownership week is fixed but it is possible to trade with other owners. Similarly, there are timesharing groups across the country and around the world which allow investors to exchange time with owners of comparable properties in other desirable locations.

Advantages

The advantages to this kind of ownership are obvious. The buyer has a vacation home without the expense of purchasing the complete home outright. This kind of plan provides access to some of the most unique and scenic property in the world. Once these very special locations are sold, they are gone: they cannot be replaced in the marketplace.

Disadvantages

On the negative side, these properties tend to be disproportionately high priced. For instance, if you multiplied the cost of one share in a week-based timeshare by an even 50, it would total much more than the market value of the property purchased. Those selling timeshares are burdened with tremendous marketing expenses. Rather than selling once, each property must be sold many times, complete with financing and paperwork.

Restrictions

A brokerage license is required to sell a timeshare package but, just as with other forms of home sales, owners have the right to transfer their ownership shares without a real estate license and have a 72-hour right of rescission.

A "Negative Declaration" is a statement by an expert affirming that a new subdivision will have NO negative impact on the environment.

The voters of California passed Proposition 20 that established the state Coastal Commission to preserve the coastline. This commission has set construction standards for private and public projects within 1,000 yards of the Pacific Ocean or any other body of water. Its purpose is to establish land use planning, which has considerable economic, social, and political overtones.

As part of this law, the commission had to establish a long-range coastal plan. No one seems to agree on the economic effects of Proposition 20, but it did have the result of reducing the number and size of coastal construction projects and required an average of six weeks to pass a project through the commission.

A. LEAD-BASED PAINT DISCLOSURE (Federal Government)

Lead-Based Paint Disclosure Pamphlet
Residential Lead-Based Paint Hazard Reduction Act

The seller or lessor must provide the buyer or lessee with a lead hazard information pamphlet (including disclosure form) and disclose the known presence of any lead-based paint.

The CAR® Residential Purchase Agreement and Joint Escrow Instructions contains a Lead Warning Statement and a statement, to be signed by the buyer, that the buyer has read the warning statement. Also, CAR® has a Lead-Based Paint Hazards Disclosure, Acknowledgment, and Addendum Form (**Figure 12-5**) that can be made a part of a Residential Purchase Agreement, Residential Lease or Month-To-Month Rental Agreement, or some other contract.

The agent, on behalf of the seller or lessor, must ensure compliance with the requirements of the law. The purchaser has a **10-day opportunity** to inspect before becoming obligated under the contract.

B. GEOLOGICAL HAZARD ZONES

Before any real estate development or large structure is built in California, a geological report must be submitted. This report must be compiled by a registered geologist and given to the city in which the development is planned. In the case of a development in an unincorporated area, the report is submitted to the county in which the planned development is located.

If the state geologist approves it, the city or county department may waive such a report as long as there is no earthquake fault activity.

The California Geological Survey (formerly called the Division of Mines and Geology) has mapped every earthquake fault that has hazardous potential or recent activity. These special study zones are found throughout California and new ones are added to the map (see **Figure 12-6**).

Any person buying within such a zone should be informed either by the seller or the real estate licensee of this fact. A buyer who is thinking of building should be cautioned as to the regulations and requirements that may have to be met to develop the land. See **Figure 12-7** for specifics on the Alquist-Priolo Special Studies Zones Act. There are approximately 205 different Geological Survey areas in California. If you want more information about these hazardous zones or copies of the maps, they can be obtained for a small fee.

www.consrv.ca.gov/cgs/index.htm
CALIFORNIA GEOLOGICAL SURVEY
801 K Street, MS 14-33
Sacramento, CA 95814-3532
(916) 445-5716

Figure 12-5

CALIFORNIA
ASSOCIATION
OF REALTORS®

LEAD-BASED PAINT AND LEAD-BASED PAINT HAZARDS DISCLOSURE, ACKNOWLEDGMENT AND ADDENDUM
For Pre-1978 Housing Sales, Leases, or Rentals
(C.A.R. Form FLD, Revised 1/03)

The following terms and conditions are hereby incorporated in and made a part of the: ☐ California Residential Purchase Agreement, ☐ Residential Lease or Month-to-Month Rental Agreement, or ☐ other: _____
_____ ,dated _____ , on property known
as: _____ ("Property")
in which _____ is referred to as Buyer or Tenant
and _____ is referred to as Seller or Landlord.

LEAD WARNING STATEMENT (SALE OR PURCHASE) Every purchaser of any interest in residential real property on which a residential dwelling was built prior to 1978 is notified that such property may present exposure to lead from lead-based paint that may place young children at risk of developing lead poisoning. Lead poisoning in young children may produce permanent neurological damage, including learning disabilities, reduced intelligent quotient, behavioral problems and impaired memory. Lead poisoning also poses a particular risk to pregnant women. The seller of any interest in residential real property is required to provide the buyer with any information on lead-based paint hazards from risk assessments or inspections in the seller's possession and notify the buyer of any known lead-based paint hazards. A risk assessment or inspection for possible lead-based paint hazards is recommended prior to purchase.

LEAD WARNING STATEMENT (LEASE OR RENTAL) Housing built before 1978 may contain lead-based paint. Lead from paint, paint chips and dust can pose health hazards if not managed properly. Lead exposure is especially harmful to young children and pregnant women. Before renting pre-1978 housing, lessors must disclose the presence of lead-based paint and/or lead-based paint hazards in the dwelling. Lessees must also receive federally approved pamphlet on lead poisoning prevention.

1. SELLER'S OR LANDLORD'S DISCLOSURE

I (we) have no knowledge of lead-based paint and/or lead-based paint hazards in the housing other than the following:
_____
_____
_____

I (we) have no reports or records pertaining to lead-based paint and/or lead-based paint hazards in the housing other than the following, which, previously or as an attachment to this addendum have been provided to Buyer or Tenant: _____
_____
_____

I (we), previously or as an attachment to this addendum, have provided Buyer or Tenant with the pamphlet *"Protect Your Family From Lead In Your Home"* or an equivalent pamphlet approved for use in the State such as *"The Homeowner's Guide to Environmental Hazards and Earthquake Safety."*

<u>For Sales Transactions Only</u>: Buyer has 10 days, unless otherwise agreed in the real estate purchase contract, to conduct a risk assessment or inspection for the presence of lead-based paint and/or lead-based paint hazards.

I (we) have reviewed the information above and certify, to the best of my (our) knowledge, that the information provided is true and correct.

_____   Date _____
Seller or Landlord

_____   Date _____
Seller or Landlord

Buyer's Initials (_____)(_____)
Seller's Initials (_____)(_____)

Reviewed by _____ Date _____

EQUAL HOUSING OPPORTUNITY

LEAD-BASED PAINT AND LEAD-BASED PAINT HAZARDS DISCLOSURE (FLD PAGE 1 OF 2)

Property Address: _____ Date _____

2. LISTING AGENT'S ACKNOWLEDGMENT

Agent has informed Seller or Landlord of Seller's or Landlord's obligations under §42 U.S.C. 4852d and is aware of Agent's responsibility to ensure compliance.

I have reviewed the information above and certify, to the best of my knowledge, that the information provided is true and correct.

_____ By _____
Agent (Broker representing Seller) Please Print   Associate-Licensee or Broker Signature   Date

3. BUYER'S OR TENANT'S ACKNOWLEDGMENT

I (we) have received copies of all information listed, if any, in 1 above and the pamphlet *"Protect Your Family From Lead In Your Home"* or an equivalent pamphlet approved for use in the State such as *"The Homeowner's Guide to Environmental Hazards and Earthquake Safety."* **If delivery of any of the disclosures or pamphlet referenced in paragraph 1 above occurs after Acceptance of an offer to purchase, Buyer has a right to cancel pursuant to the purchase contract. If you wish to cancel, you must act within the prescribed period.**

For Sales Transactions Only: Buyer acknowledges the right for 10 days, unless otherwise agreed in the real estate purchase contract, to conduct a risk assessment or inspection for the presence of lead-based paint and/or lead-based paint hazards; OR, (if checked) ☐ Buyer waives the right to conduct a risk assessment or inspection for the presence of lead-based paint and/or lead-based paint hazards.

I (we) have reviewed the information above and certify, to the best of my (our) knowledge, that the information provided is true and correct.

_____   _____
Buyer or Tenant   Date   Buyer or Tenant   Date

4. COOPERATING AGENT'S ACKNOWLEDGMENT

Agent has informed Seller or Landlord, through the Listing Agent if the property is listed, of Seller's or Landlord's obligations under §42 USC 4852d and is aware of Agent's responsibility to ensure compliance.

I have reviewed the information above and certify, to the best of my knowledge, that the information provided is true and correct.

_____ By _____
Agent (Broker obtaining the Offer)   Associate-Licensee or Broker Signature   Date

SURE TRAC
The System for Success®

Published and Distributed by:
REAL ESTATE BUSINESS SERVICES, INC.
a subsidiary of the California Association of REALTORS®
525 South Virgil Avenue, Los Angeles, California 90020

FLD REVISED 1/03 (PAGE 2 OF 2)

Reviewed by _____ Date _____

EQUAL HOUSING OPPORTUNITY

LEAD-BASED PAINT AND LEAD-BASED PAINT HAZARDS DISCLOSURE (FLD PAGE 2 OF 2)

Figure 12-6

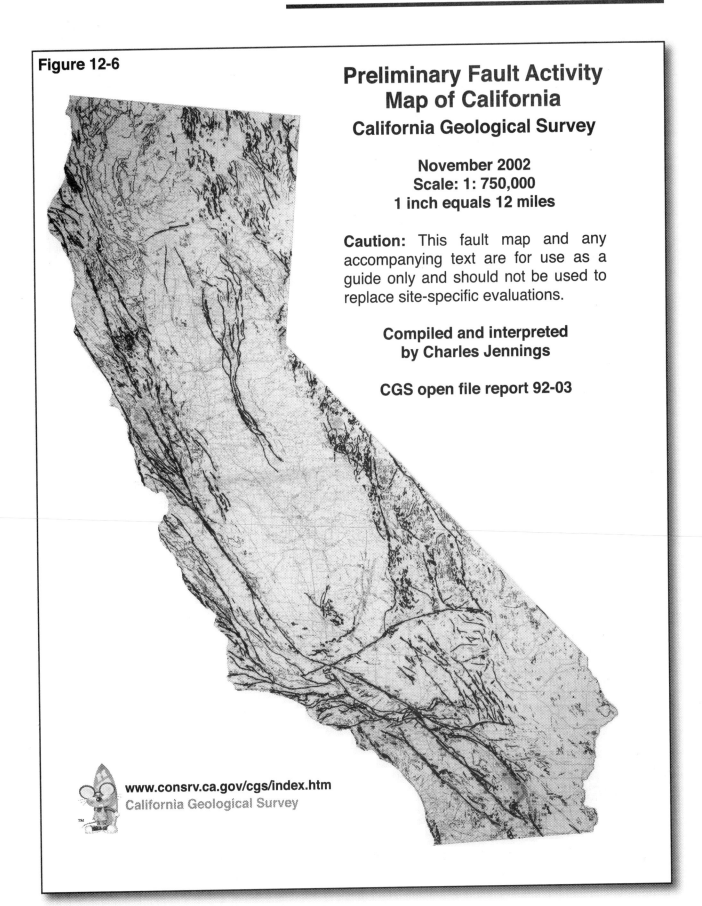

Preliminary Fault Activity Map of California
California Geological Survey

November 2002
Scale: 1: 750,000
1 inch equals 12 miles

Caution: This fault map and any accompanying text are for use as a guide only and should not be used to replace site-specific evaluations.

Compiled and interpreted by Charles Jennings

CGS open file report 92-03

www.consrv.ca.gov/cgs/index.htm
California Geological Survey

Figure 12-7

Earthquake Zones

Alquist-Priolo Special Studies Zones Act

This is a zoning act designed to control the development in the vicinity (1/4 mile wide strip) of hazardous earthquake faults for the benefit of public safety for the entire state of California.

The purpose of the Alquist-Priolo Special Studies Zones Act is to assist governmental jurisdictions in the exercise of their responsibility to prohibit the development of structures for human occupancy on top of active earthquakes faults as defined by the state geological survey maps. Developments or structures in existence prior to May 4, 1975, are not affected.

An earthquake zone normally extends one-quarter of a mile in width, centered on the trace of a fault, and includes an area that may be hazardous for development or construction of a structure for human occupancy due to surface faulting or fault creep.

Maps for Special Studies Zone

These maps can be consulted at any district office of the California Geological Survey (formerly named the Division of Mines and Geology). Individuals can obtain copies of these maps at many different local jurisdictions. As a practical matter, the local Multiple Listing Office is one of the most convenient locations to see a map.

"Any person who is acting as an agent for a seller of real estate that is located within a delineated special studies zone, or the seller who is acting without an agent, shall disclose the fact that the property is located within a delineated special studies zone."

Note – Most agents and sellers have a professional company prepare these disclosures for the buyers.

VIII. Planning Commission

The primary responsibility of a *CITY or COUNTY PLANNING COMMISSION is to prepare and adopt comprehensive, long-term general plans for the physical development of its area of jurisdiction.* These city or county organizations gather information, cite other examples, and come up with their own innovations in an attempt to make some order out of the chaos into which a city may have fallen. Commissions have discovered that preplanning exactly which types of buildings can go where, before they are constructed, saves more time and money than all the zoning laws made after the building is done. Such planning commissions make predictions to guarantee that today's residential, commercial, and industrial areas will not collide in the future due to expansion of both areas.

The primary tool used by planning commissions to implement a general plan is zoning.

A. MASTER PLAN

Every city and county must have a planning commission. The primary purpose of a Master Plan is to set forth existing and future matters concerning seismic safety, districts, streets, and highways.

Entire new cities can be pre-planned so that zoning laws exist only to enforce and execute the city's master plan. The **MASTER PLAN** *is a comprehensive guide through which zoning establishes an ideal plan for the city's development in the future.* **DIRECTIONAL GROWTH** *is the actual growth path of urban development. Properties in the direction of growth tend to increase in value especially if the growth is steady and rapid.* It is used, by smart investors, to determine where future development will be most profitable. A good example of preplanning is the Irvine Ranch in Orange County, where there is a balance between residential, recreational, commercial, and manufacturing areas. The essential elements of a master plan are:

1. The designation of proposed general distribution, location, and extent of land uses within certain areas.

2. The determination of general traffic patterns, including the extensions of existing and proposed transportation routes, terminals, and other public utility facilities.

3. The setting of standards of population density and building units per acre of various districts and the estimation of future population growth trends. A number of other elements may also be included.

IX. Zoning (Use)

Zoning is the city or county exercise of "police power"; rulings are made to control the use of private property for the protection of the public's health, safety, and welfare.

The power to zone is given by the U.S. Constitution.

ZONING LAWS *regulate the use of property by prescribing what uses that land can be put to and by establishing uniformity throughout the community.* For example, zoning laws may indicate that a specific property can be used only as a single family home, multiple family housing, or for commercial or industrial use. It is possible for the planning commission to change zoning. It can change an area from commercial to residential or change a residential area from R-4 to R-1. This is called down zoning. **DOWNZONING** *means the land will have less use density.*

Changing zoning from industrial to residential is called downzoning.

INCLUSIONARY ZONING *requires builders of new residential housing to provide a certain number of low- and moderate-income units.* No permit will be obtained if the builder does not agree. Sometimes a builder will, in lieu of setting aside inclusionary units, contribute to a fund used to provide low- and moderate-income housing.

If zoning conflicts with deed restrictions, the most restrictive controls.

Zoning laws use the "police power" granted to every county and city to regulate the use, planning, and setbacks of land. Such regulations protect the health, safety, comfort and general welfare of the community. These ordinances are public restrictions to the uses of private property. Counties and cities can set higher standards, which can be much higher than the minimums set by the state. For example, zoning which regulates the use of lands and buildings may specify the following:

1. Location and type of building
2. Height of the structure
3. Size of the building
4. Percentage of a lot the building may occupy
5. Setback requirements from front, back, and sides of the property boundaries.

Zoning changes can be initiated by local authorities, subdividers, and individuals.

Figure 12-8 is an example of a Los Angeles zoning plan. You will notice that there are many symbols that indicate the regulated uses for all the different parts of Los Angeles.

Each symbol represents a different type of zone, but it is possible to make the following generalization about some of the common zoning symbols:

A – This symbol usually indicates an *agricultural* area such as farm or ranch land. In a few isolated areas a symbol beginning with "A" stands for an airport.

C – The "C" symbol represents *commercial* areas. In these areas anything from an office building to a community shopping center may exist. There are other, more specific, "C" symbols regulating the construction of such commercial properties.

A "strip commercial development" is a single line of store buildings constructed along a major transportation route.

M – Stands for *manufacturing*. Industrial complexes must be built only in zones classified "M."

According to local zoning laws, the designation "M" most likely will refer to industrial.

P – Although there are many different interpretations of the "P" symbol, the most important categories it covers are *parking lots* and *parks*.

R – The "R" symbol stands for *residential* and is probably the most important symbol to the real estate person. This symbol (and its derivations) designates those areas in which *homes, condominiums,* or *apartments* may be built or maintained.

Each of these symbols is usually followed by a number, for example "R" may be followed by 1, 2, 3, or 4. The number indicates a higher density or use for that particular zone. The following will help explain each use:

R1 – is for a *single-family* dwelling

R2 – is for *two dwelling* units

Figure 12-8

SUMMARY OF ZONING REGULATIONS
CITY OF LOS ANGELES

CLASSIFICATION	ZONE	USE	MAXIMUM HEIGHT STORIES	MAXIMUM HEIGHT FEET	REQUIRED YARDS FRONT	REQUIRED YARDS SIDE	REQUIRED YARDS REAR	MINIMUM AREA PER LOT	MINIMUM AREA PER DWELLING UNIT	MINIMUM LOT WIDTH	PARKING SPACE	EAGLE PRISMACOLOR PENCIL CHART
AGRICULTURAL	A1	AGRICULTURAL ONE-FAMILY DWELLINGS - PARKS - PLAYGROUNDS - COMMUNITY CENTERS GOLF COURSES - TRUCK GARDENING - EXTENSIVE AGRICULTURAL USES	3	45 FT.	25 FT.	25 FT MAXIMUM 10% LOT WIDTH 3 FT MINIMUM	25 FT.	5 ACRES	2½ ACRES	300 FT.	TWO SPACES PER DWELLING UNIT	909 GRASS GREEN
	A2	AGRICULTURAL A1 USES	3	45 FT.	25 FT.	25 FT MAXIMUM 10% LOT WIDTH 3 FT MINIMUM	25 FT.	2 ACRES	1 ACRE	150 FT.	TWO SPACES PER DWELLING UNIT	912 APPLE GREEN
	RA	SUBURBAN LIMITED AGRICULTURAL USES	3	45 FT.	25 FT.	10'-1&2 STORIES 11'-3 STORIES	25 FT.	17,500 SQ. FT. ✳	17,500 SQ. FT. ✳	70 FT. ✳	TWO GARAGE SPACES PER DWELLING UNIT	910 TRUE GREEN
ONE FAMILY RESIDENTIAL	RE40	RESIDENTIAL ESTATE ONE-FAMILY DWELLINGS PARKS PLAYGROUNDS COMMUNITY CENTERS TRUCK GARDENING	3	45 FT.	25 FT	10 FT	25 FT	40,000 SQ. FT.	40,000 SQ. FT. ✳	80 FT. ✳	TWO GARAGE SPACES PER DWELLING UNIT	950 GOLD
	RE20				25 FT.	10 FT	25 FT	20,000 SQ. FT.	20,000 SQ. FT. ✳	80 FT. ✳		
	RE15				25 FT	10 FT. MAXIMUM 10% LOT WIDTH 5 FT MINIMUM	25 FT.	15,000 SQ. FT.	15,000 SQ. FT. ✳	80 FT.		
	RE11				25 FT	5'-1&2 STORIES 6'-3 STORIES	25 FT.	11,000 SQ. FT.	11,000 SQ. FT. ✳	70 FT. ✳		
	RE9				25 FT	5 FT. MAXIMUM 10% LOT WIDTH 3 FT. MINIMUM	25 FT.	9,000 SQ. FT.	9,000 SQ. FT. ✳	65 FT. ✳		
	RS	SUBURBAN ONE-FAMILY DWELLINGS - PARKS PLAYGROUNDS - TRUCK GARDENING	3	45 FT.	25 FT.	5'-1&2 STORIES 6'-3 STORIES	20 FT	7,500 SQ. FT	7,500 SQ. FT	60 FT.	TWO GARAGE SPACES PER DWELLING UNIT	911 OLIVE GREEN
	R1	ONE-FAMILY DWELLING RS USES	3	45 FT	20 FT.	5'-1&2 STORIES 6'-3 STORIES	15 FT.	5,000 SQ. FT	5,000 SQ. FT	50 FT.	TWO GARAGE SPACES PER DWELLING UNIT	916 CANARY YELLOW
	RW1	ONE-FAMILY RESIDENTIAL WATERWAYS ZONE	3	45 FT	10 FT.	4' PLUS 1' EACH STORY ABOVE 2ND 10% LOT WIDTH	15 FT.	2,300 SQ. FT	2,300 SQ. FT	28 FT.	TWO GARAGE SPACES PER DWELLING UNIT	914 CREAM
	RW2	TWO-FAMILY RESIDENTIAL WATERWAYS ZONE							1,150 SQ. FT.			
MULTIPLE RESIDENTIAL	R2	TWO-FAMILY DWELLING R1 USES TWO-FAMILY DWELLINGS	3	45 FT.	20 FT.	5'-1&2 STORIES 6'-3 STORIES	15 FT.	5,000 SQ. FT	2,500 SQ. FT	50 FT.	TWO SPACES ONE IN A GARAGE	917 YELLOW ORANGE
	RD1.5	RESTRICTED DENSITY MULTIPLE DWELLING ZONE TWO-FAMILY DWELLING APARTMENT HOUSES MULTIPLE DWELLINGS	HEIGHT DISTRICT NO.1 3 STORIES 45 FT.		20 FT.	6 FT	20 FT.	6,000 SQ. FT.	1,500 SQ. FT.	60 FT	ONE SPACE EACH DWELLING UNIT OF LESS THAN THREE ROOMS ONE AND ONE HALF SPACES EACH DWELLING UNIT OF THREE ROOMS TWO SPACES EACH DWELLING UNIT OF MORE THEN THREE ROOMS ONE SPACE EACH GUEST ROOM (FIRST THIRTY)	940 SAND
	RD2							8,000 SQ. FT.	2,000 SQ. FT.	60 FT		
	RD3								3,000 SQ. FT.			
	RD4			20 FT.	10 FT	25 FT	12,000 SQ. FT.	4,000 SQ. FT.	70 FT		
	RD5		HEIGHT DISTRICT NOS.2,3 OR 4 6 STORIES 75 FT.						5,000 SQ FT			
	RD6								6,000 SQ. FT.			
	R3	MULTIPLE DWELLING R2 USES APARTMENT HOUSES MULTIPLE DWELLINGS			15 FT.	5'-1&2 STORIE 6'-3 STORIES	15 FT.	5,000 SQ. FT.	800 TO 1,200 SQ. FT.	50 FT		918 ORANGE
	R4	MULTIPLE DWELLING R3 USES CHURCHES HOTELS - SCHOOLS	UNLIMITED ✳		15 FT.	5' PLUS 1' EACH STORY ABOVE 2ND 16 FT MAX	15' PLUS 1' EACH STORY ABOVE 3RD 20 FT. MAX.	5,000 SQ. FT.	400 TO 800 SQ. FT.	50 FT.		943 BURNT OCHRE
	R5	MULTIPLE DWELLING R4 USES CLUBS - HOSPITALS LODGES - SANITARIUMS	UNLIMITED ✳		15 FT.	5' PLUS 1' EACH STORY ABOVE 2ND 16 FT. MAX	15' PLUS 1' EACH STORY ABOVE 3RD 20 FT. MAX	5,000 SQ. FT.	200 TO 400 SQ. FT.	50 FT.		946 DARK BROWN

✳ SEE HEIGHT DISTRICTS AT THE BOTTOM OF PAGE 2

● FOR TWO OR MORE LOTS THE INTERIOR SIDE YARDS MAY BE ELIMINATED, BUT 4 FT IS REQUIRED ON EACH SIDE OF THE GROUPED LOTS.

✳ "H" HILLSIDE OR MOUNTAINOUS AREA DESIGNATION MAY ALTER THESE REQUIREMENTS IN THE RA-H OR RE-H ZONES, SUBDIVISIONS MAY BE APPROVED WITH SMALLER LOTS, PROVIDING LARGER LOTS ARE ALSO INCLUDED EACH LOT MAY BE USED FOR ONLY ONE SINGLE-FAMILY DWELLING SEE MINIMUM WIDTH & AREA REQUIREMENTS BELOW.

ZONE COMBINATION	MINIMUM TO WHICH NET AREA MAY BE REDUCED	MINIMUM TO WHICH LOT WIDTH MAY BE REDUCED
RA-H	14,000 SQ FT	63 FT
RE9-H	7,200 SQ FT	60 FT
RE11-H,	8,800 SQ FT	63 FT
RE15-H	12,000 SQ FT	72 FT
RE20-H	16,000 SQ FT	72 FT
RE40-H	32,000 SQ FT	NO REDUCTION

SHEET 1 OF 2   CP FORM 10

PREPARED BY CITY PLANNING DEPARTMENT

SUMMARY OF ZONING REGULATIONS
CITY OF LOS ANGELES

ZONE	USE	MAXIMUM HEIGHT STORIES	MAXIMUM HEIGHT FEET	REQUIRED YARDS FRONT	REQUIRED YARDS SIDE	REQUIRED YARDS REAR	MINIMUM AREA PER LOT AND UNIT	MINIMUM LOT WIDTH	LOADING SPACE	PARKING SPACE	EAGLE PRISMACOLOR PENCIL CHART
CR	LIMITED COMMERCIAL — BANKS, CLUBS, HOTELS, CHURCHES, SCHOOLS, BUSINESS & PROFESSIONAL OFFICES, PARKING AREAS	6	75 FT	10 FEET	5'-10' CORNER LOT, RESIDENTIAL USE OR ADJOINING AN "A" OR "R" ZONE SAME AS R4 ZONE	15' PLUS 1' EACH STORY ABOVE 3rd	SAME AS R4 FOR DWELLINGS OTHERWISE NONE		HOSPITALS, HOTELS INSTITUTIONS, AND WITH EVERY BUILDING WHERE LOT ABUTS ALLEY	ONE SPACE FOR EACH 500 SQ FT OF FLOOR AREA	939 FLESH
C1	LIMITED COMMERCIAL — LOCAL RETAIL STORES, OFFICES OR BUSINESSES, HOTELS, LIMITED HOSPITALS AND/OR CLINICS, PARKING AREAS				3'-5' CORNER LOT OR ADJOINING AN "A" OR "R" ZONE	15' PLUS 1' EACH STORY ABOVE 3rd RESIDENTIAL USE OR ADJOINING AN "A" OR "R" ZONE	SAME AS R3 FOR DWELLINGS EXCEPT 5000 SQ FT PER UNIT IN C1-H ZONES — OTHERWISE NONE	50 FEET FOR RESIDENCE USE OTHERWISE NONE	MINIMUM LOADING SPACE 400 SQUARE FEET	ONE SPACE FOR EACH 500 SQUARE FEET OF FLOOR AREA IN ALL BUILDINGS ON ANY LOT MUST BE LOCATED WITHIN 750 FEET OF BUILDING	929 PINK
C1.5	LIMITED COMMERCIAL — C1 USES — DEPARTMENT STORES, THEATRES, BROADCASTING STUDIOS, PARKING BUILDINGS, PARKS & PLAYGROUNDS				RESIDENTIAL USE SAME AS R4 ZONE	OTHERWISE NONE			ADDITIONAL SPACE REQUIRED FOR BUILDINGS CONTAINING MORE THAN 50,000 SQUARE FEET OF FLOOR AREA		928 BLUSH
C2	COMMERCIAL — C1.5 USES — RETAIL BUSINESSES WITH LIMITED MANUFACTURING, AUTO SERVICE STATION & GARAGE, RETAIL CONTRACTORS BUSINESSES, CHURCHES, SCHOOLS	UNLIMITED *					SAME AS R4 FOR DWELLINGS OTHERWISE NONE				922 SCARLET RED
C4	COMMERCIAL — C2 USES — (WITH EXCEPTIONS, SUCH AS AUTO SERVICE STATIONS, AMUSEMENT ENTERPRISES, CONTRACTORS BUSINESSES, SECOND-HAND BUSINESSES)			NONE	NONE FOR COMMERCIAL BUILDINGS RESIDENTIAL USES - SAME AS IN R4 ZONE	NONE FOR COMMERCIAL BUILDINGS RESIDENTIAL USES - SAME AS IN R4 ZONE			NONE REQUIRED FOR APARTMENT BUILDINGS 20 UNITS OR LESS	SEE CODE FOR ASSEMBLY AREAS, HOSPITALS AND CLINICS	924 CRIMSON RED
C5	COMMERCIAL — C2 USES — LIMITED FLOOR AREAS FOR LIGHT MANUFACTURING OF THE CM - ZONE TYPE										925 CRIMSON LAKE
CM	COMM'L MANUFACTURING — WHOLESALE BUSINESSES, STORAGE BUILDINGS, CLINICS, LIMITED MANUFACTURING, C2 USES - EXCEPT HOSPITALS, SCHOOLS, CHURCHES						SAME AS R3 FOR DWELLINGS OTHERWISE NONE				905 AQUA-MARINE
MR1	RESTRICTED INDUSTRIAL — CM USES — LIMITED COMMERCIAL & MANUFACTURING USES, HOSPITALS, CLINICS, SANITARIUMS, LIMITED MACHINE SHOPS			15 FT	NONE FOR INDUSTRIAL OR COMMERCIAL BUILDINGS RESIDENTIAL USES - SAME AS IN R4 ZONE	NONE FOR INDUSTRIAL OR COMMERCIAL BUILDINGS RESIDENTIAL USES - SAME AS IN R4 ZONE			HOSPITALS, HOTELS INSTITUTIONS, AND WITH EVERY BUILDING WHERE LOT ABUTS ALLEY	ONE SPACE FOR EACH 500 SQUARE FEET OF FLOOR AREA IN ALL BUILDINGS ON ANY LOT MUST BE LOCATED WITHIN 750 FEET OF BUILDING	901 INDIGO BLUE
MR2	RESTRICTED LIGHT INDUSTRIAL — MR1 USES — ADDITION INDUSTRIAL USES, MORTUARIES, AGRICULTURE						SAME AS R4 FOR DWELLINGS OTHERWISE NONE	50 FEET FOR RESIDENCE USE OTHERWISE NONE	MINIMUM LOADING SPACE 400 SQUARE FEET		906 COPEN-HAGEN BLUE
M1	LIMITED INDUSTRIAL — CM USES — LIMITED INDUSTRIAL & MANUFACTURING USES — NO "R" ZONE USES, NO HOSPITALS, SCHOOLS OR CHURCHES	UNLIMITED *							ADDITIONAL SPACE REQUIRED FOR BUILDINGS CONTAINING MORE THAN 50,000 SQUARE FEET OF FLOOR AREA		904 LIGHT BLUE
M2	LIGHT INDUSTRIAL — M1 USES — ADDITIONAL INDUSTRIAL USES, STORAGE YARDS OF ALL KINDS, ANIMAL KEEPING — NO "R" ZONE USES			NONE						SEE CODE FOR ASSEMBLY AREAS, HOSPITALS AND CLINICS	902 ULTRA-MARINE
M3	HEAVY INDUSTRIAL — M2 USES — ANY INDUSTRIAL USES — NUISANCE TYPE - 500 FT. FROM ANY OTHER ZONE — NO "R" ZONE USES				NONE	NONE	NONE — NOTE — "R" ZONE USES PROHIBITED	NONE	NONE REQUIRED FOR APARTMENT BUILDINGS 20 UNITS OR LESS		931 PURPLE
P	AUTOMOBILE PARKING - SURFACE & UNDERGROUND — PROPERTY IN A "P" ZONE MAY ALSO BE IN AN "A" OR "R" ZONE PARKING PERMITTED IN LIEU OF AGRICULTURAL OR RESIDENTIAL USES						NONE UNLESS ALSO IN AN "A" OR "R" ZONE	NONE UNLESS ALSO IN AN "A" OR "R" ZONE	—	—	967 COLD GREY LIGHT
PB	PARKING BUILDING — AUTOMOBILE PARKING WITHIN OR WITHOUT A BUILDING	**	—	0', 5', OR 10' DEPENDING ON ZONING IN BLOCK AND ACROSS STREET	5' PLUS 1' EACH STORY ABOVE 2nd IF ABUTTING OR ACROSS STREET FROM 'A' OR 'R' ZONE	5' PLUS 1' EACH STORY ABOVE 2nd IF ABUTTING "A" OR "R" ZONE, TO A 16' MAXIMUM	NONE	NONE	—	—	936 SLATE GREY
SL	SUBMERGED LAND ZONE — COMMERCIAL SHIPPING, NAVIGATION, FISHING, RECREATION										919 SKY BLUE
(T)	TENTATIVE CLASSIFICATION — USED IN COMBINATION WITH ZONE CHANGE ONLY - DELAYS ISSUANCE OF BUILDING PERMIT UNTIL SUBDIVISION OR PARCEL MAP RECORDED										
(F)	FUNDED IMPROVEMENT CLASSIFICATION — AN ALTERNATE MEANS OF EFFECTING ZONE CHANGES AND SECURING IMPROVEMENTS (WHEN NO SUBDIVISION OR DEDICATIONS ARE INVOLVED)										
(Q)	QUALIFIED CLASSIFICATION — USED IN COMBINATION WITH ZONE CHANGES ONLY EXCEPT WITH RA, RE, RS OR R1 ZONES - RESTRICTS USES OF PROPERTY AND ASSURES DEVELOPMENT COMPATIBLE WITH THE SURROUNDING PROPERTY										

Classification categories (left margin): RESIDENTIAL USES (EXCEPT HOTELS) PROHIBITED UNLESS CONDITIONAL USE IS APPROVED BY ZONING ADMINISTRATOR / COMMERCIAL / RESIDENTIAL USES PROHIBITED IN ALL INDUSTRIAL ZONES / INDUSTRIAL / PARKING / SPECIAL

SUPPLEMENTAL USE DISTRICTS: (ESTABLISHED IN CONJUNCTION WITH ZONES)
G ROCK AND GRAVEL • O OIL DRILLING • S ANIMAL SLAUGHTERING • RPD RESIDENTIAL PLANNED DEVELOPMENT
K HORSE - KEEPING

HEIGHT DISTRICT

*	Nº 1	FLOOR AREA OF MAIN BUILDING MAY NOT EXCEED THREE TIMES THE BUILDING AREA OF THE LOT
	Nº 1L	SAME AS Nº 1 AND MAXIMUM HEIGHT - 6 STORIES OR 75 FT
	Nº 1-VL	SAME AS Nº 1 AND MAXIMUM HEIGHT - 3 STORIES OR 45 FT
	Nº 2	FLOOR AREA OF MAIN BUILDING MAY NOT EXCEED SIX TIMES THE BUILDABLE AREA OF THE LOT
	Nº 3	FLOOR AREA OF MAIN BUILDING MAY NOT EXCEED TEN TIMES THE BUILDABLE AREA OF THE LOT
	Nº 4	FLOOR AREA OF MAIN BUILDING MAY NOT EXCEED THIRTEEN TIMES THE BUILDABLE AREA OF THE LOT

MAXIMUM PB ZONE HEIGHTS

**	Nº 1	2 STORIES AND ROOF
	Nº 2	6 STORIES
	Nº 3	10 STORIES
	Nº 4	13 STORIES

NOTE: ALL INFORMATION GENERAL - FOR SPECIFIC DETAILS CHECK WITH DEPARTMENT OF BUILDING AND SAFETY

SHEET 2 OF 2

PREPARED BY CITY PLANNING DEPARTMENT

R3 – is for *multiple-family dwellings* depending on square footage and height of apartment buildings, condos, etc. **The typical zoning for multiple-family residential units is R-3.**

R4 – is for *higher density multiple dwellings with certain square footage.*

R5 – *requirements and maximum height allowable* concerning motels, hotels, and high-rise apartments or condominiums.

Zoning restrictions reduce the buildable area by requiring setbacks from the front, back, and sides of the lot lines.

Figure 12-9 is a math problem using setbacks to determine the buildable area of a lot. Remember that all the above explanations are general and may vary. You should investigate any individual symbol for its exact meaning in your city or county before interpreting it.

Title insurance does NOT give protection for zoning changes.

A. ZONING REGULATION (Controls Use)

Zoning is police power that controls only the "use" of the property, NOT ownership.

Most planning commissions, boards, or city councils have an established procedure for a change of zoning. As part of a logical procedure, four steps are usually followed. They are:

1. Giving public notice of any proposed zoning changes.
2. Calling a public hearing where interested people can voice their opinions before any changes are made.
3. Adoption or rejection of a zoning regulation.
4. If rejected, an appeal can be made to the city council, which can overrule the planning commission.

Once zoning regulations are enacted, the objecting parties have the right to appeal to the courts on the basis that the ordinance may be arbitrary or unreasonable. The usual grounds for appeal is equal protection under the ordinance. Zoning ordinances have been held invalid when it was shown that a monopoly would be created, the new ordinance rendered an adjoining lot worthless, or when it prohibited an existing business that did not create a nuisance.

Although the intent of zoning is to create reasonable uniformity, total uniformity is not required. Spot zoning might benefit the public in some cases. *SPOT ZONING is a small area that is zoned differently from the surrounding area.* For example, controlled use of commercial stores and service stations can enhance the value and utility of the residential area.

B. NONCONFORMING USE

As conditions in the area change, the zoning of existing parcels may also change. The change may cause some of the existing structures to become nonconforming. *NONCONFORMING USE is a property that is not used according to the current zoning, but which existed legally before zoning changes were enacted.* An example of nonconforming use is an apartment building with one parking space per unit where zoning changes require two parking spaces per unit. It is a general policy to let nonconforming uses continue for a time if conformity creates unnecessary hardships. However, the growing trend is for cities to charge large fees for nonconforming properties as a source of income.

Figure 12-9

SETBACK PROBLEM
(Zoning Regulations)

BUILDABLE AREA *is the maximum allowable area of a lot that a city or county allows for a building after deducting setbacks from the front, back, and sides.*

DETERMINING USABLE AREA

Question: What is the buildable space of a lot 150 feet by 50 feet if the city zoning regulation requires deducting a 20-foot setback from the front and deducting 4 feet from each side and the back?

150 Feet x 50 Feet

4-Foot Setback

20-Foot Setback · 4-Foot Setback · 4-Foot Setback

Buildable Area?

4-Foot Setback

ANSWER:

Width: 50 feet minus (4 feet on both the left and right side) = ?
50 feet - 8 Feet = **42 feet buildable width**

Length: 150 feet minus (20-foot front setback and a 4-foot rear setback) = ?
150 feet - 24 feet = **126 feet buildable length**

TOTAL:

Width x Length = Area
42 feet x 126 feet= Area
42 feet x 126 feet= 5,292 SQUARE FEET

A "grandfather" clause is "prearranged" and allows an owner to continue using his or her property in a way prohibited by the new zoning (non-conforming use).

C. VARIANCE (For Private Hardship)

One way to provide reasonable conformity is to allow zoning variances. A *VARIANCE is an exception to the existing zoning regulations in cases of special need for circumstances that might create serious hardship for property owners.* Zoning restrictions such as setbacks may be removed by petitioning for a variance.

For example, if an individual wants to construct a building that does not comply with the local zoning rule, he or she may petition for a variance. When filing this petition, the individual must prove that the construction of the building will not be detrimental to the public. Variances are often granted with special conditions such that both plans and construction be approved and initiated within a specified time.

D. CONDITIONAL USE PERMIT (For Public Benefit)

A *CONDITIONAL USE PERMIT is an exception to the current zoning for the public welfare or benefit.* Variances, on the other hand, are based on hardship.

Since zoning ordinances may be altered, most title insurance policies do not insure against zoning changes. For a small fee, an endorsement may be added to the title insurance policy that covers any losses due to zoning changes. Zoning is an environmental control that attempts to ensure uniform land use while also meeting the occasional special needs of the community.

X. Housing, Building, and Health Laws

The basic control of housing, building, and health standards is held at the state level. Although building codes and health standards are usually enforced by the local county and city agencies, contractors, factory home builders, and house builders are always regulated at the state level.

Regulatory authority of the housing and construction industry is accomplished by the state contractor's license laws, the local building codes, and the State Housing Law.

A. STATE HOUSING LAW

California has adopted a State Housing Law that sets the minimum construction and occupancy requirements for all apartments, hotels and other dwellings. It should be noted that any city or county may impose more stringent requirements if it so wishes. Construction regulations under this law are handled by local building inspectors. Occupancy and sanitation regulations are enforced by local health officers.

B. LOCAL BUILDING CODES

If there is a building code conflict, the highest construction standard controls.

Most cities and counties have additional, more stringent construction standards than the state. The *BUILDING CODE is the basic minimum construction standard for a structure.* This code includes regulation of all the basic methods, materials, and components of a structure

from the foundation to the plumbing and electrical system. Local building inspectors enforce both the state and local building codes.

New construction or building alterations require a building permit. A *BUILDING PERMIT is an approved building application that includes plans, specifications, and a plot plan.* After an examination of the application, plans and any revisions of the plans, the building permit is issued. No construction or alteration can be started until the building permit has been issued.

C. GOVERNMENT FINANCING REQUIREMENTS

To obtain certain forms of government financing toward the purchase of a home, various construction requirements must be met. These **Minimum Property Requirements (MPRs)** are usually more restrictive than state housing or local building codes. This indirect type of regulation must be considered if any FHA, VA, or CalVet financing is needed.

D. FACTORY-BUILT HOUSING LAW

The state has preempted local building codes concerning factory-built housing (prefabricated homes). These are homes that are built in sections in a factory and assembled on site. Each section is checked at the factory by state inspectors. Local inspectors oversee only the site hookup of water lines and other on-site facilities.

1. Manufactured Housing

A manufactured home is transferred with a certificate of title.

> *MANUFACTURED HOUSING, is a transportable structure in one or more eight-foot (or more) wide by 40-foot (or more) long sections that will cover 320 or more square feet that meets HUD Code Standards.* Built on a permanent chassis, it is designed to be used with or without permanent foundation when connected to the necessary utilities. If sold in California, it must meet the California Department of Housing standards.

> Real estate salespeople can also sell, lease, or finance manufactured homes as soon as they have been transformed into real property (wheels removed, placed on a foundation, and having a building permit).

A broker can sell a manufactured home if it is registered with the Department of Housing and Community Development (HCD).

> Real Estate brokers can sell manufactured homes once they are considered real property. A real estate broker must report all sales of manufactured homes within ten calendar days to the Department of Housing and Community Development (HCD). Registration cards, title, and fees are also sent there.

An agent or licensee is able to sell any new manufactured home sold with a deed.

> A new manufactured home dealer must be licensed by the Department of Housing and Community Development.

A licensee who sells a personal property manufactured home must notify the local Department of Housing and Community Development in writing within 10 calendar days.

New manufactured homes, a growing industry, can only be sold by licensed manufactured home dealers. The **Manufactured Home Purchase Agreement and Joint Escrow Instructions** form is available from CAR® (see **Figure 12-10**).

A licensee must withdraw any advertisement of a manufactured home within 48 hours after notice that it is no longer available for sale.

E. CONTRACTOR'S STATE LICENSE LAW

Construction work of less than $500 does NOT require a contractor's license.

Contractors are licensed at the state level by the Contractor's State License Board, whose main purpose is to protect the public against incompetent building contractors and subcontractors. This protection is achieved by requiring construction to be done only by licensed persons. This includes subcontract work as well as general and engineering contract work.

The construction field is divided into general engineering, general building and specialty contracting. A license is required to perform work in any of these categories. Examinations are prepared on legal matters affecting construction and cost estimation. Each applicant is further required to have a certain amount of actual experience in his or her particular field. Only construction work done on one's own home without intent to sell or lease may be undertaken without a license, but still requires a building permit.

The state housing law, administered by the codes and standards division, is designed to provide that minimum construction and occupancy standards are met.

F. HEALTH AND SANITATION (County Function)

The California State Department of Health regulates a statewide health program. Even though the state regulates it, local health officials are required by law to be appointed in every city or county. These officials enforce either state or local health laws, whichever is stricter. Health inspectors also act as health advisors. They can close down any proposed development that may cause contamination of the water supply or drainage systems, as well as any development that would cause improper sewage disposal. Furthermore, the sanitary condition of all housing is subject to control by the health authorities.

XI. Eminent Domain

A. EMINENT DOMAIN (Involuntary Taking – Condemnation)

INVOLUNTARY CONVERSION is the legal conversion of real property to personal property (money) without the voluntary act of the owner. This occurs when property is taken by eminent domain (condemnation).

Eminent domain is an involuntary conversion process, which means that the owner receives money and is allowed to buy another property, within three years, without incurring taxes.

The owner is allowed to convert back to real property (buy another property) without paying tax on the gain from the condemnation. This must be done within a three-year period and the prices of the old and new property are considered to form a new tax base. (Tax laws are complicated and subject to change, so professional tax advice is always wise.)

Figure 12-10

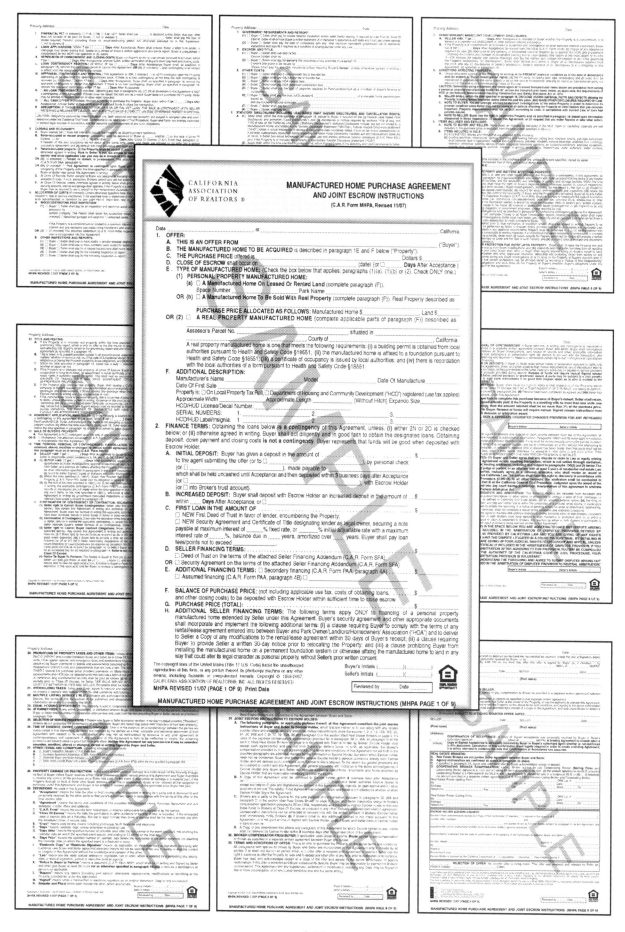

EMINENT DOMAIN is the right of the federal or state government to take private property from a landowner (with the fair market value paid as compensation to that owner) for the "public good." The use of the right of eminent domain is often referred to as "condemnation."

Property taken by the local government under the power of eminent domain must have fair and just compensation to the landowner.

If a portion of a parcel is condemned, then there may be severance damages. *SEVERANCE DAMAGE is the compensation paid an owner for "devalued remaining property" as the result of an eminent domain action.*

In some instances, the property owner will feel that the property is so devalued that he or she will file an inverse condemnation action. *INVERSE CONDEMNATION is an action whereby the property owner files suit to force the government to purchase all or part of his or her property.*

Example: Airplane flight paths cross a person's property and cause a reduction in value. The homeowner forces the government to purchase his property. This is called inverse condemnation.

The power of eminent domain can be exercised by government entities (cities and counties), utility companies, and school districts.

A renter may vacate or desert the premises when the building is condemned.

B. REDEVELOPMENT (City and County Agencies)

REDEVELOPMENT is the process of purchasing land in a run-down area (blighted) and constructing new buildings, parks, and other new construction. Early efforts at redevelopment were made by organizations such as syndication groups, realty boards, and large insurance companies. However, the difficulty of assembling the necessary parcels by negotiation alone proved to be an impossible task. There was need for a government agency that could exercise its right of eminent domain to bring, by process of law, the court condemnation orders. Redevelopment organizations have been replaced by redevelopment agencies. *REDEVELOPMENT AGENCIES are city or county-run organizations that direct the spending of federal and state money.* The cities or counties have found a new way to rebuild their areas with government money.

C. MUTUAL WATER COMPANY

A *MUTUAL WATER COMPANY is organized by water users in a given district to supply ample water at a reasonable rate.* It is usually a corporation in which the owner of each parcel of land is given a share of stock. The stock is appurtenant to the land; that is, each share of stock is attached to the land and cannot be sold separately. This enables the water company to develop uniformity and prevents speculation in the shares of stock.

Stock in a mutual water company is appurtenant to the land; it is real property.

No cash dividends are declared by these companies, but credits are given to water users if surpluses occur. On the other hand, assessments may be levied if operating revenues are not sufficient. Directors are elected by the stockholders, who usually employ one officer to operate the company, supervise the clerical help, and advise stockholders regarding any water problems.

XII. Fair Housing Laws

California first passed the Unruh Civil Rights Act (no discrimination in business, including real estate agents' services) and then the Fair Employment and Housing Act (no discrimination in housing). These were later reinforced by the Federal Civil Rights Act of 1968.

Figure 12-11 describes the different types of civil rights violations.

A. STATE LAW – UNRUH CIVIL RIGHTS ACT (No Discrimination in Business)

The Unruh Civil Rights Act was the first civil rights act in California; it prohibits "steering" and "block busting" as a real estate business practice.

The Unruh Civil Rights Act (California Civil Code Section 51) prohibits business establishments from discriminating on the basis of sex, race, color, religion, ancestry, national origin, disability, or medical condition. Assembly Bill 1400 adds marital status and sexual orientation to the list. California continues to prohibit any arbitrary discrimination.

B. STATE LAW – FAIR EMPLOYMENT AND HOUSING ACT (FEHA)

The Fair Employment and Housing Act (FEHA) (no discrimination in housing) established the Commission of Fair Employment and Housing to investigate and take action against property owners, financial institutions, and real estate licensees who engage in discriminatory practices.

It clearly defines discrimination as the refusal to sell, rent, or lease housing accommodations, including misrepresentation as to availability, offering inferior terms, and cancellations on the basis of race, color, religion, sex, family status, national origin, ancestry, and age. It also outlaws sale or rental advertisements containing discriminatory information.

Owners of three single-family homes and owner-occupied buildings that are four units or less are exempt from Fair Housing Laws under the "Mom and Pop" provision.

C. STATE LAW – HOUSING FINANCIAL DISCRIMINATION ACT

The Housing Financial Discrimination Act prohibits financial institutions from engaging in discriminatory loan practices called "redlining."

In remedying such violations, the state may force a landowner to proceed with the rental or sale in question, provide comparable housing accommodations if the original is no longer available or pay punitive damages up to $1,000. Under the **Housing Financial Discrimination Act of 1977**, the practice of redlining is specifically outlawed. *REDLINING is the practice by financial institutions of denying loans or varying finance terms based on the location of a given property, regardless of the credit worthiness of the borrower.* This law explicitly forbids discrimination because of the race of the borrower or the racial composition of the neighborhood in which the borrower's prospective home is located.

The Housing Financial Discrimination Act (no redlining) covers 1-to-4 units (at least one owner-occupied) used for residential purposes, but an owner seeking a home improvement loan need not occupy the property.

SUBDIVISIONS AND GOVERNMENT CONTROL

Figure 12-11

Fair Housing Violations and Possible Remedies

REDLINING	The refusal of a loan or insurance based upon a property's location (zip code).
STEERING	Showing a client property in only one type of neighborhood, such as a Caucasian buyer in a Caucasian neighborhood, and the refusal to communicate the availability of housing in other neighborhoods.
OWNER TELLS AGENT NOT TO SHOW PROPERTY TO MINORITY	The agent is relieved of the duty to show the property to anyone, including a minority who has requested to see the property.
CONTRACT REFUSED TO BUYER BECAUSE OF RACE	ADVISE BUYER of the right to complain to the Fair Employment and Housing (FEH) and WARN SELLER that he or she has violated fair housing laws.
RACE RESTRICTIONS	Any race restriction is UNENFORCEABLE. It has NO LEGAL effect upon a transaction.
PANIC SELLING OR BLOCK BUSTING AND PANIC PEDDLING	An agent intentionally incites existing homeowners to sell their properties by saying that property values will fall because persons of a different race or religion have targeted a move into their neighborhood.
SALE OF PROPERTY (AGENT ASKED TO DISCRIMINATE)	Agent must REFUSE the listing.

Lending institutions in violation of the Housing Financial Discrimination Act may be required to pay for damages, limited to $1,000 for each offense.

D. FEDERAL LAWS (Federal Civil Rights Act of 1968)

Federal law prohibits discrimination on the part of owners of property and their agents based on the U.S. Supreme Court case *Jones v. Mayer* (after the Civil War) and Title VIII of the Civil Rights Act of 1968.

For all practical purposes, discrimination laws evolved from the U.S. Supreme Court Case *Jones v. Mayer*, Title VIII of the Civil Rights Act of 1968 and the 13th Amendment to the U.S. Constitution.

At the federal level, the Federal Civil Rights Act of 1968 reinforced the Unruh and Fair Employment and Housing Acts: 1) Any discrimination that the two acts did not prohibit was explicitly outlawed. **THERE ARE NO EXCEPTIONS**; 2) It makes it illegal for real estate licensees to engage in discriminatory practices regardless of any instructions the agent may have received from the seller or landlord. If asked to discriminate in the sale of a property, the salesperson must refuse to accept the listing; 3) It bars real estate boards or multiple listing services from discriminating by denying participation or restricting terms and conditions of membership; 4) It requires a fair housing poster to be displayed at all real estate offices and subdivision model homes. **The poster (see Figure 12-12) must also be displayed at all financial institutions or by mortgage lenders who make loans to the general public**.

The only time an agent can refuse to show a property to a buyer is when the owner's have informed the agent that they will be out of town and, during their absence, the broker has been instructed not to show the property to anyone.

Note – A lender who charges an additional fee per annum for processing loans to non-English speaking applicants because the lender must hire non-English speaking employees, is practicing discrimination.

1. Federal Civil Rights Act Expanded in 1988
(HUD Can Initiate Housing Discrimination Cases)

A 1988 federal law allows the U.S. Government to take court action if it believes discrimination exists in home sales or apartment rentals. Landlords are explicitly forbidden to discriminate against families with children under 18 years of age. The only exemptions from this would be in retirement communities where most of the residents are more than 55 years of age.

This federal law also extends protections to handicapped home buyers or tenants. As of 1991, builders of all new apartment buildings were required to include ground floor rooms suitable for use by residents in wheelchairs.

The Housing and Urban Development (HUD) Department is authorized to bring enforcement action against sellers and landlords who defy this law. Fines of up to $10,000 have been authorized for first time violators, up to $25,000 for a second offense within five years and up to $50,000 for a third offense within seven years. Those accused of violating this tough statute would face an administrative judge unless they specifically requested a jury trial.

Complaints should be filed with Housing and Urban Development (HUD). Fair Employment and Housing will enforce any action.

When discrimination takes place (under the Civil Rights Act of 1968), the aggrieved party may file civil suit in federal, state, or local court, and file a complaint with HUD.

Figure 12-12

Equal Housing Lender

We Do Business In Accordance With The Federal Fair Housing Law

(Title VIII of the Civil Rights Act of 1968, as Amended by the Housing and Community Development Act of 1974)

IT IS ILLEGAL TO DISCRIMINATE AGAINST ANY PERSON BECAUSE OF RACE, COLOR, NATIONAL ORIGIN, RELIGION, SEX, FAMILIAL STATUS (including children under the age of 18 living with parents or legal custodians, pregnant women, and people securing custody of children under the age of 18), and HANDICAP, TO:

■ Deny a loan for the purpose of purchasing, constructing, improving, repairing or maintaining a dwelling or

■ Discriminate in fixing of the amount, interest rate, duration, application procedures or other terms or conditions of such a loan.

IF YOU BELIEVE YOU HAVE BEEN DISCRIMINATED AGAINST, YOU MAY SEND A COMPLAINT TO:

U.S. DEPARTMENT OF HOUSING AND URBAN DEVELOPMENT Assistant Secretary for Fair Housing and Equal Opportunity Washington, D.C. 20410

or call your local HUD Area or Insuring Office.

E. THE REAL ESTATE COMMISSIONER AND "NAR" ALSO ENFORCE ANTI-DISCRIMINATION

The Real Estate Commissioner

Regulations of the Real Estate Commissioner

(10177 of the Business and Professions Code)

Regulations have been issued by the Real Estate Commissioner that cover any discrimination with regard to housing. Disciplinary action will be taken against any real estate licensee who violates these regulations. This could include a suspension, fine, revocation of license, or prosecution by the local district attorney. See Chapter 14 for more about the Commissioner's Regulations.

The National Association of REALTORS®
Code of Ethics

The National Association of REALTORS® (NAR) Code of Ethics and Fair Practices forbids discrimination against any minority group. Any violation by a real estate licensee could subject that licensee to disciplinary action from the local board of REALTORS®.

Article 10 states that the REALTOR® shall not deny equal service (or be a party to any plan or agreement to deny service) to any person for reasons of race, color, religion, handicap, family status or national origin.

XIII. CHAPTER SUMMARY

There are two basic subdivision laws, including the **Subdivision Map Act** (2 or more lots) that gives cities and counties control over the physical design of a subdivision, and the **Subdivided Lands Law** (5 or more lots) that protects the purchasers of property in new subdivisions from fraud, misrepresentation, or deceit in the marketing of subdivisions.

The subdivided lands law requires a subdivider to give a buyer a copy of the public report disclosing important facts about the subdivision. A **preliminary public report** allows property reservations before the final report is issued, and a **final public report**, which must be kept by the subdivider for a three year period, is the official report that must be given to the buyer. In addition to the public reports an **environmental impact report (EIR)** may be necessary and disclosure of location within a **special studies zone** (earthquake zone).

A **master plan** is a comprehensive guide through which zoning establishes an ideal plan for the city's development in the future. **Zoning** is the city or county's exercise of **police power**, which are rulings made to control the use (not the ownership) of private property for the protection of the public's health, safety, and welfare.

Eminent domain (or **condemnation**) is the right of the government to take private property from a landowner (in exchange for fair market value) for the "public good." If any remaining property is devalued because of the condemnation, the government may pay severance damage. If the property is so devalued that a property owner feels the government should take all of the property, he or she may file an action called **inverse condemnation**.

California was one of the first states with fair housing laws. These include the **Unruh Civil Rights Act**, which prohibits steering and blockbusting in real estate, and the **Fair Employment and Housing Act (FEHA)**, which established the **Department of Fair Employment and Housing** to address housing discrimination. In addition, the **Housing Financial Discrimination Act of 1977** prohibits financial institutions from engaging in discriminatory loan practices called **redlining**.

Federal law also prohibits discrimination on the part of owners of property and their agents based on the Supreme Court Case *Jones v. Mayer*, **Title VIII of the Civil Rights Act of 1968**, and the **13th Amendment**. In 1988, the Federal Civil Rights Act was expanded to allow HUD to enforce actions against sellers and landlords who defy the law. The **DRE** and **NAR** also enforce anti-discrimination laws.

CHAPTER 12

XIV. TERMINOLOGY

A. Building Code
B. Building Permit
C. Civil Rights Act of 1968
D. Common Area
E. Community Apartment Project
F. Conditional Use Permit
G. Condominium
H. Eminent Domain
I. Environmental Impact Report
J. Housing Financial Discrimination Act

K. *Jones v. Mayer*
L. Land Project
M. Manufactured Homes
N. Master Plan
O. Mutual Water Company
P. Nonconforming Use
Q. Planned Development (PD)
R. Planning Commission
S. Public Report
T. Redevelopment Agency
U. Redlining
V. Fair Employment and Housing Act

W. Severance Damages
X. Spot Zoning
Y. Subdivided Lands Law
Z. Subdivision Map Act
AA. Unruh Act
BB. Variance
CC. Zoning Laws

1. ____ A comprehensive zoning plan to help a city grow in an orderly and sound manner, both economically and ecologically.

2. ____ A water company in which the owners are the customers.

3. ____ A permit given by a local government to construct a building or make improvements.

4. ____ A report given to a prospective purchaser(s) in a new subdivision.

5. ____ Zoning on a parcel-by-parcel basis, rather than a comprehensive general or master plan. Considered poor planning.

6. ____ The outlining in red on a map of certain "high risk" areas where lenders will not extend credit, regardless of the qualifications of the applicants (illegal practice).

7. ____ The local government board which must approve proposed building projects according to zones; it must answer to the county board or city council.

8. ____ A subdivision where there is private ownership of individual lots as well as common ownership of another lot, usually a swimming pool or a recreation room.

9. ____ A report of the probable effect of a development on the ecology of the surrounding area. The report is prepared by an independent company and follows federal, state, or local guidelines.

10. ____ An isolated rural subdivision, operating under federal guidelines, with certain rights of rescission.

11. ____ Permission to change a portion of zoning requirements without changing the entire zoning.

12. ____ Loss in value to the remaining property when part of a parcel is condemned and seized by the government for public use.

13. ____ A corporation formed for the purpose of holding title to a building. Each shareholder receives the right to occupy a dwelling unit but must pay property taxes and insurance in common with the other owners.

14. ____ The area owned in common by all the owners of condominiums or planned unit developments.

15. ____ A property that does not conform to the current zoning of the area. Usually, the property was built in conformity and then the zoning was changed.

16. ____ A structure of two or more units, the interior spaces of which are individually owned; the balance of the property is owned in common by the owners of the individual units.

17. ____ A comprehensive set of laws that control the construction of buildings, including design, materials used, repair, remodeling, and other similar factors.

18. ____ Generally, the improvement of land in accordance with a city renewal project.

19.____A governmental right to acquire private property for public use by condemnation, and the payment of just compensation.

20.____Homes that are not truly mobile but are constructed in the same manner as trailers, as opposed to conventional, on-site construction.

21.____Laws that require cities and counties to specify the uses allowable for real property in different areas or zones.

22.____An act requiring developers to obtain local government (city or county) approval for the detailed construction plan of their subdivision.

23.____A specific exception to zoning laws, granted for the general good of the community.

24.____A law requiring an acknowledgment from the Department of Real Estate that a subdivision has met the minimum requirements for filing the necessary reports.

25.____Established far-reaching federal anti-discrimination laws. Requires that fair housing posters be displayed at real estate offices and lending institutions.

26.____Civil War-era court case that was the basis for current civil rights laws.

27.____State fair housing law established to eliminate redlining.

28.____Established the California Fair Employment and Housing Act.

29.____The state fair housing law that disallowed discrimination in business, including real estate agent's services.

CHAPTER 12

XV. CHAPTER QUIZ

1. Zoning, planning and governmental land use are important examples of:
   a. encumbrances.
   b. eminent domain.
   c. deed restrictions.
   d. exercise of police power.

2. After several lots have been sold in a subdivision, the Real Estate Commissioner was informed of misrepresentation being made by a developer. The Commissioner may stop the sale of more lots by:
   a. revoking the final public report.
   b. issuing a writ of prohibition.
   c. issuing a desist and refrain order.
   d. filing an accusation in court.

3. Which of the following must be given to every buyer of a condominium unit?
   a. Copy of the CC&Rs
   b. Copy of the bylaws
   c. Copy of the most recent financial statement of the condo association
   d. All of the above

4. A timeshare company advertises the sale of timeshares on a billboard. If the billboard does not disclose the requirement to listen to a sales presentation in order to receive the promised prize, this is:
   a. legal, if the prospect is notified within 24 hours after purchasing the time share.
   b. illegal, because the broker did not disclose the requirement to listen to a sales presentation in order to receive the prize.
   c. legal.
   d. illegal, only if the timeshare company is a corporation.

5. A "Negative Declaration" is:
   a. part of the agent's section in the Transfer Disclosure Statement (TDS).
   b. issued by the title company if the property is unmarketable due to certain matters of record listed in the abstract of title.
   c. utilized by escrow if there are sufficient funds available to close escrow.
   d. a statement by an expert affirming that a new subdivision will have no significant negative impact on the environment.

6. What is the primary tool used by planning commissions to implement a general plan?
   a. Eminent domain
   b. Adverse possession
   c. Zoning
   d. Master plan

7. A change of zoning from industrial to residential is called:

    a. downzoning.
    b. spotzoning.
    c. upzoning.
    d. crosszoning.

8. What kind of manufactured home can a broker sell?

    a. Certified manufactured home
    b. Registered manufactured home
    c. Licensed manufactured home
    d. All of the above

9. Airplane flight paths cross a person's property and cause a reduction in value. If the homeowner forces the government to purchase his/her property, this is called:

    a. inverse condemnation.
    b. functional obsolescence.
    c. police power.
    d. none of the above.

10. A lender charges an additional fee of 1/8% per annum for processing loans to non-English speaking applicants since the lender must hire non-English speaking employees to communicate with these borrowers. This would be considered:

    a. good business practice.
    b. an unethical business practice as defined in the UCC.
    c. legal in the lender must pay higher wages to accommodate the non-English speaking clients.
    d. a form of illegal discrimination.

ANSWERS: 1. d; 2. c; 3. d; 4. b; 5. d; 6. c; 7. a; 8. b; 9. a; 10. d

CHAPTER 13
Taxation of Real Estate

Taxes are an important aspect of all real estate transactions. Property owners are taxed annually on the property they own. In addition, there are other state and federal taxes that must be paid in order to buy, sell, or give away real property. **Figure 13-1** illustrates the five taxes with which every taxpayer, investor, and salesperson should be familiar. The amount of tax and who must pay the tax are often major factors to consider in the transfer of real estate.

Figure 13-1

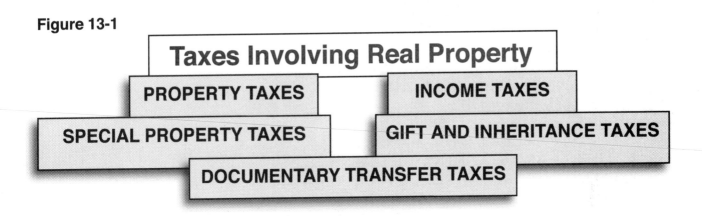

I. Real Property Taxes

A city or county receives most of its operating revenue from the assessment and collection of real property taxes. *REAL PROPERTY TAXES are taxes determined according to the value of the real property, and are paid annually or semi-annually.* These taxes are called ad valorem taxes. An *AD VALOREM TAX is a tax that is charged in proportion to the value of the property.* Property taxes are based on the concept that taxes should be assessed in accordance with a person's ability to pay. In the case of real estate, the higher the value of the property, the higher the property taxes.

"Ad valorem" means taxed "according to value." Real property is reassessed each time it is transferred (sold) at 100% of its selling price (or market value, if it is higher).

CHAPTER OUTLINE

The ***COUNTY ASSESSOR*** *is the county officer who has the responsibility of determining the assessed valuation of land, improvements, and personal property used in business.* The county assessor determines the value of both county and city properties, except in a few cities that use their own assessors. In Los Angeles County, the City of Pasadena has its own assessor who assesses the property in that city. San Francisco is unique because the city and county assessor's functions are combined.

The county assessor accumulates a list of all private owners of real property in his/her jurisdiction. The "assessment roll" is used to establish the tax base for the county.

www.co.la.ca.us/assessor
L.A. County Assessor

In general all real property, except that which is owned by the government, and all tangible personal property except inventory used in a business, is subject to property tax assessment in California. **Intangible personal property, such as shares of stock, goodwill of a business opportunity, and promissory notes, as well as tangible property, such as household furnishings and personal effects of individuals, are not assessed or taxed.**

County Assessor assesses; County Board of Supervisors sets tax rate.

The ***COUNTY TAX COLLECTOR*** *is the county officer who collects the real property taxes.* He or she only collects taxes; the county tax collector has nothing to do with determining how much tax is levied. If the real property taxes are not paid, the county tax collector will eventually require that the property be sold at a tax sale.

www.cacttc.org/start.html
List of Tax Collectors

A. PROPOSITION 13

PROPOSITION 13 *limits the amount of taxes to a maximum of 1%* of the March 1, 1975, market value of the property plus the cumulative increase of 2% in market value each year thereafter.*

Improvements made after March 1, 1975, are added to the value in the year they are made. If ownership has changed after March 1, 1975, the tax is limited to 1%* of the market value plus the 2% cumulative increase each succeeding year. (In some cases, property values came down, lowering taxes instead of raising them by 2%.) Any state-allowed exemptions are deducted after figuring the basic tax (see **Figure 13-2**).

Voted indebtedness may increase this rate beyond 1%, from area-to-area, with voter approval.

B. REAL PROPERTY TAX BASE IS TRANSFERABLE (Props 60 & 90)

Under the following conditions (based on Propositions 60 and 90), homeowners may be permitted to transfer their current Proposition 13 tax base with them when they buy a new home:

1. Homeowners over the age of 55, and

2. Home purchased within two years of original sale, and

3. Replacement home of equal or lesser value, and

4. New home must be in the same county, or another participating county (check first).

Propositions 60 and 90 allow "empty-nesters" to purchase new homes (one at a time) while holding on to their low tax base, thus freeing up larger multiple bedroom homes for younger families.

ASSESSED VALUATION is set at 100% of the property's selling price or fair market value, whichever is higher, plus a 2% increase for every year the property has been owned, but only as far back as March 1, 1975. The tax rate is set at 1% of fair market value (or selling price, whichever is higher) plus any voter-approved indebtedness. Properties that are transferred and new construction are subject to a new appraisal based upon the current market value or selling price, whichever is higher. Existing structures are given a new assessment each year as of January 1. New construction and transfers are assessed immediately upon the first day of the next month. See **Figures 13-3** and **13-4** for an example of a property tax bill.

Real property is assessed each time it is transferred (sold) at 100% of its selling price (or market value if it is higher). A "change of ownership statement" must be filed with an assessor within 45 days of change.

C. PROPERTY TAXES BECOME A SPECIFIC LIEN

Property taxes due upon real property are, in effect, liens against that specific property. Business personal property taxes (trade fixtures) also become liens against that specific real property on the same tax bill. For example, the furniture in furnished apartments is taxed as business personal property and is usually included on the property tax bill.

Property taxes for the following fiscal year become a lien against the real property on January 1 of the current year. Officially, the first installment for half of the taxes becomes due on November 1 and is delinquent after 5 P.M. on December 10. The second installment is due on February 1 and is delinquent if not paid by 5 P.M. on April 10. If either December 10 or April 10 falls on a Saturday, Sunday, or legal holiday, the delinquency date is extended to the close of the next business day.

Figure 13-2

Proposition 13

That Article XII A is added to the Constitution to read:

Section 1.

(a) The maximum amount of any ad valorem tax on real property shall not exceed one percent (1%)* of the full cash value of such property. The one percent (1%)* tax to be collected by the counties and apportioned according to law to the districts within the counties.

(b) The limitation provided for in subdivision (a) shall not apply to ad valorem taxes or special assessments to pay the interest and redemption charges on any indebtedness approved by the voters prior to the time this section becomes effective.

Section 2.

(a) The full cash value means the county assessors valuation of real property as shown on the 1975-76 tax bill under "full cash value," or thereafter, the appraised value of real property when purchased, newly constructed, or a change in ownership has occurred after the 1975 assessment. All real property not already assessed up to the 1975-76 tax levels may be reassessed to reflect that valuation.

(b) The fair market value base may reflect from year to year the inflationary rate not to exceed two percent (2%) for any given year or reduction as shown in the consumer price index or comparable data for the area under taxing jurisdiction.

Section 3.

From and after the effective date of this article, any changes in state taxes enacted for the purpose of increasing revenues collected pursuant thereto whether by increased rates or changes in methods of computation must be imposed by an Act passed by not less than two-thirds of all members elected to each of the two houses of the Legislature, except that no new ad valorem taxes on real property, or sales or transaction taxes on the sales of real property may be imposed.

Section 4.

Cities, counties, and special districts, by a two-thirds vote of the qualified electors of such district, may impose special taxes on such district, except ad valorem taxes on real property or a transaction tax or sales tax on the sale of real property within such city, county, or special district.

Section 5.

This article shall take effect for the tax year beginning on July 1 following the passage of this Amendment, except Section 3 which shall become effective upon the passage of this article.

Section 6.

If any section, part, clause, or phrase hereof is for any reason held to be invalid or unconstitutional, the remaining sections shall not be affected but will remain in full force and effect.

Voted indebtedness may increase this rate beyond 1% from local area to area with voter approval.

Figure 13-3

2007	ANNUAL PROPERTY TAX BILL	2007

CITIES, COUNTY, SCHOOLS AND ALL OTHER TAXING AGENCIES IN LOS ANGELES COUNTY

SECURED PROPERTY TAX FOR FISCAL YEAR JULY 1, 2007 TO JUNE 30, 2008

MARK J. SALADINO, TREASURER AND TAX COLLECTOR

FOR ASSISTANCE CALL 1 (213) 974-2111 OR 1 (888) 807-2111, ON THE WEB AT www.lacountypropertytax.com

ASSESSOR'S ID. NO. CK

DETAIL OF TAXES DUE FOR **4225 011 081 07 000 03**

PROPERTY IDENTIFICATION
ASSESSOR'S ID.NO.: 4225 011 081 07 000
OWNER OF RECORD AS OF JANUARY 1, 2007
SAME AS BELOW

AGENCY	AGENCY PHONE NO.	RATE		AMOUNT
GENERAL TAX LEVY				
ALL AGENCIES		1.000000	$	2,361.20
VOTED INDEBTEDNESS				
CITY-LOS ANGELES		.038051	$	89.85
METRO WATER DIST		.004500		10.63
COMMNTY COLLEGE		.008794		20.76
UNIFIED SCHOOLS		.123342		291.23
DIRECT ASSESSMENTS				
LA STORMWATER	(213) 485-2402		$	8.05
LACITY PARK DIST	(213) 978-1896			14.60
COUNTY PARK DIST	(213) 738-2983			15.38
FLOOD CONTROL	(626) 458-4337			10.09
CITY 911 FUND	(213) 978-1099			14.79
TRAUMA/EMERG SRV	(866) 587-2862			47.16
LA WEST MOSQ AB	(310) 915-7370			5.57

MAILING ADDRESS

Wolfgang Hubie
100 Internet Highway
Culver City, CA 90230

ELECTRONIC FUND TRANSFER (EFT) NUMBER
ID#: 19 4225 011 081 9 YEAR:07 SEQUENCE:000 3
PIN: 664860

For **American Express, Mastercard and Visa** payments call 1 (888) 473-0835 and have available the EFT number listed above. Service fees will be charged.

SPECIAL INFORMATION

PROPERTY LOCATION AND/OR PROPERTY DESCRIPTION

*TR=P M 72-26-27 CONDOMINIUM*UNITS
1 AND A

ASSESSOR'S REGIONAL OFFICE
REGION #07 INDEX: TRA:00067
WEST DISTRICT OFFICE
6120 BRISTOL PARKWAY
CULVER CITY CA 90230
(310)665-5300

ACCT. NO.:   PRINT NO.: 684741 BILL ID.:

TOTAL TAXES DUE		$2,889.31
FIRST INSTALLMENT TAXES	DUE NOV. 1, 2007	$1,444.66
SECOND INSTALLMENT TAXES DUE FEB. 1, 2008		$1,444.65

VALUATION INFORMATION

ROLL YEAR 07-08	CURRENT ASSESSED VALUE	TAXABLE VALUE
LAND	139,151	139,151
IMPROVEMENTS	103,969	103,969
TOTAL		243,120
LESS EXEMPTION: HOME		7,000
NET TAXABLE VALUE		236,120

THERE WILL BE A $50.00 CHARGE FOR ANY CHECK RETURNED BY THE BANK.
KEEP THIS UPPER PORTION FOR YOUR RECORDS. YOUR CANCELLED CHECK IS YOUR RECEIPT.

D. PROPERTY TAX TIME TABLE

The city or county fiscal year starts on July 1 and ends on June 30. All revenues and expenditures are planned for this period of time. **Figure 13-5** illustrates all the important dates that are associated with property taxes. Assessable property is evaluated by the assessor on January 1 for the upcoming year in the name of the property's legal owner on that date. Most cities allow the county assessor to evaluate the property in both the county and the incorporated parts of the

Figure 13-4

DETACH AND MAIL THIS STUB WITH YOUR 2ND INSTALLMENT PAYMENT
DO NOT INCLUDE NOTES WITH YOUR PAYMENT
DO NOT STAPLE, TAPE OR CLIP PAYMENT STUB OR CHECK

ANNUAL   2007

Wolfgang Hubie
100 Internet Highway
Culver City, CA 90230

ASSESSOR'S ID. NO.   CK   PK
4225 011 081 07 000   03   2

2ND INSTALLMENT DUE   INDICATE AMOUNT PAID

FOR MAILING ADDRESS CHANGE
PLEASE MARK BOX BELOW AND
COMPLETE FORM ON REVERSE SIDE
OF THIS PAYMENT COUPON.

PAYMENT DUE 02/01/08 ———————→ $1,444.65
IF NOT RECEIVED OR POSTMARKED BY 04/10/08
REMIT AMOUNT OF $1,599.11

MAKE CHECKS PAYABLE TO:
Please write the ASSESSOR'S ID. NO.
on the lower left corner of your check.

LOS ANGELES COUNTY TAX COLLECTOR
P.O. BOX 54018
LOS ANGELES, CA 90054-0018

63008

08607000342250110810000144465000015991100820410

2ND

DETACH AND MAIL THIS STUB WITH YOUR 1ST INSTALLMENT PAYMENT
DO NOT INCLUDE NOTES WITH YOUR PAYMENT
DO NOT STAPLE, TAPE OR CLIP PAYMENT STUB OR CHECK

ANNUAL   2007

Wolfgang Hubie
100 Internet Highway
Culver City, CA 90230

ASSESSOR'S ID. NO.   CK   PK
4225 011 081 07 000   03   1

1ST INSTALLMENT DUE   INDICATE AMOUNT PAID

FOR MAILING ADDRESS CHANGE
PLEASE MARK BOX AND
COMPLETE FORM ON REVERSE SIDE
OF THIS PAYMENT COUPON.

PAYMENT DUE 11/01/07 ———————→ $1,444.66
IF NOT RECEIVED OR POSTMARKED BY 12/10/07
REMIT AMOUNT OF $1,589.12

MAKE CHECKS PAYABLE TO:
Please write the ASSESSOR'S ID. NO.
on the lower left corner of your check.

LOS ANGELES COUNTY TAX COLLECTOR
P.O. BOX 54018
LOS ANGELES, CA 90054-0018

73011

07707000342250110810000144466000015891201111210

1ST

Figure 13-5

PROPERTY TAX TIME TABLE

January 1	July 1	November 1	February 1
Property tax becomes a lien on real property	Fiscal year starts	1st installment is due and delinquent after December 10 at 5 P.M.	2nd installment is due and delinquent after April 10 at 5 P.M.

county, which are the cities. In a few rare cases as stated earlier, cities may use their own assessors. County assessors complete their assessment rolls by July 1, the beginning of the government (fiscal) year. Important tax dates can be remembered by "**No Darn Fooling Around**" as follows:

N   November 1 (first installment)
D   December 10 (first installment is delinquent)
F   February 1 (second installment)
A   April 10 (second installment is delinquent)

Property taxes become a lien on real property on January 1.

E. PROPERTY TAX PRORATION PROBLEM

Proration question: Who owes whom how much?

If the seller of the subject property has paid both the 1st and 2nd installments of the property taxes for a total annual bill of $2,760, what is the proration of property taxes for both the seller and buyer if the buyer takes possession on May 1?

Remember: Escrow prorates property taxes using old (seller's) assessed value (tax bill).

The first step is to determine the amount of taxes per month. The annual tax bill of $2,760 is divided by 12 months to determine that the monthly tax is $230. Since the seller paid the property taxes through the month of June (the end of the fiscal tax year, which is July 1 through June 30), and the buyer took possession on May 1, two months of paid property taxes are owed the seller. The buyer would owe the seller for two months (May and June) that were already paid by the seller. This amount would be $460 (2 x $230).

When a property is sold, the buyer will receive one new property tax bill, but it may be followed by other updated property tax bills referred to as **supplemental property tax bills** (see **Figure 13-6**).

F. HOMEOWNER'S PROPERTY TAX EXEMPTION

Homeowner's property tax exemption is $7,000 of assessed valuation.

The *HOMEOWNER'S PROPERTY TAX EXEMPTION is a deduction on the property tax bill of the first $7,000 of assessed value of an owner-occupied property.* A homeowner's exemption on your home does the following:

1. All personal property of the homeowner is exempt from property taxes.

2. A resident owner receives a $7,000 homeowner's exemption in assessed value if the property is the principal residence on the 1st of March.

The time to file for the homeowner's exemption is from January 1 to April 15 in order to receive the full exemption. Once the exemption is filed, it remains on the property until the homeowner terminates it. If the exemption is terminated, a new claim form must be obtained from, and filed with, the assessor to regain eligibility.

Qualifying owner-occupied residential property receives a $7,000 homeowner's exemption. For example, an assessed value of $500,000 minus the homeowner's exemption of $7,000 is $493,000. (Prop. 13 tax rate is 1% of the $7,000, so the tax savings, in reality, is only $70.)

Figure 13-6

Supplemental Property Tax Bills

The law requires reassessment of property **immediately** when it changes ownership or when new construction is completed. While the amount of the supplemental assessment is still determined in accordance with Proposition 13, the actual effect is to "speed up" reassessment of property. In fact, prior to the change in the law, property was generally not reappraised until January 1.

The Office of Assessor enters the new property value onto the assessment roll as of the first of the month following the month in which the property changes ownership or new construction is completed.

Depending upon the date you purchase property or the date construction is completed, you will receive **one or more** supplemental tax bills in addition to your regular tax bill. Taxes on the supplemental tax roll become a lien against the real property on the date of change in ownership or the date new construction is completed.

G. HOMEOWNER'S AND RENTER'S PROPERTY TAX REBATE
(Senior Citizens and Disabled Persons)

This is a property tax relief law for any resident who is 62 years of age or older as of January 1, and has a household income of not more than $12,000 for the calendar year. The applicant must have owned and occupied his or her home within the fiscal year. Persons under the age of 62 who are totally disabled also qualify for this rebate. A similar program provides a rebate to elderly and disabled persons who rent their homes or apartments.

All relief is in the form of a property tax rebate granted to the applicant. The amount of the property tax rebate is a percentage of household income on the first $8,500 of assessed valuation. The exact amount of rebate is determined by the Senior Citizen's Property Tax Assistance branch of the State Franchise Tax Board.

Rebate applicants pay property taxes as usual during the year and their application must be filed between May 16 and August 31. The claim form is processed and the rebate checks are sent to the applicant. The form may be obtained from the local Franchise Tax Board office.

SENIOR CITIZEN'S PROPERTY TAX ASSISTANCE
P. O. BOX 1588
SACRAMENTO, CALIFORNIA 95807

Senior citizens may be able to defer the payment of the property taxes on their residence. In order to find out if they qualify for the program, senior citizens should contact the State Franchise Tax Board.

H. DISABLED AND SENIOR CITIZEN'S PROPERTY TAX POSTPONEMENT

Seniors who are 62 years of age or older and have a household income of $24,000 or less may qualify for this tax postponement assistance program. This program offers them the option of having the state pay all or part of the taxes on their homes. In return, a lien is placed on the property for the amount that the state has to pay. This specific lien becomes payable when the taxpayer moves or dies. In effect, the homeowner is relieved of his or her tax burden in exchange for a lien on his or her home to be paid upon death. California has extended this program to include persons under the age of 62 who are legally disabled.

I. VETERAN'S EXEMPTION

Any California resident who served in the military during a time of war is entitled to an annual $4,000 property tax exemption against the assessed value of one property. This exemption also applies to the widow, widowed mother, or pensioned father of a deceased veteran. However, the exempted property is limited to an assessed value of less than $5,000 for a single veteran or $10,000 if he or she is married. For disabled California veterans who qualify, however, the assessment limit can be raised up to $100,000.

J. TAX EXEMPT PROPERTY

In California there are some properties that are partially or totally tax exempt. All real property that is owned by the federal, state, county, or city government is automatically tax exempt. This is a huge benefit to the federal government, as it owns 45% of California land. Eastern states benefit because only about 10% of their land is owned by the federal government. **A lessee with possessory interest in oil and gas rights on government owned property is not exempt from property taxes**.

Since California has many national and state parks, the majority of land in this state is tax exempt. In addition, 50 percent of all growing crops, young orchard trees, immature timber, and young grapevines are tax exempt.

Property of nonprofit organizations used for religious, charitable, medical, or educational purposes is tax exempt.

K. PROPERTY TAX APPEALS

Over-assessments can be taken to the appeals board.

People who feel that the assessment of their property is not correct may appeal the assessment. Appeals would be directed to the Board of Equalization (the property tax assessment appeals board) in the county in which the property is located between July 2 and August 26 (in most counties). After it considers the case, the Board may reduce an assessment, or it may increase it, or it may issue a new assessment if the property has not been assessed before.

In most small and many medium sized counties, the County Board of Supervisors serves as the Board of Equalization. In larger counties with a larger number of properties to assess, a special Tax Appeals Board is usually established. This board has no control over tax rates in general, but is the government body that makes individual assessment decisions on individual properties.

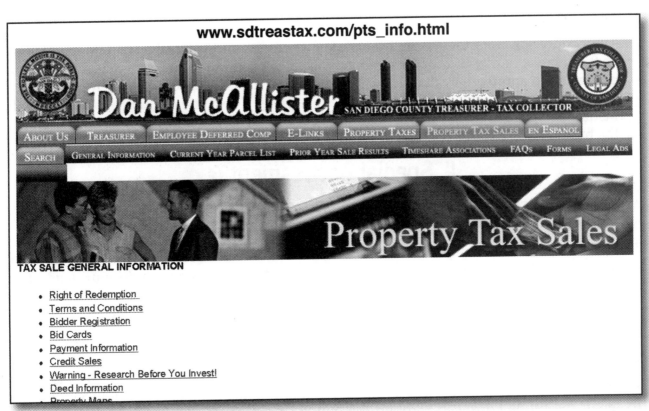

If a property owner wishes to protest the real property tax assessment, he or she can do so by contacting the appeals board office for detailed information. This Board of Equalization agency may reduce an assessed value that has been appealed.

L. DELINQUENT TAX SALE (Book Sale)

Each year, on or before June 8, the county tax collector publishes a list of tax delinquent properties. This is his or her "notice of intent to sell" all such properties on which the property taxes have not been paid for one year. *Strictly speaking, this is not a true sale but is a formality called a* **BOOK SALE**, *that starts a five-year redemption period.* If the property is not redeemed within five years, it will be deeded over to the state.

Properties may be redeemed by anyone upon the payment of taxes, interest, costs, and redemption penalties. The tax collector gives a receipt called a "**certificate of redemption**" as evidence of payment. If the owner cannot pay for all past due taxes and costs at once, he or she may pay them in five annual installment payments, providing all current taxes are paid.

If taxes are NOT paid on or before June 30, the property is sold to the state. This sale starts the running of the redemption period, which is five years.

M. SECOND SALE (After Five Years)

After five years, if the property has not been redeemed, the delinquent property is deeded to the state.

This is the official sale, and the former owner may now redeem the property only if the state has not sold the property at public auction.

N. SALE TO THE PUBLIC

The county tax collector will sell the state-owned properties to other taxing agencies or to the highest bidder at a public tax auction. The minimum bid is established by the tax collector and approved by the county board of supervisors. All such sales are for cash at the time of the sale. The purchaser then receives a tax deed. Most title insurance companies will insure the tax deed sale after one year has elapsed. But, if any difficulties are encountered, the buyer may clear title through a "quiet title" court action.

II. Special Assessment Tax

A *SPECIAL ASSESSMENT TAX is levied by a city council or a county board of supervisors, with the voters' approval, for the cost of specific local improvements such as streets, sewers, irrigation, or drainage.*

The difference between property taxes and special assessments is that special assessments are levied for the cost of specific local improvements, while property tax revenue goes into the general fund.

The official body that levies a special assessment is called a SPECIAL ASSESSMENT DISTRICT BOARD. According to state law, any self-governing area such as a city or county may establish a special assessment district for the purpose of levying a special assessment.

As a rule, a district issues its own bonds to finance particular improvements such as water distribution systems, parking facilities, street lighting, and many other types of developments. To repay the funds borrowed through the bonds issued, these districts have the power to assess all lands included in the district on an ad valorem basis. Such loans constitute liens on the land until paid. These liens can be foreclosed by sale similar to a tax sale and have priority over private property interests.

A. STREET IMPROVEMENT ACT OF 1911

According to the *STREET IMPROVEMENT ACT OF 1911, developers can use the Act to construct and improve streets and for sewer construction, however **they cannot use the Act to purchase land for subdividing.***

B. THE MELLO-ROOS COMMUNITY FACILITIES ACT

A seller must disclose the existence of a Mello-Roos bond on the property.

The Mello-Roos Community Facilities Act is another type of improvement bond. **Figure 13-7** explains Mello-Roos in detail.

> **Example:** A subdivider wanted to subdivide his property into many lots and sell individual lots to potential builders of single-family homes. To finance the off-site improvements, which include streets, sidewalks, and schools, he would institute a Mello-Roos municipal bond.

III. Documentary Transfer Tax

$.55 per $500 is paid only on the new amount of money (cash down and new financing), not on any assumed financing.

Figure 13-7

Mello-Roos Liens
DISCLOSURE REQUIRED

Failure to disclose allows buyer a 3-day right of rescission, and results in agent disciplinary action.

MELLO-ROOS LIENS are municipal bonds issued to fund streets, sewers, and other infrastructure needs before a housing development is built. This financial device allows developers to raise money to complete off-site improvements in a house or condo subdivision. The developer is usually responsible for making payments on the bond until the home is sold. The homeowner then becomes responsible for payment via a special tax.

The Mello-Roos Community Facilities Act is a way that a city or governmental district can skirt the property tax limitations of Proposition 13. The city can include the cost and maintenance of infrastructure items in the property tax bill as a special tax, which is allowed to go above the limits of Proposition 13.

This has been a boon for developers who need help financing their projects and for municipalities anxious to upgrade new developments under the restrictions of Proposition 13. The downside is that if something goes wrong with the economy or the project, the municipality may have to foreclose on the developer.

The primary responsibility for disclosure of any Mello-Roos bonds lies with the seller.

A broker must disclose to property buyers that a project is subject to a Mello-Roos special tax levy. If the agent fails to provide this disclosure, he or she is subject to discipline by the Real Estate Commissioner. A disclosure notice of the amount assessed and the amount of special tax applicable to the property is required on the sale or lease (for more than five years) of property subject to this lien. Failure to give notice before signing the sales contract permits the buyer or tenant a three-day right of rescission after receipt of the notice.

Warning: Whereas property taxes are totally deductible from state and federal income taxes, Mello-Roos taxes may only be partially deductible depending upon whether they are for maintenance or improvements. Consult with your C.P.A. before claiming such a deduction.

The *DOCUMENTARY TRANSFER TAX is a tax that is applied to the consideration paid or money borrowed when transferring property, except for any remaining loans or liens on the property.* This tax is computed at the rate of 55 cents for each $500 or $1.10 per $1,000 of consideration or any fraction thereof that exceeds $100. The consideration is any amount of cash payment plus any new loans.

However, this tax does not apply to any liens or encumbrances that remain on the property as part of the transfer. If a house were sold for $230,000 and a buyer assumed the old loan of $30,000, the documentary transfer tax would be $220 (only $200,000 is "new money" and taxable).

$$\frac{\$200,000}{\$500} \times \$.55 = \$220$$

Example: A single-family home sold for $90,750 and the buyer assumed an existing $30,000 first deed of trust. The documentary transfer tax is $67.

The documentary transfer tax is charged to the seller and is handled as part of the escrow. According to state law the county is allowed to charge this tax. However, a city within a county can charge that county for one-half of this tax. Therefore, in most cities, the county collects the documentary transfer tax and gives half of it to the city. Based on the information found at the county recorder's office, the documentary transfer tax can be used to determine a previous sale price of a property. Simply divide 55 cents into the amount of the documentary transfer tax and multiply by $500. If any loans have been assumed by the new owner, also add that amount to arrive at the total prior sale price of the property.

If any old loans or liens are to remain on the property, this fact must be stated on the deed or on a separate paper filed with the deed. Then add the value of the cash down payment and any new loans together with any remaining loan on the property to find the total selling price.

– CITY TRANSFER TAXES –

The city of Los Angeles initiated a transfer tax to be paid by sellers when a property is sold. The current charge is $4.50 per $1,000 of selling price.

– WATCH FOR A VERSION OF THIS TAX IN YOUR CITY –

IV. Gift and Estate Taxes

For federal purposes, the transfer of property by a gift or inheritance is taxed. Exemptions may reduce the taxes and sometimes eliminate them. **Figure 13-8** illustrates the federal taxes encountered by transferring property as a gift or by inheritance.

A gift of real estate may avoid federal estate taxes. So if a person wants to give a property away, it will most likely escape (the future) federal estate taxes. But, if you are to avoid federal gift taxes, usually only a fractional interest in the property should be given away each year. For example, you could give a son and daughter each a 1/30 interest in your home every year for 15 years to give the house to your children.

A. FEDERAL GIFT TAX

Frequently, as an individual family matures, the value of the real property owned by the family increases, and the owning family may consider bestowing it as a gift. When a family gives property, whether real or personal, to another individual, there may be federal gift

Figure 13-8

taxes that must be paid. If the value of the property is higher than an exempt amount, the donor must pay a gift tax. A *DONOR is the person or persons giving the property as a gift.* Generally, people give their property away to relatives on a systematic basis so that taxes are avoided. The *DONEE is the person or persons who receive the property as a gift.* The federal gift tax law also provides for an $11,000 annual exemption per donee.

B. FEDERAL ESTATE TAX

A *FEDERAL ESTATE TAX return must be filed for the estate of every resident of the United States whose gross estate exceeds $1,000,000 ($1,500,000 in 2004, $2,000,000 in 2006) in value at the date of death.* Estate tax exemptions will gradually increase the size of estates that are exempt from $1,000,000 to being repealed in 2010. However, the estate tax can be restored in 2011.

C. NO STATE GIFT AND INHERITANCE TAXES

The California State Inheritance Tax and the California State Gift Tax were repealed on June 8, 1982.

V. Federal and State Income Taxes

The annual Federal Income Tax Form 1040 (see **Figure 13-9**) and the State Income Tax Form 540 are bookkeeping or accounting summaries of the prior year's financial facts. These facts are a history and cannot be altered at the time of filing the income tax return.

www.irs.ustreas.gov
Internal Revenue Service (IRS)
www.ftb.ca.gov
Franchise Tax Board (FTB)

California has both state and federal income taxes (see **Figure 13-10**). That's right! California residents pay both income taxes, which ranks us among the most taxed people in the United States. It is no wonder that Californians are very interested in understanding the effects of income taxes on both their personal residence and income-producing property.

Under Federal Income Tax Laws, most real estate licensees are considered independent contractors. According to California Real Estate Law, most real estate licensees are considered employees of the broker.

Figure 13-9

Form **1040** — Department of the Treasury—Internal Revenue Service
U.S. Individual Income Tax Return 20XX (99) IRS Use Only—Do not write or staple in this space.

For the year Jan. 1-Dec. 31, 20XX, or other tax year beginning , 20XX, ending , 20XX

OMB No. 1545-0074

Label (See instructions on page 16.) Use the IRS label. Otherwise, please print or type.

L A B E L   H E R E

Your first name and initial — Last name — Your social security number

If a joint return, spouse's first name and initial — Last name — Spouse's social security number

Home address (number and street). If you have a P.O. box, see page 16. — Apt. no.

City, town or post office, state, and ZIP code. If you have a foreign address, see page 16.

▲ You must enter your SSN(s) above. ▲

Presidential Election Campaign ▶ Check here if you, or your spouse if filing jointly, want $3 to go to this fund (see page 16) ▶ ☐ You ☐ Spouse

Checking a box below will not change your tax or refund.

Filing Status — Check only one box.
1 ☐ Single
2 ☐ Married filing jointly (even if only one had income)
3 ☐ Married filing separately. Enter spouse's SSN above and full name here. ▶
4 ☐ Head of household (with qualifying person). (See page 17.) If the qualifying person is a child but not your dependent, enter this child's name here. ▶
5 ☐ Qualifying widow(er) with dependent child (see page 17)

Exemptions
6a ☐ Yourself. If someone can claim you as a dependent, do not check box 6a
b ☐ Spouse
c Dependents:
(1) First name Last name | (2) Dependent's social security number | (3) Dependent's relationship to you | (4) ✔ if qualifying child for child tax credit (see page 19)

If more than four dependents, see page 19.

d Total number of exemptions claimed

Boxes checked on 6a and 6b ___
No. of children on 6c who:
• lived with you
• did not live with you due to divorce or separation (see page 20)
Dependents on 6c not entered above
Add numbers on lines above ▶ ☐

Income
Attach Form(s) W-2 here. Also attach Forms W-2G and 1099-R if tax was withheld.
If you did not get a W-2, see page 22.
Enclose, but do not attach, any payment. Also, please use Form 1040-V.

7 Wages, salaries, tips, etc. Attach Form(s) W-2 | 7
8a Taxable interest. Attach Schedule B if required | 8a
b Tax-exempt interest. Do not include on line 8a | 8b
9a Ordinary dividends. Attach Schedule B if required | 9a
b Qualified dividends (see page 23) | 9b
10 Taxable refunds, credits, or offsets of state and local income taxes (see page 23) | 10
11 Alimony received | 11
12 Business income or (loss). Attach Schedule C or C-EZ | 12
13 Capital gain or (loss). Attach Schedule D if required. If not required, check here ▶ ☐ | 13
14 Other gains or (losses). Attach Form 4797 | 14
15a IRA distributions | 15a | b Taxable amount (see page 25) | 15b
16a Pensions and annuities | 16a | b Taxable amount (see page 25) | 16b
17 Rental real estate, royalties, partnerships, S corporations, trusts, etc. Attach Schedule E | 17
18 Farm income or (loss). Attach Schedule F | 18
19 Unemployment compensation | 19
20a Social security benefits | 20a | b Taxable amount (see page 27) | 20b
21 Other income. List type and amount (see page 29) | 21
22 Add the amounts in the far right column for lines 7 through 21. This is your total income ▶ | 22

Adjusted Gross Income
23 Educator expenses (see page 29) | 23
24 Certain business expenses of reservists, performing artists, and fee-basis government officials. Attach Form 2106 or 2106-EZ | 24
25 Health savings account deduction. Attach Form 8889 | 25
26 Moving expenses. Attach Form 3903 | 26
27 One-half of self-employment tax. Attach Schedule SE | 27
28 Self-employed SEP, SIMPLE, and qualified plans | 28
29 Self-employed health insurance deduction (see page 30) | 29
30 Penalty on early withdrawal of savings | 30
31a Alimony paid b Recipient's SSN ▶ | 31a
32 IRA deduction (see page 31) | 32
33 Student loan interest deduction (see page 33) | 33
34 Tuition and fees deduction (see page 34) | 34
35 Domestic production activities deduction. Attach Form 8903 | 35
36 Add lines 23 through 31a and 32 through 35 | 36
37 Subtract line 36 from line 22. This is your adjusted gross income ▶ | 37

For Disclosure, Privacy Act, and Paperwork Reduction Act Notice, see page 78. — Cat. No. 11320B — Form **1040** (2005)

Tax matters should be considered prior to buying and continued during ownership until the estate's ultimate disposition.

We will discuss only the most basic concepts of reducing the income tax bite for the average citizen. A basic knowledge of the requirements necessary to take advantage of federal and state income tax incentives is helpful. Arranging the purchase of real estate in a manner that reduces your personal income taxes is the purpose of tax planning. This may allow you to reduce the income taxes you pay, or at least postpone such taxes.

Tax shelters are the reduction in income taxes. Now is the time to start tax planning for your future income tax returns.

Figure 13-10

California vs. Federal Income Tax:
Emphasis is on the Federal

California state income tax laws tend to conform with federal laws in most respects. There are, however, several important income tax exceptions listed below:

1. State does not tax Social Security benefits.
2. State has no capital gains rates; just ordinary income rates.
3. State does not allow tax breaks for IRA plans (simple).
4. State does not tax lottery winnings.

The state taxes at a lower rate (a maximum of 9.3 percent) but tends to be more restrictive on deductions. State taxes paid are themselves deductible from the federal return.

Most state and local tax laws are considered by many insiders to be antiquated. Tax reform on these levels has become a much slower process than that by the federal government. Focus is on the federal government which taxes at higher rates and sets the tone for state and local taxes. For more detailed information on preparing personal income taxes, a tax attorney or CPA should be consulted.

Figure 13-11 shows the five main areas of the federal and state income tax laws that are incentives to owning real estate. Each area will be explained only to give the general concepts or ideas behind the laws. To obtain the exact meaning and clauses of the law, an owner or investor should seek the help of a Certified Public Accountant for advice on the accounting, or an attorney who is familiar with tax problems. Remember, these are only generalizations, and our income tax laws are more complex than the basic concepts presented here.

VI. Taxes on Personal Residence

Homeowners can deduct these three items from their income taxes based on their personal residence:

1. Mortgage Interest on Loan (Trust Deeds)
2. Property Taxes
3. Prepayment Penalties

Figure 13-11

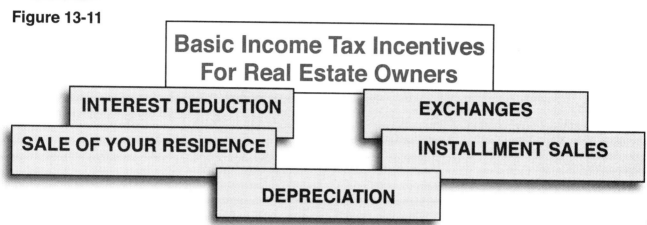

You cannot deduct the cost of personal residence repairs from your federal taxes, except for uninsured casual losses. For example, if your roof blows off and you have no insurance to cover it, the replacement cost can be deducted from your federal income taxes.

Unlike appraisals, depreciation for tax purposes is NOT based on actual deterioration, but on the calculated useful life of the property.

A. DEDUCTION OF INTEREST

Deduction of interest on your home loan from your income taxes is one of the major tax advantages of owning real estate. Buying a first and second home provides the average family with the biggest buffer against income taxes that it is likely to enjoy.

Despite recent income tax reforms, the federal tax laws still provide incentives to those who purchase a first and even a second home. When buying these homes you may finance up to $1 million ($1,000,000) with all the interest paid out during the year fully tax deductible. An additional deduction is available on the interest from home equity loans, taken for any purpose, even buying a second home, of up to $100,000 in principal. The $1,000,000 and $100,000 debit limit is a total applied against both first and second homes together or one owner-occupied home taken separately.

B. DEDUCTION OF PROPERTY TAXES

Property taxes on your first and second homes are deductible from your income taxes. This makes us feel better about paying local property taxes.

C. DEDUCTION OF PREPAYMENT PENALTIES

Prepayment penalties are also deductible from your income taxes. If you pay off or drastically reduce your home loan balance, there may be a prepayment penalty.

D. SALE OF A RESIDENCE

When selling a personal residence, the seller can deduct up to $250,000 ($500,000 if married) of any capital gain. This could be used only once every two years.

Federal income tax laws allow a taxpayer to exclude up to $250,000 of gain for each individual ($500,000 if married and on the title). This benefit may only be used once every two years for a residence.

While the law allows this deduction once every two years, you must reside in the home for two out of the last five years to qualify. In other words, if you live in the home for a year, then rent it out for three years, you would have to move back in for another year in order to take advantage of this tax break.

The only way to deduct a loss on a personal residence is to turn that property into income-producing property first by renting it. Then any loss based on its sale is deductible because it is income-producing property, not a personal residence.

VII. Taxes for Income-Producing Properties

Investors of income producing properties can annually deduct these items from income taxes:

1. Mortgage Interest on Loans (no maximum)
2. Property Taxes
3. Prepayment Penalties

In addition they can deduct:

4. Operating Expenses
5. Depreciation of Improvements

A. DEPRECIATION OF BUSINESS PROPERTY (Federal and State)

DEPRECIATION FOR TAX PURPOSES is a yearly tax deduction for wear and tear on investment property that is deducted from the taxpayer's income on his or her income tax form. This deduction applies only to investment property or property used in a business, not on a taxpayer's personal residence. Apartment buildings, commercial buildings, and any building improvements to investment property can be depreciated. The land itself cannot be depreciated.

Only the buildings and other improvements on income, trade, or business property can be depreciated. Land CANNOT be depreciated under federal income tax law.

One can only depreciate property that is improved. Since land cannot be depreciated, only the improvements can be depreciated. Currently, the straight-line method is the accepted way to depreciate buildings and other improvements.

Residential (homes and apartments) property depreciation schedule:
Minimum 27.5 years (Straight-line)
Commercial improvements depreciation schedule:
Minimum 39 years (Straight-line)

The amount of depreciation must be spread uniformly over the useful life of the property, with the same amount deducted each year (straight-line depreciation). Since most buildings in these inflationary times actually increase in value, depreciation is usually just a technique for postponing income taxes until the property is sold.

Example: An apartment building is purchased for $450,000 with land valued at $33,700. Using a 40-year straight-line depreciation schedule, the depreciated book value of the property after 16 years would be $283,480.

B. ADVANTAGES OF "SALE-LEASEBACK"
(Buyer Gets to Depreciate New Building Cost)

In a sale-leaseback for a commercial property, the buyer would be least concerned with the seller's depreciated book value of the property and more concerned with the lease amount the seller is paying, the amount the seller is receiving for the property, and the purchase price of the property.

If the owner of a business sells his or her building for cash, and then leases it back, the seller becomes a lessee and the buyer the lessor.

The advantage to the seller: all lease payments can be deducted from income taxes and he or she receives cash for the building.

The advantage to the buyer: he or she can use the purchase price as the new basis for depreciation and establish a new depreciation schedule.

Seller, now a renter, deducts 100% of future rents paid.

VIII. Sale of Real Property

A. CAPITAL ASSETS (Gains and Losses)

In real estate, a capital asset includes your personal residence (including your second home) and any other real estate because they are long-term investments. When you sell your home or other real estate, there is usually a capital gain or loss. *CAPITAL GAINS are taxed at a lower rate than is ordinary income*, but *CAPITAL LOSSES can be deducted from capital gains*. It is in the public interest to foster investment in land and buildings and other long-term assets so that businesses are encouraged to expand. This in turn creates more job opportunities for everyone.

Congress and the President have established four capital gains tax rates as follows:

20% maximum capital gains tax rate if held for more than 18 months
15% maximum capital gains tax rate if held for more than 7 years
10% capital gains tax rate if net income is less than $50,000
5% capital gains tax rate (over 7 years) if net income is less than $50,000

There should be a tax benefit to encourage entrepreneurs to risk investing long-term in things such as equipment, stocks, bonds, and real estate in order to obtain capital gains or losses. Other countries, like Japan and Germany, have very low capital gain tax rates which encourage investment in companies so that more career opportunities are generated for their employees. The size of the nation's "economic pie," which everyone enjoys, increases.

B. FEDERAL INCOME TAX RATES (Progressive)

As the old saying goes, "Nothing in life is certain, except death and taxes." One other certainty is the constant change in federal tax rates. Income tax rates are progressive. A *PROGRESSIVE TAX is a tax that charges a higher percentage of income as income rises.* So as you make more money, not only does the amount increase, but the rate at which income is taxed also increases. The end effect is that higher income families (the exact ones who usually own businesses and can expand job opportunities) pay most of the income taxes.

The *MARGINAL TAX RATE is the rate that the next dollar earned puts you into. REGRESSIVE TAXES use the same rate no matter how much is spent or earned. Sales tax is an example of a regressive tax.* The rate is the same, so in effect the poor pay a higher percent of their income.

C. ACCOUNTING FOR THE SALE OF REAL ESTATE

The method of determining a profit or loss on the sale of real property is spelled out by the Internal Revenue Service. Steps 1 and 2 must be completed before determining the profit or loss on a sale (Step 3).

"Adjusted cost basis" is the base cost, plus capital improvements, minus depreciation and sale expenses.

(1) Cost Basis (Purchase price)	**$500,000**
+ Improvements	**200,000**
	$700,000
- Depreciation (tax records)	**30,200**
= Adjusted Cost Basis	**$669,800**
(2) Sale price	**$1,000,000**
- Sale Expenses	**32,500**
= Adjusted Sale Price	**$967,500**
(3) Adjusted Sale Price	**$967,500**
- Adjusted Cost Basis	**669,800**
= Gain	**$297,700**

IX. Installment Sales and Exchanges

A. INSTALLMENT SALES OF REAL ESTATE

An *INSTALLMENT SALE is the sale of real estate in which the payments for the property extend over more than one calendar year.* Installment sales are used to spread a gain over two or more calendar years so that the entire gain is not taxed all in the first year. Our income tax system has progressive rates, which means that the higher the income, the higher the income tax rate for that year. If a person can spread a gain over more than one calendar year, the same income may be taxed at a lower rate.

By doing this the seller avoids the disadvantages of paying for his or her entire gain in one year and thereby has a substantial savings on his or her income taxes. This method is usually used when selling large tracts of land held for a period of time or large buildings owned by one individual.

A sale of a large lot for $100,000 all at once might force you into a higher tax bracket. So by having an installment sale of $25,000 for each of the next four years, you may

substantially reduce the total income taxes paid. An installment sale may be a good way to defer income taxes if your income varies from year-to-year; just arrange to get larger installment payments in years when your ordinary income is low.

B. EXCHANGES TAX-DEFERRED (FEDERAL AND STATE) (Section 1031 of the IRS Code)

In an exchange, the adjusted cost basis of the old property becomes the basis of the new property.

An **EXCHANGE** *is a transfer of real estate where one party trades property for another's property.* The property must be of "like kind" in nature or character, not in use, quality, or grade. The exchange may be a straight trade (tax-free) or one party may receive cash in addition to the property (partially tax-free). An exchange can be income tax free, partially taxed, or fully taxed, depending on the cost factors in each particular exchange. Exchanges are too detailed to explain here, but it is a way of deferring or possibly eliminating income taxes on the transfer of real estate.

Example: Able owns an apartment building and undertakes a 1031 exchange. He may exchange his apartment building for one that is more valuable, exchange loans, and pay the balance in cash.

Example: Able owned community property with a cost basis of $95,000 and a fair market value of $125,000. He exchanged this property for another property with a fair market value of $85,000 and received $30,000 cash and a $10,000 promissory note paid over four years. For federal income tax purposes, the entire purchase price of $85,000 is taxable.

To defer all current taxes, a party in an exchange would need to receive a more valuable building with a larger loan on it than the current property and pay compensation to the other party for any difference in the equities. *Any net cash or net mortgage relief that a participant in an exchange might receive in addition to the actual property is known as BOOT.* All boot is taxable to the extent of the gain in this partially tax-free exchange (see **Figure 13-12**).

"Boot" is cash or debt relief. The receiver has recognized gain. If there is no boot in an exchange, the old basis is the new basis.

Exchanges are popular among apartment owners and commercial property investors. This is because these owners are usually in high-income tax bracket, and exchanging enables them to move up to a more valuable property without paying taxes on the gain. People in higher income tax brackets usually keep their money invested in real estate, and they find exchanges to be a way of selling and buying simultaneously.

Figure 13-12

Tax-Deferred Exchanges

In a "tax-deferred" exchange, boot is defined as cash or mortgage relief given in addition to the property. Boot is the amount received to balance the equities in the exchange. Brokers often encounter the term "boot" when talking with a client about income taxes.

The person receiving boot has a net gain and has to pay taxes on it. When no boot is given or received, then the basis remains the same.

In a tax free exchange, properties must be of a "like kind" in nature or character, not in use, quality, grade, or value. "Tax free" merely means to DEFER the payment of taxes until a later time. Since you can move your equity to another property, it is almost like buying and selling without paying income taxes.

The actual techniques used to understand exchanging are too complex to be explained here, but many six-hour seminars and exchange clubs are available to interested people.

Exchanges are based on "equity value." Equity is market value minus liens.

X. We Are Now Tax Collectors (Federal and State Income Tax Laws – Escrow Usually Takes Care of This)

A. FEDERAL TAX COLLECTION REQUIREMENTS AND EXEMPTIONS (If a Foreigner) – $300,000 or More

Persons buying property from foreign investors (sellers) are required to set aside 10% of the purchase price for the Internal Revenue Service. This 10% withholding is kept by the IRS to ensure that property capital gains taxes are paid on the transaction. Both the buyer and broker share liability. If this amount is not withheld, the broker may be liable for the full amount of the tax not paid.

In effect, this law holds brokers responsible to check the citizenship of all sellers and see to it that the buyer retains either a 10% deposit, an affidavit from the seller stating that he or she is not a foreigner, or a waiver from the IRS. Residential property purchased for under $300,000 to be used as the buyer's residence is exempted from this withholding. The key points for licensees to remember are these:

1. **Inquire** into the citizenship of all sellers of residential or commercial properties priced at $300,000 or more, even if a foreigner holds only partial or syndicate interest.

2. **Require** a statement of citizenship as part of the listing agreement and then follow up in escrow by having the seller or sellers sign a sworn affidavit.

3. **Do not discriminate.** Require this information of all sellers **in transactions of $300,000 or more**. Even if someone does not appear to be an alien, they might hold foreign citizenship.

The CAR® Seller's Affidavit of Nonforeign Status and/or California Withholding Exemption is a form for the seller to sign swearing that he or she is not a nonresident alien (see **Figure 13-13**). If the seller completes the lower portion of this sworn statement, the buyer and broker may no longer be liable for any portions of unpaid taxes.

Figure 13-14 shows a Buyer's Affidavit form available from CAR®. This form states that the sales price is less than $300,000 and that the property will be used as a residence. It is signed by the buyer under penalty of perjury. If these two considerations can be met, the buyer is immediately exempted from the withholding requirement. If neither of these forms can truthfully be completed, then the broker should see to it that 10% of the sales price is withheld in escrow or that the proper waiver is obtained from the IRS. The escrow officer will help you with this matter.

B. STATE TAX COLLECTION REQUIREMENTS AND EXEMPTIONS (If a Foreigner or Resident of Another State) – $100,000 or More

Persons buying property from foreign or out-of-state investors may be required to set aside 3.3% of the sales price for the Franchise Tax Board. If this amount is not withheld, the broker and buyer may be liable for the full amount of income taxes not paid. Escrow usually handles this, but the buyer and broker are responsible.

The exemptions from the buyer withholding 3.3% of the sales price for the Franchise Tax Board are:

1. **Sales price is $100,000 or less.**
2. Property is seller's principle residence, under certain conditions.
3. Seller signs California Residency Declaration.
4. Seller receives a waiver – Franchise Tax Board Form 567A.

XI. Other Taxes Paid by Brokers

A. BUSINESS LICENSE TAXES (City Income Taxes)

A city may levy a tax against real estate brokerage firms, which is based upon the gross receipts, through a **BUSINESS LICENSE TAX**. *In most areas of California, this annual city business license tax is a nominal amount that usually starts at about $100. Other city taxes may also include employee payroll taxes.*

B. SALES TAX

Sales tax is a tax on only tangible personal property.

The maximum sales tax penalty is 35% for late filing of sales and use tax, due to fraud or evasion.

Figure 13-13

CALIFORNIA
ASSOCIATION
OF REALTORS®

SELLER'S AFFIDAVIT OF NONFOREIGN STATUS AND/OR CALIFORNIA WITHHOLDING EXEMPTION
FOREIGN INVESTMENT IN REAL PROPERTY TAX ACT (FIRPTA)
AND CALIFORNIA WITHHOLDING LAW
(Use a separate form for each Transferor)
(C.A.R. Form AS, Revised 10/05)

Internal Revenue Code ("IRC") Section 1445 provides that a transferee of a U.S. real property interest must withhold tax if the transferor is a "foreign person." California Revenue and Taxation Code Section 18662 provides that a transferee of a California real property interest must withhold tax unless an exemption applies.

I understand that this affidavit may be disclosed to the Internal Revenue Service and to the California Franchise Tax Board by the transferee, and that any false statement I have made herein may result in a fine, imprisonment or both.

1. **PROPERTY ADDRESS** (property being transferred): _____ ("Property")
2. **TRANSFEROR'S INFORMATION:**
   Full Name _____ ("Transferor")
   Telephone Number _____
   Address _____
   (Use HOME address for individual transferors. Use OFFICE address for an "Entity" i.e.: corporations, partnerships, limited liability companies, trusts and estates.)
   Social Security No., Federal Employer Identification No. or California Corporation No. _____
   Note: In order to avoid withholding by providing this affidavit, IRC Section 1445 (b) (2) requires a Seller to provide the Buyer with the Seller's taxpayer identification number ("TIN").
3. **AUTHORITY TO SIGN:** If this document is signed on behalf of an Entity Transferor, THE UNDERSIGNED INDIVIDUAL DECLARES THAT HE/SHE HAS AUTHORITY TO SIGN THIS DOCUMENT ON BEHALF OF THE TRANSFEROR.
4. **FEDERAL LAW:** I, the undersigned, declare under penalty of perjury that, for the reason checked below, if any, I am exempt (or if signed on behalf of an Entity Transferor, the Entity is exempt) from the federal withholding law (FIRPTA):
   ☐ (For individual Transferors) I am not a nonresident alien for purposes of U.S. income taxation.
   ☐ (For corporation, partnership, limited liability company, trust and estate Transferors) The Transferor is not a foreign corporation, foreign partnership, foreign limited liability company, foreign trust or foreign estate, as those terms are defined in the Internal Revenue Code and Income Tax Regulations.
5. **CALIFORNIA LAW:** I, the undersigned, declare under penalty of perjury that, for the reason checked below, if any, I am exempt (or if signed on behalf of an Entity Transferor, the Entity is exempt) from the California withholding law.
   Certifications which fully exempt the sale from withholding:
   ☐ The total sales price for the Property is $100,000 or less.
   ☐ The Property qualifies as my principal residence (or the decedent's, if being sold by the decedent's estate) within the meaning of IRC Section 121 (owned and occupied as such for two of the last five years).
   ☐ The Property was last used as my principal residence (or the decedent's, if being sold by the decedent's estate) within the meaning of IRC Section 121 without regard to the two-year time period.
   ☐ The transaction will result in a loss or zero gain for California income tax purposes. (Complete FTB Form 593-L.)
   ☐ The Property has been compulsorily or involuntarily converted (within the meaning of IRC Section 1033) and Transferor intends to acquire property similar or related in service or use to be eligible for non-recognition of gain for California income tax purposes under IRC Section 1033.
   ☐ Transferor is a corporation (or an LLC classified as a corporation) that is either qualified through the California Secretary of State or has a permanent place of business in California.
   ☐ Transferor is a partnership (or an LLC that is not a disregarded single member LLC, classified as a partnership) and recorded title to the Property is in the name of the partnership or LLC. If so, the partnership or LLC must withhold from nonresident partners or members as required.
   ☐ Transferor is exempt from tax under California or federal law.
   ☐ Transferor is an insurance company, qualified pension/profit sharing plan, IRA or charitable remainder trust.
   Certifications which may partially or fully exempt the sale from withholding:
   ☐ The Property is being, or will be, exchanged for property of like kind within the meaning of IRC Section 1031.
   ☐ The Property is subject to an installment sale, that Transferor will report as such, and Buyer has agreed to withhold on each principal payment instead of withholding the full amount at the time of transfer.

By _____ Date _____
(Transferor's Signature) (Indicate if you are signing as the grantor of a revocable/grantor trust.)

_____   _____
Typed or printed name   Title (If signed on behalf of Entity Transferor)

Buyer's unauthorized use or disclosure of Seller's TIN could result in civil or criminal liability.

Buyer _____ Date _____
(Buyer acknowledges receipt of a Copy of this Seller's Affidavit)

Buyer _____ Date _____
(Buyer acknowledges receipt of a Copy of this Seller's Affidavit)

Published and Distributed by:
REAL ESTATE BUSINESS SERVICES, INC.
a subsidiary of the California Association of REALTORS®
525 South Virgil Avenue, Los Angeles, California 90020

SURE TRAC
The System for Success®

Reviewed by _____ Date _____

EQUAL HOUSING OPPORTUNITY

AS REVISED 10/05 (PAGE 1 OF 1) Print Date

SELLER'S AFFIDAVIT OF NONFOREIGN STATUS AND/OR CALIFORNIA WITHHOLDING EXEMPTION (AS PAGE 1 OF 1)

Figure 13-14

CALIFORNIA
ASSOCIATION
OF REALTORS®

BUYER'S AFFIDAVIT
That Buyer is acquiring property for use as a residence
and that sales price does not exceed $300,000.
(FOREIGN INVESTMENT IN REAL PROPERTY TAX ACT)
(C.A.R. Form AB, 2/91)

1. I am the transferee (buyer) of real property located at _____
_____

2. The sales price (total of all consideration in the sale) does not exceed $300,000.

3. I am acquiring the real property for use as a residence. I have definite plans that I or a member of my family will reside in it for at least 50 percent of the number of days it will be in use during each of the first two 12 month periods following the transfer of the property to me. I understand that the members of my family that are included in the last sentence are my brothers, sisters, ancestors, descendents, or spouse.

4. I am making this affidavit in order to establish an exemption from withholding a portion of the sales price of the property under Internal Revenue Code §1445.

5. I understand that if the information in this affidavit is not correct, I may be liable to the Internal Revenue Service for up to 10 percent of the sales price of the property, plus interest and penalties.

Under penalties of perjury, I declare that the statements above are true, correct and complete.

Date _____   Signature _____

Typed or Printed Name _____

Date _____   Signature _____

Typed or Printed Name _____

IMPORTANT NOTICE: An affidavit should be signed by each individual transferee to whom it applies. Before you sign, any questions relating to the legal sufficiency of this form, or to whether it applies to a particular transaction, or to the definition of any of the terms used, should be referred to an attorney, certified public accountant, other professional tax advisor, or the Internal Revenue Service.

SURE TRAC
The System for Success®

Published and Distributed by:
REAL ESTATE BUSINESS SERVICES, INC.
a subsidiary of the California Association of REALTORS®
525 South Virgil Avenue, Los Angeles, California 90020

FORM AB REVISED 2/91 (PAGE 1 OF 1) Print Date

Reviewed by _____ Date _____

EQUAL HOUSING
OPPORTUNITY

BUYER'S AFFIDAVIT (AB PAGE 1 OF 1)

1. Successor's Liability

To avoid successor's liability in the sale of a business that collects sales tax, the buyer should be certain to include a provision in the purchase agreement that an amount for any sales tax collected and not yet paid is to be held in escrow until a clearance receipt is received from the State Board of Equalization.

A buyer is protected from successor's liability by obtaining a "clearance receipt" from the State Board of Equalization.

XII. CHAPTER SUMMARY

Real property taxes are determined by the value of the real property (ad valorem) and are reassessed each time a property is sold at 1% of its selling price. The **County Assessor** assesses taxes, the **County Tax Collector** collects them, and the **County Board of Supervisors** sets the rates. **Proposition 13** limits the amount of taxes to 1% of the 1975 market value of the property plus a cumulative increase of 2% in market value each year thereafter, called **assessed valuation**.

Property taxes due are, in effect, liens against that specific property. Important tax dates include **November 1** (first installment), **December 10** (first installment is delinquent), **February 1** (second installment) and **April 10** (second installment is delinquent), or **No Darn Fooling Around**.

If taxes are not paid on or before June 30, the property is sold to the state, beginning a 5-year **redemption period**. After five years, the delinquent property is deeded to the state and sold at a **public tax auction**.

The **homeowner's property tax exemption** is $7,000 of assessed valuation. And, although California has no exemption for low income families, it does have senior citizen and disabled person tax rebates and postponements, as well as veterans' and non-profit organizations' tax exemptions.

Local improvement taxes for off-site improvements like streets, sewers, irrigation, etc. are called **special assessment taxes**. Additional taxes that may be incurred include: **documentary transfer taxes**, **Mello-Roos liens** (for which disclosure is required), **federal gift taxes**, and **federal estate taxes**.

Interest, property taxes and prepayment penalties paid on a personal residence can be deducted from income taxes. Federal income tax allows a taxpayer to exclude up to $250,000 of gain for each individual ($500,000 if married and on title). When you sell your home (capital asset) a capital gain or loss results. **Capital gains** are taxed at a lower rate than ordinary income tax rates.

A loss on a sale of a personal residence can also be deducted if it is turned into **income producing property** by renting it. Income property owners can deduct **mortgage interest, property taxes**, and **prepayment penalties**, as well as **operating expenses** and **depreciation**, but not losses due to vacancies. If a business owner sells a building for cash, then leases it back (a **sale-leaseback**), the seller becomes the lessee and the buyer the lessor, and the seller can deduct 100% of future rents paid.

Federal taxes are **progressive**, meaning the percentage paid increases as the amount to be taxed increases, which is the opposite of sales taxes, which are regressive.

In addition to depreciation, two major tax benefits of owning income-producing property are **installment sales** (gain is only taxed in the year it is received) and **1031 tax-deferred exchanges** (a means of deferring or eliminating income taxes on property transfers). Cash or debt relief gained in a tax-deferred exchange is known as **boot**.

Persons buying property from **foreign investors** are required to set aside 10% of the purchase price for the IRS, to insure the property capital gains taxes are paid on the transaction. An additional 3.3% of the sales price for the Franchise Tax Board may also have to be withheld. In both cases, the burden is on the buyer and broker, not the seller. Brokers may also have to pay a **business license tax**, which is a city tax based on gross receipts.

XIII. TERMINOLOGY

A. Ad Valorem
B. Assessed Valuation
C. Boot
D. County Assessor
E. County Collector
F. Depreciation for Tax Purposes
G. Documentary Transfer Tax
H. Donee

I. Donor
J. Exchange
K. Federal and State Income Tax
L. Federal Estate Tax
M. Federal Gift Tax
N. Homeowner's Property Tax Exemption
O. Installment Sale

P. Proposition 13
Q. Real Property Taxes
R. Renter's Credit
S. Special Assessment
T. Two Out of the Last 5 Years
U. $250,000

1.____ Value placed upon property, for property tax purposes, by the tax assessor.
2.____ The sale of property in installments that spreads tax on profit from a sale of property over a number of years.
3.____ A tax charged according to the value of the property.
4.____ One who gives a gift.
5.____ A tax against the property of a deceased, based on the value of the estate.
6.____ One who receives a gift.
7.____ In a tax-deferred exchange, any cash or other property included in the transaction to make the exchange an even proposition.
8.____ The trading of parcels of real property to obtain tax benefits that might not be available in a normal sale. Generally considered tax-deferred, not tax-exempt.
9.____ An annual tax that applies to real estate that is based on the assessed valuation of the property.
10.____ The person, in a given political division within a state, who is responsible for collecting property taxes.
11.____ One who estimates the value of property for property tax purposes.
12.____ A renter's deduction allowed from state income taxes payable, under certain conditions.
13.____ A loss in value of improvements as an accounting procedure: used as a deduction on income taxes.
14.____ A lien assessed against real property in a given district, by a public authority to pay costs of special public improvements.
15.____ A tax on the sale of real property, usually based on the sales price and paid on or before the recordation of the deed.
16.____ Federal taxes paid on the giving of real property as a gift, if over an exempted amount.
17.____ Limits the amount of taxes to a maximum of 1% of the March 1, 1975 market value of the property plus the cumulative increase of 2% in market value each year thereafter.
18.____ Personal taxes paid annually on your taxable income.
19.____ A deduction of up to $7,000 from an owner-resident's assessed valuation on his or her property tax bill. Must be filed between March 1 and April 15 each year, to receive the full deduction.
20.____ The length of time a couple must live in their house to qualify for a $500,000 exclusion.
21.____ The amount that is exempt if a single person sells his or her house.

CHAPTER 13

XIV. CHAPTER QUIZ

1. The county assessor accumulates a list of all private owners of real property in his or her jurisdiction. The assessment roll is used to:
   a. set the tax rate for each year.
   b. establish the tax base for the county.
   c. determine the taxes to be paid by individual property owners.
   d. equalize the assessment throughout the county.

2. Senior citizens may be able to defer the payment of the property taxes on their residence. In order to find out if they qualify for the program, the senior citizen should contact the:
   a. Real Estate Commissioner.
   b. State Franchise Tax Board.
   c. State Housing Authority.
   d. County Tax Assessor.

3. The difference between property taxes and special assessments is that:
   a. assessment liens are always subordinate to property tax liens.
   b. assessment liens can only be levied by local improvement districts.
   c. foreclosure of assessment liens can only be achieved by court foreclosure.
   d. special assessments are levied for the cost of specific local improvements, while property tax revenue goes into the general fund.

4. The Street Improvement Act of 1911 can be used by a developer for all the following, except:
   a. constructing sewers.
   b. improving streets.
   c. constructing streets.
   d. purchase of land for subdividing.

5. The primary responsibility for disclosing any Mello-Roos bonds or assessments to a buyer when a home is sold lies with:
   a. the seller.
   b. the seller's agent.
   c. the buyer's agent.
   d. all of the above.

6. A subdivider wanted to subdivide his property into many lots and sell individual lots to potential builders of single-family homes. To finance the off-site improvements that include streets, sidewalks, and schools he would:
   a. approach the State of California for funding.
   b. ask the local governmental bodies to institute a special assessment to pay for the improvements.
   c. institute a Mello-Roos municipal bond.
   d. obtain a blanket encumbrance.

7. A home sold for $200,000. The buyer assumed an existing loan against the property for $160,000. The documentary transfer tax for this county is $.55 per $500 of consideration. The transfer tax is:

    a. $11.
    b. $22.
    c. $33.
    d. $44.

8. Under Federal Income Tax Laws, most real estate licensees are considered:

    a. employees of the broker.
    b. employees of the seller.
    c. independent contractors.
    d. any of the above.

9. Which of the following is true regarding the depreciation of land under federal income tax law?

    a. Land may be depreciated by the 125% declining balance method.
    b. Owner may deduct the accrued depreciation of land over time.
    c. Land may be depreciated by the sum of the year's digits method.
    d. Land cannot be depreciated under federal income tax law.

10. Able owns an apartment building and undertakes a 1031 exchange. He may:

    a. exchange his apartment building for one more valuable, exchange loans, and pay the balance in cash.
    b. purchase an apartment building of lesser value.
    c. purchase personal property as long as it is lesser value.
    d. none of the above.

ANSWERS: 1. b; 2. b; 3. d; 4. d; 5. a; 6. c; 7. d; 8. c; 9. d; 10. a

CHAPTER 14
Licensing, Education, and Associations

I. Department of Real Estate (DRE)

In California, all real estate agreements are under the jurisdiction of the *CALIFORNIA DEPARTMENT OF REAL ESTATE (DRE), which is the regulatory agency for real estate in California.* The main purpose of this department is to protect the public by enactment and enforcement of laws relating to real estate and by establishing requirements for real estate salespersons' or brokers' licenses.

The California Department of Real Estate is responsible for regulating real estate brokerage matters and the enforcement of real estate laws. These laws help protect both the individual citizen and the real estate profession. There are obvious benefits derived by shielding citizens from dishonest or incompetent real estate licensees. The reputation of the real estate profession is upheld by making sure that all practicing salespeople and brokers are both honest and capable of performing their jobs properly.

The California Department of Real Estate is governed by the Real Estate Commissioner. The Commissioner, who sets all the rules and regulations for the Department of Real Estate, receives his or her power from the state legislature. The legislature, in turn, used police power to create the position of Commissioner. *POLICE POWER is the right to enact and enforce laws beneficial to the health, safety, morals, and general welfare of the public.*

A. REAL ESTATE COMMISSIONER (Appointed by the Governor)

The Real Estate Commissioner will start an action against a licensee with an accusation.

www.ca.gov
Welcome to California - Online Services

In addition to his/her position as chairperson of the State Real Estate Advisory Commission, the *REAL ESTATE COMMISSIONER is the chief executive of the Department of Real Estate.* It is the Commissioner's duty, therefore, to mold the department's policy, create regulations, and to enforce Real Estate Law (found in the Business and Professions Code) so that both real estate purchasers and real estate licensed agents benefit from his or her rulings.

CHAPTER OUTLINE

The Commissioner enforces the Real Estate Law, but does not replace a court of law.

The Commissioner's other duties include:

1. Deciding the business policy of the State Department of Real Estate.

2. Informing the Governor and other state officials as to what services the department can render to the state and provide them with descriptions of the department's licenses.

3. Recommending changes in policy that may have been deemed necessary for the good of the public and the business of real estate in California.

4. Regulating the sales of subdivisions.

5. Deciding if applicants for real estate licenses have met all the experience and education requirements.

6. Investigating complaints against allegedly incompetent license holders.

7. Investigating complaints against those performing acts without the required license.

The Commissioner does not give legal advice, and do not settle commission (payment for real estate services) disputes. Commission disputes are settled by arbitration or civil lawsuits in local courts.

Example: At close of escrow the seller decided not to pay the commission. The broker/agent can file civil action in court (or in binding mediation if initialed in listing agreement).

The Real Estate Commissioner has the power to call formal hearings to discuss any issue concerning an applicant for a license, a current license holder, or a subdivider. The Commissioner may subsequently suspend, revoke or deny a license. He or she could also halt sales (desist and refrain order) in a subdivision.

The maximum fine the Real Estate Commissioner can levy against a broker who pays an unlicensed person for soliciting borrowers or negotiating loans is $10,000.

II. Real Estate License Requirements

As mentioned in the preceding section, the Real Estate Commissioner's main purpose is the regulation of the real estate business in the state of California. This regulation is accomplished by imposing mandatory licenses on those individuals who choose to work in the field of real estate. Who is required to have these licenses?

In short, any person who is actively involved in a real estate transaction at the service of another, in the expectation of receiving a commission, must be licensed.

A. WHO MUST HAVE A LICENSE

A person is required to have a license if he or she:

1. sells or offers to sell, buys or offers to buy, and solicits buyers or sellers.
2. solicits or obtains listings.
3. negotiates the purchase, sale, or exchange of real property or business opportunities.
4. leases or rents, collects rents, or negotiates the sale, purchase, or exchange of leases.
5. assists in the purchase of leases on lands owned by the state or federal government.
6. negotiates loans, collects payments, or performs services for borrowers or lenders.

Any person found to be involved in such actions without a license may be guilty of breaking the Real Estate Law, under which stiff penalties can be imposed.

B. WHEN A LICENSE IS NOT REQUIRED

It should be noted that there are a few exceptions to these regulations. The following people, because of the nature of their work, are exempt from the licensing regulations (NO LICENSE REQUIRED):

1. Employees of lending institutions
2. Lenders making federally insured or guaranteed loans
3. Certain agricultural associations
4. Licensed personal property brokers
5. Cemetery authorities
6. Collectors of loans made on real property
7. Certain clerical help

A person who is not a real estate salesperson or broker may solicit for the sale of real property (according to Section 10133 of the Real Estate Law) as long as he or she is:

1. the owner.
2. holding power of attorney for the owner.
3. an attorney at law acting on behalf of the owner.
4. a receiver or court appointee.
5. a trustee, selling under a deed of trust.

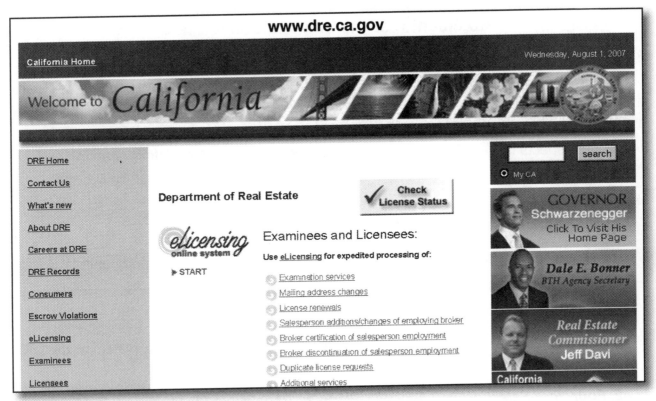

C. OBTAINING THE SALESPERSON'S LICENSE

To obtain a real estate salesperson license, you must first qualify for and pass a written examination. After passing the exam, a license application must be submitted to and approved by the Department of Real Estate (DRE).

You are now allowed to file your examination and license application at the same time.

1. **Age:** You must be 18 years of age to be licensed, but there is no age restriction for taking the exam.

2. **Residence:** Proof of legal presence in the United States is required. If you're not a California resident, refer to "Out-of-State Applicants" on the DRE website.

3. **Honesty:** Applicants must be honest and truthful. Conviction of a crime may result in denial of a license.

4. **Education:** Successful completion of the following college-level courses is required to become a real estate salesperson:

    a. **Real Estate Principles**

    b. **Real Estate Practice**

    c. One additional DRE-approved real estate course

For further information, call or write any district office of the Department of Real Estate. You can access the pamphlet, *Instructions to License Applicants* (see **Figure 14-1**) on the DRE website.

435

Applicants for the Salesperson's Exam

The original salesperson examination applicants will be required to submit evidence of completion of a three semester, or quarter unit equivalent, college-level course in **Real Estate Principles, Real Estate Practice**, and one additional course which should be chosen from the following list of courses:

Legal Aspects of Real Estate	Real Estate Office Administration
Real Estate Appraisal	Computer Applications in Real Estate
Real Estate Finance	Real Estate Economics
Property Management	Business Law
Escrows	Accounting
Mortgage Loan Brokering and Lending	Common Interest Developments

---

1. DRE to Convert to Computerized Exams

The DRE is in the process of implementing a computerized testing system at the DRE testing facilities.

2. Four-Year Salesperson's License (Regular, Renewable License)

To obtain a regular four-year salesperson's license, the applicant must:

1. complete a college level **Real Estate Principles course**, a **Real Estate Practice course**, and one other approved college level (broker-required) course;
2. pass the DRE salesperson's exam, and
3. pay the necessary fees.

3. Salesperson's Examination

To pass, an applicant must achieve a score of at least 70% in the three-hour, fifteen minute salesperson's exam, which has 150 multiple choice questions. Exams are scheduled during the morning or afternoon. A non-refundable fee is required to take the test. If you fail, you may take the exam as often as you wish, but you must pay for each exam application. See **Figure 14-2** for the salesperson's and broker's requirements.

The use of a silent, battery-operated, pocket-sized electronic calculator that is nonprogrammable and does not have a printout capability is permitted.

4. Notification of Examination Results

You will be notified of your examination results by mail, normally within five working days after the examination. You can also check your examination results using the DRE exam website (**https://secure.dre.ca.gov/elicensing**).

To pass the examination, you must correctly answer at least 70% of the questions. The examination is qualifying in nature; applicants who pass are not informed of their score. You will be notified of the actual score and the percentage of questions answered correctly in each of the seven subject areas only when unsuccessful. Those who pass will receive an application for a license. Those who do not receive a passing grade will automatically receive a re-examination form.

With the coming implementation of computerized DRE testing, an applicant will know if he or she passed or failed before leaving the testing facility.

You may not apply for a re-examination until after notification of failure of a prior test. Another application fee payment will be required. There is no limitation to the number of re-examinations you may take during the two-year period following the date of the filing of the original application. If you wish to take additional examinations after the two-year period, you must complete a new application.

Applicants for the salesperson's license must apply for a license within one year from the exam passing date, NOT the date of notification of passing.

5. Electronic Fingerprint Requirement (Salesperson and Broker)

Applicants for the salesperson's license must apply for a license within one year from the exam date.

If you have taken Principles and Practice, plus one other required course and have passed the examination, you are qualified to apply for a four-year renewable license. You must pay $120 for an active license and $56 (paid to scan service provider—fee may vary) for the live scan set of your fingerprints.

Upon completion of the real estate license exam, a copy of RE Form 237 (the Live Scan Service Request Form) will be mailed to all applicants. A list of providers of the live scan fingerprinting technique is available through the DRE website (**www.dre.ca.gov**).

D. OBTAINING THE BROKER'S LICENSE (Renewable Four-Year License)

A *BROKER'S LICENSE is required of any individual who wants to operate a real estate office.* The candidate for a real estate broker's license examination must:

1. be 18 years of age to apply for a license, although there is no age restriction for taking the exam.
2. provide Proof of Legal Presence in the United States.
3. if not a California resident, refer to "Out-of-State Applicants" on DRE website.
4. have had previous experience (two years or college education).
5. complete the required eight broker courses.
6. be honest and truthful.
7. pass the required DRE examination. (Governmental Photo ID required)

1. Broker's Qualifying Experience

A candidate must also be able to prove that he or she has experience in real estate before applying for a broker's license. Generally, two years of full-time work (104 forty-hour

Figure 14-1

Department of Real Estate (DRE)

PRINCIPAL OFFICE

SACRAMENTO
2201 Broadway, Sacramento, CA 95818-2500
(916-227-0931)

www.dre.ca.gov

All offices open 8-5 weekdays

DISTRICT OFFICES

LOS ANGELES Suite 350 (213-620-2072)
320 W. 4th St. Los Angeles, CA 90013-1105

OAKLAND Suite 702 (510-622-2552)
1515 Clay St., Oakland, CA 94612-1402

SAN DIEGO Suite 3064 (619-525-4192)
1350 Front St., San Diego, CA 92101-3687

FRESNO Rm. 3070 (559-445-5009)
2550 Mariposa Mall, Fresno, CA 93721-2273

State of California
Department of Real Estate

Instructions to License Applicants

Now Available Online Only!

Proof of Legal Presence in the United States

The **Personal Responsibility and Work Opportunity Act** (the "Act") requires states to eliminate a broad array of public benefits for illegal immigrants. The definition of a public benefit includes professional and occupational licenses issued to individuals by state agencies. For purposes of the Department of Real Estate, the term "public benefit" applies to original and renewal real estate salesperson and broker licenses, prepaid rental listing service licenses, and a payment from the Real Estate Recovery Account.

To implement the provisions of the Act, the Department has adopted Regulation 2718. This regulation requires **proof of legal presence in the United States from all applicants for a license,** and from applicants for payment from the Real Estate Recovery Account. This requirement applies to applicants for both original and renewal licenses.

Figure 14-2

EXAMINATION SUBJECT AREAS	SALESPERSON EXAM	BROKER EXAM
1. Property Ownership and Land Use Controls and Regulations	**18%**	**15%**
Classes of property; Property characteristics; Encumbrances; Types of ownership; Descriptions of property; Government rights in land; Public controls; Environmental hazards and regulations; Private controls; Water rights; Special categories of land		
2. Laws of Agency	**12%**	**12%**
Law, definition, and nature of agency relationships, types of agencies, and agents; Creation of agency and agency agreements; Responsibilities of agent to seller/buyer as principal; Disclosure of agency; Disclosure of acting as principal or other interest; Termination of agency; Commission and fees		
3. Valuation and Market Analysis	**12%**	**11%**
Value; Methods of estimating value		
4. Financing	**13%**	**13%**
General concepts; Types of loans; Sources of financing; How to deal with lenders; Government programs; Mortgages/deeds of trust/notes; Financing/credit laws; Loan brokerage		
5. Transfer of Property	**9%**	**10%**
Title insurance; Deeds; Escrow; Reports; Tax aspects; Special processes		
6. Practice of Real Estate and Mandated Disclosures	**24%**	**27%**
Trust account management; Fair housing laws; Truth in advertising; Record keeping requirements; Agent supervision; Permitted activities of unlicensed sales assistants; DRE jurisdiction and disciplinary actions; Licensing, continuing education requirements and procedures; California Real Estate Recovery Fund; General ethics; Technology; Property management/landlord-tenant rights; Commercial/industrial/income properties; Specialty areas; Transfer disclosure statement; Natural hazard disclosure statements; Material facts affecting property value; Need for inspection and obtaining/verifying information		
7. Contracts	**12%**	**12%**
General; Listing agreements; Buyer broker agreements; Offers/purchase contracts; Counter offers/multiple counter offers; Leases; Agreements; Promissory notes/securities		

Dept. of Real Estate
% of Exam Questions
Testing Emphasis

For more information:

www.dre.ca.gov
(Department of Real Estate Home Page)

www.dre.ca.gov/salesqs.htm
(Salesperson Examination Content and Test Questions)

Applicants for the Broker's Exam

1. An applicant for the broker's license examination must have completed eight courses in addition to the experience requirements. These eight courses must include the following five:

   Real Estate Practice   **Real Estate Appraisal**
   Legal Aspects of Real Estate **Real Estate Economics (or Accounting)**
   Real Estate Financing

2. The remaining three courses are to be selected from the following:

   Real Estate Principles   **Advanced Legal Aspects of R. E.**
   Business Law   **Advanced Real Estate Finance**
   Property Management   **Advanced R. E. Appraisal**
   Escrows   **Computer Applications in Real Estate**
   R. E. Office Administration   **Common Interest Development**
   Mortgage Loan Brokering and Lending

---

weeks) as a salesperson is required. This two-year requirement may be replaced by an equivalent amount of part-time salesperson work. Such experience must have been completed within the five years immediately preceding the date of application.

Sometimes the State Real Estate Commissioner will accept experience in fields other than real estate sales. These fields include contract work, lease, escrow, title insurance, bonds, mortgage company, or experience in another area directly involved in real estate.

Besides direct experience in these fields, education may qualify as full or partial experience. For example, the Commissioner has ruled that any individual with a four-year college degree is exempt from the two-year experience requirement. But, all candidates must complete the eight required real estate courses, regardless of their educational degree.

All students are encouraged to submit an equivalency request with the Department of Real Estate. All decisions made by the Commissioner are final.

B.S. or B.A. (four-year degree) = 2 years of experience

Most California colleges and universities offer courses and majors in real estate (see **Figure 14-3**).

The broker's 200-question exam takes five hours to complete. The applicant must answer 75% of the questions correctly to pass.

2. Broker's Required Education (Eight Courses)

Applicants for the real estate broker's license examination must have successfully completed the eight statutory-required, college-level courses. The required salesperson's

Figure 14-3

ADVANCED EDUCATION IN REAL ESTATE

As the study of real estate becomes more complex and more intertwined with other business disciplines, students of real estate find it rewarding to continue their studies beyond those levels required to enter the field as a salesperson or broker. Many real estate professionals, after obtaining their A.A. degrees from one of our 108 community colleges, have gone on to pursue bachelor's and master's degrees.

CALIFORNIA STATE UNIVERSITY SYSTEM

Bakersfield	Northridge
Channel Islands	Pomona*
Chico	Sacramento*
Dominguez Hills	San Bernardino
Fresno	San Diego*
Fullerton	San Francisco
Hayward	San Jose
Humboldt	San Luis Obispo
Long Beach	San Marcos
Los Angeles	Sonoma
Maritime	Stanislaus
Academy	
Monterey Bay	

Regional centers for RELUI
Real Estate and Land Use Institute
Cal State University, Sacramento
Sacramento, CA 95819

UNIVERSITY OF CALIFORNIA SYSTEM

Berkeley**	Riverside
Davis	San Diego
Irvine	San Francisco
Los Angeles***	Santa Barbara
Merced	Santa Cruz

**The U.C. Berkeley Fisher Center for Real Estate and Urban Economics (FCREUE) publishes a newsletter, Quarterly Report, which may be obtained by instructors and school libraries by writing (on college stationery) to, or contacting: Haas Real Estate Group or FCREUE: Haas School of Business, University of California Berkeley, CA 94720-1900; Tel: (510) 643-6105; Fax: (510) 643-7357; Email: creue@haas.berkeley.edu.*

***U.C.L.A. offers information on recent trends in real estate. For more information, contact the Richard S. Ziman Center for Real Estate, 110 Westwood Plaza, Los Angeles, CA 90095; Phone: (310) 206-9424; Fax: (310) 206-5455; ziman.center@anderson.ucla.edu*

EXTENSION COURSES

The UC and Cal State University campuses also offer extension programs for persons interested in a more in-depth study of certain areas of real estate without the constraints of a degree program. Classes are generally offered in the evening or on weekends.

CHAPTER 14

Filing a Ficticious Business Name

To file a fictitious business name, the broker must: 1) file a fictitious business name statement in the county where he/she intends to operate; 2) publish the fictitious business name in a newspaper of general circulation; and 3) obtain approval of the name by the Real Estate Commissioner and be issued a license in the name of the fictitious business name.

courses can be found on the list of required broker's courses, but the number of required courses is different: three for the regular salesperson's license and eight for the broker's license. An applicant's choice of eight (broker-required) courses must be taken by all broker candidates.

Once all of these requirements have been completed, a candidate may apply to take the broker's examination. By filing the examination fee, plus proof of 2 years' experience or the equivalent thereof, and transcripts showing that the eight statutory classes have been completed, the applicant will receive his or her admission card for the test. The cost of a broker's license is $165.

Members of the bar will generally qualify on the basis of their education and experience and are exempt from the college-level course requirements. Law school graduates who are not members of the state bar are required to successfully complete a college-level course in Real Estate Finance and one in Real Estate Appraisal.

E. RENEWAL OF LICENSE – EVERY FOUR YEARS (Salesperson and Broker)

If a real estate license is not renewed, the licensee has a two-year grace period and late renewal fees.

Once the license has expired, no licensed-required activity can be performed by the salesperson until the license has been renewed. The late renewal period (often referred to as the "grace" period) simply allows the licensee to renew on a late basis without retaking the examination; it does not allow the licensee to conduct license-required activity during the late renewal period. The license renewal fee for a salesperson is $120 if filed on time and $180 if filed late. A broker's renewal costs $165 if on time and $248 if late.

Whenever a real estate salesperson enters the employ of a real estate broker, or whenever the salesperson is terminated, the broker shall immediately notify the Department of Real Estate in writing.

F. CONTINUING EDUCATION (CE) REQUIREMENT
(45 Hours Every Four Years to Renew Your License)

All real estate licensees are required to attend 45 clock hours of Commissioner-approved courses, seminars, or conferences during the four-year period preceding license renewal. First time renewal for both broker and salesperson requires five separate three-hour courses in the following subjects: Ethics, Agency, Trust Fund Handling, Fair Housing, and Risk Management; a minimum of 18 clock hours of Consumer Protection Courses, and the remaining 15 clock hours related to either Consumer Service or Consumer Protection. **Figure 14-4** shows continuing education requirements for second and subsequent renewals.

Figure 14-4

45 Hours of Required Continuing Education

The required 45 hours of continuing education for second and subsequent renewals include:

12 hours of: Ethics, Agency, Trust Fund Handling, and Fair Housing **or** one six-hour course that covers the four mandatory subjects (Ethics, Agency, Trust Fund Handling, and Fair Housing);

One three-hour course in Risk Management, 18 clock hours of consumer protection courses, and the remaining clock hours to complete the 45 hours of continuing education may be related to either Consumer Service or Consumer Protection courses.

18 hours of Consumer Protection, including Agency, Ethics, Trust Fund Handling, Fair Housing, and Risk Management are all included in the required 45 hours of continuing education.

1. "Eight-Hour Continuing Education (CE) Survey" Course

The "Eight-Hour CE Survey" course can replace the 15-hour combination of five separate 3-hour courses (Ethics, Agency, Trust Fund Handling, Fair Housing, and Risk Management), starting with your second license renewal. So if a licensee takes the *Eight-hour CE Survey* course, he or she still needs an additional 36 hours of CE to complete the 45 total hours required every four years at license renewal time.

G. OTHER REAL ESTATE-RELATED LICENSES

1. Prepaid Rental Listing Service License

A *PREPAID RENTAL LISTING SERVICE (PRLS)* license is required when running a business that supplies prospective tenants with listings of residential real property for rent or lease while collecting a fee for such service. Negotiation of the rental of property is not a part of this activity. An individual may obtain, without examination, a two-year license to conduct PRLS activities.

Prior to issuance of the PRLS license, the applicant must submit, and have approved by the DRE, a contract to be entered into between the licensee and client (prospective tenant). Fingerprints and a $2,500 surety bond are required for each business location.

2. Real Property Securities Dealer (RPSD) Endorsement

A *REAL PROPERTY SECURITIES DEALER (RPSD)* is any person acting as a principal or agent who engages in the business of selling real property securities (such as promissory notes or sales contracts). RPSDs also accept or offer to accept funds for reinvestment in real property securities or for placement in an account. Before a licensed real estate broker may act in the capacity of an RPSD, he or she must obtain an RPSD endorsement on his

or her broker's license. To obtain an RPSD endorsement on a broker's license, submit the appropriate endorsement fee along with proof of a properly executed $10,000 surety bond. (For information on Real Property Securities, see Chapter 9 or call the DRE.)

www.corp.ca.gov
Department of Corporations

III. Business Opportunity Brokerage

In a sale of an existing business (Business Opportunity), the real property is transferred by "deed." If money is owed on the business, the proper financial statements are filed with the Secretary of State's office.

Personal property is transferred by a "bill of sale."

Your real estate license also authorizes you to practice in the specialized field of "Business Opportunities." This is a different area of real estate, and requires knowledge and experience beyond that which is needed for real property transactions. The business opportunity broker's transactions usually include the three items shown in **Figure 14-5**.

www.census.gov
U.S. Census Bureau
www.sbaonline.sba.gov
Small Business Administration

A. BUSINESS OPPORTUNITY SALE

A common definition of a **BUSINESS** *is an establishment whose main purpose is the buying and reselling of goods, or the performance of services, with the intention of making a profit. A **BUSINESS OPPORTUNITY** is the sale or lease of a business, including the goodwill of an existing business.* It involves the sale of personal property and must also conform to the rules and laws that govern the transfer of chattels (personal property). The most common types of business opportunities are small, locally owned neighborhood businesses like grocery stores, liquor stores, laundromats, service stations, and restaurants.

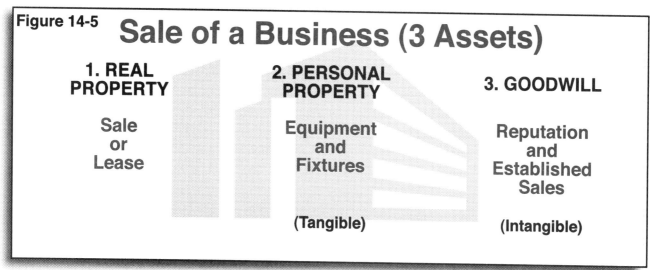

Figure 14-5

Sale of a Business (3 Assets)

1. REAL PROPERTY	2. PERSONAL PROPERTY	3. GOODWILL
Sale or Lease	Equipment and Fixtures	Reputation and Established Sales
	(Tangible)	(Intangible)

The three documents in a personal property security transaction are: 1) a promissory note; 2) a security agreement; and 3) compliance with the UCC-1 financing statement.

B. BUSINESS OPPORTUNITY LISTING

A business opportunity salesperson should have a working knowledge of business practices and a thorough understanding of accounting or bookkeeping principles. The seller of the business must give you all the pertinent information as part of the listing agreement. The accuracy of the information, however, should be validated by the listing broker.

Business opportunities can involve the transfer of both real and personal property and usually use one escrow.

The business opportunity listing should include all the information necessary for a real property sale. It should also include the:

1. name of business and owner.
2. nature and location of business.
3. price and terms of sale.
4. encumbrances and items that are to be assumed by the buyer.

In addition, if there is a lease, the terms should be stated. The important income information should detail the gross income, expenses, and net income. If there is competition in the area, it should be so stated. The usual business hours each day and the square footage of the building should also be stated. If the current employees are expected to stay, salary and any existing fringe benefits should be explained in detail.

Buyers of businesses differ. They are usually motivated by the thought of becoming their own boss or the need for a steady income, and they usually fall into one of these two categories:

1. The experienced individual with a background in the field or business he or she is buying.
2. The new buyer who is usually young and inexperienced.

The experienced individual will usually need only the basic facts in order to decide whether to purchase or not. The inexperienced buyer needs more help, but is sometimes hesitant to ask questions, so all pertinent facts should be explained in detail to that person. He or she should also be informed of applicable laws that govern that particular business.

C. BULK SALES (TRANSFER OF BUSINESS INVENTORY)
(Notice to Creditors Required)

A *BULK TRANSFER is any sale of a substantial part of the 1) inventory, items purchased for resale; 2) other supplies and equipment associated with a business.* Division 6 of the Uniform Commercial Code (UCC) requires the purchaser (transferee) in a bulk transfer to give the seller's (transferor's) creditors fair warning that a sale of all or a major part of the inventory is about to take place.

1. Buyer (Transferee) Must Comply with the UCC

If a retail or wholesale merchant transfers a substantial part of his or her materials, supplies, merchandise, or inventory, the transferee involved in the transfer must give notice by:

1. **Twelve business days prior** to transfer, recorded notice with the County Recorder's Office.

2. **Twelve business days prior** to transfer, published notice in a newspaper of general circulation in the county or judicial district.

3. **Twelve business days prior** to transfer, delivered notice (by hand or registered mail) to the County Tax Collector.

2. Protection for Creditors

This notice must include:

1. notification that the transfer is going to take place.
2. the name and any business addresses used by the seller.
3. the location and a description of the property.
4. the place and date of the transfer.

If all of the conditions of the bulk transfer notice are not met, any transfer of bulk is fraudulent and void against creditors, but valid between buyer and seller.

D. CALIFORNIA SALES TAXES (Selling Retail)

*SALES TAXES are taxes imposed on the sale of **tangible personal property** by retailers.* This is important to brokers and salespeople who are in transactions involving the sale of businesses where sales of tangible personal property is involved. A seller's permit from the State Board of Equalization is the permit that allows sellers to buy at wholesale without paying sales tax as long as they collect sales taxes from their customers and forward these taxes to the State Board of Equalization. Before selling a business, escrow should check to see if there are any past due sales taxes.

IV. Real Estate Law and Regulations

California laws affecting real estate are included in several different acts and codes. The *CALIFORNIA REAL ESTATE LAW is the portion of the Business and Professions Code that refers to licensing and subdivisions.* On the other hand, the *COMMISSIONER'S REGULATIONS are rules that form part of the California Administrative Code established and enforced by the Commissioner of Real Estate.* All licensees should be familiar with the Real Estate Law, the Commissioner's Regulations, and (as mentioned before) the Subdivided Lands Act administered by the Commissioner.

A. ENFORCEMENT OF REAL ESTATE LAW

Licensing and regulatory law is effective only to the extent that it is enforced. The Commissioner, as the chief officer of the Department of Real Estate, is duty bound to enforce the provisions of the Real Estate Law. The Commissioner may, by his or her own choice, and must upon a verified complaint in writing, investigate the actions of any person engaged in the real estate business or acting in the capacity of a licensee within this state. He or she has the power to suspend any real estate license or to revoke it permanently. The Commissioner also has the authority to deny a license to an applicant if the applicant does not meet the full requirements of the law. If, through the screening process (including the fingerprint record) of an applicant for license, it is found that he or she has a criminal record or some other record that may adversely reflect on his or her character, an investigation is made by the Commissioner's staff. A formal hearing may be ordered to determine whether or not the applicant meets the requirements of honesty, truthfulness, and good reputation.

B. HEARINGS FOR LICENSE VIOLATIONS

One function of Real Estate Law is to hold a hearing when there is a question as to the rights of persons to obtain or keep their real estate licenses. The Department of Real Estate and other licensing agencies must conduct hearings with strict regard for the rules set forth in the Administrative Procedure Act. Before denying, suspending, or revoking any license, the licensee is served a statement, and the Commissioner acts as the complainant. The licensee, or respondent as he or she is known in the hearing procedures, may appear with or without counsel. The hearing is conducted according to rules of evidence in civil matters.

A decision is made by the hearing officer based upon his or her findings. The Commissioner may reject or accept the proposed decision or reduce the proposed penalty, and then make his or her official decision. The respondent has the right of appeal to the courts. If the testimony substantiates the charges and they appear to be sufficiently serious, the license of the respondent is suspended or revoked. After a license is revoked, the person affected may not apply for reinstatement until one year has passed.

C. LICENSES: REVOKE, RESTRICT, SUSPEND

The Real Estate Commissioner can revoke, restrict, or suspend the license of any real estate agent for misconduct.

1. Child Support Obligations (150-Day License)

When the Department of Real Estate obtains live-scan fingerprints and performs a background check on a potential licensee, the Department is looking for late child support payments.

The DRE will not issue or renew a full-term license if the applicant is on a list of persons (obligors) who have not complied with a court order to provide child support payments. The DRE will issue them a 150-day license. The Department of Child Support Services compiles a list of delinquencies of over four months, and active licensees who appear on the list have 150 days to get current or have their licenses suspended. The license will not be issued or suspension revoked until a release is furnished from the district attorneys' office.

Example: A real estate salesperson owes the Department of Child Support Services for back child support payments. He may obtain a **temporary license** for 150 days.

V. Common Real Estate Law Violations

In order to obtain information about the ethical or unethical conduct of a real estate licensee, one would most likely consult the Business and Professions Code.

Section 10176 of the Business and Professions Code is the legal guideline for the licensee engaged in the practice and performance of any of the acts within the scope of the Real Estate Law. Section 10177 of the Business and Professions Code applies to situations where the licensee involved was not necessarily acting as an agent or as a licensee.

All agents must adhere to the ethical and legal requirements of Section 10176 and Section 10177 of the Business and Professions Code, which include violations such as misrepresentation and failure to disclose hidden relationships.

A. SECTION 10176: LICENSEE ACTING IN A LICENSEE CAPACITY

This section of the Real Estate Law is for violations by those licensees who are acting within the scope of their licenses (see **Figure 14-6**).

B. SECTION 10177: LICENSEE NOT NECESSARILY ACTING AS A LICENSEE

Section 10177 applies to situations where the affected party was not necessarily acting in the capacity of an agent or as a real estate licensee (see **Figure 14-7**). The vast majority of brokers and salespeople are honest and perform their services in a straightforward manner. Occasionally, a section of the Real Estate Law may be violated inadvertently and without intent. In such cases the Commissioner would most likely consider restriction of the real estate license. On the other hand, a flagrant violation would most likely cause a revocation of the license.

It is "blind advertising" if an agent gives the impression that he or she is the owner of the property for sale. The Real Estate Commissioner does not approve of pocket listings (kept within real estate office)—they are not part of the professional code and guidelines and are unethical.

> **Example:** A broker runs the following ad on his listings: "4 BR, 3 BA home with swimming pool and spa for sale for $300,000. Call 555-1234." This is called a blind ad.

C. REGULATIONS OF THE COMMISSIONER (Found in the Administrative Code)

Real Estate Law empowers the Commissioner to issue regulations to aid in the administration and enforcement of the law. These regulations, which are known formally as the Regulations of the Real Estate Commissioner, have the force and effect of the law itself. Licensees and prospective licensees should be familiar with these regulations. The California Department of Real Estate produces a factual law book entitled *Real Estate Law (Real Estate Law and Regulations of the Real Estate Commissioner)*, which can be obtained from their office.

Figure 14-6

Business & Professions Code 10176
(Real Estate Licensee _Acting_ As Licensee)
Grounds for Revocation or Suspension

Misrepresentation - 10176(a)

The licensee must disclose to his or her principal all material facts that the principal should know. Failure to do so or lying is cause for disciplinary action. A great majority of the complaints received by the Commissioner allege misrepresentation on the part of the broker or his or her salespeople.

False Promise - 10176(b)

A false promise is a false statement about what the promisor is going to do in the future. Many times a false promise is provided by showing the promise was impossible to perform and that the person making the promise knew it was impossible.

Continued and Flagrant Misrepresentation by Agents - 10176(c)

This section gives the commissioner the right to discipline a licensee for a continued and flagrant course of misrepresentation or making of false promises through real estate agents or salespeople.

Divided Agency - 10176(d)

This section requires a licensee to inform all his or her principals if he or she is acting as agent for more than one party in a transaction.

Commingling - 10176(e)

Commingling takes place when a broker has mixed the funds of his or her principals with his or her own money. A broker should keep all funds separate.

Definite Termination Date - 10176(f)

A specified termination date, in writing, is required for all exclusive listing transactions.

Secret Profit - 10176(g)

Secret profit cases usually arise when the broker makes a low offer, usually through a "dummy" purchaser, when he or she already has a higher offer from another buyer. The difference is the secret profit.

Listing Option - 10176(h)

This section requires a licensee, when he or she has used a form which is both an option and a listing, to obtain the written consent of his or her principal approving the amount of such profit before the licensee may exercise the option. This does not apply where a licensee is using an option only.

Dishonest Dealing - 10176(i)

Dishonest dealing is a catch-all section used when the acts of the person required a license, but he or she did not have a license.

Signatures of Prospective Purchasers - 10176(j)

Brokers must obtain a written (business opportunities) authorization to sell from an owner before securing the signature of a prospective purchaser to the agreement. This section strikes at what was once a common practice in some areas in the sale of business opportunities, where the prospective purchaser was forced to deal with the broker who furnished him or her the listing.

Figure 14-7

Business and Professions Code 10177
(R.E. Licensee <u>Not Necessarily Acting</u> as a Licensee)
Grounds for Revocation or Suspension

Obtaining License by Fraud - Section 10177(a)

This section gives the Commissioner the power to take action against a licensee for misstatements of fact in an application for a license and in those instances where licenses have been procured by fraud, misrepresentation, or deceit.

Convictions - Section 10177(b)

This section permits proceedings against a licensee after a criminal conviction for either a felony or a misdemeanor which involves moral turpitude (anything contrary to justice, honesty, modesty, or good morals).

False Advertising - Section 10177(c)

This section makes licensees who are parties to false advertising subject to disciplinary action. The ban extends to subdivision sales as well general property sales.

Violations of Other Sections - Section 10177(d)

This section gives the Department authority to proceed against the licensee for violation of any of the other sections of the Real Estate Law, the regulations of the Commissioner, and the subdivision laws.

Misuse of Trade Name - Section 10177(e)

Only active members of the national association or local associations of real estate boards are permitted to use the term "REALTOR®." This is a term belonging exclusively to such members, and no licensee may advertise or hold himself or herself out as a "REALTOR®" without proper entitlement.

Conduct Warranting Denial - Section 10177(f)

This is a general section of the Real Estate Law and almost any act involving crime or dishonesty will fall within it. An essential requirement for the issuance of a license is that the applicant be honest, truthful, and of good reputation.

Negligence or Incompetence - Section 10177(g)

Demonstrated negligence or incompetence, while acting as a licensee, is just cause for disciplinary action. The department proceeds in those cases where the licensee is so careless or unqualified that to allow him or her to handle a transaction would endanger the interests of his or her clients or customers.

Supervision of Salespersons - Section 10177(h)

A broker is subject to disciplinary action if he or she fails to exercise reasonable supervision over the activities of his or her salespersons.

Violating Government Trust - Section 10177(i)

Prescribes disciplinary liability for using government employment to violate the confidential nature of records thereby made available.

Other Dishonest Conduct - Section 10177(j)

Specifies that any other conduct which constitutes fraud or dishonest dealings may subject the ones involved to license suspension or revocation.

(continued)

Restricted License Violation - Section 10177(k)

Makes violation of the terms, conditions, restrictions, and limitations contained in any order granting a restricted license grounds for disciplinary action.

Inducement of Panic Selling (Blockbusting) - Section 10177(l)

It is a cause for disciplinary action to solicit or induce a sale, lease, or the listing for sale or lease, of residential property on the grounds of loss of value because of entry into the neighborhood of a person or persons of another race, color, religion, ancestry, or national origin.

Violation of Franchise Investment Law - Section 10177(m)

Violates any of the provisions of the Franchise Investment Law or any regulations of the Corporations Commissioner pertaining thereto.

Violation of Securities Law - Section 10177(n)

Violates any of the provisions of the Corporations Code or any regulations of the Commissioner of Corporations relating to securities as specified.

Violation of Securities Law - Section 10177(o)

Failure to disclose to buyer the nature and extent of ownership interest licensee has in property in which the licensee is an agent for the buyer. Also, failure to disclose ownership on the part of licensee's relative or special acquaintance in which licensee has ownership interest.

Importance of Section 10176 and Section 10177
REGULATIONS OF THE COMMISSIONER

The Real Estate Commissioner is empowered to adopt Regulations for the administration and enforcement of the Real Estate Law and the Subdivided Lands Law. Duly adopted regulations become part of the California Code of Regulations and, in effect, have the force and authority of the law itself. Therefore, all licensees, prospective licensees, and subdividers should be thoroughly familiar with the Real Estate Commissioner's Regulations.

10176. The Commissioner may, upon his or her own motion, and shall, upon the verified complaint in writing of any person, investigate the actions of any person engaged in the business or acting in the capacity of a real estate licensee within this state, and he or she may temporarily suspend or permanently revoke a real estate license at any time where the licensee, while a real estate licensee, in performing or attempting to perform any of the acts within the scope of this chapter, has been guilty of any act listed in this Section.

10177. The Commissioner may suspend or revoke the license of any real estate licensee or may deny the issuance of a license to an applicant or may suspend or revoke the license of, or deny the issuance of a license to, a corporate applicant if an officer, director, or person owning or controlling 10 percent or more of the corporation's stock has done any of the acts listed in this section.

www.dre.ca.gov
California Department of Real Estate

VI. Real Estate General Fund

All the money collected from license and exam fees goes into the REAL ESTATE GENERAL FUND. Eighty percent of this money is used for the operating expenses of the Department of Real Estate. Twenty percent of the Real Estate General Fund is set aside as follows:

1. Eight percent to the Real Estate Education and Research Fund;
2. Twelve percent to the Recovery Fund.

The *RECOVERY FUND was established for the payment of damages and arbitration awards to people who have suffered financial loss due to the wrongful act of a licensee in a real estate transaction.* To qualify for these funds, plaintiffs must first obtain a judgment in civil court (or through arbitration) against a licensee on the grounds of fraud, misrepresentation, deceit, or conversion of trust funds. If after reasonable effort the judgment remains uncollected, a claim may be filed with the Commissioner's office.

A license is suspended until the fund is reimbursed (plus interest). The maximum award from the Recovery Fund is $100,000 per individual licensee ($20,000 maximum per occurrence).

California is one of the few states that actively helps protect the public against fraudulent acts by real estate licensees.

VII. Trade and Professional Associations

A TRADE OR PROFESSIONAL ASSOCIATION is a voluntary, nonprofit organization made up of independent firms in the same industry. It is formed to promote progress, aid in solving the industry's problems, and enhance its service to the community. We will discuss the role of local boards of REALTORS®, the California Association of REALTORS® (CAR), the National Association of REALTORS® (NAR) and its Code of Ethics, and the term Realtist.

A. LOCAL REAL ESTATE ASSOCIATIONS

The *LOCAL ASSOCIATION OF REALTORS® is a voluntary organization of real estate licensees in a particular community.* A broker is entitled to full membership, a salesperson may be an associate member, and a nonrealtor (who is in a real estate related field) may be an affiliate member. For example, an affiliate member might work for a title insurance company, an escrow company, a lender, or any other business having an interest in local real estate activities.

Local boards usually provide a multiple listing service for their members so that all members can be equally informed. Most local boards provide services such as distribution of educational material, seminars, library services, and other worthwhile services for the local REALTORS®.

www.bhbr.com
Beverly Hills, California, Board of REALTORS®

California Association of REALTORS®
525 South Virgil Avenue
P. O. Box 76917
Los Angeles, California 90076

B. CALIFORNIA ASSOCIATION OF REALTORS® (CAR)

The *CALIFORNIA ASSOCIATION OF REALTORS® is the state division of the National Association of REALTORS®.* It is a voluntary organization whose membership includes local realty boards throughout the state and individual members who are not affiliated with any particular local board. With the exception of NAR, CAR is the largest REALTOR® organization in the United States, with over 100,000 members in California. The objectives of the California Association of REALTORS® are:

1. To promote high standards and unite its members.
2. To safeguard the property-buying public.
3. To foster legislation for the benefit and protection of the real estate field.
4. To cooperate in the economic growth and development of the state.

CAR has many standing committees that meet at director's meetings, seminars, and annual conventions. These committees specialize in specific areas such as education, ethics, legislation, political affairs, real property taxation, professional standards, and many other areas. There are also many divisions of CAR.

Most of the people who are successful salespeople are also members of the California Association of REALTORS®. We suggest you become a member of this or some other trade association when you are serious about selling real estate.

C. NATIONAL ASSOCIATION OF REALTORS® (NAR)

The **NATIONAL ASSOCIATION OF REALTORS®** *is the national trade association for all the state associations and local boards of REALTORS® in the United States.* NAR unifies the real estate industry at the national level. It encourages legislation favorable to the real estate industry and enforces professional conduct standards on behalf of its members across the nation.

1. Trade Name

Misuse of the name "REALTOR" is a violation of the California Real Estate Law.

Only active members of the National Association of REALTORS® (NAR) or the California Association of REALTORS® (CAR), through their local real estate boards, are permitted to use the term REALTOR®. This is a term belonging exclusively to such members, and no licensee may advertise or present himself or herself to be a REALTOR® if not associated with such a group.

Use of the term "REALTOR" without proper group affiliation is grounds for revocation of your license.

The National Association of REALTORS® has affiliated institutes, societies, and councils that provide a wide-ranging menu of programs and services that assist members in increasing skills, productivity, and knowledge (see **Figure 14-8**).

If a broker uses the term "Realtor" or "Realtist" and is NOT a member of that group, this is both unethical and unlawful.

2. Code of Ethics

See **Figure 14-9** for the National Association of REALTORS® Code of Ethics. These guidelines show not only how one should act but also how one must act.

The National Association of REALTORS® and its state and local divisions form a composite organization of brokers whose objective is to forward the interests of brokers, encourage education of practitioners and the public, raise the standard of real estate practice and increase the esteem in which brokers are held by their fellow citizens. To this end, a code of ethics has been formulated and adopted. It is the generally accepted code of ethics for real estate people and every REALTOR® swears to abide by it.

D. REALTIST DEFINED

"Realtist" is the name for a member of the National Association of Real Estate Brokers (NAREB).

The National Association of Real Estate Brokers, or "Realtist," is the oldest minority trade association in the United States. *Although composed principally of African Americans and other minority real estate professionals, the* **REALTIST** *organization is an integrated entity open to all practitioners who are committed to achieving "democracy in housing."*

The organization has local boards in the largest cities in most states. The organization in this state, called the California Association of Real Estate Brokers, has four board affiliations:

1. Associated Real Property Brokers, Oakland
2. Consolidated Real Estate Brokers, Sacramento
3. Consolidated Realty Board, Los Angeles
4. Logan Heights Realty Board, San Diego

A Realtist must be a member of a local board as well as a member of the national organization. Both on the local and national levels, Realtists work for better housing in the communities they serve. In many instances, individuals are both Realtors® and Realtists by virtue of dual membership.

E. NATIONAL ASSOCIATION OF HISPANIC REAL ESTATE PROFESSIONALS (NAHREP)

The National Association of Hispanic Real Estate Professionals (NAHREP) is a national non-profit trade association made up primarily of Hispanic members. This association was created to establish a venue where members can congregate, exchange ideas, and formulate an agenda beneficial to the collective well-being of the Hispanic segment of the industry. The mission statement of NAHREP is "To increase the Hispanic homeownership rate by empowering the real estate professionals that serve Hispanic consumers."

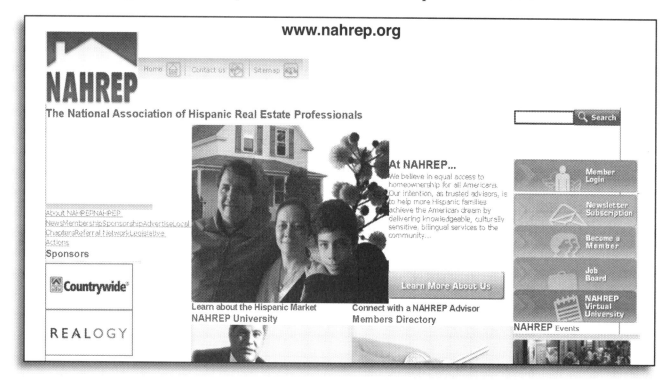

F. ASIAN REAL ESTATE ASSOCIATION OF AMERICA (AREAA)

The Asian Real Estate Association of America (AREAA) is a national trade association committed to enhancing business opportunities and success of real estate professionals serving the Asian American community. AREAA is dedicated to promoting homeownership opportunities among the many Asian American communities throughout the nation.

Figure 14-8

NAR Affiliates

1. American Society of Real Estate Counselors (ASREC)

This division of NAR offers the CRE (Counselor of Real Estate) designation.

2. Commercial Investment Real Estate Institute (CIREI)

CIREI enhances the professional development of those engaged in commercial investment real estate. Offers the CCIM (Certified Commercial Investment Member) designation.

 www.ccim.com

3. Realtors® National Marketing Institute (RNMI)

RNMI promotes professional competence in real estate sales and brokerage, and real estate brokerage management. It has two councils:

A. Council of Real Estate Brokerage Managers (CRB)

Recognized throughout the industry as the professional peer organization for managers of residential, commercial, industrial, relocation, appraising and property management companies. The CRB designation is available for members who meet experience requirements and complete a series of courses.

 www.crb.com

B. Counselors of Real Estate (CRE)

The Counselors of Real Estate is a professional membership organization established exclusively for leading real property advisors.

 www.cre.org

4. Certified Residential Specialists (CRS)

This designation is awarded to the top producing agents in the country who complete advanced training in selling and listing.

 www.crs.com

(continued)

5. Graduate Realtor® Institute (GRI)

The GRI symbol is recognized nationwide, showing buyers, sellers, and other real estate industry members that you are a true professional, and have a solid grasp of real estate fundamentals. It is the dominant real estate designation in California.

 www.edesignations.com

6. Real Estate Buyer's Agent Council (REBAC)

REBAC (Real Estate Buyer's Agent Council) serves Realtors® members who wish to devote all or part of their business to the practice of buyer's agency.

7. Society of Industrial and Office Realtors® (SIOR)

An international organization whose members specialize in a variety of commercial real estate activities. They offer the SIOR designation.

 www.sior.com

8. Women's Council of Realtors® (WCR)

WCR offers opportunities for developing leadership skills as well as a Referral and Relocation Certification (RRC). This is the only referral and relocation certification offered by NAR.

9. Professional Real Estate Executive (PRE)

The PRE designation is available for corporate real estate executives who meet experience and course completion criteria.

 www.realtor.org
NAR - All these affiliates can be accessed here

10. Seniors Real Estate Specialist (SRES)

A Seniors Real Estate Specialist® (SRES) is experienced and knowledgeable in meeting the specific needs of clients 45 years or older. SRES has demonstrated requisite knowledge and expertise to counsel senior clients through major financial and lifestyle transitions involved in relocating, refinancing, or selling the family home.

 www.seniorsrealestate.com

11. The Institute of Real Estate Management (IREM)

This is an organization, within NAR, of professional property managers. They offer a number of designations including:

A. Certified Property Manager (CPM)
B. Accredited Residential Manager (ARM)
C. Accredited Management Organization (AMO)

 www.irem.org/home.cfm

Figure 14-9

Code of Ethics and Standards of Practice of the National Association of REALTORS® Effective January 1, 2007

Where the word REALTORS® is used in this Code and Preamble, it shall be deemed to include REALTOR-ASSOCIATE®s.

While the Code of Ethics establishes obligations that may be higher than those mandated by law, in any instance where the Code of Ethics and the law conflict, the obligations of the law must take precedence.

Preamble

Under all is the land. Upon its wise utilization and widely allocated ownership depend the survival and growth of free institutions and of our civilization. REALTORS® should recognize that the interests of the nation and its citizens require the highest and best use of the land and the widest distribution of land ownership. They require the creation of adequate housing, the building of functioning cities, the development of productive industries and farms, and the preservation of a healthful environment.

Such interests impose obligations beyond those of ordinary commerce. They impose grave social responsibility and a patriotic duty to which REALTORS® should dedicate themselves, and for which they should be diligent in preparing themselves. REALTORS®, therefore, are zealous to maintain and improve the standards of their calling and share with their fellow REALTORS® a common responsibility for its integrity and honor.

In recognition and appreciation of their obligations to clients, customers, the public, and each other, REALTORS® continuously strive to become and remain informed on issues affecting real estate and, as knowledgeable professionals, they willingly share the fruit of their experience and study with others. They identify and take steps, through enforcement of this Code of Ethics and by assisting appropriate regulatory bodies, to eliminate practices which may damage the public or which might discredit or bring dishonor on the real estate profession. REALTORS® having direct personal knowledge of conduct that may violate the Code of Ethics involving misappropriation of client or customer funds or property, willful discrimination, or fraud resulting in substantial economic harm, bring such matters to the attention of the appropriate Board or Association of REALTORS®. (Amended 1/00)

Realizing that cooperation with other real estate professionals promotes the best interests of those who utilize their services, REALTORS® urge exclusive representation of clients; do not attempt to gain any unfair advantage over their competitors; and they refrain from making unsolicited comments about other practitioners. In instances where their opinion is sought, or where REALTORS® believe that comment is necessary, their opinion is offered in an objective, professional manner, uninfluenced by any personal motivation or potential advantage or gain.

The term REALTOR® has come to connote competency, fairness, and high integrity resulting from adherence to a lofty ideal of moral conduct in business relations. No inducement of profit and no instruction from clients ever can justify departure from this ideal.

In the interpretation of this obligation, REALTORS® can take no safer guide than that which has been handed down through the centuries, embodied in the Golden Rule, "Whatsoever ye would that others should do to you, do ye even so to them."

Accepting this standard as their own, REALTORS® pledge to observe its spirit in all of their activities whether conducted personally, through associates or others, or via technological means, and to conduct their business in accordance with the tenets set forth below. (Amended 1/07)

Duties to Clients and Customers

Article 1

When representing a buyer, seller, landlord, tenant, or other client as an agent, REALTORS® pledge themselves to protect and promote the interests of their client. This obligation to the client is primary, but it does not relieve REALTORS® of their obligation to treat all parties honestly. When serving a buyer, seller, landlord, tenant or other party in a non-agency capacity, REALTORS® remain obligated to treat all parties honestly. (Amended 1/01)

Standard of Practice 1-1

REALTORS®, when acting as principals in a real estate transaction, remain obligated by the duties imposed by the Code of Ethics. (Amended 1/93)

Standard of Practice 1-2

The duties imposed by the Code of Ethics encompass all real estate-related activities and transactions whether conducted in person, electronically, or through any other means.

The duties the Code of Ethics imposes are applicable whether REALTORS® are acting as agents or in legally recognized non-agency capacities except that any duty imposed exclusively on agents by law or regulation shall not be imposed by this Code of Ethics on REALTORS® acting in non-agency capacities.

As used in this Code of Ethics, "client" means the person(s) or entity(ies) with whom a REALTOR® or a REALTOR®'s firm has an agency or legally recognized non-agency relationship; "customer" means a party to a real estate transaction who receives information, services, or benefits but has no contractual relationship with the REALTOR® or the REALTOR®'s firm; "prospect" means a purchaser, seller, tenant, or landlord who is not subject to a representation relationship with the REALTOR® or REALTOR®'s firm; "agent" means a real estate licensee (including brokers and sales associates) acting in an agency relationship as defined by state law or regulation; and "broker" means a real estate licensee (including brokers and sales associates) acting as an agent or in a legally recognized non-agency capacity. (Adopted 1/95, Amended 1/07)

Standard of Practice 1-3

REALTORS®, in attempting to secure a listing, shall not deliberately mislead the owner as to market value.

Standard of Practice 1-4

REALTORS®, when seeking to become a buyer/tenant representative, shall not mislead buyers or tenants as to savings or other benefits that might be realized through use of the REALTOR®'s services. (Amended 1/93)

Standard of Practice 1-5

REALTORS® may represent the seller/landlord and buyer/tenant in the same transaction only after full disclosure to and with informed consent of both parties. (Adopted 1/93)

Standard of Practice 1-6

REALTORS® shall submit offers and counter-offers objectively and as quickly as possible. (Adopted 1/93, Amended 1/95)

Standard of Practice 1-7

When acting as listing brokers, REALTORS® shall continue to submit to the seller/landlord all offers and counter-offers until closing or execution of a lease unless the seller/landlord has waived this obligation in writing. REALTORS® shall not be obligated to continue to market the property after an offer has been accepted by the seller/landlord. REALTORS® shall recommend that sellers/landlords obtain the advice of legal counsel prior to acceptance of a subsequent offer except where the acceptance is contingent on the termination of the pre-existing purchase contract or lease. (Amended 1/93)

Standard of Practice 1-8
REALTORS®, acting as agents or brokers of buyers/tenants, shall submit to buyers/tenants all offers and counter-offers until acceptance but have no obligation to continue to show properties to their clients after an offer has been accepted unless otherwise agreed in writing. REALTORS®, acting as agents or brokers of buyers/tenants, shall recommend that buyers/tenants obtain the advice of legal counsel if there is a question as to whether a pre-existing contract has been terminated. (Adopted 1/93, Amended 1/99)

Standard of Practice 1-9
The obligation of REALTORS® to preserve confidential information (as defined by state law) provided by their clients in the course of any agency relationship or non-agency relationship recognized by law continues after termination of agency relationships or any non-agency relationships recognized by law. REALTORS® shall not knowingly, during or following the termination of professional relationships with their clients:

1) reveal confidential information of clients; or
2) use confidential information of clients to the disadvantage of clients; or
3) use confidential information of clients for the REALTOR®'s advantage or the advantage of third parties unless:
a) clients consent after full disclosure; or
b) REALTORS® are required by court order; or
c) it is the intention of a client to commit a crime and the information is necessary to prevent the crime; or
d) it is necessary to defend a REALTOR® or the REALTOR®'s employees or associates against an accusation of wrongful conduct.

Information concerning latent material defects is not considered confidential information under this Code of Ethics. (Adopted 1/93, Amended 1/01)

Standard of Practice 1-10
REALTORS® shall, consistent with the terms and conditions of their real estate licensure and their property management agreement, competently manage the property of clients with due regard for the rights, safety and health of tenants and others lawfully on the premises. (Adopted 1/95, Amended 1/00)

Standard of Practice 1-11
REALTORS® who are employed to maintain or manage a client's property shall exercise due diligence and make reasonable efforts to protect it against reasonably foreseeable contingencies and losses. (Adopted 1/95)

Standard of Practice 1-12
When entering into listing contracts, REALTORS® must advise sellers/ landlords of:

1) the REALTOR®'s company policies regarding cooperation and the amount(s) of any compensation that will be offered to subagents, buyer/tenant agents, and/or brokers acting in legally recognized non-agency capacities;
2) the fact that buyer/tenant agents or brokers, even if compensated by listing brokers, or by sellers/landlords may represent the interests of buyers/tenants; and
3) any potential for listing brokers to act as disclosed dual agents, e.g. buyer/tenant agents. (Adopted 1/93, Renumbered 1/98, Amended 1/03)

Standard of Practice 1-13
When entering into buyer/tenant agreements, REALTORS® must advise potential clients of:

1) the REALTOR®'s company policies regarding cooperation;
2) the amount of compensation to be paid by the client;
3) the potential for additional or offsetting compensation from other brokers, from the seller or landlord, or from other parties;
4) any potential for the buyer/tenant representative to act as a disclosed dual agent, e.g. listing broker, subagent, landlord's agent, etc., and
5) the possibility that sellers or sellers' representatives may not treat the existence, terms, or conditions of offers as confidential unless confidentiality is required by law, regulation, or by any confidentiality agreement between the parties. (Adopted 1/93, Renumbered 1/98, Amended 1/06)

Standard of Practice 1-14
Fees for preparing appraisals or other valuations shall not be contingent upon the amount of the appraisal or valuation. (Adopted 1/02)

Standard of Practice 1-15
REALTORS®, in response to inquiries from buyers or cooperating brokers shall, with the sellers' approval, disclose the existence of offers on the property. Where disclosure is authorized, REALTORS® shall also disclose whether offers were obtained by the listing licensee, another licensee in the listing firm, or by a cooperating broker. (Adopted 1/03, Amended 1/06)

Article 2
REALTORS® shall avoid exaggeration, misrepresentation, or concealment of pertinent facts relating to the property or the transaction. REALTORS® shall not, however, be obligated to discover latent defects in the property, to advise on matters outside the scope of their real estate license, or to disclose facts which are confidential under the scope of agency or non-agency relationships as defined by state law. (Amended 1/00)

Standard of Practice 2-1
REALTORS® shall only be obligated to discover and disclose adverse factors reasonably apparent to someone with expertise in those areas required by their real estate licensing authority. Article 2 does not impose upon the REALTOR® the obligation of expertise in other professional or technical disciplines. (Amended 1/96)

Standard of Practice 2-2
(Renumbered as Standard of Practice 1-12 1/98)

Standard of Practice 2-3
(Renumbered as Standard of Practice 1-13 1/98)

Standard of Practice 2-4
REALTORS® shall not be parties to the naming of a false consideration in any document, unless it be the naming of an obviously nominal consideration.

Standard of Practice 2-5
Factors defined as "non-material" by law or regulation or which are expressly referenced in law or regulation as not being subject to disclosure are considered not "pertinent" for purposes of Article 2. (Adopted 1/93)

Article 3
REALTORS® shall cooperate with other brokers except when cooperation is not in the client's best interest. The obligation to cooperate does not include the obligation to share commissions, fees, or to otherwise compensate another broker. (Amended 1/95)

Standard of Practice 3-1
REALTORS®, acting as exclusive agents or brokers of sellers/landlords, establish the terms and conditions of offers to cooperate. Unless expressly indicated in offers to cooperate, cooperating brokers may not assume that the offer of cooperation includes an offer of compensation. Terms of compensation, if any, shall be ascertained by cooperating brokers before beginning efforts to accept the offer of cooperation. (Amended 1/99)

Standard of Practice 3-2

REALTORS® shall, with respect to offers of compensation to another REALTOR®, timely communicate any change of compensation for cooperative services to the other REALTOR® prior to the time such REALTOR® produces an offer to purchase/lease the property. (Amended 1/94)

Standard of Practice 3-3

Standard of Practice 3-2 does not preclude the listing broker and cooperating broker from entering into an agreement to change cooperative compensation. (Adopted 1/94)

Standard of Practice 3-4

REALTORS®, acting as listing brokers, have an affirmative obligation to disclose the existence of dual or variable rate commission arrangements (i.e., listings where one amount of commission is payable if the listing broker's firm is the procuring cause of sale/lease and a different amount of commission is payable if the sale/lease results through the efforts of the seller/landlord or a cooperating broker). The listing broker shall, as soon as practical, disclose the existence of such arrangements to potential cooperating brokers and shall, in response to inquiries from cooperating brokers, disclose the differential that would result in a cooperative transaction or in a sale/lease that results through the efforts of the seller/landlord. If the cooperating broker is a buyer/tenant representative, the buyer/tenant representative must disclose such information to their client before the client makes an offer to purchase or lease. (Amended 1/02)

Standard of Practice 3-5

It is the obligation of subagents to promptly disclose all pertinent facts to the principal's agent prior to as well as after a purchase or lease agreement is executed. (Amended 1/93)

Standard of Practice 3-6

REALTORS® shall disclose the existence of accepted offers, including offers with unresolved contingencies, to any broker seeking cooperation. (Adopted 5/86, Amended 1/04)

Standard of Practice 3-7

When seeking information from another REALTOR® concerning property under a management or listing agreement, REALTORS® shall disclose their REALTOR® status and whether their interest is personal or on behalf of a client and, if on behalf of a client, their representational status. (Amended 1/95)

Standard of Practice 3-8

REALTORS® shall not misrepresent the availability of access to show or inspect a listed property. (Amended 11/87)

Article 4

REALTORS® shall not acquire an interest in or buy or present offers from themselves, any member of their immediate families, their firms or any member thereof, or any entities in which they have any ownership interest, any real property without making their true position known to the owner or the owner's agent or broker. In selling property they own, or in which they have any interest, REALTORS® shall reveal their ownership or interest in writing to the purchaser or the purchaser's representative. (Amended 1/00)

Standard of Practice 4-1

For the protection of all parties, the disclosures required by Article 4 shall be in writing and provided by REALTORS® prior to the signing of any contract. (Adopted 2/86)

Article 5

REALTORS® shall not undertake to provide professional services concerning a property or its value where they have a present or contemplated interest unless such interest is specifically disclosed to all affected parties.

Article 6

REALTORS® shall not accept any commission, rebate, or profit on expenditures made for their client, without the client's knowledge and consent.

When recommending real estate products or services (e.g., homeowner's insurance, warranty programs, mortgage financing, title insurance, etc.), REALTORS® shall disclose to the client or customer to whom the recommendation is made any financial benefits or fees, other than real estate referral fees, the REALTOR® or REALTOR®'s firm may receive as a direct result of such recommendation. (Amended 1/99)

Standard of Practice 6-1

REALTORS® shall not recommend or suggest to a client or a customer the use of services of another organization or business entity in which they have a direct interest without disclosing such interest at the time of the recommendation or suggestion. (Amended 5/88)

Article 7

In a transaction, REALTORS® shall not accept compensation from more than one party, even if permitted by law, without disclosure to all parties and the informed consent of the REALTOR®'s client or clients. (Amended 1/93)

Article 8

REALTORS® shall keep in a special account in an appropriate financial institution, separated from their own funds, monies coming into their possession in trust for other persons, such as escrows, trust funds, clients' monies, and other like items.

Article 9

REALTORS®, for the protection of all parties, shall assure whenever possible that all agreements related to real estate transactions including, but not limited to, listing and representation agreements, purchase contracts, and leases are in writing in clear and understandable language expressing the specific terms, conditions, obligations and commitments of the parties. A copy of each agreement shall be furnished to each party to such agreements upon their signing or initialing. (Amended 1/04)

Standard of Practice 9-1

For the protection of all parties, REALTORS® shall use reasonable care to ensure that documents pertaining to the purchase, sale, or lease of real estate are kept current through the use of written extensions or amendments. (Amended 1/93)

Standard of Practice 9-2

When assisting or enabling a client or customer in establishing a contractual relationship (e.g., listing and representation agreements, purchase agreements, leases, etc.) electronically, REALTORS® shall make reasonable efforts to explain the nature and disclose the specific terms of the contractual relationship being established prior to it being agreed to by a contracting party. (Adopted 1/07)

Duties to the Public

Article 10

REALTORS® shall not deny equal professional services to any person for reasons of race, color, religion, sex, handicap, familial status, or national origin. REALTORS® shall not be parties to any plan or agreement to discriminate against a person or persons on the basis of race, color, religion, sex, handicap, familial status, or national origin. (Amended 1/90)

REALTORS®, in their real estate employment practices, shall not discriminate against any person or persons on the basis of race, color, religion, sex, handicap, familial status, or national origin. (Amended 1/00)

Standard of Practice 10-1

When involved in the sale or lease of a residence,

REALTORS® shall not volunteer information regarding the racial, religious or ethnic composition of any neighborhood nor shall they engage in any activity which may result in panic selling, however, REALTORS® may provide other demographic information. (Adopted 1/94, Amended 1/06)

Standard of Practice 10-2
When not involved in the sale or lease of a residence, REALTORS® may provide demographic information related to a property, transaction or professional assignment to a party if such demographic information is (a) deemed by the REALTOR® to be needed to assist with or complete, in a manner consistent with Article 10, a real estate transaction or professional assignment and (b) is obtained or derived from a recognized, reliable, independent, and impartial source. The source of such information and any additions, deletions, modifications, interpretations, or other changes shall be disclosed in reasonable detail. (Adopted 1/05, Renumbered 1/06)

Standard of Practice 10-3
REALTORS® shall not print, display or circulate any statement or advertisement with respect to selling or renting of a property that indicates any preference, limitations or discrimination based on race, color, religion, sex, handicap, familial status, or national origin. (Adopted 1/94, Renumbered 1/05 and 1/06)

Standard of Practice 10-4
As used in Article 10 "real estate employment practices" relates to employees and independent contractors providing real estate-related services and the administrative and clerical staff directly supporting those individuals. (Adopted 1/00, Renumbered 1/05 and 1/06)

Article 11
The services which REALTORS® provide to their clients and customers shall conform to the standards of practice and competence which are reasonably expected in the specific real estate disciplines in which they engage; specifically, residential real estate brokerage, real property management, commercial and industrial real estate brokerage, real estate appraisal, real estate counseling, real estate syndication, real estate auction, and international real estate.

REALTORS® shall not undertake to provide specialized professional services concerning a type of property or service that is outside their field of competence unless they engage the assistance of one who is competent on such types of property or service, or unless the facts are fully disclosed to the client. Any persons engaged to provide such assistance shall be so identified to the client and their contribution to the assignment should be set forth. (Amended 1/95)

Standard of Practice 11-1
When REALTORS® prepare opinions of real property value or price, other than in pursuit of a listing or to assist a potential purchaser in formulating a purchase offer, such opinions shall include the following:

1) identification of the subject property
2) date prepared
3) defined value or price
4) limiting conditions, including statements of purpose(s) and intended user(s)
5) any present or contemplated interest, including the possibility of representing the seller/landlord or buyers/tenants
6) basis for the opinion, including applicable market data
7) if the opinion is not an appraisal, a statement to that effect (Amended 1/01)

Standard of Practice 11-2
The obligations of the Code of Ethics in respect of real estate disciplines other than appraisal shall be interpreted and applied in accordance with the standards of competence and practice which clients and the public reasonably require to protect their rights and interests considering the complexity of the transaction, the availability of expert assistance, and, where the REALTOR® is an agent or subagent, the obligations of a fiduciary. (Adopted 1/95)

Standard of Practice 11-3
When REALTORS® provide consultive services to clients which involve advice or counsel for a fee (not a commission), such advice shall be rendered in an objective manner and the fee shall not be contingent on the substance of the advice or counsel given. If brokerage or transaction services are to be provided in addition to consultive services, a separate compensation may be paid with prior agreement between the client and REALTOR®. (Adopted 1/96)

Standard of Practice 11-4
The competency required by Article 11 relates to services contracted for between REALTORS® and their clients or customers; the duties expressly imposed by the Code of Ethics; and the duties imposed by law or regulation. (Adopted 1/02)

Article 12
REALTORS® shall be careful at all times to present a true picture in their advertising and representations to the public. REALTORS® shall also ensure that their professional status (e.g., broker, appraiser, property manager, etc.) or status as REALTORS® is clearly identifiable in any such advertising. (Amended 1/93)

Standard of Practice 12-1
REALTORS® may use the term "free" and similar terms in their advertising and in other representations provided that all terms governing availability of the offered product or service are clearly disclosed at the same time. (Amended 1/97)

Standard of Practice 12-2
REALTORS® may represent their services as "free" or without cost even if they expect to receive compensation from a source other than their client provided that the potential for the REALTOR® to obtain a benefit from a third party is clearly disclosed at the same time. (Amended 1/97)

Standard of Practice 12-3
The offering of premiums, prizes, merchandise discounts or other inducements to list, sell, purchase, or lease is not, in itself, unethical even if receipt of the benefit is contingent on listing, selling, purchasing, or leasing through the REALTOR® making the offer. However, REALTORS® must exercise care and candor in any such advertising or other public or private representations so that any party interested in receiving or otherwise benefiting from the REALTOR®'s offer will have clear, thorough, advance understanding of all the terms and conditions of the offer. The offering of any inducements to do business is subject to the limitations and restrictions of state law and the ethical obligations established by any applicable Standard of Practice. (Amended 1/95)

Standard of Practice 12-4
REALTORS® shall not offer for sale/lease or advertise property without authority. When acting as listing brokers or as subagents, REALTORS® shall not quote a price different from that agreed upon with the seller/landlord. (Amended 1/93)

Standard of Practice 12-5
REALTORS® shall not advertise nor permit any person employed by or affiliated with them to advertise listed property in any medium (e.g., electronically, print, radio, television, etc.) without disclosing the name of that REALTOR®'s firm in a reasonable and readily apparent manner. (Adopted 11/86, Amended 1/07)

Standard of Practice 12-6
REALTORS®, when advertising unlisted real property for sale/lease in which they have an ownership interest, shall disclose their status as both owners/landlords and as REALTORS® or real estate licensees. (Amended 1/93)

Standard of Practice 12-7
Only REALTORS® who participated in the transaction as the listing broker or cooperating broker (selling broker) may claim to have "sold" the property. Prior to closing, a cooperating broker may post a "sold" sign only with the consent of the listing broker. (Amended 1/96)

Standard of Practice 12-8
The obligation to present a true picture in representations to the public includes information presented, provided, or displayed on REALTORS®' websites. REALTORS® shall use reasonable efforts to ensure that information on their websites is current. When it becomes apparent that information on a REALTOR®'s website is no longer current or accurate, REALTORS® shall promptly take corrective action. (Adopted 1/07)

Standard of Practice 12-9
REALTOR® firm websites shall disclose the firm's name and state(s) of licensure in a reasonable and readily apparent manner.

Websites of REALTORS® and non-member licensees affiliated with a REALTOR® firm shall disclose the firm's name and that REALTOR®'s or non-member licensee's state(s) of licensure in a reasonable and readily apparent manner. (Adopted 1/07)

Standard of Practice 12-10
REALTORS®' obligation to present a true picture in their advertising and representations to the public includes the URLs and domain names they use, and prohibits REALTORS® from:

1) engaging in deceptive or unauthorized framing of real estate brokerage websites;
2) manipulating (e.g., presenting content developed by others) listing content in any way that produces a deceptive or misleading result; or
3) deceptively using metatags, keywords or other devices/methods to direct, drive, or divert Internet traffic, or to otherwise mislead consumers. (Adopted 1/07)

Standard of Practice 12-11
REALTORS® intending to share or sell consumer information gathered via the Internet shall disclose that possibility in a reasonable and readily apparent manner. (Adopted 1/07)

Article 13
REALTORS® shall not engage in activities that constitute the unauthorized practice of law and shall recommend that legal counsel be obtained when the interest of any party to the transaction requires it.

Article 14
If charged with unethical practice or asked to present evidence or to cooperate in any other way, in any professional standards proceeding or investigation, REALTORS® shall place all pertinent facts before the proper tribunals of the Member Board or affiliated institute, society, or council in which membership is held and shall take no action to disrupt or obstruct such processes. (Amended 1/99)

Standard of Practice 14-1
REALTORS® shall not be subject to disciplinary proceedings in more than one Board of REALTORS® or affiliated institute, society or council in which they hold membership with respect to alleged violations of the Code of Ethics relating to the same transaction or event. (Amended 1/95)

Standard of Practice 14-2
REALTORS® shall not make any unauthorized disclosure or dissemination of the allegations, findings, or decision developed in connection with an ethics hearing or appeal or in connection with an arbitration hearing or procedural review. (Amended 1/92)

Standard of Practice 14-3
REALTORS® shall not obstruct the Board's investigative or professional standards proceedings by instituting or threatening to institute actions for libel, slander or defamation against any party to a professional standards proceeding or their witnesses based on the filing of an arbitration request, an ethics complaint, or testimony given before any tribunal. (Adopted 11/87, Amended 1/99)

Standard of Practice 14-4
REALTORS® shall not intentionally impede the Board's investigative or disciplinary proceedings by filing multiple ethics complaints based on the same event or transaction. (Adopted 11/88)

Duties to REALTORS®

Article 15
REALTORS® shall not knowingly or recklessly make false or misleading statements about competitors, their businesses, or their business practices. (Amended 1/92)

Standard of Practice 15-1
REALTORS® shall not knowingly or recklessly file false or unfounded ethics complaints. (Adopted 1/00)

Standard of Practice 15-2
The obligation to refrain from making false or misleading statements about competitors' businesses and competitors' business practices includes the duty to not knowingly or recklessly repeat, retransmit, or republish false or misleading statements made by others. This duty applies whether false or misleading statements are repeated in person, in writing, by technological means (e.g., the Internet), or by any other means. (Adopted 1/07)

Article 16
REALTORS® shall not engage in any practice or take any action inconsistent with exclusive representation or exclusive brokerage relationship agreements that other REALTORS® have with clients. (Amended 1/04)

Standard of Practice 16-1
Article 16 is not intended to prohibit aggressive or innovative business practices which are otherwise ethical and does not prohibit disagreements with other REALTORS® involving commission, fees, compensation or other forms of payment or expenses. (Adopted 1/93, Amended 1/95)

Standard of Practice 16-2
Article 16 does not preclude REALTORS® from making general announcements to prospects describing their services and the terms of their availability even though some recipients may have entered into agency agreements or other exclusive relationships with another REALTOR®. A general telephone canvass, general mailing or distribution addressed to all prospects in a given geographical area or in a given profession, business, club, or organization, or other classification or group is deemed "general" for purposes of this standard. (Amended 1/04)

Article 16 is intended to recognize as unethical two basic types of solicitations:

First, telephone or personal solicitations of property owners who have been identified by a real estate sign, multiple listing compilation, or other information service as having exclusively listed their property with another REALTOR®; and

Second, mail or other forms of written solicitations of prospects whose properties are exclusively listed with another REALTOR® when such solicitations are not part of a general mailing but are directed specifically to property owners identified through compilations of current listings, "for sale" or "for rent" signs, or other sources of information required by Article 3 and Multiple Listing Service rules to be made available to other REALTORS® under offers of subagency or cooperation. (Amended 1/04)

Standard of Practice 16-3
Article 16 does not preclude REALTORS® from contacting the client of another broker for the purpose of offering to

provide, or entering into a contract to provide, a different type of real estate service unrelated to the type of service currently being provided (e.g., property management as opposed to brokerage) or from offering the same type of service for property not subject to other brokers' exclusive agreements. However, information received through a Multiple Listing Service or any other offer of cooperation may not be used to target clients of other REALTORS® to whom such offers to provide services may be made. (Amended 1/04)

Standard of Practice 16-4
REALTORS® shall not solicit a listing which is currently listed exclusively with another broker. However, if the listing broker, when asked by the REALTOR®, refuses to disclose the expiration date and nature of such listing; i.e., an exclusive right to sell, an exclusive agency, open listing, or other form of contractual agreement between the listing broker and the client, the REALTOR® may contact the owner to secure such information and may discuss the terms upon which the REALTOR® might take a future listing or, alternatively, may take a listing to become effective upon expiration of any existing exclusive listing. (Amended 1/94)

Standard of Practice 16-5
REALTORS® shall not solicit buyer/tenant agreements from buyers/ tenants who are subject to exclusive buyer/tenant agreements. However, if asked by a REALTOR®, the broker refuses to disclose the expiration date of the exclusive buyer/tenant agreement, the REALTOR® may contact the buyer/tenant to secure such information and may discuss the terms upon which the REALTOR® might enter into a future buyer/tenant agreement or, alternatively, may enter into a buyer/tenant agreement to become effective upon the expiration of any existing exclusive buyer/tenant agreement. (Adopted 1/94, Amended 1/98)

Standard of Practice 16-6
When REALTORS® are contacted by the client of another REALTOR® regarding the creation of an exclusive relationship to provide the same type of service, and REALTORS® have not directly or indirectly initiated such discussions, they may discuss the terms upon which they might enter into a future agreement or, alternatively, may enter into an agreement which becomes effective upon expiration of any existing exclusive agreement. (Amended 1/98)

Standard of Practice 16-7
The fact that a prospect has retained a REALTOR® as an exclusive representative or exclusive broker in one or more past transactions does not preclude other REALTORS® from seeking such prospect's future business. (Amended 1/04)

Standard of Practice 16-8
The fact that an exclusive agreement has been entered into with a REALTOR® shall not preclude or inhibit any other REALTOR® from entering into a similar agreement after the expiration of the prior agreement. (Amended 1/98)

Standard of Practice 16-9
REALTORS®, prior to entering into a representation agreement, have an affirmative obligation to make reasonable efforts to determine whether the prospect is subject to a current, valid exclusive agreement to provide the same type of real estate service. (Amended 1/04)

Standard of Practice 16-10
REALTORS®, acting as buyer or tenant representatives or brokers, shall disclose that relationship to the seller/landlord's representative or broker at first contact and shall provide written confirmation of that disclosure to the seller/landlord's representative or broker not later than execution of a purchase agreement or lease. (Amended 1/04)

Standard of Practice 16-11
On unlisted property, REALTORS® acting as buyer/tenant representatives or brokers shall disclose that relationship to the seller/landlord at first contact for that buyer/tenant and shall provide written confirmation of such disclosure to the seller/landlord not later than execution of any purchase or lease agreement. (Amended 1/04)

REALTORS® shall make any request for anticipated compensation from the seller/landlord at first contact. (Amended 1/98)

Standard of Practice 16-12
REALTORS®, acting as representatives or brokers of sellers/landlords or as subagents of listing brokers, shall disclose that relationship to buyers/tenants as soon as practicable and shall provide written confirmation of such disclosure to buyers/tenants not later than execution of any purchase or lease agreement. (Amended 1/04)

Standard of Practice 16-13
All dealings concerning property exclusively listed, or with buyer/tenants who are subject to an exclusive agreement shall be carried on with the client's representative or broker, and not with the client, except with the consent of the client's representative or broker or except where such dealings are initiated by the client.

Before providing substantive services (such as writing a purchase offer or presenting a CMA) to prospects, REALTORS® shall ask prospects whether they are a party to any exclusive representation agreement. REALTORS® shall not knowingly provide substantive services concerning a prospective transaction to prospects who are parties to exclusive representation agreements, except with the consent of the prospects' exclusive representatives or at the direction of prospects. (Adopted 1/93, Amended 1/04)

Standard of Practice 16-14
REALTORS® are free to enter into contractual relationships or to negotiate with sellers/landlords, buyers/tenants or others who are not subject to an exclusive agreement but shall not knowingly obligate them to pay more than one commission except with their informed consent. (Amended 1/98)

Standard of Practice 16-15
In cooperative transactions REALTORS® shall compensate cooperating REALTORS® (principal brokers) and shall not compensate nor offer to compensate, directly or indirectly, any of the sales licensees employed by or affiliated with other REALTORS® without the prior express knowledge and consent of the cooperating broker.

Standard of Practice 16-16
REALTORS®, acting as subagents or buyer/tenant representatives or brokers, shall not use the terms of an offer to purchase/lease to attempt to modify the listing broker's offer of compensation to subagents or buyer/tenant representatives or brokers nor make the submission of an executed offer to purchase/lease contingent on the listing broker's agreement to modify the offer of compensation. (Amended 1/04)

Standard of Practice 16-17
REALTORS®, acting as subagents or as buyer/tenant representatives or brokers, shall not attempt to extend a listing broker's offer of cooperation and/or compensation to other brokers without the consent of the listing broker. (Amended 1/04)

Standard of Practice 16-18
REALTORS® shall not use information obtained from listing brokers through offers to cooperate made through multiple listing services or through other offers of cooperation to refer listing brokers' clients to other brokers or to create buyer/tenant relationships with listing brokers' clients, unless such use is authorized by listing brokers. (Amended 1/02)

Standard of Practice 16-19
Signs giving notice of property for sale, rent, lease, or exchange shall not be placed on property without consent of the seller/landlord. (Amended 1/93)

Standard of Practice 16-20
REALTORS®, prior to or after terminating their relationship with their current firm, shall not induce clients of their current firm to cancel exclusive contractual agreements between the client and that firm.

This does not preclude REALTORS® (principals) from establishing agreements with their associated licensees governing assignability of exclusive agreements. (Adopted 1/98)

Article 17
In the event of contractual disputes or specific non-contractual disputes as defined in Standard of Practice 17-4 between REALTORS® (principals) associated with different firms, arising out of their relationship as REALTORS®, the REALTORS® shall submit the dispute to arbitration in accordance with the regulations of their Board or Boards rather than litigate the matter.

In the event clients of REALTORS® wish to arbitrate contractual disputes arising out of real estate transactions, REALTORS® shall arbitrate those disputes in accordance with the regulations of their Board, provided the clients agree to be bound by the decision.

The obligation to participate in arbitration contemplated by this Article includes the obligation of REALTORS® (principals) to cause their firms to arbitrate and be bound by any award. (Amended 1/01)

Standard of Practice 17-1
The filing of litigation and refusal to withdraw from it by REALTORS® in an arbitrable matter constitutes a refusal to arbitrate. (Adopted 2/86)

Standard of Practice 17-2
Article 17 does not require REALTORS® to arbitrate in those circumstances when all parties to the dispute advise the Board in writing that they choose not to arbitrate before the Board. (Amended 1/93)

Standard of Practice 17-3
REALTORS®, when acting solely as principals in a real estate transaction, are not obligated to arbitrate disputes with other REALTORS® absent a specific written agreement to the contrary. (Adopted 1/96)

Standard of Practice 17-4
Specific non-contractual disputes that are subject to arbitration pursuant to Article 17 are:

1) Where a listing broker has compensated a cooperating broker and another cooperating broker subsequently claims to be the procuring cause of the sale or lease. In such cases the complainant may name the first cooperating broker as respondent and arbitration may proceed without the listing broker being named as a respondent.

When arbitration occurs between two (or more) cooperating brokers and where the listing broker is not a party, the amount in dispute and the amount of any potential resulting award is limited to the amount paid to the respondent by the listing broker and any amount credited or paid to a party to the transaction at the direction of the respondent.

Alternatively, if the complaint is brought against the listing broker, the listing broker may name the first cooperating broker as a third-party respondent. In either instance the decision of the hearing panel as to procuring cause shall be conclusive with respect to all current or subsequent claims of the parties for compensation arising out of the underlying cooperative transaction. (Adopted 1/97, Amended 1/07)

2) Where a buyer or tenant representative is compensated by the seller or landlord, and not by the listing broker, and the listing broker, as a result, reduces the commission owed by the seller or landlord and, subsequent to such actions, another cooperating broker claims to be the procuring cause of sale or lease. In such cases the complainant may name the first cooperating broker as respondent and arbitration may proceed without the listing broker being named as a respondent. When arbitration occurs between two (or more) cooperating brokers and where the listing broker is not a party, the amount in dispute and the amount of any potential resulting award is limited to the amount paid to the respondent by the listing broker and any amount credited or paid to a party to the transaction at the direction of the respondent. Alternatively, if the complaint is brought against the listing broker, the listing broker may name the first cooperating broker as a third-party respondent. In either instance the decision of the hearing panel as to procuring cause shall be conclusive with respect to all current or subsequent claims of the parties for compensation arising out of the underlying cooperative transaction. (Adopted 1/97, Amended 1/07)

3) Where a buyer or tenant representative is compensated by the buyer or tenant and, as a result, the listing broker reduces the commission owed by the seller or landlord and, subsequent to such actions, another cooperating broker claims to be the procuring cause of sale or lease. In such cases the complainant may name the first cooperating broker as respondent and arbitration may proceed without the listing broker being named as a respondent. Alternatively, if the complaint is brought against the listing broker, the listing broker may name the first cooperating broker as a third-party respondent. In either instance the decision of the hearing panel as to procuring cause shall be conclusive with respect to all current or subsequent claims of the parties for compensation arising out of the underlying cooperative transaction. (Adopted 1/97)

4) Where two or more listing brokers claim entitlement to compensation pursuant to open listings with a seller or landlord who agrees to participate in arbitration (or who requests arbitration) and who agrees to be bound by the decision. In cases where one of the listing brokers has been compensated by the seller or landlord, the other listing broker, as complainant, may name the first listing broker as respondent and arbitration may proceed between the brokers. (Adopted 1/97)

5) Where a buyer or tenant representative is compensated by the seller or landlord, and not by the listing broker, and the listing broker, as a result, reduces the commission owed by the seller or landlord and, subsequent to such actions, claims to be the procuring cause of sale or lease. In such cases arbitration shall be between the listing broker and the buyer or tenant representative and the amount in dispute is limited to the amount of the reduction of commission to which the listing broker agreed. (Adopted 1/05)

Standard of Practice 17-5
The obligation to arbitrate established in Article 17 includes disputes between REALTORS® (principals) in different states in instances where, absent an established inter-association arbitration agreement, the REALTOR® (principal) requesting arbitration agrees to submit to the jurisdiction of, travel to, participate in, and be bound by any resulting award rendered in arbitration conducted by the respondent(s) REALTOR®'s association, in instances where the respondent(s) REALTOR®'s association determines that an arbitrable issue exists. (Adopted 1/07)

The Code of Ethics was adopted in 1913. Amended at the Annual Convention in 1924, 1928, 1950, 1951, 1952, 1955, 1956, 1961, 1962, 1974, 1982, 1986, 1987, 1989, 1990, 1991, 1992, 1993, 1994, 1995, 1996, 1997, 1998, 1999, 2000, 2001, 2002, 2003, 2004, 2005 and 2006.

Explanatory Notes
The reader should be aware of the following policies which have been approved by the Board of Directors of the National Association:

In filing a charge of an alleged violation of the Code of Ethics by a REALTOR®, the charge must read as an alleged violation of one or more Articles of the Code. Standards of Practice may be cited in support of the charge.

The Standards of Practice serve to clarify the ethical obligations imposed by the various Articles and supplement, and do not substitute for, the Case Interpretations in Interpretations of the Code of Ethics.

Modifications to existing Standards of Practice and additional new Standards of Practice are approved from time to time. Readers are cautioned to ensure that the most recent publications are utilized.

G. INDEPENDENT BOARDS

There are also several "independent" boards in California, some of which are large in membership and influential in their communities. Most of these boards are organized for some particular purpose, such as a multiple listing service. Many members of independent boards are also members of boards affiliated with CAR. Examples of independent boards are:

1. Chinese American Real Estate Professionals Association of Southern California
2. Chinese Real Estate Association of America
3. Korean Real Estate Brokers of Southern California
4. Women in Real Estate (WIRE)

H. OTHER ASSOCIATIONS

In addition to the above-mentioned organizations, there are many trade associations and professional bodies that are related to the real estate business, such as:

1. American Bankers Association
2. American Savings and Loan Institute
3. Building Owners and Managers Association
4. Mortgage Bankers Association
5. National Association of Home Builders
6. National Association of Mutual Savings Banks
7. Prefabricated Home Manufacturers Institute

I. REAL ESTATE INSTRUCTOR AND LICENSING ASSOCIATIONS

In addition to the above mentioned organizations, there are real estate instructor organizations and other professional bodies that are related to real estate education and licensing (see **Figure 14-10**).

J. NO AFFILIATION NECESSARY

A real estate licensee need not be a member of any trade or professional association. In this case, he or she is simply referred to as a salesperson or broker. There is no compulsion for any licensee of the Department of Real Estate to join or affiliate with any local or state organization. That decision is strictly individual and personal.

Figure 14-10

Real Estate Teacher's Groups

California Real Estate Educators Association (CREEA)

Real estate instructors from throughout the state have come together with the formation of CREEA, the California Real Estate Educators Association. This organization constitutes a chapter of REEA, the Real Estate Educators Association, a private trade association, which is international in scope. REEA has a reputation throughout the world for its comprehensive representation.

**California Real Estate
Education Association
P.O. Box 1230
Costa Mesa, CA 92628
714-751-2787 Ext. 204**

**Real Estate Educators Association (REEA)
407 Wekiva Springs Road, Suite 241
Longwood, FL 32779
407-834-6688**

**www.creea.org (CREEA)
www.reea.org (REEA)
www.ccsf.edu/Resources/Real_Estate_Education_Center/
(California Community Colleges Real Estate Education Center)
www.arello.org (Association of Real Estate License Law Officials - ARELLO)**

CALIFORNIA COMMUNITY COLLEGES
REAL ESTATE EDUCATION CENTER

The California Community Colleges Real Estate Education Center is a real estate instructors' group sponsored by the California Department of Real Estate. The Center publishes a quarterly newsletter and sponsors educators' conferences three times a year in cooperation with the California Community College Chancellor's office. The newsletter, called *The Informer*, is a useful reference source to keep educators up to date on new laws and real estate practices. The conferences are held in the San Francisco Bay area, the Los Angeles area, and the San Diego area. For information about The Informer and Endowment Fund contact:

**Michele E. Hagan, J.D., Director
California Community Colleges
Real Estate Education Center
City College of San Francisco - Downtown Campus
800 Mission Street
San Francisco, California 94103
415-267-6550
mhagan@ccsf.edu**

**Association of Real Estate
License Law Officials (ARELLO)
P. O. BOX 230159
Montgomery, AL 36123-0159**

VIII. CHAPTER SUMMARY

A person who is actively involved in a real estate transaction at the service of another, in the expectation of receiving a commission must be licensed by the **Department of Real Estate (DRE)**, which is the regulatory agency for real estate in California. The DRE is governed by the **Real Estate Commissioner**, who is appointed by the governor and defended by the state Attorney General. The Commissioner does not settle commission disputes, take the place of a court of law, nor give legal advice, but the rules and regulations he or she issues do have the force and effect of law.

To obtain a **salesperson's license**, a candidate must: be 18 or over, honest and truthful, and complete a Real Estate Principle's course, a Real Estate Practice course, and one other required college-level course real estate course and pass the state exam. The salesperson exam takes 3 hours and 15 minutes, has 150 questions and requires a 70% or better to pass.

Applicants must apply for a license within one year from passing the exam date, at which time he or she will have to submit an electronic **fingerprint scan**.

A **broker's license** is required to operate a real estate office. A broker must be 18 years old, have had two years previous experience or college education, complete the required 8 broker courses, be honest and truthful, and pass the required examination. A four-year degree (B.S. or B.A) = 2 years experience.

The **continuing education requirement of 45 hours every four years** for a license renewal, includes three hours each of **Ethics, Agency, Trust Fund Handling, Fair Housing,** and **Risk Management**. After a second license renewal, these four three-hour courses can be replaced with a **six-hour CE survey course** plus additional courses in Risk Management and Consumer Service and Consumer Protection courses.

In a sale of a business, (**Business Opportunity**) the real property is transferred by deed and the personal property by bill of sale. The three documents in a **personal security transaction** are: 1) a promissory note; 2) a security agreement, and 3) compliance with the UCC-1 financing statement. A **bulk transfer** involves the sale of a substantial part of the 1) inventory, items purchased for resale; 2) other supplies and equipment associated with the business. If tangible personal property is involved, escrow should check to be sure there are no past sales taxes due to the **State Board of Equalization**.

California Real Estate Law is the portion of the **Business and Professions Code** that refers to licensing and subdivision. The **Commissioner's Regulations** are rules that form part of the **California Administrative Code** and are enforced by the Real Estate Commissioner. The Commissioner can revoke, restrict, or suspend the license of any real estate agent for misconduct.

All agents must adhere to **Section 10176** (acting in a licensee capacity) and **Section 10177** of the **Business and Professions Code**, which have the force and effect of the law itself.

IX. TERMINOLOGY

A. Broker's License
B. Business
C. Business Opportunity and Bulk Sales
D. California Association of REALTORS®
E. Commissioner's Code of Ethics (2785)
F. Commissioner's Regulations

G. Continuing Education Requirements
H. Department of Real Estate (DRE)
I. Local Board of REALTORS®
J. NAR Code of Ethics
K. ARELLO
L. National Association of REALTORS® (NAR)

M. Police Power
N. Real Estate Advisory Commission
O. Real Estate Law
P. Realtist
Q. REALTOR®
R. Recovery Fund
S. Trade Association

1.____ A national trade association of real estate professionals who call themselves Realtors®.
2.____ The sale of a business.
3.____ The right of the government to enact laws for the protection of the general public. Laws such as zoning ordinances, building codes, and health and safety requirements are common in real estate.
4.____ Any legitimate activity by which people expect to earn money.
5.____ The division of the state government responsible for the licensing and regulation of persons engaged in the real estate business. Heading the department is the Real Estate Commissioner.
6.____ Composed of ten members, it recommends and makes suggestions to the Commissioner.
7.____ A voluntary, nonprofit organization made up of independent firms in the same industry. CAR and NAR are examples.
8.____ A license that allows a person to represent, for compensation, one or more parties in a real estate transaction.
9.____ Established to compensate people who have suffered financial loss due to the wrongful act of a real estate licensee.
10.____ Rules that form part of the California Administrative Code. Established regulations are enforced by the Commissioner of Real Estate.
11.____ The portion of the Business and Professions Code that refers to licensing and subdivisions.
12.____ A local voluntary organization in a given community, made up of real estate licensees.
13.____ The state division of the National Association of REALTORS®.
14.____ The 45 clock hours of Commissioner-approved courses that must be taken by all real estate licensees during the four-year period preceding license renewal.
15.____ The association made up of real estate license law officials.
16.____ Standards of professional conduct and business practices established by the Commissioner to enhance the professionalism of the California real estate industry.
17.____ A term reserved for active members of the National Association of REALTORS® or the California Association of REALTORS®.
18.____ Members of the National Association of Real Estate Brokers.
19.____ In order to be a realtor, a person must swear to uphold this code.

CHAPTER 14

X. CHAPTER QUIZ

1. The Real Estate Commissioner will start an action against a licensee with:

    a. an injunction.

    b. a lawsuit.

    c. an accusation.

    d. a lis pendens.

2. The maximum fine the Real Estate Commissioner can levy against a broker who pays an unlicensed person for soliciting borrowers or negotiating loans is:

    a. $2,000.

    b. $5,000.

    c. $10,000.

    d. $20,000.

3. To file a fictitious business name, the broker must:

    a. file a fictitious business name statement in the county where he or she intends to operate.

    b. publish the fictitious business name in a newspaper of general circulation.

    c. obtain approval of the name by the Real Estate Commissioner and be issued a license in the name of the fictitious business name.

    d. all of the above.

4. Which of the following is included as part of the required 45 hours of continuing education?

    a. Agency and Ethics

    b. Trust Fund Handling and Fair Housing

    c. 18 hours of Consumer Protection

    d. All of the above are included in the 45 hours of continuing education

5. When the Department of Real Estate obtains live-scan fingerprints and performs a background check on a potential licensee, the Department is looking for:

    a. late child support payments.

    b. past job history.

    c. credit report.

    d. all of the above.

6. A real estate salesperson owes the Department of Child Support Services for back child support payments. He may:

    a. obtain a temporary license for 150 days.

    b. not obtain a license until the past due funds are paid.

    c. obtain a license after a hearing by the Real Estate Commissioner.

    d. not obtain a license.

7. A broker runs the following ad on his listings: "4 BR, 3 BATH home with swimming pool and spa for sale for $154,000. Call 555-1234." This is called:

    a. misleading.

    b. a false ad.

    c. a blind ad.

    d. a violation of Regulation Z.

8. In order to obtain information about the ethical or unethical conduct of a real estate licensee, one would most likely consult:

    a. the "REALTOR'S® Golden Rule."

    b. the Business and Professions Code.

    c. the California Criminal Code.

    d. generally accepted business practices of highly trained real estate professionals.

9. The maximum recovery from the Recovery Fund is:

    a. unlimited.

    b. $100,000 per individual licensee ($20,000 maximum per occurrence).

    c. $20,000 per individual licensee.

    d. None of the above.

10. Misuse of the name "REALTOR®" is:

    a. a violation of the California Real Estate Law.

    b. a violation of the Business and Professions Code.

    c. a violation of the Civil Code.

    d. a violation of common law.

ANSWERS: *1. c; 2. c; 3. d; 4. d; 5. d; 6. a; 7. c; 8. b; 9. b; 10. a*

_{TM}

CHAPTER 15
Real Estate Math

Real Estate, as you have learned, can be an extremely profitable profession. The licensee who is able to compute quickly and accurately the mathematics underlying most transactions will be in a better position to capitalize on opportunities as they arise.

This chapter will illustrate and explain some basic mathematical skills useful to a career in real estate. Familiarity with fundamental arithmetic and a few simple formulas along with plain common sense will provide the necessary background. Such knowledge will not only assist in the practice of real estate, but should also prove advantageous in passing the licensing exam. **Figure 15-1** is a table of common measurements.

It might also prove to your advantage to bring a calculator with you when taking the salesperson's examination. The state permits applicants to use electronic calculators as long as they are battery operated, non-programmable, silent, and without printout capability. Such a device will free you from tedious and time-consuming arithmetic work in order to concentrate on the reasoning behind the problems you will encounter.

I. Area Measurement

LAND AREA is the surface space between lot lines measured in square feet.

A. AREA OF A RECTANGULAR LOT

A RECTANGULAR LOT is a four-sided parcel whose opposite sides are equal in length and right angles are formed by the intersection of the sides. The dimensions of a rectangle are equal on two sides. Most lots encountered will be rectangular in shape.

1. How Do We Get "Square" Measurement?

The area of a rectangular or square lot is determined by multiplying the length by the width. The result is expressed in square feet, square yards, or some similar expression. The formula is:

$$A = L \times W$$
$$AREA = LENGTH \times WIDTH$$

CHAPTER OUTLINE

EXAMPLE: How many square feet would there be in a rectangular parcel 100 feet long and 50 feet wide?

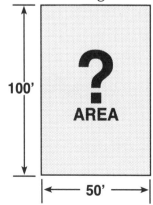

A = L x W

AREA = LENGTH x WIDTH

AREA = 100 FEET x 50 FEET

A = 100 x 50

A = 5,000 SQUARE FEET

ANSWER: The area of this lot is calculated to be 5,000 square feet.

Figure 15-1

Measurements

(A Salesperson Should Be Familiar With These)

LINEAR

1 foot (ft.) = 12 inches (in.)
1 yard (yd.) = 3 feet (ft.)
1 rod = 16.5 ft. = 5.5 yd.
1 mile = 5,280 ft. = 1,760 yd. = 320 rods

SQUARE

1 sq. ft. = 144 sq. in. (12 in. x 12 in.)
1 sq. yd. = 9 sq. ft. (3 ft. x 3 ft.)
1 acre = 43,560 sq. ft. = 4,840 sq. yd. = 160 sq. rods
1 sq. mile = 5,280 ft. x 5,280 ft.

CUBIC

1 cu. ft. = 1,728 cu. in. (12 in. x 12 in. x 12 in.)
1 cu. yd. = 27 cu. ft. (3 ft. x 3 ft. x 3 ft.)

LAND DESCRIPTION

1 link = 7.92 inches
1 rod = 25 links
1 chain = 100 links = 66 ft. = 4 rods
1 mile = 80 chains
1 acre = 43,560 sq. ft.
1 township = 36 sections = 36 square miles = 23,040 acres
1 section = 1 mile square = 640 acres = 1/36 of a township
1 circle = 360 degrees (°)
1 quadrant = 90 degrees (°)
1 degree (°) = 60 minutes (′)
1 minute (′) = 60 seconds (″)

B. AREA OF A TRIANGULAR LOT

A *TRIANGULAR LOT is a three-sided parcel.*

In order to determine the area of a triangular parcel, we must know the measurements of its base and height.

The *BASE OF A TRIANGULAR LOT is the side that is horizontal.* The *HEIGHT OF A TRIANGULAR LOT is the perpendicular distance from the base to the highest point.*

The area of a triangular parcel is determined by multiplying the base by the height, and then dividing by two. This is normally expressed by the formula:

$$A = \frac{B \times H}{2}$$

$$AREA = \frac{BASE \times HEIGHT}{2}$$

Here is a sample exercise for you to try:

EXAMPLE: How many square feet would there be in a triangular lot with a 150 foot base and a height of 100 feet?

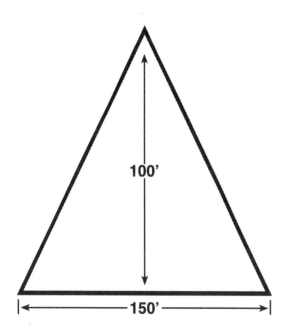

100'

150'

$$A = \frac{B \times H}{2}$$

$$AREA = \frac{BASE \times HEIGHT}{2}$$

$$AREA = \frac{150 \text{ FEET} \times 100 \text{ FEET}}{2}$$

$$A = \frac{150 \times 100}{2}$$

$$A = \frac{15{,}000}{2}$$

A = 7,500 SQUARE FEET

ANSWER: The area of this lot is 7,500 square feet.

C. AREA OF AN IRREGULAR LOT

An *IRREGULAR LOT is a parcel that does not consist of a single known shape.* Often the area of an irregular or circular parcel cannot be measured accurately without the help of a land measurement expert, such as a surveyor. Many times, though, an irregular lot is simply made up of a series of rectangles and triangles, the combined measures of which make up the measure of the whole. In these cases the square footage of the parcel can be determined through the use of techniques already described in this chapter.

The area of an irregular parcel is determined by breaking the lot up into the various rectangles and triangles which comprise it, and totaling their areas.

1. An Irregular Lot Problem

EXAMPLE: What would be the total area of the irregular lot shown below? Use the dimensions given to calculate your answer.

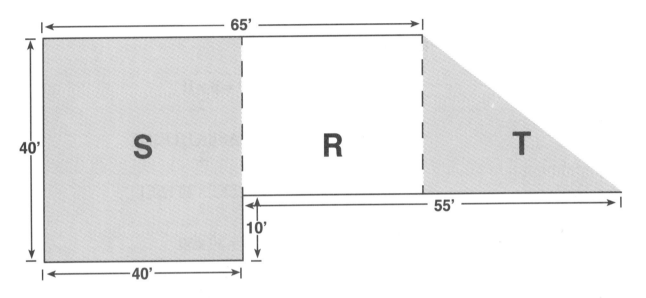

ANSWER: The irregular lot is broken up into a square, a rectangle, and a triangle. The area of the parcel is the total of the areas of each of these.

$$\text{TOTAL AREA} = \text{AREA (S)} + \text{AREA (R)} + \text{AREA (T)}$$
$$\text{TOTAL AREA} = \text{AREA SQUARE} + \text{AREA RECTANGLE} + \text{AREA TRIANGLE}$$

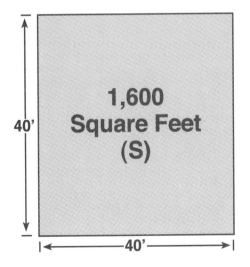

AREA (S) = L x W

AREA (S) = LENGTH x WIDTH

AREA (S) = 40 FEET x 40 FEET

AREA (S) = 40 x 40

AREA (S) = 1,600 SQUARE FEET

The area of the square (S) is 1,600 square feet.

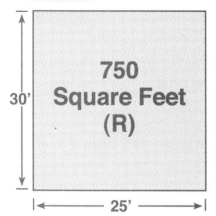

30'

750
Square Feet
(R)

25'

AREA (R) = L x W

AREA (R) = LENGTH x WIDTH

AREA (R) = 30 FEET x 25 FEET

AREA (R) = 30 x 25

AREA (R) = 750 SQUARE FEET

The area of the rectangle (R) is 750 square feet.

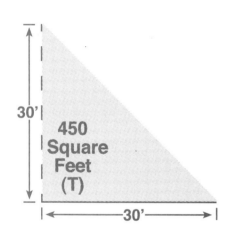

30'

450
Square
Feet
(T)

30'

$$\text{AREA (T)} = \frac{B \times H}{2}$$

$$\text{AREA (T)} = \frac{\text{BASE} \times \text{HEIGHT}}{2}$$

$$\text{AREA (T)} = \frac{30 \text{ FEET} \times 30 \text{ FEET}}{2}$$

$$\text{AREA (T)} = \frac{30 \times 30}{2}$$

$$\text{AREA (T)} = \frac{900}{2}$$

AREA (T) = 450 SQUARE FEET

The area of the triangle (T) is 450 square feet.

Irregular Problem Solution

AREA (S) = 1,600 SQUARE FEET

AREA (R) = 750 SQUARE FEET

AREA (T) = 450 SQUARE FEET

TOTAL AREA = AREA (S) + AREA (R) + AREA (T)

TOTAL AREA = 1,600 + 750 + 450

TOTAL AREA = 2,800 SQUARE FEET

ANSWER: The total area of this irregular lot is 2,800 square feet.

Conversion: Square Feet to SquareYards

Many questions on area will ask that you present the answer in square yards, rather than square feet. Conversion of square feet to square yards is a simple matter of dividing the answer by nine, because there are nine square feet in a square yard.

(3 feet x 3 feet = 9 square feet or 1 square yard)

Square yards, likewise, may be converted into square feet through multiplication by nine.

SQUARE YARDS = $\dfrac{\text{SQUARE FEET}}{9}$

SQUARE FEET = SQUARE YARDS x 9

D. VOLUME OF A STRUCTURE

STRUCTURAL VOLUME is the square or cubic measure of the space within a structure. Structural volume measurement is generally used when renting space in a warehouse type structure. Square measure is the area of the floor space, and it is determined through the use of the same techniques that apply to finding the square footage of a lot. *CUBIC MEASURE is the area volume or total air space.* The cubic volume of a structure is determined by multiplying the interior length by the width and the height. This can be expressed by the formula:

$$V = L \times W \times H$$
VOLUME = LENGTH x WIDTH x HEIGHT

EXAMPLE: How many cubic feet would there be in a room that is 15 feet long, 10 feet wide, and 10 feet high?

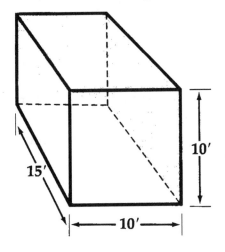

$V = L \times W \times H$
VOLUME = LENGTH x WIDTH x HEIGHT
VOLUME = 15 FEET x 10 FEET x 10 FEET
VOLUME = 15 x 10 x 10
VOLUME = 150 x 10
VOLUME = 1,500 CUBIC FEET

ANSWER: The cubic volume of this room would be 1,500 cubic feet.

II. Percentage Problems

The majority of math problems that you will encounter in real estate involve the use of percent. It is important, therefore, for you to understand certain general rules about percentage problems before dealing with any of the particular types. There are three factors in any percentage problem:

1. The amount *PAID (P) is the amount invested.*
2. The *RATE (%) is the percentage.*
3. The amount *MADE (M) is the amount earned.*

In percentage problems, **one** of the three factors is missing. There are three rules for finding the missing factor:

1. To find the amount **PAID (P)**, divide **MADE (M)** by the **RATE (%)**.
2. To find the amount **MADE (M)**, multiply **PAID (P)** by **RATE (%)**.
3. To find the **RATE (%)**, divide **MADE (M)** by (**PAID (P)**.

A. OTHER FACTOR TERMS

MADE	PAID	RATE %
Return	Investment	Rate of return
Profit	Cost	Rate of profit
Commission	Price	Rate of commission
Net income	Value	Rate of capitalization
Interest	Principal	Rate of interest

Whenever you are working a percent problem, you will be dealing with one of these equations or a modification of one of them. The typical percent problem will supply you with two of the variables. You may easily determine the third through the use of the proper equation.

B. HUBER'S PYRAMID

If you feel that you might have trouble committing the percent equations to memory, you might want to make use of Huber's percent problem pyramid instead. Shown in **Figure 15-2**, this diagram points out what operation is required to find each of the variables.

To use the Huber Pyramid, simply cover the chamber you are trying to find and then perform the required math:

1. **To find M, cover M and multiply P x %**

2. **To find P, cover P and divide M by %**

3. **To find %, cover % and divide M by P**

When doing a math problem involving three or more variables, first draw the Huber Pyramid and plug in the available figures, then perform the required action.

Figure 15-2

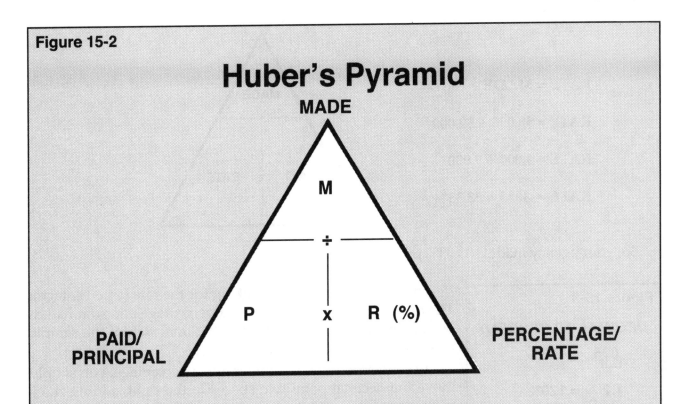

Huber's Pyramid

The Huber Pyramid consists of three sections, or chambers (which can be modified to four chambers for certain problems). The top chamber is the **MADE (M)** chamber. It is separated from the other two chambers by a **division sign**. The bottom left chamber is the **PAID** or **PRINCIPAL (P)** chamber. The bottom right chamber is the **RATE (%)** chamber. It is separated from the PAID chamber by a **multiplication sign**.

Your success in solving percentage problems will depend largely on your ability to spot and identify the three variables as they are presented. In most problems the **PAID** and the **MADE** will both be labeled as money. But the **PAID** (generally the larger amount) will usually be given as a base amount such as a price, investment, or loan balance. The **MADE**, on the other hand (generally the smaller amount), will be a sum made or lost from the **PAID**. Returns, profits, net income, taxes, interest, and commissions are all common labels identifying the **MADE**. The rate is easy to identify because it will always be given as some form of a percentage (%).

Here is a sample percent exercise for you to try:

EXAMPLE: Your agency purchases a lot for $9,000. In selling it later, you made a profit of $3,000. What was your percentage of profit?

ANSWER: The first step is to identify the variables. The principal (paid) is the purchase price of $9,000. The result (made) is the $3,000 margin of profit that resulted from the transaction. The rate is the percentage that we are asked to determine. To find it we use the rate equation:

CHAPTER 15

% = $\dfrac{M}{P}$

RATE = MADE ÷ PAID

RATE = $3,000 ÷ $9,000

RATE = 3,000 ÷ 9,000

RATE = .3333 = 33.33%

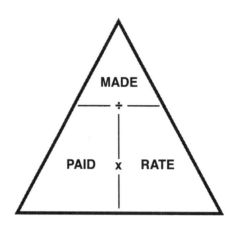

So, your agency made a 33.33% profit on the transaction.

Figure 15-3

DECIMAL TO PERCENT

.095 = 9.5%

1.2 = 120%

.009 = .9%

The above problem was looking for the rate (a percentage). The decimal number .3333 is not a percentage and so it had to be converted into a percentage in the final step of the sample exercise.

To convert a decimal number into a percentage, you simply move the decimal point two spaces to the right, adding zeros if needed. **Figure 15-3** gives some examples of this type of conversion.

In problems where you are asked to compute the results (paid) and the principal (made) it will be necessary for you to multiply or divide by the rate. In these cases you will have to convert the percentage into a decimal before completing the operation. This is done by reversing the process above: Move the decimal point two spaces to the left, and drop the percent sign. This changes a percent into its equivalent decimal form. **Figure 15-4** demonstrates this process.

Another simple way to remember percents is to relate them to dollars and cents.

Figure 15-4

PERCENT TO DECIMAL

8.5% = .085

50.% = .5

110% = 1.1

10 cents	= .10	10%	=	.10
50 cents	= .50	50%	=	.50
$1.50	= 1.50	150%	=	1.50

C. DETERMINING COMMISSIONS AND SELLING PRICE

A *COMMISSION RATE is a percentage of the selling price that is used to calculate the commission. The **COMMISSION** is the dollar amount received by a real estate agent for completing the sale. A real estate agent wants to know how much he or she will be paid for doing his or her job. Most real estate salespeople are paid on a commission basis. As a licensed real estate agent, one of your most pleasant duties will be determining your commission.*

482

When dealing with math problems in real estate, it is important to translate "words" into "math words" and "math symbols."

WORD	MATH WORD	MATH SYMBOL
OF (Means)	**MULTIPLY**	x
IS (Means)	**EQUALS**	=

In commission problems you are supplied with the **PRINCIPAL (PAID)**, which is the property selling price, and the **RATE (%)**, which is the rate of commission, and asked to find the **RESULT (MADE)**, the agent's commission. Such problems use the result equation: **M = P x %.**

EXAMPLE: You have completed the sale of a $100,000 home. The rate of commission is 6%. How much money have you made?

M = P x %

MADE = PAID x RATE

MADE = $100,000 x 6% (.06)

MADE = $6,000

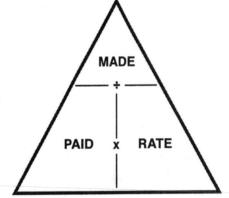

ANSWER: Your commission is $6,000.

1. Splitting Commissions

Most often when you have completed a sale, your brokerage will not be entitled to the entire commission. If you were representing the seller, for example, you might very likely split your commission with a broker and salesperson for the buyer. You will have earned a percentage of the amount earned by your broker, depending on the percentage both of you have agreed to in advance. The rates here are negotiable and usually vary with your experience and success.

When determining the splits of a commission, you use the result **(MADE)** equation. The total commission represents the principal **(PAID)** and the percentage **(RATE)** is whatever rate of commission was agreed to between the parties. **Figure 15-5** illustrates how a commission might be split.

D. PROFIT AND LOSS

When dealing with profit and loss problems, you must establish the value, or cost, before profit (+), or loss (-).

The terms "value" and "cost" are interchangeable in real estate math problems; **it is what you paid for the property.**

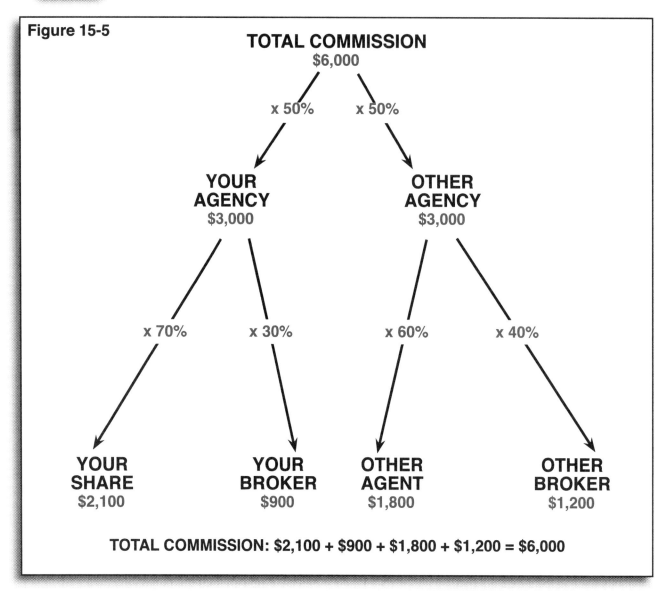

Figure 15-5

Key terms when working profit and loss problems:

1. **SELLING PRICE** – the dollar value after the profit or loss has been added or subtracted from the original cost.

2. **COST** – the dollar value before the profit or loss has been added or subtracted. Cost is often stated as purchase price or original price.

3. **1 + % PROFIT** – in a profit problem, the percent used in the formula will always be greater than 100%; in other words, the original cost (100%) plus the percent of profit. If you sold your property for 40% more than you paid for it, your selling price (100% + 40% = 140%) would be the cost x 140 % (1.40). To find the amount of profit (+40%), you would subtract the cost from the selling price.

4. **1 - % LOSS** – for a loss problem, the percent used will always be less than 100%; in other words, the original cost (100%) minus the percent of loss. If you sold your

property for 25% less than what you paid for it, your selling price (100% - 25% = 75%) would be the cost x 75% (.75). To find the amount of loss (- 25%), you would subtract the selling price from the cost.

The key to working these types of problems is to determine what percent to use.

EXAMPLE: Ms. Smith sold her home for $250,000, which was 8% more than she paid for the property. How much did Ms. Smith pay for the property?

SOLUTION: Remember that profit is **always a %** **of cost**. If we use the Huber Pyramid, we know the Selling price (MADE) is $250,000 and the rate (%) is 108% (100% + 8%). To find the cost (PAID), we would **divide MADE by %**.

ANSWER: (rounded) $250,000 divided by 108% (1.08) = **$231,481**

Ms. Smith paid $231,481 for her property.

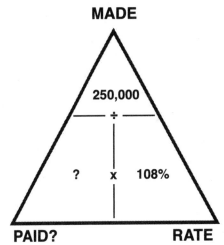

Let's try another problem:

EXAMPLE: Mr. Bush bought a new home on January 14 for $280,000. On July 6, he was transferred to a new city and sold his home for $270,000. What was his percent of loss?

REMEMBER: the percent of loss is based on what the home cost, not what it sold for.

SOLUTION: First we determine the amount of loss: $280,000 - $270,000 = $10,000.

Now we plug in the figures: MADE ($10,000) divided by PAID ($280,000) = percent (%) of loss.

ANSWER: Mr. Bush's percent of loss was 4% (.03572, or .04).

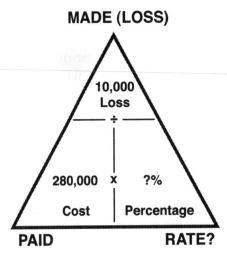

Remember: In profit problems, percent will always be greater than 100%. In loss problems, percent will always be less than 100%.

E. PRINCIPAL AND INTEREST CALCULATIONS

Use a 30-day month (banker's month) in calculating interest payments; thus 1 year = 360 days (statutory year).

Great amounts of capital are necessary to complete most real estate transactions. As a licensed real estate agent, financing will often be one of the major concerns of your clients. It will be advantageous, therefore, for you to be able to provide loan counseling as a part of your services. Essential to this service will be your ability to readily calculate principal and interest payments.

INTEREST is a fee paid for the use of other people's money, stated in dollars and cents. When one leases an apartment, he or she pays rent to the landlord for the use of the property. Similarly, when one borrows money he or she pays "rent" to the lender for the use of the money. This "rent" is called interest. *SIMPLE INTEREST is the term used to describe interest on the unpaid balance.*

Most interest problems will supply you with the principal **(PAID)**, which is the amount borrowed, and the rate **(%)**, which is the percentage being charged. You are asked to determine the interest **(MADE)**. We learned this formula earlier:

$$M = P \times R \, (\%)$$

There is an extra variable that is a factor in all interest problems: time. The duration of the loan determines how much interest is owed at the annual rate. One year equals one, one month equals 1/12, and one day equals 1/360. In order to take this factor into consideration, we modify the MADE equation slightly, with **MADE (M)** becoming **INTEREST (I)**:

$$I = P \times R \times T$$

INTEREST (MADE) = PRINCIPAL (PAID) x RATE (%) x TIME

When doing principal and interest problems, you are trying to find one of four unknowns: **INTEREST (I), PRINCIPAL (P), INTEREST RATE (R),** or **TIME (T)**.

We will use this modified Huber Pyramid to work these types of problems:

Remember: To use the Huber Pyramid, simply cover the chamber you are trying to find and then perform the required math.

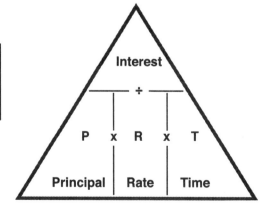

1. Interest Problem

Interest is the payment made for using other people's money. The formula for finding interest is:

$$I = P \times R \times T$$

Here is a sample exercise for you to try:

EXAMPLE: What would be the interest due on a loan of $10,000, borrowed at 9%, for a period of 2 years?

I = P x R x T

INTEREST = PRINCIPAL x RATE x TIME

INTEREST = $10,000 x 9% x 2 YEARS

INTEREST = $10,000 x .09 x 2

INTEREST = $900 x 2

INTEREST = $1,800

ANSWER: The interest would be $1,800.

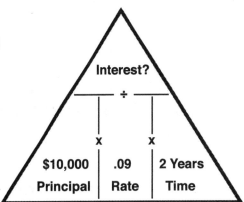

2. Principal Problem

As used in real estate finance problems, ***PRINCIPAL*** *is the amount borrowed in dollars.* To find the principal (amount borrowed), we would use the following formula:

$$P = \frac{I}{R \times T}$$

EXAMPLE: Mr. Johnson has a trust deed loan with annual interest payments of $5,200. If the rate of interest is 10%, how much did he borrow?

SOLUTION: We know that the interest (I) is $5,200, the rate (%) is 10% (.10) and the time (T) is 1 year. Using the above formula:

$$P = \frac{\$5,200}{.10 \times 1} = \frac{\$5,200}{.10} = \$52,000$$

ANSWER: Mr. Johnson borrowed $52,000.

3. Interest Rate Problem

The ***INTEREST RATE*** *is the percent of interest charged.* The purpose of principal and interest problems is to determine what we are paying **(INTEREST)** for the use of the amount borrowed **(PRINCIPAL)** and expressing that amount as a percentage **(INTEREST RATE)**. We use the following formula to find the interest rate:

$$R = \frac{I}{P \times T}$$

EXAMPLE: Ms. Bishop borrows $150,000 from 1st Bank to purchase a condominium. If, after the first year, she owes the lender $15,000 interest, what is the rate of interest?

SOLUTION: We know that the **INTEREST (I)** is $15,000, the **PRINCIPAL (P)** is $150,000 and the **TIME (T)** is one year.

Using the above formula:

$$R = \frac{\$15,000}{\$150,000 \times 1} = \frac{\$15,000}{\$150,000} = (.10) \text{ or } 10\%$$

ANSWER: Ms. Bishop's rate of interest is 10%.

Unless stated otherwise, the interest rate is assumed to be in annual terms.

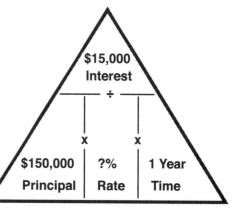

Figure 15-6 explains some useful terms in calculating interest rate problems.

Figure 15-6

In Calculating Interest Rate Problems:

Annual = once a year
Semiannual = twice a year at 6 month intervals
Biannual = twice a year
Bimonthly = 6 times a year (every 2 months)
Monthly = 12 times a year
Semimonthly = twice a month
Biennial = once every 2 years
1 Year = 12 months = 52 weeks = 360 days
1 Month = 30 days

---

4. Time Problem

TIME is used for periods less than or greater than one year. Time is expressed as a fraction or percent of a year (1/12th or .0833) if a payment is to be made monthly. As stated earlier, **interest rates** are assumed to be annual unless otherwise stated. However the payment of **principal and interest** is usually done on a monthly basis. The previous problems used a one year time period. If the time period is more or less than a year, then **TIME (T)** takes on a different value:

Monthly payment: T = 1/12 or .0833
Semiannual payment: T = 1/2 or .5

EXAMPLE: Mr. Philips borrows $200,000 at 9.5 % interest. What is the monthly interest payment?

SOLUTION: **PRINCIPAL (P)** is $200,000, **RATE (R)** is 9.5% and **TIME (T)** is 1/12 or .0833.

$$I = P \times R \times T$$

I = $200,000 x .095 x .0833 = $1,583

ANSWER: Mr. Philips makes a monthly interest payment of $1,583.

F. DISCOUNT POINTS ("Points")

1 discount point = 1% of the loan amount

> DISCOUNT POINTS *are charges made by a lender to increase the yield on a loan: one point equals 1% of the loan.*
>
> **EXAMPLE:** Mr. and Mrs. Majors are purchasing a house for $155,000. They will put $30,000 down and borrow the rest, which will include a 4 point charge by the savings bank. How much will the points cost them?
>
> **SOLUTION:** First we must determine the amount being borrowed:
>
> **$155,000 - $30,000 = $125,000**
>
> Next we compute the discount rate:
>
> **1 point = 1% of the loan amount = .01 x $125,000 = $1,250**
>
> Finally, we calculate the amount of discount:
>
> **4 x $1,250 = $5,000**
>
> **ANSWER:** The Majors will pay $5,000 for the discount points from the borrowed $125,000.

III. Determining Prorations

Buyer's ownership starts on the day of closing.

PRORATION *is the process of proportionately dividing (prorating) expenses or income to the precise date that escrow closes, or any other date previously agreed upon.* Its purpose is to apportion income and expense items correctly between the parties of a sale. These are divided (or **prorated**) in proportion to the time that each owned or will own the property.

In analyzing proration problems, you will first need to determine **who** will be credited with a dollar amount at closing. It is obvious that a seller has owned the property for the period *before* the day of closing and that the buyer will own the property *after* the day of closing. But who owns the property on the day of the closing itself? The real estate contract will usually answer this question.

If the contract determines prorations "to the day of closing," the buyer is considered the owner for that day. But if the contract reads "through the day of closing," the seller is considered the owner for that day for the purpose of determining proration calculations.

The contract will also specify the type year to be used for prorations (a calendar-- 365 day year or a banker's statutory year—360 days).

The next thing that you need to consider is **how much** will be credited. Items that are normally prorated include mortgage interest, taxes, homeowners' association dues, rent, and assessments. In some areas, prorations are also known as **adjustments** or **apportionments**.

Proration involves dividing the dollar amount associated with the time an expense or income occurred between two parties (the buyer and seller). Rent and interest are usually paid in one month intervals, while property taxes are paid once a year. An important question that must be answered is who gets credit for an item. The rules are simple.

On an escrow statement a CREDIT is something that is received and a DEBIT is something that is owed.

A. Rents (Income)

In determining the proration of rents, it is important to know what type year is being used (banker's year or calendar year). The calendar year is generally used. The portion of income that is granted to each party can be represented as a fraction. The denominator will be the number of days in the month, while the numerator will vary depending upon what day in the month escrow closes.

EXAMPLE: If the escrow closes on the 20th day of 30-day month, how would you divide a prepaid rent of $1,500 between the seller and the buyer?

ANSWER: The seller's share would be 20/30 of the whole, because he holds ownership through the 20th day. The share of the other 10 days (10/30) would go to the buyer.

SELLER'S SHARE	BUYER'S SHARE
$\dfrac{20}{30} \times 1,500 = \$1,000$	$\dfrac{10}{30} \times 1,500 = \$500$

So, the seller would receive $1,000 of the rent money, while the buyer would be prorated $500.

B. PROPERTY TAXES (EXPENSES) – BUYER'S AND SELLER'S

Property taxes are prorated either from July 1, the beginning of the fiscal year, or January 1, the middle of the fiscal year. Since each of these two installments covers a six-month period, the portion of the expense prorated to each party is represented as a fraction with a denominator of 6. The numerator varies depending upon what month in the six-month period escrow closes.

Buyer's and Seller's Settlement Statements
(Also See Chapter 7)

DOUBLE-ENTRY BOOKKEEPING is the balancing procedure used to complete a settlement statement. (Accountants will find this the opposite of true accounting.) The statement consists of two parts: a **buyer's statement** and a **seller's statement**. Each of these is divided into a **debit column** and a **credit column**.

A **DEBIT** is something that is owed. A debit entry for a buyer is anything charged against or subtracted from his or her account. The purchase price of the property is an example of something debited to the buyer. A debit entry for a seller means the same thing. Unpaid property taxes are a good example.

A **CREDIT** is something that is received. A credit entry for a buyer is anything received or added to his or her account. The deposit made on the property is a good example of something credited to the buyer. A good example of a credit entry for the seller would be prepaid property taxes.

If an item was **paid** before closing, the buyer's closing statement will be debited and the seller's statement will be credited. If **income** was received before closing, the buyer's statement will be credited and the seller's statement will be debited. Though items on closing statements follow no set order of entry, **the purchase price is usually the first entry and the amount due from/to buyer to close, and the amount due to/from seller to close are the last entries**.

EXAMPLE: The second installment of property tax on a home is $500. The seller has paid this tax, which covers a six-month period ending July 1. If he sells this property and escrow closes on April 1, how much of the $500 is his share in the expense? How much would the buyer have to reimburse?

ANSWER: The seller's share would be 3/6 of the tax bill, while the buyer would also be responsible for 3/6. This is because both the seller and the buyer owned the property for three months during the six-month period.

SELLER'S SHARE	BUYER'S SHARE
$\frac{3}{6} \times 500 = \$250$	$\frac{3}{6} \times 500 = \$250$

Each would be responsible for $250 of the property tax; the buyer having to reimburse the seller, who already paid the entire property tax bill.

CHAPTER 15

IV. Depreciation (For Tax Purposes)

DEPRECIATION *(for income taxes)* *is a diminishing (loss) in the value of buildings and other improvements.* All new depreciation schedules for normal income tax purposes involving real property must be straight-line.

A. STRAIGHT-LINE DEPRECIATION

STRAIGHT-LINE DEPRECIATION is a method of computing depreciation on assets other than land for income tax purposes in which the difference between the original cost and salvage value is deducted in installments evenly over the life of the asset. It is based upon the assumption that depreciation is dependent solely on the passage of time. Depreciation is spread uniformly over the useful life of a property (building).

When doing depreciation problems, it is important to remember that land does NOT depreciate.

To find depreciation using the straight-line method use:

ANNUAL DEPRECIATION (A) = VALUE (COST) OF IMPROVEMENTS (V)
ECONOMIC LIFE (E)

or simplified:

$$A = \frac{V}{E}$$

Let's try a problem using straight-line depreciation:

EXAMPLE: Mr. and Mrs. Roberts purchased some income property for $475,000. The land was valued at $200,000. The improvements had an estimated economic life of 27.5 years. What would be the depreciated value of the property after 17 years?

ANSWER: We must first determine the value of the depreciable asset (improvements) because land is not depreciated.

$475,000 (land and improvements)
- 200,000 (land)
$275,000 (COST of improvements)

$A = \frac{V}{E} = A = \frac{\$275,000}{27.5} = \$10,000$ **depreciation per year**

$10,000 x 17 years = $170,000 accumulated depreciation
$275,000 - $170,000 = $105,000 depreciated value of the improvements only
$105,000 + $200,000 (value of land) = $305,000

$305,000 is the depreciated value of the property.

492

The IRS allows a minimum of 27.5 years straight-line depreciation on residential properties and 39 years on commercial properties.

V. How to Find the Value of a Parcel

PROBLEM: The NW¼ of the SW¼ of Section 7 is valued at $800 per acre. The N½ of the NE¼ of Section 4 is valued at $500 per acre. What is the difference in value between the two parcels?

NW		NE	SECTION 7
160 Acres			
■	40 Acres	SE	

NW		
		■
		80 Acres
SW		SE

SECTION 4

SOLUTION:

1 section = 640 acres
¼ section = 160 acres
¼ of ¼ section = 40 acres   40 acres x $800 per acre = $32,000
½ of ¼ section = 80 acres   80 acres x $500 per acre = $40,000
$40,000 - $32,000 = $8000

ANSWER: $8,000

I wish you the best of luck in your real estate career, whether it be as a homeowner, investor, or salesperson. The future is yours!

– Walt Huber

P.S. – Real Estate cycles go up and down. As a professional, it's up to you to turn challenges into opportunities.

VI. CHAPTER SUMMARY

This chapter illustrates some of the basic mathematical skills useful for a career in real estate. Familiarity with fundamental arithmetic and a few simple formulas, along with plain common sense, will provide the necessary background. Such knowledge will not only assist in the practice of real estate, but should also prove advantageous in passing the licensing exam. You should know the following common measurements:

LINEAR

1 foot (ft.) = 12 inches (in.)
1 yard (yd.) = 3 feet (ft.)
1 rod = 16.5 ft. = 5.5 yd.
1 mile = 5,280 ft. = 1,760 yd. = 320 rods

SQUARE

1 sq. ft. = 144 sq. in. (12 in. x 12 in.)
1 sq. yd. = 9 sq. ft. (3 ft. x 3 ft.)
1 acre = 43,560 sq. ft. = 4,840 sq. yd. = 160 sq. rods
1 sq. mile = 5,280 ft. x 5,280 ft.

CUBIC

1 cu. ft. = 1,728 cu. in. (12 in. x 12 in. x 12 in.)
1 cu. yd. = 27 cu. ft. (3 ft. x 3 ft. x 3 ft.)

LAND DESCRIPTION

1 link = 7.92 inches
1 rod = 25 links
1 chain = 100 links = 66 ft. = 4 rods
1 mile = 80 chains
1 acre = 43,560 sq. ft.
1 township = 36 sections = 36 square miles = 23,040 acres
1 section = 1 mile square = 640 acres = 1/36 of a township
1 circle = 360 degrees (°)
1 quadrant = 90 degrees (°)
1 degree (°) = 60 minutes (´)
1 minute (´) = 60 seconds (´´)

The agent needs to know measurements. The buyer wants to know how much land and building space he or she is buying. **Area measurements (length times width)** in square feet gives him or her that information.

Land area is the surface space between lot lines measured in square feet. **Building area** is the space enclosed by the exterior walls, measured in square feet.

Rectangular Lot: 4-sided parcels. Opposite sides are equal in length and right angles are formed by the intersection of the sides. Area equals Length times Width: $\mathbf{A = L \times W}$.

Triangular Lot: 3-sided parcel. Area equals Base (horizontal side) times Height (perpendicular distance from base to highest point) divided by 2: $\mathbf{A = B \times H \div 2}$.

Irregular Lot: Parcel that does not consist of a single known shape. Area is determined by breaking lot into rectangles and triangles and totalling the areas: **Total Area = Area (S) + Area (R) + Area (T).**

Structural Volume is the cubic measure of the space within a structure. Structural volume measurement is generally used when renting space in a warehouse type structure. **Cubic Measure** is determined by multiplying the interior length by the width and the height: $\mathbf{V = L \times W \times H}$.

The majority of math problems that you will encounter in real estate involve the use of **percentages**. It is important, therefore, for you to understand certain general rules about percentage problems before dealing with any of the particular types.

Percentage problems: Factors are: (1) Amount invested is the amount **Paid (P)**; (2) The rate is the **Percentage (%)**; and (3) The amount **Made (M)** is the amount earned. One of the three factors is usually missing. To compute the missing factor:

Amount Paid (P) = **Amount Made (M) ÷ Percentage Rate (%)**
Amount Made (M) = **Amount Paid (P) x Percentage (%)**
Percentage Rate (%) = **Amount Made (M) ÷ Amount Paid (P)**

The **commission** is the dollar amount received by a real estate agent for completing the sale.

Determining Commissions and Selling Price: The **Commission Rate** is a percentage of selling price. The **Commission** is the dollar amount received for completing the sale:

Commission = Principal Paid x Percentage Rate

Profit and Loss: Profit is the excess of revenues over expenses. **Loss** is the excess of expenses over revenues. **Profits = Revenues minus Expenses.**

Large amounts of capital are necessary to complete most real estate transactions. As a licensed real estate agent, financing will often be one of the major concerns of your clients. It will be advantageous for you to be able to provide loan counseling as a part of your services. Your ability to readily calculate **principal and interest payments** will be essential to this service.

CHAPTER 15

> **Principal and Interest Calculations:** Interest is the fee paid for the use of other people's money.
> **Interest (Amount Made) = Principal (Amount Paid) x Percentage Rate (%) x Time (T).**
>
> **Determining Prorations:** Dividing expenses (property taxes) or income (rents) to a specified date, close of escrow or other agreed upon date, in proportion to time each owned or will own the property is called **proration**. In determining the proration of rents, it is important to remember that all escrow companies use a **30-day base month** (banker's month) and a **360-day statutory year**. The portion of income that is granted to each party can be represented as a fraction. The denominator will be 30, while the numerator will vary depending upon what day in the month escrow closes. **It is important to remember that the buyer's ownership starts on the day of closing.**
>
> **Straight-line depreciation** is the difference between original cost of improvements and salvage value that is deducted in even installments over the life of the asset. When doing depreciation problems, it is important to remember that land does not depreciate, just the cost of improvements depreciate. The IRS allows straight-line depreciation of 27.5 years on residential properties and 39 years on commercial properties.
>
> **Annual Depreciation (A) = Cost of Improvements - salvage value (V) ÷ Economic Life (E)**

VII. TERMINOLOGY

A. Area
B. Commission
C. Credit
D. Cubic Area
E. Debit
F. Depreciation

G. Discount Points (Points)
H. Interest
I. Interest Rate
J. Irregular Lot
K. Principal (Amount Paid)
L. Proration

M. Rectangular Lot
N. Result (Amount Made)
O. Straight-Line Depreciation
P. Triangular Lot

1.____ The amount of money borrowed.
2.____ Money owed as it is shown on the settlement statement.
3.____ The up-front charge by a lender to obtain and to increase the yield on a loan.
4.____ The amount paid to a real estate broker usually expressed as a percentage of the sale price.
5.____ To divide property taxes, insurance premiums, rental income, etc. between buyer and seller proportionately to time of use or the date of closing.
6.____ Decrease in value to real property improvements by any cause.
7.____ The rent or charge for the use of money.
8.____ The surface of land or building. Length (in feet) times width (in feet).
9.____ The area of this shaped lot is obtained by multiplying base times height and dividing by 2.
10.____ Money received; it is shown as what on the settlement statement.
11.____ Principal (paid) times rate (%) equals?
12.____ The percentage paid for the use of borrowed money. Usually expressed as an annual percentage.
13.____ Equal amount of depreciation each year. A loss in the value of improvements, used as an accounting (income tax) procedure.
14.____ A lot with an unusual shape.
15.____ The result of multiplying length times width times height.
16.____ Four-sided figure with opposite sides equal in length and intersecting corners forming right angles.

VIII. CHAPTER QUIZ

1. Ms. Donaldson exchanged her fourplex (fair market value $100,000 with a loan of $52,000) for a larger building (fair market value $150,000 with a loan of $42,000). Using only the above figures, how much money did Donaldson have to pay to complete the exchange?

    a. $48,000
    b. $52,000
    c. $60,000
    d. $108,000

2. Carol borrowed $5,200 and signed a straight note with an interest rate of 7% per annum. If she paid $1,125 in interest during the term of the note, what was the term of the note?

    a. 22 months
    b. 27 months
    c. 32 months
    d. 37 months

3. A woman owns a rental unit that nets her $450 per month. She realizes a 10% return on her investment each year. What is her investment in the property?

    a. $45,000
    b. $48,500
    c. $54,000
    d. None of the above

4. The assessed value of a piece of property is $48,700. The tax is $1.02 per $100 of assessed valuation. The tax is:

    a. $496.74.
    b. $489.60.
    c. $584.40.
    d. $594.14.

5. How much would have to be invested at 7% in order to provide an investor with $640 monthly income?

    a. $9,143
    b. $91,429
    c. $109,714
    d. $53,760

6. The second quarter interest on a $7,600 term loan at 8% interest is:

    a. $76.
    b. $152.
    c. $608.
    d. none of the above.

7. An apartment complex cost $450,000. It brings in a net income of $3,000 per month. The owner is making what percentage of return on her investment?

    a. 7%

    b. 8%

    c. 11%

    d. 12%

8. Broker Jones negotiates a lease for 3,000 square feet of warehouse storage space at a monthly rental of $0.50 per square foot. Jones commission is 8% of the first year's gross. Jones will receive:

    a. $1,180.

    b. $1,340.

    c. $1,440.

    d. none of the above.

9. Frank holds a five-year trust deed and note that was paid off at 7.2% interest per annum. If the total interest he received from the borrower was $4,140, what, approximately, was the original amount of the loan?

    a. $11, 500

    b. $29,700

    c. $33,650

    d. $57,500

10. A builder constructed a home for $350,000 and sold it for a 20% profit. What is the amount of profit?

    a. $17,500

    b. $20,000

    c. $35,000

    d. $70,000

ANSWERS: 1. c; 2. d; 3. c; 4. a; 5. c; 6. b; 7. b; 8. c; 9. a; 10. d

A

ALTA Title Policy (American Land Title Association): A type of title insurance policy issued by title insurance companies that expands the risks normally insured against under the standard type policy to include unrecorded mechanic's liens; unrecorded physical easements; facts a physical survey would show; water and mineral rights; and rights of parties in possession, such as tenants and buyers under unrecorded instruments.

ALTA Owner's Policy: An owner's extended coverage policy that provides buyers or owners the same protection the ALTA policy gives to lenders.

Abatement of Nuisance: Extinction or termination of a nuisance.

Absolute Fee Simple Title: Absolute or fee simple title is one that is absolute and unqualified. It is the most complete title one can have.

Abstract of Judgment: A condensation or summary of the essential provisions of a court judgment.

Abstract of Title: A summary or digest of the conveyances, transfers, and any other facts relied on as evidence of title, together with any other elements of record which may impair the title.

Abstraction: A method of valuing land. The indicated value of the improvement is deducted from the sale price.

Acceleration Clause: Clause in trust deed or mortgage giving lender right to call all sums to be immediately due and payable upon the happening of a certain event.

Acceptance: When the seller's or agent's principal agrees to the terms of the agreement of sale and approves the negotiation on the part of the agent and acknowledges receipt of the deposit in subscribing to the agreement of sale, that act is termed an acceptance.

Access Right: The right of an owner to have ingress and egress to and from his/her property.

Accession: Gaining title when property is added to a property by another or a natural action.

Accretion: An addition to land from natural causes as, for example, from gradual action of the ocean or river waters.

Accrued Depreciation: The difference between the cost of replacement new as of the date of the appraisal and the present appraised value.

Accrued Items of Expense: Those incurred expenses that are not yet payable. The seller's accrued expenses are credited to the purchaser in a closing statement.

Acknowledgment: A formal declaration before a duly authorized officer by a person who has executed an instrument that such execution is his/her act and deed.

Acoustical Tile: Blocks of fiber, mineral or metal, with small holes or rough textured surface to absorb sound, used as covering for interior walls and ceilings.

Acquisition: The act or process by which a person procures property.

Acre: A measure of land equaling 160 square rods, or 4,840 square yards, or 43,560 square feet, or a tract about 208.71 feet square.

Adjustments: A means by which characteristics of a residential property are regulated by dollar amount or percentage to conform to similar characteristics of another residential property.

GLOSSARY

Affiant: A person who has made an affidavit.

Administrator: A person appointed by the probate court to administer the estate of a person deceased.

Ad Valorem: A Latin phrase meaning, "according to value." Usually used in connection with real estate taxation.

Advance: Transfer of funds from a lender to a borrower in advance on a loan.

Advance Commitment: The institutional investor's prior agreement to provide long-term financing upon completion of construction.

Advance Fee: A fee paid in advance of any services rendered.

Adverse Possession: Claiming based on the open and notorious possession and occupancy, usually under an evident claim or right, in denial or opposition to the title of another claimant.

Affidavit: A statement or declaration reduced to writing sworn to or affirmed before some officer who has authority to administer an oath or affirmation.

Affidavit of Title: A statement in writing, made under oath by seller or grantor, acknowledged before a Notary Public in which the affiant identifies himself/herself and his/her marital status certifying that since the examination of title on the contract date there are no judgments, bankruptcies or divorces, or unrecorded deeds, contracts, unpaid repairs or improvements or defects of title known to him/her and that he/she is in possession of the property.

Affirm: To confirm, to aver, to ratify, to verify.

AFLB: Accredited Farm and Land Broker.

Agency: The relationship between principal and agent which arises out of a contract, either expressed or implied, written or oral, wherein the agent is employed by the principal to do certain acts dealing with a third party.

Agent: One who represents another from whom he/she has derived authority.

Agreement of Sale: A written agreement or contract between seller and purchaser in which they reach a meeting of minds on the terms and conditions of the sale.

Air Rights: The rights in real property to use the air space above the surface of the land.

Alienation: The transferring of property to another; the transfer of property and possession of lands, or other things, from one person to another.

Allodial Tenure: A real property ownership system where ownership may be complete except for those rights held by government. Allodial is in contrast to feudal tenure.

Alluvion (Alluvium): Soil deposited by accretion. Increase of earth on a shore or bank of a river.

Amenities: Satisfaction of enjoyable living to be derived from a home; conditions of agreeable living or a beneficial influence arising from the location or improvements.

AMO: Accredited Management Organization.

Amortization: The liquidation of a financial obligation on an equal installment basis; also, recovery over a period of cost or value.

Amortized Loan: A loan that is completely paid off, interest and principal, by a series of regular payments that are equal or nearly equal. Also called a **Level Payments Loan**.

Annuity: A series of assured equal or nearly equal payments to be made over a period of time or it may be a lump sum payment to be made in the future.

Anticipation, Principle of: Affirms that value is created by anticipated benefits to be derived in the future.

Appraisal: An opinion of value as of a certain date; a conclusion resulting from the analysis of facts.

Appraiser: One qualified by education, training and experience who is hired to estimate the value of real and personal property based on experience, judgment, facts, and use of formal appraisal processes.

Appurtenance: Something annexed to another thing that may be transferred with it. Your real property is burdened with an easement, water rights, or improvements that a person may use.

Architectural Style: Generally the appearance and character of a building's design and construction.

ASA: American Society of Appraisers.

Asbestos: A fibrous insulation and construction material that causes serious lung problems.

Assessed Valuation: A valuation placed upon property by a public officer or board, as a basis for taxation.

Assessed Value: Value placed on property as a basis for taxation.

Assessment: The valuation of property for the purpose of levying a tax or the amount of the tax levied.

Assessor: The official who has the responsibility of determining assessed values.

Assignment: A transfer or making over to another of the whole of any property, real or personal, in possession or in action, or of any estate or right therein. (The transfer of an entire leasehold estate to a new person.)

Assignor: One who assigns or transfers the claim, benefit, or right in property.

Assigns; Assignees: Those to whom a lease shall have been transferred or assigned.

Assumption Agreement: An undertaking or adoption of a debt or obligation primarily resting upon another person.

Assumption Fee: A lender's charge for changing over and processing new records for a new owner who is assuming an existing loan.

Assumption of Mortgage: The taking of title to property by a grantee, wherein he/she assumes liability for payment of an existing note secured by a mortgage or deed of trust against the property; becoming a co-guarantor for the payment of a mortgage or deed of trust note.

Attachment: Seizure of property by court order, usually done to have it available in event a judgment is obtained in a pending suit.

Attest: To affirm to be true or genuine; an official act establishing authenticity.

Attorney-in-Fact: One who is authorized to perform certain acts for another under a power of attorney; power of attorney may be limited to a specific act or acts, or be general.

Avulsion: The sudden tearing away or removal of land by action of water flowing over or through it.

Axial Growth: City growth which occurs along main transportation routes. Usually takes the form of star-shaped extensions outward from the center.

B

Backfill: The replacement of excavated earth into a hole or against a structure.

Balloon Payment: Where the final installment payment on a note is greater than the preceding installment payments and it pays the note in full, such final installment is termed a balloon payment.

Bargain and Sale Deed: Any deed that recites a consideration and purports to convey the real estate; a bargain and sale deed with a covenant against the grantor's acts is one in which the grantor warrants that the grantor has done nothing to harm or cloud the title.

Baseboard: A board placed against the wall around a room next to the floor.

Base and Meridian: Imaginary lines used by surveyors to find and describe the location of private or public lands.

Base Molding: Molding used at top of baseboard.

Base Shoe: Molding used at junction of baseboard and floor. Commonly called a carpet strip.

Batten: Narrow strips of wood or metal used to cover joints, interiorly or exteriorly; also used for decorative effect.

Beam: A structural member transversely supporting a load.

Bearing Wall or Partition: A wall or partition supporting any vertical load in addition to its own weight.

Bench Marks: A location indicated on a durable marker by surveyors.

Beneficiary: (1) One entitled to the benefit of a trust; (2) One who receives profit from an estate, the title of which is vested in a trustee; (3) The lender on the security of a note and deed of trust.

Bequeath: To give or hand down by will; to leave by will.

Bequest: That which is given by the terms of a will (applies to personal property).

Betterment: An improvement upon property that increases the property value and is considered as a capital asset or distinguished from repairs or replacements where the original character or cost is unchanged.

Bill of Sale: A written instrument given to pass title of personal property from vendor to the vendee.

Binder: An agreement to consider a down payment for the purchase of real estate as evidence of good faith on the part of the purchaser. Also, a notation of coverage on an insurance policy, issued by an agent, and given to the insured prior to issuing of the policy.

Blacktop: Asphalt paving used in streets and driveways.

Blanket Trust Deed or Encumbrance: A single mortgage that covers more than one piece of real estate.

Blighted Area: A declining area in which real property values are seriously affected by destructive economic forces, such as encroaching inharmonious property usages, infiltration of lower economic inhabitants, and/or rapidly depreciating buildings.

Board Foot: A unit of measurement of lumber; one-foot wide, one-foot long, one-inch thick; 144 cubic inches.

Bona Fide: In good faith, without fraud.

Bond: An obligation under seal. A real estate bond is a written obligation issued on security of a mortgage or trust deed.

Bracing: Framing lumber nailed at an angle in order to provide rigidity.

Breach: The breaking of a law, or failure of duty, either by omission or commission.

Breezeway: A covered porch or passage, open on two sides, connecting house and garage or two parts of the house.

Bridge Loan (Gap Loan/Swing Loan): Short-term loan between construction loan and permanent financing.

Bridging: Small wood or metal pieces used to brace floor joists.

Broker: A person employed by another, to carry on any of the activities listed in the license law definition of a broker, for a fee.

B.T.U. (British Thermal Unit): The quantity of heat required to raise the temperature of one pound of water one degree Fahrenheit.

Building Code: A systematic regulation of construction of buildings within a municipality established by ordinance or law.

Building Line: A line set by law a certain distance from a street line in front of which an owner cannot build on his/her lot. (**Setback Line**)

Building Paper: A heavy waterproofed paper used as sheathing in wall or roof construction as a protection against air passage and moisture.

Built-In: Cabinets or similar features built as part of the house.

Bundle of Rights: Beneficial interests or rights attached to the ownership of real property.

Buy-Down Loan: A loan where the seller pays points to a lender so that the lender can offer below market financing.

Buyer's Agent: An agent representing the buyer rather than the seller.

C

CCIM: Certified Commercial Investment Member.

CC&Rs: Abbreviation for covenants, conditions, and restrictions.

CPM: Certified Property Manager, a designation of the Institute of Real Estate Management.

Capital Assets: Assets of a permanent nature used in the production of an income, such as: land, buildings, machinery, and equipment, etc. Under income tax law, it is usually distinguishable from "inventory" which comprises assets held for sale to customers in ordinary course of the taxpayers' trade or business.

Capital Gain: Income from a sale of an asset rather than from the general business activity. Capital gains are generally taxed at a lower rate than ordinary income.

Capitalization: In appraising, determining value of property by considering net income and percentage of reasonable return on the investment. Thus, the value of an income property is determined by dividing annual net income by the capitalization rate (see below).

Capitalization Rate: The rate of interest that is considered a reasonable return on the investment, and used in the process of determining value based upon net income. It may also be described as the yield rate that is necessary to attract the money of the average investor to a particular kind of investment. In the case of land improvements which depreciate to this yield rate is added a factor to take into consideration the annual amortization factor necessary to recapture the initial investment in improvements.

Casement Window: Frames of wood or metal, which swing outward.

Cash Flow: The net income generated by a property before depreciation and other noncash expenses.

Caveat Emptor: "Let the buyer beware." The buyer must examine the goods or property and buy at his own risk.

Certificate of Reasonable Value (CRV): The federal Veterans Administration appraisal commitment of property value.

Chain: A unit of measurement used by surveyors. A chain consists of 100 links equal to 66 feet.

Chain of Title: A history of conveyances and encumbrances affecting the title from the time the original patent was granted, or as far back as records are available.

Change, Principle of: Holds that it is the future, not the past, which is of prime importance in estimating value.

Characteristics: Distinguishing features of a (residential) property.

Chattel Mortgage: A claim on personal property (instead of real property) used to secure or guarantee a promissory note. (See definitions of **Security Agreement** and **Security Interest**.)

Chattel Real: A personal property interest related to real estate, such as a lease on real property.

Chattels: Goods or every species of property movable or immovable that are not real property.

Circuit Breaker: An electrical device that automatically interrupts an electric circuit when an overload occurs; may be used instead of a fuse to protect each circuit and can be reset.

Civil Rights Act of 1866: The first federal fair housing act (applied to race only).

Civil Rights Act of 1968: Federal fair housing act that expanded the Civil Rights Act of 1866.

Clapboard: Overlapping boards usually thicker at one edge used for siding.

Closing Statement: An accounting of funds made to the buyer and seller separately.

Cloud on the Title: Any conditions revealed by a title search that affect the title to property; usually relatively unimportant items, but which cannot be removed without a quitclaim deed or court action.

Collar Beam: A beam that connects the pairs of opposite roof rafters above the attic floor.

Collateral: This is the property subject to the security interest. (See definition of **Security Interest.**)

Collateral Security: A separate obligation attached to contract to guarantee its performance; the transfer of property or of other contracts, or valuables, to insure the performance of a principal agreement.

Collusion: An agreement between two or more persons to defraud another of his/her rights by the forms of law, or to obtain an object forbidden by law.

Color of Title: That which appears to be good title, but which is not title in fact. Example: title under a forged deed.

Commercial Acre: A term applied to the remainder of an acre of newly subdivided land after the area devoted to streets, sidewalks, and curbs, etc., has been deducted from the acre.

Commercial Paper: Bills of exchange used in commercial trade.

Commission: An agent's compensation for performing the duties of his/her agency; in real estate practice, a percentage of the selling price of property, percentage of rentals, etc.

Commitment: A pledge or a promise or firm agreement.

Common Law: The body of law that grew from customs and practices developed and used in England. (Based on court decisions, not statutes.)

Community: A part of a metropolitan area that has a number of neighborhoods that have a tendency toward common interests and problems.

Community Property: Property accumulated during marriage that is owned equally by husband and wife.

Compaction: Ability of the soil to support a structure. Compaction tests are important as to filled land.

Comparable Sales: Sales that have similar characteristics as the subject property and are used for analysis in the appraisal process.

Compensator Damages: Damages to reimburse an injured party for the actual loss suffered.

Competent: Legally qualified.

Component: One of the features making up the whole property.

Compound Interest: Interest paid on original principal and also on the accrued and unpaid interest which has accumulated.

Conclusion: The final estimate of value, realized from facts, data, experience and judgment.

Condemnation: The act of taking private property for public use. Also a declaration that a structure is unfit for use.

Condition: A qualification of an estate granted which can be imposed only in conveyances. They are classified as conditions precedent and conditions subsequent.

GLOSSARY

Condition Precedent: A condition that requires certain action or the happening of a specified event before the estate granted can take effect. **Example:** most installment real estate sale contracts require all payments to be made at the time specified before the buyer may demand transfer of title.

Condition Subsequent: When there is a condition subsequent in a deed, the title vests immediately in the grantee, but upon breach of the condition the grantor has the power to terminate the estate if he/she wishes to do so. **Example:** A condition in the deed prohibiting the grantee from using the premises as a liquor store.

Conditional Commitment: A commitment of a definite loan amount for some future unknown purchaser of satisfactory credit standing.

Condominium: A system of individual fee ownership of units in a multi-family structure, combined with joint ownership of common areas of the structure and the land. (Sometimes referred to as a **Vertical Subdivision.**)

Conduit: Usually a metal pipe in which electrical wiring is installed.

Conduits: Individuals or firms that purchase loans from originators to resell to investors.

Confession of Judgment: An entry of judgment upon the debtor's voluntary admission or confession.

Confirmation of Sale: A court approval of the sale of property by an executor, administrator, guardian or conservator.

Confiscation: The seizing of property without compensation.

Conforming Loans: Loans that meet the purchase requirement of Fannie Mae and Freddie Mac.

Conformity, Principle of: Holds that the maximum value is realized when a reasonable degree of homogeneity of improvements is present.

Conservation: The process of utilizing resources in such a manner that minimizes their depletion.

Consideration: Anything of value given to induce entering into a contract; it may be money, personal services, or anything having value.

Constant: The percentage which, when applied directly to the face value of a debt, develops the annual amount of money necessary to pay a specified net rate of interest on the reducing balance and to liquidate the debt in a specified time period. For example, a 6% loan with a 20-year amortization has a constant of approximately 8.5%. Thus, a $10,000 loan amortized over 20 years requires an annual payment of approximately $850.00.

Contingent Remainder: A remainder interest that can be defeated by the happening of an event.

Construction Loans: Loans made for the construction of homes or commercial buildings. Usually funds are disbursed to the contractor/builder during construction and after periodic inspections. Disbursements are based on an agreement between borrower and lender.

Constructive Eviction: Breach of a covenant of warranty or quiet enjoyment, e.g., the inability of a lessee to obtain possession because of a paramount defect in title, or a condition making occupancy hazardous. A lessee can treat it as cause to void a lease.

Constructive Notice: Notice given by the public records.

Consummate Dower: A widow's dower interest which, after the death of her husband, is complete or may be completed and become an interest in real estate.

Contour: The surface configuration of land.

Contour Lines: Lines on a map that indicate elevation. When lines are close together, it indicates a steep stoop, but if the lines are far apart, it indicates the land is relatively level.

Contract: An agreement, either written or oral, to do or not to do certain things.

Contribution, Principle of: Holds that maximum real property values are achieved when the improvements on the site produce the highest (net) return commensurate with the investment.

Consumer Goods: These are goods used or bought for use primarily for personal, family or household purposes.

Conventional Mortgage: A mortgage securing a loan made by investors without governmental underwriting, i.e., which is not FHA insured or VA guaranteed.

Conversion: Change from one character or use to another. Also, the wrongful appropriation of funds of another.

Conveyance: This has two meanings. One meaning refers to the process of transferring title to property from one person to another. In this sense it is used as a verb. The other meaning refers to the document used to effect the transfer of title (usually some kind of deed). In this last sense, it is used a noun.

Cooperative Ownership: A form of apartment ownership. Ownership of shares in a cooperative venture which entitles the owner to use, rent, or sell a specific apartment unit. The corporation usually reserves the right to approve certain actions such as a sale or improvement.

Corner Influence Table: A statistical table that may be used to estimate the added value of a corner lot.

Corporation: A group or body of persons established and treated by law as an individual or unit with rights and liabilities or both, distinct and apart from those of the persons composing it. A corporation is a creature of law having certain powers and duties of a natural person. Being created by law it may continue for any length of time the law prescribes.

Corporeal Rights: Possessory rights in real property.

Correction Lines: A system for compensating inaccuracies in the Government Rectangular Survey System due to the curvature of the earth. Every fourth township line, 24 mile intervals, is used as a correction line on which the intervals between the north and south range lines are remeasured and corrected to a full 6 miles.

Correlate the Findings: Interpret the data and value estimates to bring them together to a final conclusion of value.

Correlation: To bring the indicated values developed by the three approaches into mutual relationship with each other.

Correlative User: Rights of an owner to reasonable use of nonflowing underground water.

Cost: A historical record of past expenditures, or an amount that would be given in exchange for other things.

Cost Approach: One of three methods in the appraisal process. An analysis in which a value estimate of a property is derived by estimating the replacement cost of the improvements, deducting therefrom the estimated accrued depreciation, then adding the market value of the land.

GLOSSARY

Counterflashing: Sheet metal used around chimneys, at roof line and in roof valleys to prevent moisture entry.

Covenant: Agreements written into deeds and other instruments promising performance or nonperformance of certain acts or stipulating certain uses or nonuses of the property.

CPM: Certified Property Manager. IREM's highest designation.

Crawl Space: Exterior or interior opening permitting access underneath building (**minimum 18˝**), as required by building codes.

CRB: Certified Residential Broker.

CRE: Counselor of Real Estate. Members of American Society of Real Estate Counselors.

CRS: Certified Residential Specialist (a NAR designation).

Cubage: The number or product resulting by multiplying the width of a thing by its height and by its depth or length.

Curable Depreciation: Items of physical deterioration and functional obsolescence that are customarily repaired or replaced by a prudent property owner.

Curtail Schedule: A listing of the amounts by which the principal sum of an obligation is to be reduced by partial payments and of the dates when each payment will become payable.

D

Damages: The indemnity (amount) recoverable by a person who has sustained an injury, either in his person, property, or relative rights, through the act or default of another.

Data Plant: An appraiser's file of information on real estate.

Debenture: Bonds issued without specific security.

Debtor: This is the party who "owns" the property that is subject to the security interest.

Deciduous Trees: Trees that lose their leaves in the autumn and winter. (Regarded as hardwoods.)

Deck: Usually an open area on the roof, or off a ground or higher floor. Similar areas are called porch, patio, lanai, veranda.

Dedication: A conveyance of land by its owner for some public use, accepted for such use by authorized public officials on behalf of the public.

Deed: Written instrument which, when properly executed and delivered, conveys title.

Deed in Lieu of Foreclosure: Mortgagor gives a quit claim deed to mortgagee. There could be a problem as to junior liens.

Deed Restrictions: This is a limitation in the deed to a property that dictates certain uses that may or may not be made of the property.

Default: Failure to fulfill a duty or promise or to discharge an obligation; omission or failure to perform any act.

Defeasance Clause: The clause in a mortgage that gives the mortgagor the right to redeem his/her property upon the payment of his obligations to the mortgagee.

Defeasible Fee: Sometimes called a "base fee" or "qualified fee"; a fee simple absolute interest in land that is capable of being terminated upon the happening of a specified event.

Deferred Maintenance: Existing but unfulfilled requirements for repairs and rehabilitation.

Deficiency Judgment: A judgment given when the foreclosure sale of the security pledge for a loan does not satisfy the debt.

Depreciation: Loss of value in real property brought about by age, physical deterioration or functional or economic obsolescence. Broadly, a loss in value from any cause.

Depth Table: A statistical table that may be used to estimate the value of the added depth of a lot.

Desist and Refrain Order: An order directing a person to desist and refrain (stop) from committing an act in violation of the real estate law.

Desk Cost: The cost of operation of a real estate office expressed on a per salesperson basis.

Deterioration (Physical): Impairment of condition. One of the causes of depreciation and reflecting the loss in value brought about by wear and tear, disintegration, use in service, and the action of the elements.

Devisee: One who receives a bequest made by will.

Devisor: One who bequeaths by will.

Directional Growth: The location or direction toward which the residential sections of a city are destined or determined to grow.

Discount: An amount deducted in advance from the principal before the borrower is given the use of the principal. (See **Points**.)

Disintermediation: The relatively sudden withdrawal of substantial sums of money savers have deposited with savings and loan associations, commercial banks, and mutual savings banks. This term can also be considered to include life insurance policy purchasers borrowing against the value of their policies. The essence of this phenomenon is financial intermediaries losing within a short period of time billions of dollars as owners of funds held by those institutional lenders exercise their prerogative of taking them out of the hands of these financial institutions.

Disposable Income: The after-tax income a household receives to spend on personal consumption.

Dispossess: To deprive one of the use of real estate.

Documentary Transfer Tax: A state enabling act allowing a county to adopt a documentary transfer tax to apply on all transfer of real property located in the county. Notice of payment is entered on face of the deed or on a separate paper filed with the deed.

Dominant Tenement: Estate benefited by an easement right of use.

Donee: A person to whom a gift is made.

Donor: A person who makes a gift.

Dower: The right that a wife has in her husband's estate at his death.

Dual Agency: An agent who has agency duties to both buyer and seller.

Duress: Unlawful constraint exercised upon a person whereby he/she is forced to do some act against his/her will.

E

Earnest Money: Down payment made by a purchaser of real estate as evidence of good faith.

Easement: Created by grant or agreement for a specific purpose, an easement is the right, privilege or interest which one party has in land of another. **Example:** right of way.

Easement by Necessity: Easement granted when lands were formerly under a single owner and there is not other ingress or egress.

Easement by Prescription: An easement obtained by open, notorious and hostile use.

Easement In Gross: Easement personal to the easement holder where there is no dominant tenement (such as the right of a utility company to run power lines across a property).

Eaves: The lower part of a roof projecting over the wall.

Economic Life: The period over which a property will yield a return on the investment, over and above the economic or ground rent due to land.

Economic Obsolescence: A loss in value due to factors away from the subject property but adversely affecting the value of the subject property.

Economic Rent: The reasonable rental expectancy if the property were available for renting at the time of its valuation.

Effective Age of Improvement: The number of years of age that is indicated by the condition of the structure, not its actual chronological age.

Effective Date of Value: The specific day the conclusion of value applies.

Effective Interest Rate: The percentage of interest that is actually being paid by the borrower for the use of the money.

Electromagnetic Fields: Possible harmful magnetic fields surrounding high capacity electrical transmission lines.

Eminent Domain: The right of the government to acquire property for necessary public or quasi-public use by condemnation; the owner must be fairly compensated. The right of the government to do this and the right of the private citizen to get paid is spelled out in the 5th Amendment to the United States Constitution.

Encroachment: The building of a structure or construction of any improvements, partly or wholly on the property of another. A form of trespass.

Encumbrance: Anything which affects or limits the fee simple title to property, such as mortgages, easements or restrictions of any kind. Liens are special encumbrances which make the property security for the payment of a debt or obligation, such as mortgages and taxes.

Environmental Impact Report (EIR): A report as to the effect of a proposed development on the environment.

Equity: The interest or value which an owner has in real estate over and above the liens against it; branch of remedial justice by and through which relief is afforded to suitors in courts of equity.

Equity of Redemption: The right to redeem property during or after the foreclosure period, such as a mortgagor's right to redeem within a set period after foreclosure sale (some states).

Erosion: The wearing away of land by the action of water, wind or glacial ice.

Escalation: The right reserved by the lender to increase the amount of the payments and/or interest upon the happening of a certain event.

Escalator Clause: A clause in a contract or lease providing for the upward or downward adjustment of payments.

Escheat: The reverting of property to the State when heirs capable of inheriting are lacking.

Escrow: The deposit of instruments and funds with instructions to a third neutral party to carry out the provisions of an agreement or contract; when everything is deposited to enable carrying out the instructions, it is called a complete or perfect escrow.

Estate: As applied to the real estate practice, the term signifies the quantity of interest, share, right, equity, of which riches or fortune may consist, in real property. The degree, quantity, nature, and extent of interest which a person has in real property.

Estate of Inheritance: An estate which may descend to heirs. All freehold estates are estates of inheritance, except estates for life.

Estate for Life: A freehold estate, not of inheritance, but which is held by the tenant for his own life or the life or lives of one or more other persons, or for an indefinite period which may endure for the life or lives of persons in being and beyond the period of life.

Estate from Period-to-Period: An interest in land where there is no definite termination date but the rental period is fixed at a certain sum per week, month, or year. Also called a **Periodic Tenancy**.

Estate at Sufferance: An estate arising when the tenant wrongfully holds over after the expiration of his term. The landlord has the choice of evicting the tenant as a trespasser or accepting such tenant for a similar term and under the conditions of the tenant's previous holding. Also called a **Tenancy at Sufferance**.

Estate of Will: The permissive occupation of lands and tenements by a tenant for an indefinite period, without a rental agreement.

Estate for Years: An interest in lands by virtue of a contract for the possession of them for a definite and limited period of time. A lease with a definite termination date may be said to be an estate for years.

Estate Tax: Inheritance tax.

Estimate: To form a preliminary opinion of value.

Estimated Remaining Life: The period of time (years) it takes for the improvements to become valueless.

Estoppel: A doctrine which bars one from asserting rights which are inconsistent with a previous position or representation.

Ethics: That branch of moral science, idealism, justness, and fairness, which sets out the obligations a member of a profession or craft owes to the public, to his clients or patron, and to his professional brethren or members.

Eviction: Dispossession by process of law. The act of depriving a person of the possession of lands, in pursuance of the judgment of a court.

Exclusive Agency Listing: A written instrument giving one agent the right to sell property for a specified time but reserving the right of the owner to sell the property himself without the payment of a commission.

Exclusive Right to Sell Listing: A written agreement between owner and agent giving agent the right to collect a commission if the property is sold by anyone during the term of his agreement.

Execute: To complete, to make, to perform, to do, to follow out; to execute a deed, to make a deed, including especially signing, sealing, and delivery; to execute a contract is to perform the contract, to follow out to the end, to complete.

Executor: A person named in a will to carry out its provisions as to the disposition of the estate of a person deceased.

Expansion Joint: A fiber strip used to separate units of concrete to prevent cracking due to expansion as a result of temperature changes.

Expenses: Certain items which may appear on a closing statement in connection with a real estate sale.

F

Facade: Front of a building.

Facilitator: A person who acts to bring parties to an agreement but is the agent of neither.

Fair Market Value: This is the amount of money that would be paid for a property offered on the open market for a reasonable period of time with both buyer and seller knowing all the uses to which the property could be put and with neither party being under pressure to buy or sell.

Farm Service Agency (FSA): An agency of the Department of Agriculture. Primary responsibility is to provide financial assistance for farmers and others living in rural areas where financing is not available on reasonable terms from private sources.

Federal Deposit Insurance Corporation (FDIC): Agency of the federal government which insures deposits at commercial banks and savings banks up to $100,000.

Federal Home Loan Bank (FHLB): A district bank of the Federal Home Loan Bank system that lends only to member savings and loan associations.

Federal Home Loan Bank Board (FHLBB): The administrative agency that charters federal savings and loan associations and exercises regulatory authority over the FHLB system.

Federal Housing Administration (FHA): An agency of the federal government that insures mortgage loans.

Federal National Mortgage Association (FNMA - "Fannie Mae"): A private corporation whose primary function is to buy and sell FHA and VA mortgages in the secondary market.

Fee: An estate of inheritance in real property.

Fee Simple: In modern estates, the terms "Fee" and "Fee Simple" are substantially synonymous. The term "Fee" is of Old English derivation. "Fee Simple Absolute" is an estate in real property, by which the owner has the greatest power over the title which it is possible to have, being an absolute estate. In modern use, it expressly establishes the title of real property in the owner, without limitation or end. He may dispose of it by sale, trade, or will, as he chooses.

Fee Simple Determinable: An estate that ends automatically when a condition is breached.

Feudal Tenure: A real property ownership system where ownership rests with a sovereign who, in turn, may grant lesser interests in return for service or loyalty. In contrast to allodial tenure where ownership is complete.

Feuds: Grants of land.

Fidelity Bond: A security posted to insure the honesty of a person.

Fiduciary: A person in a position of trust and confidence, as between principal and broker; broker as fiduciary owes certain loyalty which cannot be breached under the rules of agency.

Filtering Down: The process of housing passing down to successively lower income groups.

Financial Intermediary: Financial institutions such as commercial banks, savings and loan associations, mutual savings banks and life insurance companies which receive relatively small sums of money from the public and invest them in the form of large sums. A considerable portion of these funds are loaned on real estate.

Financing Statement: This is the instrument which is filed in order to give public notice of the security interest in personal property and thereby protect the interest of the secured parties in the collateral. See definitions of Security Interest and Secured Party.

Finder's Fee: A fee for introducing the parties to a transaction.

Finish Floor: Finish floor strips are applied over wood joists, and plywood before finish floor is installed; finish floor is the final covering on the floor: wood, linoleum, cork, tile or carpet.

Fire Stop: A horizontal board between studs placed to prevent the spread of fire and smoke through such a space.

First Mortgage: A legal document pledging collateral for a loan (see "mortgage") that has first priority over all other claims against the property except taxes and bonded indebtedness.

Fiscal Controls: Federal tax and expenditure policies used to control the level of economic activity.

Fixity of Location: The physical characteristic of real estate that subjects it to the influence of its surroundings.

Fixtures: Appurtenances attached to the land or improvements, which usually cannot be removed without agreement as they become real property. **Examples:** plumbing fixtures built into the property.

Flashing: Sheet metal or other material used to protect a building from seepage of water.

Footing: The base or bottom of a foundation wall, pier, or column.

Foreclosure: Legal procedure whereby property pledged as security for a debt is sold to pay the debt in event of default in payments or terms.

Forfeiture: Loss of money or anything of value, due to failure to perform.

Foundation: The supporting portion of a structure below the first floor construction, or below grade.

GLOSSARY

Franchise: A specified privilege awarded by a government or business firm which awards an exclusive marketing.

Fraud: The intentional and successful employment of any cunning, deception, collusion, or artifice, used to circumvent, cheat or deceive another person, whereby that person acts upon it to the loss of his property and to his legal injury.

Freehold: An estate of indeterminable duration, e.g., fee simple or life estate.

Frontage: Land bordering a street.

Front Foot: Property measurement for sale or valuation purposes; the property measures by the front foot on its street line—each front foot extending the depth of the lot.

Front Money: The minimum amount of money necessary to initiate a real estate venture.

Frostline: The depth of frost penetration in the soil. Varies in different parts of the country. Footings should be placed below this depth to prevent movement.

Fructus Naturales: Naturally growing plants and trees.

Functional Obsolescence: A loss of value due to adverse factors built into the structure which affect the utility of the structure.

Funding Fee: A fee paid to the Department of Veterans Affairs for a VA loan.

Furring: Strips of wood or metal applied to a wall or other surface to even it, to form an air space, or to give the wall an appearance of greater thickness.

Future Benefits: The anticipated benefits the present owner will receive from his property in the future.

G

Gable Roof: A pitched roof with sloping sides.

Gambrel Roof: A curb roof, having a steep lower slope with a flatter upper slope above.

General Lien: A lien on all the property of a debtor.

General Warranty Deed: The warranty deed where the seller guarantees that the title is marketable.

Gift Deed: A deed for which the consideration is love and affection and where there is no material consideration.

Girder: A large beam used to support beams, joists and partitions.

Grade: Ground level at the foundation.

Graduated Lease: Lease which provides for a varying rental rate, often based upon future determination; sometimes rent is based upon result of periodical appraisals; used largely in long-term leases.

Grant: A technical term made use of in deeds of conveyance of lands to import a transfer.

Grant Deed: A deed in which "grant" is used as the word of conveyance. The grantor impliedly warrants that he has not already conveyed to any other person, and that the estate conveyed is free from encumbrances done, made or suffered by the grantor or any person claiming under him, including taxes, assessments, and other liens.

Grantee: The purchaser; a person to whom a grant is made.

Grantor: Seller of property; one who signs a deed.

GRI: Graduate, Realtors Institute.

Grid: A chart used in rating the borrower risk, property, and the neighborhood.

Gross Income: Total income from property before any expenses are deducted.

Gross Domestic Product (GDP): The total value of all goods and services produced in a economy during a given period of time.

Gross Rate: A method of collecting interest by adding total interest to the principal of the loan at the outset of the term.

Gross Rent Multiplier: A figure which, times the gross income of a property, produces an estimate of value of the property.

Ground Lease: An agreement for the use of the land only, sometimes secured by improvements placed on the land by the user.

Ground Rent: Earnings of improved property credited to earnings of the ground itself after allowance is made for earnings of improvements; often termed economic rent.

Growing Equity Mortgage (GEM): A mortgage with payments that increase in steps resulting in a rapid payback.

H - I

Habendum Clause: The "to have and to hold" clause in a deed.

Hard Money Loan: A cash loan by a noninstitutional lender.

Header: The horizontal beam above doors or windows.

Highest and Best Use: An appraisal phrase meaning that use which at the time of an appraisal is most likely to produce the greatest net return to the land and/or buildings over a given period of time; that use which will produce the greatest amount of amenities or profit. This is the starting point for appraisal.

Hip Roof: A pitched roof with all four sides sloping to the eaves.

Holder in Due Course: One who has taken a note, check or bill of exchange in due course:

1. Appears good on its face
2. Before it was overdue;
3. In good faith and for value;
4. Without knowledge that it has been previously dishonored without notice of any defect at the time it was negotiated to him.

Holdover Tenant: Tenant who remains in possession of leased property after the expiration of the lease term.

Homestead: A home upon which the owner or owners have recorded a Declaration of Homestead. As provided by Statutes in some states, it protects home against judgments up to specified amounts.

Hundred Percent Location: A city retail business location which is considered the best available for attracting business.

Hypothecate: To give a thing as security without the necessity of giving up possession of it.

Impounds: A trust-type account established by lenders for the accumulation of funds to meet taxes and future insurance policy premiums required to protect their security. Impounds are usually collected with the note payment.

Inchoate Right of Dower: A wife's interest in the real estate of her husband during his life which upon his death may become a dower interest.

Income Approach: One of the three methods in the appraisal process; an analysis in which the estimated net income from the subject residence is used as a basis for estimating value by dividing the net by a capitalization rate.

Incompetent: One who is mentally incapable of contracting; judged to be of unsound mind, therefore lacking contractual capacity.

Incorporeal Rights: Nonpossessory rights in real estate.

Increment: An increase. Most frequently used to refer to the increase of value of land that accompanies population growth and increasing wealth in the community. The term unearned increment is used in this connection since values are supposed to have increased without effort on the part of the owner.

Indenture: A formal written instrument made between two or more persons.

Indorsement: The act of signing one's name on the back of a check or note, with or without further qualification.

Injunction: A writ or order issued under the seal of a court to restrain one or more parties to a suit or proceeding from doing an act which is deemed to be inequitable or unjust in regard to the rights of some other party or parties in the suit or proceeding.

Input: Data, information, etc., that is fed into a computer or other system.

Installment Contract: Purchase of real estate wherein the purchase price is paid in installments over a long period of time; title is retained by seller; upon default the payments are forfeited. Also known as a land contract.

Installment Note: A note which provides that payments of a certain sum or amount be paid on the dates specified in the instrument.

Installment Reporting: A method of reporting capital gains by installments for successive tax years to minimize the impact of the totality of the capital gains tax in the year of the sale.

Instrument: A written legal document; created to effect the rights of the parties.

Interest: The charge in dollars for the use of money for a period of time. In a sense, the "rent" paid for the use of money.

Interest Rate: The percentage of a sum of money charged for its use.

Interim Loan: A short-term loan until long-term financing is available.

Intermediate Theory: That a mortgage is a lien but title transfers to mortgagee automatically upon default.

Interstate Land Sales Full Disclosure Act: Disclosure requirements for unimproved land sales made in interstate commerce.

Intestate: A person who dies having made no will, or one which is defective in form in which case his estate descends to his heirs at law or next of kin.

Involuntary Alienation: Involuntary transfer such as foreclosure for eminent domain.

Involuntary Lien: A lien imposed against property without consent of an owner. **Example:** taxes, special assessments, federal income tax liens, etc.

Inwood Tables: Concept of using present value of income in a perpetuity table to help appraisers.

IREM: Institute of Real Estate Management. Part of NAR.

Irrevocable: Incapable of being recalled or revoked; unchangeable.

J

Jalousie: A slatted blind shutter or window, like a venetian blind but used on the exterior to protect against rain as well as to control sunlight.

Jamb: The side post or lining of a doorway, window or other opening.

Joint Note: A note signed by two or more persons who have equal liability for payment.

Joint Tenancy: Joint ownership by two or more persons with right of survivorship; all joint tenants own equal interest and have equal rights in the property and are formed at the same time by the same instrument.

Joint Venture: Two or more individuals or firms joining together on a single project as partners.

Joist: One of a series of parallel horizontal beams to which the boards of a floor and ceiling laths are nailed, and supported in turn by larger beams, girders, or bearing walls.

Judgment: The final determination of a court of competent jurisdiction of a matter presented to it; money judgments provide for the payment of claims presented to the court, or are awarded as damages, etc.

Judgment Lien: A legal claim on all of the property of a judgment debtor in the county where recorded, which enables the judgment creditor to have the property sold for payment of the amount of the judgment.

Junior Mortgage: A mortgage second in line to a previous mortgage.

Jurisdiction: The authority by which judicial officers take cognizance of and decide causes; the power to hear and determine a cause; the right and power which a judicial officer has to enter upon the inquiry.

L

Laches: Delay or negligence in asserting one's legal rights.

Land Contract: A contract ordinarily used in connection with the sale of property in cases where the seller does not wish to convey title until all or a certain part of the purchase price is paid by the buyer; often used when property is sold on small down payment.

Landlord: One who rents his property to another.

Lateral Support: The support which the soil of an adjoining owner gives to his neighbors' land.

Lath: A building material of wood, metal, gypsum, or insulating board fastened to the frame of a building to act as a plaster base.

Lead-Based Paint Disclosure: Federally mandated disclosure for residential property built prior to 1978.

Lease: A contract between owner and tenant, setting forth conditions upon which tenant may occupy and use the property, and the term of the occupancy.

Leasehold Estate: A tenant's right to occupy real estate during the term of the lease. This is a personal property interest.

Legal Description: A description recognized by law; a description by which property can be definitely located by reference to government surveys metes and bounds or approved recorded maps.

Lessee: One who contracts to rent property under a lease contract; a tenant.

Lessor: An owner who enters into a lease with a tenant.

Level Payment Mortgage: A loan on real estate that is paid off by making a series of equal (or nearly equal) regular payments. Part of the payment is usually interest on the loan and part of it reduces the amount of the unpaid balance of the loan. Also sometimes called an **Amortized Mortgage**.

Leverage: Maximizing net by using borrowed funds.

Lien: A form of encumbrance which usually makes property security for the payment of a debt or discharge of an obligation. **Example:** judgments, taxes, mortgages, deeds of trust, etc.

Lien Theory: A mortgage theory that a mortgage creates only a lien.

Life Estate: An estate or interest in real property which is held for the duration of the life of some certain person.

Limited Partnership: A partnership composed of some partners whose contribution is financial and liability is limited to their investment.

Lintel: A horizontal board that supports the load over an opening such as a door or window.

Lis Pendens: Suit pending, usually recorded so as to give constructive notice of pending litigation.

Liquidated Damages: A sum agreed upon by the parties to be full damages if an agreement is breached.

Listing: An employment contract between principal and agent authorizing the agent to perform services for the principal involving the latter's property; listing contracts are entered into for the purpose of securing persons to buy, lease or rent property. Employment of an agent by a prospective purchaser or lessee to locate property for purchase or lease may be considered a listing.

Loan Administration: Also called **Loan Servicing**. Mortgage bankers not only originate loans, but also "service" them from origination to maturity of the loan.

Loan Application: The loan application is a source of information on which the lender bases his decision to make the loan, defines the terms of the loan contract; gives the name of the borrower, place of employment, salary, bank accounts, and credit references; and, describes the real estate that is to be mortgaged. It also stipulates the amount of loan being applied for, and repayment terms.

Loan Closing: When all conditions have been met, the loan officer authorizes the recording of the trust deed or mortgage. The disbursal procedure of funds is similar to the closing of a real estate sales escrow. The borrower can expect to receive less than the amount of the loan, as title, recording, service, and other fees may be withheld, or he can expect to deposit the cost of these items into the loan escrow. This process is sometimes called "funding" or "settlement."

Loan Commitment: Lender's contractual commitment to a loan based on the appraisal and underwriting.

Loan-To-Value Ratio (LTV): The percentage of a property's value that a lender can or may loan to a borrower. For example, if the ratio is 80% this means that a lender may loan 80% of the property's appraised value to a borrower.

Long-Term Gain: Capital gain on sale of property held over 18 months.

Louver: An opening with a series of horizontal slats set at an agle to permit ventilation without admitting rain, sunlight, or vision.

M

MAI: Designates a person who is a member of the Appraisal Institute.

Margin of Security: The difference between the amount of the mortgage loan(s) and the appraised value of the property.

Marginal Land: Land which barely pays the cost of working or using.

Market Data Approach: One of the three methods in the appraisal process. A means of comparing similar type residential properties, which have recently sold, to the subject property.

Market Price: The price paid regardless of pressures, motives or intelligence.

Market Value: (1) The price at which a willing seller would sell and a willing buyer would buy, neither being under abnormal pressure; (2) as defined by the courts, is the highest price estimated in terms of money which a property will bring if exposed for sale in the open market allowing a reasonable time to find a purchaser with knowledge of property's use and capabilities for use.

Marketable Title: Merchantable title; title free and clear of objectionable liens or encumbrances.

Material Fact: A fact is material if it is one which the agent should realize would be likely to affect the judgment of the principal in giving his consent to the agent to enter into the particular transaction on the specified terms.

Mechanic's Lien: A lien created by statute which exists against real property in favor of persons who have performed work or furnished materials for the improvement of the real estate.

Meridians: North-south surveyor lines which intersect base lines to form a starting point for the measurement of land.

Metes and Bounds: A term used in describing the boundary lines of land, setting forth all the boundary lines together with their terminal points and angles.

Mid-Term Gain: Gain on sale of property held over one year but less than 18 months.

Mile: 5,280 feet.

Mineral, Oil, and Gas Rights: The right to minerals, oil and gas in the ground and the implied easement to enter to mine or drill.

Minor: All persons under 18 years of age who are not emancipated.

Misplaced Improvement: Improvements on land which do not conform to the most profitable use of the site.

Mitigation of Damages: Duty of lessor to attempt to rent to keep defaulting tenant's damages down.

Manufactured Home: A home constructed and then transported on its own chassis.

Modular: A building composed of modules constructed on an assembly line in a factory. Usually, the modules are self-contained.

Moldings: Usually patterned or curved strips used to provide ornamental variation of outline or contour, such as cornices, bases, window and door jambs.

Monetary Controls: Federal Reserve tools for regulating the availability of money and credit to influence the level of economic activity.

Monument: A fixed object and point established by surveyors to establish land locations.

Moratorium: The temporary suspension, usually by statute, of construction or the enforcement of a debt.

Mortgage: An instrument recognized by law by which property is hypothecated to secure the payment of a debt or obligation; procedure for foreclosure in event of default is established by statute.

Mortgage Guaranty Insurance: Insurance against financial loss available to mortgage lenders from Mortgage Guaranty Insurance Corporation (MGIC), a private company organized in 1956.

Mortgage Loan Broker: A broker who charges borrowers for loans arranged.

Mortgagee: One to whom a mortgagor gives a mortgage to secure a loan or performance of an obligation, a lender. (See definition of **Secured Party**.)

Mortgagor: One who gives a mortgage on his property to secure a loan or assure performance of an obligation; a borrower. (See definition of **Debtor**.)

Multiple Listing: A listing, usually an exclusive right to sell, taken by a member of an organization composed of real estate brokers, with the provisions that all members will have the opportunity to find an interested client; a cooperative listing.

Mutual Water Company: A water company organized by or for water users in a given district with the object of securing an ample water supply at a reasonable rate; stock is issued to users.

N

Naked Legal Title: Title held by a trustee until the terms of trust deed and note have been met.

NAREB: National Association of Real Estate Brokers.

NAR: National Association of REALTORS®.

Narrative Appraisal: A summary of all factual materials, techniques and appraisal methods used by the appraiser in setting forth his value conclusion.

Negative Amortization: Loan payments that do not cover the interest due so that the loan principal increases.

Negative Declaration: A statement that a development will not adversely effect the environment.

Negotiable: Capable of being negotiated, assigned, or transferred in the ordinary course of business.

Net Listing: A listing which provides that the agent may retain as compensation for his services all sums received over and above a net price to the owner. (Illegal in many states)

Nominal Interest Rates: The percentage of interest that is stated in loan documents.

Notary Public: An appointed officer with authority to take the acknowledgment of persons executing documents, to sign the certificate, and affix his seal.

Note: A signed written instrument acknowledging a debt and promising payment.

Notice: Actual knowledge acquired by being or knowing of the occurrence.

Notice of Nonresponsibility: A notice provided by law designed to relieve a property owner from responsibility for the cost of work done on the property or materials furnished therefor; when contracted by a tenant or vendee on a land contract notice must be verified, recorded and posted.

Notice to Quit: A notice to a tenant to vacate rented property.

Nuncupative Will: Oral will. Not generally valid.

O

Obligating Advance: Required advance on a construction loan as work progresses.

Obsolescence: Loss in value due to reduced desirability and usefulness of a structure because its design and construction become obsolete.

Occupancy Permit: Required from building inspector prior to occupancy of a new unit.

Offset Statement: Statement by owner of property or owner of lien against property, setting forth the present status of liens against said property.

Open-End Mortgage: A mortgage containing a clause which permits the mortgagor to borrow additional money without rewriting the mortgage.

Open Housing Law: See **Civil Rights Act of 1968**.

Open Listing: An authorization given by a property owner to a real estate agent wherein said agent is given the non-exclusive rights to secure a purchaser; open listings may be given to any number of agents without liability to compensate any except the one who first secures a buyer ready, willing and able to meet the terms of the listing, or secures the acceptance by the seller of a satisfactory offer.

Opinion of Title: An attorney's evaluation of the condition of the title to a parcel of land after his examination of the abstract of title to the land.

Option: A right given for a consideration to purchase or lease a property upon specified terms within a specified time.

Oral Contract: A verbal agreement; one which is not reduced to writing.

Orientation: Placing a house on its lot with regard to its exposure to the rays of the sun, prevailing winds, privacy from the street and protection from outside noises.

Overhang: The part of the roof extending beyond the walls, to shade buildings and cover walks.

Over Improvement: An improvement which is not the highest and best use for the site on which it is placed by reason of excess size or cost. An improvement that will not reasonably contribute to income or market value.

P

Packaged Mortgage: A mortgage covering both real and personal property.

Parquet Floor: Hardwood flooring laid in squares or patterns.

Participation: In addition to base interest on mortgage loans on income properties, a percentage of ownership is given to the lender.

Partition Action: Court proceedings by which co-owners seek to sever their joint ownership.

Partnership: A contract of two or more persons to unite their property, labor or skill, or some of them, in prosecution of some joint or lawful business, and to share the profits in certain proportions.

Party Wall: A wall erected on the line between two adjoining properties, which are under different ownership, for the use of both properties.

Patent: Conveyance of title to government land.

PCPs: A carcinogenic substance used in insulating fluids in electrical transformers.

Penalty: An extra payment or charge required of the borrower for deviating from the terms of the original loan agreement. Usually levied for being late in making regular payment or for paying off the loan before it is due.

Penny: The term, as applied to nails, serves as a measure of nail length and is abbreviated by the letter "d."

Percentage Lease: Lease on the property, the rental for which is determined by amount of business done by the lessee; usually a percentage of gross receipts from the business with provision for a minimum rental.

Perimeter Heating: Baseboard heating, or any system in which the heat registers are located along the outside walls of a room, especially under the windows.

Personal Property: Any property which is not real property.

Physical Deterioration: Impairment of condition. Loss in value brought about by wear and tear, disintegration, use, and actions of the elements.

Pier: A column of masonry, usually rectangular in horizontal cross section, used to support other structural members.

Pitch: The incline or rise of a roof.

Planned Unit Development (PUD): A land use design with private unit ownership and common areas shared equally with all owners.

Plate: A horizontal board placed on a wall or supported on posts or studs to carry the trusses of a roof or rafters directly; a shoe, or base member as of a partition or other frame; a small flat horizontal board placed on or in a wall to support girders, joists, rafters, etc.

Pledge: The depositing of personal property by a debtor with a creditor as security for a debt or engagement.

Pledgee: One who is given a pledge or a security. (See definition of **Secured Party**.)

Pledgor: One who offers a pledge or gives security. (See definition of **Debtor**.)

Plottage Increment: The appreciation in unit value created by joining smaller ownerships into one large single ownership.

Plywood: Laminated wood made up in panels; several thickness of wood glued together with grain at different angles for strength.

Point of Beginning (POB): Beginning point for a metes and bounds description.

Points: Each point is one percent of the loan. They are charged by lenders to make the loan more attractive. For buyers they are treated as prepaid interest.

Police Power: The right of the State to enact laws and regulations and enforce them for the order, safety, health, morals, and general welfare of the public.

Power of Attorney: An instrument authorizing a person to act as the agent of the person granting it, and a general power authorizing the agent to act generally in behalf of the principal. A special power limits the agent to a particular or specific act, as a landowner may grant an agent special power of attorney to convey a single and specific parcel of property. Under the provisions of a general power of attorney, the agent having the power may convey any or all property of the principal granting the general power of attorney.

Prefabricated House: A house manufactured, and sometimes partly assembled, before delivery to building site.

Prepaid Items of Expense: Prorations of prepaid items of expense which are credited to the seller in the closing statement.

Prepayment: Provision made for loan payments to be larger than those specified in the note.

Prepayment Penalty: Penalty for the payment of a mortgage or trust deed note before it actually becomes due if the note does not provide for prepayment.

Present Value: The lump sum value today of an annuity. A $100 bill to be paid to someone in one year is worth less than if it were a $100 bill to be paid to someone today. This is due to several things, one of which is that the money has time value. How much the $100 bill to be paid in one year is worth today will depend on the interest rate that seems proper for the particular circumstances. For example, if 6% is the appropriate rate, the $100 to be paid one year from now would be worth $94.34 today.

Presumption: A rule of law that courts and judges shall draw a particular inference from a particular fact, or from particular evidence, unless and until the truth of such inference is disproved.

Prima Facie: Presumptive on its face.

Principal: This term is used to mean either the employer of an agent or the amount of money borrowed or the amount of the loan.

Principal Note: The promissory note which is secured by the mortgage or trust deed.

Prior Appropriation: The superior rights of the first user of flowing water (in some states).

Private Mortgage Insurance (PMI): A policy of Private Mortgage Insurance usually required for a conventional loan where the down payment is less than 20 percent.

Privity: Mutual relationship to the same rights of property, contractual relationship.

Procuring Cause: That cause originating from series of events that, without break in continuity, results in the prime object of an agent's employment producing a final buyer.

Progression, Principle of: The worth of a lesser valued residence tends to be enhanced by association with many higher valued residences in the same area.

Promissory Note: Following a loan commitment from the lender, the borrower signs a note, promising to repay the loan under stipulated terms. The promissory note establishes liability for its repayment.

Property: The rights of ownership. The right to use, possess, enjoy, and dispose of a thing in every legal way and to exclude everyone else from interfering with these rights. Property is generally classified into two groups, personal property and real property.

Proprietary Lease: The lease that goes with stock in a cooperative authorizing occupancy of a specific unit.

Proration: Adjustments of interest, taxes, and insurance, etc., on a prorate basis as of the closing date. Fire insurance is normally paid for in advance. If a property is sold during this time, the seller wants a refund on that portion of the advance payment that has not been used at the time the title to the property is transferred.

Proration of Taxes: To divide or prorate the taxes equally or proportionately to time of use.

Proximate Cause: That cause of an event is that which, in a natural and continuous sequence unbroken by any new cause, produced that event, and without which the event would not have happened. Also, the procuring cause.

Public Trustee: The county public official whose office has been created by statute, to whom title to real property, in certain states, e.g., Colorado, is conveyed by Trust Deed for the use and benefit of the beneficiary, who usually is the lender.

Punitive Damages: Damages in excess of compensatory damages to punish the wrongdoer for an outrageous action.

Purchase and Installment Sale-Back: Involves purchase of the property upon completion of construction and immediate sale-back on a long-term installment contract.

Purchase of Land, Leaseback, and Leasehold Mortgages: An arrangement whereby land is purchased by the lender and leased back to the developer with a mortgage negotiated on the resulting leasehold of the income property constructed. The lender receives an annual ground rent, plus a percentage of income from the property.

Purchase and Leaseback: Involves the purchase of property subject to an existing mortgage and immediate leaseback.

Purchase Money Mortgage or Trust Deed: A trust deed or mortgage given as part or all of the purchase consideration for property. In some states the purchase money mortgage or trust deed loan can be made by a seller who extends credit to the buyer of property or by a third party lender (typically a financial institution) that makes a loan to the buyer of real property for a portion of the purchase price to be paid for the property. (In many states there are legal limitations upon mortgagees and trust deed beneficiaries collecting deficiency judgments against the purchase money borrower after the collateral hypothecated under such security instruments has been sold through the foreclosure process. Generally no deficiency judgment is allowed if the collateral property under the mortgage or trust deed is residential property of four units or less with the debtor occupying the property as a place of residence.)

Q - R

Quantity Survey: A highly technical process in arriving at cost estimate of new construction, and sometimes referred to in the building trade as the price takeoff method. It involves a detailed estimate of the quantities of raw material lumber, plaster, brick, cement, etc. used, as well as the current price of the material and installation costs. These factors are all added together to arrive at the cost of a structure. It is usually used by contractors and experienced estimators.

Quarter Round: A molding that presents a profile of a quarter circle.

Quiet Enjoyment: Right of an owner to the use of the property without interference of possession.

Quiet Title: A court action brought to establish title; to remove a cloud on the title.

Quitclaim Deed: A deed to relinquish any interest in property which the grantor may have, without claiming to have an interest.

Radiant Heating: A method of heating, usually consisting of coils or pipes placed in the floor, wall, or ceiling.

Radon: A colorless odorless, naturally occurring hazardous gas. Measured using a **Spectrometer**.

Rafter: One of a series of boards of a roof designed to support roof loads. The rafters of a flat roof are sometimes called roof joists.

Range: A strip of land six miles wide determined by a government survey, running in a north-south direction.

Ratification: The adoption or approval of an act performed on behalf of a person without previous authorization.

Real Estate Board: An organization whose members consist primarily of real estate brokers and salespeople.

Real Estate Settlement Procedures Act (RESPA): A federal disclosure law effective June 20, 1975 requiring new procedures and forms for settlements (closing costs) involving federally related loans.

Real Estate Trust: A special arrangement under Federal and State law whereby investors may pool funds for investments in real estate and mortgages and yet escape corporation taxes.

Realtist: A real estate broker holding active membership in a real estate board affiliated with the National Association of Real Estate Brokers (NAREB).

REALTOR®: A real estate licensee holding active membership in a real estate board affiliated with the National Association of REALTORS® (NAR).

Recapture: The rate of interest necessary to provide for the return of an investment. Not to be confused with interest rate, which is a rate of interest on an investment.

Reconveyance: The transfer of the title of land from one person to the immediate preceding owner. This particular instrument of transfer is commonly used when the performance or debt is satisfied under the terms of a deed of trust, when the trustee conveys the title he has held on condition back to the owner.

Recording: The process of placing a document on file with a designated public official for everyone to see. This public official is usually a county officer known as the County Recorder. He designates the fact that a document has been given to him by placing his stamp upon it indicating the time of day and the date when it was officially placed on file. Documents filed with the Recorder are considered to be placed on open notice to the general public of that county. Claims against property usually are given a priority on the basis of the time and the date they are recorded with the most preferred claim status going to the earliest one recorded and the next claim going to the next earliest one recorded, and so on. This type of notice is called "constructive notice" or "legal notice."

Redemption: Buying back one's property after a judicial sale.

Refinancing: The paying-off of an existing obligation and assuming a new obligation in its place.

Reformation: An action to correct a mistake in a deed or other document.

Rehabilitation: The restoration of a property to satisfactory condition without drastically changing the plan, form, or style of architecture.

Release Clause: This is a stipulation that upon the payment of a specific sum of money to the holder of a trust deed or mortgage, the lien of the instrument as to a specific described lot or area shall be removed from the blanket lien on the whole area involved.

Release Deed: An instrument executed by the mortgagee or the trustee reconveying to the mortgagor the real estate which secured the mortgage loan after the debt has been paid in full. Upon recording it cancels the mortgage lien created when the mortgage or trust deed was recorded.

Reliction: The addition to land by the permanent recession of water.

Remainder: An estate which takes effect after the termination of the prior estate, such as a life estate.

Remainder Depreciation: The possible loss in value of an improvement which will occur in the future.

Replacement Cost: The cost to replace the structure with one having utility equivalent to that being appraised, but constructed with modern materials, and according to current standards, design and layout.

Reproduction Costs: The cost of replacing the subject improvement with one that is the exact replica, having the same quality of workmanship, design and layout.

Request for Notice of Default: Recorded request so junior lienholder will be notified of foreclosure action.

Request for Notice of Delinquency: When filed, mortgagee must notify junior lienholder that mortgagor is delinquent in payments.

Required Provider: A lender requiring particular service providers.

Rescission of Contract: The abrogation or annulling of contract; the revocation or repealing of contract by mutual consent by parties to the contract, or for cause by either party to the contract.

Reservation: A right retained by a grantor in conveying property.

Restriction: The term as used relating to real property means the owner of real property is restricted or prohibited from doing certain things relating to the property, or using the property for certain purposes. Property restrictions fall into two general classifications--public and private. Zoning ordinances are examples of the former type. Restrictions may be created by private owners, typically by appropriate clauses in deeds, or in agreements, or in general plans of entire subdivisions. Usually they assume the form of a covenant, or promise to do or not to do a certain thing. They cover a multitude of matters including use for residential or business purposes, e.g. houses in tract must cost more than $150,000 etc.

Retrospective Value: The value of the property as of a previous date.

Reversion: The right to future possession or enjoyment by the person, or his heirs, creating the preceding estate.

Reversionary Interest: The interest which a person has in lands or other property, upon the termination of the preceding estate.

Ridge: The horizontal line at the junction of the top edges of two sloping roof surfaces. The rafters at both slopes are nailed to a ridge board at the ridge.

Ridge Board: The board placed on edge at the ridge of the roof to support the upper ends of the rafters; also called roof tree, ridge piece, ridge plate or ridgepole.

Right of First Refusal: A right to buy or lease only if an owner wishes to sell or lease to another party. (Rights holder must match the offer.)

Right of Survivorship: Right to acquire the interests of a deceased joint owner; distinguishing feature of a joint tenancy.

Right of Way: A privilege operating as an easement upon land, whereby the owner does by grant, or by agreement, give to another the right to pass over his land, to construct a roadway, or use as a roadway, a specific part of his land, or the right to construct through and over his land, telephone, telegraph, or electric power lines, or the right to place underground water mains, gas mains, sewer mains, etc.

Riparian Rights: The right of a landowner to flowing water on, under, or adjacent to his land.

Riser: The upright board at the back of each step of a stairway. In heating, a riser is a duct slanted upward to carry hot air from the furnace to the room above.

Risk Analysis: A study made, usually by a lender, of the various factors that might affect the repayment of a loan.

Risk Rating: A process used by the lender to decide on the soundness of making a loan and to reduce all the various factors affecting the repayment of the loan to a qualified rating of some kind.

S

Sales Contract: A contract by which buyer and seller agree to terms of a sale.

Sale-Leaseback: A situation where the owner of a piece of property wishes to sell the property and retain occupancy by leasing it from the buyer.

Sandwich Lease: A leasehold interest which lies between the primary lease and the operating lease.

Sash: Wood or metal frames containing one or more window panes.

Satisfaction: Discharge of mortgage or trust deed lien from the records upon payment of the evidenced debt.

Satisfaction Piece: An instrument for recording and acknowledging payment of an indebtedness secured by a mortgage.

Scribing: Fitting woodwork to an irregular surface.

Seal: An impression made to attest the execution of an instrument in some states, particular documents require seals.

Secondary Financing: A loan secured by a second mortgage or trust deed on real property. These can be third, fourth, fifth, sixth—on and on ad infinitum.

Secured Party: This is the party having the security interest. Thus the mortgagee, the conditional seller, the beneficiary, etc., are all now referred to as the secured party.

Security Agreement: An agreement between the secured party and the debtor which creates the security interest.

Security Interest: A term designating the interest of the creditor in the personal property of the debtor in all types of credit transactions. It thus replaces such terms as the following: chattel mortgage; pledge; trust receipt; chattel trust; equipment trust; conditional sale; inventory lien; etc.

Section: Section of land is established by government survey and contains 640 acres.

Seizin: Possession of real estate by one entitled thereto.

Separate Property: Property owned by a husband or wife which is not jointly owned.

Septic Tank: An underground tank in which sewage from the house is reduced to liquid by bacterial action and drained off.

Servicing: Supervising and administering a loan after it has been made. This involves such things as: collecting the payments, keeping accounting records, computing the interest and principal, foreclosure of defaulted loans, and so on.

Servient Tenement: The property that is burdened by an easement. It must "serve" the dominant tenement.

Setback Ordinance: An ordinance prohibiting the erection of a building or structure between the curb and the setback line.

Severalty Ownership: Owned by one person only. Sole ownership.

Shopping Center, Regional: A large shopping center with 250,000 to 1,000,000 or more square feet of store area, serving 200,000 or more people.

Shake: A handsplit shingle, usually edge grained.

Sharing Appreciation Mortgage: A loan where a lender shares in the value appreciation. It usually requires a sale or appraisal at a future date.

Sheathing: Structural covering usually boards, plywood, or wallboards, placed over exterior studding or rafters of a house.

Sheriff's Deed: Deed given by court order in connection with sale of property to satisfy a judgment.

Short-Term Gain: Gain on sale where property was held for one year or less.

Sill: The lowest part of the frame of a house, resting on the foundation and supporting the uprights of the frame (mud sill). The board or metal forming the lower side of an opening, as a door sill, window sill, etc.

Sinking Fund: Fund set aside from the income from property which, with accrued interest, will eventually pay for replacement of the improvements.

SIR: Society of Industrial Realtors®.

Soft Money Loan: Seller financing where cash does not change hands.

Soil Pipe: Pipe carrying waste out from the house to the main sewer line.

Sole or Sole Plate: A member, usually a 2 by 4, on which wall and partition studs rest.

Span: The distance between structural supports such as walls, columns, piers, beams, girders, and trusses.

Special Assessment: Legal charge against real estate by a public authority to pay cost of public improvements such as: street lights, sidewalks, street improvements, etc.

Special Warranty Deed: A deed in which the grantor warrants or guarantees the title only against defects arising during his ownership of the property and not against defects existing before the time of his ownership.

Specific Liens: Liens which attach to only a certain specific parcel of land or piece of property.

Specific Performance: An action to compel performance of an agreement, e.g., sale of land.

Standard-Depth: Generally the most typical lot depth in the neighborhood.

Standby Commitment: The mortgage banker frequently protects a builder by a "standby" agreement, under which he agrees to make mortgage loans at an agreed price for many months in the future. The builder deposits a "standby fee" with the mortgage banker for this service. Frequently, the mortgage banker protects himself by securing a "standby" from a long-term investor for the same period of time, paying a fee for this privilege.

Starker Exchange: A delayed tax deferred exchange.

Statute of Frauds: State law which provides that certain contracts must be in writing in order to be enforceable at law. **Example:** real property lease for more than one year; agent's authorization to sell real estate.

Statutory Warranty Deed: A short form warranty deed which warrants by inference that the seller is the undisputed owner and has the right to convey the property and that he will defend the title if necessary. This type of deed protects the purchaser in that the conveyor covenants to defend all claims against the property. If he fails to do so, the new owner can defend said claims and sue the former owner.

Straight-Line Depreciation: A method of depreciation under which improvements are depreciated at a constant rate throughout the estimated life of the improvement.

Strict Foreclosure: Foreclosure without a sale if the debt has not been paid after statutory notice. The court transfers title to the mortgagee (a few states).

String, Stringer: A timber or other support for cross members. In stairs, the diagonal support on which the stair treads rest.

Studs or Studding: Vertical supporting timbers in the walls and partitions spaced 16″ on center.

Subjacent Support: The duty of an excavator or miner to support the surface.

"Subject To" Mortgage: When a grantee takes a title to real property subject to mortgage, he is not responsible to the holder of the promissory note for the payment of any portion of the amount due. The most that he can lose in the event of a foreclosure is his equity in the property. See also **Assumption of Mortgage**. In neither case is the original maker of the note released from his responsibility.

Sublease: A lease, given by a lessee, transferring less than the entire leasehold. Original lessee is primarily liable for the rental agreement.

Subordinate: To make subject to, or junior to.

Subordination Clause: Clause in a junior or a second lien permitting retention of priority for prior liens. A subordination clause may also be used in a first deed of trust permitting it to be subordinated to subsequent liens as, for example, the liens of construction loans.

Subpoena: A process to cause a witness to appear and give testimony.

Subrogation: The substitution of another person in place of the creditor, to whose rights he succeeds in relation to the debt. The doctrine is used very often where one person agrees to stand surety for the performance of a contract by another person.

Substitution, Principle of: Affirms that the maximum value of a property tends to be set by the cost of acquiring an equally desirable and valuable substitute property, assuming no costly delay is encountered in making the substitution.

Sum of the Years Digits: An accelerated depreciation method.

Supply and Demand, Principle of: Affirms that price or value varies directly, but not necessarily proportionally with demand, and inversely, but not necessarily proportionately with supply.

Surety: One who guarantees the performance of another: Guarantor. A surety bond guarantees contract performance.

Surplus Productivity, Principle of: Affirms that the net income that remains after the proper costs of labor, organization and capital have been paid, which surplus is imputable to the land and tends to fix the value thereof.

Survey: The process by which a parcel of land is measured and its area is ascertained.

Syndicate: A partnership organized for participation in a real estate venture. Partners may be limited or unlimited in their liability.

T

Takeout Loan: The permanent loan arranged by the owner or builder developer for a buyer. The construction loan made for construction of the improvements is usually paid from the proceeds of this loan.

Tax-Deferred Exchange: Income property exchanged on for other income property which does not have to pay a capital gain tax at the time.

Tax Roll: Total of taxable property assessments in taxing district.

Tax Sale: Sale of property by a taxing authority after a period of nonpayment of taxes.

Tax Shelter: Use of depreciation to shelter income from taxation.

Teaser Rate: An initial rate on an adjustable rate loan less than the index figure plus margin. It is usually only given for a relatively short period of time.

Tenancy in Common: Ownership by two or more persons who hold undivided interest, without right of survivorship; interests need not be equal.

Tenants by the Entireties: Under certain state laws, ownership of property acquired by a husband and wife during marriage which is jointly owned and cannot be separately transferred. Upon death of one spouse, it becomes the property of the survivor.

Tentative Map: The Subdivision Map Act requires subdividers to submit initially a tentative map of their tract to the local planning commission for study. The approval or disapproval of the planning commission is noted on the map. Thereafter a final map of the tract embodying any changes requested by the planning commission is required to be filed with the planning commission.

Tenure in Land: The mode or manner by which an estate in lands is held.

Termites: Ant-like insects which feed on wood.

Termite Shield: A shield, usually of noncorrodible metal, placed on top of the foundation wall or around pipes to prevent passage of termites.

Testator: One who leaves a will in force at his death.

Threshold: A strip of wood or metal beveled on each edge and used above the finished floor under outside doors.

Third Party Originator: A party that prepares loan packages for borrowers for submission to lenders.

Time is of the Essence: A requirement that performance be punctual and that any delay will breach the contract.

Title: Evidence that owner of land is in lawful possession thereof, an instrument evidencing such ownership.

Title Insurance: Insurance written by a title company to protect property owner against loss if title is imperfect.

Title Report: A report which discloses condition of the title, made by a title company preliminary to issuance of title insurance (**Preliminary Title Report**).

Title Theory: Mortgage arrangement whereby title to mortgaged real property vests in the lender.

Topography: Nature of the surface of land; topography may be level, rolling, or mountainous.

Torrens Title: System of title records provided by state law (no longer used in California).

Tort: A wrongful act; wrong, injury; violation of a legal right.

Township: A division by government survey that is six miles long, six miles wide and containing 36 sections, each one mile square.

Trade Fixtures: Articles of personal property annexed to real property, but which are necessary to the carrying on of a trade and are removable by the owner of the fixtures.

Treads: Horizontal boards of a stairway on which one steps.

Trim: The finish materials in a building, such as moldings, applied around openings (window trim, door trim) or at the floor and ceiling (baseboard, cornice, picture molding).

Trust Account: An account separate and apart and physically segregated from broker's own funds, in which broker is required by law to deposit all funds collected for clients.

Trust Deed: Just as with a mortgage, this is a legal document by which a borrower pledges certain real property or collateral as guarantee for the repayment of a loan. However, it differs from the mortgage in a number of important respects. For example, instead of there being two parties to the transaction, there are three. There is the borrower who gives the trust deed and who is called the trustor. There is the third, neutral party (just as there is with an escrow) who receives the trust deed and who is called the trustee. And, finally, there is the lender who is called the beneficiary since he is the one who benefits from the pledge arrangement in that in the event of a default the trustee can sell the property and transfer the money obtained at the sale to him as payment of the debt.

Trustee: One who holds property in trust for another to secure the performance of an obligation.

Trustor: One who deeds his property to a trustee to be held as security until he has performed his obligation to a lender under terms of a deed of trust.

U - V

Under Improvement: An improvement which, because of its deficiency in size or cost, is not the highest and best use of the site.

Underwriting: The technical analysis by a lender to determine if a borrower should receive a loan.

Undue Influence: Taking any fraudulent or unfair advantage of another's weakness of mind, distress, or necessity.

Unearned Increment: An increase in value of real estate due to no effort on the part of the owner; often due to increase in population.

Uniform Commercial Code (UCC): Establishes a unified and comprehensive scheme for regulation of security transactions in personal property, superseding the existing statutes on chattel mortgages, conditional sales, trust receipts, assignment of accounts receivable and others in this field.

Unit-In-Place Method: The cost of erecting a building by estimating the cost of each component part, i.e. foundations, floors, walls, windows, ceilings, roofs, etc. (including labor and overhead).

Urban Property: City property; closely settled property.

Usury: On a loan, claiming a rate of interest greater than that permitted by law.

Utilities: Refers to services rendered by utility companies, such as: water, gas, electricity, and telephone.

Utility: The ability to give satisfaction and/or excite desire for possession.

Valid: Having force, or binding force; legally sufficient and authorized by law.

Valley: The internal angle formed by the junction of two sloping sides of a roof.

Valuation: Estimated worth or price. Estimation. The act of valuing by appraisal.

Vendee: A purchaser; buyer under a contract of sale (land contract).

Vendor: A seller; one who disposes of a thing in consideration of money. Used in a land contract.

Veneer: Thin sheets of wood glued to other wood products to form a surface.

Vent: A pipe installed to provide a flow of air to or from a drainage system or to provide a circulation of air within such system to protect trap seals from siphonage and back pressure.

Verification: Sworn statement before a duly qualified officer to correctness of contents of an instrument.

Vested: Bestowed upon someone; secured by someone, such as a title to property.

Vested Remainder: A certain remainder interest.

Void: To have no force or effect; that which is unenforceable.

Voidable: That which is capable of being adjudged void, but is not void unless action is taken to make it so.

Voluntary Lien: Any lien placed on property with consent of, or as a result of, the voluntary act of the owner.

W - Z

Wainscoting: The covering of an interior wall with wood (usually panels), tiles, etc., from the floor to a point about half way to the ceiling. The remaining portion is painted, wallpapered or covered with another material different from the lower portion.

Waive: To relinquish, or abandon; to forego a right to enforce or require anything.

Warranty Deed: A deed used to convey real property which contains warranties of title and quiet possession, and the grantor thus agrees to defend the premises against the lawful claims of third persons. It is commonly used in many states, but in others, the grant deed has supplanted it due to the practice of securing title insurance policies which have reduced the importance of express and implied warranty in deeds.

Waste: The destruction, removal, material alteration of, or injury to premises by a tenant for life or years.

Water Table: Distance from surface of ground to a depth at which natural groundwater is found.

Wrap-Around Mortgage: A second trust deed with a face value of both the new amount it secures and the balance due under the first trust deed. A wrap-around can take the form of a land contract or a deed of trust.

Yield: The interest earned by an investor on his investment (or bank on the money it has lent). Also called **Return**.

Yield Rate: The yield expressed as a percentage of the total investment. Also called **Rate of Return**.

Zone: The area set off by the proper authorities for specific use; subject to certain restrictions or restraints.

Zoning: Act of city or county authorities specifying type of use to which property may be put in specific areas.

INDEX

INDEX

APPENDIX A: MATCHING TERMINOLOGY ANSWERS

Chapter 1

1. P
2. K
3. V
4. I
5. L
6. N
7. E
8. H
9. M
10. F
11. U
12. Q
13. G
14. A
15. R
16. T
17. S
18. C
19. D
20. O
21. J
22. B

Chapter 2

1. K
2. N
3. P
4. Q
5. O
6. T
7. C
8. V
9. G
10. I
11. DD
12. M
13. J
14. A
15. W
16. H
17. S
18. E
19. BB
20. X
21. D
22. Y
23. AA
24. EE
25. F
26. CC
27. U
28. R
29. Z
30. L
31. B

Chapter 3

1. J
2. P
3. N
4. U
5. X
6. B
7. Q
8. Y
9. D
10. E
11. H
12. T
13. V
14. A
15. S
16. CC
17. G
18. C
19. W
20. F
21. AA
22. M
23. K
24. I
25. DD
26. Z
27. L
28. R
29. O
30. BB

Chapter 4

1. C
2. S
3. D
4. U
5. A
6. Y
7. AA
8. H
9. N
10. V
11. E
12. P
13. Z
14. M
15. I
16. J
17. R
18. F
19. W
20. L
21. O
22. Q
23. BB
24. B
25. K
26. G
27. T
28. X

Chapter 5

1. HH
2. H
3. P
4. BB
5. FF
6. V
7. W
8. D
9. B
10. T
11. L
12. X
13. C
14. J
15. M
16. S
17. E
18. JJ
19. LL
20. AA
21. Z
22. Y
23. A
24. K
25. F
26. GG
27. U
28. EE
29. CC
30. DD
31. Q
32. I
33. N
34. II
35. O
36. KK
37. R
38. G

Chapter 6

1. T
2. M
3. P
4. C
5. J
6. N
7. O
8. X
9. I
10. E
11. H
12. V
13. U
14. F
15. A
16. G
17. K
18. D
19. S
20. Q
21. B
22. Y
23. W
24. R
25. Z
26. L

Chapter 7

1. N
2. F
3. B
4. L
5. H
6. G
7. A
8. C
9. D
10. J
11. E
12. M
13. K
14. I
15. O

Chapter 8

1. AA
2. OO
3. K
4. O
5. J
6. X
7. F
8. Y
9. A
10. L
11. II
12. S
13. GG
14. C
15. V
16. N
17. MM
18. EE
19. LL
20. D
21. NN
22. U
23. T
24. W
25. R
26. I
27. P
28. JJ
29. HH
30. H
31. M
32. G
33. FF
34. E
35. B
36. KK
37. Q
38. CC
39. BB
40. DD
41. Z

Chapter 9

1. R
2. M
3. S
4. J
5. W
6. C
7. F

8. O
9. N
10. P
11. Z
12. I
13. L
14. K
15. U
16. B
17. E
18. V
19. D
20. Q
21. Y
22. X
23. T
24. H
25. A
26. G

Chapter 10

1. D
2. L
3. O
4. N
5. K
6. P
7. F
8. A
9. J
10. M
11. B
12. S
13. E
14. U
15. H
16. G
17. I
18. V
19. T
20. C
21. Q
22. R

Chapter 11

1. X
2. D
3. T
4. N
5. M
6. E

7. J
8. G
9. O
10. W
11. R
12. S
13. U
14. C
15. B
16. H
17. V
18. P
19. K
20. F
21. Q
22. A
23. I
24. L

Chapter 12

1. N
2. O
3. B
4. S
5. X
6. U
7. R
8. Q
9. I
10. L
11. BB
12. W
13. E
14. D
15. P
16. G
17. A
18. T
19. H
20. M
21. CC
22. Z
23. F
24. Y
25. C
26. K
27. J
28. V
29. AA

Chapter 13

1. B
2. O
3. A
4. I
5. L
6. H
7. C
8. J
9. Q
10. E
11. D
12. R
13. F
14. S
15. G
16. M
17. P
18. K
19. N
20. T
21. U

Chapter 14

1. L
2. C
3. M
4. B
5. H
6. N
7. S
8. A
9. R
10. F
11. O
12. I
13. D
14. G
15. K
16. E
17. Q
18. P
19. J

Chapter 15

1. K
2. E
3. G
4. B
5. L

6. F
7. H
8. A
9. P
10. C
11. N
12. I
13. O
14. J
15. D
16. M

Textbooks From
Educational Textbook Company

etctextbooks.com, etcbooks.com, or appraisal-etcbooks.com

Order
Department

Having trouble finding any of our textbooks?

If your bookstore does not carry or is out of our textbooks, send us a check or money order and we'll mail them to you with our 30-day money back guarantee.

Other Great Books from Educational Textbook Company:

California Real Estate Principles, 12th ed. by Huber. . . . . $65.00 _____
California Real Estate Practice, 5th ed., by Huber & Lyons. . . . . $50.00 _____
How To Pass The Real Estate Exam (850 Exam Questions), by Huber . . . . $50.00 _____
California Real Estate Law, 6th ed., by Huber & Tyler. . . . . $50.00 _____
Real Estate Finance, 6th ed. by Huber & Messick. . . . . $50.00 _____
Real Estate Finance: Appraiser's Edition, 6th ed. by Huber & Messick. . . . . $50.00 _____
Real Estate Economics, 4th ed., by Huber, Messick, & Pivar . . . . $50.00 _____
Real Estate Appraisal – Principles & Procedures, 3rd ed., by Huber, Messick, & Pivar . $50.00 _____
Residential Real Estate Appraisal, 3rd ed., by Huber & Messick. . . . . $50.00 _____
Mortgage Loan Brokering, 3rd ed., by Huber, Pivar, & Zozula . . . . $50.00 _____
Property Management, 4th ed. by Huber, Lyons, & Pivar . . . . $50.00 _____
Escrow I: An Introduction, 3rd ed., by Huber & Newton. . . . . $50.00 _____
Real Estate Computer Applications, by Grogan & Huber. . . . . $50.00 _____
Homeowner's Association Management, by Huber & Tyler . . . . $50.00 _____
California Business Law, 2nd ed. by Huber, Owens, & Tyler. $65.00 _____
Hubie's Power Prep 700 CD – 700 Questions, by Huber . . . . $50.00 _____

Subtotal _____
Add shipping and handling @ $5.00 per book _____
Add California sales tax @ 8.25% _____
TOTAL _____

Name: _____

Address: _____

City, State, Zip: _____

Phone: _____

For faster results, order by credit card from the Glendale Community College Bookstore:
1-818-240-1000 x3024
1-818-242-1561 (Direct)
www.glendalebookstore.com

552